PASTORAL MINISTRY IN A TIME OF CHANGE

Pastoral Ministry

in a

Time of Change

Eugene J. Weitzel, C.S.V., S.T.D.

PARTICIPATING EDITOR

THE BRUCE PUBLISHING COMPANY · MILWAUKEE

IMPRIMI POTEST:

JOHN W. STAFFORD, C.S.V.
Provincial

NIHIL OBSTAT:

JOHN A. SCHULIEN, S.T.D.
Censor librorum

IMPRIMATUR:

✝ WILLIAM E. COUSINS
Archbishop of Milwaukee
September 20, 1966

Library of Congress Catalog Card Number: 66–29713

To Christ
the Eternal
High Priest,
and to
my father
Frank J. Weitzel
R.I.P.

Foreword

THE LATE BISHOP WILLIAM STANG IN HIS BOOK STATED THAT "PASTORAL Theology is the science which teaches the proper discharging of the various duties of the priest in the care of souls and prepares the young ecclesiastic for his sublime destiny to worthily represent Christ among the people of God and continue the work of His redemption."

Today Vatican Council II in the *Decree on Priestly Formation* repeats what Bishop Stang stated but spells out in greater detail how to meet the needs of this modern world. "Pastoral concern which should thoroughly penetrate the entire training of seminarians also requires that they be carefully instructed in those matters which have a special bearing on the sacred ministry. . . . Let them receive careful instruction in the art of guiding souls, so that they can lead all sons of the Church, before everything else, to a Christian life which is fully conscious and apostolic. . . ."

The same Council concludes the document on priests with these words: "The ministers of the Church and even, at times, the faithful themselves feel like strangers in this world anxiously looking for appropriate ways and words with which to communicate with it." The priest today must not and cannot feel like a stranger, but he must be ready to meet the challenge that the world offers. He must recognize the social changes in the contemporary world and the necessity for the clergy to relate themselves to it intelligently. Professor Warren A. Quanbeck's comment on the decree, *Priestly Formation,* applies to all engaged in pastoral work. "The repeated instruction that seminaries are to learn from modern sociology, psychology, and pedagogy prods the theologians to grapple with the problem of communication and forbids them contentment with repetition of theological formulas."

PASTORAL MINISTRY IN A TIME OF CHANGE aims at presenting some aspects of the priests' problems. In this volume the priest may not necessarily find a complete solution to his problem but certainly he will find intelligent advice from others especially trained and experienced.

The priest of yesterday, the newly ordained, and the seminarian in these changing times are grateful for Father Weitzel's contribution to a better fulfillment of their pastoral ministry.

VERY REVEREND WALTER J. SCHMITZ, S.S., S.T.D.
Dean, The School of Sacred Theology
The Catholic University of America

vii

Introduction

THE PEOPLE OF GOD, IF THEY ARE EVER TO EXPERIENCE A "THREE-cornered Christianity" involving God, self, and neighbor, need priests who can bring them a theology that is in harmony with the times, participate with them in a living liturgy, provide pastoral counseling as well as sacramental absolution and inspire them with sermons and homilies filled with divine revelation and human wisdom. Therefore, the priest of today and tomorrow, like those who have served before him, must be totally dedicated to the apostolate so that he can be a true witness to Christ, the Sacrament of man's encounter with God. But to achieve this total dedication, whether it be to the parish, the classroom, the hospital, the correctional institution, or the battlefield, a priest, "over and above sanctity and proper science (i.e., intellectual knowledge) . . . needs a detailed and absolutely complete preparation for the dutiful performance of his apostolic ministry"; therefore, he ". . . must beget and nourish a real skill and dexterity in properly carrying out the manifold duties of the Christian apostolate."[1]

That every seminarian and priest, regardless of his apostolate, shall be properly and adequately prepared is clearly the mind of the Church, for throughout the whole of its existence, the Church has continually taught that the priesthood is a social sacrament, and that those who embrace it must be faithful "dispensers of the mysteries of God,"[2] and "ready for every noble work."[3] Consequently, the Church requires that her priests, "chosen by our brethren to be helpers in the ministry,"[4] be possessed of knowledge and skill sufficient to meet the ministerial obligations that flow from the social character of this sacrament. Though many popes in every age of history have strongly emphasized the social character of the sacrament of orders, none has been more articulate on this point than Pius XII, who wrote:

> Priests are the "stewards of the mysteries of God" (1 Cor. 4:1); therefore they must serve Jesus Christ with perfect charity and consecrate all their strength to the salvation of their brethren. . . . [They] are apostles of grace and pardon; therefore they must consecrate themselves entirely to the salvation of men and draw them to the altar of God in order that they may nourish themselves with the bread of eternal life.[5]

---

[1] Pius XII, *The Apostolic Constitution Sedes Sapientiae and the General Statutes Annexed to It* (trans. The Catholic University of America Press), p. 12.
[2] 1 Co 4:1.
[3] 1 Co 3:9.
[4] *The Rite of Ordination* (trans. A. Biskupek, S.V.D.), p. 76.
[5] Pius XII, *Menti Nostrae* (trans. N.C.W.C.), p. 21.

Furthermore, as is evident from the many constitutions and decrees issued by the Second Vatican Council, the Council Fathers place great stress on the pastoral formation of seminarians and priests and have established clear and definite norms and goals for the pastoral training of all seminarians and priests. Thus, in the *Decree on Priestly Training* they state:

> That pastoral concern which ought to permeate thoroughly the entire training of the students also demands that they be diligently instructed in those matters which are particularly linked to the sacred ministry, especially in catechesis and preaching, in liturgical worship and the administration of the sacraments, in works of charity, in assisting the erring and the unbelieving, and in the other pastoral functions. They are to be carefully instructed in the art of directing souls, whereby they will be able to bring all the sons of the Church first of all to a fully conscious and apostolic Christian life and to the fulfillment of the duties of their state of life. Let them learn to help, with equal solicitude, religious men and women that they may persevere in the grace of their vocations and may make progress according to the spirit of their various Institutes.
>
> In general, those capabilities are to be developed in the students which especially contribute to dialogue with men, such as the ability to listen to others and to open their hearts and minds in the spirit of charity to the various circumstances and needs of men.
>
> They should also be taught to use the aids which the disciplines of pedagogy, psychology, and sociology can provide, according to correct methodology and the norms of ecclesiastical authority. Likewise let them be properly instructed in inspiring and fostering the apostolic activity of the laity and in promoting the various and more effective forms of the apostolate. Let them also be imbued with that truly Catholic spirit which will accustom them to transcend the limits of their own diocese, nation, or rite, and to help the needs of the whole Church, prepared in spirit to preach the Gospel everywhere.[6]

Though PASTORAL MINISTRY IN A TIME OF CHANGE does not presume to treat of every possible aspect of the priestly ministry, or to say all that could be said about a particular apostolate — volumes would be needed to do this — the contributors to this work and the editor-author have endeavored to present the fundamental principles, problems, and possible solutions to these problems affecting the various ministerial tasks or the various apostolates. In so doing, they have sought to provide both the young priest embarking upon his first pastoral assignment and the older priest who is entering into a new apostolate with a starting point for acquiring the necessary knowledge and skills for the work he has been called upon to do.

Each contributor to this work is a person of considerable knowledge and skill in the area which he treats, but over and above this, each author is personally convinced that considerable progress would be made in

---

[6] Vatican Council II, *The Decree on Priestly Training* (trans. N.C.W.C.), p. 9.

converting the world to Christ if the apostolic principles that are inherent in divine revelation permeated the individual's preparation for all phases of the pastoral ministry. For the divine truths which have been revealed to us by the patriarchs and prophets of the Old Testament, and by Jesus Christ and his Apostles in the New Testament, contain all of the power needed to inspire in future priests a picture of Christian life which includes not only man's final end but also his responsibility to labor continually for the betterment of the temporal order in accord with the whole plan of God.

It now becomes my happy task to thank all of those who have in any way contributed toward the publication of this work. Special acknowledgement is due to the Very Reverend John W. Stafford, C.S.V., provincial superior of the clerics of St. Viator, for his generous approval of this undertaking. The editor-author is also indebted to the Very Reverend Walter J. Schmitz, S.S., dean of the School of Sacred Theology at the Catholic University, for his advice and encouragement, to the Reverend John J. Wood, C.S.V., and to Brothers John L. Corredato, C.S.V., and Thomas E. Long, C.S.V. for their assistance in preparing some of the material, and to Mr. Aloysius Croft, of the editorial department of the Bruce Publishing Company, whose interest and counsel were invaluable.

EUGENE J. WEITZEL, C.S.V.

Viatorian Seminary
Washington, D. C.

Contents

PASTORAL MINISTRY IN A TIME OF CHANGE

1

The Pastoral Ministry

EUGENE J. WEITZEL, C.S.V.

ON SEPTEMBER 12, 1960, POPE JOHN XXIII WAS "ONCE AGAIN BACK AT OUR seminary after more than fifty years of priestly life" to address the seminarians assembled in the chapel of the villa of the Roman seminary. This was a happy moment in the life of Angelo Giuseppe Roncalli and he spent several minutes recalling ". . . the fruitful years of Our preparation for the priesthood, . . . the trepidation while awaiting (Our approach) to the altar, . . . (and) the atmosphere of piety, of study, of joy that surrounded Our life as a seminarian." His thoughts then turned to St. Peter's, "where, in the quiet and modest intimacy of the crypt of the Confession, we celebrated our first holy Mass," to his audience with the Holy Father, Pius X, ". . . who laid his august hand on Our head, like a consecration of the humble but fervent intention of priestly life," and to "the celebration of our second Mass here on this altar, exactly on the 12th of that month of August, the feast of St. Clare of Assisi."

Though time would not permit him to detail the fifty years that had passed since those happy days at Roccantica, the Pope did hint at ". . . many other precious and sweet memories . . . since We left it to tread in obedience the roads of the world, practicing the sacred ministry with the most humble functions, to that of the 'Servant of the servants of God,' reserved for Us by Providence for these last years."

But Pope John had not returned to Roccantica merely to reminisce. Rather he had come back to speak to the hearts and minds of young men who within a few short months or years would be actively engaged in the priestly ministry in a time of change. To them, and to all of us who are spending our lives laboring zealously as parish priests, teachers, retreat masters, hospital and convent chaplains, military and correctional institution chaplains, he said:

> Beloved sons, with reverence and almost trembling, We pronounce these words: sacred ministry; sacred priestly, pastoral ministry *"In Christo Jesu et in Ecclesia sancta,"* (In Christ Jesus and in the Holy Church). They summarize one's whole life; your life, dear sons, as hope and beginning, and the life expressed on all levels of the hierarchy of orders and of jurisdiction, for which is raised the prayer of the Major Litanies, which is pervaded with anxious trepidation: *"Ut Domnum apostolicum et omnes ecclesiasticos ordines in sancta religione conservare digneris, te rogamus audi nos,"* (We pray you to hear us and preserve in the holy religion the Pope and all orders of the ecclesiastical hierarchy).
>
> Yes, Jesus Christ is at the center of our Faith and of our life. He is the "nobiscum Deus." It is He in the Gospel; it is He still living with us, in the Blessed Sacrament. Priestly life draws its support and vigor, its beauty and its glory from this twofold luminous and divine source. The priestly preparation that begins in the seminary, is it not all an inspiration of this intense faith, which is intimate and ardent love, poured out in an ascetic uplifting of the spirit, in an enjoyment of contemplation, sweet familiarity, in an effort of imitation and like a transfiguration with the patient and suffering Jesus "unto death"?[1]

Since we, as Christ's priests have dedicated our lives to "the sacred priestly, pastoral ministry," it is of the greatest importance that each of us have a profound love for and understanding of the pastoral ministry in the contemporary situation. Though many theologians and spiritual writers have written volumes on this topic, few can compare with the magnificent treatment of this important topic provided by the popes of recent years who have from time to time expressed their minds on the nature and function of the priesthood and the pastoral ministry. Nor, can we ignore the inspiring exhortation of the Fathers of Vatican II who were so deeply concerned about this priesthood, and this ministry in a time of change.

One of the most valuable of these considerations of the pastoral ministry is found in the Encyclical letter *E supremi apostolatus* issued by Pope St. Pius X in 1903. In this encyclical on the mission of the priest, the saintly Pope, while professing a strong preference for pastoral, spoke quite clearly on the nature of the pastoral ministry when he said that "On the other hand, we cannot hide the fact, indeed we declare it quite openly, that our own preference will always be for the priest who, without neglecting sacred or profane learning, devotes himself particularly to the welfare of souls by discharging various functions of the ministry which are par-

---

[1] John XXIII, "To Seminarians," *Addresses of His Holiness Pope John XXIII,* (trans. N.C.W.C.), pp. 8–9.

ticularly fitting for the priest who is animated by zeal for the glory of God."[2]

Many years later, another pontiff, Pope Pius XI, in his Encyclical letter *Ad catholici sacerdotii fastigium,* touched upon the very nature of the priesthood itself when he said, "The priest, in the magnificent definition of St. Paul, is a man taken from among men, yet appointed for men in the things that pertain to God (Heb 5:1). His office does not concern itself with human and transitory things, important and praiseworthy though these may seem, but with things that are divine and eternal." A few paragraphs later, the pontiff spoke specifically about the Christian priesthood when he said, "The Apostle of the gentiles sums up concisely and exactly all that can be said of the greatness, the dignity and the duty of the Christian priesthood when he writes: 'Let a man so account of us as ministers of Christ and the dispensers of the mysteries of God' (1 Cor 4:1)."[3]

However, one of the clearest explanations of the nature of the priestly ministry was given by Pius XII in *Menti Nostrae,* an Apostolic Exhortation to the Catholic clergy on the sanctification of priestly life, which was published on September 23, 1950. After a brief exposition of the exalted ministry of the divine Redeemer, the Holy Father explained that,

> To carry out this exalted ministry is the mission of priests. For they not only secure the life and grace of Jesus Christ and communicate them to the members of his Mystical Body; they also contribute to the development and increase of that Body, because they must, without ceasing, give new children to the Church, rear them, instruct them and guide them.
>
> Inasmuch as they are dispensers of the mysteries of God, they should serve Jesus Christ with perfect charity and devote all their energies to the salvation of their brethren. Since they are the apostles of the light, they must illuminate the world with the teaching of the Gospel; they must be themselves so strong in the Christian faith that they can communicate it to others, and they must so follow the example and abide by the teaching of the divine Master that they may be able to lead all to him. They are apostles of grace and of pardon, and so they must dedicate themselves completely to achieving the salvation of men, summoning them to the altar of God where they can be nourished by the bread of eternal life. They are apostles of charity, and so they must promote charitable works and undertakings, especially since the wants of the needy have increased immensely in these days.[4]

A little over a year later, the same pontiff, in a discourse to the First World Congress of the Apostolate of the Laity, again spoke about the role of the clergy, and on this occasion he insisted that ". . . the clergy must reserve themselves primarily for the exercise of their specifically

[2] Pius X, *E supremi apostolatus, ASS* 36 (1903), p. 130.
[3] Pius XI, *Ad Catholici sacerdotii fastigium, AAS* 28 (1936), pp. 9–10.
[4] Pius XII, *Menti Nostrae, AAS* 42 (1950), p. 675.

priestly functions, where no one else can take their place."[5]

Few words on the nature and function of the priesthood and the pastoral ministry are more inspiring than those of Pope John XXIII spoken in praise of St. John Vianney in the Encyclical *Sacerdotii nostri primordia.* In the third part of this Encyclical which tells of the Curé d'Ars' care in preaching and teaching, the Pope says,

> The first thing that strikes Us is the very high esteem in which he held his pastoral office. He was so humble by disposition and so much aware through faith of the importance of the salvation of a human soul that he could never undertake his parish duties without a feeling of fear.
>
> "My friend" — these are the words he used to open his heart to a fellow-priest — "you have no idea of how fearful a thing it is for a priest to be snatched away from the care of souls to appear before the judgment seat of God."[6]

In later paragraphs, the saintly pontiff spoke about the three great pastoral duties — preaching, catechizing, and hearing confessions. "Because, as it is recorded," said the Pope, " 'He was always ready to care for the needs of souls,' St. John M. Vianney, good shepherd that he was, was also outstanding in offering his sheep an abundant supply of the food of Christian truth. Throughout his life, he preached and taught catechism." Then, the Pope went on to remind his readers that "The Council of Trent pronounced this to be a parish priest's first and greatest duty. . . ."[7] Speaking about the priest's obligation to teach, the Father of Vatican Council II said,

> So it is easy to realize what great joy it brought Our predecessors to point out an example like this to be imitated by those who guide the Christian people; for the proper and careful exercise of the teaching office by the clergy is of great importance. In speaking of this, St. Pius X had this to say: "We want especially to pursue this one point and to urge strongly that no priest has any more important duty or is bound by any stricter obligation."[8]

Having pointed out the greatness of preaching and teaching, the Pope then turned his attention to John Vianney's ministry in the confessional. On this point he said, "All that remains for Us to do is to recall at a little greater length the pastoral ministry of St. John M. Vianney, which was a kind of steady martyrdom for a long period of his life, and especially his administration of the sacrament of penance, which calls for special praise for it brought forth riches and most salutary fruits."[9] After

---

[5] Pius XII, *Discourse to the First World Congress of the Lay Apostolate, AAS* 43 (1951), p. 784.

[6] John XXIII, *Sacerdotii nostri primordia, AAS* 51 (1959), p. 568.

[7] *Ibid.,* p. 570.

[8] *Ibid.,* p. 572.

[9] *Ibid.,* p. 573.

touching on the saint's anguish over sins and his concern for sinners, the Vicar of Christ spoke about the seriousness of confession. "Let the example of the Curé of Ars," he said, "stir up those who are in charge of souls to be eager and well-prepared in devoting themselves to this very serious work, for it is here most of all that divine mercy finally triumphs over human malice and that men have their sins wiped away and are reconciled to God."[10]

Several months before the Encyclical letter *Sacerdotii nostri primordia* was issued, Pope John XXIII addressed the Apostolic Union of the Clergy in commemoration of the 100th anniversary of the death of St. John Vianney on priestly vocations. In this inspiring address he said:

> Therefore, may your life be impregnated with the sweet perfume of Christ, in the ardent love of Him, which leads us to the Father. This is the real basis of a priestly life full of intimate peace and of irresistible enchantment of souls. We therefore say to you: "Amor Christi et amor silentis." May Jesus Christ be your only friend and comforter, in the vigils before the tabernacle or at the work table, in the care of the poor and of the sick, in the ministry of sacred preaching. Seek only Him, considering the human things in His light, so as to conquer them through Him. Take upon yourselves His gentle yoke and His light weight, practicing the virtues proper to every consecrated life: dedication to the Lord and to souls, tireless work for the Church, practice of the fourteen works of mercy, prompt and sincere obedience to the bishop, respectful of manly tenderness for sacred things.[11]

Pope Paul VI also spoke at length about his great love and esteem for pastors of souls and offered words of encouragement:

> We take this occasion to show Our highest esteem, Our special benevolence, Our fraternal and great encouragement for the pastors of souls. This special recognition, which your distinguished pastoral study arouses in Us, is due to them, for We Ourself have been a pastor, first in a diocese, which seems to have been an experimental field of typical and positive pastoral importance in past centuries under St. Ambrose and St. Charles, and as it still is today after the servants of God, Cardinals Ferrari and Schuster. And We are a pastor today on this Chair of Peter to which We have been called by Christ to feed the flock of His Church.
>
> Our expression of affectionate devotion is due to them because the pastoral ministry binds them to complete dedication as the word and example of Jesus our Master teaches us: "The good shepherd lays down his life for his sheep." It is due to them because their dedication touches the summit of charity, as again Christ Himself admonishes us: "Greater love than this no one has, that one lay down his life for his friends."
>
> Our encouragement is due to the pastors of souls, to the bishops and the pastors especially, and to all others who are dedicated to pastoral cares, because We know under what conditions they labor today. The spiritual

---

[10] *Ibid.,* p. 574.

[11] John XXIII, *Discourse to the Apostolic Union of the Clergy on Priestly Vocations, AAS* 51 (1959), pp. 199–200.

state of the world today presents enormous difficulties, some of which were unknown until yesterday.

We know what apprehensions weigh so often on the heart of a bishop, what sufferings often afflict him, not only for the poverty of means even now so grave and mortifying, but because of the deafness of those who should hear his words, for the diffidence which surrounds him and isolates him, for the indifference and lack of respect which disturb his ministry and paralyze him. We know how many pastors and assistant pastors exercise the care of souls in vast and populated areas where the number, mentality, the exigencies of the inhabitants force them to unceasing and tiring labors. We also know how many priests must exercise their ministry in the hidden little towns, without companionship, without help and the comforts that would result from these.

Both the former and the latter often must live in dire economic conditions, often opposed and misunderstood and forced to live on their own resources. Their pay is only to find in the humble who surround them, in the sacred book of their prayers and in the tabernacle, the mystery of the Divine Presence.

We feel obliged to assure these dear and venerated brothers, overworked laborers of the Gospel, these modest and persevering ministers of the Church of God, that the Pope thinks of them, understands them, esteems them, assists them, loves them, and therefore follows them with his prayers and blessings.[12]

On December 24, 1965, the Pope, in a brief talk to a group of newly-ordained American priests who are students at Rome's North American College, said:

We are happy to welcome you here today because you, as newly ordained priests, are a cause of much joy and satisfaction. The fields are white for the harvest, and you will be precious new workers to reap the harvest of God's graces.

These are challenging days for your ministry. The world has changed and you will have to bring the message of Christ to a troubled, searching, and seemingly confused society. You have studied in Rome during the Second Vatican Council which has given us the Decree on the Priestly Ministry. According to this important document "the purpose which priests pursue in their ministry and by their life is to procure the glory of God the Father in Christ. That glory consists of this — that men working freely and with a grateful spirit receive the work of God made perfect in Christ and then manifest it in their whole lives." Study this document well, and make every effort to make it the touchstone of your ministry to the People of God. Your stay in Rome has produced a special affection for the Church, and we are confident that you will be worthy stewards of the Gospel and ministers of the word. Have courage; have faith; give yourselves whole-heartedly to the task at hand and your fruits will be rich.[13]

Several of the decrees of Vatican Council II also provide some interesting and helpful insights into the nature and function of the priesthood and

---

[12] Paul VI, *Address to the 13th Pastoral Up-dating Week*, AAS 55 (1963), pp. 753–754.

[13] Paul VI, *A Talk to a Group of Newly-ordained American Priests Who Are Students at Rome's North American College*, Documentary Service, N.C.W.C. (1965).

the pastoral ministry. Thus, in that portion of the Decree on Priestly Training in which the Fathers of the Council discuss the importance of a careful development of the spiritual training of future priests, they clearly
point out that the students must be so saturated with the Mystery of the
Church that they will readily learn to take part with a generous heart in
the life of the whole Church, and understand most clearly, "that they are
not destined for domination or for honors, but are given over totally to
the service of God and to the pastoral ministry."[14]

This same document also points out that the seminarian and consequently the priest must be deeply concerned about the pastoral ministry,
and have a thorough knowledge of those matters which are connected
to the pastoral ministry. These are, of course, catechetics, preaching,
liturgical worship, the administration of the sacraments, works of charity,
assisting the erring and unbelieving, and other pastoral functions. It also
urges that clerics be capable of directing souls so that they will be able
to bring the faithful first of all to a fully conscious and apostolic life, and
secondly to the fulfillment of the duties of their state in life. The decree
also encourages priests to help religious men and women so that they
will persevere in their vocation and make progress in accord with the
spirit of their various institutes.[15]

Of the conciliar documents which stress the importance of the pastoral
ministry, the *Decree on the Priestly Ministry,* promulgated on December
17, 1965, is an extremely valuable document for those who will carry on
the work of pastoral theology in future years. For, this decree, as the
preface clearly states, ". . . applies to all priests, especially those devoted
to the care of souls, . . . in order that their ministry be carried on more
effectively and their lives be better provided for, in pastoral and human
circumstances which very often change so profoundly. . . ."[16]

Chapters I and II are of special interest to those concerned with the
care of souls. In Chapter I, the Council Fathers treat in considerable detail the office of priests, pointing out that "The purpose, therefore, which
priests pursue in their ministry and by their life is the glory of God the
Father in Christ." They also observe that:

> Priests of the New Testament, by their vocation and ordination, are in
> a certain sense set apart in the bosom of the People of God. However,
> they are not to be separated from the People of God or from any person;
> but they are to be totally dedicated to the work for which the Lord has
> chosen them. They cannot be ministers of Christ unless they be witnesses
> and dispensers of a life other than earthly life. But they cannot be of service
> to men if they remain strangers to the life and conditions of men. Their

---

[14] Vatican Council II, *Decree on Priestly Training* (trans. N.C.W.C.), p. 7.
[15] *Ibid.,* p. 14.
[16] Vatican Council II, *Decree on the Priestly Ministry* (trans. N.C.W.C. News
Service), p. 1.

ministry itself, by a special title, forbids that they be conformed to this world; yet at the same time it requires that they live in this world among men. They are to live as good shepherds that know their sheep, and they are to seek to lead those who are not of this sheepfold that they, too, may hear the voice of Christ, so that there might be one fold and one shepherd.[17]

In Chapter II the Council Fathers turn their attention to the ministry of priests and discuss the various priestly functions, the priests' relationships with others and the distribution of priests and vocations to the priesthood.

However, for priests laboring in the various apostolates, Chapter III seems to be the most important chapter of the document, for in this chapter, under section three — "Aids for the Life of Priests" — the Fathers of Vatican II urge priests to continue their studies and to acquire more comprehensive pastoral knowledge:

> Priests are admonished by their bishop in the sacred rite of ordination that they "be mature in knowledge" and that their doctrine be "spiritual medicine for the People of God." The knowledge of the sacred minister ought to be sacred because it is drawn from the sacred source and directed to a sacred goal. Especially it is drawn from reading and meditating on the Sacred Scriptures, and it is equally nourished by the study of the Holy Fathers and other Doctors and monuments of tradition. In order, moreover, that they may give apt answers to questions posed by men of this age, it is necessary for priests to know well the doctrines of the magisterium and the councils and documents of the Roman pontiffs and to consult the best of prudent writers of theological science.[18]

The Council Fathers then point out that inasmuch as there has been considerable progress in both the theological sciences and human culture in the present age, priests should continue to perfect their knowledge of divine things and human affairs in a suitable manner. By so doing, they will be better prepared to enter into dialogue with their contemporaries. On this point, they make the following recommendation:

> Therefore let priests more readily study and effectively learn the methods of evangelization and the apostolate. Let opportune aids be prepared with all care, such as the institution of courses and meetings according to territorial conditions, the erection of centers of pastoral studies, the establishment of libraries, and the qualified supervision of studies by suitable persons. Moreover, let bishops, either individually or united in groups, see to it that all their priests at established intervals, especially a few years after their ordination, may be able to frequent courses in which they will be given the opportunity to acquire a fuller knowledge of pastoral methods and theological science, both in order that they may strengthen their spiritual life and mutually communicate their apostolic experiences with their brothers. New pastors and those who have newly begun pastoral work, as well

---

[17] *Ibid.*, p. 2.
[18] *Ibid.*, p. 17.

as those who are sent to other dioceses or nations, should be helped by these and other suitable means with special care.[19]

The *Decree on the Adaptation and Renewal of the Religious Life* contains several points that are of interest to priests charged with the care of souls. This decree recognizes that while some religious institutes are entirely dedicated to contemplation, many others, both clerical and lay, devote themselves to apostolic tasks. The Council Fathers remind the active communities that they have received many and various gifts according to the grace which has been given to them, to carry out these tasks. They also state quite clearly that apostolic and charitable activity belongs to the very nature of religious life, because it is a holy service and a work characteristic of love, which has been given to them by the Church to be carried out in its own name. Consequently, they observe, ". . . the whole religious life of their members should be inspired by an apostolic spirit and all their apostolic activity formed by the spirit of religion."[20]

The various religious communities throughout the world are admonished to adjust their rules and customs so that they will better serve the apostolate to which they are dedicated. On this important point, the Fathers of Vatican II observe that "The fact however that apostolic religious life takes on many forms requires that its adaptation and renewal take account of this diversity and provide that the lives of Religious dedicated to the service of Christ in these various communities be sustained by special provisions appropriate to each."[21]

At a much later point in the document, the authors also point out that religious communities must continue to maintain and fulfill the ministries proper to them. They also encourage the various religious communities, after due consideration of the needs of the universal Church and individual dioceses, to adapt themselves to the requirements of time and place and to employ appropriate and even new programs that are relevant to the spirit and authentic nature of the community. They are advised to abandon those that are less relevant.[22]

In this decree, the Council Fathers also remind religious communities of the necessity of preserving the missionary spirit, and admonish them that it should be adapted according to the nature of each community, and to modern conditions so that the preaching of the Gospel can be carried out more effectively in every nation.[23]

Two other decrees must also be mentioned, for while they are not directly concerned with priestly training or priestly life, they are of con-

---

[19] *Ibid.,* p. 17.
[20] Vatican Council II, *Decree on the Adaptation and Renewal of the Religious Life,* (trans. N.C.W.C. News Service), p. 4.
[21] *Ibid.,* p. 4.
[22] *Ibid.,* p. 9.
[23] *Ibid.,* p. 9.

siderable value to a more complete understanding of the pastoral ministry. The first of these decrees is the *Decree on the Apostolate of the Laity;* the second is the *Decree on Pastoral Office of Bishops.* The first of these two decrees is important because as the lay apostolate grows, more and more priests will be needed to assist in every way possible laymen engaged in various apostolic works. The second of the two decrees derives its importance from the fact that it is precisely the bishop who must bear the full burden of the care of souls, and who must direct the training of both seminarians and priests who will assist him in this work.

In the *Decree on the Apostolate of the Laity,* the Vatican Council reminds bishops, pastors of parishes, and other priests of both branches of the clergy to bear in mind that all of the faithful have a part in the apostolate, and that the laity have their own roles in building up the Church. Therefore, say the Fathers, all priests should work fraternally with the laity in and for the Church, and take special care of them in these apostolic works.[24] However, they also recommend that bishops select and train suitable priests who are capable of promoting particular forms of the apostolate of the laity for this important work.

In this same decree, the Council reminds those who are engaged in this ministry that they represent the hierarchy in their pastoral activity, and should, therefore, always adhere faithfully to the spirit and teaching of the Church, and promote proper relations between the laity and the hierarchy. These same priests are also admonished to devote themselves to nourishing the spiritual life and an apostolic attitude in the Catholic societies entrusted to them. The Fathers also remind priests associated with the laity in apostolic work to contribute their wise counsel to the apostolic activity of these associations and promote their undertakings, and, through continuous dialogue, determine which forms make apostolic activity more fruitful, while continually striving to promote the spirit of unity within the association as well as between it and others.[25]

Since many of the pastoral duties of bishops must of necessity be delegated to priests of both branches of the clergy who "to the best of their ability assume the bishops' anxieties and carry them on day by day so zealously,"[26] it will be of value to list briefly the various duties that have been ascribed to diocesan bishops in the *Decree on the Pastoral Office of Bishops.* In Chapter II, under the title "Diocesan bishops," the Fathers of Vatican II admonish those bishops "who have been entrusted with the care of a particular church — under the authority of the supreme pontiff —" to:

[24] Vatican Council II, *Decree on the Apostolate of the Laity* (trans. N.C.W.C. News Service), p. 15.

[25] *Ibid.,* p. 16.

[26] Vatican Council II, *The Decree on the Pastoral Office of Bishops* (trans. N.C.W.C. News Service), p. 6.

1. Dedicate themselves to their apostolic office as witnesses of Christ before all men.
2. Exercise the duty of teaching, which is one of their principal duties, and present Christian doctrine in a manner adapted to the needs of the times.
3. Seek out men and both request and promote dialogue with them, since it is the mission of the Church to converse with the human society in which it lives.
4. Make use of the various media available at the present time for proclaiming Christian doctrine. These media include preaching and catechetical instruction, presentation of Christian doctrine in schools, academies, conferences, and meetings of every kind, and the dissemination of Christian doctrine through public statements at public events and through the press and various other media of communication.
5. Take care that catechetical instruction is given with sedulous care to both children and adolescents, youth and adults.
6. See that catechists are properly trained for their work.
7. Develop new and better ways of instructing adult catechumens.
8. Remember that they are the principal dispensers of the mysteries of God, as well as the governors, promoters, and guardians of the entire liturgical life in the diocese, with the responsibility to promote liturgical practices among the people.
9. Foster holiness among their clerics, religious, and laity, according to the special vocation of each.
10. Stand in the midst of their people as those who serve.
11. Strive to become duly acquainted with the needs of the people in the social circumstances in which they live, so that they can better look to the welfare of the faithful according to the conditions of each one.
12. Deal lovingly and kindly with the separated brethren and encourage the faithful to conduct themselves toward them with great kindness and charity.
13. Foster ecumenism as it is understood by the Church.
14. Have a place in their hearts for the non-baptized.
15. Encourage various forms of the apostolate, and foster the coordination and close connection of all apostolic works in the whole diocese or in any particular area of it.
16. Encourage the laity to assume their duty in carrying on the apostolate.
17. Adopt forms of the apostolate that meet the needs of the present day with regard not only for man's spiritual and moral circumstances but also for his social, demographic, and economic conditions.

18. Show special concern for those Catholics who because of their way of life cannot sufficiently make use of the common and ordinary pastoral care of parish priests or are quite cut off from it — the majority of migrants, exiles and refugees, seafarers, air travelers, gypsies and others of this kind, and those who go to other lands for a time for the sake of recreation.

19. Have regard to the social and civic progress and prosperity of the faithful.

20. Be solicitous for the spiritual, intellectual, and material welfare of priests, and pursue those who are involved in any danger or who have failed in certain respects.[27]

From all that has been said above, it becomes immediately evident that the mission of every priest actively engaged in pastoral work is to carry out the exalted ministry of Jesus Christ by laboring zealously for the salvation of souls. But, if the priest of today and tomorrow is to become effectively involved in that "dialogue with the world," which has been much discussed ever since Pope John XXIII first announced that he planned to call an ecumenical council, then seminarians and priests must continually strive, through formal and informal study, to prepare themselves most adequately for that portion of the apostolate in which they will be assigned to labor. In other words, it should be the primary goal of every cleric to continually prepare himself for effective leadership in the Church's ministry in the world.

Though it is quite true that this priestly ministering must be firmly based in the biblical, theological, and historical witness of the Church, nevertheless, the pastoral ministry can only be made proficient and effective by the careful development of the ministering arts both during the years of seminary training and in the years immediately after ordination. In this regard, perhaps, the efforts at renewal and reform that are taking place in our seminaries and the development of various pastoral programs — workshops, institutes, summer sessions, etc. — for priests already actively engaged in some phase of pastoral work, are two of the great blessings of the *"aggiornamento"* inaugurated under the guidance of the spirit of love by Pope John XXIII of happy memory.

---

[27] *Ibid.*, pp. 4–7.

2

The Proper and Fruitful Celebration
of the Sacred Liturgy

ROY FRANCIS AIKEN

THE AIM AND PURPOSE OF THE PASTORAL MINISTRY IS THE SANCTIFICATION of those whom God has chosen and called apart. The ordinary means of accomplishing this is through the sacred liturgy. To say this is to classify every other means as extraordinary, as being beyond or out of the common method of achieving holiness. The main concern, then, of the pastor, or indeed of all those who are involved in pastoral work, should be the proper and fruitful celebration of the sacred liturgy.

The most remarkable impetus has been given to this all-important work by Vatican II in its *Constitution on the Sacred Liturgy,* promulgated by Pope Paul VI on December 4, 1963, almost three years ago. To say that there is much still to be done in implementing the provisions of this decree is to put it mildly indeed. We have done fairly well, I think, in what might be called the mechanics of liturgy — in getting people to stand or sit at certain designated times, in having them recite the Gloria, the Creed, and make other responses from time to time and — indeed miracle of miracles! — even in getting them to sing occasionally! But it is going to take a very long time to reorient our people so thoroughly that there will be real depth underlying what they do at the sacred functions.

This reorientation, if it is to have maximum effect, must proceed along all lines. The whole structure of the parish must be reorganized to focus on the liturgy — its devotional life, the teaching of religion both in the parish school and in the Confraternity classes, all phases of parish work — everything — must be thoroughly integrated with the liturgy for, as the *Constitution on the Sacred Liturgy* tells us, this "is the summit toward which the activity of the Church is directed."[1] A halfhearted commitment to the proper celebration of the liturgy and to liturgically related practices in every phase of parish life will not be sufficient. It must be a complete and total commitment. In this way, through the years to come, we will develop depth and maturity in our understanding of what it is that we do at the sacred functions. It is extremely unfortunate that such an understanding is in so large a measure lacking at the present time.

The permission to use the vernacular and for the people to assume their proper role at Mass had been so eagerly awaited and, when it finally came, was so gratefully received that I am afraid we all rushed into it rather haphazardly. Some seem to think that the job is complete when we have the people making the responses and perhaps singing a few hymns. These are but the outward manifestations of liturgical worship and if all this is to mean anything and bear fruit in a more fervent and intelligent Christian life, "it is necessary that the faithful come to it with proper dispositions, that their minds should be attuned to their voices, and that they should cooperate with divine grace lest they receive it in vain."[2] This involves a vast amount of study and reflection on the part of both priests and people. That we are all so unprepared is not altogether our fault.

Our limited purpose here will be to consider the liturgical functions in the normal parish church, not as they might be in the larger and more complicated structures, in great cathedrals and basilicas; and not as they might be in places that have the advantage of cultivated and professional musicians and choirs. We will deal with the Low Mass as it might be celebrated in anyone's parish church. Without pretensions to liturgical scholarship, but with nearly a score of years in the pastoral ministry, I would like to make a few observations.

Efforts are being made now to make a clear separation between the Service of the Word and the Eucharistic part of the Mass. Good beginnings have been made in this area but I am afraid that we are not going to achieve the proper distinction until the Mass structure is revised. Perhaps this revision could proceed somewhat along the following lines.

The priest should not in the fore-Mass be clothed in Eucharistic vestments. In cassock, surplice, and stole he should enter the church in procession through the main body of the building. During this time the choir and congregation, the celebrant and those with him in the procession, should sing the entrance hymn or psalm. On entering the sanctuary,

---

[1] *Constitution on the Sacred Liturgy*, p. 10.
[2] *Ibid.*, p. 11.

after making the proper reverence, the celebrant should go to his chair. The hymn or psalm should be concluded at the first convenient place. The priest then begins the "Lord have mercy" to which all others respond. Next he leads in the *Gloria*. After greeting the people he prays in clear and measured tones the prayer of the Mass. There should almost invariably be but one prayer here. Perhaps once in a great while, in the time of clear and imminent tragedy or catastrophe, one other could be added for a brief time. The celebrant and congregation then seat themselves while someone reads the first Scripture lesson. This should be done by someone in the sanctuary vested in cassock and surplice.

I have not said anything up to now about the commentator. I know this is an "in" thing at the present time but, even so, one must be courageous and I am going to be bold enough to say that I do not like the commentator. I have never seen it done really well anywhere. The commentator, though I know that he has been given a true liturgical role, officially recognized, still strikes me as something artificial and extraneous to the celebration of Mass. Liturgical worship should be a free and spontaneous interplay between the celebrant and the people. The sacred functions must never appear as something that must be directed or explained. If this is the case, then there is something wrong with the way in which we are celebrating the sacred mysteries. The worship of God should never be theatrical, nor should it ever have any of the characteristics of a stunt. We should not have to be coached when we assemble for the worship of God. God's holy people gathered in their Father's house to do him honor should do so, each in his own place, with spontaneous dignity. A very large proportion of our people, I think, share these sentiments. Except for an elite few whom I have met at various liturgical gatherings, I have never met a layman who thought the commentator was anything but an unnecessary distraction.

As I have said, it is desirable to have someone other than the celebrant read the Epistle. This should be someone who can read well in public, one who can give the reading the proper inflections and emphasis. And as I have mentioned, he should be vested in cassock and surplice. It is indecorous to have a man standing at the lectern in the sanctuary, taking an important and official part before the liturgical assembly, wearing a business suit.

There should be an interlude between the Epistle and the Gospel. The Graduals, Tracts, Sequences, Alleluias that we now have are urgently in need of revision. Very often the few verses of the psalm do not make sense to the average man in the pew. Above all, the liturgy should be intelligible and thoroughly relevant. Many of our graduals and other interludes at this point do not fit these aims except perhaps to Scripture scholars and theologians who are thoroughly familiar with the context and need only a few words or phrases to bring to mind the intent and meaning of the whole passage. So often what is perfectly clear to such scholars is not at all clear to the man in the pew. Careful, even scrupulous, effort must be made not only here but all through the liturgy to use images, words, phrases, descriptions, etc., that can be immediately understood and appreciated by most people. The liturgy must never be only for the initiated, the elite few, but rather for the average man who constitutes the vast majority of the human race. If he cannot understand it, if he cannot grasp its symbolism, there is something wrong with it and it must be redone.

Why could we not develop these interludes along the line of responsorial reading by the people? They should be very brief, of course, but meaningful to every one, and should relate in some way to the readings and to the theme of the Mass. Perhaps a short psalm or hymn sung by the people would be desirable here. To have some moments of reflection at this point in the act of worship is surely a good tradition that should be preserved.

Now we come to the central feature, to the most sacred part, of the Service of the Word — the Gospel. Appropriately enough, this is read by the priest. Surely it is hardly necessary to point out that this should be read with the gravity and dignity that befits the very words of Christ. It should be a very good practice to have a lectionary, suitably bound and tastefully decorated, left permanently at the lectern or ambo, certainly at the ambo where there is one.

This might be the proper place in our discussion to bring up the whole matter of the lecterns. The current thought seems to prefer but one, in order to emphasize the unity of the word. I am not in total agreement with this. Two seem more appropriate to me. I do not think that this would sacrifice the symbol of unity. While it is important to stress the oneness of the Sacred Scriptures, it is also desirable to safeguard the unique character and dignity of the Gospels. The ancient tradition assigns to the Gospels a primacy of honor. This could be secured by employing an ambo where only the Gospel is proclaimed and the homily, which is ideally an extension of the Gospel, is given. Nothing else should take place there. Anything else should be done at the lectern on the opposite side of the sanctuary.

Perhaps a word should be said here about the responses at the end of both readings. Frankly, I find them very awkward and I think they should be dropped altogether. I don't see how it will be possible ever to get whole congregations to say them in unison or in any meaningful way. Even with the immediate assistants at the altar they seldom come out well. Let us hope that they will be eliminated in time.

Announcements or whatever else should be said apart from the homily should be taken care of before the procession enters the church. Better still, it could all be put in a weekly bulletin or parish newspaper or newsletter. Certainly there should be no interval between the Gospel and the homily. The homily should flow naturally from what has been read. Reading long discourses at Mass does not achieve the desired results and certainly they should never take the place of the homily. Other ways must be found to communicate letters, instructions, and the like, to the people.

The homily, as I have said, should flow naturally from the Gospel. Perhaps on occasion it could be taken from the Epistle or some other portion of the Scriptures. It would be preferable, when possible, to bring both readings into the homily in some sort of organic unity.

We Catholics are emphasizing these days the power of the Word of God as contained in the Scriptures. But, unfortunately, we have yet to go on from there to see and appreciate the importance of the preached word. The homily is an important and integral part of the fore-Mass. It should have power, it should say something relevant and specific to man and his present needs. It should be substantial fare. Many homilies that I have heard and some that I have read have been little more than innocuous drivel. Surely it should never be this.

How long should the homily be? It is hard to give a definitive answer to this question. It all depends. Perhaps on formal occasions it would run a little long. But ordinarily in the usual parish church, on a typical Sunday, ten or fifteen minutes would be ample; hardly ever more than this. Yet, on the other hand, we might ask ourselves why we are always so time conscious in regard to the Mass. This seems to be a peculiarly Catholic problem. Our Protestant friends do not seem to be bothered by it. Why should it assume such proportions with us?

I think probably there are a number of reasons for this. One undoubtedly is the silent Latin Mass that was in vogue for so long. The congregation, for the most part, had come merely to witness the Mass. They were spectators at something the priest was doing and all too often he was doing it very quickly. Everything was very mechanical. It was difficult to feel really involved and many people were only physically present there in obedience to a law. Another reason is the crowded schedule on Sunday morning. Now that Mass can be celebrated at any time it seems hardly necessary to press all Masses into the few hours on Sunday morning. Why not spread them out through the day? No doubt there are many other reasons that we haven't time to go into here. But I am sure that as our understanding of the Mass deepens we will not be so preoccupied with time but will consider the forty-five or fifty minutes little enough to give to God once in a week.

Immediately after the homily the priest should lead the congregation in the profession of faith. I would like to suggest that in place of the Nicene Creed we adopt the Apostles' Creed. The former is much too theological and polemical while the latter is simple and forthright, admirably suited for public worship. The priest could remain at the ambo after the homily and lead the assembly in the creed, or return to his chair and lead from there.

After the creed, the priest greets the people and then leads them in the prayer of the faithful, or the bidding prayers, or the general prayer of the Church, whatever one wishes to call them. These should be short and to the point and, above all, we should resist the tendency to add to them. Four or five petitions would seem to be adequate most of the time. These prayers, in the Mass arrangement that I am suggesting, would take the place of the present offertory prayers, which should be eliminated altogether.

The prayer of the faithful as we now have it, tacked on to the existing structure of the Mass, is very unsatisfactory. Moreover, many of the prayers are repetitious. There is already a place in the Mass for the pope and the bishop, for the faithful and the deceased. Why bring these in again? There is a growing tendency to add to these prayers and, at least in the present Mass structure, I think this bears all the earmarks of a nascent abuse which, as we know so well from past experience, once it develops, will be extremely difficult to correct. I would say, let us forego these prayers until the Mass is restructured, desirable as they may be.

Now that we have reached the end of the fore-Mass, or the Service of the Word, we are ready for the Eucharistic rite itself. A hymn should be sung at this point by the choir, the congregation, and most of the assistants at the altar. Meanwhile, the priest with one or two assistants retires to the sacristy, or to some other convenient place, to put on the eucharistic vestments. While the hymn is being sung and the celebrant is vesting, the ushers should take up the collection.

In my view, the collection represents the real offering of the people in these times. It is of their substance and, on very rare occasions and in some places, it might even represent a sacrifice on their part. This is what they wish to give for God's work. It should be an integral part of their act of worship. It is their portion given to the Lord. We have failed to give to the collection the spiritual dimension that it deserves and should have. We should begin to remedy this defect. The monetary contribution of the faithful can, and should, become for each of them a real religious act.

While the priest vests and the ushers take up the collection, someone prepares the altar. Nothing should be on the altar until now. The chalice, the ciboria, the missal are all arranged. The cruets and other appurtenances are put in their proper place.

After the priest has vested, he returns to the sanctuary, goes to the center. The hymn stops. The ushers now come forward with the baskets and place them on a table in the sanctuary. They remain there while the priest with an appropriate prayer asks God to accept the gifts. The ushers return to their places and the priest ascends the altar, simply asks God to accept the bread and the wine, and begins the preface.

I have said nothing about an offertory procession, or about anyone bringing up the altar breads or the cruets. I know this is another "in" thing. If one wishes to appear really avant garde, he must have someone bring these articles to the altar; preferably a well balanced group should do this, someone from each continent would be just the right composition. Frankly, this leaves me rather cold. It has about it the aura of a stunt, something that has been staged. Liturgical worship should be natural, honest, genuine. I cannot see that having a group of people bring the breads and the cruets to the altar, when this is not necessary, is anything but theatrical. I have discussed this with numerous lay people and have found that most of them share these views. The genuine offertory procession, in the context of these times, is the bringing to the altar the real gifts of the people, part of their own possessions which they have freely given over to God's work in the world.

Now to get back to the preface for just a further word. We should have more of them. This will tax our ingenuity but certainly we have enough competent people to compose them. And while we are at it, let us by all means revise the *Preface of the Holy Trinity*. This is entirely too theological and nonpastoral. It might be a very desirable reading for a classroom but it is hardly a meaningful prayer for public worship.

If any Latin is to be preserved in the Mass, surely the Canon is the place for it. For my part, I would like to see the whole Mass in the language of the people. The aim and purpose of the liturgy is to lift our minds and hearts to God in corporate prayer, through Christ, the unique mediator; to unite our human minds and hearts with his human mind and heart as he offers the supreme and eternal act of worship to God the Father under the signs and symbols of the Eucharistic sacrifice. This we were deputized to do, and constituted for, in the holy sacrament of baptism. How can we do this in any significant human way if we do not understand the signs and symbols, or the language, in which it is done? The liturgy, above all, must be intelligible, and not just to an elite, but to the average man in the pew. If he misses it, there is something wrong with it. Thank God we have come a long way toward making the sacred functions understandable and relevant. Thank God for so much of our own language! How could we really pray in any other? Can anyone honestly say that *Pater Noster* has as deep a meaning for him as *Our Father?*

Because of the vernacular and other revised forms, the Mass has a far deeper meaning to the people of this generation and to those yet to come than has been the case in many a century. In this connection I am reminded of an incident recorded by Father Bouyer as follows:

". . . dialog between Cranmer and Gardiner, held when both men were still orthodox Catholic priests. Cranmer said, 'How sad it is that the people in the nave of the church do not understand anything about what is being celebrated in the sanctuary!' And Gardiner answered, 'Don't worry about that, it has never occurred to them that they might want to understand it!' "[3]

Father Bouyer goes on to observe, "How distressing it is for us now to consider that it was the future heretic who had the more truly Catholic reaction!" Such a dialogue as that between Cranmer and Gardiner could not take place now. The language battle, and many others as well, has been won, but we must not rest. There must be a continuing effort to make the liturgy ever more meaningful. It must never again be allowed to become static but must be at all times a dynamic and invigorating force in the Christian life.

In any case, even if the Canon is to remain in Latin, let us hope that we will be permitted to say it aloud. Then let us read it slowly, deliberately, and with the proper voice inflections. The celebrant's actions, his voice, his manner — everything that he does at the altar — must manifest the faith that is in him, and this is no less true of the people in their places; the faith of the entire assembly must be revealed in its actions.

No one wishes to abolish or to change in any substantive way the present Canon. It has a cherished and venerable place. Nevertheless, there are a few excisions that should be made for pastoral reasons. The first of these should be the conclusions with an *amen* that inflict four of the prayers and disrupt the even flow of the thought. The Canon should be thought of as a single prayer, the prayer of consecration, and it should be brought to a glorious conclusion with the Great Amen fervently said by everyone in the church. Of all the responses this seems to be the most difficult for the people. Somehow they can't seem to remember it or don't give it the proper enthusiasm. Yet this is one of the most important of all their responses. I think one problem is the Latin Canon. They cannot follow or keep up with the priest. If they could hear him and understand what he says, the conclusion would mean more to them. They would be ready for the great act of faith.

Another excision that should be considered is in the two listings of saints. Many of these saints are unknown to most people. Even their feast days are no longer celebrated. They should be eliminated from the Canon and there should be left only those who have meaning for the

---

[3] Louis Bouyer, *Liturgical Piety* (Univ. of Notre Dame Press, 1957), p. 2.

universal Church such as the Blessed Mother, the Apostles, and St. John the Baptist.

The two elevations came about as a result of a theological controversy in the thirteenth century. This dispute, important enough at the time, has long since been settled and has no meaning for our time. The vestige of it that yet remains should be eliminated so that the Canon could end with the single elevation at the Great Doxology.

The multiplication of kisses and the signs of the cross should be done away with. So many of these are not pleasing to the senses; they are very awkward and lack dignity and grace. Perhaps the kiss at the *te igitur* could be left and the one at the end of Mass just before the Last Blessing. The sign of the cross should be used only where there is a real blessing involved. This would mean that it would be retained at the *"Benedicas"* in the *Te igitur,* at *"benedictam"* in *Quam oblationem,* at *"benedixit"* in the consecrations.

Following the Canon with its Great Amen, the Communion Service begins with the Lord's Prayer. This, by all means, should be retained. There is little that needs to be changed in this rite, in my opinion. However, there are one or two observations to be made in regard to the mechanics of receiving Communion. The custom now in many places is for the people to stand. Though this is surely the more ancient way, we must not fall into a trap. *Mediator Dei* roundly and emphatically condems what might be called "liturgical archaism."

> But ancient usage must not be esteemed more suitable and proper, either in its own right or in its significance for later times and new situations, on the simple ground that it carries the savor and aroma of antiquity. The more recent liturgical rites likewise deserve reverence and respect.[4]

In revising and formulating liturgical practices we must always first seek out the ancient forms but alongside these we must place current theological development, the thought patterns and customs of the people, then the ever present question, "Is this meaningful to people now?" It seems to me that nowadays, at least in this country, most of us do not consider standing as the proper posture for prayer, except in exceptional circumstances, and least of all is it considered appropriate for receiving Holy Communion. We almost instinctively kneel to pray in church. There is a very old tradition behind this attitude. At least I would regard as old something that has been in existence for well over 1100 years. The Council of Tours in 813 recognized this as the fundamental characteristic posture of the faithful. Since kneeling is thoroughly in accord with the standards of good liturgical practice, there would seem to be no reason for making a big issue out of getting everyone to stand while receiving Holy Communion.

---

4 Pius XII, *Mediator Dei,* p. 61.

There are many problems connected with administering Communion under both species. It is impossible to go into all these here. This could be the subject for another essay, but let us indicate a few of them. Such matters as safeguarding the reverence and dignity due the Sacred Species, hygiene, esthetics, and the difficulty in determining how much wine to consecrate and what to do with large quantities of it that might be left over, are far from extraneous. Moreover, there is the problem as to how both can be given to large numbers of people in a reasonable period of time. These matters must engage the immediate attention of liturgical scholars so that some practical solutions can be found.

The communion antiphon as we know it is hardly significant to most people. It would be better to have a good hymn or psalm sung by the entire congregation. This should begin right after the *Agnus Dei* and while the priest is saying his preparatory prayers. Sung all through the Communion, it should be terminated about the time the priest is finishing the ablutions. If one hymn or psalm is not sufficient, there is no reason why two cannot be sung at this point.

There should be a great variety of hymns for all parts of the Mass and for the different seasons of the year. Though much excellent work has been done in this field in recent years, we have yet to achieve the richness in variety that we so urgently need. The main concern should be pastoral; to get everyone — both priests and people — singing at all the Sunday Masses, not just at one or two of them, and indeed at every Mass every day when this is possible. These hymns and psalms should be brought together in one volume. The books now available, the result of an admirable effort to produce in one place all the prayers and hymns that will ever be needed in church, good as they are, are not the ultimate solution to the problem. The psalms and hymns that we need are too numerous, too vast in their variety, to be combined with all the other liturgical functions. Better to have two books, a hymnal and the other with the Masses and other prayers.

Following the ablutions, the priest says the Postcommunion prayer, greets the people, says the *Placeat* — aloud and in the vernacular! — then gives the blessing. The celebrant and his assistants, after the proper reverence, go out through the main body of the church while the entire congregation, the priest and those in procession with him, all sing a recessional hymn.

We have all rejoiced in the extensive use of our own language in the Mass and the sacraments. But for many of us I am sure that our joy is not full because of the poor quality of the English used. This is a very serious defect and should be corrected at the earliest possible moment. The worship of God deserves nothing less than the very best literary efforts. The language should never be trite, commonplace, colloquial, but should be elegant, inspiring, uplifting. Translations that we now have are far from this. It is obvious that the rather considerable literary talent within the Church was not tapped for these texts. This is particularly true, and glaringly so, of the Epistles and Gospels. Certainly the Scripture scholars who worked on the New Confraternity Version are extremely competent men in their fields and they may have succeeded in rendering one of the most accurate translations, but this is not sufficient for the proclamation of God's word in church. A clear distinction must be made between private reading in one's home and public reading as part of the act of worship. What might be perfectly satisfactory for the one need not be at all suitable for the other.

Before I leave this commentary on the Mass, let me say one further word about the homily. I have said previously that I thought it should be substantial fare, hard-hitting, relevant. The Gospels, and other portions of Scripture as well, should be related to the times in which we are actually living and to the problems that we are facing. The homily should come to grips with the realities of the latter half of the twentieth century. Such problems as civil rights and, indeed, of every form of social justice should occupy our attention in the pulpit as well as problems of nuclear war, poverty, and the continuing effort so to renovate the city of man that it might become a truer reflection of the city of God. This involves a principle that should become firmly established, namely, freedom of the pulpit. This does not mean freedom to depart from the norms of Christian doctrine proposed to us by the infallible teaching authority of the Church or of the magisterium but rather freedom of the priest, within this framework, to bring to bear on the issues of the day the results of his prayerful study and reflection. It should be expected that he would have some contribution to make toward the solution of these perplexing problems. Can we afford not to seek the answers wherever they might be found?

While it is, of course, perfectly true that the priest must be loyal to the ecclesiastical authority, it must also be borne in mind that he has not ceased to be an individual human person with ideals and ideas; that he should have the liberty to express his Christian commitment in his own personal way along with every other Christian; that he not only may, but should, address himself to the crucial problems of these disturbed times. Ecclesiastical authority should recognize this and, apart from well defined doctrine and the teachings of the magisterium, the priest should have the same rights as those cherished by any other free man. The laity who are now demanding so much freedom for themselves, and rightly so, should expect and encourage the same for their priests.

There is one other problem begging for attention. The *ordo* too frequently calls for repeating the Sunday Mass on weekdays. In my opinion, this should never be done. It is indicative of a poverty that does not exist. It is only that we have not used the wealth that is available to us. We have, as I have mentioned elsewhere, plenty of people with the competence, the imagination, the ingenuity to provide the vast variety and richness that we urgently need in the ferial Masses. This not only can be done; it should be done.

We should celebrate only those saints who have meaning for the universal Church. Those whose lives and works have only a local or national relevance should be observed only in those places. Why would it not be a very good plan to have one feast during the year for each category of saint? For instance, one day could be set aside as the feast of the holy martyrs. All of them could be commemorated in this one Mass except, of course, the Apostles who deserve their own day. The same could be done for confessors, doctors, and other classes. All other Masses would be ferial but each would be distinctive and individual.

As one who has had the benefit of many years of pastoral experience, I have dealt quite frankly with what I would like to see in the Mass of the future. That some revision is necessary is admitted by all. Indeed a commission already is working on the restructuring of the Mass. Let us hope that we might have the benefit of their work realized in our time.

Now to turn our attention very briefly to the sacraments. There is not space, unfortunately, to go into this matter in any detail but only to point out one or two of the most urgent needs.

First of all, in the sacrament of baptism let us cut out the disturbing reference to the little child, or indeed to anyone, as having been held in the "snares of Satan." Surely this is an affront to the innocent child lying before us. I am embarrassed when in the exorcism I have to treat the child as though he were possessed of the devil. When these prayers were in Latin, perhaps it did not matter so much, because so few understood what was being said, but now that the language barrier has been removed, there is all the more reason to eliminate the objectionable references. Moreover, such thoughts are repugnant to our sensibilities and irrelevant to our times. They would, of course, be perfectly in order in cases of true possession but certainly not in regard to a newborn baby.

Another problem that we should confront honestly and realistically is the putrid water that we have to use. Why can we not use fresh water? This would be much more symbolic of the effects of the sacrament. This is so obviously the way to do it that it is very difficult to understand why the change has not been made.

Much thought should be given to the sacrament of penance by liturgical scholars and theologians. Here is an area that is in urgent need of profound study, reevaluation, and reorientation. For instance, our simplistic understanding of sin as simply an infraction of the laws of God or of the Church does not seem to be adequate for these times. Sin should be seen in a much broader and more positive context, such as love and its effects in the Mystical Body. This is far more satisfying and appealing. These studies should be correlated with the findings of modern psychology and psychiatry. These sciences have much to tell us about human acts that should be taken into account when trying to assess the morality of an action. But this would be the subject for another essay.

Getting back to the pastoral aspects of going to confession, let me say that, by all means, I hope we will soon have a new formula for absolution. The one now in use is much too juridical, too wordy, and out of step with current thinking. Why not the simple words, readily grasped by everyone, "I absolve you from your sins, in the name of the Father, and of the Son, and of the Holy Spirit." Need anything else be said?

The act of going to confession has become much too mechanical for all of us. This is probably inevitable in view of the large numbers of people receiving the sacrament and the necessity of adhering to some sort of schedule. But it is one of the problems that deserves our attention. I know of one parish in which three priests heard confessions for a total of twenty-nine hours on the 23rd and 24th of December. Though there was plenty of good will on the part of all, I wonder if any of us can say that the maximum benefit was received. In other words, did the sacrament do for these people all that it could do? There is no question here, of course, of the validity of the sacrament but only of its possibilities. Confessions should be made in a more relaxed situation, free from external pressures, and in a more comfortable place. Why do confessionals have to be so unmindful of such ordinary human comforts as light, air, and space?

Should not the whole matter of confessions of devotion be looked into very carefully? Would it not instead be better to have more time for personal counseling? Some have said that we should counsel in the confessional, that we should take time to do this even though there are a number of others waiting in line outside. I could not disagree with this more. The confessional is no place, in my opinion, for counseling. It is, as I indicated previously, too uncomfortable. There must be comfortable and relaxed surroundings for such important consultations. How and where should this be done? Perhaps there should be an office somewhere in the church, small but attractively furnished, that is used exclusively for this purpose. If this is not possible or practical, perhaps a suitable arrangement could be made in the rectory, though this seems to me to be the least desirable of all places. We should look toward some time in the future to separating the priest's official work from his living quarters. There should be a distinct division here. In view of this, I would not advocate setting up counseling services in the rectory unless this is a last resort. Where there is a school, an office might be set up there. In any case, we should be more conscious of the value of personal counseling, and we should find some way of providing time and space for it.

All priests, but especially those who are destined for pastoral work, should receive special training in the seminary in the art of counseling. This would fit in very well and, indeed, should become a major part of our studies in moral and pastoral theology. I know there are all sorts of suggestions being made these days as to what should be added to the seminary curriculum but surely everyone will agree that for those who are going to work in parishes the art of counseling should be a necessary requirement. The priest himself should be fitted for this kind of work. He should have a real interest in people and their problems. He should have sufficient leisure to enable him to get the proper rest and relaxation so that he can enter into this demanding and perplexing work with the calmness and patience that are necessary. Many priests are caught up in a welter of all sorts of activities so that there is often little time to think of and care for his own humanity. In these circumstances, pressures build up that have a deleterious effect on his own personality. This should be avoided.

Let us get back to the problems of confessions of devotion. This is an area in which the thought and study of theologians and liturgical scholars are urgently needed. Sometimes many hours in the course of a week are spent just hearing children's confessions and those of religious. Then there are the inevitable schedules for confessions in every church. Can we not, without emotion or sentimentality, look into this matter to see if we are doing with it the very best that can be done? Is there not another way that would be more beneficial to everyone, more human, more in accord with what we now know about the vast complexity of the human mind and heart? Is not the present method too juridical, too cut-and-dried, too matter-of-fact, too streamlined, too much like a slot machine?

The chief work in every parish should be the reverent and fitting celebration of the sacred liturgy by both priests and people. The Mass and the sacraments are the center around which all the activities of the Church are directed, as we have learned so well from the *Constitution on the Sacred Liturgy*. Every liturgical celebration should be a profound experience for everyone who assists at it. We should all come away from it with much the same feeling that Peter and James and John must have had as they came down from Mount Tabor and with them we should be able to say, "Lord, it is good for us to be here!"

3

Architecture, the Architect, and the Priest

EUGENE F. KENNEDY, JR., F.A.I.A., A.N.A.

AND WHEN CHURCHES ARE TO BE BUILT, LET GREAT CARE BE TAKEN THAT they be suitable for the celebration of liturgical services and for the active participation of the people. — *Constitution on the Liturgy*

In the course of his priestly life, the cleric frequently comes into contact with men and women of the various professions. Some of these professional people, he may contact for purely personal reasons. Others, he may contact for both personal and apostolic reasons. When a priest contacts his physician or his lawyer regarding personal matters, few others are even indirectly affected. But, when he discusses a medico-moral problem with an obstetrician, a robbery case with a criminal lawyer, a school problem with an educator, or a community problem with local government leaders, the consequences of the discussion may have far-reaching effects touching the lives and activities of many others. Since a priest rarely engages an architect for personal reasons, it is almost certain that this relationship will have far-reaching and lost-lasting effects upon himself, his parishioners, his neighbors, and his entire community. His choice of a painting or a piece of sculpture need never be seen, or, at the worst may be avoided; his choice of music need offend only his own ears, but his influence upon the church he builds, the school he erects, the convent, rectory, or parish center he establishes will ultimately delight or distress him and everyone about him. A piece of architecture, like a Mt. Everest, is there for all to see in its felicitous distinction or its awful embarrassment; an enduring monument to his wisdom or to his folly.

Even the umbrageous charity of nature may, in the course of time, mitigate but will never fully conceal an architectural mistake.

As patrons of architecture, the Catholic bishop and the priest have been preeminent for more than a thousand years, and their reputations as builders of superb architecture have been questioned only in the past two centuries. Every building erected under their auspices is an enduring statement, though sometimes an inferior statement, of their aspirations and their influence. This statement must be made to be intelligent, meaningful, sacramental, and beautiful. This much, at the very least, we owe to the Church, to ourselves, our neighbors, and to God.

Architecture has been called an art, a science, and a profession. Separately these definitions are neither wholly correct nor entirely inaccurate; together they but hint at its complexity. It cannot be doubted that architecture is an art; indeed, it has long been known as the "Mother of the Arts." But architecture is even more than that, for among all of the fine arts it is the only one that is primarily utilitarian. Like painting and sculpture it is a visual art, but its quality depends as much on its practical functions as it does upon the excellence of its esthetic values. The most visually satisfactory building that fails to fulfill its intended function or comfortably to house its occupants becomes no more than stage scenery — a one-dimensional facade suitable only for a moving picture set. Nor does the soundest structure with the most perfect air-conditioning system add up to architecture if beauty of design is not an inherent part of it.

More than any other art, architecture reflects, and sometimes even influences, the attitudes and ideals of society. It mirrors the social customs, the cultural attainments, the spiritual values of its time and its milieu. Even now while it frantically searches for an ultimate and inevitable expression, giving us on the one hand the sleek, sheer, well-ordered rigidity of a Seagram Building, and on the other the brutesque, agitated, restless accumulation of concrete boxes of a La Tourette, it may unconsciously be reflecting the complexities and confusions of our own time.

The man who creates this art, the architect, differs from the painter, the sculptor, the musician, and the poet, not because he is less the artist, but because he is, at the same time, the practical technician, the master builder, the astute businessman. Since his is the single utilitarian art, he must maintain an equal allegiance to considerations of practicality and of beauty.

The practice of architecture involves inspired design, skilled planning, an understanding of sound economical construction and of structural, mechanical, and electrical engineering. It involves proficiency in the production of working plans and specifications and administration of construction; a familiarity with business practices, finance, and law. The practice of this complex art may theoretically be the work of a single individual, but it is more likely to be undertaken by a well-balanced team of experts, each especially proficient in one or more aspects of practice, whose skills are coordinated and balanced by the architect.

It follows that this creator, this architect, must combine many available talents since he must blend the ingredients of structure, function, and good design if the building he creates is to be considered a successful work of art. The architect must be endowed with — or otherwise have acquired — the ability to analyze and interpret the building problems of his client, for which he must possess the knowledge, training, experience, and ability to find the proper solutions. He must be able to develop buildings that will satisfy the functional requirements of these problems and provide, in addition, stable structures to enclose an atmosphere in which man may live, learn, and pray in inspiration and comfort — and, more often than not, within the confines of an all too limited budget. Moreover, all of this must be done to the end that the ultimate result will please the eye and elevate the spirit of the occupant and the beholder.

The architect alone, by virtue of his prolonged training, experience, and special ability, commands the disciplines and possesses the skills to achieve these goals. The priest, confronted with the task of selecting an architect to endow his proposed building with all the essential qualities of architecture, comes suddenly face to face with the first and most compelling of all his construction problems.

It should be unnecessary to state that all architects are not equally talented nor equally capable of creating outstanding architecture. Some are exceptionally able; others have an average proficiency; and some, unfortunately, are of very mediocre ability. This revelation should cause no astonishment; we are aware that similar patterns exist in all professions, all trades, all businesses, and in all arts. Nor should any client presume that he can, by virtue of his own force of personality, extract any kind of desired building from any architect. If you, as a client, admire the work of a Le Corbusier or a Frank Lloyd Wright, you will hardly be satisfied with the results emanating from the office of John Smith if John Smith is confirmed in the idea that all good architectural design was arrested following the completion of the last great Gothic cathedral.

How should an architect be selected? Occasionally, design competitions are held in which a number of architects are invited to submit their solutions to a particular problem. Such competitions for the purpose of selecting an architect or an architectural design are assured of validity only when the competition conforms to the rigid conditions laid down for such procedures by the American Institute of Architects. Competitions are admittedly somewhat unwieldy and time-consuming methods of selection generally employed in connection with the largest and more important architectural projects, but they have been instrumental in the discovery of great talents hitherto unrecognized.

More frequently, an architect is selected on the basis of his reputation and past performance. His buildings, and, if they exist, the ones that have encountered problems similar to the client's, should be examined with care. Is it a satisfyingly beautiful building? Is it pleasant to look at; to be in? Does it function as it should? Are its occupants comfortable within its atmosphere? Is it well built, or does it show signs of premature age or deterioration? Since selection of an architect is the priest's initial and the most vitally important step toward achieving his own building goals, he should spare neither effort nor time to see that he engages the best man for his particular job.

A word of caution may be indicated at this point to warn against selection based upon the amount of fee to be paid. Naturally enough, not all architects perform their professional services for the same fee schedule. It is appropriate, however, to point out that the architect who receives a fee of one or two percentage points higher than another may, by virtue of his greater natural ability and the additional time and effort he can afford to expend on study, research, and design, save his client many thousands of building dollars. It is quite possible to imagine that the architect employed because of his lower fee may ultimately prove to be the costlier professional.

Almost without exception, every satisfying building depends for its success upon the close, intimate teamwork of architect and client. Learning how to be a good client to your architect is a lesson that may ultimately reap innumerable benefits and great satisfaction. First of all, your architect must know what you have in mind for your building project. He must know your ideals and your goals. A written program of your ideas and objectives will be most beneficial in establishing the nature of the problems he must meet and solve, and the good architect may help by pointedly delving into the background for facets of information you may think can be taken for granted. You must be able to let him know not just what you need but what you like. Every human being is endowed with individual tastes, reactions, and prejudices but you should be prepared to see some of yours sacrificed for reasons of economy or because they are structurally, functionally, or esthetically wrong, or unsuitable, for the project. You must learn to listen to your architect and depend upon his judgment, his experience, and his talents, but you should demand to know why he is reluctant to follow certain suggestions, and why he advocates certain materials, certain structural principles, and certain designs. He, in turn, must rely upon you to acquaint him with all sides and shadings of the problem and, having selected him with care, you must have confidence in his ability to solve your building problem and create for you a structurally sound, a perfectly functioning and an esthetically beautiful building.

No building type destined for the service of humanity should summon more of man's ingenuity, studied consideration, and artistic inspiration than the church building, for it is also destined for the service of God. From the beginning of recorded history we know that man has expressed his dependence upon and his fear and love of God by lavishing upon his temples and his churches his greatest artistic talents and energies. For the glorification of his Creator he has been inspired to create outstanding monuments of his own genius. He has sought to make his place of worship an abode fitting for the God he hopes will abide there. The perfected elegance of the Grecian temple; the stately grandeur of the Roman temple, the resplendent glory of the Byzantine interior, and the aspiring sinews of the Gothic Cathedral are all witness to man's intense devotion to God. It is significantly true that the inspiration of the Christian idea has produced over the ages an art which is the proudest accomplishment of the human spirit. And it still endows the countenance of Europe with dignity and great beauty! Pope Pius XII, speaking to a group of artists and architects, paid tribute to these accomplishments when he said,

> . . . the great masters of Christian Art became interpreters, not only of beauty but also of the goodness of God, the Revealer and Redeemer. A marvelous exchange of services between Christianity and art! From their faith the artist drew sublime inspiration. They drew hearts to the Faith when for continuous centuries they communicated and spread the truths contained in the Holy Scripture, truths inaccessible, at least directly, to the humble people.

We need not believe this type of communication no longer necessary because of the sophistication of our present society.

It has been claimed that this idea and these ideals have vanished from the heart and the mind of modern man and he has now relinquished his affection for his place of worship and has bestowed it on his banks, his office buildings, and his clubs. This may be partially true and the appearance of modern office buildings, banks, and clubs may lend credence to this point of view. But I cannot imagine the priest who will not approach the task of building a church with eager ambition, lofty ideals, and anxious concern; nor the architect who will not be impelled to plumb the very limits of his ability when confronted with the responsibility to execute such a commission.

Of all building types the church is unique and very special. Not only is it a place where the community of the faithful may periodically meet for worship or where the Sacred Liturgy can be effectively celebrated, it is also a place which should teach Christian values in its own way and in its own language. The atmosphere within its walls should convey the import of the holy mysteries celebrated therein, and of the very transcendence of God. Much of the current literature pertaining to church buildings will extol the form and the functional "perfection" of certain new churches or the architect's singular solution of some of its problems; but it is exceedingly rare to read of the creation of this intangible spiritual atmosphere and, these days, it is rarer still to encounter it.

We are now in an age of great scientific achievement. The boundaries of structural possibilities for buildings of all kinds have expanded far beyond yesterday's limited horizon. We can now design buildings in virtually any shape or in any mold; whatever limitation still exists is formed only by the exigency of budget. Expanding scientific knowledge as well as the recent changes in the liturgy both suggest a reevaluation of the familiar architectural forms of the churches which are the heritage from our forefathers. Indeed, a continuing appraisal is dictated both by wisdom and history; wisdom, because we must never assume satisfaction with what we shall ever be inspired to do, and history which reminds us that at least one past structural discovery has already given us the glory of the Gothic. Yet, who among us will, despite the masterpieces of the past, dare to determine beyond all question that any past or present form or shape embodies the ideal expression of our faith; not just the most perfect that has yet been found, but the most perfect that can be created?

We need avoid but one pitfall lurking insidiously within the wealth of the new knowledge, materials, and systems we have fallen heir to. We must not allow ourselves to be misguidedly trapped into the conclusion that what is now structurally possible must now, therefore, be erected. The search for form cannot be made the excuse to show off flights of undisciplined imagination or to astound or shock by exhibiting our mastery of the gymnastic possibilities of concrete, steel, or laminated wood. Nor, in our enthusiasm for all that is new, should we neglect to further explore the possibilities still inherent in the very materials God himself has given us. We have but to look about in order to discover the seemingly endless variety of architectural form, shape, and expression man has already wrought with so simple a material as articulated stonework, for example; surely, we would demean all our potentialities were we now to assume that its possibilities have at last been exhausted. Particularly in the expression of our churches, it may be as valid for us to question occasionally whether or not everything that matters for us began the day before yesterday, as it is to inquire into the possibilities of what we shall receive tomorrow.

The development of the new liturgy will by its very nature dictate new dimensions to church design; our sanctuaries, at least, will never again look the same. It is not the intention of this chapter to suggest the ideal location for the altar, the tabernacle, the ambo, the celebrant's chair, or bishop's throne; time, trial, and experience will settle them all comfortably in their most ideally appointed places, and we shall have forgotten the consternation with which we initially faced the problem of disposing them. The more active participation of the faithful in the sacred ceremonies and the revived significance of the baptistry, among other things, will soon, if they have not already done so, make their impact felt on the shape of the church as they have in the minds and hearts of the people. But these are only a few among the challenges to be met and conquered.

There should be no anxious concern because changes in our previous conceptions are now indicated; that we shall soon be confronted by now unfamiliar ecclesiastical surroundings; but there may be just concern that these very differences themselves serve as the justification to build a "different" church. It does not follow that because the liturgical movement has already produced churches of unconventional form that an unconventional church is an expression of the revised liturgy. The desire to bring the congregation closer to the center of the Holy Sacrifice has, for example, produced several round churches with the people surrounding the altar. This may have been an easy solution to that problem but sober consideration reveals that this type of plan raises many more problems than the one it has solved.

There will, of course, be no simple answer, nor will there ever be but one nearly perfect solution. Every church building, like every other piece of architecture, will require its unique approach based upon considerations even beyond those of liturgy and science; available funds, topography, character of surroundings, traffic patterns, and personal taste (still a valid principle) are some of these. And in our search for the design of the ideal church let us also remember that it is as much a place for private worship, meditation, and inspiration, the place to go when we have need to feel very close to the comforting presence of God, as it is for the accommodation of the assembled faithful at the holy Sacrifice of the Mass on a Sunday morning.

It has been the purpose of this chapter to raise questions as it intends to warn against the slick and easy solutions that flow from the facile hand rather than from the understanding mind. Nowhere have we attempted to set down instructions or directions; to have done so would be as futile as it is impossible. One thing only has been stressed and that is the importance of the architect's role in relation to the building problems of the priest. Pope Paul VI, opening the Fourth National Congress of the Catholic Union of Italian Artists, said, "We ask only that your art serve us in reality and in dignity, that it possess dynamism, that we be able to understand it. We ask further that it may assist us, that it may speak truly, and inspire people with authentic religious emotion." These words may well be the ultimate charge to your architect.

4

The Liturgical Elements
of the Church Interior

VIGGO F. E. RAMBUSCH

UNTIL RECENTLY, WHEN THE SECOND VATICAN COUNCIL PLACED A NEW
and dynamic emphasis on the liturgy, many priests and architects, as
well as interior designers, were not altogether conscious of the precise
function of the church building. Many priests, for example, considered it
to be a place where they would "say Mass" and where the parishioners
would be "out in the pews" looking on and worshiping privately, and as
a place to hold novenas and other devotions throughout the week.
According to this view, all that was needed was a building that would
hold a specified number of people, with room for an impressive high
altar for Mass, and two side altars with tabernacles. Large and colorful
stations of the cross were strung along the side walls, and the baptistry
was frequently squeezed into one of the corners at the rear of the church
or placed in a small room adjacent to the vestibule.

Frequently, the parishioners had little to say about the design or decoration of their church; their responsibility was to provide the funds for
construction. Usually the pastor placed the architect's sketch of the new
church in a convenient place where all could see and "approve." Often
enough the sketches they saw were a compromise between the pastor's
wishes and the architect's standards.

Efforts at church renovation followed similar patterns, and except for
a new coat of paint on the walls and statues, a few new light fixtures, and

34

perhaps some new furniture in the sanctuary, little change was made in the basic form of the building or the order of its interior. Renovation as a rule did not include placing a new emphasis on the liturgical elements of the interior.

Fortunately, however, the *Constitution on the Sacred Liturgy,* the *Decree for Implementation of the Constitution on the Sacred Liturgy,* and the *Notitiae* from the Commission for the Implementation of the Liturgy Constitution have, in recent years, forced pastors and architects, engineers and interior designers to take a new look at church design and furnishings. Now, pastor and architect must plan for the altar and for the full participation of the people of God, and then enclose these areas within a suitable structure. The day of the massive high altar, the hidden baptistry, and the choir loft in the rear has passed, for the conciliar documents allow for no false dichotomies — for example, the sanctuary as the place of liturgical activity, the nave as the place of liturgical passivity. On the contrary, all the liturgical elements of the church must be emphasized so that all who are present will comprehend the reality of these elements and be drawn to greater participation.

Thus, a church is correctly designed or renovated when all elements of liturgical worship are appropriately placed and properly related in a manner that is best suited to the celebration of the liturgical services.[1] In a word, it is primarily for the celebration of the liturgy — the Mass and the sacraments — that churches are built. However, without sacrificing this primary purpose, those planning church construction or church renovation — the pastor and his assistants, the architect and his staff, and the lay advisers — should allow for the paraliturgical functions and the non-liturgical devotions. Having provided for the basic liturgical needs of the parish, the architect is free to use his talents to plan and design structures that will enrich the church and make it a beautiful place to house a worshiping community.

Since it is impossible to discuss the various aspects of church elements and decoration for all types of structures such as cathedrals, chapels, and oratories, this chapter is limited to a consideration of those elements that are essential for the planning and design of new parish churches or the renovation of old ones.

Because the catechumen makes his first formal commitment to Christ in baptism where he is reborn of water and of the Holy Spirit, and where he becomes a member of the Church, it seems appropriate to place the baptistry first on the list of considerations. It should preferably be the first liturgical element that the people of God see when they come to their church, so that all will be continually reminded of their rebirth

[1] Vatican Council II, *Constitution on the Sacred Liturgy* (trans. N.C.W.C.), n. 124, p. 39.

in Christ and of their eventual resurrection with him. Therefore, it is fitting to locate the baptistry at the entrance to the church. For example, the baptistry may be placed in the vestibule, or at the end of a widened center aisle, at all times in plain view of the members of the community. When provisions cannot be made for the baptistry at or near the church entrance, it may properly be placed in a forward area, for example, in a transcept. No matter where the baptistry is located, however, ample space must be provided to guarantee the unencumbered performance of the baptismal rite. Therefore, there must be adequate room for the principal participants without obstructing the view of family and friends who will actively share this liturgical experience, or for parish participation during the Holy Saturday services when the new fire is kindled and the water blessed. A decorative plaque on which the Apostles' Creed has been inscribed could be hung on a nearby wall in such a way that it is visible to all as a constant reminder of their faith and dedication.

The second sacrament by which the Christian is cleansed is Penance. Thus, it seems natural and logical to place the confessional or confessionals near the baptistry. Where this cannot be done, they may be placed along the side walls. Both locations are well suited to remind the community that confession is another step leading them closer to Christ in the Eucharist. Under no conditions should the confessionals be located in an obscure area of the structure; they should always be in full view of the community. When designing and locating the confessionals, architects and designers should make adequate provision for privacy and for the unhampered movement of lines of penitents. Confessionals should also be equipped with adequate lighting, signaling, heating, and ventilating facilities.

Liturgists also recommend that the sacristy, or at least a small vesting room, be located at the entrance of the church. Such a location will make processions to and from the altar much more effective and convenient. It will also encourage more processions, and experience has shown that processions are an effective means of participating and symbolizing the movement of the Christian toward the altar of sacrifice.

Furthermore, when the sacristy or vesting room is located near the entrance of the church, the pastor can more easily greet the arriving or departing parishioners. The immediate effect of such greetings on the occasion of a liturgical celebration is the development of a community spirit which will bring priest and people as close together socially as they are spiritually through the Eucharist.

Where it is extremely difficult, or impossible, to locate the sacristy or a vesting room near the entrance, the same results can be achieved by placing a small hinged vesting table at the rear of the church. Liturgists encourage this practice for Sunday masses and more solemn occasions.

Since the *Decree for Implementation* places great emphasis on communal singing, the choir loft which was usually located at the rear of the church is no longer needed for this purpose; therefore the gallery may be excluded from the plans. Rather, since full, active participation requires that all participants join in the songs and chants of the celebration, it would be helpful and certainly more in accord with the spirit of the decree if choir members joined the community of worshipers and took places in various sections of the church to assist and encourage those around them. On those occasions when a choir is needed to sing a special Mass, a small group may be placed toward the front of the church, with the director visible to all at all times. Since the use of an organ is highly recommended in the *Constitution on the Sacred Liturgy*,[2] provision must be made for it in the early stages of church planning. If necessary, authorities in the field of acoustics should be consulted.

The familiar "cry room" which was an important fixture in many churches seems to be falling into disuse. In preference to a "cry room," today, pastors in increasing numbers are requesting their architect to include a funeral chapel as part of the floor plan of the church. This use of a funeral chapel is especially appropriate in those communities where evening funeral Masses are becoming more common. It might be well to mention here that an evening funeral Mass allows for far greater attendance and participation. This chapel might also be used for an overnight resting place for the corpse in localities where funeral Masses will be celebrated in the morning hours. Some liturgists have also suggested that when the church does not have a funeral chapel and it is desirable to bring the remains to the church several hours before the time of the evening funeral Mass, the coffin could be placed in the baptistry and be returned to the baptistry after the Mass, remaining there until the following morning when the family comes to accompany the deceased to the cemetery. This chapel might be suitably designated "All Souls Chapel," and provisions made for holding at least one day of the "visitation" here, where all members of the community could assemble for the Office of the Dead or the recitation of the rosary. When the chapel is too small to accommodate this practice, the body could be placed in the center aisle, with the family and friends taking their places in the adjacent pews.

Since more and more people are taking an active part in the liturgical celebration, including the reception of Holy Communion, architects are advised to provide wider aisles, and allow for a greater space between the pews. Such changes will facilitate the movement of people at Communion time, as well as during processions and at the end of the liturgical celebration.

[2] *Ibid.*, n. 120, p. 37.

Though all the points thus far touched upon are of considerable importance, the sanctuary deserves the architect's and interior designer's fullest attention, for it is the focal point of all liturgical activity. In recent years, architects experimenting with church design have attempted to place the sanctuary in the mathematical center of the church. In most cases, however, the results have been less than satisfactory, for when the sanctuary is located in the center of the structure, a sizeable portion of the worshiping community will probably be deprived of "Mass facing the people." The ideal place for the sanctuary is in or near the optical center of the structure opposite the main entrances.

But, regardless of where the sanctuary is located, it should have sufficient floor space and the proper levels to assure that all the various rites and services can be properly carried out with full decorum in the full view of the worshiping community.

Liturgists point out that there are three important elements in the sanctuary, namely, *the altar, the chair,* and *the ambo (pulpit).* These elements derive their importance primarily from the *Constitution on the Sacred Liturgy* which provides for an altar facing the people, the use of the president's chair, and the more frequent use of the ambo by priests, deacons, and lectors. A lectern is desirable for the commentator and the leader of song. The various liturgical reforms lay special stress on the function of the altar of sacrifice. As more and more priests and people envision the altar as the communal table, fewer and fewer demands will be made for side altars.

The altar of sacrifice should be placed as close to the front of the sanctuary as possible to assure maximum visibility. However, it should not be so close to the front edge of the sanctuary as to interfere with the necessary movements of the ministers, especially at solemn Masses. It is, nevertheless, a good rule of liturgy that the celebrant must be seen by everyone regardless of whether he is standing behind the altar or sitting in the president's chair.

It is no longer necessary to place the altar three or more steps above the floor. Most authorities in this field say that the altar should not be elevated too far above the eye level of persons sitting or kneeling in the pews. Therefore, they recommend that the altar be placed only one step above the sanctuary level. Difficulties frequently arise concerning the placing of the altar when planning the renovation of a church. The altar should preferably not be put on a split level directly over the old steps. This has frequently been attempted in the renovation of those churches where the sanctuary is too shallow, and where the existing predella must be used. The split level effect makes the altar look too tall and the priest too short. One solution to this problem is to relocate or eliminate some of the front pews and extend the sanctuary forward.

The material out of which the altar is to be constructed must be such that it will harmonize with the interior decorating scheme and the other sanctuary furnishings and be in accordance with the rubrics relating to a portable or a fixed altar; the fixed altar should be constructed of a natural material, i.e., stone, marble or limestone. The mensa should be executed from one piece of stone. Though the altar should be simple in design, it should be beautifully executed by an expert craftsman as is befitting the sacred use to which it will be put.

The sepulcher should preferably be located in the edge of the mensa. However, it may also be placed elsewhere, for example in the front or rear edge on one of the supports. By locating the sepulcher in one of these places, the top of the mensa remains unmarred except for the five crosses which symbolize the five wounds of Christ and designate the points for anointing.

Since the altar of sacrifice is actually a table, it may well look like one. It should be tall enough for the priest to perform the sacred rites conveniently, but never so tall or so short as to interfere with those portions of the service that take place at the altar. Many liturgists suggest 39 inches as the ideal height. Since most of the ceremonies are now performed at the center of the altar, there is no longer need for altars that are six, eight, or even ten feet long. An altar five feet in length is sufficiently long to accommodate the chalice, ciboria, and missal. Candlesticks, reliquaries, and flowers should not be placed on the altar of sacrifice. The altar should be deep enough to accommodate the altar cards and a small crucifix, in those instances where a processional cross is not used. Many recommend that the altar should not be more than 30 inches deep. However, the size of the church, the style of architecture, and the motif of the interior can be important guidelines for determining the exact size and shape — square or rectangular — of the altar. The guiding principle in altar design is that it should be of a noble and solid character.

The center section below the mensa may be open. The advantage of such a solution is that the people can see the complete figure of the priest standing and genuflecting. If there is an open space below the mensa, the congregation will also be able to look beyond the altar to the rear of the sanctuary where the president's chair is ideally placed.

Though it is preferable to place the tabernacle on an altar or pedestal or in a chapel, or off to the side of the sanctuary, if necessary, it may be placed on the altar of sacrifice. When the latter position is resorted to, a small precious tabernacle that will not interfere with the people's view of the Mass should be used. When the tabernacle is placed on the mensa, it may be desirable to increase the depth of the altar.

The predella on which the altar rests should be of sufficient size to permit the celebrant and the other ministers to perform their various functions, including genuflections, with dignity and solemnity. The rubrics for solemn Masses and for concelebrated Masses should be kept clearly in mind when determining the size of this platform. It should also be spacious enough to accommodate the six tall floor candlesticks that will be placed to the right and left of the altar. Though the candlesticks can be placed on the mensa, they are more properly placed on the floor to form a setting, as it were, for the altar and celebrant, and provide the outer boundaries of an area of special sacredness in the church. The predella should also be large enough to accommodate the processional cross, and provide a suitable place for the celebrant to receive the nuptial vows and carry out other functions, and for the bishop to confer the sacrament of confirmation. In view of the various uses to which the front and rear portions of the predella will be put, it is recommended that it be at least nine feet six inches deep and thirteen feet wide.

A well designed and executed canopy or testor can greatly enhance the beauty of the sanctuary and articulate the location of the altar of sacrifice. It can be put to a very practical use too, if the architect desires to design it in such a way that lights and amplifiers can be built into it. However, it is not a necessary appointment of the sanctuary, and can readily be dispensed with if it does not give emphasis to the altar or the overall decorating scheme.

If the crucifix to be used for Mass must be placed on the altar, it should be very small and narrow so as not to interfere with the people's visibility, or with the celebrant's dialogue with the congregation. However, the most effective solution to the problem of providing a crucifix for Mass is the processional cross. One of the advantages of using the processional cross is that it can be kept in its place at all times when not being carried in procession. When Mass is not being celebrated, the processional cross can be turned so that the *corpus* faces the people.

Since the processional cross is frequently carried by young accolytes, it should be made of a light but durable material that harmonizes with the floor candlesticks and the rest of the sanctuary appointments. The lower end of the shaft should be so designed that it can be fitted into a floor socket or a portable base placed on the predella. The crucifix portion of the processional cross should be large enough to produce a significant silhouette that will pleasantly dominate the scene. However, it must never overshadow the altar. The shaft of the processional cross should be at least six feet in length so that the crucifix portion of it will not block the celebrant's or the congregation's vision. All surfaces of the crucifix, including the edges, if it is a very thick one, may be ornamented to harmonize with the sanctuary decor. The corpus which may represent either the crucified Christ or the glorified Christ should be attached to the cross in bold relief and not be recessed into the cross.

The floor candlesticks should be constructed in such a way that the bobeches and the upper section can be removed for use in processions. The floor candlesticks should be as high as the mensa, and preferably the new, short, thick candles should be used. When it is impossible to use the floor candlesticks, very low candlesticks may be arranged along the edge of the altar nearest the people, or at both ends. Very short candles should be used in these holders also. All candlesticks that are not to be used during a particular celebration should be removed from the sanctuary. If there is a tabernacle on the altar of sacrifice, or if the Bible is to be enthroned on the altar or at the ambo, two candlesticks may honor these locations.

The credence table serves additional needs in the new liturgy. Therefore it must be large enough to hold the chalice(s) and unconsecrated hosts which are kept there until the offertory, and the missal and missal stand which may be placed there until needed before the secret prayer. At concelebrated Masses, it may also be desirable to place ablution cups on the credence table for the use of the concelebrating priests. Of course, the cruets and *lavabo* basin are kept on this table. The credence table should be of a sufficient height; however, it should not be as high as the altar itself. Though convenience and necessity will for the most part dictate its size, the overall dimensions of this table as well as its distance from the altar will be determined in part by the size of the sanctuary. Needless to say, it should harmonize with the other sanctuary appointments.

With the introduction of the new liturgy, the president's chair which was important in the ancient rites as the presiding bishop's throne has been returned to its proper place in the sanctuary.[3] Unlike the *sedilla,* which was merely a convenient seat for the celebrant and other ministers to use during the singing of long chants or during the sermon, the president's chair is a fitting seat for the celebrant who is the leader of the assembly and who directs and unifies the people of God during this celebration.

In view of the significant role which this chair plays in the revised liturgy, it is important that it be given a place of prominence in the

[3] *Ibid.,* n. 7, p. 5; n. 41–42, p. 15; Sacred Congregation of Rites, *Instruction for the Proper Implementation of the Constitution on the Sacred Liturgy* (Washington, D. C.: The National Catholic Welfare Conference, 1964), n. 92, p. 33; The Commission for Implementation of the Liturgy, *The Ordinary of the Mass* (Liturgical Press: Collegeville, 1965), n. 7, p. 11; The Commission for Implementation of the Liturgy, *The Rites to Be Observed for the Celebration of Mass, op. cit.,* n. 23, p. 61; Sacred Congregation of Rites, *The Rite To Be Observed in the Concelebration of Mass and the Rite for Communion Under Both Kinds With the Text of the Canon of the Mass and Chants for Concelebration* (New York: Joseph F. Wagner, Inc., 1965), n. 87, p. 22.

sanctuary. Therefore, whenever possible it should be placed directly behind the altar of sacrifice on a platform two or three steps higher than the *predella* so that the seated celebrant wil be clearly visible to every member of the worshiping community. Though it is not required that the celebrant be seen in his entirety while sitting in the president's chair, his head and the upper portions of his body should be clearly visible.

The president's chair should be an impressive sanctuary appointment befitting the dignity of the celebrant; it must not, however, have the appearance of a throne. The platform on which the chair is placed should be large enough to allow the president of the assemby to stand and even genuflect. If space permits, the platform and the steps leading to it should be constructed in such a way that two smaller chairs or stools can be placed on either side of the president's chair for the use of the other ministers. If possible these chairs or stools should be placed on a lower level. In churches where concelebrated Masses will be celebrated, additional chairs or stools should be provided for the use of the concelebrants. These additional seats should match the other furnishings in the sanctuary.

If the sanctuary is so small that the president's chair cannot be placed directly behind the altar, it may be placed in a prominent position either to the right or the left of the altar. However, since this chair represents the authority which the celebrant exercises over the assembly during the celebration, this concept must always be kept in mind when choosing a place for this chair. The architect should always consider the importance of providing adequate lighting over this chair, as well as outlets for microphones. (These should also be provided at the altar, the ambo, the lectern, and at the forward portion of the predella for the bishop at Confirmation and for the priest at weddings.)

The third most important element in the sanctuary is the lectern. Its importance, according to the liturgical decrees of Vatican II, derives from the fact that it is the place where the written Word of God is proclaimed. For this reason, it becomes a holy place where the greater portion of the Liturgy of the Word is celebrated. The lectern or *ambo* may be located on either side of the altar preferably as near to the front edge of the sanctuary as possible. If the architectural design of the church will not allow the lectern to be placed in this position, it may be located near the president's chair. The lectern should be elevated one step from the sanctuary floor to give it greater dignity.

To emphasize the importance of the Liturgy of the Word, many liturgists recommend that the Scriptures be displayed in a prominent place in the church during those times when services are not in progress by enshrining them either on the altar of sacrifice or in a niche built into the front of the ambo. When the Bible is enthroned on a lectern, the lectern should be so constructed that it can be turned around so that the opened Bible would face the people.

While the modern architect must be conscious of many things when he designs a contemporary church edifice — adequate heating and air-conditioning systems, adequate lighting for both the sanctuary and the body of the church, a sufficient number of exits, storage space, etc. — few appointments are more important than good acoustics. If it is the duty of the celebrant to proclaim the Word of God, it is the right of the people of God to be able to hear him. Therefore, architects and interior designers should carefully plan for a building that is accoustically sound, and as part of this planning they should make provisions for an adequate sound system if needed.

The proper place for the tabernacle seems to be one of the more delicate questions facing liturgists today. Though many liturgists suggest that the tabernacle should not be placed on the altar of sacrifice, some priests feel that it should not be removed from its traditional place. They argue that to place it in a less prominent location is disrespectful. However, this argument is at least debatable for, as Godfrey Diekmann, O.S.B., the Editor of *Worship* and a member of the Postconciliar Commission on the Liturgy, observes, "Liturgists have been generally unhappy about the tabernacle on the altar. Why?" Perhaps the most weighty reason for this feeling was broadly indicated by Pope Pius XII in his address to the Assisi Liturgical Congress in 1956:

> One is fully justified (he said) in distinguishing between the offering of the sacrifice of the Mass and the Latreutic cult (that is, adoration), the supreme form of worship offered to the God-Man hidden in the Eucharist. A decision of the Sacred Congregation of Rites, dated July 27, 1927, limits as much as possible the exposition of the Blessed Sacrament during Mass; but this is easily explained by the desire of keeping habitually separate the act of sacrifice and the worship of simple adoration in order that the faithful would clearly understand their respective proper character.[4]

To assure identity to each, and to assure that the Blessed Sacrament reserved in the tabernacle will continue to have a prominent place in the sanctuary, liturgists suggest that the tabernacle be placed on an appropriately designed shelf or pedestal near the back wall of the sanctuary, or recessed into the back wall itself. If this solution is adopted, it is permissible to place the president's chair in front of the tabernacle. However, the tabernacle must be placed high enough so that at least a portion of it can be seen over the head of the priest standing. The chair should be moved forward a few feet to provide easy access to the tabernacle. The chair may also be placed slightly to the left of the tabernacle.

---

[4] Pius XII, "Allocution to the Congress," *The Assisi Papers* (Collegeville: Liturgical Press, 1957), p. 233.

An ideal solution for renovated churches is to place the tabernacle on a remodeled side altar. This altar then becomes the altar of reservation. One of the advantages of this solution is that it brings the Blessed Sacrament nearer to the adoring community. Regardless of where the tabernacle is placed, it must under all conditions be visible to those within the church, even when located in a newly created Blessed Sacrament chapel.

Former legislation governing the construction and permanent erection of the tabernacle, the lock, lining, etc., are still in effect. Church law also requires that a modest sanctuary lamp of clear or white glass be located near the tabernacle. This lamp may be mounted on a floor stand, suspended from a wall bracket, or hung from the ceiling. The two latter solutions seem preferable since they leave the sanctuary floor unencumbered.

Many of the new churches are eliminating the usual communion railing, for though it was originally intended as a communion table, in the opinion of many liturgists, it has gradually become a physical and psychological barrier between the celebrant and the people of God. Instead, the use of communion stations is becoming more acceptable. These are stands about four feet tall, behind which the priest stands to distribute Communion to those standing. In dioceses where it is still customary for the communicants to kneel, priedieux may be used or the communicants may kneel along the elevated front edge of the sanctuary. This latter solution presents a serious disadvantage to the old and the infirm, who could be favored with a short rail at the far ends of the communion area.

In existing churches or where altar rails are to be used, architects and interior decorators have successfully eliminated the "barrier" effect by removing the center gates and widening the opening from the usual 5 feet to 12 or 13 feet. Such modifications of the communion railing have proved very effective in establishing contact between priest and people and in encouraging greater participation during Mass, weddings, confirmation, and other services. Furthermore, a properly designed and appointed sanctuary will also allow for or add beauty and dignity to the ceremonies and, by providing ample room, facilitate the movement of priest, bishop, and ministers.

In the new decrees, there are few directives regarding the use and placement of shrines, statues, and the stations of the cross, or the design and use of stained glass windows. However, this is no indication that they are to be eliminated. Rather, it means that prudence and good taste should guide the architect and interior decorator in their choice of design, materials, and location. While statuary and stained glass windows certainly have a place in the contemporary church, they should contribute to the *raison d'etre* for which the church is being built or renovated, namely, for the Service of the Word and the Service of the Eucharist. In a word, they should enhance the liturgical celebration by directing the attention of the people to it, rather than detract from it. Therefore, it is important to remember that while the multiplication of shrines and statues is to be avoided, it is not necessary to exclude them altogether. If needed, group or place them in or toward the rear where they will be readily available to those seeking them.

The modern architect and interior designer has at his disposal a wide range of forms, materials, colors, textures, and lighting effects to work with. Used effectively, they can create a truly communal and religious atmosphere which will aid in drawing the individual worshiper closer to God.

5

The Priest As Confessor and Spiritual Director

JOHN E. CORRIGAN

THE PROMISE OF SPIRITUAL RENEWAL AS THE FLOWER OF VATICAN Council II lays upon confessors a special obligation that is both satisfying and challenging. They should bring to the celebration of the sacrament of penance the spirit that imbues the *Constitution on the Sacred Liturgy* — the Council's first and perhaps most luminous contribution to meaningful worship.

The Constitution has promised that "the rite and formulas for the sacrament of penance are to be revised so that they may more clearly express the nature and the effect of sacrament." But even as confessors await the revision, they should endeavor to infuse a deeper meaning in the sacrament of reconciliation in line with the directions pointed out in the Constitution.

The Council's decree underscores the necessity for the liturgy to reflect "the mystery of Christ in His Church." How much more necessary is it for the priest in celebrating the sacraments to be a reflector of Christ conveying to us the Father's love. If this ideal is to become a motivating conviction in the confessor's life, he must free himself from an excessively juridical attitude toward the penitent and penance which sees the priest solely as judge. Though the element of judging can never be absent, the priest's primary role is that of Christ announcing forgiveness to Magdalene, bringing peace to the fear-filled apostles in the Upper Room, restoring the physical vigor as well as forgiving the sins of the helpless paralytic. He is the father of the prodigal — loving and trusting more than rebuking.

The role of the priest-confessor as spiritual director is a clouded area of discussion. There are many who would insist upon a sharp distinction between confession and direction, maintaining that the anonymous confession is the better practice. Of course, there is a latent danger that confession to a trusted priest-counselor may obscure the sacred and sacramental act, making it seem like just another talk with a friend. There are three reasons, however, why I believe that this is an incomplete view. As a practical approach, one of the pastoral facts of life is that only a few persons come to a priest for regular spiritual direction. Whether the fault belongs to priest or penitent does not greatly matter. The reality remains. If the great majority of Christians are to receive any person-to-person word of encouragement and counsel, it is going to be heard in the confessional. In any event, if most of the people did come for personal direction in a large parish, the priest just could not find time to counsel them.

Next, although the confessional is not the place for any prolonged discussion of problems and a priest may often have to urge that the penitent visit him at another time, there is a certain amount of direction inherent in the sacrament itself. The Roman Ritual clearly states that an instruction should accompany the celebration of the sacrament. In what better way could the confessor fulfill this mandate than by speaking relevantly to the penitent concerning his faults and encouraging him to look to the future with concrete resolutions? It is necessary to understand that in this dialogue the priest is not acting directly as an instrument of Christ, as in giving absolution, but in his own name as a pastor of his people.

The third reason for encouraging priests to use the occasion of confession for brief spiritual direction is linked to the human workings of God's grace. Ordinarily the more deeply a person experiences the love and forgiveness of Christ in confession, the more fully will he respond to the workings of God's grace in his life. As the noted psychiatrist, Dr. E. Mark Stern, observes:

> In like fashion the priest must try to regard each penitent as a subject, not an object. In so doing he shows that he *cares* for the person who has come to him; he is genuinely interested in that person's life. And he will better feel the penitent's hunger if he realizes that by the very fact of coming to confession the penitent is seeking fulfillment.
>
> . . . the priest must be a companion in the penitent's pilgrimage, a participant in his revelations about himself. He must be willing to hear out the penitent's doubts, willing to accompany him in his gropings and strivings.[1]

[1] E. Mark Stern, "Psychoanalysis and Confession," *Jubilee* (May, 1965).

This is not to say that the priest should function in the confessional as a psychiatrist. Nonetheless an understanding of the basic attitudes that are part of psychiatric interviews would have great value for the confessor. He can learn from the psychiatrist the value of listening and observing and believing with a Christian optimism that God's grace can work its wonders in a person's life.

In this view of penance there is a greater value to both penitent and priest when the priest knows who the penitent is. Aside from the fact that we tend to have a greater respect for persons we know and whose opinions we appreciate, there is the value to the penitent in seeing the confessor as a man and not solely as an authority figure. In the incarnation God became man and showed us what the Father's love was like in association with other men. So in the sacrament of penance, the confessor becomes man in order to make God's forgiveness more real and personal, thereby achieving a real human meeting with a common bond of interest and sympathy. This conclusion is supported by modern research in psychology that has demonstrated that people will reveal their serious faults only to close friends or complete strangers. In psychotherapy patients are free in admitting their faults. As the therapy progresses they stop for awhile and then resume after a real friendship has been established. The priest-confessor has much to learn from these research findings. In addition, the testimony of the early Church seems to second this. We read in some of the ancient rituals that as part of the public penance the celebrant of penance would kneel with the penitent, pray with him, fast with him, and even weep with him. Surely this was human support. This communicated the solicitude that the confessor really had for the penitent, sharing and understanding his feelings. It must have made the rigors of public penance somewhat more bearable. A true spiritual benefit also accrues to the priest when the sacrament of reconcilition is a true human encounter. The attitude of the penitent toward him as a person — not an anonymous absolution machine — cannot but awaken his ability to respond meaningfully to another's life.

Although the attitude of the priest toward the sacrament is the key to its fruitfulness, there is a corresponding need for instructing the laity in its significance — now and in prospect — lest the developments in the liturgy lead merely to a new formalism. The spiritual potential inherent in a renewal of the ritual of penance emphasizes the advisability of such training by seminars, at meetings of parish organizations, and in parish workshops and discussion groups. Perhaps most important of all, the instruction should be embodied in Sunday sermons on the liturgy when the whole Christian assembly is present. An explanation of the elements of the rite of penance should be part of any program of instruction.

Examination of Conscience

Priests should instruct their parishioners that penance, like any sacrament, is first of all a meeting with Christ in the Church. The first step in preparing for penance is to place oneself in contact with Christ. We might suggest that an ideal way of doing this is to take a Bible or missal along to church and to spend a few minutes before entering the confessional in reading, slowly and carefully, a passage from the Bible or the liturgy which tells of Christ's love, the response he desires of Christians, or his willingness to raise up again those who have failed him.

The important thing is that this reading should be meditative and personal. This is Christ's word — spoken to the penitent here and now. What is Christ saying about himself, about the Father, about the divine plan of salvation? What reply does Christ expect here in prayer and later in everyday action?

Each of the following readings could be recommended as an excellent preparation for penance:

Hosea, Chapter 2: the Christian's love for God must be as personal and intimate as the love between a man and a woman.

Joel, Chapter 2: the prophet of repentance encourages the penitent to live by the interior law of love rather than the external forms.

Isaiah, Chapter 58: true penance is grounded in the practice of love for neighbor.

Jeremiah, Chapter 7: the call to conversion.

Jeremiah, Chapter 31: a prophecy of the new covenant to be established in Christ and a promise of the forgiveness Christ will bring.

Matthew, Chapters 5–7: the sermon on the Mount provides an ideal examination of conscience for every Christian; this is no mere list of duties, but an invitation to grow constantly toward the fullness of Christian life.

Matthew, Chapter 9: the sinner is the paralytic; he can do nothing to help himself, but depends entirely on the aid of other Christians and the unbounded mercy of Christ.

Matthew, Chapter 18: a lesson in forgiveness and an invitation to forgive others as the Father has forgiven us.

Luke, Chapter 18: the story of the pharisee and the publican is a sobering lesson on true sorrow for sin.

John, Chapter 20: having conquered sin and death, Christ leaves to his Church the power to reconcile sinners.

Finally, any part of the accounts of Christ's suffering, death, and resurrection given by the Evangelists would always be appropriate.

The Blessing

For most penitents the formal, "Bless me, Father," is simply a rather meaningless mechanical "starter" for the confession, no more than a salutation. Few realize that it is an actual request for a blessing — a sacramental to aid the penitent in making a good confession and the Church's official welcome to this contrite sinner. It might roughly be compared to the atrium or vestibule of the ancient Roman basilica which served to effect a transition from this world to God's special presence. The blessing, properly given, could help to create the atmosphere of calmness in which God's grace could more effectively work.

Unfortunately, even among priests the significance of this custom is overlooked, and the giving of a blessing is often neglected. With a minimum of instruction penitents can be taught to pause after the request for the blessing while the priest gives it in English: "May the Lord be in your heart and on your lips, that you may properly confess all your sins in the name of the Father. . . ." The words are reminiscent of the blessing which the celebrant at a solemn Mass bestows on the deacon who will proclaim the Gospel. In the sacrament the penitent also witnesses the good news of salvation and God's merciful love.

Penitent's Accusation

Use of English in the sacrament necessitates some continuing instruction of the people, so that they may not only understand the ritual change but also profit from the greater intelligibility of the form of absolution. Such instruction would provide an opportunity for suggesting ways in which the telling of one's sins could be done more personally and with greater meaning. The following check list could be given to penitents as a guideline for an examination of conscience and could be so entitled:

Do I realize that in penance I am brought into a personal meeting with Christ — friend and brother?

Do I understand that even in the privacy of the confessional I am engaged in a public act, acknowledging my faults before the whole community of Christians in the person of the priest?

Do I examine my conscience not only according to the commandments of God and his Church but also in fulfillment of God's invitation to seek perfection?

Do I give some identification of myself in confession at least according to age, state in life, and profession?

Do I realize that every sin is unique, and does my confession indicate this by detailing the circumstances and motivation of my actions?

Does my confession manifest the totality of my life with God, and others? Would my friends recognize this confession as mine and only mine?

Have I made specific resolutions regarding my faults and spoken them in the confessional?

Do I go to the confessor who is best able to guide me even though this may put me to some inconvenience?

PRIEST'S INSTRUCTION

The advice in the Roman Ritual that the celebration of every sacrament should be accompanied by an instruction, as indicated earlier, is particularly appropriate for this sacrament. The priest-confessor is both judge and physician, father and friend. In many cases his words will deepen the gift of true contrition in the penitents. Even for the devout a brief word of counsel specifically related to the faults just confessed will aid penitents in receiving the healing grace of the sacrament.

To give a spiritual exhortation with no relevance to the confession just made is apt at best to lead the faithful to confuse the sacrament and general spiritual direction and perhaps at the worst to leave the penitents with the empty feeling that their confessions were not heard. Such a practice diminishes the official and public character of the forgiveness of sins in and through the Church.

Likewise, if we believe that the celebration of penance is true worship, we then see that the important thing is that God is praised and glorified and that forgiveness of sins is granted. This occurs even when material integrity is not present in the confession. Thus questions which presuppose theological sophistication should surely be avoided. Although the Council of Trent enjoined penitents to confess serious sins according to the number and kind, this must often give way to the penitent's inability to meet that requirement in a literal enumeration.

In view of the large numbers of confessions to be heard, should not our pastoral efforts be in the direction of the quality of confessions rather than frequency? Guidelines about frequency, of course, may be given, but ultimately this should be a personal matter that each person should decide for himself. To confess with deep sorrow and understanding once every two months would surely be better than a more frequent but less personal reception.

In counseling penitents with habits of sin we must depend in part on the insights of modern psychology. It should be clear that it is as much a mistake to consider every wrong action as a matter of personal responsibility as it is to believe that in most cases there is no freedom at all — that every action can be explained through psychological pressures. In this connection subjective mortal sin needs to be reappraised. St. Augustine's advice, "What sins are mortal and what sins are venial, only God knows," should be kept in mind by every confessor, and our penitents should also know that when people commit habitual sins, their freedom and responsibility are diminished. To commit mortal sin means to make a free, full, and final decision to separate oneself from God, to leave the Father's home for good. In the view of Father Marc Oraison, the French priest-psychiatrist, "it is rare in the life of a Christian for him to break so completely with God that he is obliged to go to confession before approaching the Lord's Table." Appropriate counsel for persons struggling with a sinful habit could be given in the words of Father Adrian Van Kaam, professor of psychology at Duquesne University:

> If I desire to survive spiritually, there is only one way, namely, not to identify myself with my sinful or neurotic habit, but to assume some attitude against it whenever and to the degree that I am still able to do so. It is necessary for me to maintain some areas of freedom of thought and activity, however insignificant and seemingly ineffective, against the onslaught of passion, habit, and neurosis. I must hold on to this last possibility of 'not totally consenting interiorly' to that which seems to draw me in without the possibility of resistance. This preservation of a conviction of freedom, even if it does not help me to transcend totally the symptoms of neurosis and sin, will at least preserve my awareness of a last vestige of that human dignity which extends as far as freedom does. Without this awareness, everything seems lost. It is in this last outpost and refuge of my disturbed existence that grace may move me to turn to God in a dialogue between humble contrition and infinite mercy. *The Power and the Glory,* a novel by Graham Greene, which reports the dialogue between the weak will of a priest and his Lord, is representative of such a boundary situation which tomorrow may be mine.[2]

The target of spiritual direction, in the example cited in Father Van Kaam's moving diagnosis, should be the root of the sin rather than the immediate sin itself. Giving the penitent counsel that would encourage within him a sense of interim responsibility that could be the first step toward spiritual health and wholeness.

In those cases where the penitent seems to be indisposed to receive the sacrament, great care must be taken in judging too definitely his dispositions. The refusal of absolution should occur in only the rarest of cases when there is no doubt whatever that the penitent has come with no true sorrow and no intention of amendment. In all doubtful cases absolution should be granted, explaining carefully the conditional nature of all absolution — that forgiveness depends on what is in the penitent's heart and not necessarily in his words.

The admonition given in many writings about confession that penitents who have been away from penance for three months or more should be directly asked whether they have anything on their conscience re-

---

[2] Adrian Van Kaam, C.S.Sp., *Religion and Personality,* © 1964. By permission of Prentice Hall, Inc., Englewood Cliffs, N. J., pp. 101–102.

garding the responsiblities of marriage seems to involve a violation of the rights of conscience. Obviously, this question was devised to trap married people who are practicing birth control and have decided not to confess it. To those whose confessions are integral in every sense such an inquiry could be a serious affront. This suggests that we accept in the confessional even the incorrect subjective conscience of our people and use our other pastoral opportunities for teaching correct moral attitudes.

PENANCES

Is it possible to broaden our scope beyond the traditional "five Our Fathers and five Hail Marys"? Obviously, great care is needed in this area lest enthusiasm to aid the penitent cause bewilderment and uncertainty as to what the penance really is or how it is to be fulfilled. This would be especially true of the elderly, the uneducated, and the very young. But many would welcome both instruction on the nature of satisfaction and an opportunity to do greater and more pertinent penances than are commonly given.

The penance should be purposeful insofar as the confessor has reached an understanding of the penitent's problem of sin — by omission or commission. A penitent who has been away from Mass and the sacraments for almost a year and is making his Easter duty could be instructed, for example, that his penance is aimed not simply at aiding him to be "debt-free" with God, but at preparing him for reinitiation into the life of the Christian community. A confessor might ask such a person to take part in some specifically named parish activity as his penance. It might be possible to enlist the penitent's help by asking him to suggest remedial penances. For penitents who are open to suggestions a penance could be chosen that would in some way be suited to aid in healing the weakness caused by this person's sins or his predominant fault. The penitent would have the opportunity to "stretch" spiritually. It would also provide the occasion for a concrete resolution for action by the penitent — an act of charity toward a person about whom malice has been spoken, an apology to a wife injured by an unfair criticism, a promise by an engaged man to talk over with his fiancee the particular resolutions needed to avoid occasions of sin, or an extra hour's work by an employee who habitually wastes time. All these could serve as possible healing penances for particular faults, and they would also achieve the primary purpose of reparation.

But sin involves the whole man: therefore, penance need not be confined to prayers and scripture readings, but could include appropriate physical activity. The penitential practices exemplified in the Bible and recommended by the Church — fasting and almsgiving — should not be neglected. For sins of the flesh bodily penances could be recommended in certain carefully judged cases. After absolution, weakness remains and discipline is needed — a rosary said with arms outstretched, kneeling on the bare floor for a five-minute meditation, no food or drink between meals for one day. These are mortifications which could strengthen one's weaknesses. Although these options are not customary in our present practice, they are consistent with the counsel to the confessor in the Roman Ritual: "Wherefore, he should strive so far as possible to enjoin as penances practices which are opposed to the sins confessed, for example, almsgiving in the case of the avaricious, fasting or other mortifications of the flesh for the dissolute, acts of humility for the proud, exercises of piety for the lax."

For those persons to whom it would be difficult to assign a directly appropriate penance, the best suggestions might be a reading assignment, a short visit to the blessed sacrament, or one prayer said prayerfully and devoutly. In some parishes Bibles have been set up on prie-dieus for the use of parishioners going to confession. In others prayer books, including selections from the psalms, are available in the pews near the confessionals. In this situation a confessor could recommend specific passages if the confession suggested a particularly appropriate passage as a proper meditation.

In all these efforts at selecting more relevant penances the confessor should not be too quick to put aside simpler forms. Preferably he should gradually and selectively initiate the custom of meaningful variety. Helpful instruction in this area could be given occasionally in a Sunday sermon.

ABSOLUTION

With the permission to absolve in English there has arisen the question of when the act of contrition is to be said. Several possibilities have been tried. In the instruction on the sacrament it could be proposed that the penitent make an act of contrition at the end of the examination of conscience immediately preceding confession. It could be in one's own words or according to a suggested formula. This would prepare him for the confessional and help bring the confession itself to a more harmonious end. In the past the conclusion of the sacrament was indeed strange and somewhat cacophonous. The important words of forgiveness in Latin — the divine pardon — were intermingled with the penitent's seeming counterattack with his expression of sorrow for sin.

A simple solution would be for the penitent to conclude his confession with a personal expression of sorrow. "I am truly sorry for all my sins and particularly for my lack of patience with my family during the past week" is an example. It would not be necessary then for the penitent to recite another act of contrition at the time of absolution. Instead he would listen attentively to the words of forgiveness. We could also emulate in penance the present practice of reciting "amen" before receiving communion by instructing penitents to answer "amen" to the words of absolution. This would sum up in a single word his sorrow and desire for amendment — his assent to this sign of Christ's forgiving love.

The prayer *"Passio,"* also said in English, extends the penance assigned to and accepted by this person. In effect, it makes all the subsequent life of the Christian one of penance.

Generally the priest completes the celebration of the sacrament by simply saying, "God bless you," or some similar formula. Perhaps it would be better to use the words of Christ himself — effective, biblical words of power: "Your sins are forgiven; go in peace." This also recalls the words used by the bishop in the ancient penitential practices.

SAMPLE CONFESSION

In practice the resulting dialogue might be something like this:

Penitent: Give me your blessing, Father, for I have sinned.

Priest: May the Lord be in your heart and on your lips, that you may properly confess all your sins, in the name of the Father and of the Son and of the Holy Spirit. Amen.

Penitent: My last confession was two weeks ago. I am a housewife and mother of two small children. My resolution for the last few months has been to curb my tendency to nag my husband and to be more cheerful with him. I think I did better during this period.

I have incurred unnecessary debts and have managed the home finances poorly and selfishly.

I learned last week that I am pregnant. It has made me depressed and resentful because it was unexpected. I think I have overcome these feelings now.

I am only gradually adjusting to our new neighbors. I find it hard to meet people and have been lacking in friendliness in failing to visit them.

My Lenten resolution to read the New Testament every day has suffered because of the company that we had last week. I'll begin again. I shall also continue my resolution about being more considerate of my husband.

Priest: Remember that each of the things you have just mentioned offers you an opportunity now for a real promise to God. Before you leave the Church today try to make these promises. Also thank God for the graces in being faithful to your resolution in regard to your husband. Perhaps it would be helpful for you to discuss with your husband the home finances and to seek his advice and help.

For your penance express your love for God by praying the Our Father once. In addition would you be willing to accept as part of your penance the responsibility to visit your new neighbors during this coming week and show your charitable interest in them?

Penitent: Yes, Father, I'll be happy to do that.

Priest: Now to express your sorrow for these sins and to show your acceptance of God's forgiveness answer "amen" at the end of this absolution.

May our Lord Jesus Christ absolve you; and by his authority I absolve you from every bond of excommunication and interdict, to the extent of my power and your need. Finally, I absolve you from your sins, in the name of the Father and of the Son and of the Holy Spirit.

Penitent: Amen.

Priest: May the passion of our Lord Jesus Christ, the merits of the Blessed Virgin Mary and of all the saints, and also whatever good you do and evil you endure be cause for the remission of your sins, the increase of grace, and the reward of everlasting life. Amen. Your sins are forgiven — go in peace.

In this ecumenical age of search and sharing, we may also profit from the current pastoral practice of confession among some Protestants. The Reverend Earl Jabay presented early in 1965 in the Reformed Church publication, *The Church Herald,* a moving description of confession adapted to the task of spiritual direction. His method is outlined in this manner:

He has a table facing a wall, on the table covered with white linen is an opened bible and a nine-inch high bronze cross. The penitent sits at this table, facing a blank wall. The pastor then says to the penitent, "You and I are now in the presence of God. Let your body relax completely for a few minutes and open your spirit to experience God's presence. (Pause) What we talk about here will always be a secret with us. I assure you that you are completely safe in my presence to reveal anything to God. (Pause) I encourage you to speak of anything which has been hidden, anything for which you feel regret, anything for which you feel guilty. This is a time to be completely open with God. (Pause) You may begin when you wish, or wait for a time. We have plenty of time. There is no hurry.

"No pastor would ever divulge what he hears," Pastor Jabay says of the confession, "but I can say this. The depth of revelation is far greater in the confessional than I have ever experienced in face-to-face counseling." The pastor remains silent during the confession. When the confession is finished— one may take only minutes, another may last an hour — the pastor speaks. He describes the conclusion in this fashion:

Up to this point in the confessional I have been an ear hearing a soul speak to God, but now I become a voice witnessing to the forgiveness of God in Christ. That is all I am — a voice. Not the source of forgiveness; not the dispenser of grace; not the absolver of sins — just a voice speaking somewhat as follows:

'I am a witness to your confession to God. God has promised forgiveness and pardon to those who sincerely confess their sins, as I believe you have done. The Holy Scriptures tell us: If we confess our sins, God is faithful and just and will forgive our sins and cleanse us from unrighteousness. Do you believe this with all your heart?'

When he gets the answer he then has the penitent place his hand on the Bible before him and hold the cross in the other hand. The pastor then prays for the penitent, having the penitent repeat the following words after him:

Lord Jesus Christ: Thou hast heard me speak of my sins. I ask Thee to pardon them completely through Thy blood shed on Calvary. Remove every spot of guilt, and save my soul by Thy perfect atonement. I thank Thee for this salvation. Thou art now my leader and my God. I am Thy follower. In the name of the Father and of the Son and of the Holy Spirit.

After this, says Pastor Jabay, he counsels the penitent in a face-to-face talk.

SPIRITUAL DIRECTION

In the primitive Church personal words of counsel were not a part of the sacrament of reconciliation. The Scripture readings and instruction that preceded the sacrament were the ordinary vehicle of spiritual direction. The present usage is otherwise. In the sacrament of penance spiritual direction consists of a personal word directly related to the penitent's confession, which the confessor should give immediately before absolution. It should not be a mere moral exhortation to a better life, but an aid to the penitent in becoming a better member of Christ's mystical body, the Church. Just as reading certain passages of Scripture would be an excellent preparation for confession, so too the priest's counsel would best be the Word of God as applied to this Christian's real life problems.

Obviously, the value of counsel given in the sacrament is to a significant degree dependent on the priest's closeness to God. His mature perceptivity will reflect the relationship the penitent establishes with the confessor. The average Catholic's vision of penance as a sort of spiritual laundromat has caused the positive aspect of spiritual growth inherent in the sacrament to be overlooked. Most penitents on a given Saturday are in search of the shortest line rather than a specific priest confessor's guidance.

It should be clear that a regular confessor can be a great help as an instrument in bridging the gap between Christ and the penitent. The confessor has often been termed a "physician of the soul," and his function as healer and consoler underscores that idea. Most of us would be reluctant to try our luck with a different doctor every time we needed medical care, and we ordinarily would avoid the one with the "shortest line." Should not the same judgments guide the penitent's approach to the reception of the medicine of divine forgiveness?

It is the penitent's initiative that establishes this relationship. After careful thought on the basis of experience the penitent would ask the priest in confession to act as his spiritual guide. The relationship would be carried on in one of three ways.

1. The penitent would not identify himself by name but merely indicate a designation of his state in life and relevant circumstances. The confessor would gradually come to recognize that this was the same person who had spoken to him last month about that question.
2. The penitent would be known to the priest and introduce his confession with an opening statement such as, "Your blessing, Father, this is John Smith. . . ."
3. The third possibility is that the penitent, in addition to going to the same priest regularly for confession, would occasionally seek his counsel outside the confessional.

The advice given by the priest in this last situation is called spiritual direction. Actually it is something we do all the time. Most of us regularly talk over decisions, problems, and courses of action with trusted friends, spouse, or parent. In fact, in our day the concept of spiritual direction must be broadened to embrace many related situations. In several parishes there exist small lay apostolate groups or similar bodies which through the dynamics of discussion actually afford the opportunity for mutual spiritual direction. This is a valuable and even necessary adjunct to our own reflection on a situation, and it is true that any person with faith, wisdom and prudence can be a helpful guide in matters relating to Christian life. The danger to be avoided lies in the possibility of such discussions degenerating into a sort of pious gossiping about oneself. If the confidant is chosen only because he will readily nod assent, the meetings surely will be fruitless. They may result in a psychological lift to one's ego, but little else.

This same obstacle has to be honestly faced in any kind of spiritual direction undertaken by one's confessor. In this personal and even brotherly relationship, it is of key importance to be open to the Holy Spirit. Sometimes it is only in this setting that a person can talk about his deepest concerns. Often the most basic problems go unmentioned in a routine confession for they do not seem to fit into the category of sins or faults. Because complete honesty is of great significance, the penitent should only choose someone with whom he can truly be himself and speak freely. With this condition verified, the penitent is able to seek the

Lord's desire for him here and now in this very concrete situation. Yet the aid which direction brings usually is beyond the necessities of an immediate problem. Instead the focus ordinarily is on the Christian's ever expanding readiness to respond to God's call in fulfilling the ever-present demands of his vocation and enlarging his vision to reach out to his neighbor in needs of every description.

THE COMMUNITY CELEBRATION OF PENANCE

Of the many areas of needed renewal regarding penance perhaps the greatest need is an understanding of the community aspect of the sacrament. In the Constitution on the Church the bishops of the world speak about the community effect of sin and the Church's consequent presence in reconciliation:

> Those who approach the Sacrament of Penance obtain pardon from the mercy of God for the offense committed against Him and are at the same time reconciled with the Church which they have wounded by their sins, and which by charity, example, and prayer seeks their conversion.

When we have sinned we only return to the grace of God in the community of our fellow Christians. This community is the Church.

The medieval theologians taught that the first effect of penance, as with the Eucharist, is the unity of the Church. Reconciliation with the Church is the immediate effect of the sacrament. Sin, then, is an estrangement not only from God but also from God's people. The prodigal in the gospel parable becomes a son again only when he enters into the house of the father and is able to take part in the family feast.

In recent years a desire has been growing among both the clergy and laity to experience the community aspect of penance through a public celebration. This may be done at any gathering of the parish or by a small group at a retreat. In this celebration certain points need clarification:

Absolution in the present discipline of the Church may not be given to several penitents simultaneously except in emergencies — in time of war, for example.

The private character of penance is not to be abandoned and public confession of faults is, in general, not to be encouraged.

The celebration of penance is particularly appropriate on penitential days during the liturgical year. Included in these days would be Advent, Lent, Ember days, vigils of major feasts, Ash Wednesday, Holy Week.

In a parish the service might be conducted in place of a traditional evening devotion or occur during the regular hours for confessions.

In a meaningful community celebration the service opens with a series of short readings from Scripture — from the prophets and psalms of the Old Testament, and from the Gospels and Epistles of the New. These should be chosen to conform with the liturgy of the season or to center the service on a particular theme such as Christian unity.

Following a prayer to the Holy Spirit, the people are seated and make an examination of conscience; the parish priest leads this aloud but with appropriate silences for personal self-examination by each individual participating. This examination of conscience may also be centered on a particular theme, according to the circumstances and needs of the parish or group. This kind of "conducted" preparation for confession is seen as an aid to forming the individual conscience, reminding individuals of failings they might otherwise overlook.

Next, the people say together the *Confiteor,* the Act of Contrition, or one of the psalms of penance.

Then the priests present go to the confessionals to hear each individual's private confession and give absolution. This should go fast, depending on the number of priests and people present. In many cases only a short confession of sins is called for and admonitions only when really necessary.

Meanwhile, the faithful waiting before or after confession listen to scriptural or other inspirational reading by a priest or lay lector. Occasional hymns and periods of silence may be used to vary the service.

When all the confessions are completed, the service concludes with some appropriate prayer of penance, with the common recitation of a "penance" (if a uniform one has been imposed; individuals, of course, may have private penances to perform afterwards) and with a psalm or hymn of thanksgiving.

The advantages of such a common celebration of penance are obvious. The faithful receive spiritual formation that goes much deeper than anything usually possible in the rushed method of the private confession. They are offered the opportunity to obtain new insights into the meaning of penance and the ritual of the confessional. They are made to realize the communal value of penance, of sorrow for sin and repentance. Individuals who do not go to confession can participate in the service, joining the parish community in a joint act of penitence. Finally this kind of celebration restores the good aspects of the public penance of ancient times without disturbing the present laws of private confession.

There are added advantages in the common celebration of penance during a retreat, and the parish service becomes a less startling idea if it is looked at as a "retreat in miniature" insofar as its purpose is the same: the conversion of sinners.

In a retreat, however, there is opportunity for preparing participants well in advance for their common and private act of penance. Conferences will give retreatants orientation on sin and on the sacrament of penance. Private spiritual reading can be suggested for meditation. The retreat can lead naturally into a parish service similar to the one described above.

Whenever possible the celebration of penance in common should be followed by the Mass and the reception of Holy Communion by all.

CHILDREN'S CONFESSIONS

Is there anything more deadening to the spirit than hearing several hundred children's confessions each month on the eve of first Friday? Is there value in the practice? Many today would question the value. The one advantage most often mentioned — establishing good habits — seems not to be present, apart from the danger of lifeless formalism that carries over into adulthood. How else can we explain the common pastoral experience that most of the children who go to confession in September were last to confession when school was in session? However, if these children's confession days cannot be eliminated, then at least some shortened version of the community celebration of penance should be used to assure the children as much benefit as possible from the penance experience.

Another question of real moment today is the age when children should first receive penance. The virtue of penance reinforced with an understanding of God's forgiving love through Christ should be instilled at an early age. But there are good reasons why our present practice could profit from some change. An experience going on in the Diocese of Roermond in the Netherlands sheds light on the problem and possible solutions. Since 1962 studies have been made of the age for the reception of both the Eucharist and penance and the relationship between them. Parents, priests, and teachers are responsible for suggestions which were implemented in a directive of Bishop Petrus Moors that took effect at the beginning of the 1964-1965 school year. The instruction is as follows:

1. The responsibility for the religious education of children rests primarily with the parents. If the preparation for first Communion and Confession is given in school, the parents should be involved as much as possible. The parents should receive instruction and help so that they recognize their task in all its dimensions and are able to fulfill it as well as possible.
2. The preparation for children's first Communion, insofar as it is school-related, shall take place in the second grade.
3. The introduction to the sacrament of Penance is best done gradually. In this way the development of the child will be taken into account; he can be led to Confession with a proper disposition — namely, a conversion of heart. Likewise, proper attention can be given to the social and ecclesial aspects which are essential to the sacrament of Penance.
4. The preparation for first Confession, when it is given in school, will start in the year following the first Communion. In third grade, a non-sacramental penance celebration would be held a few times. In fourth grade, the child would approach the sacrament occasionally in the form of a communal celebration where he confesses and receives absolution individually. From the fifth grade on, in addition to the communal celebration, there would be opportunities for private Confession.

If the emphasis on the gradualness of the introduction may suggest a tendency to temporize with the sacrament of penance, it should be kept in mind that sustained and continuous guidance directs the children's education in both sacraments. Undoubtedly the result is a better understanding among the children of what they are doing than they obtain from a sink-or-swim immersion in the sacramental life.

It is worth noting that the Roermond legislation is the first diocesan action of its kind. But the practice it sanctions is not entirely new. Children in many places in Europe and some places in the United States are introduced to the sacrament of penance after they have received First Communion.

The committee that worked on the new legislation has explained their reasoning:

> We must remember that the knowledge of good and evil is still very defective in the young school child. His conscience is in an unformed state. As long as the child is in the world of imaginary realism (between 5.5 and 7 years) it is not advisable to confront him prematurely with Confession because a sense of objectivity is still lacking.
>
> . . . We agree that the young child has a certain knowledge of good and evil. But is he able to commit the kind of sin that begs forgiveness in Confession? The wide acceptance of Confessions of devotion gained over the centuries must not blind us to the practice, commonly understood by the faithful, whereby venial sin is forgiven principally through prayer and fraternal charity.
>
> . . . It is much more important that a child discovers slowly by means of instruction and prayer where the root of sin lies, what sin is, and how forgiveness is possible. In the measure that understanding grows, the child's words will express his misdeeds and will beg forgiveness. At the same time he has discovered the social aspects of his sin and his repentance.
>
> . . . Let us conclude with a remark of Van Haaren: "Confession is not properly the concern at the time of preparation for the first Communion. It is rightly a concern that befits life in the adult Christian community." So that Penance's true perspective is realized by those coming to adulthood, however, we must first provide for their sound initiation to the sacrament. How otherwise can we expect that adult Christians will comprehend its significance?

It may be several years before a new ritual of penance is introduced into the Roman rite. However, it is in the situation here and now that the priest must make decisions, impart absolution, and offer counsel. The priest today, in the absence of specific direction from the Church, must nonetheless look to the attitudes clearly taught in the documents of the Vatican Council II and embody them in his approach to the sacrament of penance. The emphasis on Christ as the agent of reconciliation, the importance of the personal meeting between priest and penitent, the realization of the community aspect of private confession — all these call for a continuing sensitivity on the part of the priest in his understanding of his office as confessor.

Thus in the renewal of the Church the role of the priest as confessor is emerging as ever more significant. The insecurity bred of changes in society and the Church and the increasing educational level of Catholics conspire to demand more and more of the persons entrusted with the spiritual guidance of the faithful. Priests should consider that their effectiveness as confessors is related — in addition to their human gifts and spiritual perception — to their continuing efforts to update their own theological and psychological knowledge. Insofar as possible a good confessor must be all things to all men.

6

The Confessor Focuses
on the Adolescent

BERNARD A. MEYER

"BLESS ME, FATHER, FOR I HAVE SINNED . . . I FEEL SO MISERABLE, I wanted to be good and I tried, really I tried, but I've been a failure," stammered the teen-age girl. "The last time I went to confession, I promised God that I was going to improve, but I didn't!" she almost shouted. With an emotionally filled voice, she hauntingly whispered, "Life is so confusing . . . it's so difficult . . . being good is such an effort. . . . at times I want to give up trying . . . everything is such a struggle . . . such a struggle!"

The one word which the teen-age penitent used to describe her state, and that of many teen-agers like her, was the word "struggle." For it is in the teen years that the youth find themselves deeply immersed in the struggle toward self-expression, independence, intellectual growth, and emotional control. The artist does not turn toward the teen-ager when he seeks to depict the "good things of life." It is through the child that he projects security, the carefreeness and charm of the young, not the teen! We, too, with a certain envy, look at these "little ones" and dream dreams of carefreeness that was ours once, many years ago. It is to this image of the child, who has no struggles, not the teen, that we are tempted to retreat when we encounter the difficulties of the world.

"Life is impossible," states the teen when confronting the difficulties of his world; and within a few moments, with bubbling enthusiasm, he is

64

capable of saying, "Ain't life grand!" To the teen belongs the world of contradiction and change. To him belongs the problems of friction and adjustment which are caused by change. In his world, there is no choice, no opportunity to reject change, for the intellectual, emotional, and physical changes that he experiences are of the very essence of his life. Not only is he forced to face the problems that are caused by his own personal development, but at this time, he must face a new challenge entering into his personal arena of growth, the modern complex society. Exiting from the neat, packaged world of childhood security, he stands on the threshold of the turmoil of growing up. Despite the energy of his youth, his own sense of insecurity in these new surroundings pervades his youthful vitality to the extent that at times he is paralyzed. He vacillates daily from complete optimism concerning his capabilities to utter dejection and frustration at the thought of failure. His world at one time can appear as the land of opportunity, yet on another occasion, as a deep foreboding unknown. Advice from adults penetrates his consciousness, but his natural tendency to be independent encourages him to reject it. His sense of idealism conflicts vehemently with his selfish interests. Amid this sea of confusion stands the teen-ager, surrounded by many people, but often feeling very much alone.

The paradoxes of the teen-age life pose a great mystery for him. His own moods are unintelligible to him. His natural bent toward independence makes it difficult for him to communicate with adults, especially his parents, concerning problems that he cannot solve. It is to his friends that he turns for knowledge and solutions, but after many experiences he realizes that they, too, are engulfed in misunderstanding and are unable to aid him. During these moments of confusion, he can easily become the prey of a sophisticated companion, only to become misled, misinformed, and disillusioned.

It is this type of world that the confessor has a unique opportunity to enter. The entrance by the priest is facilitated by many factors. The fact that the priest symbolizes security to the youth is important. The priest, as confessor, can become the rock of security to which the youth can anchor with confidence. Another factor is the confessional itself, which provides an appealing atmosphere in which the teen can reveal his fears, apprehensions, faults, and failing, without the fear of public recriminations for failure. The newly found sensitivity and idealism of the teen can develop him into a most vital receptacle for the idealism of Christ. These factors enable the priest-confessor to penetrate with knowledge the conscious life of the teen, which will prepare the way for the troubled soul to be soothed by the grace of Christ.

The efforts expended by the priest to mentally recapture his youth can pay great dividends for the confessor of the teen-ager. These mental gymnastics, which will be quite strenuous for some, will help give him an insight into the problems of youth which stem from human nature. Such efforts will necessarily instill sympathy into the confessor and motivate him to act and speak with a personal concern to the troubled youth. Thus, to represent the Divine Physician in the confessional with maximum success, it is important that the confessor strive to understand the adolescent as a human person. This understanding does not apply merely to the intellectual faculty of the youth, but to the *whole person*. As Cardinal Tisserand has said, "It is a grave mistake to treat people as though they were merely minds. The emotive forces of nature, physical and animal, must not be forgotten, so often driving them blindly in contrary directions."[1] With this in mind, then, the primary effort exerted in this chapter will be to understand the intellectual and emotional factors of adolescence, in order that the confessional advice might become more effective in helping the teen acquire sanctity.

Focus on the Expanding Imagination

With the advance of adolescence, no new powers of the soul are developed since the ability to think, will, and feel are possessed by the child. These powers do begin to develop rapidly when the adolescent reaches puberty. The transition from childhood to adolescence is a major step. The child is concerned with neither the past nor the future, but only with the present. That is why childhood is carefree and happy. But adolescence brings about an important change, for the powers of sensation now have a far deeper meaning because of the wider background of experiences. Experiences no longer affect only the present, but are now capable of affecting the future, and can be recalled. This causes an increased sensitivity in the teen ager. For example, he becomes aware of much more than mere physical injury in the act of falling; he now views this act in relation to the society in which he lives. If his friends laugh, he is humiliated and embarrassed. Of eminent importance, therefore, will be the opinions of others concerning him. He will become increasingly prone to pass judgments upon his own actions depending upon how they will reflect upon him. Should an act possibly bring ridicule upon him, no price is too great to avoid it; but if it is an opportunity to bathe in the praise of his friends, no danger is too great! Such praiseworthy acts, as viewed by the adolescent, can be discussed only in the most glowing terms. Thus, his vocabulary becomes infiltrated with extremes, such as "the greatest" or "the worst."

All of this is partially the result of the youth's expanding imagination, which is the power of recalling past sensations, of reliving them in the

---

[1] Very Rev. Fernand Van Steenberghen, *Psychology, Morality and Education* (Great Britain: Burns Oates Ltd., 1958).

memory, and of building them into new combinations. Controlled, the imagination can be a great asset to youth in developing their powers of creativity. But uncontrolled, it can distort the naturally active youth into inactivity, e.g., when he dwells on past failures or future difficulties. Realizing that the imagination can be a great motivating factor in the teen's life, the confessor should be aware of the great powers of this faculty. Through the power of the imagination, the teen is quite capable of seeing himself sacrificing all for the good of others. Certainly, the saints must have had their creative powers stimulated by their imagination to perform their heroic acts. Must we not dream dreams in order to see the challenges of Christ in our lives? Here, then, in the imagination lies the instrument which the alert confessor can use to broaden the horizons of youth to encourage him to go beyond the limited bonds of self-concern to the desperate needs of humanity throughout the world. It will be this type of creativity, through which the youth can visualize himself as Christ's ambassador to the mission fields of the world, that will inspire him to undergo degradation and poverty willingly, and to bring the peace of Christ to the "least of his brethren."

Focus on the Intellectual Struggle

The security of the pre-adolescent's world was greatly enhanced by his intellectual immaturity. Truth was identified with a person, not a fact! His whole process of searching for the truth was very simple, for the value of a statement was determined by *who* made it rather than by *what* was expressed. After all, his parents had said that there is a Santa Claus and that was good enough for him! There existed no intellectual curiosity in the child which encouraged him to probe beyond the authority behind the statement, v.g., parents, teacher, priest. The only requirement was that the authority be someone accepted by the child. But this process of evaluation changes when the child becomes an adolescent.

At this stage of the teen's development, a maze of half-truths, myths, and facts are being carefully sorted out in the search for truth. The awakened intellectual curiosity forces him to transcend the superficial understanding of childhood. His developing spirit of independency is now being applied to his intellectual life. He wants to do things on his own, find out for himself. His primary concern becomes *what* is said instead of *who* said it! The over-simplified answers of the past are no longer sufficient since he is developing the ability to grasp ideas in their relationship to one another. With the broadening of his intellectual horizons, new ideas emerge and he struggles to place them into a coherent system of thought, thus developing his logical thinking processes. As his intellectual appetite is stimulated, he begins to probe beneath the surface of the statement, and another word in his vocabulary takes on serious meaning

— *'why!'* The answers to these questions must be reasonable so that they may be absorbed into his logical thinking processes. If the answers do not follow logically from what he has been previously told, they will soon be discarded. Now, becoming an experienced member in this new world of ideas and actions, he quickly perceives the discrepancies between the ideas and actions of many adults. Pressure upon the adult world begins to mount, from its youthful adherent, to make ideas conform to actions. The adolescent, being idealistic, is mystified when they don't. Failure by an influential adult to live by his ideas can destroy the confidence between the teen and the adult world.

Just as the adult world can fail the youth at this crucial time of his life, so might the adolescent fail himself. Readily, he realizes that his expectations of the adult world to harmonize their ideas and actions now becomes his responsibility as well! As he became aware of the contradictions between profession and action in the lives of others, he now becomes aware of self-contradiction. St. Paul aptly described this state of mind when he said: "For I do not understand what I do, for it is not what I wish that I do, but what I hate, that I do!" (Rm 7:15.) The searching nature of the teen forces him to look into the recesses of his own being for the answers to his own personal conflict between ideas and actions. This search will be in vain, if the youth is left to his own resources. There are so many factors in his life, v.g., physical, emotional, and intellectual change, that without help, he could not understand. His groping for answers will force him to find someone who can be his guiding light, someone who can present truth and its relationship to him in an intelligible manner. It will be someone who is sympathetic, in whom the teen can have confidence, whose ability he respects, and whose guidance he cherishes. This "someone" can be the confessor of the teen-ager!

This confessor, indeed, has a delicate role. He must be able to project through the confessional screen the image of patience and kindness. By so doing, he will provide the opportunity for the youthful penitent to articulate the questions that are stirred up in him by his interminable struggle. These virtues dispose the penitent to become on the one hand open and frank, and on the other, receptive of advice. They create the image of a confessor who is concerned. Patience and kindness help the youth to have confidence in the confessor, thus transforming the youth into a vital receptacle. But the disposition of the youth, despite its importance, is not enough. The confessor must be able to communicate. In order to do this successfully, his own powers of creativity will be taxed to their fullest. By the creative confessor is meant one who has the interest, enthusiasm, and spiritual depth to translate the Christian way of life into concepts which can be grasped by the teen. This is no small task, particularly when one considers the practical difficulties regarding time, or really the lack of it, and the large numbers of penitents. The confessor, then, in a very short span of times, will have to analyze the problems of the individual, and then graphically and dynamically project the solutions on an intellectual level that can be comprehended by the youth.

Should the advice of the confessor, filtering its way through the confessional screen to the penitent, sound as though it were coming from a record being played for the hundredth time, it obviously is not dynamic. Despite the excellence of the advice, it lacks that very essential quality which only the human voice can give to it — *conviction!* This quality of conviction can only come from the soul which is deeply immersed in the realities of life, secular and spiritual. From these depths, in which he himself has faced the personal struggle of fusing together the spiritual and secular world into a practical daily way of life, will come the confessor's personal dynamism. He will not be satisfied to utter trite, meaningless phrases, but from the depths of his own spiritual life ideas and words will come which will possess and convey this quality of conviction.

The ideas and words which are a sounding of the depths of his own spiritual life, must be presented graphically to be understood. They must be formed into an image which can be easily grasped. In order that this image be meaningful, it is necessary to analyze the penitent himself. If the words that are used are beyond the comprehension of the hearer, no matter how distinctly or how convincingly they are said, they will not be understood. In the confessional, the analysis of the penitent is limited. Yet, a significant clue to the confessor is the vocabulary, manner of speech, etc., that the penitent himself uses. It will not be too difficult for the confessor to phrase his words into an intelligible image if he listens alertly to the penitent. Despite the fact that the penitent says relatively little in the confessional, he does project an impression of his own spiritual, intellectual, and emotional development. It is on this basis that the confessor must accommodate his words and expressions so that they are understood by this particular penitent. The confessor's own awareness of the problems of adolescence will give him the foundation upon which he can construct his confessional advice. Indeed, it would be unfortunate if the youthful penitent, upon leaving the confessional, marveled at the vocabulary of the priest, but at the same time was not able to be edified and helped by what was said, simply because he didn't understand the words the priest used!

The natural phenomenon of the teen's striving for intellectual maturity will pose a challenge for the confessor. It may be that the "Santa Claus" answers to questions in the sphere of religion were once accepted, but with the arrival of a certain degree of maturity the adolescent finds that these answers of the past are no longer sufficient; the partial truths of preadolescence in religious matters, as in secular affairs, will no longer suffice; he wants all the truth, uncontaminated by myth. This challenge should often cause the confessor to reflect upon his confessional advice and his ability to communicate with youth. This is indeed healthy, for it is only through this internal questioning and searching that the confessor can hope to remain relevant to the teen-ager in our modern society. On these occasions, it most probably would be advisable for the confessor to take a personal inventory, to see if he is using the powers of *creativity* which God gave him to communicate the ideals of Christ to the teen, who is so capable of idealism.

Focus on the Emotional Struggle

Most men eulogize activities that are guided by reason, but they usually guide their own personal lives by their feelings. In the majority of cases the heart plays a more prominent role than the head. This may not be the ideal, but it is a fact, and as such, we must face it. It would, indeed, be unfortunate if we viewed the emotions as being bad or dangerous in themselves. True, they can become destructive if they are misused; but properly channeled, they add vitality to life itself. The world would be a drab place if there were no love and sympathy for the unfortunate, or hatred of what is evil. The emotions, then, must be trained, not killed.

The goal of training the emotions is this: to develop the ability to respond with the particular emotion that the situation calls for. This response is not to be overdone; rather, it ought to be measured, both in degree and duration, by the situation itself. This goal is not easily achieved, but attained only through much practice. The training program is initiated in the very first years of infancy and lasts throughout one's life.

The effort expended by the adolescent is particularly important because this is the time of dramatic emotional change. He will establish emotional patterns which will affect his adult life. During the teen years he is in the process of breaking with the past. It is with the advent of puberty that he becomes capable of feelings that are different, both in kind and intensity, from those he knew as a child. Since he is developing intellectually, his emotional life becomes more involved. He not only has participated in more of life's experiences, but his mental development enables him to read deeper meanings into them. Another reason for the change is physical. At this period, the mutual interaction of the body and soul becomes quite obvious. He becomes, v.g., very sensitive about his physical appearance, and any deficiency in this area can cause him many anxious moments. Thus for the teen the opportune time for the emotions to grow fuller and richer has arrived. An added note of importance lies in the fact that this emotional training, or the lack of it, will establish patterns of emotional expression that will profoundly affect himself and his relationship to others.

A new set of values is derived by the adolescent from his deepened insight, vivid imagination, and greater capacity for reasoning. The teen's increased awareness of his own developing capabilities enable him to elicit deeper meanings from his experiences. His relationship to others, his social consciousness, becomes increasingly important in his life, and flowing from this, a keen sense of justice to which he is delicately sensitive. Frequently, his sense of justice toward himself is grossly exaggerated — e.g., when he develops a persecution complex — and this will cause him many hours of discomfort.

Emotional unrest promotes instability within youth. The teen's desire for thrills and excitement is heightened, regardless of the effects upon himself or others. If he is permitted to overindulge in this desire, he then develops a greater excitability; yet, if he is forced to repress it too sternly, he may end up brooding or rebelling. The instability of the teen is frequently exemplified when he begins a task with energy and enthusiasm, only to abandon it because his efforts are not met with immediate success. The initial enthusiasm may soon change into despondency when he meets some unexpected obstacle. Teen-age is often characterized by a vacillation between inactivity and over-activity.

To be frivolous, too, is characteristic of youth! The goal of his life is "to have a good time." This is the focal point, and seems to be the determining factor of the success or failure of any event. He seems to regard as sacred his right to fill his life with as many thrills as possible despite the consequence. As a child, he treated many people, ideas, and objects with great respect; now, as an adolescent, he treats these same people, ideas, and objects in a flippant and light-hearted way. All seems justified to the youth if it brings from his companions convulsive laughter. Yet, almost instantaneously, the mood can change from delight to depression. He becomes engrossed in his own inadequacies which generate an overpowering fear of failure stymying any positive action on his part. Due to the teen's increased awareness of and dependency upon others, he fears not only his own personal incompetency, but the possibility of being rejected by the "crowd." This emotional vacillation can lead him into a state of confusion. It is at this time that patience and sympathy from adults are so necessary for the teen's well being.

The adolescent views himself in a very serious light. Yet, being a product of diverse emotional drives, he can at one moment have a very lofty trust in his own ability, exuding cockiness, and in the next moment, sulking for fear of what his friends might think. His arrogance most frequently is merely an effort to hide his insecurity. Despite his own personal views of himself and the image that he tries to project to the crowd, he is, in reality, a most uncertain and timid creature. The clown of the group performs constantly within the group, where nothing is considered sacred; but to get him to exercise his talents on a stage is a near impossibility. And notwithstanding the fact that his antics rarely meet with silence from the crowd, he becomes speechless when introduced to someone new, particularly an adult. His sensitiveness, at times, contributes to the youth's reluctance to express himself, for fear of saying something in an ill-advised manner or at the wrong time. This self-consciousness is a constant source of agitation, being quite obvious when the teen is at his worst, and merely lurking beneath the surface when he is at his best.

The selfishness of childhood is part of the life of the teen. He frequently displays this childishness by wanting his own way or by ignoring completely the rights of others. Another part of the adolescent's life, though, is the development of his social consciousness. This, too, is displayed by the teen by his many acts of courtesy and his earnest desire to help others. It is at this time that most religious vocations bud, but they need nourishment which the confessor can readily provide. It is important, however, that ideas about the religious life be presented to the youth, not merely in esoteric terms, but in a comprehensible manner. If the vocation to the religious life is presented in a sanctimonious way, the youth, because of his own internal turmoil, will feel the necessity of rejecting it. But if the religious vocation is presented in the light of a spiritual struggle toward sanctity, similar to his personal struggle toward adulthood, it becomes meaningful to him. The religious vocation will not have a superficial image of an accomplished state of perfection, but a true image insofar as it is a way or means toward perfection. This will help the youth to understand that the primary requisite for the religious vocation is the desire and willingness to expend his effort in this way, to seek perfection. He will not think that a high degree of personal sanctification is required prior to his acceptance of the challenge of the religious vocation. If the idea of the vocation when presented to the adolescent contains this element of *striving* for perfection, then it will be in much greater accord with the nature of the youth who, too, is constantly *striving* in his relationships with himself, his parents, and his friends.

The atmosphere generated by the confessional is one of introspection in the appealing calm of the church — an atmosphere quite foreign to the teen's regular schedule of intense activity. But it is only in this setting of external calm that he has a chance to find and understand himself amid the complexities of adolescent life. Of itself, however, this calm is not sufficient since the teen cannot divorce himself from the internal struggles caused by a liberation from the clearly defined world of "do's and don'ts" of childhood to the greater independency of adolescence. But the external calm of the church, plus the demands of preparing for confession, will force the youth to be introspective; it will, therefore, help to dispose the teen to seek the advice of the confessor concerning his problems. Then the confessor, assisted by his own awareness of the emotional turmoil of the teen, can help him to develop emotional patterns which will be advantageous to his spiritual maturity. The confessor can present practical goals to the youth to enable him to understand himself, his experiences, and his social consciousness. Goals become more practical the more intimately they are based upon the nature of the adolescent.

Thus, the teen's sensitivity about *his* rights can be utilized by the confessor to make him sensitive about the rights of others. Appealing to the indignation of the teen, who reacts quickly when his rights are infringed upon, the confessor has a good basis to explain how the teen himself violates the rights of others by his sins. Even the youth's emotional reaction of anger against an offender can be utilized, by way of contrast, to illustrate God's mercy demonstrated by giving us the sacrament of penance. In this manner, the priest, using the emotions as a springboard, helps the youth to obtain a concrete appreciation of God and his kindness. In so doing, the confessor can project the goal of being Christ-like regarding self-control. Using examples from the life of Christ and the saints, the confessor graphically illustrates, in terms understandable by the teen, the harmony which should exist between the emotions and self-control. Thus, he helps the youth to establish emotional patterns which will be conducive to spiritual maturity.

Within the context of the teen's struggle for independence, the priest can emphasize God's goodness in making him free. Since freedom has become personalized in his life, the teen can appreciate God's goodness in this manner. Stressing the fact that God has made us free, so that we become personally responsible for our own actions, will help the youth to understand the interrelationship between freedom and his personal responsibility.

Furthermore, the teen's propensity to identify with others should enable him to understand Christ's identifying himself with men. As the youth suffers from the constant fear of rejection by his own friends, the rejection of Christ by his friends becomes more real and meaningful. It becomes easier, then, for the teen to see and understand his own rejection of Christ by sin, since this rejection is the same thing that he most probably has experienced himself. The emotions, then, properly used by the confessor, become instruments to illustrate what being Christ-like really means. In the example of the life of Christ, the confessor has the perfect illustration of goals for the teen's life.

The social consciousness of the youth can aid him to understand his relationship with his own family, often an area of difficulty for the teen. The confessor can aid him to discover that just as the words and actions of others affect his life, so too his words and actions affect the lives of others, especially his family. As he is inspired by the example of others, so too, must he become a source of inspiration. The idealism of youth, properly focused by the confessor upon Christ, can be the youth's greatest asset in making major strides spiritually. Accentuating the life of Christ, particularly his passion, the confessor can help the teen to understand that true idealism can become a reality only through great personal effort and sacrifice.

It is within the providence of the confessor to help the teen realize that Christianity is not merely a set of dogmas and abstruse laws, but a person — Christ. Christ then becomes real, vital, alive, not because of the intellectual knowledge alone that the teen has of Christ's life, but because the teen realizes that what he is experiencing, Christ has experienced. The adolescent's subjection to authority was part of Christ's life, too! When Christ, as an adolescent, was lost and eventually found in the temple, St. Luke said that, "He went down with them and came to Nazareth and was subject to them. . . . And Jesus advanced in wisdom and age and grace before God and men" (Lk 2:51–52). Authority in the life of the teen, as in Christ's Life, is actually an opportunity for developing maturity; in accepting the authority expressed by his parents, the teen too can grow in age, grace, and wisdom. As the teen lives in a world of insecurity, resulting partially from a fear of rejection by others, so did Christ, since he was rejected by one of his best friends, Peter. . . . "And after a little while the bystanders for their part said to Peter: 'You are certainly one of them; why, you are a Galilean!' Then he burst out cursing and swearing: 'I have nothing to do with this man Christ you are talking about' " (Mk 14:70–71). The natural feelings of despondency and loneliness which periodically invade the teen's life were certainly a part of Christ's life, especially when he was on the cross and said, "My God, my God, why do you abandon me?" (Mt 27:47.) Through such examples, the youth will comprehend that his personal struggle with life is the same as Christ's. Christ becomes something more than just a pious image to imitate; he becomes a person who is capable of concern and sympathy for the struggling teen. Christ now becomes alive and capable of igniting the passions of loyalty and dedication within the youth. Christ is his friend! The confessor, therefore, founding his guiding efforts on the emotional experiences of the youth, can assist the teen to develop into a dynamic follower of Christ.

FOCUS ON THE CONSEQUENCES OF THESE STRUGGLES

Having acquired an insight into the complexities of adolescent development, we must now focus our attention upon the natural consequences arising from the teen's intellectual and emotional struggles. It becomes increasingly important, then, for the confessor to perceive clearly the difference within youth between the *natural,* i.e., properties common to all adolescent development, and the *unnatural,* i.e., the peculiarities of an individual adolescent, so that the supernatural life can be built upon the teen's *natural* mode of development. It is an axiom of theology that grace builds upon nature, and by understanding the nature of the teen, the confessor can more adequately help him build the superstructure of divine life. Youth has many natural tendencies which exist for his well-being, social and spiritual. In his advice the confessor should utilize these natural tendencies to help the teen to understand himself, and to follow more easily the spiritual director's advice. For example, if it is understood that it is natural for the teen to associate with a particular crowd, then despite its evil effect upon the teen, the confessor should not tersely say, "drop the crowd!" To the teen this advice would be impractical since it is natural and necessary for him to be identified with a group. The confessor can use this natural tendency of *group identification* to advise him to find a new group of friends. Now the advice is practical to the teen since it follows the natural trend, at this age, to be identified with a particular group. The confessor has demonstrated, by his practical advice, his ability to understand the teen and his problems. Consequently, there develops a bond of confidence between the teen and the confessor, which will enable the latter to become a more effective instrument of grace.

Focus on "The Gang"

The very young child naturally turns toward himself. He is egotistical, self-willed, and self-interested. In the process of growth, he begins to realize his dependency upon others. In the quest for survival, he needs his parents. The classroom teacher aids him to learn. Eventually, his awareness of this dependency develops into a social consciousness which ordinarily reaches the apex in the teen years. It is natural for the adolescent to expend considerable energy in seeking and appeasing his companions. Mutual companionship among teens is usually expressed in terms of "the crowd" or "the gang."

This pattern of development among boys is obvious because their activities are more sensational than those of girls. But girls, too, have the same natural tendency to form closely knit groups. The center of interests shifts from the home to the gang, with whom they are closely associated and identified. The select group fosters a spirit of loyalty and exacts certain standards from each participating member. This pervading influence is easily demonstrated in the lives of most teens. Once established, the gang dictates styles of dress, preference of entertainment, mannerisms in speech, etc. Being considered a member of the "in-group" can become so necessary to the teen that it affects his every waking moment. The total value and moral structure of this group will affect the individual in proportion to the importance he places upon being considered one of its members. The gang exerts an influence upon its members to an extent far greater than is often realized; and if an abnormal difficulty develops within the home life, the gang's influence will develop proportionally. This identification with the gang is a natural tendency for the adolescent, but its influence for good or evil will depend upon the members of the gang.

Awareness of the natural tendency of youth to be a member of a gang will be of great value to the confessor. He will realize that the youthful penitent in the confessional will frequently be reflecting the influences of his companions upon his life. It will become readily apparent to the confessor when these influences have become spiritually detrimental to the youth. At this juncture, the confessor's prudential judgment will be necessary to determine the capabilities of the penitent and the approach which will appeal most naturally to this individual. The priest could appeal to the idealism of youth and endeavor to enkindle the ideal or desire of having a positive influence for good upon his companions. This approach might take the form of citing examples from the life of St. Paul, who strove to instill Christian principles in his pagan and Jewish contemporaries. The relating of the ideal to a person is important because the ideal of itself is vague, but when it becomes identified with someone, the ideal becomes alive. This is the technique that Christ used so frequently. He did not speak in terms of "goodness" itself, but told the story of the "Good Samaritan," nor did he give a dissertation on the evil of injustice, but talked about the "Unjust Steward" and "The Rich Man and Lazarus." In this way the advice becomes practical since it is not projected in some lofty, almost unapproachable, way; and it becomes real and vital since it is firmly anchored in a person with whom the youth can easily identify himself.

The influence of the gang might be so great that the confessor deems it necessary for the youth to seek out new friends, a new crowd. Making the adjustment from one group to another will be difficult, so the confessor should use the youth's natural tendency toward independency to implement the transferral of allegiance. The confessor can appeal to the heroic instincts of the teen by emphasizing Christ's unwillingness to follow the crowd into error, and his determination to choose the more difficult path of the crucifixion to live by his principles.

FOCUS ON THE SEXUAL STRUGGLE

Sexlessness characterizes the relationship in the early years of life between boys and girls. Their primary concern is that of having a playmate. This is obvious from the behavior of the children themselves, for they do not differentiate between their playmates, regardless of race or sex. In this idyllic setting, equality reigns supreme. If at this age, the boys should show deference or special consideration for girls, it is only the result of training or imitation, not of any natural instinct. In fact, if nature held complete sway, all boys would be boys and most girls would be tomboys; but there is another factor that must be considered, and this is the influence of the adult world in which they live. As the children continue to grow the environmental influence develops proportionately and effects a partial separation of the sexes. For the child at this age, the differentiating characteristics, such as interests, manners of expression, games played, exist because they are fostered by adults. Were these differences not fostered, the children in their behavior and interests would be very much the same.

Natural segregation develops between boys and girls immediately prior to adolescence. Two factors contribute to this natural segregation; the gang influence upon the boys and the early age of puberty for the girls. The gang influence encourages the boys to treat all girls with complete disdain. The early age of puberty causes the girls to surpass the boys in their physical and mental development, particularly during the first few years of adolescence. This superiority of the girls continues until about the age of fifteen. Until this approximate age, it is most natural for the sexes to be apart. This alienation between the sexes, which lasts until a physical and mental balance develops, seems to be a wise provision of nature since it provides an excellent opportunity for them to develop the qualities of manliness and femininity. Once this period of balance sets in, it becomes natural for them to seek each other's companionship, which, if properly utilized, will have a healthy effect upon them. In this period of development, mutual companionship will affect the refinement of the boys and broaden the horizons of the girls. They become aware that particular qualities lacking in themselves can be found in the other. These differentiating, but complementing, qualities rooted in their nature, contribute to their radically different outlooks on life, to the disparity of their emotional lives, and the diversity of temperamental characteristics and interests. An awareness of these diverse, yet complementary, qualities in each other, plus the wisdom garnered from the world of experience, assist the teen to choose his future mate more wisely.

Realizing the influence of the adult society on the early stages of childhood will aid us to become more aware of the influence of the affluent society on the teenager of today. The second half of the twentieth century has frequently been referred to as the "Sex Saturated Society." A quick perusal of the movie advertisements or corner newspaper stands in most communities will prove the point. The continual exposé of adolescent sex by various magazines and newspapers makes one wonder, at times, who is exposing whom. The names of those who, in the United States, have expressed themselves with deep concern about this problem, *via* the printed word, television, and radio, would read like a "who's who" list. The problem of sex, society, and the teen has occasioned many spoken and written words.

One author has succinctly expressed the problem in these terms, "The percentage of adolescents in trouble is up. . . . Since World War II the time table of sex activity has been set ahead by approximately three years."[2] The priest, dealing with the ever increasing number of teen-age marriages, is forced to echo these same sentiments. Despite any personal views concerning the exposé of *sex and the teenager* in the communication media, it is, and certainly will remain for some time, a fact that the sex saturated society is a reality and must be dealt with as such!

The confessor must struggle with this society and the complexities of adolescent development, for he is in a position of imparting to teenagers something of far greater value than mere biological information regarding sex, namely, the proper attitudes toward sex. To be of value, these attitudes must be related to God; and to be meaningful, they must be personally understood. This is the goal toward which the confessor of youth must strive.

The development of attitudes does not depend completely upon what is said, but also upon the situation in which it is expressed. To make a serious statement in a situation which calls for levity runs the risk not only of the statement being ineffectual, but of creating an adverse attitude toward what is said. For example, the fellow who, at the office Christmas party, climbs upon the soap box to convince his fellow workers of the great opportunities of sanctification contained within the Christian way of life, is wasting his time and most probably creating many enemies. Despite the validity of what he says, the situation is inappropriate. Quite to the contrary though, the confessional situation is ideal for developing attitudes. The penitent voluntarily embraces the situation of secrecy and sacredness of the confession. The secrecy imposed upon the confessor helps the teen to be honest and receptive. The sacredness of the act, in which the teen participates, enables him to prize highly the advice of the confessor as a means toward sanctification. It is this situation, created by the sacrament of penance, which readily disposes the youthful penitent to grasp the Christian attitudes toward sex.

"But Father, I love him . . ." is the frequent explanation by the teen when confessing the sin of fornication. Love is a many splendored thing and so are its expressions, but premarital sex relations is not one of them. Through the confessor's efforts in cultivating the proper attitudes toward love, the youth will understand that love's proper expression lies not in personal pleasure alone, but more realistically in personal

---

[2] Ann Landers, *Talks To Teen-Agers About Sex* (Englewood Cliffs, N. J.: Prentice-Hall, 1963).

sacrifice. "Greater love than this no one has, that one lay down his life for his friends" (Jn 15:13). Real love must have its climax in the spiritual and physical good of the beloved. Love helps the teen to overcome the seemingly insurmountable natural inclination toward selfishness, to become concerned about the welfare of others. In human relationships, particularly those of youth, love is immersed within an emotional context. Consequently, as the word *love* is used and viewed by the teen, it is a subjective experience to be felt, rather than an objective fact to be analyzed. It will be necessary for the confessor to emphasize frequently the difference between love and passion, by particularly stressing the fact that true love is expressed in such a way as to be for the spiritual and physical welfare of the beloved. This advice by the confessor must be relevant to the teenage mentality in order that it may be absorbed by the penitent in terms of conviction which will dynamically influence his life. There are many ways in which the confessor can assist an adolescent to understand love and sacrifice. The ideal example will be the expression of the love of Christ for all humanity in his sacrificial act. Sometimes the ideal example is not always effective, so the confessor must be prepared with supplementary examples from the lives of the saints or from the lives of heroic figures of today, to be used as a vehicle for illustrating the proper attitudes, i.e., the attitudes of love and sacrifice. These attitudes are the key which will unlock the door of mystery barring the youth from a proper understanding of sex in relationship to others and himself.

Since the natural culmination of the complete use of the sexual faculties results in children, the teen needs to realize that the responsibility to the children can only be fulfilled in a stable society, the family. The proper rearing and education of the children is the function of the parents. Thus the desired image, to be presented to the youth by the confessor, is the intimate relationship of sex-and-marriage. For only in marriage can the youth properly exercise the use of his sexual faculties and also fulfill his responsibilities to the offspring. The confessor can project this image of sex-and-marriage to the mind of the teen through his terminology. If the confessor uses such terms as marital intercourse, premarital, and extra-marital, then he helps the teen to realize that sexual activity must be intimately bound to marriage. Once this bond is firmly established in the youth's mind, the confessor will be able to focus all preliminary sexual activity, v.g., petting, necking, etc., to the ultimate act of marital intercourse. Since the final act must take place in marriage, so, too, must the preparatory acts. In so doing, the confessor helps the teen to relate all sexual activity to marriage.

When a group of young adults were asked, "In a dating situation, how can the couple help each other regarding sex?" they were stunned! One girl explained that she had never thought in a *positive* way about sex, for in her four years in a Catholic high school, all she had ever heard about the sixth and ninth commandments was "Don't . . . don't . . . don't!" By always speaking of sex in relation to marriage, the confessor can aid the youth to think *positive!* Being positive means, e.g., that the priest should insist that sex can help the husband and wife in their personal relationships, and that the teens, too, possess the ability to be helpmates to each other by being aware of biological facts concerning sexual stimulation. One of the most important facts is that the boy is more quickly stimulated to passion than the girl. The advice of the confessor should stress the contribution the girl can make to the boy, especially by her modest dress and actions. Since she naturally has greater self-control sexually, she can assist him in his quest for the virtue of purity. On the other hand, the confessor should stress that the boy, treating the girl with respect, gives her an image to aspire to. In being positive, the confessor presents a challenge to his youthful penitents and is expressing confidence in their ability to meet it. The confessor should demonstrate to the teen that he expects the best behavior from him and most likely he will get it.

It is the teen years that present to the youth the greatest opportunity to develop the virtue of self-control. Since no virtue is acquired without a struggle, nature has provided a battle ground of sexual temptation upon which the teen can prove his heroism and gain for himself the laurel of self-mastery. To be victorious, the youth must understand sexual temptation in terms of an opportunity to mature, both physically and spiritually. That nature should allow the sexual instinct to be aroused and cause the resulting temptations, should not be viewed with alarm by the youth, but merely seen as an indication of his approaching physical maturity. The youth's spiritual nature will enable him to be properly clad for the battle. The spiritual protection of the frequent reception of the sacraments will enable him to overcome sexual temptations with confidence. It is this confidence that the confessor is able to help the teen acquire by stressing the naturalness of the temptations and the supernatural armor that he has to defend himself — the sacraments! Poised on the battlefield of life, the teen is thus prepared to attain the goal of self-control.

The teen's social consciousness contributes to his natural respect for the opinions of others and provides another link in his armor of defense on the battlefield of sexual temptations. In fact, the more he associates with those whose opinions he respects, the easier the struggle for self-control becomes. Since respect is a prelude to love, this battle for self-control will be a practical way for him to acquire a true perspective of the relationship between love and sacrifice.

Youth, being extremely sensitive, is easily influenced by other people and their writings. The confessor can stress the influence of obscene literature upon him, that it places serious obstacles in his path toward self-control. It is only reasonable to take the easier path toward a goal, i.e., the one with the least number of obstacles. The priest should explain that the teen's own maturity and common sense should persuade him to remove the obstacle of obscene literature from his life.

Sexuality indulged in by the adolescent outside its proper context of marriage is an expression of his immaturity and a deterrent from maturity. A judgment of moral responsibility should take into consideration that an act such as masturbation is one performed by a relatively immature person. In the case of masturbation we should in no sense approve of the activity; rather we "should encourage him to develop himself as a human being and to put aside the disequilibrium and tensions which accompany adolescence and to grow to adulthood. We must judge the adolescent's guilt according to his present structure of personality and psychological maturity."[3] It would seem that the confessor may be lenient in judging the guilt of the youthful masturbator who is making a sincere effort to cooperate with the advice of the confessor and whose general moral life is praiseworthy. The youth who is truly making an effort to overcome the problem, by the frequent reception of the sacraments, will naturally be depressed by repeated failure to conquer the problem. Bearing this in mind, the confessor's most effective instrument to aid the youth will be encouragement. The confessor encourages the teen by indicating that the problem of masturbation is not uncommon, that others who had the same problem were able to overcome it through continued effort, and that frequent reception of the sacraments will be an indication of effort.

CONCLUSION

Sanctity through sanity has been the effort that the author has sought to convey to the readers of this chapter. It is hoped that through the sane approach of utilizing the natural tendencies of the teen, the confessor can direct the youth more effectively to his goal of sanctity. It is the conviction of the author that the resources of youth for sanctity lie waiting to be tapped by the confessor. Hopefully then, the ideas expressed in this chapter will contribute to some degree in aiding the confessor to tap these natural resources to develop the adolescent into a vibrant reproduction of Christ for the twentieth century.

---

[3] George Hagmaier, C.S.P. and Robert Gleason, S.J., *Counseling the Catholic* (New York: Sheed and Ward, Inc., 1959).

7

Hearing the Confessions of Nuns

Eugene J. Weitzel, C.S.V.

In the united states today, there are more than 180,000 nuns effectively serving the needs of the Church in schools, colleges and universities, hospitals, orphanages and infant asylums, homes for the aged, and other vital institutions. Each Sister ordinarily (some are obliged by the statutes of their particular institute) goes to confession at least once a week, and presents herself to the extraordinary confessor, at least for a blessing, whenever he comes to the convent to exercise his office. Consequently, there is a good possibility that before too many of your priestly years have passed you will be approved as an ordinary, extraordinary, or supplementary confessor of nuns by the ordinary of the diocese in which you are carrying on your apostolate.

Unfortunately, many priests do not look forward to this aspect of the sacramental ministry, for they find that, as Father Gerald Kelly, S.J., points out in his book, *The Good Confessor,* the time for hearing Sisters' confessions "comes round with a boring regularity; . . . 'interferes' with other work; . . . [and] deprives one of pleasant recreations."[1] Other priests regard it as a most trying, monotonous, and even distasteful task. However, contrary to what you may have heard or read about this matter, hearing the confessions of Sisters can be one of the most soul-satisfying and rewarding tasks of your priestly ministry. Early in my priestly life I was assigned as an ordinary confessor at the Motherhouse of a community of Dominican Sisters. Each week I heard the confessions

---

[1] G. Kelly, S.J., *The Good Confessor* (New York: Sentinal Press, 1951), p. 8.

of approximately seventy religious. Though frequently tired after having put in a full day in the classroom (I taught in a neighboring high school), I found my weekly assignment to be spiritually rewarding and satisfying. I also found it to be a very important avenue for my own religious and priestly growth and development.

Developing Proper Attitudes

In this matter, much depends on the attitude of the confessor toward his assignment. Many factors can contribute toward the development of positive attitudes concerning the task of hearing Sisters' confessions. But, perhaps the three most important are: 1) a deeper appreciation of the necessity for spiritual advancement; 2) a constant awareness of the effects of penance, especially the symbolic reality of the sacrament (*res et sacramentum*); and 3) an appreciation of the value of confessions of devotion.

First of all, a confessor of nuns must have a deep appreciation of the religious life and of the obligations assumed by those who embrace it. All religious are obliged to lead an exemplary life and to practice acts of worship, penance, and piety. By their entrance into religious life, they have freely accepted the duty of using special means which are only of counsel for other Christians in order to attain special perfection. Consequently, they are no longer free in the choice of the means to be used to arrive at perfection, but must tend toward it by keeping the vows of poverty, chastity, and obedience, and by observing the practices of piety and the exercises of virtue prescribed by the rules of this particular institute. The Fathers of Vatican Council II spoke quite clearly about these matters in the *Decree on the Adaptation and Renewal of the Religious Life* when they stated that:

> Members of each institute should recall first of all that by professing the evangelical counsels they responded to a divine call so that by being not only dead to sin (cf. *Rom.* 6, 11) but also renouncing the world they may live for God alone. They have dedicated their entire lives to His service. This constitutes a special consecration, which is deeply rooted in that of baptism and expresses it more fully.
>
> This service of God ought to inspire and foster in them the exercise of the virtues, especially humility, obedience, fortitude and chastity. In such a way they share in Christ's emptying of Himself (cf. *Phil.* 2, 7–8) and His life in the spirit (cf. *Rom.* 8, 1–13).
>
> Faithful to their profession then, and leaving all things for the sake of Christ (cf. *Mark* 10, 28), Religious are to follow Him (cf. *Matt.* 19, 21) as the one thing necessary (cf. *Luke* 10, 42) listening to His words (cf. *Luke* 10, 39) and solicitous for the things that are His (cf. *1 Cor.* 7, 32).[2]

---

[2] Vatican Council II, *Decree on the Adaptation and Renewal of the Religious Life* (trans. N.C.W.C.), pp. 4–5.

Needless to say, one of the most important means of attaining perfection in the religious life is the sacrament of penance. The Church itself has always considered penance as a means most suited to religious perfection, and it is for this reason that the weekly reception of this sacrament has been recommended. It follows then, that if a religious is urged to employ this means to perfection each and every week of her religious life, then the confessor must strive in every way possible to make confession an effective and efficacious means to "seek and love above all else God who has first loved us (cf. 1 Jn 4:10)," and to "foster in all circumstances a life hidden with Christ in God (cf. Col 3:3)."[3]

Secondly, the confessor of nuns, through his continued study of sacramental theology, ought to strive for a deeper appreciation of the symbolic reality of the sacrament of penance, the *res et sacramentum,* so that they can better understand the sacramental grace of this sacrament.

In a booklet entitled *Sacraments of Healing and of Vocation,* Paul F. Palmer, S.J., discusses symbolic reality at some length. He points out that the symbolic reality of the sacrament of penance is at one and the same time a reality and a sacrament or sign of a new relationship with Christ and his Church. Many theologians are of the opinion that penance, like baptism, produces an effect which, though not prior in time, is prior in nature to the grace of divine forgiveness. Though the symbolic reality of the sacrament of penance may be understood in several ways, Father Palmer prefers to find it in "peace and reconciliation with the Church, a spiritual bond which disposes the soul for the life of grace which flows through the Church, Christ's mystical body." In a word, the immediate effect of the sacrament of penance is reconciliation with the Church.

Such a view as this emphasizes the social or ecclesial character of the sacrament of penance, and makes it clear that salvation ordinarily comes to the sinner in and through the Church. But, if it is true that the penitent benefits through the Church, that is, is reconciled with the Church in which and through which he is reconciled to God, it is also true that the Church benefits through the penitent. This is so because the spiritual advancement of each member of the Mystical Body has an effect on the life of the Mystical Body itself. The People of God are so intimately joined in the Mystical Body of Christ that what affects the individual member of the Body affects the life of the whole body. In other words, when a particular soul advances toward perfection, the life of the whole Church is imperceptibly intensified. Therefore, when a confessor helps a Sister make a more fruitful confession and when he guides and directs her toward that perfection to which she is called in her particular community, the effects of the sacrament of penance are not

---

[3] *Ibid.,* p. 5.

restricted solely to the individual Sister, but have a profound influence on the whole Church.

As for the grace of the sacrament, it is important for the confessor to remember that while it is true that penance, like the other sacraments, either confers the life of grace on the soul or increases it, there is a special modality to sanctifying grace that is conferred in this sacrament. In penance the recipient of this sacrament receives the grace of reconciliation. Closely associated with this modality of sanctifying grace, which is the principal effect of penance, is the special virtue of penance which is infused into the soul. This virtue moves the penitent to make reparation for his sins. However, if this virtue is to become operative in works of reparation, the recipient of the sacrament needs a special actual grace that will always be available to him, since he, having been reconciled, will always remain a penitent.[4]

Thirdly, the confessor for religious must be aware of the great value of confessions of devotion. To fully understand and appreciate the confession of devotion, the confessor must first of all keep in mind that the Church itself introduced the practice of the devotional confession, that is, the confession in which only venial sins or sins already forgiven are confessed. Furthermore, he must remember that while it is true that venial sins do not destroy the bond of charity that unites the individual to God and to his Church, and that consequently there is no need of reconciliation, nevertheless, venial sins do weaken the bond of charity that exists between God and the individual Christian. Added to this, venial sins are an offense against the whole Mystical Body of Christ, for it is the mission of the Church to be a witness to the truth of its claim to be the Church of Christ by the outstanding sanctity of its members. In a word, every sin, mortal or venial, has a social or ecclesial dimension inasmuch as it affects the Church's mission to teach and sanctify the world, and therefore it is proper to confess even venial sins to the confessor who represents both God and the Church.[5] Finally, the confessor of religious must keep in mind the reason why a person can again receive sacramental forgiveness for a sin already forgiven. On this point theologians teach that a penitent can receive from the sacrament of penance the grace which would forgive this sin if it were still on his soul because he can be, in this particular confession, truly sorry for it.[6]

The confessor who recognizes the religious' need for spiritual advancement and who understands and appreciates the symbolic reality of this sacrament and the value of the devotional confession will soon come to

---

[4] P. Palmer, S.J., *Sacraments of Healing and of Vocation* (Westminster: Newman, 1960), pp. 34–37.   [5] *Ibid.*, pp. 37–38.
[6] F. Connell, C.SS.R., *Outlines of Moral Theology* (Milwaukee: Bruce, 1958), pp. 208–209.

regard his sacramental ministry to religious women as no small matter. In fact, he will quickly develop a truly supernatural outlook and conviction regarding the importance of frequent confession for Sisters. Whereas he once found it difficult to listen to the continual repetitions of the same small faults, many of which are not sins at all, and whereas he once felt that he lacked the ability to grasp the small problems and difficulties of the religious life, now he will be eager to help each one of his Sister-penitents to eradicate even little faults and imperfections. Furthermore, he will see the importance of preparing well for this task, for he will understand that the more he helps a Sister live out her vocation, the greater will be her witness to Christ and the more she will contribute to the life of the Church.

In his efforts to develop proper attitudes and to perfect himself as a confessor of Sisters, a priest can do no better than to reflect on those words which Pope John XXIII spoke in praise of the Curé of Ars as a confessor in his Encyclical *Sacerdotii nostri primordia:* "All that remains for us to do is to recall at a little greater length the pastoral ministry of St. John M. Vianney, which was a kind of steady martyrdom for a long period of his life, and especially his administration of the sacrament of Penance, which calls for special praise for it brought forth riches and most salutary fruits. . . . Let the example of the Curé of Ars stir up those who are in charge of souls to be eager and well prepared in devoting themselves to this very serious work, for it is here most of all that divine mercy finally triumphs over human malice and that men have their sins wiped away and are reconciled to God."[7]

QUALITIES OF A GOOD CONFESSOR OF SISTERS

Church law prescribes that confessors of Sisters must be distinguished by the probity of their lives and by their prudence. In other words, they must be priests who have acquired considerable experience in the spiritual life, who are learned in matters of faith and morals, and whose personal life is characterized by its holiness. Furthermore, they should be distinguished for their patience and charity. Concerning these qualities, Gerald Kelly, S.J., once wrote:

> Such is the ideal, it is not always realized in practice. Ecclesiastical superiors have no special charism that prevents them from making mistakes in their appointments; and at times they must appoint ordinary confessors who, they realize, do not measure up perfectly to the canonical standards. Like the rest of us, they cannot give what they do not have. In these situations the sisters must be both fair-minded and patient. If possible, they can avail themselves of the other privileges given by canon law; when this is impossible, they have every reason to trust in God.[8]

---

[7] John XXIII, *Sacerdotii nostri primordia,* AAS 51 (1959), p. 574.

[8] G. Kelly, S.J., *Guidance for Religious* (Westminster: Newman, 1956), p. 165.

Though a priest, when he is given the responsibility of hearing Sisters' confessions, may feel that both as a person and as a priest he is a long way from meeting these ideals, there are a number of steps that he can take that will eventually, and sometimes quickly, bring him close to this ideal. These steps might be regarded as a remote preparation for hearing Sisters' confessions.

First of all, it goes without saying that every priest must strive for that holiness of life which aims at virtue, sacrifice, and renunciation, and that he must strive to acquire self-mastery, solid personal maturity, and all the other dispositions of mind and heart that can aid the ordered and fruitful mission of the Church.

Secondly, the confessor must continually perfect his knowledge of divine things and human affairs so that he will be "mature in knowledge" and that his doctrine will be "spiritual medicine for the People of God."[9] On this point, the *Decree on Priestly Life and Ministry* observes that "the knowledge of a sacred minister should be sacred, since it is drawn from a sacred fountain and is directed to a sacred goal. Hence that knowledge should be drawn primarily from reading and meditating on the Sacred Scriptures. But it should also be fruitfully nourished by a study of the Holy Fathers and Doctors and other annals of tradition."[10] The Council Fathers also pointed out that "in addition, that they may be able to provide proper answers to the questions discussed by men of this age, priests should be well acquainted with the documents of the Church's teaching authority and especially of Councils and the Roman pontiffs. They should consult, too, the best, approved writers in theological science."[11]

In an article entitled "Nuns' Confessions: the Human Side," Charles Dollen emphasizes the importance of the continual study of theology on the part of the confessor of Sisters when he points out that one of the important tasks of the confessor is to "re-present basic dogma."

> The unsettled times in the world and in the Church are reflected in even the most cloistered communities. The terribly needed and much desired *aggiornamento* has effects within convent walls, too. Here the confessor gives the stability and security of the familiar truths of the Faith upon which all the modernization of the Church rests. Charity is still the summit of perfection and it is the firm basis upon which all the newness of modern spirituality must be built. The painful re-evaluations that many communities have to make, that many individual Sisters are making, must proceed along the lines of Christ-like charity, a spiritual commodity that is never dated or out-moded.[12]

---

[9] Roman Pontifical, "Ordination of Priests."

[10] Vatican Council II, *Decree on Priestly Life and Ministry* (trans. *The Documents of Vatican II*, ed. W. Abbott, S.J.), p. 571.

[11] *Ibid.*, p. 571.

[12] C. Dollen, "Nuns' Confessions: the Human Side," *Pastoral Life*, 13, 11 (November, 1965), pp. 619–620.

Thirdly, the confessor of Sisters should strive to understand the spirit of the religious community to which he has been assigned as confessor. He should be knowledgeable concerning the life of the foundress, the rules, customs, and the specific apostolates of the institute. On this point, William F. Hogan, C.S.C., asks:

> Where do the religious find this special spirit which is supposed to be theirs? In some measure it can be found in the practises and customs of the community, but these change with time and are concerned for the most part with externals. Any writings of their founders which have been preserved will yield some knowledge of it, but the Book of Constitutions is the most valuable source, for ultimately the Constitutions can be traced back to the pen of the founder — and even when they have been changed over the course of time, Rome never permits them to depart basically from the original spiritual heritage of the founder.
>
> It is not correct to conceive of the Constitutions of a religious community as a book of "do's and don'ts" or as just a collection of particular laws governing external conduct; they are much more than that. In the Constitutions of the more recently founded communities and the revised editions of them in older religious groups a great deal of spiritual wealth is to be found. There are sections on certain basic virtues to be stressed, spiritual maxims, the peculiar devotions and special feasts of the community, etc., all of which indicate what should be the spiritual emphasis and special spirit of the particular community. A comparison of the Constitutions of several communities, even those engaged in the same type of apostolate, will indicate differences of emphasis and make it manifest that each group has its peculiar spirit from the founder according to which the members are to develop their lives.[13]

PROXIMATE PREPARATION FOR HEARING NUNS' CONFESSIONS

The proximate preparation required for the hearing of Sisters' confessions is equally as important as the remote preparation outlined above. Perhaps the most important aspect of this preparation is the scheduling of sufficient time for this important work. It is impossible for any priest to hear the confessions of five Sisters in ten minutes; on occasion it is difficult even to hear the confessions of five Sisters in twenty-five minutes. One of the most frequent, and perhaps, most justified complaints of religious women is that: "Father is always so rushed. We seldom have an opportunity to talk to him, or to seek advice and direction." As a rule, Sisters make very few demands on priests, and especially on confessors. In fact, too frequently just the opposite is true; it is we priests and confessors who make too many demands on our Sisters. Therefore, it is hardly asking too much of any confessor of Sisters that he so arrange his schedule on the day he is to hear nuns' confessions that each religious will have an opportunity to make a con-

---

[13] W. Hogan, C.S.C., "The Sisters' Confessor," *The Priest*, 20, 6 (June, 1964), p. 509.

fession that is not only valid, but one that really gives her peace and serenity of conscience, and even an overwhelming consolation of spirit. If a confessor keeps in mind that few of his waking hours will be better spent than those he spends in the convent confessional, he will have little difficulty in providing sufficient time for this task. Charles Dollen reflects these same sentiments when he writes:

> When this comes to spiritual matters, the Sisters need time to talk to their confessor, and time to ask questions. Obviously, this does not mean 25-minute confessions per Sister, but it is equally obvious that the confessions of six sisters cannot be heard in three minutes. Some of the nuns have harrowing tales to tell of priests who either race through a whole community in three minutes, or who take the opportunity to catch up on their reading. It is necessary to be alert and interested, not to mention awake.[14]

Not only are Sisters justifiably annoyed by the "hasty confessor," but they are also quite understandably irritated by the "always late" or the "never there" confessor. Ordinarily, the daily schedule of most convents is filled with activities — prayers, work, study, meals, recreation, etc. — and therefore it is of the greatest importance that the confessor be prompt in arriving to hear his Sisters' confessions. Sisters, like anyone else, can understand and excuse an occasional delay, but, like the rest of us, they are hard pressed to understand and accept the "always late confessor." Usually, with little or no effort, the priest can plan his departure from the rectory or religious house so that he will arrive on time.

Occasional forgetfulness is excusable in all of us, but when the superior of the Sisters is compelled to phone Father week after week to remind him that this is confession day, perhaps there is cause to wonder about his sense of responsibility and his devotion to duty. There are instances, of course, when through no fault of his own the confessor will not be able to hear confessions at the time or on the day assigned. When such circumstances arise, or when a priest can reasonably foresee that they will arise, he should make every effort to inform the Sisters of this situation, and strive to see that a supplementary confessor will be available. Unless it is absolutely unavoidable, Sisters should not be deprived of the opportunity for weekly confession on the day and at the time appointed.

THE CONFESSOR AND SPIRITUAL DIRECTION

Though every theologian realizes that the sacramental value of absolution can never take second place to spiritual advice, and that the sacrament of penance is the source of graces that are more beneficial for

---

[14] C. Dollen, *op. cit.*, p. 618.

the human soul than is spiritual direction, yet, almost every author who has written about the confessor of Sisters stresses the great need they have for sound, prudent spiritual direction. Ordinarily, the only spiritual direction which Sisters receive is that which they obtain in the confessional. Therefore the time spent by the confessor of Sisters in giving advice and encouragement, and in answering questions before giving a penance and absolution is of the greatest importance for the religious striving for perfection, and it behooves every priest to use this time as profitably as possible. As Gerald Kelly observes:

> Religious, however, are not ordinary penitents. They belong to the spiritual elite of the Church. They are supposed to strive after perfection, and they are entitled to the means conducive to perfection. One of these means is the opportunity of having expert spiritual guidance. True, to some extent this guidance is embodied in their rule, for the rule contains the plan of a perfect life. Also, guidance is frequently available through their superiors. Despite these helps, however, all will experience, at least at times, the need of counsel which only a priest can give.[15]

In the matter of spiritual direction, it is the mind of the Church that ordinarily priestly counsel should be given to the Sisters by the ordinary confessor, who will advise them in a manner that is competent, consistent, and uniform. Competency is demanded of the confessor-director because of his position in the Church. Consistency is required because this quality is usually essential for progress in the spiritual life. Uniformity is essential because of the uniformity that is so much a part of the religious life, and because great variations in direction could be a cause of disagreeable situations in the convent life.

Though uniformity is an essential characteristic of good direction, uniformity does not require that the confessor give the same spiritual nosegay or the same words of encouragement to every Sister. Every good confessor of women religious knows that different Sisters have different problems and that it is useless to give the same advice to each, if real help is to be given them. Father Hogan, C.S.C., gives a very helpful explanation of the kind of uniformity that the Church requires when he writes:

> Could it be that the uniformity of spiritual direction to be given by the ordinary confessor to the members of the religious house might have something to do with the special spirit of the community as gleaned from the Constitutions? The author feels that while this may not be precisely what the commentators on canon 520 have in mind, nevertheless the solution of the problem of giving this direction is contained therein; for it will allow for helping the individual with personal problems while at the same time giving a basic, profitable uniformity to the direction of all.
> If the confessor becomes acquainted with the spirit of the founder and

---

[15] G. Kelly, S.J., *Guidance for Religious* (Westminster: Newman, 1956), p. 164.

the special spiritual emphasis of the community, he can, while giving advice in relation to peculiar spiritual problems, often orientate their solution in relation to the precise spiritual characteristics of the community which the religious should be attempting to develop within their lives. Indeed, unless the direction is given in this vein, it could prove harmful to the penitent, who may become a spiritual eclectic, not being concerned with developing the precise spirit of her vocation as she should be.[16]

On the problem of uniformity, my own views are that, while a confessor must strive for general uniformity of direction, he should never sacrifice the personal needs of a penitent for the sake of it. Actually, if a confessor strives to give wise and prudent direction that is tailored to the needs and the capacity of each Sister, he will have little cause for worry about uniformity. After all, in the confessional he is not dealing with a community, he is dealing with an individual. Furthermore, if a confessor has made an adequate remote preparation for this task, uniformity of direction will be almost automatic. Finally, as he gains experience as a confessor of Sisters he will achieve not only the desired uniformity of direction but also acquire an evident capability and consistency.

However, in the matter of confessional direction, there is another area that is of even greater importance than that just considered, for it involves the proper subject matter of direction. On this point Henry Davis, S.J., once wrote that:

> In the concrete and in actually dealing with Sisters in religion, the confessor will urge the fullest observance of vows and rules, insist that the exact time should be given to spiritual duties, exhort to purity of intention, avoidance of particular friendships and enmities, abhorrence of divisions in the community, tale-bearing to the Superior, criticism of rules or customs, care of all matters confided to individuals, contentment in religious vocation, religious silence and complete detachment from the world, and worldly conversations.[17]

Though this listing of topics and others similar to it can be useful, they are by no means to be regarded as complete. Perhaps, the best source of information regarding the subject matter of direction is the many good books which are now being published which take up the various problems of religious. The neophyte confessor of Sisters can also obtain valuable advice from experienced confessors, especially those who are members of religious communities since many of the problems which confront Sisters are similar to those which must be faced by the members of religious communities of men. However, the best source of information in this area will ever and always be the penitent herself. Father Dollen

---

[16] W. Hogan, C.S.C., *op. cit.,* pp. 509–510.
[17] H. Davis, S.J., *Moral and Pastoral Theology* [Vol. III, Sacraments (1)] (New York: Sheed and Ward, 1958), pp. 308–309.

makes an important contribution to our understanding of the subject matter of direction when he writes that:

> Every religious community is a busy place, and the Sisters have little opportunity to bring live new ideas into the convents. It is terribly easy for them to go round-and-round in circles, if they only have a small community in which to exchange ideas. In the average parish convent the time for spiritual reading (or for recreation even) can be precious little on any workday, and if there is no one to inject new thinking and suggest new books, spiritual sloth creeps in. Nothing will kill the spirit so quickly.
>
> The life of a religious Sister has no meaning without positive growth in her spiritual life. Is it any wonder that modern American women grow restless when spiritual aridity sets in? Too many vocations are lost some years after final profession because the light of life has grown dim. And these nuns can hardly inspire young people to join a community which offers nothing but hard work and spiritual drudgery. The first is a challenge; the second defeats it.
>
> This is certainly where the confessor fits in and, as a spiritual advisor, it would seem to be the prime reason why the Church insists on such frequent confession. Precisely as women, the Sisters need a safety valve, a discipline, and a guide.[18]

Though it may be impossible to supply a complete list of topics that can be regarded as suitable subject matter for direction, it is very easy to specify the areas which must never be the concern of the confessor of Sisters, for Church law clearly specifies that he *should not in any way interfere in the internal or external rule of the community* (c. 524, par. 3). Many years ago, Charles Augustine, O.S.B., explained that this regulation positively forbids confessors to censure the religious or settle affairs or reserved cases which require an ecclesiastical trial.[19] The points which he makes on censuring the religious and on settling affairs should be of especial concern to the confessor in his role as spiritual director, for under no circumstance should he meddle in community affairs. Therefore, in giving advice or in answering questions, he should avoid any response that would constitute a direct or indirect violation of this law. However, as John A. Abbo and Jerome D. Hannon point out in their book, *The Sacred Canons,* "on request, the confessor may give advice. Superioresses should refrain, however, from making such requests, especially in regard to the transfer or the dismissal of religious or in reference to their attitude in council meetings on matters of discipline."[20] Nevertheless, even in those instances when advice is legitimately requested, confessors should act with the utmost prudence and discretion.

---

[18] C. Dollen, *op. cit.,* pp. 618–619.
[19] C. Augustine, O.S.B., *A Commentary on Canon Law* [Vol. III] (St. Louis: B. Herder), p. 165.
[20] J. Abbo and J. Hannan, *The Sacred Canons* (St. Louis: B. Herder, 1953), p. 540.

Kindness and Understanding

In his first epistle to the Corinthians, St. Paul said: "And I point out to you a yet more excellent way. If I should speak with the tongues of men and of angels, but do not have charity, I have become as sounding brass or a tinkling cymbal. And if I have prophecy and know all mysteries and all knowledge, and if I have all faith so as to remove mountains, yet do not have charity, I am nothing. . . . Charity is patient, is kind . . . is not provoked; . . . bears with all things, hopes all things, endures all things" (13:1–7). If these words of the Apostle of the Gentiles have a special meaning for all Christians, they ought to have an even greater meaning for all confessors, but especially for the confessors of Sisters. For, no matter how experienced in the spiritual life a confessor of women religious might be, or how learned, or prudent, his hours in the convent confessional will bear little fruit if he be lacking in kindness and understanding. Consequently, few suggestions that can be given the nuns' confessor are more important than those that have to do with kindness and understanding. Sisters, like all penitents, will joyfully tolerate many of our faults and weaknesses if they know that in us they will always find a truly Christ-like spirit of understanding and kindness. Therefore, allow me to bring this chapter to a conclusion by making an earnest and sincere plea that you, as a confessor and director of Sisters, will always strive to be the kindest and most understanding of confessors.

8

Co-Workers In the Lord

A Woman Religious

First and foremost, religious women and priests are co-workers, living out in the world of today the pattern indicated in Genesis 2:18. Woman is a helper for man and like him, as both are like God and help him. In fact, this is verified in Christian living in two ways: in marriage and in the life of service in the Church, and in the special service of those who live a celibate life, a life which has its own glory and its own love. And if, in this chapter, we are following the tradition of the Church which sees the priest more as helper of women in religious life than being helped by them, it will not be out of place to indicate the mutual helpfulness. And perhaps this article may be seen in itself as one aspect of the helpfulness of dialogue between men and women in Christ striving to understand one another better, and to understand their own vocations more fully.

The Feminine Mystique

In the past, much of Catholic thinking about women has been identified with the mentality of the feminine mystique so sharply condemned by Betty Friedan.[1] According to this point of view, woman is defined primarily by her sexual role as wife and mother, and every aspect of her being is stamped by this basic orientation. Such for example is the attitude of Gertrud von le Fort who sees woman as pure mystery inaccessible to

---

[1] Betty Friedan, *The Feminine Mystique.*

the ordinary scrambling climb of reason, accessible only to the higher flights of something approaching a special kind of mystical intuition.[2] Thus man is aggressive, rational, and concerned with abstractions, while woman in the depth of her being is passive, receptive, intuitive, emotional, and people-centered. If most of this romanticizing came out of the 1940's it is by no means dead today, especially among some of the younger priests who have "discovered" woman, and such thinking can be found among some women also.[3]

The Kinder-Küche-Kirche picture of woman is still found as a relic among some of the women's orders, while for married women it is becoming more and more unworkable. Too many married women are working, on the professional level as well as on the secretarial level, and are enjoying their work. They do not have the mystical attachment to the myriad duties of the home, but a very practical appreciation of them, of their children, and of their husbands. Professional women today are no longer ardent feminists, for they are secure as persons, and do not need to fight for their right to work side by side with men.

If the old stereotype remains to some extent with regard to the Sisters, it is in part tied up with the uniformity that has been felt to be the ideal of religious life. It is tied up too with the image of " 'Ster" who is in her element with her grade school children, and who ceases to be of importance with the fading of one's childhood. Thus the Sister seems to reflect the sociological position of women some generations ago, though the situation is certainly improving.

Yet in the Gospels and Epistles, we find an extraordinary respect given to women who seem to have accompanied the Lord and later his Apostles

---

[2] Gertrud von le Fort, *The Eternal Woman* (Milwaukee: Bruce, 1962).

[3] To belabor the point a little, let me quote from two authorities. The first is Teilhard de Chardin who wrote in 1950, "The most vital aspect of the Tangible is Flesh, and for man, flesh is woman. Involved in the pursuit of the heart of matter from childhood, it was inevitable that one day I should come face to face with woman. The curious thing is that the encounter had to wait until my thirtieth year. So great was my fascination with the impersonal and the general." (From "Le Feminin, ou l'unitif," an unpublished excerpt dated Oct. 30, 1950.)

The second quotation is taken from a paper given by Sr. Annette Walters to a group of priests on the topic at hand, unpublished: "Destined by nature to conceive and foster children, a woman has concomitant traits to help her. I mention three. First, a woman is naturally sensitive, both in herself and for the feelings of others; she is compassionate. In brief she is tinged with emotion throughout the whole of her being. Second, to enable her to care for a home and children she has a capacity for detail, a willingness to do routine tasks, a preference for what is tangible. Third, because of her maternal role, she has a greater need than a man to love and to be loved. Within the context of maternity — physical or spiritual — these qualities perfect a woman; out of that context they may weaken or harm her. For the religious woman, who lacks the natural objects of these outgoing qualities their exercise and regulation are more difficult."

on their journeys, and even to have shared in their teaching.[4] (cf. Mt 27:55; Rom 16:1 f.). But in the time of the religious communities in the middle ages, women were entirely cloistered, and helped their male counterparts who preached the gospel only by their silent and hidden prayer. Thus the dichotomy between prayer and action that seems to have its roots in the Greek conception of man as body and soul was further emphasized in the duality of roles of men and women. At the same time there were a few exceptional women in their monasteries who were comparable to the medieval ladies who presided over huge households with extraordinary competence, and a few women of intense intellectual penetration. Some of these, like the abbess Hilda of Whitby, even ruled over a double monastery, a kind of co-institutional structure combining a monastery of monks with a convent of nuns. At the other extreme, taking on a masculine responsibility that was so bold that it became an excuse to have her burned as a heretic was Joan of Arc, the simple peasant girl, who could inspire a demoralized army with courage, and could out-theologize the theologians on the question of grace.

Throughout the middle ages, however, formal education for women generally was minimal, as indeed it was for men. Later, with a decadent scholasticism, and the fear generated by the Protestant reformation, religious education become the repetition of doctrinal formulas which long ceased to have any vitality. In religious life, this sterility was manifested in the construction of rules which attempted to regulate the minutest details of life, and perfection then became the achievement of a vast mass of regulations. This was the ideal even among the men's orders, so that John Berchmans, for example, was canonized for the perfect observance of his religious rule.[5] The attempt was the more understandable if it is seen as the sincere attempt to maintain the original spirit of reform, a reform that was in fact the base of many of the post-Tridentine religious institutes. Some of the later orders of the nineteenth century even tried to make the regulations absolutely explicit and binding, so that renewal might be a permanent reality in the community, in the original prophetic insight of the founder or foundress, but in fact, the letter had already killed the spirit. This legalism was aggravated further in the women's orders by the fact that their members never had any formal training in theology, though they usually did have some kind of guidance from priests. This legislated uniformity of religious life, held up as the ideal, contained its own built-in sanctions, for the Sister who failed to reach it

---

[4] As far as I know, the implications of the Lord's dealings with women, the work of the women in the apostolic Church, and the respect accorded to them has never been dealt with theologically.

[5] There is the apocryphal story of his contemporary, St. Aloysius, who seems to have had a similar devotion, that when the day of a great picnic came, as the community journal tells it, "Luigi stayed home, D.G."

had to consider herself as a failure as a religious. Nor did she have the breadth of experience that would enable her to reach beyond that ideal. The stereotype for men has been less successful as a religious mask, since men have always mingled freely in the world, and have never been held to one place in the same sense as women, since this is inconsistent with their mission as priests and preachers of the gospel. If they were narrow and provincial, this was within the Catholic ghetto, where the priest commanded an extraordinary amount of respect due to the mystique of his priesthood.[6]

The crisis of the religious orders of women today, as Cardinal Suenens has pointed out,[7] is the result of their emancipation in the Church. Today the Sister is coming into her own as her secular counterpart is, and this is true above all if she is professionally trained. She is aware of her power as a woman, as a thinking person, and she respects both people and ideas, and in turn expects respect. But this education is not purely or primarily a secular education, for she has become aware of new theological currents in the Church, and of the need for Sisters trained as theologians. She must face something of a struggle in herself to reconcile the "spiritual" life with the "intellectual" life as if the intellectual life were somehow hostile to the spiritual and alien to it. This struggle is not hers alone, of course, but that of the educated Christian generally, who is often treated as if he were on the fringe of the Church. The Christian, however, must think as well as pray, and even think in order to pray and to act as Christ in the world.

Because of the very complexity of the world in which Sisters live, they are aware of their obligations to that world in conscience, and they are aware also that they do not agree. In part, this very sense of obligation brought them to religious life, and determined their entrance into a particular order, for example, in their desire to nurse the sick poor, or to educate the underprivileged. But a conflict can arise insofar as the communal obligation is thought to cancel any individual obligation, so that the individual need only conform to the decision of the community, that her conscience is sufficiently taken care of by the community. Thus, Sisters are questioning the work of religious orders as we know them at present because they are too much tied up with middle class suburban Catholic life. There are vast areas of human living crying out for the Christian witness, as the poor in the inner city, or the campuses of secular universities, or the apostolate of scholarship. Women can and must in the

---

[6] I do not mean to disparage the sacramental nature of the priesthood, but rather to suggest that the exaggerated respect we have given our priests has been rather a disservice than an encouragement to the building up of the people of God. For our priests forgot their humanity, and our people forgot their priesthood as faithful believers.

[7] Cardinal Suenens, *The Nun in the World*.

plan of Christ take their share of responsibility for the proclamation of the Gospel each in her own way. Though good example is important, it alone is not always an adequate means of communicating the message of Christ in a world of technology, of rapid communication, of insecurity. The old security of religious life is even being felt by some of the younger Sisters as a betrayal of the world and of Christ; the security of a settled scheme of thought is not necessarily the same as faith in the good news of Jesus Christ.

Insofar as this questioning is felt to be disloyalty to the order and to the ideal of religious life, the modern Sister has more and different problems than her counterpart of the past in normal circumstances. Then, only a Teresa of Avila or a Margaret Mary, or a foundress like Thérèse Couderc, or on the other hand (though it often must have seemed disconcertingly similar!) the poor neurotic souls that seem to exist in every religious community — both the Sisters who are asking basic questions about their religious life, and the Sisters who have not been able to meet the demands of this life for one reason or for another — need the help and understanding of the priest. But equally in need of assistance are the Sisters who cling to the security of traditional ways, and traditional modes of thought that bear all the security of being "Catholic." Such people may have an almost pathological fear of change, since they are unable to distinguish the externals from the inner meaning of faith. Thus the changes in the liturgy struck many as being "Protestant" because the singing sounded like a revival meeting. But though one might not like revival meetings, there is nothing necessarily un-Catholic about them. In such a state of fear and anxiety, the suggestion of change (or the lack of it for the other group) can bring about a disproportionate reaction. The old sense of peaceful "supernatural" community where criticism and real disagreements were cut off by the label "natural" is no longer possible, and people are often afraid of the kind of community that requires them to be real people.

THE SISTER AND THE "FEMININE PERSONALITY"

Is there then such a thing as feminine personality? The answer to that seems to be both yes and no. There are very real and obvious physiological and psychological differences between men and women. But the psychological differences, though real, seem to be dependent upon the culture and the education within the culture. There are aggressive men and aggressive women, thoughtful men and thoughtful women, and so on. Yet the differing cultural patterns for men and women, though not directly founded on reality necessarily, do point to the mutual need of man for woman and woman for man. Men who are somewhat impersonal in their dealings with one another can benefit from the thoughtfulness that is required in their dealings with women. Women who can be very petty, and take each other for granted, can grow as they find themselves appreciated by men, and needed to provide understanding. Community life for both sexes becomes fuller and richer as the people who come to it have the sense of being welcomed and appreciated for what they are. Thus, priests and brothers who have been deprived of a full and real contact with others frequently develop a real bachelor syndrome, whereas Sisters who have been afraid of their own loving nature frequently develop a spinster complex.

If in the past (and indeed the movies today are full of little else) woman is for man so often an ambivalent figure, either wife and mother or sexual symbol, in neither case is she really seen as she is. She is seen only in her sexual role, in her relation to man. Nor were women really capable of taking on any other role until Christianity provided an alternative for the virgin consecrated to God, who was a person precisely in her response to God. The personhood of women is being seen much more clearly today, and with that awareness is the consciousness of her own likeness to man. Their mutual likeness is the ground of her sexual polarity, which then becomes secondary. As the awareness of likeness grows, the possibility of friendship between the sexes grows, and in fact, the witness of Christian friendship that is outgoing and inclusive may well be a real witness to a cynical world. Prudence and common sense will show how the balance between deep respect and simplicity is to be achieved, together with a healthy and humorous sense of human frailty, both one's own and other people's.

THE PRIEST AS LEITOURGOS

As in the past, superiors and communities of women have relied heavily on priests, and they will continue to do so. The priest may function as chaplain, confessor, spiritual director, retreat master, teacher, friend and co-worker in the apostolate. The difficulty is that there are far too few priests who are trained adequately, a fact that the priests themselves are perhaps more conscious of than anyone, especially in the area of liturgical celebration in convents, though the massive work of the Liturgical Conferences has been invaluable.

On the whole, Sisters have probably taken more easily to the liturgical changes than to any other areas of change. There is singing at the Mass, they receive communion standing, they even (until, alas, it was forbidden) read the epistle and commented. Yet these changes are done with something less than enthusiasm on the whole, as it becomes evident that a new set of rubrics is replacing the old. And to speak very frankly, part of the Sisters' difficulty in trying to become aware of the meaning of the Eucharist is that so often the convent chaplain is elderly, deaf, or for some other reason available for them, rather than in a parish.[8] He does his best to conform to the new regulations, but it is nonetheless simply that, a conformity to regulations. (The same problem, of course, often exists in the parishes under the present structure.)

A priest who has thought through the Constitution on the Liturgy, however, and who sees it as the gospel proclaimed and made effective today, can do a great deal to help a community of Sisters achieve a sense of fellowship and community, a *koinonia* as it is described of the early Church (Acts 2:42; 4, 32). A short homily on the day's gospel, with a penetration of the meaning of the word and action of the Lord as it applies today, can make this Eucharistic celebration a special event. A willingness to experiment, to vary the celebration from day to day, or week to week, can give the community a sense of freedom and enthusiasm. After all, the people of God still expect their priests to lead them, and it will take them some time before they will feel free to express their own initiatives. But the priest's own sense of ease with his people, his deep sense of reverence before the mystery enacted here in their midst, this will have a profound effect. He need not feel that he has to make suggestions here that directly touch the life of the community, but as he speaks the gospel message, and tries to make it relevant, this itself will have its own impact on the community as they seek to live out the message more and more fully. In fact, many communities resent priests who seem to be interfering, and this is always a possible source of friction. Yet an open and friendly manner with the Sisters, the deeply reverent celebration of the Eucharist, the reverent and relevant speaking of the Word, all these can mean a new outpouring of the Spirit for a religious community, and can help to heal the sense of disunity that strikes so many as a threat coming from the changes, and to give encouragement to the Sisters who feel that their order is perhaps less Catholic than the Church.

The priest by his own manner can show Sisters how to be people during the celebration, by the expression of Christian unity in the peace greeting, and by their greeting one another after the celebration in a true spirit of joy. Perhaps silence in leaving the Church after the challenge, Go, you are sent forth, or whatever else the *Ite missa est* means, is not as meaningful in this instance as speech would be. Yet he shows, too, by his manner and by his prayer, after the celebration, that the Eucharist is a deeply interior mystery, a prayerful communion with Christ as well as with others.

---

[8] In some cases, Sisters might be integrated effectively into parish life, and help in the parish celebration. Where hospitals, colleges, Newman work, etc., require a resident chaplain, a man of understanding and enthusiasm ought to be available.

Perhaps some Sisters who still fear too much that prayer and a genuine human, Christian love are incompatible or impossible will learn to see them as two sides of a single consecration.

THE PRIEST AS CONFESSOR

Perhaps the place where Sisters experience most difficulties in their Christian lives is confession. It can so easily be a matter of routine as one recites the same list of sins every Thursday afternoon as one has for the past ten, twenty, or thirty years. It would be a great help if the confessor could show the true nature of confession as sign of God's mercy rather than the IBM recitation of faults. It would be a great help if the link could be made with the Sunday Gospel, or with one or other gospel text, to show the transcendental meaning of the sacrament, and if the homily at the Eucharist in turn could show the sacramental dimension of the gospel, if the biblical theologians are right that the signs and miracles that Jesus works are in fact continued in the sacraments.

Confession is a transcendental thing, an act here and now that carries a divine depth of meaning. There is then a double aspect to it, the full human reality which yet must carry and mean in its finite value, the infinite. This is, of course, the problem in all our contact with God, but perhaps most especially here. As sign, it means the confrontation of the sinner with the all-holy God, and the confession of our utter inadequacy, that we are man and not God. Sin is seen there in the light of God, and is found to be a basic category of human being, the "fallenness" inherent in the depths of ourselves.

This transcendental recognition, though it is the deepest meaning of sin, is not, however, the first awareness we have of the reality of sin, but only comes as man learns to confront God in prayer. The understanding of sin begins more naturally in the psychological awareness of our failures in human relationships, our lack of love, recognized in the reaction of others to us. This is a valid experience of sin, since love of the brother is closely tied up with love of God. If the sinner comes to confession to manifest his conscience quite simply, less in the sense of describing the sins committed as isolated atomic acts committed x number of times, but rather to mention the actual faults in context and indicating what might be done to remedy the situation, the experience of oneself as sinner in need of God's mercy might be more readily achieved. The work of the priest would then be to clarify the situation if need be, by prudent questioning, to encourage the penitent, and to increase a sense of generosity by showing the love of the Lord.

There have been objections to this psychological dimension of confession on the grounds that it focuses the penitent's concern on himself, or that it takes away from the sign value of the confession to reduce it to a psychological pep talk or to counseling.[9] It must be understood that as *sign*, confession is an encounter between God and the Christian who experiences his own sinfulness, an encounter mediated by the priest by way of the confession of the concrete sin-acts which in themselves point to a deeper fallenness in us. In this encounter, the priest takes part in a personal way, so that he himself is sign of the divine mercy, in what he says and does, not just in the ritual words, but in the words he actually says to this penitent here and now. His words must speak on two levels, the sign on the human experimental level and the deeper reality to which it points on the divine level.[10] What must be clarified is that the human is both sign and place of this confrontation with the mercy of God.

If there is this sensitivity to God and to his work in the Spirit on the part of the confessor, the concern would be for the real sinfulness and the real growth, and less on the nature of the act committed as such. There would be a deep respect for the other as person, an unwillingness to pry, and a deep respect for God before whom all stand as sinners redeemed in Jesus Christ.

But there are certain difficulties inherent in the confession situation for women that are perhaps not adequately spoken about. It is difficult for many women to speak to men about their sins, especially if these are sexual, and if there is a real problem. It may be a help in such cases for a Sister to talk the matter over with someone of her own sex who is experienced in counseling, and then to mention the matter only briefly in the confessional in order to obtain sacramental absolution. Yet where there has been a Jansenistic spirit in communities of women in sexual matters, the sound common-sense counsel of a priest can restore a sense of balance, and can show that sexuality is a natural part of our being human, and that the awareness of sexual desire is normal. Along this line of thought, it might be possible to substitute for the old categories of confession, "impure thoughts and desires," a language that is more conformed to the present understanding of sexuality, that there is impure thinking only when the person deliberately engages in what is less than fully personal and conformed to the holiness to which he is called, a holiness that is expressed in the respect for oneself and others in chastity. For the Sister, or priest, this holiness is the total attitude before God of utter self-giving, an attitude far deeper than merely ethical behavior and the non-performance of certain acts.

As confessor, the priest is a sign of the forgiving Christ, as he clarified the sin-act ("You have had five husbands"), for all sin is in a sense in-

9 Thus Louis Monden, S.J., "Confession: Psychology is not enough," *Jubilee,* Nov., 1965, pp. 14–19.

10 These two levels are not equivalent to nature and grace, since in the present order, grace penetrates the human through and through. The relation between them is rather that the divine is to be manifested and incarnated in and through the human.

fidelity to him who loved man, as he healed and forgave freely ("Go your sins are forgiven you," Mk 2:9), and who did not condemn (Has no man condemned you? Neither will I condemn you," Jn 8:11). He is friend, yet can be demanding, though the demand is nearly always felt as invitation to come nearer, to do better, as encouragement that the struggle has been worthwhile and that one is not alone.

There may be dangers in the situation, though normally these are dealt with simply and prudently. If the confessor is himself overly conscious of sexual difficulties, this is bound to carry over to his penitents, especially if they are women. In such a case, it might be better for him not to act as confessor at all. Another difficulty is that the relation between confessor and penitent may become over emotional, all the more if both are zealous, and if the penitent has a real need of his counsel. The advantage of natural sympathy between the sexes and a similar point of view here may become too much of a good thing. The solution may be that the relation between confessor and penitent should not normally be one of friendship, or that some impersonality should remain. Such an "impersonality" or "psychic distance" then becomes part of the sign value of confession as encounter with Christ, and not primarily with the confessor. This distance is then the manifestation of the confessor's transparence to the transcendent Christ who chooses to act personally, yet through the mediation of men.

Perhaps part of the difficulty here is that we women expect our Fathers in Christ to do everything for us. As there are women in the Church who have more and more adequate theological and psychological training, it may be possible to speak of the manifestation of one's conscience to a friend or counselor, so that the sacramental confession becomes the seal of God's pardon. Such contact with one's peers may well be of more service in the way of spiritual direction than the more formal guidance from superiors (though this will remain for the younger members of the community to some extent) or from priests.

THE PRIEST AS RETREAT MASTER

If confession is really seen as the opening of oneself in all one's sinfulness to the all-holy God, it is already prayer and leads to the prayer of love expressed both in the liturgy and in contemplation. The whole concept of the Ignation retreat which begins with the prayer on the beginning and foundation of Christian life leads from reverence, and the sense of one's own sinfulness, to understanding of God as he has revealed himself in his son Jesus Christ through to the prayer of Communion. Ignatius himself, though he was sometimes noticeably hampered by a platonic anthropology,[11] was profoundly in tune with modern theological develop-

---

[11] As for example, when in the meditation on sin, he describes the soul as imprisoned in a vile and loathsome body.

ments. *The Exercises* are scriptural in their inspiration, and are intended to lead the retreatant to a meeting with the Lord where he is able to make a decision with the full freedom and power of his being, in order to share in the dying and rising of the Lord. This life is profoundly contemplative and active, a life hidden in Christ and lived in the world where God manifests himself and works continually in love.

Or the retreat master may use the exercises of the Better World Movement to broaden the horizons of the Sisters and to show them how to speak their hearts to one another. Such a retreat can be one of the most helpful ways of showing what the Lord is asking of Christians today: a greater concern for the needs of the Church and of the whole world, and a greater willingness to communicate with others, to say honestly what each one thinks in love. Since these retreats bring in men and women from other religious communities and lay people, there is a real expanding of one's understanding of the work of the Church, a growth in openness. If the need for dialogue were more explicitly balanced by a sense of silence, the need for dialogue and stillness before God, such a retreat could very well be a real integration of prayer and action.

Both in retreat and in spiritual direction, Sisters are crying out for the living water, strong and solid teaching on prayer that meets their needs and their problems. They need to know ways of praying the scriptures, to see the Lord present, to know him as loving. For women, methodical prayer may be useful to give a needed discipline to the mind, where this has not been already disciplined by study, but they can be shown too how to make their prayer gradually more affective. If they read good spiritual books, books which combine the intellectual and affective aspects of the person, as do many of the new books on theology and scripture, a slow meditative reading of these will itself lead to prayer.

THE PRIEST AS SPIRITUAL DIRECTOR

Yet it would seem that there is still room for something like the traditional view of spiritual direction, though not necessarily in the form that was traditional. There is a need to talk about prayer, to grow in the understanding of Scripture, and for a woman, it is a great help to have a man's point of view. There is the need to talk over theological questions as these arise in life situations, and especially the problem of religious in this time of transition. Because of his greater involvement in the world, the priest tends to take people and things less seriously, to be less sensitive to emotional problems than women more or less enclosed in their convent situation. His attitude may be a sign of male insensitivity, but it can also help to restore a sense of balance, provided that he realizes that the situation of Sisters is different from his own. But as the way of life of women religious approximates that of men more and more, in education, for example, in type of work, in presence in the world, in the freedom to be oneself, the narrowness of perspective and the emotional imbalance resulting therefrom will to some extent disappear. Spiritual direction will then be more a talking out of mutual problems whether in the life of prayer, in the spiritual direction of others, or problems of the apostolate in any sense.

In the meantime, the priest will be able to help the Sister achieve a sense of self-possession even in an atmosphere where she does not really feel free to be herself. He will help her to accept the sense of risk and of insecurity, as the order itself gradually moves from a more or less rigid structure to greater personal responsibility for each Sister. Both the individual and the whole community must learn to accept the responsibility of freedom, to see rules in the context of Christ and the Church, and not as self-sufficient means for perfection. This growth in understanding will take time, however, and can only take place in the context of great mutual understanding and love all the greater because of great differences within communities. These very differences are themselves the challenge to a deeper and stronger community, a *real* community.

THE DISCERNMENT OF THE SOUL

For the spiritual director of all times, there is no more vexing problem than the determination of the spirit by which a person is led. In the so-called ages of faith, the normal problem of prayer (beyond ordinary prayer, that is) was the phenomenon of ecstacy, visions, raptures, and the like, which today poses a problem for very few of us, whether fortunately or not. Yet the problem of the discernment of the Spirit is as urgent as it ever was, and perhaps more so, with the increasing "secularity" of the world, and the consequences of this for the Church. The age itself is so much in transition that stability seems a thing of the past, and there seem to be few norms to guide Christians attempting to live their self-giving to the full. Even the norms set up by Ignatius of thinking with the Church do not seem to be entirely satisfactory, for if the Church must confess that she is a Church of sinners, that she may fail, though not ultimately, how is the Christian to know where his responsibility lies with any degree of assurance?

If every thinking Christian is haunted by this sense of insecurity, the Sister is more so than anyone, since it goes counter to the security and dependence that has been bred into her from childhood and in her religious life. Practically, the problem boils down to this for the Sister: either she feels that renewal is a threat to her religious life altogether, and hence every kind of change is a traumatic experience, or she feels that she has a real responsibility both for her own response to God and to some extent the response of her community, according to the norms laid down in the new decree. It becomes difficult to accept the idea that obedience to religious superiors, right or wrong, is identical with obedience and fidelity to God. For most, the tensions will lead to a desire to serve the Church more fully, by working for the necessary changes within the order, a work that will vary in intensity with different communities. Each one accepts in advance the friction and disagreement, and the very real suffering that this will cause both to herself and those in the community who fear change, and each chooses her community in love. Out of the struggle, there is the real possibility of a new understanding and a much deeper sense of community, and it is this hope that gives the Sisters the courage and persistence necessary. But even where we grant that tension can be fruitful for life, for a deeper sense of unity, and for work, there may come the point where friction is positively destructive, where it leads to the disintegration of the person or to the suppression of personality and/or to defection from the order.

The confessor or spiritual director can do a great deal here. In the first place, he can, as confessor, clarify the situation for the individual, and simply state what the order may not be able to admit, that the present state of affairs is not objectively according to the plan of God for today, though it may have been so in the past. At the same time, he will be able to show that the order is in fact moving ahead, compared to other orders, or compared to the *status quo* ten years ago. This reassurance will be all the easier in the light of the new schema for religious, which if it does not actually spell out reforms, certainly indicates the general lines of reform very strongly. Secondly, he may point out to the Sister the relevant sections of canon law, which is actually a required study for many religious congregations today.

The matter of guidance here is obviously a very delicate matter, because while he can and must give the necessary reassurance, it must not be done in such a way as to prejudice the Sister's actual religious life, to make it more difficult for her to live in her community. This is where his own attitude and balance will be very important, and his counseling here will perhaps be more like Rogers' nondirective method. He must know how to admit the less good and still point out the very real communications of grace within the order, and perhaps also to suggest ways in which the Sister might manifest the problem to her superiors and work toward a solution.

A new discernment of spirits is needed here, both for the confessor and the superiors, to test whether the difficulty in question is a personal maladjustment, or whether it is a sign of a real work of God (cf. Acts 5:39). The lesson in Acts might be relevant, where Gamaliel says of the Christians whom the Jews do not know how to handle: "Keep clear of these men, I tell you; leave them alone. For if this idea of theirs or its execution is of human origin, it will collapse; but if it is from God you will never be able to put them down, and you risk finding yourselves at war with God" (Acts 5:38 f.). One of the signs of a work of God will then be its ultimate success, but there are other signs too.

Ignatius says that one can discern the Spirit in the life of an evil man by the disturbance he causes, since such a man must be shocked into a new life. For the good man, the Spirit will work by way of peace. The difficulty with this as a sign is that today it is not always good enough. It is adequate as a sign where the will of God and the *status quo* are identical, as for Ignatius they were on the whole, for then the Spirit moves the individual to harmony with the whole. The Lord himself did not promise this as an infallible sign, however, since he gave the assurance of bringing not peace but the sword, and the reminder that his peace is not of this world. As one reads the prophets, the Gospels, and the lives of the saints, peace is not always evident, and one finds very real self-doubt and self-questioning. Wherever one must protest against an established order of things when it is not in order to protest, then the experience will be that of the sword. We are too much bound to the community as human persons to find ourselves at ease against it. This is particularly true of women, and perhaps this is why there have been so few women in the prophetic role. To be willing to take on this burden of protest itself requires a great care for the community, so that in the end it may be true that protest is a form of communion.[12]

If peace is not an infallible sign, and if the truth of the message is not immediately evident, not even fully to the one speaking it, are there any other signs? It would seem that a good sign for Sisters in the struggle for renewal would be the desire for prayer, that is, a real hunger and thirst for God, who absolutely transcends every particular expression of his will, and the willingness to accept the present difficulty as part of that will here and now, as revealing the presence of God. The basic attitude is then a waiting on God's will, a surrender even while one does everything in one's power to realize that will in the awareness that it is God's initiative, God's time, and God's victory that matters.

Another sign is a dialectical one, a double fidelity, that means suffering in the measure that the two values do not coincide: the fidelity to truth and the fidelity to the community, a fidelity that has the shape of the cross. Perhaps this double fidelity is the ultimate sign, the sign of Jesus who loved to the end and would not come down from the cross. When this happens, there must be Christians who stand by to encourage one another to this fidelity, as a witness to the world that God keeps faith. And in one way or another, it seems that this fidelity will be required of every Christian today.

---

[12] Tillich, *Systematic Theology* I.

If the confessor feels he has the duty to advise a Sister to leave, this can only be after much prayer on the part of all, and in some cases, after she has received psychological help, which would make it possible for her to see the situation more clearly. The work of the priest or the superior in this case is to clarify the situation, to advise a possible trial period of further effort within the community, to see whether some adjustment might not be made. If this is impossible, it may be necessary to ask for a degree of exclaustration, permission to live as a secular outside the order for a period of a year, after which a final decision might be made with a sense of assurance that this is God's intention for this person, and not a hasty move under the pressure of emotional strain. Such a situation, which is unfortunately not rare, requires real dialogue, in order to understand the situation as it is, and ultimately the decision must be the Sister's own in as much freedom as is possible.

THE DEMANDS MADE ON THE PRIEST

More is asked of the priest today than ever before, and this is especially true of his work with Sisters. It is true of every apostle today, for all Christians are called to give of themselves more fully. The priest must be a real man of God, deeply rooted in Christ in the celebration of the Eucharist which is the priestly act par excellence, and in prayer. His training in prayer, in scripture, in dogmatic and pastoral theology, and liturgy must be both solid and deep, and above all, must be integrated into his life. Over and above this, he must have a sensitivity to women that can only come from a real knowledge of them as persons, a knowledge which presupposes real and matter-of-fact contact with them. He must have a profound sense of his own gift of himself to the Lord and to his work in chastity, and a sensitivity to the Holy Spirit, coupled with a sense of humor and common sense. Then he can go ahead quite simply to do this work as one who hopes to serve, and in turn as he works with the Sisters he will find that he himself is helped by them. They and he are then truly co-workers with the Lord to bring the more abundant life that he promised.

9

The Modern Renewal of Preaching

WILLIAM TOOHEY, C.S.C.

A MAN WOULD PROBABLY BE CONSIDERED SOMEWHAT FACETIOUS, IF HE replied to the question, "What do you think of the preacher in America today?" with the words of Martha: "Lord, he stinketh" (Jn 11:39). And yet it seems only fair to acknowledge, with the majority of observers, that all is not well in the American pulpit. Preaching is presently in a critical state — an urgent, practical problem.

At the same time, however, there are evident signs of resuscitation. For some years now, particularly in Europe, a body of scholars has realized that the sad state of preaching can be altered only by a serious study of all the facets of the communication of the Word of God. Taking the lead from other movements of renewal (biblical, liturgical, catechetical), these men sought for the doctrinal basis of the Christian message; in short, they attempted to construct a theology of preaching. This investigation, conducted by Protestants and Catholics alike, has contributed significantly to a fresh awareness of all that is involved in preaching.

Few preachers face their congregations these days with the conviction that they are the instruments through which God himself speaks to his people, inviting them to respond with a deep and abiding commitment and to enjoy new life in him. As an obvious consequence, as George Tavard notes, few laymen listening to sermons consider that "the same Word of God who spoke by the prophets and guided the Apostles is now speaking to them."[1] François Mauriac was once asked what he expected from a preacher. "Dare I admit," he replied, "that I am mistaken enough to expect nothing? I only ask him to give me God, not to talk to me about Him."[2]

Mauriac was indeed mistaken; but only because he failed to realize

---

[1] George Tavard, "Reunion and Liturgy," *Worship*, December, 1962, p. 72.
[2] Quoted by A. Liege, "The Ministry of the Word: From Kerygma to Catechetics," *Lumen Vitae*, March, 1962, p. 26.

that being given God is precisely what one expects from a genuine preacher. As a matter of fact, Mauriac was requesting just what the Church has always insisted on from her preachers. St. Paul, for instance, realized that Christian preachers were called upon by Christ to continue an operation of vocal instrumentality; he gives to himself and to the other Apostles the title "prophet" (Eph 2:20; 3:5). A prophet was a tool in the hands of one upon whom he was completely dependent; vividly conscious that the words coming from his mouth were not just his own, the prophet was aware that his message was formally the Word of God. The preacher, Paul insists, has this prophetic task: God himself continues to reach men through the instrumentality of his chosen spokesmen. The preacher is the mouthpiece of Christ; the preaching of the Apostles is the preaching of Christ himself (Eph 2:17).

Should a professor of preaching dare to inform his students that he is training them to be prophets, he may be immediately consigned to the lunatic fringe; but this does not change the fact that he is simply disclosing the full implications of being a real preacher. Although the appreciation of the prophetical nature of preaching has sadly declined in recent centuries, it was a pivotal truth for the apostolic preachers. For them, preaching was God in action. St. Paul does not hesitate to address the Thessalonians as "God-taught." "God chose you from the beginning unto salvation through sanctification of the Spirit and credence of the truth. It was to this end he called you through our Gospel" (2 Thes 2:12-13). The Lord is the one who calls (1 Thes 5:24), even though the actual words used are those of a preacher. "We are ambassadors, therefore, on Christ's behalf since God is entreating through us" (2 Cor 5:20). When Peter speaks to Cornelius, he refers to God "preaching good news of peace by Jesus Christ" (Acts 10:36). "The apostles," E. Schillebeeckx points out, "did nothing but transmit the Word of Christ,"[3] which means they permitted Christ himself to address men through them.

Authentic Christian tradition has always insisted on the prophetical nature of preaching, and we discover an impressive agreement on the issue by Protestants and Catholics alike. Protestantism has done rather well in maintaining a sound appreciation for the fact that in a real sermon Christ is the preacher. Calvin, for example, insisted that genuine preachers spoke "not only in His name and by His command, but as it were, in His own person," so that their preaching "is justly ascribed to none other than Christ Himself."[4] Heinrich Bullinger, instrumental in unifying the Luther-Zwingli-Calvin conception of the presence of God's Word in the preached word, formulated what became common Reformation doctrine: "The

---

[3] E. Schillebeeckx, "Revelation in Word and Deed," *The Word: Readings in Theology* (New York, 1964), p. 260.

[4] Cf. Donald G. Miller, *Fire in Thy Mouth* (Nashville, 1954), p. 17.

preaching of the Word of God *is* the Word of God." One hears echoes here of Luther's: "Yes, I hear the sermon; but who is speaking? The minister? No, indeed! You do not hear the minister. True, the voice is his; but my God is speaking the Word which he preaches or speaks."[5]

One of the great benefits of the recent renewal of preaching in Catholicism has been this same insistence upon its prophetical nature. Louis Bouyer has pointed out that authentic preaching has always been an occasion when "everything the people heard was received by them as a living Word, always present, destined for them, addressed to them by Christ Himself present among them."[6] "Preaching," Jean Danielou says, "is not discourse on God, it is the Word of God."[7] In one of the most significant passages in the Constitution on the Sacred Liturgy, the Council Fathers insist that in the liturgy "Christ is still proclaiming His Gospel" (art. 33). This principle holds for the sermon at Mass (the homily) as well as for the public reading of the Word, a point emphasized in that marvelous Liturgical Conference publication, *Priest's Guide to Parish Worship*: "When the Scriptures are read in the liturgical community, it is Christ speaking to each of us, and when the meaning of the Scriptures here and now is explained by the priest as president of the community and minister of the Word, it is Christ who addresses each of us directly in our daily lives."[8]

All who presume to preach need to grapple with these fundamental truths. Too long have preachers trembled with trepidation, or stumbled with blindness, at the threshold of authentic prophetic preaching. A priest finds no difficulty in acknowledging the power of the sacraments; there is no problem in admitting that it is truly Christ who baptizes, absolves, and speaks the words of consecration. Unfortunately, however, it has long been a different story when the question of the sacramentality of God's Word in preaching arose (the fact that God also acts here); there is real reluctance to extend an act of faith that far.

A major first step towards remedying this deficiency is reached when the preacher appreciates the credentials of Revelation. These are not romantic notions — when we read of a Word that is "alive, full of energy," which can "penetrate deeper than any two-edged sword" (Heb 4:12). This Word is creative; it goes to the heart of a man, stimulating faith (1 Co 2:4), effecting sanctification (1 Tim 4:5). "The Word of God increased and multiplied," we read in Acts (12:24); and St. Paul expresses it this way: "It (the preached Gospel) is the power of God unto

---

[5] Martin Luther, *Werke, Kritische Gesamtansgate* (Weimar, 1883 f.), Vol. 47, p. 229.

[6] Louis Bouyer, "The Word of God Lives in the Liturgy," *The Liturgy and the Word of God* (Collegeville, 1959), p. 60.

[7] Jean Danielou, *Christ and Us* (New York: Sheed and Ward, 1961), p. 180.

[8] *Priest's Guide to Parish Worship* (Washington, D. C., 1964), p. 41.

salvation to everyone that believes" (Rm 1:16). St. Paul goes so far as to proclaim that he begets Christians in Jesus Christ, *by the Gospel* (1 Co 4:15). It is absolutely essential for the preacher to think of the Word as Isaiah did: "Once fallen from the sky, does rain or snow return to it? No, it refreshes earth, soaking into it and making it fruitful, to provide the sower with fresh seed, the hungry mouths with bread. So it is with the Word by these lips of mine once uttered; it will not come back, an empty echo . . ." (Is 4:10-11).

Because the Word of God is just that — God's own Word — most scholars insist that there is something here that goes beyond ordinary discourse. Preacher and faithful, Charles Davis writes, "are engaged in a sacred event, a mystery; the power of the Spirit is here."[9] Hence, careful study of the biblical notion of the Word of God has led theologians to the conclusion that preaching is capable of directly causing grace. This grace is not sanctifying grace (preaching is not the eighth sacrament), but the grace of faith.

The Word of the preacher is a personal call from God; in the sermon God turns toward man and addresses him, invites him to surrender, to believe. If a man is to respond to this invitation, he must be given the grace to do it — his mind must be enlightened and his will drawn by grace. In short, there are two testimonies needed: the outward testimony of the preacher and the interior testimony (the grace) of the Spirit. It is precisely the point of those theologians who hold that preaching is a direct cause of grace that preaching does not merely offer the Christian message outwardly, but gives at the same time the interior testimony, the grace necessary for that real assent, which is faith. "We mediate the Word in its fullness," Father Davis notes, "the living Word, which means the Word illuminated by the action of the Spirit."[10] The Word bears with it a power reaching to the heart at the very moment it is heard. This was the case with Lydia, a seller of purple, who was listening to St. Paul, and the Lord "touched her heart to give heed to what was being said by Paul" (Acts 16:14).

The preacher must force himself to advance one step further. He must realize that it is this very Word of God which he is privileged to proclaim in his preaching; and that when he does, he becomes the vehicle for God's communication with man. If the preacher holds to the apostolic tradition of preaching, he realizes, with Von Allmen, that "God is not so much the object as the true source of Christian preaching. Preaching is thus speech by God rather than speech *about* God."[11]

---

[9] Charles Davis, "The Theology of Preaching," *Clergy Review,* September, 1960, p. 533.

[10] *Ibid.,* p. 536.

[11] Jean-Jacques Von Allmen, *Preaching and Congregation* (Richmond, 1962), p. 7. Italics added.

Preaching is thus an incarnational activity.[12] God, in his wisdom, has always chosen to communicate with man through a perceptible means; he incarnates himself in what is tangible, and this sensible thing becomes a communicator of the divine. This is true of the hypostatic union, of the sacraments, and of preaching. In preaching, the personal Word of Christ resounds again through the weak, fallible instrumentality of his minister.

> It is the old story of Balaam's ass [C. K. Barrett suggests] through which the Lord condescended to speak: He can express Himself through very unworthy means. There is no excuse here for slovenly workmanship, but there is very solid ground for hope, and for the earnest prayer, that God will allow His Word to be clothed in our weak, ignorant, and inadequate language, and not to be obscured by it. May God deliver us from the false humility, and from the subservience to routine, which allow us to forget, when we enter the pulpit, that we are to assist at a miracle, and that God will communicate Himself through our speech to those who sit before us.[13]

I am becoming thoroughly convinced that full awareness of and appreciation for these points is absolutely indispensable for any appreciable renewal of preaching. The preacher who is oblivious to the prophetical nature of preaching and the authentic power of the Word he is privileged to communicate becomes susceptible to numerous pitfalls. He may, for example, wonder why his words do not convert more people, or influence a deepening of faith, without realizing that the failure occurs precisely because they *are* his words, instead of God's. Only God's Word carries with it the efficacy to touch men's hearts; no merely human word can penetrate like a knife. And yet so many preachers avoid real contact with this Word. They stand on the outside looking in: they talk around the Word, comment on it, discuss it, defend it, offer their personal opinions about it. Regretfully, they do not *preach* it; Christ is not allowed to speak to men through them.

This is why awareness of all that is involved in preaching can sometimes terrify a man. The interior grace, so necessary if preaching is to lead to faith, follows upon what is outwardly offered, and will only be present to the extent the genuine Word of God is preached and not some imposture — like the preacher's own word. So, if the grace of faith is given, it is because of God's Word, not the eloquence of the preacher; but he does determine whether or not the process ever gets that far. In other words, the Word of God will not be present without the cooperation of the preacher, since he has to construct the sermon, compose and form the expression of the Word for his listeners. Hence, there is greater dependence upon the minister in preaching than there is, say, in administering the sacraments.

---

[12] Schillebeeckx, *op. cit.*, p. 261.

[13] C. K. Barrett, "Biblical Preaching and Biblical Scholarship," a lecture from: *Biblical Problems and Biblical Preaching* (Philadelphia: Fortress Press, 1964), pp. 47–48.

Any departure from the function of explaining, expounding, and unfolding the Word of God itself, as contained in Scripture, can mean, of course, that a man becomes a nonbiblical preacher — a contradiction in terms. We see this sort of thing in "springboard preaching," where a preacher draws a topic, theme, or subject from a biblical text, and then proceeds to develop his "talk" any way he wants, usually along lines suggested by the principles of public speaking. But to the extent he is guided by the laws of secular oratory rather than the biblical text, his preaching suffers. As Von Allmen warns: "The history of preaching proves that the introduction of rhetoric into homiletics works to the disadvantage of exegesis."[14] This is to deny nothing to the important role of rhetorical theory; it is simply to insist that preaching the word of God demands full penetration of the biblical text, not avoidance of it.

The deleterious effect of "springboard preaching" has been particularly apparent in the field of liturgical preaching. For example, some diocesan series of sermons have frequently incorporated topics totally unrelated to the theme of the Mass. And even when some connection with the Mass texts was attempted, it often meant simply stretching the texts to fit a preconceived series of doctrinal or moral topics. In one recent series, for instance, the results become embarrassingly ludicrous when, on the third Sunday of Advent, the text, "I am the voice . . ." becomes the springboard for the topic: God Speaks to Us Through Tradition; and the text, "I will, be thou made clean," from the third Sunday after Epiphany, is taken for the subject: The Sixth and Ninth Commandments.[15] The sad thing about so much of this "theme" preaching is that it has distorted the Mass into a mere occasion for preaching. Happily, the Liturgy Constitution has clearly affirmed that the sermon at Mass must always remain in context — within the general context of worship, and within the exegetical context of the texts of the particular Mass being celebrated.

There are more subtle dangers in thematic or topical preaching, beyond cases where there is a clear twisting of the text. A topic may be actually mentioned in the text, but it may not be the main concern of God's message, not really the principal point He is trying to communicate. A typical instance of this occurs frequently on the first Sunday of Lent. The Gospel text (the temptations of Christ) is a profound revelation of the personality of Jesus. Unfortunately, the preacher may not get this far: the passage, you see, mentions fasting, so he may launch into an exhortation on the practice of fasting — and another opportunity to preach Christ loses out to moralizing.

Although moralizing can infect any type of preaching, it seems to

---

14 Von Allmen, *op. cit.,* p. 54.
15 Joseph Kellner, S.J., *One Year's Preaching the Good Tidings* (Manila, 1962), p. 8.

cause particular havoc with liturgical preaching, demonstrating again and again a profound misapprehension of theological principle. Preaching to assist full participation in Mass does not seem an adequate achievement. Regretfully, St. Pius X's famous statement about the liturgy being the primary and indispensable source of the Christian spirit is oft-quoted but rarely appreciated. Christian action must be the outward expression of the inward vitality — the Christlife we share; and the supreme source of this transformation is to be found in the Mass.

Many preachers identify practical sermons with the promotion of religious practices, when in reality the most practical sermon possible first of all works in the service of faith. As Cardinal Suhard declared, "The purpose of our preaching is to give the faith or to make it grow."[16] Activists, so impatient with the liturgy, fail to realize the necessity for this sequence. The initial effort must be to form believers who, having heard the Word and responded in faith, react in their lives in a new and dynamic way. We must not be fooled by appearances: the liturgy may seem unconcerned with action outside the assembly; but actually, in accord with the principle of Christian action (*operatio sequitur esse*) the liturgy is designed to extend beyond the limits of any specific celebration. As Guardini put it, the liturgy "knows that those who live by it will be true and spiritually sound, and at peace to the depths of their being; and that when they leave its sacred confines to enter life they will be men of courage."[17] The faith that has been deepened through participation in Mass must overflow in subsequent action. A man has more fully become dominated by Christ; he has the spiritual disposition to do what is right when action is demanded. It is imperative that preachers realize that the faith their preaching has helped engender influences dynamically the life of the hearer. They must see that a homily that aids worship leads the people to the possession of "the Spirit who will lead them, as Jesus promised, 'into the full range of truth' (Jn 16:13). The words of the preacher, uttered as successor of the Apostles, evoke in his hearers that inner Word, the Gospel in the fullest sense (as Paul was so well aware), spoken by the Spirit in the depths of their hearts."[18]

Closely related to topical and moralistic preaching is the so-called "cult of the relevant," or "tonic preaching," a combination of a problem of the moment and the "positive thinking" of the preacher. This "problem-centered, moral-uplift talk," as *Time* magazine labelled it, does not begin with the Gospel at all, but with the suspected needs of the people. The cart is placed before the horse: the audience becomes the source for

---

[16] Emmanuel Cardinal Suhard, *Priests Among Men* (Chicago, 1950), p. 47.

[17] Romano Guardini, *The Church and the Catholic, and the Spirit of the Liturgy* (New York, 1935), p. 211.

[18] David M. Stanley, S.J., "The Fonts of Preaching," *Worship*, February, 1963, p. 172.

preaching instead of the recipient. As a result, rather than trusting to the Gospel to deal with ultimate needs, which it always does, the preacher begins to "compete with the psychiatrists on their own level, and to offer people the kind of 'comfort' they are looking for in these less-than-ultimate needs."[19] I am reminded of the preacher who reported not so long ago that he was preparing his next Sunday's sermon on the big problem of the day: his people had been going to see *The Night of the Iguana*.

Only a lack of appreciation for the power and never failing relevance of the Gospel of Jesus Christ can cause what H. A. Oberman refers to as "the frantic search for a vital message for our time."[20] No one denies that we must be up to date — fully contemporary and timely with our proclamation of the good news of salvation; but "this does not mean that we should have a 'nice modern gospel,' which is specially tailored to meet the requirements of our less exacting contemporaries. We cannot cut the gospel to 'what Jones likes.' "[21] One starting point must always be the Gospel: What does Christ want to say to this audience here and now? His Word is not supposed to fit in and blend and soothe, necessarily; it has always been revolutionary and transforming. To water down the Word to the "crust" needs of the people is to cheat them. "Christ does not meet man's needs. He alters them. After a man has met Christ, he finds his needs have changed. He needs forgiveness; he needs a task; he needs someone to love in Christ's name."[22]

The current renewal of preaching has not only considered the content of the message; it has also disclosed that the unique quality of this content determines the method for its communication. Just before beginning her Adventures, Alice, who was looking over her sister's shoulder, said: "What is the use of a book without pictures or conversation?" We might say the same thing of our preaching; for we preach revelation, the Unseen, the suprasensible, the ineffable mystery of God's love. And the only way we can express these realities is by way of imagery — figures, similies, metaphors, analogies, parables, and so on. The language of faith is the image; thus, the method of communicating the content of our message is the same one God himself used in his own catechism, the Bible.

No doubt the image is only a tool of accommodation, as all language must be that attempts to speak of the ineffable, but there is no satisfactory alternative. You cannot get around it; it is impossible to speak of divine reality except through comparison with things of the world. It is, St.

---

[19] Reginald H. Fuller, *What is Liturgical Preaching?* (London, 1957), pp. 16–17.

[20] H. A. Oberman, "Reformation, Preaching, and Ex Opere Operato," D. Callahan (ed.), *Christianity Divided* (New York, 1961), p. 235.

[21] W. Norman Pittenger, *Proclaiming Christ Today* (Greenwich, 1962), p. 45; cf. also P. Hitz, *To Preach the Gospel* (New York, 1963), pp. 165–166.

[22] Thomas H. Keir, *The Word in Worship* (London, 1962), p. 142.

Thomas insists, the law of our limited reason. How silly for a preacher to presume that God can best be expressed in the abstract when he himself has always expressed himself in the concrete.[23] Witness the biblical imagery on almost every page of Scripture, that superb book of pictures and conversations. "For since the beginning of the world the invisible attributes of God have been plainly discernible through things which he has made and which are commonly seen and known" (Rm 1:20).

Just look at the way Christ employed the method of imagery in his preaching. "Christ taught by vision rather than imperatives," Aelred Graham once remarked.[24] Christ fully realized that the human mind is not a debating hall but a picture gallery; and so, following the laws of learning, he adapted himself to the people and the surroundings of Palestine, and therefore penetrated to the primary target for all preaching — the listener's imagination. He spoke in concrete terms of fields, pearls, fig trees, wedding feasts, harvests, coins, storms, kings and kingdoms, fathers and sons, farmers, merchants, tax-collectors, the rich and the poor, sick and healthy. To these images he attached a religious significance; by means of these he communicated divine truth.

This is why Newman was so critical of a preaching that entailed the mere transmission of abstract general definitions and facts, theological theses and syllogistic formulas. He knew that truth presented in this fashion could elicit an apprehension and assent that is only notional; and though this assent might be absolute and unconditional, it is not one that results in a person living in accord with it; it is not that real assent which alone is true faith. As Newman himself said: "The heart is commonly reached, not through the reason, but through the imagination. . . . Many men will live and die upon a dogma; no man will be a martyr for a conclusion."[25]

The method for preaching, then, is imagery in its various forms: parable, analogy, simile, metaphor, and so on. Imagery makes the shadowy things clear, and brings out the supernatural in the visible. Because preaching is related to particular audiences, the imagery will always have to be suitably adapted for comprehension. Christ is also our exemplar here: "So he taught them his message with many parables according as they were able to understand it" (Mk 4:33). A preacher will thus often have to use his own analogies and illustrations to make the imagery God has used in the Bible fully meaningful and relevant — just as long as he remembers that the biblical imagery is inspired, his is not. Failure to give first priority to the biblical expression, which, after all, contains the revelation, has resulted all too often in a preacher attempting to structure

---

[23] *Ibid.,* p. 53.
[24] Aelred Graham, *Christian Thought and Action* (New York, 1958), p. 91.
[25] John H. Newman, *A Grammar of Assent* (New York, 1903), p. 93.

his own analogies and illustrations without any reference at all to God's. Consequently, one hears grace being "revealed" as "juice in the wires," a very nice image perhaps, but no revelation of the reality involved.

There is more involved in adapation, however, than clarity and comprehensibility. In addition to being understood, the Word of God must be appreciated and loved; that is, it must strike the hearer as personal and crucially pertinent for him. The preacher wishes to lead his listener from presentation through explanation to assimilation. The first two steps lead from the historical word (the biblically-oriented imagery) to the eternal Word (God's message); for example, from the story of the lost sheep to the lesson — God searches for and rejoices in the recovery of the sinner. But at this point, the listener is still a full step away from being the recipient of authentic preaching. Recognition of story and identification of message do not suffice; the hearer must recognize himself as the lost sheep and the present moment as his opportunity to be found.

It is no great accomplishment to afford our people familiarity with biblical narrative and even the spiritual point contained, if they are never impressed by the penetrating relevance of the Word: "This is God's message to ME, his message to me NOW!" We have to be like modern Nathans, bringing the Davids of the world from a simple story to the searing revelation: "That man is you" (2 K 12:7). The secret of the "that man is you" approach lies in the fact that in the explanation we do not move from the passage to the people, trying to get something to fit them. We illustrate, rather, how they are already contained in some way in the text itself. Let me illustrate. In the very explanation of the miracle of the widow's son, the preacher attempts to confront his listeners with the fact that Christ is speaking to them here and now; that, in a spiritual sense, they are being told, "Young man, I say to you, arise!" The application is *in* the explanation: the people pass from a mere hearing and understanding of the Word to an appreciation and love for it, they recognize it as being for them, now! Through the prophetical character of preaching, Christ speaks to the present audience, seeing in them a similarity with the original audience: *they* are like Lazarus, the lepers, the daughter of Naim, Martha, the Pharisee, Zaccheus, or Magdalene.

Campion Gavaler's "unredeemed situation" technique is quite similar to this.[26] In many scriptural passages we see an unredeemed human situation that Christ enters and transforms. The preacher attempts to help the present audience recognize that their own situation is similar to the one depicted in the Bible, and that Christ, here and now, invites them to a salvific transformation. A fuller demonstration of these various principles will be given in the final section of this essay.

---

[26] Campion Gavaler, O.S.B., "Theology of the Sermon as Part of the Mass," *Worship,* March, 1964, p. 207.

Once the general principles of preaching are appreciated, specific attention can be given to the types of preaching, determined on the basis of the circumstances and situations within which the communication of God's message takes place. Since all preaching works in the service of faith, its purpose will always be either to gather up or build up; that is, it will be an operation of transmitting the Christian message in order to lead to first faith or the further development of a faith already initiated.

The first type of preaching is missionary preaching, or evangelization. Here we have the prospective believer, whether already baptized or not, and the aim is to lead to conversion, that initial, free, personal response to Christ's invitation for commitment. The content of the communication is the kerygma — the essential core of the Christian message, the announcement of an event of critical importance for the hearer. Non-detailed and more emotional than coldly rational in format, it is the revelation of basic salvation history — a striking summons, an imperative call.

Because man does not automatically feel or acknowledge the need for conversion, attention will often have to be paid to pre-evangelization. This is an effort to dispose the listener and set the stage for evangelization, an attempt to remove any obstacles to the reception of the good news. Yves Congar refers to this as an "apostolic preamble" — "the disinfecting of men in their secular social structures, in their actual life as persons, so that the faith may strike root, grow and bear fruit."[27] This phase of missionary preaching, needed probably more today than ever before, attempts to dispel the fantasies and illusions of life and to declare the fundamental facts of life. It is never done in an angry way: it is given, however, with urgency, prophetic surety, and supreme earnestness. The preacher does not intend to leave his audience at this point; he merely wants to ready them to give full acceptance to the good news to follow: "Fear not, I bring you tidings of great joy; there has been born for you a Savior."

All other varieties of preaching are efforts to build up the faith engendered through evangelization. The content shifts to the "explicit Word," the full implications of the basic message, its organic development and continuation. If the audience (whether in a CCD classroom or rectory parlor) is made up of believers being led to a deeper faith through a series of instructions, we have an instance of the second type of preaching — catechetical. A third category — special preaching — takes in a great number of situations where a similar activity of nourishing and enriching the faith takes place; e.g., retreats, days of recollection, forty hours, cursillos, conferences, and the like.

Thorough consideration of these three types of preaching is beyond the scope of this essay. There is a fourth category, however, about which I

---

[27] Yves Congar, O.P., *Lay People in the Church* (Westminster: Newman, 1956), pp. 364–365,

wish to offer some extended comments — liturgical preaching.

Preaching at Mass must be viewed from the perspective of sacramental theology. It is here that we discover the immediate utility of the word: it is absolutely indispensable to lend significance to the sacramental gesture or action. As St. Augustine said, "The word is added to the action and then it becomes a sacrament." Baptism, for example, is a mere bathing without the signifying words; and a priest is just holding bread until Christ's consecratory words are spoken. The word, then, is necessary for validity; but we are concerned with more than this. Validity, let us admit it, is simply not sufficient when it comes to the sacramental involvement of the faithful. We need a "full sacrament," a celebration so meaningful that the people are stimulated to join themselves to it efficaciously. There is a chain reaction at work here: worship necessitates faith, and faith demands the Word. As F. X. Durrwell put it, "There is no substitute for faith in the work of our salvation. The sacrament works by its own power, *ex opere operato*, yet remains without effect in us in the absence of faith. For though the power to nourish us is in the bread of the sacrament, it is faith that eats, digests, and assimilates it."[28] Our major concern in sacramental celebration is that man be caught up by God's word of invitation and respond to it with a loving surrender.

Hence the word is essential for fruitfulness; and here is where we see the great utility of the readings of the Mass, especially the Gospel and Epistle. The readings, if properly selected, are supposed to be saying something about the central mystery being celebrated. Some will do this more readily than others, the Gospels being the most dependable for opening up the sign of the liturgical action. Think of the selection of the Mass texts in relation to a Bible Service. The theme of the Service or Vigil is chosen first, then the readings that most appropriately support this; in this way, it is obvious each one of the texts is speaking about the same theme. Looking at the Mass from the same point of view, it will be logical to believe that the texts for a particular celebration are likewise chosen to help establish and sustain a central theme, in this instance the redemptive passover of Christ, re-presented in the Mass.

Consequently, you always know the answer to the question: What is this text all about? It must be understood in the light of the redemptive act of Christ. Each passage is revealing some aspect of this paschal event; that is why it is in the Mass in the first place. Some, for example, will be identity texts, revealing Christ, the chief actor in the eucharistic drama (Cana, Epiphany, "But who do you say I am?"). Others will unfold some characteristic of the Lord who works in our midst: the extraordinary events (feeding the 5000) present Jesus as acting with power and compassion. The healing miracles proclaim spiritual salvation: the individual

---

[28] F. X. Durrwell, *In the Redeeming Christ* (London, 1963), p. 126.

miracle is a sign of the one great miracle of redemption that Christ principally came to accomplish. For example, raising Lazarus from the dead is a sign of his raising all men to new life in him. And then there are the parables, many of which, like the miracles, speak of the kind of God we have (the laborers in the vineyard, the lost sheep). Some will throw light on the nature of the Kingdom to which man is invited (treasure in the field, precious pearl), while others will point to the dispositions requisite for men of this Kingdom (pharisee and the publican). The "be prepared" parables all fall into this latter category: in these (ten maidens, thief in the night, householders waiting for their master's return) the focus is on the need for the people to respond to Christ, present and active in the Eucharistic Banquet.

At this juncture, we discover the necessity of the homily. It is a simple application of the law of communication: the Word must be "explained" and "expounded,"[29] in order that the people may truly appreciate its continuity with and relevance to the celebration they are participating in. The preacher must discover the particular way the reading refers to the central mystery, and pass this "revelation" along to the congregation. In doing this, he has to observe the following priority of contexts: the Word, the Eucharistic Sacrifice it helps "signify," and, finally, the liturgical feast or season. Failure to follow this sequence has done immeasurable harm to liturgical preaching in past years. Serious rethinking must be given to the lamentable practice of "using" the Mass for a multitude of festive occasions. All too often the Mass loses out to the occasion, providing a kind of background or ceremonial filler, during which a talk is delivered on a topic disassociated from either the Eucharist or the texts of the Mass being offered. The Mass does not play second fiddle to any event: the people (should) have come to worship, and so references to any seasonal setting (Mother's Day) must be made with extreme caution. Even references to the liturgical feast must be discriminately made; after all, there is a vast difference in significance between the feast of Easter and that of some little-known saint.

Giving first attention to the text means uncovering the literal meaning, and this involves the preacher in the task of exegesis. Without sound exegesis there will never be true preaching. Although it should not be a mere sharing of technical notes, "it must be scientific in the sense of solidly founded in a grasp of the problems involved in the meaning of the text in question and an understanding of the limits of even the specialist's appreciation of the passage."[30]

---

[29] These are the precise words used to describe the homily in the *Constitution on the Sacred Liturgy,* art. 24, and art. 52.

[30] Thomas Barrosse, C.S.C., "The Preacher's Role as Exegete," *Preaching,* Spring, 1965, p. 10.

There is a good deal of terror over recent scriptural advances; but this need not be. If anything, the new approach to the Bible is a simplified one: the fundamental unity is being brought out more and more. The Bible is a book of signs; symbolic language is used over and over again in order to reveal God's wonderful plan of love, reaching its crescendo in Christ. For example, God wishes to say, "I love men." He gets His point across through a story (the prodigal), a sign (feeding the 5000), and actual events (the passion-death-resurrection). The job of the homilist is to share this with the people and proclaim that this God who loves men is here to be encountered in the Eucharist.

For assistance in discovering the literal meaning of the text, the preacher has a number of helpful commentaries at his disposal, e.g., *The New Testament Reading Guide* pamphlets, *the Interpreter's Bible,* A. M. Hunter's *Interpreting the Parables.* He will also have personal notes he can refer to, either from his seminary Scripture classes, Bible Institutes, or study days he has attended, or from personal reading of periodicals, like *The Bible Today,* or books, such as John McKenzie's *The Power and the Wisdom.* There are also sample homilies or outlines available, but the preacher must use these with great reserve. They are final products — not just the basic analysis of the biblical text — and the reader is likely to be impressed with what he finds without realizing that it may be simply a good specimen of "springboard preaching," having little or no connection with authentic exegesis. One of the better collections is E. Lawrence's *Homilies for the Year.*

It is important for the preacher to begin his preparation early. In preaching weekly homilies, for instance, he should at least look at the readings of the next Sunday's Mass the preceding Sunday night or Monday. He next turns to the exegetical material to discover what particular aspect of the paschal mystery is treated in the pericope. It is helpful to constantly ask the key questions: What does this text have to say about the central mystery we are now celebrating? What connection or continuity is there with this text and what is taking place at Mass? How can I legitimately say about this passage what Christ said in his famous homily: "This Scripture I have just read is today fulfilled"? In that renowned Synagogue scene, you will recall, Christ presented himself as the fulfillment of the Isaian prophecy. It is the same with the Mass: the encounter in the Eucharist is the full actualization of what is announced, promised, "signified" in the reading and homily — the Word of salvation followed by the Work of salvation.

Once the teacher has applied the literal meaning of the text to the Mass, I would suggest he attempt to formulate an outline of just what he is going to say. This can come only from deep reflection on the message itself, taking into consideration the audience situation, desired style of approach, supplementing examples, and other factors. At this point, he should preach it to himself, that is, attempt to actually say it all the way through, working with nothing more than his outline. Frequent repetition will polish style, familiarize content, rehearse delivery. This will give the preacher an extemporaneous presentation, which alone captures the directness, freshness, and spontaneity so vital in effective preaching. Most homilies would be vastly improved with just a few more rehearsals.

It may prove helpful now to exemplify the various features of homily preparation. Let us take the Gospel for the nineteenth Sunday after Pentecost, the parable of the king who gave a marriage feast for his son (Mt 22:1-10). Exegetical research immediately shows that the final scene (the man without the wedding garment) is a separate parable appended to the first; so the preacher, in his concern to keep his scope properly narrowed, is free to choose not to treat it at this time. The symbolism is clear: the king and his son denote the Father and Christ; the use of the image "marriage feast" refers to the Hebrew sense of the union with God as similar to marriage; consequently, Christ is the bridegroom and mankind the bride (the Church as bride). The basic message comes clearly through: the Father is calling all men to everlasting life, through their union with Christ; but if God invites men into the Kingdom, their salvation depends on their accepting his invitation.

The biblical analysis also uncovers the influence of the apostolic times, when the emphasis was on the rejection of the Old Testament prophets (the first servants sent forth), and also the New Testament preachers who were martyred (the second wave of servants), whose death God avenged by the destruction of Jerusalem. This reference to "their city" is a redaction inserted later in the oral communication of the parable, and a demonstration of how the early preachers adapted the story to fit their particular audience situation.

The continuity of this text with the Mass is only too obvious: the liturgy of the Word is the "wedding invitation" and the sacramental action the Messianic Banquet itself. The biblical image of a wedding is still a timely one; so the preacher can quite effectively modernize and personalize the revelation. He might ask the congregation to imagine they were actually inviting friends and relatives to the marriage of one of their children; that these invitations had been ignored or, worse, answered with snide remarks and insults — all of this despite the fact that the people were being invited to something that would mean for them an occasion of great happiness. With regard to God's invitation, there is a feature that makes it even more appalling to refuse: we are called to be not mere guests at somebody else's wedding but guests of honor — it is our own wedding with God, through union with Christ in the Mass, to which we are being invited,

For a final example we will turn our attention to Quinquagesima Sunday. This Gospel (Lk 18:31-43) depicts the third prediction of the passion and the miraculous cure of the blind man at Jericho. Here in a more finalized form is how the fruit of exegesis might be structured for the homily.

Why the passion prediction? It seems a pity Christ decided to shatter the lighthearted mood of the Apostles, bringing them to earth with such a jolt. He had issued these dire predictions twice before, at what must have seemed the worst possible times: immediately following Peter's profession of faith (Lk 9:22), and while they marvelled at the healing of the epileptic boy (Lk 9:44). One might suppose Christ was trying to prepare them for any eventuality well before it happened. It is true he offered sufficient testimony of his power and promises of eternal life, and only then revealed that he must suffer. But despite his efforts, they refused to take what he said seriously. There is another alternative: perhaps Christ expected his warnings to strengthen and support the Apostles *during* his passion, inasmuch as it would mean fulfillment of something he had predicted — another sign of his power. But this did not work either. They panicked and scattered, thinking all was lost. It can only mean then, that the prediction was to provide substance for faith *after* the passion. Our Lord knew the Spirit would bring all things to their minds, helping them understand the significance of his forewarnings — and also the momentous "sign" he had worked for them in curing the blind man.

While they were still on their way to the city and Jesus' passover to the Father, he works a sign of this ultimate miracle of salvation. Luke has the blind man call Christ by a messianic title — "Son of David" — and, as a result, is himself called by our Lord. He received his request for sight because he had faith in the beneficence God has for the outcasts of life.

Precisely because the full significance of these events come in retrospection, they are just as meaningful for us today as for Luke's original audience. Men were impressed with the terrific impact from both the Old Testament prophecies and Christ's own predictions only after the resurrection: "And their eyes were opened and they recognized him" — (Lk 24:31); "These are the words which I spoke to you while I was yet with you, that all things might be fulfilled that are written in the Law of Moses and in the prophets and the psalms concerning me" (Lk 24:44). Now we realize that he went to his passion with complete knowledge and deliberation; he was not surprised at its occurrence, nor compelled to its climax. It is amazing that he would foretell all these things just that we might know how great his desire was to liberate us; he wanted no mistaking the fact that love was the motive — for this, he realized, would stimulate our own love in return.

Christ's strategy is to capture our loving commitment. His "going up" to

Jerusalem refers to the Cross and the bosom of the Father. And we are each of us a part of this; as a matter of fact, *we* are the blind man on the way. Only now does the full force of Luke's words hit home. Luke records Jesus saying, "Your faith has *saved* you," suggesting something more than a mere physical cure. Here is the sign of promise: through our reaching out in faith, as we offer Eucharist (thanks) for his loving redemption, we will personally join in the rescue he offers the world of darkness and blindness, and we will pass with him to the Father.

10

Contemporary Catechesis

CARL J. PFEIFER, S.J.

THE DAY OF QUESTION-ANSWER, MEMORY-CENTERED CATECHESIS IS rapidly passing; significant advances in catechetical theory and practice have resulted since the "catechetical movement" began in Germany and Austria at the turn of the century. Yet a number of questions and problems today coexist with the seemingly secure position of the so-called "kerygmatic" approach to catechesis. Growing pains are being experienced in catechetical circles throughout the world. Perhaps a brief focusing of the problem will help.

In the early years of this century considerable attention was given to catechetical methodology by German-speaking catechists. Gradually a consensus was reached regarding a method proper to catechetical instruction. The "Munich Method," also known as the psychological method, with its formal steps of presentation-explanation-assimilation, has dominated catechetical practice up to the present. Most modern catechisms are constructed according to this plan which is a notable advance over the previous "text-explanatory" method which concentrated so much on the rational powers of the students.

Slowly, however, catechetical thinking turned to a consideration not only of how to teach (methodology) but of what to teach (content). As early as 1936 Josef Andreas Jungmann, S.J., directed attention to the need for a thorough reconsideration of the catechism. His work was widely popularized by Johannes Hofinger, S.J., and today there is international agreement on the fundamentals of kerygmatic catechesis. For example, the entire content centers on Christ; every aspect of doctrine and morals is related to him as the very center of the history of salvation. Catechesis is seen as a message, a joyful message to be proclaimed, rather than doctrine to be learned and memorized. Events rather than words are the primary carriers of revelation, and the central event is the paschal mystery, the dying and rising of Christ in a self-oblation to the Father on behalf of mankind. Man, aware of the divine initiative of love, responds in faith and obedient love. Most contemporary catechisms incorporate these principles agreed upon by catechetical experts at the International Study Week on Mission Catechetics held at Eichstätt, Germany, in 1960 and again in 1962 at Bangkok.

Yet there is today further questioning, deeper probing. A reflective reading of the flood of new catechisms, the frequently disheartening picture of CCD programs, the radical needs of inner-city dwellers, all tend to shatter a bit of the self-complacency and security that seem to have settled on the catechetical scene. One may legitimately ask why the consideration of salvation history almost always ends with the early Church. If God does reveal and save through events, are not current events equally part of the working out of God's plan? Often catechisms seem to replace the older philosophical structure of concepts with a more theological structure of concepts, namely, that of salvation history. In practice, then, students learn and memorize facts and events of the past instead of abstract definitions; the history of salvation is reduced to historical study. Is this what is meant by the catechetical tradition that God taught and formed his people through the history of salvation?

Is it surprising then, that American adolescents, particularly those in CCD programs, find little challenge in a rather stereotyped progression from Abraham to Moses to David to the Prophets to Christ? Especially if they have gone through this before? Certainly such an approach is of more interest than the analysis and memorization of abstract doctrinal formulae, but what does it have to do with their lives, lives filled with anxiety, automobiles, space exploration, sex? It appears that a major catechetical problem today is the meaningful relating of God's Word to contemporary Americans. The advances of the catechetical movement have largely centered on the kerygma, on content; today, attention must be focused more on man, on situations of life.

This is not a question merely of method; nor is it just a matter of content. It extends the theology already inherent in the salvation history approach to its implied conclusion. God does form and teach through salvation history, but primarily in the events of history and the facts of cosmos and only secondarily through the verbal interpretation of such facts and events. And therefore God is teaching and forming his people in and through the events and experiences of today. Life itself is holy; to be is itself a blessed thing. Life is mystery, the world, a divine milieu, where one encounters God and the powers of darkness. Contemporary situations, life experiences, events of importance for the individual, for the Church, for society — all are signs of the mysterious presence of God, all are Christic, bearers of God's life and love in Christ. Salvation history is today. The struggle for racial equality, the Vatican Council, are signs of God's saving presence, just as were the sufferings of the *anawim* in Israel and the Jerusalem Council of apostolic times. Hence the catechist's role is not merely to communicate information about the past interventions of God in history, but also to initiate the students into the mystery of God present and active in their lives, and lead them to the change of mentality demanded by this meeting with the divine. Or to put it another way, the catechist's task is to point to and interpret the signs of God in the world and its history. He has a prophetic role, a mediatorial role, in the context of God's self-communication to the students.

This aspect of God's plan is beautifully expressed by the prophet Osee, in a text which can be the background for the study of catechesis.

> So I will allure her [Israel]; I will lead her into the desert and speak to her heart. . . .
> She shall respond there as in the days of her youth, when she came up from the land of Egypt.
> On that day, says the Lord, she shall call me "My husband," and never again "My baal". . . .
> I will espouse you to me forever: I will espouse you in right and in justice, in love and in mercy; I will espouse you in fidelity, and you shall know the Lord (Ho 2:16–22).

God speaks to the freedom of men, to their hearts, in the events of the desert, the time of pilgrimage, this world. His message is that of love, revealed in the communication of his life through the historical experiences of his people. His purpose is to unite men with himself in a union so intimate that marriage is the only adequate symbol. His word is addressed to mankind through the power of the Spirit in history and cosmos, progressively revealing the divine plan of love until the fullness of its revelation in Christ (Heb 1:1–4).

The catechist stands between God and man, a prophet pointing out and interpreting the Word operative in human events through signs. His task, then, is to help the students read the signs, to recognize and interpret the action of God in their lives; that is, to interpret their life experiences in the light of faith, to discover a Christian meaning in their lives, to come to a personal union with God in Christ, and hence a constantly deepening conversion rooted in their commitment and communion with Christ, the Word. His task is to introduce them to the mystery of Christ, operative in the most profane experiences of their lives as well as in the more sacral.

To do this he must both know the Word and the hearers of the Word and be able to speak to the heart as well as to the mind. His knowledge of the Word, of Christ, must be intimate, personal, experiential, arrived at through prayer and love as well as through study. And he must have a genuine fellowship with those he teaches, marked by understanding and appreciation, and reverent trust — again developed not only from study of psychology, but through personal dialogue motivated by love. Then the catechist can be mediator, prophet, introducing those he loves to friendship with him who loves them even more.

Perhaps what has been said can be clarified and further developed from the very example of Christ and the Apostles. The story in Acts 8 of Phillip and the Ethiopian eunuch is a good example of the principles of modern catechetics, but perhaps an even better passage is that of the meeting of the Risen Lord with the two disciples on the road to Emmaus (Lk 24). Luke portrays Christ himself, risen yet recognizable only through faith, in a situation quite similar to the catechetical situation.

The starting point of Christ's catechesis is the life experience, the concrete situation of his two friends. They are sad, disillusioned, and with good reason. They had placed all their hopes on Jesus of Nazareth, apparently the Messiah, and now he is dead, crucified. Their hopes shattered, their lives seem empty, without meaning. And yet the truth of the matter is that Jesus is very much alive, very much the Messiah; in fact he is there with them, alive with a fullness of life, filled with the Spirit, victorious over death itself. But as yet their faith is not vital enough to recognize him in the stranger who walks along the road with them.

Notice Christ. Sensitive to their feelings, respectful of the sorrow that is part of the uniqueness, the mystery of their lives, he manifests concern through a genuine attempt to understand these two sad, puzzled, suffering men. And so he listens, not just to their words, but to yearnings of their hearts, to their feelings, their hopes, their sorrow. He listens with his heart as well as with his ears, and so they trusted him with their fears and doubts and desires. The beginning of all catechesis is exemplified here by Christ. The catechist must meet his students with a similar respect and trust, a reverent understanding that allows them to be free, enables them to freely express their deepest desires and doubts. Such love is at the heart of the catechetical process, according to Augustine (fifth century), Fleury (seventeenth century), Dupanloup (nineteenth century), to cite but three of the great catechists of the past, and is the major factor of what today is called preevangelization. This is one of the most fruitful areas of contemporary research and experimentation in catechetics, prominent in the Bangkok Study Week, and popularized by Alfonso Nebreda, S.J. Genuine human love, incarnating God's love, and enlightened by modern studies in anthropology, psychology, and sociology, is the key to effective catechesis.

Only after the disciples have freely responded to his respectful concern does Christ speak. Understanding precedes proclamation. With a sureness and strength expressed with the gentleness born of suffering, he proceeds to interpret their experiences of the past three days. This he does in such a way that they are led gradually to find again the true meaning of their lives, a meaning which is not a datum of conceptual definition, but in terms of value. This is a central factor of catechesis relative to the task of conversion or formation, namely the emphasis on value or personally appreciated meaning. And the value must somehow be experienced and appreciated in terms of one's unique life situation. Christian interpretation of life must be not merely cognitive but evaluative, not only conceptual but vital, personal as well as general. For this very reason, the interpretation, the reading of the signs of God's active presence, must be concrete and experiential — while thereby no less spiritual — rather than merely abstract.

Christ does precisely that, for his interpretation of their harrowing experiences of the past days is given in terms of the life experience of their own people, Israel. He does not philosophize, he elaborates no theory, but he turns their consideration to the repeated experience of the Jewish people in their dealings with their God in the course of history. He opens to them the Scriptures, which record and interpret the historically situated and developing dialogue of man and God. Beginning with Moses, and then the prophets, he explains the Scriptures, to find in the record of the past communal religious experience an interpretation of the disciples' present experience, so that a divine meaning is discernible in their present disheartening situation. The entire experience of God's people as interpreted by God's spokesman indicated that the Messiah's experience would be marked by rejection, suffering, death as the means of entry to victory and glorious new life. The implication is that their sadness is in fact without objective foundation, for the death of Jesus was not defeat but victory, and a sign that he was indeed the Messiah and that they had done well to give him their trust and their lives.

Contemporary catechesis, along the same lines as indicated by Jesus' example on the road to Emmaus, is concerned with life, with experience, with situation and value. Not that the catechist need always begin with a situation in which the students find themselves, but the total orientation must be in the direction of their lives, so that Christ may be encountered there, and so that Christian values be vitally perceived and appreciated. The catechist must help the student meet Christ in his daily life, to interpret his life and tasks in the light of the experience of Christ and the Church. This experience is recorded and interpreted in the Church's living Tradition, biblical and doctrinal. Catechesis, then, must be biblical and doctrinal — the interpreted experience of God's people as the basis of interpretation of our experience of God today. In other words, learning to read the biblical and doctrinal signs of God's action is the partial means toward learning to read the signs of God's present action in our own lives, since God's activity manifests fundamental patterns and characteristics.

Turning back to Luke and the Emmaus incident we find Christ at table with the two after being persuaded to stay with them. Up to this point they had responded warmly to him. Already on the road, as they would afterwards reflect, their hearts were burning as he opened the Scriptures to them. But as yet they did not recognize him. Much of their sadness had been dispelled; perhaps an inkling into the meaning and hopes of their lives had been achieved. But it was not till he broke bread with them that their eyes were opened and they recognize him. Then the full meaning of the past three days, already partially perceived through the Scripture, came home: He is not dead! He is alive, risen! He is here! Through the experience of the liturgical sign of the Eucharist their faith penetrated the mystery of Jesus, and the mystery of their own lives, too. He had been with them all the time, and through the interpretation of Scripture had partially made his presence felt. Now in the rich experience of his presence realized through faith as they joined with him in the Eucharist they were aware of the value and meaning of their lives. No longer empty, their sadness was replaced by a joyful peace. Rising up from table they hastened back to the community of Apostles — to be met with the same joyful message: He is risen!

A similar experience is an integral part of catechesis. The life of the student is partially interpreted in a Christian way through the recorded experience of God's people. The past communal religious experience of Israel and the Church is normative for a penetration into the plan and meaning of human life and history. Yet the history of salvation continues today in human events, and particularly in the sacraments. Here Christ is encountered most immediately and personally, within the communal experience of God's people, the Church. Here ideally there is the most intense union with the Father through Christ, and with one's fellow Christians in the Spirit of love. But again, experience, not merely abstract concepts, is the operative element toward communion with Christ and the formation of a Christian mentality for the interpretation and evaluation of one's life through the liturgy. For what God did in the past in Christ is actually reenacted in the liturgical experience. It is Christ who acts, Christ whom we recognize through faith. Therefore, community worship should be a peak moment in the religious experience of the Christian — an experienced moment of union with God present and acting on behalf of his people today. Such experiences are particularly formative of a Christian mentality flowing from communion with Christ in the fellowship of the Christian community. And so it is that modern catechesis has a strong liturgical emphasis, together with the biblical and doctrinal. It is another of the signs students must learn to read and interpret in order to learn to read the signs of God's saving presence in the rest of their lives. And thus the widespread mediocrity of parish worship is a considerable problem facing the catechist.

A final and closely related facet of the Emmaus story is the element of catechesis called today "Christian witness." Two aspects are evident in the Gospel account, the witness of the community of disciples and the personal witness of Jesus himself. This is the area of the most vital of the signs of God's saving presence. For the objective of catechesis is faith, a mature, living faith, a total entrusting of self to God in Christ. Now normally faith grows through contact with lived faith. Luke hints at this as the two disciples return to Jerusalem and are met with the joyful message of faith in the risen Christ. The faith of all was deepened through their mutual witness. Today, in terms of catechetical problems, one of the greatest appears to be the lack of clear witness of the Christian community — in the liturgical assembly, in social movements, in notable examples of Christian life. Yet it is in the fellowship of believers that the faith of the individual must find nourishment and support. It must never be forgotten that the goal of catechesis is not just information but communion with God and the formation of Christian value-judgments in a sound interpretation of one's life situation. And for most men and women and children the most vital sign of the effective presence of God and his saving plan is is the manifest faith, hope, and love of the Christian community, first of all in worship, and secondly in lives lived within contemporary society in the spirit of Christ.

It is in this context also that the past or distant witness of Christians has an important place in catechesis. Authentic documents of outstanding Christians can be most helpful catechetically, especially for adolescents; examples might be the letter of Martin Luther King from the Birmingham jail, or of imprisoned Thomas More to his daughter, or of Tom Dooley, writing from his hospital in Laos. The documents must be genuine and exemplify values relevant to the lives and problems of the students. Much more important than textbook knowledge is that appreciative and evaluative cognition based on confrontation with authentic documentation of real Christian men and women. Today's world is filled with examples of such real Christians — "heroes" — who are witnesses in the truest sense, and they need be presented to youth together with great Israelites and Christians of old.

But by far the most important witness of Christian faith for the student is —next to his parents — the catechist. He or she is to the student the most tangible and moving sign of the saving presence of God. The catechist incarnates, or fails to incarnate the effect of the message he proclaims, and the students read authentic faith, hope, and love much more accurately than they read words about these virtues. They tend to identify with the catechist and assimilate his attitudes. The honesty and joy and courage of the catechist are a source of hope and strength to students who are confused and anxious — a hope and strength rooted in the love and presence of the Risen Christ in the midst of a seemingly threatening world.

But the chief element of the catechist's witness is the love he manifests, and mature love expressed in trust and acceptance, in the invitation and challenge to grow. Understanding is essential, an understanding which penetrates the heart of the student and discovers goodness and resources unknown even to himself, hidden often under a mask of apathy or hostility. Particularly today, in inner-city poverty as in wealthy suburbia, is such Christian love required of the catechist, for so many children and adolescents experience so little of it. The catechist's love for them incarnates God's love. Even discipline must be experienced as an expression of care and concern, and not merely as arbitrary adult domination.

To summarize, then, catechesis as the proclaiming and interpreting of God's Word, aims at the deepening of faith, the more vital awareness of Christ in the situations of daily living, commitment to Him, and the consequent change of mentality this requires. As Osee put it, "and you shall know the Lord." Faith-knowledge. "Now this is everlasting life, that they may know thee, the only true God, him whom thou has sent, Jesus Christ" (Jn 17:23). "Knowledge" in these texts is not the intellectual concept of Greek mentality, but is best symbolized by the Hebrew mind in terms of marriage. It is a deeply, intimately, personal knowledge, and very practical; a knowledge that is experiential and personal, rather than abstract. Arising in the atmosphere of love, it moves to action, to living. Such knowledge involves the giving of oneself to another, and therefore requires constant adjustment of self to the desires of the other. It is communion, commitment, conversion. Hence the inadequacy of an exclusively conceptual, intellectual approach to catechesis.

> Where can I go from your spirit? from your presence where can I flee? If I go up to the heavens, you are there; if I sink to the nether world, you are present there. If I take the wings of the dawn, if I settle at the farthest limits of the sea, even there your hand shall guide me, and your right hand hold me fast (Ps 138:7–10).

Such is the living faith which catechesis strives to awaken and deepen. Symbolically it is summed up in the Emmaus story — Christ walks with us along the road of our lives; our spiritual perception must grow, through the interpretative reading of the signs of his presence. "He is not dead; He is here with us, risen."

But how recognize him? Catechesis aims at recognition by helping the students learn to read the signs of Christ's presence. Penetration of the sacral signs of Scripture, liturgy, doctrine, mediated through the sign of Witness, lead to an ability to recognize in the profane events of life the mysterious presence of God. One meets Christ through the four signs of the Church's experience of Christ, present and past, and through this "knowledge" learns to find him in the divine milieu of the seemingly profane. At all events it is imperative that salvation history is not taught as something merely past, but as continuing in the present, in life, in experience, sacred and profane. Our God is a living God, and our Savior is Emmanuel, God-with-us.

With these principles in mind, further thought must be given to the catechist and his relation to the student. As prophet, mediator, his action must be similar to that of God who, as Osee states, "leads," "allures," "speaks to the heart." All catechizing must be marked with the profoundest respect for the freedom of the person. And the catechist, in reverent awe at the mystery of God, must equally respect and reverence the mystery of the human person and his freedom. Christ on the road to Emmaus gives us the ideal example. So, too, the catechist must struggle to leave the other free, to foster and nourish, to encourage freedom. Faith is a gift of self, and no catechist can force or demand or program it. One must seriously question in this regard the enforced routine in many Catholic schools concerning the reception of the Sacraments and the exaggerated cult of discipline.

The catechist then will attempt to challenge, to stir up that freedom in a spirit of openness. If life is mystery, the place and moment of encounter with the living God, then the full attractiveness, the challenge and joy of living in a world where Christ is always just around the corner must be presented to the child or adolescent. The Church is on the march; an open spirit must be fostered. Life lived fully and humanly with Christ is the goal of catechesis — not the memorization of doctrine in an atmosphere of security, fearful of the realities of contemporary life. The full challenge of continuing and sharing the creative and redemptive work of God should be presented. The world is to be created, to be redeemed, and the task rests with the Christian by right. Not only does one meet Christ in the world, but one shares with him in the very redemption of that world. This is the task of the Christian rather than merely to "save his soul" by "keeping the commandments."

To foster this freedom, to effectively challenge and inspire, the catechist, like God, must "speak to the heart" of the students. In biblical terms, the heart is the seat of life, the core or center of one's person, where one can freely give oneself in love. To speak to the heart involves reaching the person in his depth, at the core of his person; it means communicating to the whole personality. With the heart one "knows" in the biblical sense considered above, a knowledge that is personally experienced, is the fruit of a love-experience, and the dynamic source of a life of love. Such knowledge is the aim of catechesis; therefore serious consideration must be given to the means of communicating, of reaching the heart.

So often catechesis is mainly in verbal terms — words, descriptions, explanations, questions, answers. Much of this is necessary since a person is intellectual. But as one knows from modern psychology as well as from experience of friendship and love, the deepest communication, the most involving knowedge is achieved more often on a nonverbal level. Hence it is extremely important that the catechesis create in the students a sense of awe at the mystery of God, a sense of wonder at the mystery of themselves, their bodies and whole persons, their freedom; a sense of community, of fellowship; a sense of reality, a sense of responsibility. Atmosphere, attitude, gesture, play as important a part, or a more important part, than words. There must be a capacity for silence, of receptivity — not passivity, but the full concentration of one's powers on some other person or thing, allowing him or it to penetrate one's being.

Scripture is replete with examples of such atmosphere or attitude which communicates more than words can. One thinks of Moses, shoes off, bowed low to the ground, before the holiness of Jahweh manifesting Himself in the burning bush (Ex 3). Or Job, humbled, silent, before the powerful intimacy of Jahweh: "I had heard of you by word of mouth, but now my eye has seen you" (Jb 42:3). And David dancing before the ark of the Lord (2 S 6). A sense of reverence, of wonder, of awe, of peace and joy communicates more than words the presence of the mighty yet gracious God. A gesture, a moment of silence — not just a pause between noises, but a moment of stillness pregnant with the simple awareness of the presence of the living, loving God — says more to the heart than a dozen explanations of omnipresence. It is perhaps the ability to communicate this sense of the sacred in an atmosphere of love that marks the most successful catechist. For the catechism class itself partakes in the mystery of life, it is a graced hour in itself, a time of meeting God as well as a time of preparation to meet him in daily life. It is within this context that one must use and evaluate audio-visual aids and other techniques. Music is an often neglected medium of penetrating the heart, of creating an atmosphere; similarly neglected is creative dance and dramatics. In Europe much use is made of "celebrations," which are somewhat constructed as a Scripture service (reading song-prayer) but with gesture and action added. Creative photography is a further means available. For small children one of the most effective methods of interiorizing the catechesis is drawing. Whatever the particular means, it is extremely important that this interiorization take place, that the whole person, the heart be involved,

Finally, the most important form of interiorization is prayer, not prayers formally recited before and after class, but prayer, silent awareness of God's presence and openness to him. Catechism class should climax in such moments of prayer, still, silent union with God and with each other in Christ; but this must not be artificial. Genuine prayer should flow from the dynamics of the catechesis itself, as it is but another manner of defining the purpose of catechesis. Silence before God is so much neglected, yet so important, that it should be an element of catechetical procedure on every level. The human conditioning for such silence should be a part of the first years of religious formation. Small children must learn to be still. They must learn to be receptive, observant, to see, hear, touch. For true Christian prayer is basically contemplative, union with God through the signs of his presence. It is through the world of sense that contact with God is possible, and an important part of early catechetical work involves the human preconditioning for contemplative prayer.

Particularly helpful for growth in prayer is the effective use of the psalms. They are God's own way of teaching us to pray, and have been the Church's prayer throughout the centuries. Concrete, sapiential language, symbol and image, multiplicity of human situations — all communicate the deep faith in God's presence and power and love. They are addressed to the heart and reverently express the heart's response. Communal recitation of the psalms fosters the sense of fellowship of God's children united in Christ. And sung to appropriate melodies the psalms can be an excellent means of formation toward contemplative prayer, particularly when sung responsorially, with the verses sung by a cantor, after each of which the people sing an antiphon. A gentle rhythm is created of silent hearing of the Word followed repeatedly by the antiphonal response to the Word. But none of this is automatically effective. Much care must be had in choosing proper psalms or parts of psalms that will be meaningful to a particular group or situation. And needed explanations of words or symbols must be given. The recitation or singing must be genuine and reverent; gesture or action may be used to further engage the whole person. In this way one can gradually learn to pray with one's whole being.

This chapter has outlined the principles of contemporary catechetical theory. What is greatly needed today is catechists who are grounded in sound theological and scientific principles and who have the courage to experiment, trusting the Spirit of Christ, themselves, and their students. And one senses that the direction of the experimentation will lie in the area of the human and the secular, in accord with the above principles which are in terms of the history of salvation. Christ is in the world; he is risen; he is here. But how meet him?

11

Needs and Problems of the Modern Parish

PART I

HENRY J. YANNONE

THE OFFICE OF PASTOR IS NOT CONFINED TO THE CARE OF THE FAITHFUL as individuals, but in a true sense is extended to the formation of a genuine Christian community. Yet the spirit of the community should be so fostered as to embrace not only the local Church, but also the universal Church. The local community should promote not only the care of its own faithful, but, filled with a missionary zeal, it should prepare also the way of Christ for all men.[1]

In order to understand the needs and problems of the modern parish, it seems proper that we should establish first what a parish is. In the canonical sense a parish is a territory entrusted to a pastor by his bishop for the spiritual care of the faithful living within specific territorial boundaries. Such a parish is called a territorial parish as against the so-called national parish, presently very few in number. Though the Church formerly favored stable parishes, that is parishes with permanent pastors, the Decree on the Pastoral Office of Bishops does away with the distinction between unremovable and removable pastors and makes a pastor transferrable either at his own request or upon the suggestion of the Ordinary concerned with the needs and conditions of certain areas which make the change advisable.

Unlike national parishes, that is, parishes consisting of one particular

[1] Vatican Council II, *The Decree on the Priestly Ministry* (trans. N.C.W.C.), p. 5.

national group with its own national language and its own customs, most American parishes represent a cross-section of many national strains living in the same community, and more or less united. From the pastoral standpoint *all* the people living within the territorial boundaries of a parish make up that parish, including Christians of other religious denominations. With respect to the whole Church of God a parish is a unit of the universal Church. In a narrower sense, it is a portion of one of the many dioceses into which the universal Church is organized.

Besides this classification of parishes, there is another classification which must be considered in any study of the needs and problems of the modern parish. This latter is based on location, and classifies parishes as urban parishes, suburban parishes, and rural parishes. Though it is not necessary here to consider each of these in detail, it is worthwhile noting there are three kinds of urban parishes that are being singled out for special consideration by many churchmen today. The first of these is the giant-sized city parish, sometimes referred to as the "macroparish," having thousands of inhabitants who form a rather anonymous mass. Frequently the pastor of the macroparish is unacquainted with even the relatively small circle of churchgoers. The second type is the downtown parish where the number of permanent residents is declining while the number of transients is on the rise. The third type is the well-known center-city or inner-city parish.

Perhaps some mention should be made here too of the so-called "vacation parish" — the parish located in a resort area. This parish is characterized by marked increases and decreases in members and activities depending upon the season of the year.

Though every territorial parish, regardless of classification, is a unit, it is also a complex entity inasmuch as it is made up of individuals with the most diverse national, cultural, economic, and social backgrounds who are tending toward the same ultimate goal — citizenship in God's eternal Kingdom. Nevertheless, despite the complexities, the chief function of the parish is to teach man today, to save man today, to make man holy today. It is in this process of teaching, saving, and sanctifying that the parish is confronted with a variety of problems. However, the ultimate goal of the parish can only be achieved by the proper development of parish life in all of its various aspects — liturgical, catechetical, ecumenical, missional, social, lay, and religious. Or to state it another way:

> The parish is the center of religious life. The faithful must look to it for the administration of the sacraments, at least baptism, confirmation and matrimony. It is a good thing to attend to the other practices of religious life in one's own parish.
> The parish is also the main center where religious instruction in the family is integrated by catechism for children and adults, missions for the people, ordinary preaching.

The parish is also a center for Catholic Action and charitable welfare activities. The success of these groups and their activities depends on the cooperation displayed by individuals, on the means at the disposal of the parish church, and on the parish societies. Parents should direct their children to look upon the parish as a center where spiritual life is nourished and developed and where they receive the proper guidance for their own apostolic work.[2]

THE PASTOR

From a canonical point of view, a pastor is a priest or legal person who has been entrusted with the care of souls in a parish. He exercises this responsibility under the jurisdiction of the local Ordinary. To meet his responsibilities, a priest charged with the care of souls in a parish must carry out a considerable number of pastoral functions which are quite clearly stated in either the Code of Canon Law or the decrees of the diocesan statutes and therefore need not all be listed here. However, it does seem well to point out that a pastor has several important obligations, besides those consequent upon his office, which bind in justice. These include: residence in the parish house, application of Mass for the people on certain prescribed days, and careful preservation of the parish records.

Inasmuch as he is a father and pastor of souls, he should also use every means available to him for the instruction and religious formation of the faithful, and strive to promote the practice of Christian virtues and charitable works. He should also labor zealously to organize Catholic Action groups and associations, and provide spiritual assistance for all those in his parish who are most in need, especially the young, the poor, the sick, and the orphans.

THE ASSISTANT PASTOR

Most parishes with more than 500 families need at least one curate, to aid the pastor in carrying out the great variety of parochial tasks — guiding the parish organizations, assisting the parochial school, organizing CCD programs, census work, caring for the spiritual needs of the sick, administering the sacraments, recruiting workers for parish projects, and other important functions — which he must perform but which it is almost impossible for him to handle alone. Furthermore, the need will be even greater as we begin to implement the provisions of renewal and reform decreed by Vatican Council II. Pastors of large parishes know well how difficult a task it is just to keep up with the present day-to-day activities. In fact, quite often this very fact prevents them from getting a total view

---

[2] P. Felici, "Parish," *Dictionary of Moral Theology* (Eng. trans. H. J. Yannone), p. 872.

of the parish, that is, a view which starts from the very essence of the parish, namely, the administration of the sacraments, and embraces all the other areas that are proper to the parish for its fuller development and fulfillment.

Consequently, it is quite disconcerting, to say the least, to read at times generalized criticisms of the quality of clerical performance which appear to go beyond the limits of fact. One criticism leveled against the clergy is that "This is the age of the shoddy performance, the task poorly done, the privilege sought, the responsibility ignored, the easy way out, 'don't bother me,' and 'I don't want to get involved.' " Another is that "this is the era of the poorly-prepared sermon and the slovenly-taught CCD class, the hurried absolution, and the ill-concealed impatience in the rectory parlor." If these criticisms were generally true, the Church would certainly be in a terrible shape. But thank God, for the most part, they are not so. The fact of the matter is that the person who wrote those words probably never worked in a parish, certainly not in a modern suburban parish where parochial activity goes on from early in the morning to the late evening hours. Indeed it is a common complaint of priests that there are too few hours in the day for all the things that they would like to do for and with the people of God.

CLERICAL "RESTLESSNESS"

However, no life, including that of the priest, is free from problems and difficulties. There are problems involving personalities, problems of adjustments to be made when one is transferred from one type of social community to another, and from one household to another. Certainly, there is restlessness among the clergy, particularly the younger clergy, but it is a restlessness which exists in many other quarters in the world. There seems to be no reason to isolate the restlessness existing among the clergy from the general unrest and make it exclusively a "clergy crisis." It has been stated, and quite properly, that "we are in the midst of a revolution." It is a general type of revolution; one which is expressed in the form of a reaction against conformism, stability, and set rules; or as "antipathy toward obedience and the law, and a sympathy for the voluntaristic system of thought," or as "refusal to accept (blindly) whatever comes to us by way of tradition, of custom, of habit." But this is not all bad. Great reforms have always been preceded by this type of "revolution." The important thing is not to look the other way as if it did not exist but to deal with it intelligently, generously, and confidently. It could be tragic only if those who are in a position of leadership fail to recognize the signs of the time and do not deal with it courageously as a phenomenon that can lead mankind to a brighter and happier world.

The specific restlessness of the clergy as a phenomenon of our time is, at least partially, curable. By way of specific remedy we would suggest that what is needed (in fact, it is a fundamental requirement) is a greater degree of mutual confidence and better communication between bishops and pastors and between pastors and assistants. However, when speaking of mutual confidence, the emphasis must be placed on the word "mutual," for not only must those in positions of leadership have confidence in those who assist them, but subjects must also have confidence in their superiors. This mutual trust must be built on two things: first, recognition of the fact that we are all striving for the attainment of the same goal, namely, the restoration of the world to Christ; and secondly, that this can best be attained by concerted effort of all the members of "the people of God" working together with a united hierarchy and clergy. Perhaps, Father Charles W. Paris touches upon a vital point when he writes:

> It seems logical to ask, "Why give a priest so much in education and power if toward him— for 15 or 25 or more years — there will be shown so little confidence, and asked of him so small a contribution?" Yet what greater asset does the Church have than these educated, dedicated, zealous young priests? . . . Perhaps the time is long past for a change from the "pastor-assistant" concept to one of "associate pastor" in the multi-priest parish?[3]

Though there are many solutions to the problem of restlessness in young priests, one possible solution might be to have those newly ordained priests who did not major in a particular field before entering the major seminary return to a college or university for further study while assigned to a parish as a part-time assistant. Such an arrangement would give the young priest the opportunity to work toward a specific goal while at the same time finding fulfillment in parish work. Competence in one or even two specific fields would give him, as it does to every person, a feeling of justifiable self-assurance and a greater effectiveness in his work in this age of specialization. It would also give him a sense of humility growing out of an awareness of his limitations, as he realizes that he is more at ease with matters relating to his own particular field of work, and that he would be better advised to refer people with serious problems to more experienced persons especially when the problem is outside the area of his professional competence. The benefits accruing to a parish with assistant priests who are professionally competent, each one in his own field, are inestimable. Furthermore, there is reason to believe that such an arrangement would make for better harmony in the household and for greater effectiveness in handling the workload of a medium or large size parish. This, of course, would be true not only in a modern suburban parish, but in a center-city parish as well. The good, for instance, which a young priest with a degree in social science and/or economics could do

---

[3] C. Paris, "Preventing Frustration of Priests," *Pastoral Life,* 14 (February, 1965), p. 97.

among poverty stricken people or the underprivileged of a center-city parish, is literally inestimable.

Another solution, perhaps not easily achieved, is the establishment of parishes so small that each could be properly staffed by the pastor and one assistant. This arrangement offers many advantages — not the least of which is that it would allow priests to become pastors at an earlier age. Under the present seniority system, in some dioceses, some may never become pastors, or if they do, only at an age when their capacity for work has passed the peak of its effectiveness and their administrative ability has all but vanished. It is a well established fact that a training period of ten years is sufficient to prepare an assistant pastor who has conscientiously done his work to take charge of a parish. Considerable discouragement for the priest and disedification for the flock flows from a longer than normal waiting period.

Furthermore, it might also be desirable to replace the seniority system with one that is based on talent and performance. Such a system would be based on an "efficiency rating" report made annually to the Ordinary by each pastor. This system has been used very effectively by the civil government, and might prove equally effective within the Church. Father Paris makes a similar suggestion when he writes:

> To put it briefly, one aspect of what I see as a cause of clerical frustration, which has the effect of paralyzing priestly efforts, even driving some priests to unwholesome, if not actually sinful, escape mechanisms, is the present prevalent method of dealing with manpower utilization. Allowing for the exception that one gratefully notes here and there, clerical advancement seems to be based on a seniority system rather than on the basis of talent and performance. The bestowal of a pastorate thereby becomes, not so much a challenge to do a job, but a recognition of one's length of service. Not infrequently this outlook generates the attitude — shown toward assistant priests and parishioners alike — of personal possession: my parish, my assistants, my parishioners, etc. An encroachment, real or imaginary, against this assumed personal domain by initiative on the part of the laity or by capability and zeal in the efforts of the assistant is jealously watched for and promptly crushed, if it appears.[4]

Today a modern parish needs more than anything else a clergy that is not only completely aware of the problems of modern society, but also well prepared and competent to deal with them. The people of a modern parish look to the priests for spiritual nourishment and guidance. To the priest they bring their problems, social, moral, or spiritual, and expect that he will help them. The task facing the priest of a modern parish is a momentous one. Therefore, he must use every lawful means available to him to prepare himself to serve the needs of his people; and first on his list of means must be his own spiritual and religious growth and development.

---

[4] *Ibid.,* pp. 96–97.

The Liturgical Aspects of the Parish

Liturgy can be defined in many ways. The definition which seems to be more appropriately pastoral is that which describes liturgy as "man's response to God's saving deeds." The history of salvation, which consists of the great acts by which God has redeemed man, calls for a response from man. This man gives through the liturgy which is the unfolding of man's response to God's saving acts and to his promises. But like all human acts, man's response expressed in the form of a religious rite has been in the course of time manifested in different forms, and at times in ways that have even been more or less remote and incomprehensible. The efforts made in recent times to make this rite (particularly the Mass) more attractive and meaningful have been chiefly the work of the liturgical movement, which originated in France in the nineteenth century through the work of Dom Gueranger, abbot of the monastery of Solesmes. The continuing work of those involved in this movement led ultimately to the liturgical renewal decreed by the Second Vatican Council.

The promulgation on December 4, 1963, of *The Constitution on the Liturgy* set in motion a long range program of reform in the worship of the Church, particularly a reform of the Mass. The aim of the reform is to make the Mass a conscious gathering in the Lord, a grace-filled encounter with God in Christ, as well as the great worshiping prayer of the People of God which it has always been. In the words of the Council, "The liturgy is the summit toward which the activity of the Church is directed; at the same time it is the fount from which all her power flows. For the aim and object of apostolic work is that all who are made Sons of God by faith and baptism should come together to praise God in the midst of His Church, to take part in the sacrifice and to eat the Lord's supper."[5]

The emphasis in the work of restoration and promotion of the liturgy is clearly on "participation." "The Church earnestly desires that all the faithful should be led to the full conscious, active participation in liturgical celebrations that is demanded by the very nature of the liturgy." Still emphasizing the importance of participation, the Constitution continues: ". . . This full and active participation by all the people is the aim to be considered before all else; for it is the primary and indispensable source from which the faithful are to derive the true Christian spirit. . . ."[6]

Though apparently new, this program of renewal of the Vatican Council is but an echo of the liturgical principle enunciated at the beginning of our century by the pastoral pontiff, St. Pius X, who declared that ". . . the first and necessary font of a truly Christian spirit for the faithful is their active participation in the most holy and sacred mysteries and in the

---

[5] Vatican Council II, *The Constitution on the Liturgy* (trans. N.C.W.C.), p. 6.
[6] *Ibid.*, p. 7.

solemn and common prayer of the Church." Emphasizing participation, Pius asked that we should bring "before God the whole individual man in the whole Christian community." This the holy pontiff endeavored to do through the *Motu proprio* issued to correct and develop the texts and rites of worship and by the reform of Church music. Viewing liturgical life as the vital center of Christian life itself, Vatican Council II has officially adopted the apostolate of the liturgical reform and has decreed renewal in light of the scholarly and pastoral works of three popes, Pius X, Pius XII, ard John XXIII, and of the liturgical, biblical, and doctrinal studies of illustrious liturgical reformers, including Beauduin, Parsh, Jungmann, and others, who paved the way to the present work of renewal and reform.

Well aware of the necessity for clerical leadership in the implementation of the work of reform and renewal, the Constitution calls for active participation:

> . . . pastors of souls must zealously strive to achieve it [i.e. active participation] by means of the necessary instruction in all their pastoral work. . . . Yet, it would be futile to entertain any hopes of realizing this unless pastors themselves in the first place, became thoroughly imbued with the spirit and power of the liturgy, and undertake to give instruction about it.[7]

Finally, after describing the various provisions of a liturgical nature recommended in the training of future priests, the Constitution concludes:

> With zeal and patience, pastors of souls must promote the liturgical instruction of the faithful, and also their active participation in the liturgy both internally and externally taking into account their age and condition, their way of life and standard of religious culture. By so doing, pastors will be fulfilling one of the chief duties of a faithful dispenser of the mysteries of God; and in this manner they must lead their flock not only in word but also by example.[8]

If one were to question why the Council gave such importance to the work of liturgical reform and renewal, he would find the answer in the words of Pope Paul: "The Church is no longer seen as something particular . . . it is not merely one person, it is a family." This applies to the Church at large as well as to the parish which is "the Church" in miniature. The central concept is that the parish is a family, not a collection of individuals, but a family of worshipers, a real worshiping community, united with Christ in the worship of the Father.

Ultimately, a true liturgical renewal must be one which will produce a spirit of prayer, of union, and of love among the members of the Mystical Body of Christ. The liturgy is the Mystical Body at Prayer, that is Christ and his members united in prayer to worship the Father. It is the union of men with God in Christ. When we pray and sing together, though we are many, we are one. Liturgy unites in a real sense. It unites physically by

---

7 *Ibid.*, p. 7.   8 *Ibid.*, p. 8.

the very fact that men gather together in a specific place, join their voices, and coordinate their actions. It unites spiritually because "it focuses the minds of the worshipers in common on the central Christian realities and seeks to elicit from all the same interior acts of adoration and love." Finally, and more important, "it unites men sacramentally; eating the same bread, they live the same life." This is the sacrament of fellowship, the sacrament which gives the grace of fellowship and really unites. But the gift becomes an obligation. This is what the new liturgy is trying to teach. We are branches of one Vine, stones of a living Temple, members of one Body. But the fruits of this union must not end here. Rather, they must increase our social awareness as well as our compassion for the less fortunate members of the Body of Christ; they must teach all that kneeling together means opening our hearts to one another and loving one another in God through Jesus Christ. This is true liturgy. It is little wonder that the Vatican Council expects so much from the liturgical renewal. Actually, the life of the parish, too, must be renewed through the liturgy. The corporate response to God's saving deeds must rise from the heart of the whole parish as a hymn of praise to the Father through Jesus, his Son and our brother, who by his incarnation continued in time completes our incompleteness and fills our insufficiency, enabling us to form a community of worshipers worthy of the Father.

TEACHING THE WORD IN THE PARISH

The ministry of the Word is an extremely important aspect of the priestly life. This is even more true today when a great desire for good preaching is felt among the people of God.

> I charge thee, in the sight of God in Christ Jesus, who will judge the living and the dead by his coming and by his kingdom, preach the word, be urgent in season, out of season; reprove, entreat, rebuke with all patience and teaching . . . but do thou be watchful in all things, bear with tribulation patiently, work as a preacher of the gospel, fulfill thy ministry.[9]

By this injunction, St. Paul laid down the ground rules for Timothy, his disciple, as well as for all those who would follow him in the ministry as preachers of the Gospel.

In his first Encyclical letter, "His Church," Pope Paul VI underscores the importance of the preaching of the Word.

> Preaching is the primary apostolate. Our apostolate . . . is above all the ministry of the Word. We know this very well, but it seems good to remind ourselves of it now, so as to direct our pastoral activities aright. We must go back to the study, not of human eloquence or empty rhetoric, but of the genuine art of the Sacred Word.
>
> We must search for the laws of its simplicity and clarity, for its power

_____
[9] 2 Tm 4:15.

and authority, so as to overcome our natural lack of skill in the use of the great and mysterious spiritual instrument of speech and to enable us worthily to compete with those who today exert so much influence through their words by having access to the organs of public opinion.

We must beg the Lord for the great and uplifting gift of speech (cf. Jer. 1, 6), to be able to confer on faith its practical and efficacious principle (cf. Rom. 10, 17) and to enable their words to reach out to the ends of the earth (cf. Ps. 18, 5 and Rom. 10, 18).[10]

There are those who think that preaching in Catholic churches has greatly deteriorated in our time. Whether or not this is true, or to what extent it may be true, is difficult to say. It would certainly be true if we were to compare today's preaching with the preaching of Lacordaire, or the great Bossuet. However, those who argue that preaching has deteriorated are unable to establish in a positive way whether the alleged deterioration is due to lack of sufficient preparation in the seminary or to new habits of the priest regarding the use of television, the overemphasis on sports, the numerous and varied social activities, and the like. It may be that all these causes, and perhaps others, are contributing factors to the lower quality of preaching in our churches today.

Our people do expect good preaching, in fact they need it, the young and the old, the learned and the unlearned, the strong and the weak. Though meaningful sermons should be the goal of every priest, it seems that in suburban parishes the need for well-prepared, formative and informative sermons is even greater, for many of the parishioners are college graduates — scientists, teachers, doctors, or members of other professional groups. In a word, it may be said that, generally speaking, churchgoers in a suburban parish have a more sophisticated attitude and are undoubtedly interested in the view of the Church about such contemporary problems as the pill and birth control, outer-space exploration, the existence of intelligent beings on other planets and the question of their salvation, the possession and lawful uses of nuclear power for peaceful, defensive or offensive purposes, the extent of the obligations of affluent nations to the underprivileged or emerging nations of the world, the degree of responsibility of the rich to the millions of underprivileged, deprived and destitute individuals of the same nation, or the problem of modern patriotism with the new trend of a self-immolating practice dictated by political or nationalistic purposes. Many of these problems as well as questions concerning the civil rights marches and the campus agitations by and large remain unanswered because they are kept out of Sunday sermons. To ignore these issues leaves the field wide open to newspaper and magazine writers who attempt answers which at times leave much to be desired as they are dictated by philosophical principles often at variance with Christian moral principles. Hence, the importance of good, sound, enlightened preaching,

---

[10] Pope Paul VI, *Encyclical Letter Paths of the Church* (trans. N.C.W.C.), p. 91.

having a firm basis in Scripture and the teachings of the Church.

This problem is felt quite strongly at the parish level where people, hungry for guidance and in search for the right answer, are left bewildered and confused at the failure of religion to offer them proper enlightenment and guidance in these difficult times. Therefore, the wisdom of Pope Paul's exhortation to the clergy to "carry out the prescriptions of the Council's constitution on sacred liturgy with zeal and ability," expressing at the same time the wish that the catechetical teaching of the faith to the Christian people and to as many others as possible *"be marked by the aptness of its language, the wisdom of its method, the zeal of its exercise supported by the evidence of real virtues,"* and that the clergy may *"strive ardently to lead its hearers to the security of faith, to a realization of the intimate connection between the divine word and life and to the illumination of the living God,"* is not without relevance in our age.

The course, as traced by the Pope, is clear. What is needed is a true appreciation by the ministers of the Word of the cry of the people for the kind of homily that can lead the world to a better understanding of its relationship to God, in whom all things converge as to their beginning and their end.

12

Needs and Problems of the Modern Parish
PART II

Henry J. Yannone

Teaching the Word in the Parish

IN THE TEACHING OF CHRISTIAN DOCTRINE, THE PARISH HAS TWO important responsibilities. The first involves the formation and perfection of those already members of the Church; the second involves bringing the faith to those outside the Church. Though the Church at the parish level has always been concerned with this twofold aspect of her teaching responsibility, greater efforts must be made in both areas and new programs and procedures must be developed.

The Church in America has, over the years, developed an excellent school system, which until recently has served its purpose quite adequately. However, because of the increased birthrate after World War II, the recent drop in vocations, the higher cost of construction, and other factors the Church has become less and less able to meet the needs of her people in the field of education. In fact, there is a grave danger that because of the increased cost of Catholic education those who need it most are being deprived of it. Though this is especially true at the secondary and college levels, it is also true at the elementary level. Only too frequently the cost of Catholic education excludes the underprivileged. But, even in wealthier suburban areas, high costs of construction and teacher shortages often make it impossible for the parish to provide Catholic education for the youngsters.

However, none of the problems mentioned excuse the pastor from his grave responsibility for the religious education and formation of his parishioners. The pastoral directive to instruct the people in matters of faith and morals was seen quite clearly by the saintly pontiff, Pope Pius X, who, appalled by the lack of religious knowledge on the part of the people, requested that the Confraternity of Christian Doctrine be canonically instituted in each parish.[1] The Confraternity would spread the knowledge and practice of the faith by the following means:

1. religious instruction of Catholic elementary and high school children not attending Catholic schools,
2. religious discussion clubs for adult groups,
3. religious education of children by parents in the homes,
4. instruction of persons other than Catholic.

Obviously, the chief purpose of the Confraternity of Christian Doctrine is to assist the pastor in instructing and training children, young people, and adults in a knowledge and practice of Christian Doctrine. Inasmuch as the parish represents the primary cell of the great Christian family, which is the Church, and inasmuch as every man has a primary duty to possess an adequate knowledge of religion, it is logical to hold that the CCD should have a primary place in the life of every parish.

The CCD, which is governed by statutes approved by the local Ordinary, usually consists of: (1) teachers or catechists who teach Christian doctrine to the various parish groups, (2) home visitors, whose task it is to seek candidates for enrollment in religion classes, promote regular attendance at such classes, make family visits, etc., (3) benefactors or helpers, who serve in whatever way they can to promote the work of the Confraternity and to make it as effective as possible. Frequently, these benefactors arrange transportation to religion classes, act as baby-sitters for adults eager to attend inquiry classes or discussion clubs, distribute literature and the like.

The primary responsibility of CCD members is to assist the parish clergy in the instruction and preparation of candidates for first Communion and confirmation, and to promote and carry out all the various liturgical activities that enhance the religious life of the parish. Thus, in a word, this organization affords every member of the parish an excellent opportunity for developing a lay apostolate, which is of the greatest importance for the preservation and promotion of the faith, especially in parishes which have no parochial school or where no provision can be made for Catholic secondary education.

Though the Confraternity is an effective catechetical organization for providing religious instruction, inquiry classes or discussion clubs for young people and adults, and is extremely useful for combating the dan-

---

[1] Canon 711, § 2 provides for this.

gerous effects of religious ignorance in family and social life, it is not without its problems.

It is generally agreed, for instance, that one area of the parish CCD program that calls for complete re-examination is the method by which public high school students are trained. One hears that the matter is under study in some places. While this is an encouraging sign, one would wish that positive action on a national or at least a regional level be inaugurated in the very near future. But whatever plan is developed, it is my hope that it will provide for the greater participation of all of the members of the family. A program in which the parents can participate, at least from time to time, could be extremely effective. The impact made on the children by the interest and at least the occasional presence of their parents attending and even participating would be a great incentive to young people. Furthermore, at least a part of religious education of the children would be restored to those to whom it rightfully belongs. This program would also keep the parents abreast of new developments in the field of religious education and religious practice.

Another process which needs to be re-examined is that by which we receive inquirers in the Catholic instruction class and lead them to baptism. We appear at times to be more concerned with numbers than with quality of teaching. To improve the quality of convert instruction a much longer period of instruction for prospective converts is needed. Perhaps a catechumen should attend weekly Mass and weekly instructions for at least a year before he is admitted to baptism. During the year, he would, of course, take part in all the nonsacramental activities of the parish.

Another serious problem in a modern parish involves the training of lay catechists. A program of broader spiritual formation is greatly needed. It is quite clear in any medium-size or large parish that the work of convert instruction cannot be left to two or three priests assigned to the parish, who must be involved in a variety of activities, including the care of parish organizations, the administration of the sacraments, the parlor calls, the home visitation, etc. The need in every parish today is to develop a sufficient number of instructors in religion if the parish is to meet the needs of all those within its boundaries. This, of course, requires the awakening of the Catholic laity to a sense of responsibility growing, not so much out of the new call for *aggiornamento,* inaugurated by Pope John and developed by Vatican Council II, as out of the basic precept of Christianity, "love your neighbor as you love yourself." It is a matter of sharing the knowledge and blessing of true love. Frequently, it seems that in preaching and teaching, and in ordinary conversation or occasional talks, priests are at a loss to find convincing reasons to back up the call to the apostolate for our laity when it can be found in the simple, yet majestic and divine injunction, *"from this you shall be known as my followers if you love one another as I loved you."* The astounding value of the call of Pope John is its simplicity, that is, returning the whole Christian people to the observance of the most basic, fundamental, and essential tenet of Christian living, "love your neighbor as you love yourself," not by words but by deeds, not theoretically, but practically, not by wishing it, but by actually doing it every hour of every day. So every effort in a modern parish should be directed to developing all aspects of the commandment which Christ our Lord called his own, "love your neighbor as you love yourself." The carrying out of this program must extend not only to those of the household of the faith who appear to be well established on the path to salvation, but also and especially to those who are running away from Christ and who are heading for the blind alleys of indifference and despair; to those hiding behind a wall of complacency and self-contentment.

It seems that many of the personal problems of the laity that exist today arise from a lack of vision on the part of certain of the clergy. They are responsible to a great degree for the aloofness and indifference of many of the laity, and unless those pastoral techniques aimed at preserving the faith and loyalty of the Church are quickly and properly overhauled and revitalized, and brought in keeping with the needs of the twentieth century, the Church will be faced with problems of such magnitude as to make the loss of the laboring class to the French Church seem insignificant by comparison. Where does one find God and the things of God in this world? Where is the voice of his priests? Cardinal Suhard, in a pastoral letter, gave the answer when he said:

> A new world is in the making, forming even faster than we anticipated. The world is being driven toward a general remolding of civilization. Christians cannot look upon the ever-increasing number of modern inventions as accidental or scientific curiosities. They have to be integrated into an apostolic vision of the world's redemption. For indeed they do not merely ornament the world, but are actually building a new universe. And it is that very universe and no other that we are called upon to save.[2]

The Ecumenical Aspects of the Parish

As the Church Universal looks outward "at those who have not been evangelized and at those who are not of her unity," so, too, does the parish.

> When the parish looks outside its own membership it finds not only the great masses of the unchurched, it also finds that large number of sincere Protestants who make up the congregations of the neighboring churches — men and women whose vocation has cast them as Committed Christians

---

[2] Cardinal Suhard, Pastoral Letter, *Priests Among Men,* issued April 14, 1949.

with a denominational allegiance, who are hearing God's word and receiving God's graces through these bodies.[3]

This is a typical ecumenical setting. Nearly every parish in America is ecumenically constituted, which means that every parish is torn by the scandal that is division. And what can a parish do about the ecumenical problem with which it is confronted? Actually, it isn't so much what it can do as what it must do to hasten the time when the prayer of the Lord may be fulfilled, that there may be "one flock and one shepherd." Vatican Council II, after taking a long look at this scandalous division in Christendom, under the guidance of the Holy Spirit declared: "The concern for restoring unity (in Christendom) involves the whole Church, faithful and clergy alike. It extends to everyone."[4] As a result of the decree the ecumenical movement is now taking hold in many Catholic communities. The establishment in Rome of a Secretariat for Christian Unity has been a great step forward in the hopeful prospect of healing the strained relations between the various Christian communions. Happily a new climate now exists in the world's communities. The animosities which had developed in the course of the centuries are gradually giving way to understanding, respect, and friendliness, and even to cooperation in some fields. Under the guidance of the Holy Spirit, hopes and desires for unity have been stirred up within and without the Church.

Now, the important question is, what can the parish do to foster ecumenism? First of all the "parish prayer-life can be directed to a spirit of contrition on the part of Catholics for our share in the schism, and to a spirit of faithful entreaty that the day may be hastened when the prayer of the Lord (for unity) may be fulfilled."[5] In other words, in all public and private prayers of the parish the intention for restoration of unity should be included. All Catholics should endeavor, through a deeper study of their own positions, to bear better witness to the truth that has been given to them. The parish clergy has a very important role to play in this work by providing courses of instruction and spiritual formation through appropriate classes on Church history, liturgy, and sacred Scriptures, and by suggestion of the *Decree on Ecumenism:* "in certain special circumstances such as prayer for unity and during ecumenical gatherings it is allowable, indeed desirable, that Catholics should join in prayer with their separated brethren," leaving the "concrete course to be adopted" to the prudent judgment of the local Ordinary. Joint participation of Catholic groups with other Christian groups of the community in promoting social and welfare community projects should be encouraged. Such joint efforts

---

[3] J. M. Connolly, "The Parish: A Total View," *The Revival of the Liturgy* (ed. F. R. McManus), pp. 132–133.

[4] Vatican Council II, *Decree on Ecumenism, The Documents of Vatican II* (ed. W. Abbott, S.J., trans. ed. J. Gallagher), p. 351.

[5] *Ibid.,* p. 352.

will contribute much to the solution of community problems, particularly "illiteracy and poverty, lack of housing, and the unequal distribution of wealth." "Through such cooperation all believers in Christ are able to learn easily how they can understand each other better and esteem each other more and how the road to the unity of Christians may be made smooth." In view of this a council or committee of parishioners of all ages should be organized in every parish to study and organize the various ecumenical activities. In cooperation with the diocesan Commission on Christian Unity and the Liturgical Commission, books, periodicals, and pamphlets on ecumenism should be made available to the laity in parish publications, pamphlet racks, and parish libraries. In addition to the *Decree on Ecumenism,* priests and people should familiarize themselves with the better works published in the ecumenical field by Catholics, Protestants, and Jews. The following periodicals are especially recommended: *The Ecumenist,* Paulist Press quarterly; *Voices of Our Brothers,* a bi-weekly summary of 150 non-Catholic publications, O.S.V. Press; *Ecumenical News Notes,* monthly; *The Grail; The Christian Century,* a Protestant weekly journal, Chicago. Informal conversations with the clergy of other denominations and association with local ministerial groups are of inestimable value in promoting ecumenical understanding.

The problem of a divided Christianity has been felt for a long time in the life of every parish, particularly in the areas of mixed marriages and the related problems of conversion of the non-Catholic party to the Catholic faith, the rearing of children, in the loss of Catholics to other Christian denominations, and in the area of community activities. Difficulties will continue, perhaps, for some time to come. Nevertheless, no one should lose sight of the goal of effecting Christian unity or making any contribution toward that goal. Therefore, "when unity with our brethren becomes difficult let us not break, but bend . . . until love works the miracle of one heart and one mind" and of "one flock under one shepherd."

THE PARISH AND THE POOR

"The Church must present herself to the world as she is and desires to be: The Church of all, but in particular the Church of the poor." This statement of the beloved Pope John XXIII has given the Church a fresh new impetus in its work of helping to solve the problems of poverty and of bringing the Gospel to the poor. Though this rekindled concern for the poor must involve the whole Church at all levels, it is especially important at the parish level. Theoretically, at least, the parish is the ideal institution for bringing spiritual and material comfort to needy persons. Furthermore, as the basic unit in the organizational structure of the Church and as an integral part of the local community, the parish is in a strategic position to give dynamic leadership to the assault on poverty. In practice, however, this leadership is not always given. There are those who believe that their communities and their parishes have no poor to care for. While conceding that such a situation may exist in certain more fortunate areas, the fact remains that those who hold such views are ignoring the facts and depriving themselves of the opportunities available to every parish, regardless of its condition, to practice love of neighbor through help given to the less fortunate. If a parish is a unit of the Mystical Body of Christ bound by love to the rest of the Body, it follows that individuals, families, and organizations in the well-to-do parishes have an excellent opportunity to carry out one of the basic tenets of Christianity, love of neighbor for the sake of God, even to the point of going beyond parish boundaries to surrounding communities, and of assisting wherever assistance is needed without regard to race, color, origin, or creed. One such project in which they might participate consists of collecting donated food in a parish center under the leadership of the St. Vincent de Paul Society, to be distributed, as need may arise, to center-city parishes, thereby helping to alleviate the needs of the less fortunate members of the Body of Christ. A few of the very many activities in which both priests and laymen could easily participate include:

1. Visiting the poor and the infirm in their homes, in hospitals and in nursing homes.
2. Assisting the unemployed to obtain full- or part-time employment.
3. Purchasing books and First Communion outfits for poor children.
4. Providing budgeting services.[6]
5. Helping with debt adjustments.
6. Offering material assistance to the poor of the parish, including supplementary relief, food, coal, clothing, rent, payment of utilities.
7. Caring for the needs of the blind, deaf, and handicapped.
8. Helping the indigent to secure admission to hospitals, charitable homes, and institutions.
9. Providing or helping to provide free legal service for the poor.
10. Arranging for housekeeper service for the sick and elderly.[7]

The planning of modern communities has become very cold and impersonal. Frequently those responsible for community planning and development have had little regard for the problems of the poor. It must have been with these thoughts in mind that the most Reverend Raymond J. Gallagher, Bishop of Lafayette, Indiana, and former Secretary of the

---

[6] Cf. "Helping Families Manage Their Finances," *Handbook of Budgetary Guidance and Financial Management,* available through the Society of St. Vincent de Paul and the Ladies of Charity, Archdiocese of Washington, Washington, D. C. An excellent aid in carrying out the work of charity. This book is available upon request.

[7] The list of activities of the Society of St. Vincent de Paul from which these suggestions were taken was prepared by the Milwaukee Particular Council and was published by the Superior Council of the United States Society of St. Vincent de Paul.

National Conference of Catholic Charities, in an article "A Plea for Personal Charity," underscores the great need for personal contact and personal service. In this article the bishop suggests a program in which fathers would help fathers gain employment and provide their know-how for household repairs; mothers would help mothers with problems of child care, budgeting, and housekeeping; teenagers would help teenagers through advice in social behavior and good grooming, and would staff parish tutoring centers for slow learners and the culturally underprivileged. There would also be programs in which the whole parish community would help the housebound, the aged, or the ill. The adults would take shut-ins to church and provide them with meals and housekeeping services, while young people could perform such services as visiting the sick, writing letters for them, and running errands.

Under the category of the less fortunate members of a parish or a community, the following ought to be included: (1) the timid poor, (2) the honest poor, (3) the aggressive poor, and (4) the spiritually poor.

1. *The Timid Poor.* The timid poor may be those who because of some disability are unable to provide for themselves so as to live comfortably in an affluent society. With full realization of their limitations they manage to live within their means, often suffering privation and at times even a certain degree of embarrassment because they are unable to participate in the activities of the parish or the community. These people ought to be carefully sought out and, with greatest care, helped through guidance and counselling. Such people are to be found in practically every parish. They are the people who fear to come to the rectory lest there be others worse off than themselves and they would be depriving others whose needs are more imperative than their own. Who doesn't know such persons?

2. *The Honest Poor.* The honest poor are members of the parish or the community at large who, having suffered reverses or having made mistakes in the handling of their earnings or possessions, are temporarily unable to meet their financial obligations. These people are deserving of help despite their errors, and the parish can assist them in arranging for a loan either from the parish credit union or from private banking agencies, guaranteeing payments for them, thus enabling them to solve their problem and resume an honorable place in the community. It is distressing at times to hear uncharitable remarks made about them such as, "They deserve no sympathy," "They should have known better," and "It is up to them to get out of it." This is the antithesis of Christian behavior. The honest poor who come to the rectory and admit their mistakes as well as their needs are deserving of every consideration and have a right to the love and support of the parish. If the honest poor are not to be supported, who, then, in God's name, should we help?

3. *The Aggressive Poor.* This class includes those people who unfortunately think that the community owes them a living and that if they are now in distress it is not their fault but rather, the fault of others. Obviously these people need help, but not necessarily financial or material help. They need to be counseled and guided, so as to better understand themselves and the community in which they live. They must be helped to regain confidence in their own ability to overcome their problems, one by one, so that eventually they, too, may take an honorable place in the community. The process of guidance and rehabilitation may be long. A social worker filled with the spirit of Christ would be of immeasurable aid to the parish priest in this important work. An assistant priest with a degree in psychology and/or sociology would be of invaluable help in restoring parishioners with problems to a worthy position in the community. Today no parish in the center-city or in suburbia should be without the services of a full-time or part-time social worker and perhaps also of a psychologist unless this service can properly be supplied by a priest professionally trained in these fields. Without minimizing in the least the importance and necessity of prayer and the sacraments, the time is long past when a priest, faced with individuals with psychological problems, can help them by counselling them to go home, say their prayers, and be good, and that "everything will be all right."

4. *The Spiritually Poor.* This category includes those Christians who grew up without a solid Christian education and formation and who, in the course of time, have set up their own personal scale of values. At one time or another, perhaps during adolescence, they decided what would be good for them, and as they grew older and made their way in the world, they came to equate their own standard of living with the divinely established requisites for salvation. These are Christians who find reason to criticize the Church and its teachings; the bishops and their administration of the diocese. These are the ones who are contented with attending Sunday Mass and by abiding by certain moral restraints, but who are also convinced that the Church is a clerical affair and has little or no interest in lay people except for what it can get out of them. Those are spiritually poor who see a skeleton in every closet and predict crises of faith and troubles for the Church in every field, while remaining outside of it, lest they become involved. The spiritually poor are also those Christians who remain on the fringe of parish or community activities, or take part only in fund raising activities and similar ventures. The spiritually poor must also include those who always find reasons for being lax in the practice of their faith.

How can these be helped? What is the answer to this problem? In times past some pastors might have thought that a parish mission would correct these ills. Without discounting such a possibility, it would seem that personal contact with such parishioners might prove much more effective. Furthermore, the various members of the family might be invited to make either a day of recollection or a weekend retreat or to join a study club. These spiritually poor might also be helped by what has now become known as a neighborhood mobilization followed by the organization of a group of men well trained in the teaching of the Church and able to answer in a satisfactory way most of the questions raised by the spiritually poor and the half-hearted Catholics. This could be done with or without the assistance of a priest as a part of the apostolate of the layman.

THE PARISH AND VOCATIONS

From time immemorial the parish has been the primary source of vocations to the priesthood and the religious life. For a long time, the "Altar Boys" organization has served as one of the great sources of vocations. In recent times, much concern has been voiced in various quarters about a decline in the number of vocations both to the priesthood and the religious life. Statistics seem to have established this as a fact. Quite understandably, however, though there is considerable agreement concerning the decline in vocations, there is much disagreement about the possible causes of the decline. Is it the home? Or the school? Or the environment? Or is it due to the failure of the parish clergy? This is a difficult question to answer in a definitive way, and probably there is no one single answer.

There are those who point to the materialistic trends of modern society as the greatest single influence on young men just out of high school who are deciding upon their future. To a large extent, today, the choice of a career is decided mainly on the basis of "what's in it for me?" even when considering the questions of vocations to the priesthood and the religious life. Furthermore, regard for spiritual and intangible values has, to a large extent, lost its time-honored appeal, and where such regard does exist, it seems to hold no more than a casual place in the human scale of values. This, they say, is quite noticeable in modern suburban communities from which candidates to the priesthood and the religious life have come in larger number. Here, prosperity and material comfort seem to have become the yardstick of social progress and individual success. Bigger houses, more cars, more television sets, more expensive vacations, and more and better clothes are, unfortunately, the status symbols of our time. Religion, although it is conceded a place, is looked upon chiefly as a necessary ingredient for respectability. Such attitudes and behavior are hardly conducive to the fostering of a genuine religious vocation in children.

Then there are those who think that in its present form the priesthood and religious life have become irrelevant to modern society. If this is so, why should a young man go into a way of life which no longer meets needs of modern man? Others think that the decline in the number of vocations and the irrelevancy of the priesthood and religious life to a modern society are due to the failure on the part of the clergy to present their way of life both as a unique challenge and as the medium through which the perfecting of the city of man is accomplished. They charge that there has been too much watering down of the traditional principles of Christian asceticism in favor of modern pragmatism. If what is convenient for me is "good," becomes the yardstick of one's moral behavior, then, it is quite clear that a distinct inversion of values has taken place here, with the net loss on the side of "the good." In other words, the time-honored principle "what is good is worth all honest effort to achieve it," is no longer the dominant principle in schools and seminaries, and it scarcely finds a place in the philosophy of life of modern society. It seems that an ever-increasing number of people who should strive toward higher goals are quite satisfied to remain on the monotonous plateau of mediocrity. This is particularly disturbing when one realizes that in other fields of endeavor, for instance in the sciences and medicine, the emphasis is on superior achievement. So much for the negative side.

Looking to the positive side, it seems that the present decline in vocations can be offset in a number of ways: (1) by a better utilization of the existing manpower, and by a system of temporary loaning of priests from one diocese to another, and of religious from one religious community to another and to the dioceses that are in greater need; (2) by an intensive program of re-education of our people at the national, diocesan, and parochial levels, about the true values of life and the means of applying them in everyday life; (3) by an intensive and sustained program of education at all academic levels concerning the worthwhileness and the beauty of the life of a priest or religious as a life of total dedication, a life filled with the challenges and unsurpassed joys for one who offers sacrifice and leads souls to Christ; (4) by a much greater selectivity and more stringent screening in the selection of candidates for the priesthood and the religious life, including social and psychological screening of the home background, habits, tendencies, and attitudes of possible candidates; (5) by placing the emphasis on quality rather than on quantity. (6) Finally, the wide utilization for parochial work of the many thousands of Brothers until now engaged exclusively in the teaching profession should be considered. Why not open to them the great opportunities that parish work offers at the present time? Their solid religious and educational background makes them a truly competent source from which pastors can draw effective assistance in preparing the laity and in guiding them in their many new roles in the Church and in society. Better yet, why not confer on them the deaconate and employ them in the administration of some of the sacraments? Our communities of Brothers are truly the largest untapped source of manpower at the parish level in the work of preparing the laity. In this way communities of Brothers would help solve a very perplexing problem in the modern parishes. It would also fill a void in the lives of many individual Brothers who, like many other educated men and women of our time, are looking restlessly for new avenues into which to channel their energies and new fields of interest for their zeal.

A mediocre priest or religious does harm to the cause of religion and to the society he is supposed to help. Religion today needs not simply more spokesmen but more articulate and competent witnesses. It needs men who, because of their profound spiritual and scientific preparation, are able to shed the light of the supernatural on the path of human science and of all human endeavor. This must be the role of the priest in our times, and there could hardly be a more exalted one.

The stories of the lives of priests and religious who have valiantly served the cause of Christ in all parts of the world must, once again, arouse the kind of interest needed to make young men proud to tread in their footsteps, as they endeavored to tread in the footsteps of the Master. In the words of the Holy Father Paul VI,

> The duty of fostering vocations pertains to the whole Christian community. . . . The teachers and all those who are in any way in charge of the training of boys and young men, especially Christian associations, should carefully guide the young people entrusted to them so that they will recognize and freely accept a divine vocation (Pope Paul VI, October, 1965).[8]

In the final analysis, the fostering of vocations in the parish depends to a large extent upon the image of the priesthood which each priest of the parish reflects in his own life as he performs his mission of ambassador of Christ and distributor of the mysteries of God to God's people.

PARISH AND FUND RAISING ACTIVITIES

One of the problems perennially facing the modern parish is the high cost of operation. The rates of services and maintenance, construction and repairs are constantly rising, as is the number of services demanded today as compared to the past. Besides this, the number of volunteer workers for the parish has greatly diminished. In fact, in many places volunteers have vanished altogether. The increased and ever increasing cost of living, the big salaries of government and private industry, union wages and union rules have made it difficult for churches to compete in the labor market. Even retired persons willing to work are hard to find. Then, too, the

---

[8] Vatican Council II, *Decree on Priestly Formation, The Document of Vatican II, op. cit.,* p. 439.

demands for efficiency in our society require the employment of persons who are skilled in their particular field — teacher or secretaries, custodians or stationary engineers. All these conditions have caused the cost of operation of the modern parish to rise to an unprecedented high level.

Unfortunately, however, the amount of church contributions has not increased in proportion to the increased cost of operation. Consequently, there is a serious need in many places for extraordinary income to supplement the ordinary income. To meet this need, parishes frequently resort to various types of fund raising activities. Some of these are certainly legitimate enough, but the morality of others is questionable. Frequently, the latter type are defended on the dubious ground that they are serving a good cause. These activities have not escaped criticism, and rightly so, within as well as outside the Catholic sphere. Though the criticisms are not always valid, the fact remains that the use of questionable practices is responsible for the bad image that the Catholic Church has in many localities. In fact, many are convinced that the Church has two standards of morality. But an even greater evil connected with fund raising, and one that is seldom mentioned, is that of the diversion of so much of the energy of so many young priests from the important work of the ministry to promotional activities, some of which are of questionable moral value. Fortunately, whether because of the extensive criticism leveled against them in the public press or an awakened sense of the value of the ministry benefit-fund-raising activities are declining in some places, it seems that wherever this de-emphasis has taken place, the moral tone of the life of the parish has improved considerably. Of late, thanks to the courageous action of a few bishops, certain types of fund raising activities have been curtailed, and in at least one diocese, all such undesirable activities have been forbidden. A pertinent question may be asked at this point. Has the financial condition of these dioceses or parishes suffered from this prohibition? If the Archdiocese of Chicago, which is one of the largest in the world, is any proof, the answer is definitely no. The consensus of some pastors concerning this matter, and this includes our own view, is that once the people are made aware of the various needs of the parish, and are informed concerning the various aspects of the operation of the parish, they will provide the proper support of the parish and the clergy.

Does elimination of all benefit fund-raising activities mean the end of all social activities in the parish? Not at all. The development of the social life of the parish is as important as that of any other aspect. The city of man, whose citizens the parish endeavors to sanctify through its ministration, needs to be sanctified in all its aspects and activities. If they are human activities, they can be made holy, or at least conducted in such a way as not to detract from the overall effort made in directing the city of men to its supernatural destiny.

13

Management Responsibilities of the Pastor

BROTHER LEO V. RYAN, C.S.V.

THOUGH A FEW SEMINARIES — TEN TO BE EXACT — OFFER COURSES IN bookkeeping and church administration, many priests are not adequately prepared to assume the various responsibilities involved in the administration of a parish when they receive their first appointment as pastor. It is, therefore, the purpose of this chapter to discuss the role of the pastor as manager, and to establish some guidelines for administrative efficiency at the parish level.

THE PASTOR AS MANAGER

Pastors, or parishioners, seeking guidelines for administrative efficiency will not find them in Canon Law. Canon Law deals quite explicitly with the manifold acts of ecclesiastical administration (cc. 1518–1528), but deals quite generally with the numerous pastoral duties in temporal management. Yet every pastor is a type of businessman as well as a parish administrator. His role as manager of parochial temporalities makes him comparable to the executive of a business enterprise. Bouscaren, Ellis, and Korth note that "the fundamental principle of all good administration is contained in and illustrated by Canon 1523: administrators of Church property are obliged to fulfill their office with the care and diligence of a good *paterfamilias*. Hence, they must observe the following:

1. Be *vigilant* that the church property entrusted to their care suffer no harm or perish in any way;

2. *Observe the regulations* of canon and civil law, as well as regulations imposed by a founder or donor or by legitimate authority;
3. *Collect the income* and fruits accurately and in due time, keep them in a safe place, and use them according to the mind of the founder or according to established laws or norms;
4. With the permission of the Ordinary, to lay out or use for the benefit of the Church (moral person) money which may be left over after all expenses are paid and which can be invested profitably;
5. *Keep well ordered accounts* of receipts and expenditures;
6. *Keep in good order* in the archives or in a convenient safe *all documents and legal papers* upon which the rights and property of the moral person depend.[1]

The business-management aspects of parish administration constitute one phase of parish work for which the priest is generally least prepared by experience, general education, or seminary training. That many priests fulfill these responsibilities admirably is a matter of record, but their success is often due to personal acumen, skills, and talent, rather than to professional preparation. There is almost universal recognition of the fact that parish administration today is big business. The business management of any parish consumes more time than most priests care to admit or like to give to it. Management responsibilities represent a major challenge to every pastor.

A. *Managerial Functions Performed by Pastors*

What are the managerial responsibilities of the pastor? They are in most respects similar to the managerial responsibilities of corporation presidents, plant managers, or self-employed entrepreneurs. Management principles may differ in application between the parish and the business enterprise, but the principles themselves are universal. However, managerial responsibilities must be differentiated from the host of detailed tasks which every manager performs. Though a priest in his role as pastor may supervise the custodian, order the candles, and purchase the floor wax, control buying for the school, bank the Sunday collection, submit claims to the insurance company, write checks for the utilities, make interest payments on parish borrowing, and perform a hundred other acts of administration, these details, important as they are, are not to be confused with the concept of managerial responsibilities. In his role as manager, the pastor (1) plans, (2) organizes, and (3) controls, for these are the basic responsibilities of any business executive.

1. The Pastor Must Plan

Planning is a definitive function of management which consists in

---

[1] T. Lincoln Bouscaren, S.J., Adam C. Ellis, S.J., and Francis N. Korth, S.J., *Canon Law: A Text and Commentary,* Fourth Revised Edition, Second Printing, 1966 (Milwaukee: The Bruce Publishing Company), p. 833.

formulating the objectives of the enterprise and selecting the means, methods, and techniques by which these objectives may be achieved.

Planning may include the construction of a church, the building or expansion of the parish educational facilities, or the operation of a parish center. However, regardless of the project, the pastor should in cooperation with his people establish parochial objectives. He will, of course, take the initiative since parishioners look to the pastor for leadership.

Next, the pastor determines how to go about realizing these plans for, whatever the project might be, he, as manager, must specify the means, methods, and techniques to be employed. Since most priests have limited business experience and cannot possibly know every modern technique successfully employed by businessmen, he should solicit assistance from those in his parish who make similar decisions daily as part of their managerial responsibilities. Establishing objectives, selecting means, methods, and techniques is a unique pastoral and managerial responsibility.

2. The Pastor Must Organize

Organizing is the implementing function of management which involves securing suitable personnel and capital and arranging them in such a way that they may be controlled. People and funds are both needed. With regard to personnel, the pastor should exercise a quality of leadership that inspires confidence, motivates, marshals enthusiasm and support so that all those associated with the parish enterprise work together. For example, the principal of the parish school is the parish authority on education. Pastor and principal, therefore, must work together with teachers and parents in order that the educational efforts of the school contribute to the accomplishment of the academic and spiritual goals of the parish, identified in the master plan.

Concerning capital, the pastor must seek maximum return on the parish investment through proper utilization of the physical plant (an example of fixed capital), and make the most judicious use of funds in the acquisition of equipment and supplies, maintenance of plant and equipment, care of the grounds, and a host of similar acts of supervision. Furthermore, as a manager, the pastor will exercise control over these undertakings and will see that the business affairs of the parish are efficiently and systematically organized. He probably should not, from the viewpoint of good manager, perform these tasks himself. Rather, he should delegate most of them. Nevertheless, although the pastor may divest himself of the organizational details, he still remains responsible for their successful outcome. In this area, he will make the greatest contribution if he performs well the executive functions of organizing, that is, the securing of proper personnel and adequate funds, and the uniting of them in a way that they can be controlled.

3. The Pastor Must Control

Controlling is a regulative function of management which consists in verifying performance according to the plan and measuring its effectiveness. In this area, many people equate accounting and business management. However, accounting is only a tool of management which records the historical fact of expenditures in order that an analysis can be made to determine how well the funds were expended. The question "how well?" is answered by whether or not the expenditures helped achieve the original plan. Therefore the pastor must continually say to himself: "This is what we planned to do, and this is what we accomplished; are the results satisfactory?" A true manager will continuously ask and be prepared to answer this question.

In reviewing these three principles, it must be evident by now that there is much more to managing than merely doing. Persons who perform the detailed tasks of business are not necessarily managers. The manager masterminds, and accomplishes goals through others, without getting "bogged" down in details.

The formula of planning, organizing, and controlling is simple, and basic; it is the very essence of management responsibility. Every pastor is challenged to be a good manager, and he will increase his executive efficiency in proportion as he understands and exercises these basic business-management functions.[2]

PASTORAL RESPONSIBILITY FOR THE MANAGEMENT OF PARISH INCOME

The assessment of the financial needs of the parish in terms of both capital and operating funds, and an evaluation of income sources represent a major responsibility. The financial needs of any parish are manifold, and vary considerably depending on whether the parish is a new venture or an existing plant; and if the latter, how long the parish has been in operation. Capital needs include those demands for fixed or permanent assets, both in terms of physical plant and equipment. Operating needs include the funds required to meet ordinary costs of parish operation and maintenance. These capital and operating needs and the raising of funds to meet them constitute a major demand on the time and business acumen of the pastor.

A. *Capital Needs*

The need for funds to finance new buildings or to rehabilitate an existing parish plant grows out of the present status of the parish as well

---

[2] The definitions of planning, organizing, and controlling are adapted from Walter A. Gast, *Principles of Business Management* (St. Louis: St. Louis University, 1953), p. 55.

as the immediate and long-range plans for the development of the parish plant and program.

1. The New Parish

Volumes could be written about procedures to be followed in the establishment of a new parish. This chapter will not attempt even to outline the problems connected with such a venture. What is suggested here are some considerations the pastor should incorporate into any system of estimating the necessary income for parish development and operations. First of all, the physical needs of the parish must be considered, and these should be developed according to immediate, short-term (one to two years), intermediate (three to five years), and long-term (five years and more) plans. The scope of the parish program — spiritual, educational, and social — will dictate the number of buildings required. Once the physical needs have been determined and a parish program has been designed, it is possible to translate this program into capital costs (facilities), and to gather data regarding the costs involved in operating and staffing a parish from a similar parish already in operation. Defining goals, establishing plans are difficult; gathering data is relatively easy.

Developing the financial plan or estimating construction costs follows rather naturally, once a decision has been made as to what will or should be done and a timetable has been drawn up. To perform these tasks effectively, it is wise to consult published sources, experienced pastors, the chancery office, responsible specialists among the laity (preferably from among parishioners), who can advise on the realism of the plans, provide cost estimates and related data about resources available and the finances required for the projected parish.

Financing the proposed plan represents a real challenge. Therefore, it is important to remember that the professional manager will establish his objectives, translate them into a realistic plan, assess the dollar costs of fulfilling the plan, and then consider how the financing will be accomplished. Any effort that begins with the presumed number of dollars available is usually shortsighted and doomed to failure. The preliminary census will reveal the number of persons to be served and will provide a good indication of the socioeconomic status of the parishioners. But valuable statistical data revealing the financial profile of persons in a given area is also available from public sources. Plans must be realistic in terms of the people served; but to scale-down efforts or to revise plans based on some personal judgment that the people cannot afford the total program is to reflect a lack of confidence in the generosity of the people and in their commitment and to suggest a lack of administrative leadership on the part of the pastor himself.

2. The Existing Parish

The existing parish constitutes a much more restricted situation. Any pastor assigned to an established parish usually takes inventory of the situation. Sometimes the inventory is more personal than professional and physical. A pastor newly appointed would naturally be interested in a review of the objectives of the parish and in securing an estimate of how well these objectives are being met. Frequently, this appraisal leads to an amendment, modification, or revision of the parish spiritual and educational program. After that appraisal has been accomplished, there is also need for an examination of the physical plant.

Every pastor should have a comprehensive plan for maintaining the parish plant. It should be developed in some detail; records should be kept. Many parishes do not have their original blueprints, inventories of original purchase of plant and contents, but the absence of such records does not prevent a pastor from inaugurating appropriate records and maintaining them in a safe place. A review of the existing plant from the viewpoint of preparing a current status report on the condition of buildings and contents is a valuable guide for planning ordinary and special programs of maintenance and/or rehabilitation. Ordinary maintenance alone makes heavy demands on most parish budgets. Delay or postponement of maintenance only intensifies problems and ultimately increases the cost of any work required. Important areas deserving of attention in every parish and usually requiring a cycle plan for proper maintenance include: painting and wall washing, preservation of church interior and/or periodic redecorating, maintenance of electrical, heating, and cooling systems, roof and shingle care, sidewalk, steps, and cement upkeep, grounds care, and landscaping. Certainly all of this work could not be done at once; a project of replacing lights, in the school for example, could be cycled over a period of years; systems should be developed for all major areas based on a priority of needs and availability of funds.

Rehabilitation costs should be carefully estimated. In most cases, it is possible to have specialists examine the problem area and submit estimates or quotations. Usually three estimates represent a good business approach for gathering a range of cost estimates and for securing competitive advantages. Maintenance management that is planned is always less costly than maintenance management by crises.

Once costs have been approximated and a schedule of major maintenance has evolved, the plan is quite well developed. Advantage can be later taken of seasonal factors in a program that is planned on an annual or long term basis. Where approvals are required because of the total anticipated expenditure, it is usually easier to secure authorization when the proposal reflects a systematic approach to solving a problem. Some parishes require year around attention to major maintenance needs; others have so many needs it is hard to develop priorities. Parish objectives, demands of the apostolate, local circumstances, special needs, and those possibilities of special parish support are all factors to be weighed in establishing maintenance priorities. The managerial skill of the pastor becomes especially evident through his efforts in planning preventative maintenance and rehabilitation, in organizing the personnel and raising the necessary capital, and in controlling or evaluating the effectiveness of these efforts.

Major rehabilitation costs sometimes involve borrowing funds, or the raising of funds through special collections or through parish fund raising efforts for this specific purpose; occasionally a gift is earmarked for a particular phase of the program. Probably the most ordinary means of paying for these programs comes from the use of surplus funds, depreciation reserves, or a contracted agreement to pay the supplier a specified amount from current operating revenues over a period of time.

B. *Operating Needs*

The total dollars needed to operate the parish plant and program will be governed by the size of each. It is important for a pastor to calculate what it costs each day to operate the parish; the sum is often quite startling, but expressed in this manner it becomes personal and real to parishioners. The cost of operating should be calculated by computing annual expenditures over a period of years and achieving an average divisible by the days of the year. It is also desirable in larger parishes to compute similar data for segments of the program (i.e., the grade and/or high school) or plant (i.e., gym operation).

1. For the Church

Since our churches are usually open daily and throughout the day, daily costs even for small items add up to a substantial sum annually. There are costs associated with the Divine Services, ranging from vestments, and sacred vessels, hosts, candles, incense, laundry to cite a few; fuel; custodian services; utilities; premiums for property, contents, and personal liability insurance are a few operational expenses associated with the church itself. The pastor as manager defines the services to be provided and he must be able to translate those services into estimated dollar costs. The proper grouping of these related expenses in the parish books makes it easier each year to make these projections of income needed more accurate.

2. For the Rectory

Parishioners recognize their own costs of household operation, and so are rather acutely aware of reasonable rectory costs. In addition to the help factor (housekeeping, cleaning, and laundry personnel, and perhaps a part-time parish secretary with an office in the rectory), there are expenses associated with the table. These costs will vary from parish to parish, but they can be identified and can be estimated with considerable accuracy. Here again averages developed over a number of years represent a trend and reflect cost of living increases. There are also ordinary expenses of maintaining a house ranging from incidental kitchen, cleaning, and laundry needs to insurance and utilities. Where the parish is large enough to maintain an office, the costs associated with that function can be estimated with considerable accuracy.

3. For the Schools

Parish educational costs make one of the heaviest demands on the parish budget. A great portion of parish income is usually channelled into the educational program. The elementary and high school programs are the usual consideration here, but as the concept of life-long learning grows in acceptance and the parish as a community of the people of God becomes more meaningful, additional educational programs are becoming a part of the parish effort. Confraternity instructions, adult education courses, programs for young adults, convert instructions, study-clubs, lectures for special groups (pre-Cana, Cana, married couples, young parents), and activities for senior citizens are all examples of a growing phase of the parochial apostolate. Every program or service requires some degree of funding. The income necessary to cover these educational endeavors must be estimated quite accurately. Poor management would simply assign specific funds to each activity; good management involves cooperative planning of the objectives of each effort, an estimate of personnel required and dollars necessary to implement the programs, and then some degree of evaluation of results related to funds and efforts.

The Elementary School.[3] Since the Council of Baltimore (1884) advocated a grade school in each parish, this commitment has formed the backbone of many parish operations. Parish grade schools have usually been free schools; their financial support came out of ordinary parish income. Frequently, school costs were simply lumped together in the annual report with little effort to apply accounting methods to these expenditures, much less an analysis of school costs. The parish grade school is an example of an early form of centralized financing since everyone who contributed to the parish was, in effect, supporting the school. Today a moderate tuition and a schedule of fees are quite common for parish elementary schools. While this income can be estimated, it usually covers only a fraction of the actual costs of operation. The pastor as manager, in

---

[3] For a more detailed discussion of "Financial Aspects of the Parish School," by Brother Leo V. Ryan, C.S.V., consult John P. Treacy (ed.), *The Pastor and the School* (Milwaukee: Bruce, 1966).

conference with the principal or educational specialists, should reach an early agreement on the educational program that insures both academic excellence and religious formation. This program then should be translated into dollars; and subsequently, a financial plan for the school evolves based on some ratio between general parish underwriting from current operating funds and from funds generated by the school itself.

The manner in which the pastor approaches educational planning, his recognition of the principles of good organization in developing a professional staff, in providing for adequate equipment and supplies and for continuous cooperation in evaluating and understanding the school as an educational institution as well as a parish project, all indicate his effectiveness as an administrator.

The Secondary School. Many parishes operate high schools. Those parishes without their own secondary school are usually linked together with other parishes in the support of area, regional, and interparish high schools. Because of their interparochial nature often these schools are diocesan high schools, and because of the concept of a common educational service and geographical location, are frequently called central high schools.

For the parish high school, the pastor and principal again must cooperate in determining the educational program and its cost and then reach some understanding on how much of the needed school income will be paid directly from the parish as a subsidy and how much will be generated by the school itself. Only by making these decisions in that order will a defensible program be developed. Today there are so many outside agencies establishing objective standards for schools, that arbitrary and subjectively based decisions regarding the schools are simply inappropriate.

High schools are usually operated from tuition and fee collections to a much greater extent than elementary schools. But facts indicate that no secondary school can operate on tuition income alone. Central diocesan-wide financing of secondary schools is not a reality yet, but appears on the horizon as perhaps the only solution to the survival of these schools, if accreditation, certified teachers, adequate curriculum choices, and related educational standards are to be maintained.

In the case of parish involvement in diocesan high schools the option of support and the degree of contribution is predetermined. Diocesan high schools usually operate on either a tuition only, tuition assessment, or assessment only basis.[4] Hence, it is possible for the pastor again to estimate the income necessary on each parish level to finance the parish contribution to the central school.

---

[4] Edward F. Spires, *The Central Catholic High School* (Washington, D. C.: The Catholic University of America Press, 1951), pp. 96–107.

4. For the Convent

Convent operational costs assumed by the parish are really costs associated with the educational program. While the salaries of teaching Sisters are still quite modest and will probably increase in the future, to this basic payment must be added those parish financial costs for convent operation. These costs may vary from one parish to another depending on the arrangements previously agreed upon by the parish and the religious congregation. Here again the average of annual expenditures over the period of several years will provide the pastor-manager with an indication of the dollars and percentage of parish income that must be earmarked for this purpose. The income necessary for convent operating expenses should then be identified as a supplemental educational cost.

5. Other Parish Facilities

Whatever other facilities exist in the parish also require income to operate. The parish hall or parish center is a common facility in many areas of the country. Frequently in the past these facilities stood idle for long periods of time each year; today the trend is toward constant use. Idle facilities are most costly in terms of deterioration; active facilities require budgeting allocations and place a further demand on parish resources. Sometimes such facilities do generate some income that can be used to offset particular costs related to their operation; usually the parish subsidizes these facilities from current revenues. Here again the pastor must exercise his insight and make accurate estimates of the income necessary to carry out the programs approved for these adjuncts to parochial life.

Throughout this section one theme has been underscored; the role of the pastor as manager in establishing objectives for various programs, selecting the means, methods, and techniques most suited to his parish to achieve these programs, the need to estimate the manpower and current income required to implement the programs, and the desirability of evaluating the final product in terms of objectives and means (personnel and capital). All that has been suggested stresses the necessity of determining the income necessary to accomplish properly the goals deemed essential for parish life. Having established the programs, and estimated the financial resources required, the pastor's talent as a manager is further challenged as he proceeds to explore sources of funds to support these programs in the manner which they require and deserve.

C. *Sources of Income*

Once the parish program has been defined and translated into elements of cost, the pastor faces the necessity of raising the revenues required to meet the obligations essential to the program and incurred by the parish.

1. Capital Sources

Major sources for parish financing must come from major efforts on the part of pastor and parishioners. Such activities constitute extraordinary acts of administration and require the observance of diocesan regulations.

Campaigns to secure funds for capital expenditures are quite common. These campaigns may either be parish based, drawing on talented personnel within the parish, or they may be directed by professional fund raisers who specialize in this service. Both types of campaign demand well defined goals, leadership, good communications, objective analysis of the financial potential of parishioners, and a systematic approach employing both public relations and business management skills. Parish based drives for capital gifts too frequently lack a comprehensive design, reflect considerable subjectivity, are loosely organized, lag in intensity, depend too much on all volunteer services, and often fail to inspire sufficient gifts to meet the proposed goals. Professional fund raising programs are generally thoroughly designed, rely on objective data, are highly organized, stress interest building and timeliness, involve professional direction, and often oversubscribe original goals. The decision to use one method over another must be based on local circumstances and on an objective comparision of the two methods.

Ordinary and extraordinary bequests represent another source of funds for either general parish needs or for specific phases of the parish program (cc. 1513-1517 consider gifts and bequests for pious causes). Parishioners should be periodically reminded of the desirability of remembering the parish and parish programs in their wills. Gifts made to rectors of churches are presumed to be given to the Church, unless the contrary can be established (c. 1536).

Diocesan assistance is a growing source of funds for new parishes and also for parishes in areas of declining economic support (i.e., inner-city parishes, or parishes involving severe relocation of parishioners, decline in membership, and severe financial readjustments). Diocesan plans vary. Support is often provided in the form of loans as a basic contribution to new parishes; loans are likewise usually available under special circumstances to assist parishes in meeting specific obligations.

2. Current Operating Sources

The Church has the right to expect and demand support from the faithful (c. 1496). Ordinary parish revenues are secured through some system of family pew-rent payments and/or seat offerings based on presumed ability to pay, usually gauged on some estimate of annual income. Many parishioners are not registered and hence do not contribute through the Sunday and holyday envelope system. Silver collections are a regular feature of parish life and serve to supplement membership dues envelopes. Pastors should make every effort to encourage parish enrollment by all families and single individuals earning separate incomes. Membership dues assessments should be reviewed regularly to adjust for new earning power and shifting dollar values.

Special collections are another regular feature of parish life. Special collections may be either diocesan or local in character. The former are usually annual collections (Peter's Pence, Propagation of the Faith, Indian and Negro Missions, etc.) predictable in advance and usually operating on a minimum quota basis. Local collections can be organized for specific parochial purposes; this method has genuine appeal provided the project is widely accepted and represents a real need and is properly approached. This method of collecting funds, however, can also be abused by too frequent use for projects of lesser importance, less widely known and recognized and inadequately planned. Sometimes requests are made for ordinary and extraordinary expenditures of a relatively current nature; quite a few requests are unrestricted (cc. 1513-1517).

No one has ever catalogued all the possible programs of fund raising undertaken by parishes. Aids, bake sales, bazaars, card parties, carnivals, dramatics are among the best known possibilities. Such activities should not be multiplied needlessly; they should be truly organized with social as well as economic objectives and should yield a return proportionate to the time and effort required for their execution.

Parish organizations represent an important source of funds and support, particularly for specific parish ventures. The Altar and Rosary Society, the Holy Name Society, parent groups involved in educational interest, study clubs, young married couple groups (CFM for example), and others are sources of support for specialized programs of the parish. The projects undertaken by these organizations should be coordinated, necessary, and useful. Parish organizations should not be exploited, nor should they be used primarily as fund raising agents; they all have other acknowledged objectives; it is their objectives that lend themselves quite naturally to related parish efforts and financial support.

Interest earned on parish funds (c. 1543) or on parish long-term investments or short-term securities (usually governmental) may make a modest contribution to parish revenues initially but in some parishes and over a period of time interest has a way of accumulating large sums of money in the parish checking account. Many keep a balance in excess of needs. A reasonable balance would be a sum equal to one and one-half times average monthly expenditures. It is the duty of the administrator to invest all money not needed for current expenses (c. 1523 § 4). Because investment constitutes an act of extraordinary administration it requires consent of the ecclesiastical superior. Funds may occasionally be transferred from one source to another on a temporary or permanent basis, depending on circumstances. It is important here to exercise caution and to observe whatever regulation may be involved. The use of cemetery funds in many states is regulated by law and such funds cannot be transferred at will to current operating use for activities other than those permitted.

Tithing has become a popular means of parish support in many dioceses, and the movement is growing in acceptance and use. Tithing means giving the first 10 percent of gross earnings before deductions and taxes to the church through offertory collections.

The usual approach involves assigning the first five percent of gross earnings to the parish and allowing the remaining five percent for other parish, diocesan, or other religious and civic charities. Advocates point out that tithing is possible, specific, based on ability to give, and rooted in historical precedents. Tithing has been described as a challenge, as a way of life, a means of giving a priority of thanks to God, of maintaining a sense of values in a materialistic world, and a desirable way to fulfill the precept of church support. Various firms have specialized in introducing tithing programs at diocesan and parish levels and frequently conduct, at diocesan invitation, workshops for pastors to demonstrate the purpose, success, and value of tithing plans.

Every parish has a variety of revenue sources arising from special sources. As mentioned earlier elementary and secondary schools generate income, but rarely earn any funds to be transferred to the parish; rather the parish must supplement school efforts. Auxiliary enterprises (bookstore, cafeteria, uniform sales, etc.) of the school should be self-supporting and should contribute something to the overhead of the school. The parish itself may regularly or periodically sell religious goods or operate a bookrack and magazine stand. Funds from various offerings; candles, votive lights, poor box must all be separately accounted for and appropriately used.

Pastoral Responsibilities for the Management of Parish Expenditures

Proper planning of objectives, accurate assessment of revenue sources, and effective accumulation of funds all presuppose efficient, economical, and effective management of parish funds. This section of the chapter will consider specific areas of managerial responsibility and suggest management tools which will enable the pastor to achieve success as administrator. The specific areas which will be considered briefly include: accounting, auditing, budgeting, cost analysis, financing, insurance management, personnel, purchasing, and reporting.

A. Accounting

Accounting is an important management tool if it is properly understood and utilized. A good accounting system is a real asset to every administrator. Good accounting is not synonymous with good administration, but it is one of the acceptable barometers. Accounting is more than record keeping. Recording the income and expenditures of the parish is only one aspect of accounting. Parish records, financial or nonfinancial, are simply historical evidence of past transactions. If these data are properly classified and recorded, and if they can be analyzed as a basis for future decision making, then the parish possesses a good accounting system. Rather than concentration of the details and mechanics of recording, the pastor as manager should be concerned how the recorded information can indicate guidelines, identify trends, and provide other facts which reveal patterns of giving and expenditure trends of value in financial planning and in controlling expenditures.

Frequently, the accounting system is dictated by financial reports required at a higher level. Occasionally, special ledger forms are available that have been prepared for this purpose. Sometimes, dioceses supply pastors with a daybook and report forms. Usually, the pastor must rely on some competent person who will design and develop an accounting system which employs uniform accounts, standard classifications, and well defined procedures, and apply these accounting norms to the circumstances and need of the parish. Again the pastor provides the guidelines, advising what data he needs and indicating how he proposes to use the information, what reports are required of him (at the local, diocesan levels), so the system will be able to yield the information easily and systematically in uniform and standard terms. Such a system has already been developed for Catholic schools.[5] Pastors would do well to employ the services of a professional accountant on a regular retainer basis to insure a proper set of books and to guarantee accuracy and consistency of recording practice, to provide for proper adjusting entries, calculation of accrued and deferred payments, and the preparation of reports. Every parish has a number of qualified laymen who do similar work for their livelihood, and who would be able and willing to assist in this area.

An important point to emphasize beyond the need for standard accounting procedure and a uniform system is the need for separate accounts or ledgers or sometimes different books for various aspects of parish life; accounts for the parish proper should be separated from school and related educational accounts, i.e., convent, CCD, etc.; rectory accounts

---

[5] Brother Leo V. Ryan, C.S.V., *Accounting Manual for Catholic Elementary and Secondary Schools* (Washington, D. C.: National Catholic Education Association, 1963).

should also be kept separately, as should the funds of parish organizations. The totals of these operations can be consolidated at the time of auditing and preparing parish reports.

Even with the strongest determination to gather cost data, the establishment of separate books of account for parish and school, and the systematic classification of expenditures, there develop a number of knotty questions which can easily appear burdensome to a pastor. One problem which appears in parish accounting arises from the vast number of expenditures which cannot be easily assigned to either the church, convent, rectory, or school. Many expenditures can be classified easily as school or church, but a large number of expenditures affect both segments of the parish. Such expenditures should be prorated, recording against the church and school the amounts appropriate to each, based on some formula that is reasonable and simple to administer. The question of prorating expenditures is not new; it involves a rather common accounting procedure.[6]

As long as the disbursement is for a single purpose, the problem is simple. Most disbursements in the typical parish situation fall into this category. A salary paid to a full-time elementary teacher presents no classification problem, not does a salary paid to the parish housekeeper. However, the case of the custodian often presents a different situation. Here, a simple expenditure — the custodian salary — is made for services rendered to both the church (and church related plants, i.e., rectory) and the school (and school related plants, i.e., convent). The problem of prorating is to determine what part of the salary payment should properly be charged against the church account and what amount should properly be recorded in the school account. That the salary should be prorated is the first point.

No pastor really interested in cost analysis and in accurate cost data can afford to overlook or ignore the problem of prorating expenditures. The alternative to prorating is simple enough — recording the total amount of an expenditure to one or another convenient and logical account. The custodian or janitor's salary could be charged against either church or the parish school, without regard for the proportion of time spent caring for either of the two physical plants. Or, the amount may be charged to the area which absorbs the bulk of the expenditure (or time, in the case of the custodian).

Methods of prorating expenditures vary from the relatively simple procedure of approximating time to the more complex time-flow-area formula. Methods of prorating are usually considered to be: (1) time; (2) average daily membership or average daily attendance; (3) time-flow area; (4) hour-consumption; (5) number of pupils; (6) mileage- and/or quantity-consumed. These methods apply to various expenditures and not all meth-

---

[6] *Ibid.,* pp. 59–65.

ods can be applied in every case. Local modification can and should be made as long as the method of prorating remains consistent and simple.

The *time* formula consists in prorating or allocating a part of the expenditure to a given activity in proportion to the time spent in the activity (salaries).

The *average-daily-membership* method consists in allocating a part of the expenditure to a given activity in proportion to the average-daily-membership of the pupils engaged in the activity (instructional supplies).

The *time-flow-area* method of prorating consists of allocating a part of an expenditure to a given activity in proportion to the gross floor area used by the activity and the length of time the floor area is used (an allocation for costs of operation between school and parish use of a parish hall, or dividing fuel costs between the grade and high school and the church).

The *hour-consumption method* of prorating consists in allocating a part of an expenditure to a given activity in proportion to the length of time the activity uses facilities and the hourly rate at which the utility is consumed in the use of such facilities (water, electricity, heat). When various facilities are metered separately, the hourly rate of consumption can be obtained from meter readings. When facilities are not on separate meters, it becomes desirable to estimate the hourly rate of consumption. (The rental of parish facilities should take such guidelines into consideration.) Local utility companies can and will readily provide assistance in making such estimates.

The *number-of-pupils* for prorating applies within the school and consists in the allocation of a part of the expenditures for a given activity in proportion to the actual number of pupils involved (transportation expenditure).

The *mileage* method for prorating consists of allocating an expenditure to a given activity in proportion to the mileage traveled for the activity (transportation expenses again).

The *quantity-consumed* method for prorating consists of allocating a part of the expenditure to a given activity in proportion to the actual consumption of supplies or other commodities (sweeping compound, floor wax, etc.)

A rapid review of the systems of prorating will diminish any fear that might have been planted initially about the complexity of the techniques. The methods are simple, a few will cover most situations; and once established, they can be administered with ease. By prorating the pastor ensures himself a more professional approach to costing, a more accurate index of costs by activity, and contributes to a more factual and realistic understanding of real costs. Even on a modest scale the introduction of a simple system of prorating will be a rewarding experience and at the same time a helpful basis for better understanding parish disbursements, and will contribute directly to per pupil costing.

B. Auditing

Every parish should have an annual accounting and financial audit. Administrators of every church must provide the ordinary with an account of their administration annually (c. 1525). The bishop will review the parish accounts and records on the occasion of his visitation, but this policy should not substitute for the annual audit. Handled by a professional accountant, the audit verifies the accuracy and consistency of accounting procedures, makes appropriate adjusting and closing entries, and serves as a basis for annual reports. Auditors should be engaged on an annual basis, and invited to work on the books periodically throughout the year, reducing their annual audit time and providing professional counsel to the bookkeeper. The fee for such service is moderate; the assistance of competent and professional work is great, and the confidence it generates among pastor and parishioners is substantial.

C. Budgeting

Throughout the discussion on pastoral responsibilities for determining parish needs, the recurring theme concerned itself with planning ahead, translating plans into dollar estimates, and arranging them in an orderly, coordinated manner into a total parish program. The budget is a type of plan, a plan which reveals anticipated income and expenditures. A budget neither earns money nor reduces deficits, but it is a valuable blueprint of the parish program, a guide to what is possible, an index of expectations, a norm for performance and forms an intelligent basis for estimating income and expenditures by classification.

Budgets as a type of plan should correspond in length to parish program plans; thus, there should be annual, intermediate, and long-range budgets, each translating into dollars the plans for their respective period. The budget as a plan helps to "develop sound policies of administration, encourage cooperation, coordinate effort, fix responsibility, and control expenses."[7] The parish budget serves several functions: it is a servant of the program; provides an overview of the entire parish activity; aids in analysis of old and new programs; develops cooperation; stimulates confidence among parishioners; estimates receipts; determines the pew-rent (or membership) levy; authorizes expenses; aids in administering the parish economically; improves accounting procedures; and projects the parish into the future.[8]

The budget also has limitations. The budget is not a watchdog of the treasury; cannot be substituted for good administration; will be only as

---

[7] Francis J. Corrigan, "Do Hospitals Need Budgets?" *Hospital Progress,* XXXV, December, 1954, p. 65.

[8] Adapted from Chris De Young, *Budgeting in Public Schools* (Chicago: John S. Swift Co., Inc., 1946), pp. 9–14.

good as the executive makes it; improves as administration improves; should not be discarded because of failure to use it advantageously; should not be followed blindly; should involve judgment (for a budget is based on estimates); should not be allowed to kill initiative; is to good administration what bookkeeping is to good accounting.[9]

Preparation, presentation, adoption, and administration are the four stages of budgeting. Budget estimates are made by persons most acquainted with the particular area of parochial life involved and these estimates are presented according to the various accounting classifications and calculated by the pastor into a single document, reviewed, revised (upward or downward as necessary), and later adopted as the dollar plan required to meet the program of the parish. Budget preparation is a cooperative venture, planned over a period of months, discussed and developed in substantial detail; presented to the proper authorities; adopted and administered by the chief administrator of the parish or by his delegate.

D. Costing Parish Operations

With the budget as the basic financial plan, and with separate ledgers for distinct projects, standard account classifications, and uniform accounting, it becomes possible for the pastor to extract pertinent data that will make it possible to secure cost information by area, by specific activity or appropriate groupings. The accumulation of cost data makes it possible to analyze costs, to detect trends, to formulate recommendations, to enhance decision making, and to provide for the possibility of developing a cost index and meaningful comparisons with like or dissimilar institutions. Cost analysis of this type is especially useful in evaluating expenditures for education against national norms, experience, and local circumstances. Per pupil diocesan cost information is a valuable index of economy, efficiency, and educational effectiveness.

E. Parochial Financial Needs

Emphasis has been placed on the role of the pastor in defining parish goals and in translating those goals into a viable program. Emphasis has been placed on the pastor's responsibility for identifying the financial needs and income sources and governing the management of specific areas of parish affairs. Sometimes, especially in the case of capital needs, and occasionally, and in some geographical areas in particular, it will be necessary for the pastor to have recourse to others for parish assistance. The chancery office in many dioceses has in operation financial plans designed to assist or even support parish programs; direct appeal to persons outside the parish has been undertaken by some home missions; financial institu-

---

[9] Adapted from N. L. Englehardt and Fred Englehardt, *Public School Business Administration* (New York: Bureau of Publications, Teachers College, Columbia University, 1927), p. 553.

tions have proven to be a source of financial assistance. Banks are one such source; occasionally, and more at the diocesan or religious community level, bond brokers have been helpful in the issuance and sale of bonds, serial notes, or other debentures. The pastor who must go outside his parish for financial support should take counsel with the proper authorities and with finance specialists.

F. The Insurance Portfolio

That insurance coverage is necessary no pastor denies. Questions arise about the kind of insurance necessary and the extent of coverage desirable. A wide range of policies are necessary to cover the parish adequately. The pastor should develop a comprehensive program of insurance coverage; aided by specialists, he should plan a total program of protection. But personal liability coverage and property insurance are vital. Employee coverage is an important area. Workman's compensation, accident and health, major medical; life insurance and retirement benefits for parish employes and school personnel, lay and religious, should be included in any comprehensive program. The increasing accountability of eleemosynary corporations for their actions and for personal injuries sustained by individuals while on the property of charitable, educational, and religious organizations makes personal liability coverage essential.

Because needs vary according to the risks taken and the size and contents of plants, it is well to design a comprehensive uniform program. Provision should be made for periodical reviews and revisions. An inventory should be undertaken to establish a value basis for covering contents of parish buildings. Estimates for insurance should be based on factual data, not educated guesses. Coverage should be provided against fire, and physical damage by wind, rain, hail and other acts of God. Additional property insurance may be recommended by local circumstances.

Sources of coverage vary. In some dioceses, insurance coverage is provided by the chancery office and the degree of pastoral involvement in determining the type or extent of coverage may be restricted or regulated. Self-insurance or co-insurance by dioceses is increasingly common. In other areas, a single insurance broker handles all coverage of all institutions of the diocese, including parishes. In these cases, the insurance broker is a professional who renders service to the entire diocese. The relationship between such a person and the pastor should be one of confidence and cordiality; frequent conferences are desirable in achieving a comprehensive insurance portfolio tailored to the special conditions, needs, and wishes of a given parish. In other parishes, the pastor contracts individually with insurance agents and brokers for the necessary coverage. Here again a continuing relationship with one or several persons is desirable. Shopping around for excellence of coverage and services is one thing, but shopping around on insurance based on price is undesirable and dissatisfying. The more thoroughly an insurance agent understands the individual parish situation, the more professional the advice, and the more satisfying the coverage, the explanation of the coverage, the protection provided, and the service performed.

G. Personnel Administration

One of the very important responsibilities of the pastor is for personnel management. The pastor is responsible for policies governing the procurement, development, utilization, and remuneration of all employees of the parish. Today the number of lay persons involved in teaching and nonteaching roles (i.e., choir director, clerical, custodian, and domestic roles) and the number of religious in both teaching and nonteaching roles also increases, if not in number, in importance. The pastor must determine policies related to recruiting and selecting (including hiring, placing, orientating, and evaluating), provide for adequate in-service education and opportunities for further development, insure proper utilization of staff, and arrange to compensate them fairly. Provision must be made for essential fringe benefits (social security; various forms of personal insurance, such as: health and accident, major medical, and life insurance; holidays, holydays, and vacation periods, and retirement), and a system of two-way communication between employees and their respective supervisors is essential. Periodic conferences, effective communications, and opportunities for consultation are all essential elements of a good personnel program.

H. Purchasing Management

Purchasing has rapidly advanced from the simple level of buying to purchasing to the more involved concept of procurement (purchasing plus transportation) to the current idea of materials management (purchasing plus transportation plus supplies distribution). The pastor can find in efficient purchasing management a real key to economy, a realistic means of making the purchase dollar stretch, and of insuring savings while at the same time procuring necessary goods and services in proper quality and quantity. Purchasing is essentially having the right quality of goods, in the right quantity, in the right place, at the right time, and secured at the right price.

Some norms, guidelines, and techniques may be suggested to improve purchasing management at the parish level.

1. *Purchasing efficiency is not judged by price alone.* Price is an important factor in purchasing, so important that it often overshadows every other consideration. The scarcity of institutional dollars, frequent pressure on the checkbook, the need to stretch dollars to respond to so many demands, and rising costs all argue for a special weight to the accorded

price. The essence of purchasing is to balance the need for right price with the other important factors in the purchasing function, i.e., quality, quantity, timing, delivery service, care, maintenance, and special factors involved in the use of the materials.

2. *Establish quality standards.* Consider such questions as: (1) What is the purpose of the purchase? (2) Who will use the material? (3) How will it be used? (4) What results are expected from the purchase? and (5) What general and special characteristics should the material possess to achieve the desired results? Involve the users; evolve standards for products; establish product specifications. Remember quality standards depend on availability, standardization, specifications, and ability to test the quality of goods as specified. Developing specifications can be a detailed, technical job. In major purchases it is essential; in routine purchases, it is also important, but need not be so formal or detailed.

3. *Use standard purchasing lists.* Reduce the type of goods purchased by agreeing with users on the products to be specified, and develop a standard listing of these items which can serve as the basis for ordering. A standard list itemizes products traditionally purchased by the organization, arranged in an orderly manner, identified by description and number, containing unit prices, allowing space for quantity designation and price extensions. The standard list eliminates multiple purchases, minute distinctions, reduces man-hours of selection, description, and requisition effort, provides accurate cumulative data, reduces sporadic buying, restricts indiscriminate ordering, and allows for quantity buying and bulk economies.

4. *Develop a schedule for ordering.* Adequate lead time is a key point in efficient purchasing. The "right time" refers to order timing as well as delivery time. Design a schedule for parish buying; different units have varying needs, but they are usually reoccurring needs and predictable in time. Frequency of ordering can be reduced by periodic orders with more frequent shipping and spaced billing. Proper lead time makes it possible to take advantage of market trends, manufacturer's slack periods, variable shipping schedules, price changes, and insures delivery before needed, avoiding delays and costly retail replacement purchases and disappointments.

5. *Develop multiple sources of supply.* The decision concerning the company from whom to purchase is influenced by the types of items to be purchased. Reliability of vendors should be established. Know your vendor's past performance record. Ability to produce or perform is vital. Vendors come highly recommended; many vendors will be local persons, including parishioners. Purchasing should be motivated by principles, not personalities. Parishioners respect a pastor who is objective in his business dealings; the criteria for reputable vendors and quality products should apply equally to all persons. Considerable emotional pressure often is brought to

bear on the pastor to purchase from some person or another. Only by establishing specifications and adopting good procedures can the buyer be assured of good quality and good price.

6. *Use bids and quotations.* In making purchases of any quantity or consequence ask several competitors to *quote* prices on specifications given to all. To ask them to *bid* is to imply intention to award the contract to the lowest bidder. Pastors usually gather quotations on most items and bids on major projects. Establishing a system in this area provides legal protection, invites price savings, regularizes relationship, and results in efficient and economical purchasing.

7. *Organize a system for receiving merchandise.* The parish plant is usually complex. It is important to have a delivery area, or several areas where purchases may be delivered and accepted, receipted and contents verified. There should be a central location where purchases are stored, together with a system (however simple) for controlling storage and distribution of purchases. The principles involved in purchasing management are universal. Their application will vary. Probably the parish school will have the most highly developed system. Complexity of system is to be avoided; what is needed in every case is a policy decision, a procedure developed that balances needs with resources and thus insures prudent and profitable use of the purchasing dollar.

I. *Reporting on Parish Operations*

The pastor enjoys considerable autonomy in the operation of the parish. Good communication between the pastor and the parishioner involves some accountability for the income and expenditure of the parish. Reports are common enough to both ecclesiastical superiors and the people. Reports to both can be either oral or written and may be of many types. A study by McCleary reveals the common practice in most dioceses of requiring annual reports to be filed with the chancery.[10] These reports vary but usually involve an annual balance sheet, an asset and liability schedule, an income and expenditure schedule, an insurance schedule, and a cemetery schedule.

Reports to parishioners are frequently oral, mostly in periodic sermons. The annual parish report is usually a printed document. For many years and in many parishes these reports were limited to a general statement of income and expenses, complete with a listing of parishioners, and their Sunday, holyday, and special-collection contributions. Essential as this information may be, it is insufficient and places the emphasis only on the material relationship between the church and people, not on the essential spiritual nature of this assembly of the People of God.

---

[10] Dumas McCleary, C.S.V., *Parish Accounting* (Washington, D. C.: The Catholic University of American Press, 1948), pp. 7–20,

An increasing number of parishes have begun to prepare annual reports, complete with charts, graphs, and pictures, reporting on the spiritual, educational, social, and financial status of the parish. Patterned after some of the corporate annual reports, these documents are artistic yearbooks telling of the activities of the parish, reporting on both the spiritual and material stewardship of the parochial administration, featuring spiritual statistics, information on parish activities, especially educational endeavors, organizational data, and financial information. Such reports are to be encouraged; teams of dedicated and professionally qualified lay persons would consider an invitation to prepare such a report a real opportunity to serve.

Annual or periodic reports of parish organizations should be prepared for the members and the pastor. Perhaps a relatively simple but uniform report could be developed, so that the financial data of these organizational reports could be included as supplements to any composite financial report prepared by the auditors.

Conclusion

The pastor, as manager, has a wide range of responsibilities. The pastor must know and understand his abilities for planning, organizing, and controlling, must appreciate his obligation to define needs, to seek qualified persons, to generate funds, and to expend those funds efficiently and economically. The pastor need not do all these things, nor should he attempt to do so. His greatest contribution lies in defining parochial goals and in exercising leadership that motivates others to achieve those goals. By determining goals cooperatively with others in parish administration, by conferring with specialists, and by serving parishioners, the pastor reflects an understanding of his unique role as ecclesiastical administrator and evidence of managerial responsibility.

14

Pastoral Law

WILLIAM R. CONSEDINE

THE PASTOR, FROM TIME TO TIME, WILL ENCOUNTER PROBLEMS involving civil law. Law is a highly specialized science, and expert opinion of a lawyer is necessary when any decision requires the application of legal principles. Emphatically, the pastor should not attempt to render legal interpretations, either for an inquiring parishioner or on a matter of Church business.

In an increasing number of states, the Catholic Ordinaries are establishing State Catholic Conferences patterned on the National Catholic Welfare Conference. As with the latter, the State Conference has a legal section, or general counsel, available to pastors and officials of Catholic institutions for information on points of state law affecting their fields of responsibility. Each Ordinary, including those in states where there is as yet no Conference, has a diocesan counsel. This latter is usually an attorney in general practice of law, and to what extent he might be in position to furnish advice to pastors and others will depend on the circumstances of the particular case.

Needless to say, litigation should never be incurred, nor any action taken which might precipitate legal difficulties, unless the matter has been referred to the chancery.

Subject to the foregoing, a general knowledge of the civil law as it applies to aspects of parish administration will be helpful.

The pastor should make a point of locating one or more reliable lawyers within the parish borders, or in some other area, who are readily accessible. Such individuals might find it necessary to charge for services consuming substantial periods of time or requiring legal research. After all, time is the lawyer's principal asset, and if he is an employee or member of a law firm or partnership, he might not have complete freedom in the disposal of his business hours. However, the pastor will find that most conscientious lawyers, if properly approached, will gladly furnish informal advice and assistance without charge, either on the relation of one professional man to another, or from higher motives. If it appears that the matter at hand is one requiring a substantial amount of time or extensive legal research, they will tell him, advising if it is necessary to charge a fee, and undoubtedly making the charge as minimal as possible.

A lawyer, resident in the parish, will prove valuable as a member of a board of trustees, school board, St. Vincent de Paul Society, and for service on committees and societies generally.

CIVIL STATUS OF PASTOR

The status of the pastor is unique in civil law. He has been described as "one who has been installed according to the usage of some religious denomination in charge of a specific church or body of churches" (45 American Jurisprudence 741, article, "Religious Societies").

His relation to the Ordinary and to the Church as a whole, is governed entirely by canon law, and the same applies to his curates and all others in holy orders. All questions of appointment, transfer, dismissal, and discipline are regarded as matters within the internal government of the Church, and civil courts will not interfere with any action regularly taken by properly constituted ecclesiastical authority. The Catholic Church has been singularly free from litigation as to authority of its Ordinaries, but decisions involving other denominations would be held applicable.

In *Watson* vs. *Jones,* 13 Wallace 679, 20 L. Ed. 666, (1871), a landmark case in Church-State relations, the Supreme Court of the United States said: "All who unite themselves to such a body [the Presbyterian Church in that case] do so with an implied consent to this government and are bound to submit to it. But it would be a vain consent and would lead to the total subversion of such religious bodies if anyone aggrieved by one of their decisions could appeal to the secular courts and have them reversed." (At page 729, Wallace, and 676, L. Ed.) This general principle was reaffirmed by the Supreme Court in *Kedroff et al* vs. *St. Nicholas Cathedral,* 344 U.S. 94, 73 S. Ct. 143 (1952) and remains secure as a guiding principle in American Church-State relations.

Thus, in *Kinder* vs. *Webb,* 96 S.W. 2d 823 (1965), the Supreme Court of Arkansas refused to accept jurisdiction in an action by a minister against a regional church association to prevent cancellation of his credentials.

Civil courts will not enforce the authority of ecclesiastical bodies in spiritual matters; however, where there is a defiance of orders issued by church officials which involves usurpation of church property or funds, the courts will accept jurisdiction. Thus, a minister might be enjoined from attempting to exercise his functions after removal by superior officials of the Church, *Williams* vs. *Wilder,* 397 S.W. 2d 696 (Court of Appeals, Missouri, 1965); *Collins* vs. *Sims,* 118 S.E. 2d 402 (Supreme Court of North Carolina, 1961).

Although the pastor in the exercise of his spiritual functions is governed by canon law and the statutes of his diocese, his actions may in certain areas be affected by civil law.

Performance of Marriage

In a few jurisdictions it is required that a minister of the Gospel must be registered with the state, or a local subdivision, in order to perform the marriage ceremony. The validity of such regulation was sustained in at least one case *Ladd* vs. *Commonwealth,* 233 S.W. 2d, 517 (Court of Appeals, Kentucky, 1950).

While the issue does not appear to have been judicially determined, at least insofar as Catholic clergy are concerned, the pastor must take note of civil regulations on marriage, such as the requirement for the marriage license, and in some states, the waiting period, medical examination of parties, and similar restrictions. A particular problem is posed by laws in a number of states prohibiting marriage between persons of different races. Questions of conscience which might arise as the result of such statutes should be referred to the chancery.

Libel

A pastor must also be cautious that his public utterances do not contravene the law of libel. He is permitted great latitude in denouncing wrong doing and social injustice, even from the pulpit. However, he must be careful that his statements do not expose specific individuals to public shame or ridicule. Thus, in *Morasse* vs. *Brochu,* 151 Massachusetts, 567, the Supreme Judicial Court of Massachusetts in 1890 sustained a judgment for libel against a priest for intemperate words spoken from the pulpit against a Catholic physician who had been divorced and remarried out of the Church. If a pastor feels it necessary publicly to denounce any individual, either by name or implication as to identity, he should clear his remarks with the chancery and legal counsel.

Health and Safety Regulations

The pastor must maintain the church building, parochial school, and parish premises generally in conformity with local regulations on safety and sanitation. If he feels that any such regulation is arbitrary or unreasonable, the matter should be cleared with local counsel.

Other Relations With Civil Law

Following are more detailed discussions of other situations in which the pastor may find himself involved with civil law.

TENURE OF CHURCH PROPERTY

The pastor is, of course, concerned with the ownership of the parish plant in civil law. The pattern for legal title to Catholic Church property differs from one state to another. In general, there are three basic forms of tenure prevailing in the United States: (1) the trustee system, (2) the corporation sole, and (3) the parish corporation.

The trustee system which is the oldest, had its origin in early times when Catholics were in a decided minority, and the law in numerous states made it difficult to administer Church property in accordance with canon law. Largely to avoid difficulties inherent in these circumstances, the Ordinary took title to Church property in his name, as trustee for religious uses, invoking certain commonly accepted principles of the general law of trusts. The system has been continued in operation in numerous states, even though the necessity which led to its creation has ceased with the better relationship now existing among the various religious denominations. On the Ordinary's death, Church property held by him in trust passes to his successor in the episcopal office, rather than to his heirs. To minimize possible legal complications, it is customary for the Ordinary to execute a last will and testament, leaving Church property to whomever may be his successor in the episcopate. Property acquired by the Church is deeded to the Ordinary as trustee, and in this capacity he executes deeds of conveyance, or any mortgage or deed of trust necessary to secure a loan.

The corporation sole, as the term implies, is a corporation composed of a single individual. It is found in about twenty-one jurisdictions; namely, Alabama, Alaska, California, District of Columbia, Florida, Georgia, Hawaii, Idaho, Illinois, Kentucky, Maine, Maryland, Massachusetts, Montana, Nevada, Oregon, New Hampshire, Rhode Island, South Carolina, Utah, Washington. It is a technique peculiar to ecclesiastical practice and recognized in English common law. The Ordinary, of course, is the individual constituting the corporation. In most states where the corporation sole is in existence, it has been created by statute; but in at least two, Florida and Georgia, it was evolved by the courts from the trustee pattern. In some states the statute in question is applicable only to the Catholic Church, and in others, available to any denomination which desires to make use of it.

It might be mentioned at this point that in some states having two or more dioceses, different systems of tenure may prevail. Thus, in Illinois the Archbishop of Chicago is a corporation sole, while some of the other Ordinaries hold property in trust, and numerous parishes are separately incorporated. There is likewise variation in the tenure systems followed by dioceses in Kentucky, Louisiana, Oregon, and perhaps in some other states.

The corporation sole is somewhat similar to the trustee, in that the Ordinary in his corporate capacity holds title to Church property, accepts conveyances, and executes deeds, mortgages, and deeds of trust. It provides a greater degree of continuity than the trustee system, and statutes creating the office in some jurisdictions spell out the rights and obligations of the incumbent in considerable detail. It might be noted that in some states where the trustee pattern is followed, it has been modified by statute or judicial decision to a point where there is little to distinguish the Ordinary as trustee, from a corporation sole, except the title.

The parish corporation predominates in about twelve jurisdictions; namely, Colorado, Connecticut, Delaware, Iowa, Michigan, Nebraska, New Jersey, New York, North Dakota, Vermont, Wisconsin, and Wyoming. However, parishes may be found separately incorporated in some states where the trustee or corporation sole system is principally followed. Parish corporations are provided for by statute, there being considerable variation among such statutes. As a general thing, the essence of the system is that each parish constitutes a separate corporation in civil law. Its membership is usually composed of the Ordinary as president, the vicar general, and the pastor. There may be provision for two or more laymen of the parish as additional members, these being either appointed by the Ordinary or elected at annual parish meetings. The parish corporation places a greater responsibility on the pastor because, subject to the supervision of the Ordinary, he has the effective local management of the corporation. It must be remembered that religious orders, colleges, hospitals, and other Catholic institutions are normally incorporated separately, and thus hold and manage their property apart from that of the diocese as a whole.

Whatever may be the pattern of tenure for Church property, it is safe to say that a standing operating procedure in this regard has been evolved in every diocese. It will be necessary for the pastor to familiarize himself with the arrangements actually in effect and govern his conduct accordingly.

1. Income taxes

a. Vow of Poverty

The income tax obligation of a pastor will depend on whether or not he is a member of a religious order subscribing to the vow of poverty. The federal government recognizes the canonical effect of the vow of poverty, and if the religious acquires property or money by reason of his religious status, it is viewed as passing immediately to his order. Thus, the salary of a parish priest subscribing to the vow is not subject to federal income tax, and the same applies to his Mass stipends and other sums received in connection with priestly ministration. (Office Decision 119, U.S. Treasury, 1919.)

In general, any compensation which the religious receives for services performed on assignment by his superior will be regarded as passing immediately to his order. However, there is question regarding compensation for services other than in connection with his religious status, even though *permitted* by his superior. For instance, local treasury agents have refused exemption for fees received by a religious priest for service as executor of the estate of a deceased relative. Any question arising in this doubtful area should be referred to a lawyer for advice prior to disposition of funds received, so as to avoid embarrassment, if there should be demand for tax accountability.

The states, in the administration of their own income tax laws, are not required to follow this federal doctrine on the vow of poverty, and in some of them religious pay state income taxes, at least where income is derived from state sources, such as teaching in public schools or employment in a public hospital or other institution. A lawyer should be consulted as to the rule in effect in the religious pastor's state of residence.

b. Tax Liability of Secular Priests

A secular priest, or one belonging to an order not requiring the vow of poverty, is subject to federal and state income tax laws. Secular priests frequently affiliate with a secular institute. Some secular institutes prescribe a vow of poverty in modified form, but such a vow as taken in the secular institutes does not qualify for the exemption accorded to the total vow of the religious orders.

The pastor — and the same applies to his curates — is subject to income tax on his salary. It is specified additionally that income tax liability accrues on "marriage fees and other contributions received by a clergyman for his services . . ." (Sections 161–62, Federal Tax Regulations). While priests have occasionally urged that the use of the term "marriage fees" should be construed as a limitation of tax liability to that specific category, inquiry at the Treasury has revealed that the concurrent expression "other contributions" is intended to cover all sums received in connection with administration of clerical functions.

It is a general principle that *bona fide* gifts are not subject to income tax. It has been said that: "If the payment is intended to represent payment, whether designated as compensation or otherwise, for services rendered either in the past, present, or future, the amount received will be taxable income to the recipient. If, on the other hand, the payments are made to show good will or a mere kindliness toward the recipient and are not intended as a recompense for services rendered, then the payments represent gifts and should be exempt. A payment may be compensation for services rendered although made voluntarily and without legal obligation." (Merten, *Law of Federal Taxation,* Section 6:03).

It may be conceded that the foregoing attempt at clarification probably raises more questions than it answers. If a parishioner encloses a five dollar bill with his Christmas card to the pastor, the latter may with reasonable safety consider it as a tax free gift. However, if there exists a custom whereby the pastor and his curates share in the annual Christmas collection, this would be taxable income, even designated as a "free will gift," or by some similar title, the Treasury viewing this as financial remuneration which the priest may expect in due course. Examples might be multiplied, but the fact would remain that the line of demarcation between a *bona fide* gift and taxable income may sometimes be very indistinct. An attorney should be consulted in doubtful cases.

The pastor and his curates ordinarily live rent free in the parish rectory, which as an economic fact represents an element of compensation for services performed. Section 107 of the Internal Revenue Code specifically exempts from taxable income the value of either a residence furnished for a minister of the Gospel, or a rental allowance in lieu of such residence.

Besides, there is a general provision of the Internal Revenue Code which exempts from taxable income "the value of any meals or lodging furnished" to an employee "for the convenience of the employer" (Section 119, supra). It is necessary that the employee live on the premises so furnished and partake of his meals therein to qualify for the exemption. A pastor and his curates who are required to live in the rectory and take their meals there in order to be available on call for the priestly obligations, come within this provision.

Hence for federal income tax purposes the priest need not list the value of his lodging in the rectory, nor of food furnished by the parish and consumed therein. As a general thing, it is of academic concern only whether he considers the exemption relative to the value of his living quarters to accrue under Section 107, 119, or both. This exemption does not apply to services of a personal nature which, as a matter of custom, might be furnished in some localities at parish expense, such as his laundry or the cleaning and pressing of his suit. Technically, he should add the value of such personal items if furnished by the parish to his taxable income.

A different rule pertains relative to the social security contributions of a priest who has elected voluntary coverage on a self employment basis. As noted in the section on social security, the value of food and lodging furnished, even if on parish premises and for the convenience of the parish, is an element of compensation for this purpose, and the reasonable value thereof must be set out on the priest's return for self-employment income.

In a few instances, local district directors of internal revenue have asserted that a pastor was liable for income tax on the value of the service of his housekeeper on the theory, it seems, that she occupied a position analogous to that of a maid in a private family. This is an erroneous assumption in view of the actual status of the "housekeeper" in a Catholic rectory. The question has not been resolved definitively at the national level. If demand for tax accounting is made on a pastor relative to this issue, he should take it up with counsel for clarification.

A taxpayer may ordinarily deduct for certain expenses incurred in connection with his occupation and for which he is not reimbursed. These would include for the pastor necessary travel expenses, both away from home such as attendance at a diocesan meeting, and local transportation in connection with his ministry, for instance, on sick calls. The rules for deduction of expenses are very complicated and it would be impracticable to attempt any detailed discussion here. The Catholic Mutual Relief Society of America, 4223 Center Street, Omaha, Nebraska, 68105, as of this date, issues a very helpful booklet on income tax information for priests.

It might be noted that while a minister of religion is subject to income tax, as indicated, his salary is specifically exempted from the requirement of "withholding" (26 U.S. Code 3401 [a] [9]). Previously the minister had been permitted to pay his entire income tax at the time of making his annual report on April 15th. Under the Tax Adjustment Act of 1966 ministers of religion, and self-employed persons generally, must file a declaration of estimated income tax, which in the case of ministers who have elected social security coverage, will include social security charges, and pay same in quarterly installments. Any deficiency between the estimated tax, and that found actually due on the April 15th report, must be paid when filing such report.

As previously indicated, states need not follow federal norms in administering their own income taxes. However, it appears that in practically all states, substantially similar treatment is accorded the income of a clergyman, as to both tax liability and exemptions. If the instructional material issued by most states to accompany their printed income tax returns indicates a different treatment, the matter should be clarified with a local attorney.

2. Tax Status of Church Property

This is a field in which the Ordinary has a vital interest and any questions arising should be referred immediately to the chancery. However, some general knowledge on the subject will be of value to the pastor.

It may be stated that in all states there is exemption from general property tax for the church and parochial school, together with their furnishings.

Rectories are exempted from property tax by statute in at least twenty-six states and the District of Columbia, and in most others by custom or under judicial decision. However, there are a few in which the rectory is subject to property tax (see *Tax Exemption for Rectories, The Jurist,* Catholic University of America, April, 1953.) If a tax bill is received for the rectory, the pastor should refer it to the chancery unless taxation of rectories is an accepted fact in the state in question.

Convents occupied by teaching sisters are tax exempt in most states, generally on the theory of being an integral part of the parochial school establishment. However, in a few they have been held liable for property tax on the theory of being used primarily for residential purposes. Here again the pastor should contact the chancery on receipt of a tax bill for the parish convent, unless such taxability is an accepted fact in the state.

If any Church-owned property is used for income producing purposes, either by way of rental or the pursuit of business activity, such premises would in most jurisdictions be subject to the general property tax. The income received would be exempt from federal income tax, but might be subject to income tax in some states.

Benefit assessments. A distinction must be drawn between general taxation and the assessment of property for specific benefits, such as street paving. Very frequently there is no exemption from benefit assessments, even for property dedicated to religious and charitable uses. The rationale is that the specific benefit involved adds to the market value of the property, and the assessment is to a certain extent a part of the purchase price, rather than a tax in the strict sense of that term. The law on this subject is highly conflicting from one state to another, and legal counsel should be consulted if the pastor receives a bill for benefit assessment against church property.

3. Lotteries, Bingo, and Similar Activities

If the parish, either for the benefit of its parochial school or for other Church purposes, conducts lotteries, bingo, and other forms of games of chance, there should be coordination with state law, both as to general legality and tax status. In some states all forms of gambling are prohibited, even for charitable and religious purposes, although police often "look the other way" if proceeds are intended for religion or charity. In others, such activities are lawful when conducted by religious and charitable organizations, being specifically regulated by a statute in a few — New York, for instance.

Ordinarily, the proceeds of such games of chance are not subject to state taxation. Likewise, they are normally exempt from federal taxation.

However, if the *modus operandi* is analogous to "accepting wagers," there may be liability under the federal wagering tax (Section 4401, Internal Revenue Code). The issue of taxability under this section is highly technical. The traditional "raffle," for instance (of an automobile or television set), the bingo game, the parish bazaar are not subject to the wagering tax. However, the tax becomes effective if the operation approaches the connotation of "policy" as the same is (nearly always illegally) conducted by commercial interests. Therefore, any form of game of chance, other than those traditionally sanctioned by long standing local custom, should be cleared with a lawyer relative to both general legality and taxability.

Reporting on winnings. Of additional concern to the pastor is Section 6041, Internal Revenue Code, which provides that "all persons engaged in a trade or business and making payment in the course of such trade or business to another person . . . of $600 or more in any taxable year," . . . must report thereon to the Treasury. This provision does not apply to compensation paid for work and labor. However, the term "engaged in a trade or business" as used therein has been construed as applicable to churches and other nonprofit entities. The award of money or prizes won at a church bazaar was specifically held subject to reporting (*Sykes* vs. *Commissioner,* 24 Tax Court 1156). Thus a report should be made as to any cash prize awarded in amount of $600 or more, or of any article of property — an automobile, for instance — valued in such amount. The report to the district director of internal revenue is made on Treasury Form 1096.

4. Mass Stipends

As indicated, the priest must include Mass stipends in his income tax report. The issue of whether a bequest for Masses is subject to state inheritance tax, or federal estate tax, is one of considerable confusion. In most states, a bequest to a priest by name for the saying of Masses has been held subject to state inheritance tax on the rationale that the money was intended, actually, for the individual with a condition annexed for the performance of the religious service. Where the Will provides that the bequest shall go to a designated church, no priest being named, there is conflict among judicial decisions of record as to application of inheritance tax. It would not be helpful, in a work of this kind, to attempt to discuss the numerous decisions with their conflicting conclusions, and the discordant legal theories on which they are based. A local lawyer should be consulted when the question of taxability becomes an issue.

The federal estate tax is applicable only to estates in excess of $60,000. There are no judicial decisions relative to Mass bequests, and the current administrative thinking in the Treasury seems to hold a Mass bequest includable in the taxable estate except where it is to a religious order or institution, all priest members of which subscribe to the vow of poverty, the rationale being that in such event the money involved goes to the tax exempt entity, rather than to the priest who says the Mass.

PARISH LIABILITY

Today, there is an ever-increasing number of court cases involving claims against the parish for injuries which have occurred on church premises. For a long time, most of the states had a charitable immunity doctrine which prevented injured claimants from collecting a judgment against a religious, charitable, or educational organization.

For the most part, this immunity was not embodied in any statute. On the contrary, it was judge-made law. Several states have, through their higher court, repudiated the charitable immunity. In these instances, a pastor may no longer rely upon this privileged position.

However, if a given state still has an immunity doctrine, there is no guarantee that it will prevail in a judicial test for the trend is very definitely against the retention of charitable immunity. This suggests the prudence of church authorities to provide adequate liability insurance. The term "adequate" must be emphasized for judgments in damage cases are now quite large. Certainly a judgment of $150,000 in an individual case is not unusual.

Much of this will be handled through the chancery office. However, where this situation does not prevail, the pastor should be very certain that the parish is covered by liability insurance. Furthermore, all injuries should be promptly reported to the insurance carrier and to the parish attorney. Frequently, this will result in the avoidance of litigation or mitigation of damages.

What has been said of the church generally applies also to the school premises. Moreover, since they house a large number of children, very substantial liability insurance should be carried upon the premises. Additionally, the children's parents should be encouraged to take out individual liability insurance for accidents occurring on the playground or on the way to and from school. If the majority of the children have these policies, it will frequently eliminate litigation involving the parish school.

Similar principles apply to lay employees of the parish. Under common law an employee could recover damages for injury on the job only if the injury was occasioned through the negligence of the employer. In all states, this doctrine has been superseded by workmen's compensation statutes, under which an injured workman can recover regardless of negligence. Recovery under workmen's compensation statutes is geared to the actual wage loss of the employee, his medical costs, and in event of death, reasonable compensation for his dependents. Excessive financial awards, possible in general litigation, are not available.

Although churches may be exempt from the application of workmen's compensation statutes in a very few states, the tendency is to make them applicable to all categories of employment. In Iowa, for instance, it was held that a nun teaching in the parochial school could recover from the parish for an injury resulting from falling while at work (*Sister Mary Benedict* vs. *St. Mary's Corporation,* 124 N.W. 2d 548, Supreme Court of Iowa, 1963).

Insurance is available to cover liability under the workman's compensation statute.

SEAL OF CONFESSION

All priests are familiar with their canonical obligation of secrecy on matters revealed in confession. However, the penitent's sin may also constitute a violation of the penal law — homicide, theft, and so on — and the confessor might be interested in knowing to what extent he is legally protected against possible efforts by the state to compel him to testify to such admission of guilt. In at least 33 jurisdictions there are statutes safeguarding the confidentiality of such communications (Alaska, Arizona, Arkansas, California, Colorado, Hawaii, Idaho, Indiana, Iowa, Kansas, Kentucky, Louisiana, Michigan, Minnesota, Missouri, Montana, Nebraska, Nevada, New Jersey, New Mexico, New York, North Dakota, Ohio, Oklahoma, Oregon, South Dakota, Utah, Vermont, Washington, West Virginia, Wisconsin, Wyoming, District of Columbia).

These statutes are designed to apply to clergymen of all denominations. They differ considerably as to phraseology; referring to statements made "in the course of discipline" of the clergyman's church, "in his professional character," or "by one seeking his spiritual advice or consultation." In all cases, the statutory protection is applicable to sacramental confession. In the broader aspect most of them will cover statements made, even if not of a sacramental character, by one seeking spiritual advice or consolation. However, in some states courts have held that the communication "must be made pursuant to a duty enjoined by the rule or practice of that particular church," *Sherman* vs. *State,* 279 S.W. 3535 (Supreme Court of Arkansas, 1926).

The essence of all such statutes is that the communication must be made in confidence and in secret. The known presence of a third party ordinarily abrogates any legal protection. At least one statute, that of the District of Columbia, makes specific mention of marriage counseling, where both spouses may be present. In at least one case, *Cimijotti* vs. *Paulsen,* 219 F. Supp. 621, 230 F. Supp. 39, a Federal District Court construed a privileged communication statute as protecting statements made in a diocesan marriage tribunal, even though in the presence of other persons summoned as corroborating witnesses. Nevertheless, in the absence of specific provision to the contrary in the statute, it should not be assumed that privilege would apply relative to an interview where others than the minister and penitent, or person seeking spiritual assistance, were present.

Another qualification, even in states where there is no requirement relative to a denominational "course of discipline," is that the statement must be made by one seeking spiritual advice or consolation. It does not apply to conversations on other matters.

In the absence of statute, courts have differed in according privileged status to such communications. The courts of New Jersey and New York refused to grant it prior to the enactment of statutes on the subject. In a Mississippi case involving homicide, evidence of incriminating statements by the accused to a clergyman were accepted by the trial court, but this issue was not stressed on appeal (*Barnes* vs. *State,* 23 S. 2d 405, Supreme Court of Mississippi, 1945). The courts of the United States have uniformly refused to require a clergyman to testify as to statements made by one seeking spiritual advice (*Totten* vs. *Administrator,* 92 U.S. 105, 23 L Ed 605 Supreme Court, 186; *Mullen* vs. *United States,* 263 F 2d 275, Court of Appeals, 1958).

The First Amendment of the Constitution of the United States prohibits any official prohibition on the free exercise of religion. While this amendment has never been cited in a case involving the seal of confession, a plausible contention could be urged that legal pressure on a clergyman to reveal confidential communications constituted a prohibition on the free exercise of religion for both clergyman and penitent.

If demand is made on a priest by attorneys, or public authority, relative to communications received in the course of his priestly ministration, he should contact legal counsel to learn his rights at civil law.

ANTE-NUPTIAL PROMISE BEFORE MIXED MARRIAGE

Recently, Pope Paul VI modified the rule requiring the non-Catholic party to execute a promise to rear the children as Catholics as a condition for marriage with a Catholic. According to the new ruling which shifts the burden of rearing the children as Catholics to the Catholic partner in a mixed marriage, a local bishop may decide whether oral or written promises to raise the children as Catholics will be required of the non-Catholic partner. Since some bishops may choose to continue the practice of requiring written promises, it is still useful to consider the extent to which civil courts will enforce such promises.

Efforts looking toward civil enforcement of the promise may have their origin in the breakup of the marriage, or death of one or both of the spouses. American courts in awarding custody of children in divorce or separation proceedings are guided largely by two norms of long standing — one that the welfare of the children is the predominant consideration, and the other that children of tender age should be awarded to the mother, unless her unfitness has been clearly demonstrated. Moreover, it is considered that the spouse receiving an award of custody should have control of the child's education and rearing, which includes religious training.

In a succession of cases, courts of several states have refused to recognize the ante-nuptial promise as justification for taking action contrary to any of the foregoing (*Boerger* vs. *Boerger,* 97 A. 2d 419, New Jersey, 1953; *Dumais* vs. *Dumais,* 122 A. 2d 322, Maine, 1956; *Lynch* vs. *Uhlenhopp,* 78 N.W. 2d 491, Iowa, 1956; *Hackett* vs. *Hackett,* 150 N.E. 2d 431, Ohio, 1958; *Stanton* vs. *Stanton,* 100 S.E. 2d 289, Georgia, 1957; *McLaughlin* vs. *McLaughlin,* 132 A. 2d 420, Connecticut, 1957).

If the Catholic spouse dies, it is highly improbable that a court would compel a surviving, and unwilling, non-Catholic spouse to rear a child as a Catholic. This was most emphatically held by the Missouri courts in *Brewer* vs. *Cary,* 127 S.W. 685 (1910).

Where both spouses are dead, the law is sympathetic to the premise that, "their care and supervision (the children) should be entrusted to persons of the same religious faith as that of the minors or to an institution controlled by persons of their faith, when practicable." The foregoing language is typical of statutes on the subject in a substantial number of States. It will be noted that the general requirement is qualified by the words "when practicable." This proviso appears in all but a very few of these statutes, and under it, if in the court's opinion there are other considerations relative to the child's welfare which strongly suggest different action, the religious test may be disregarded.

It would be impracticable to discuss in detail either of these statutes, or the numerous, and often conflicting, decisions construing them. It must be noted that although the child might have been reared as a Catholic because of the ante-nuptial promise, the promise itself is not considered a vital factor. Where the child is of such a tender age as to have no perception as to religion, the tendency of the courts, in the absence of substantial considerations to the contrary, is to consider that introduction into a religious denomination, by baptism or other prescribed ritual, brings it within the statute. Thus a New York Court of Domestic Relations stated, regarding a child of four, that: "If the child is Jewish, it cannot be deprived of its Jewishness by an exposure to the culture of another religion prior to the age of reason" (*In re Dennis Glavin,* 121 N.Y.S. 2d 12, 1953).

WELFARE

"The poor you have always with you." No one knows this better than the pastor. He should have active lay groups for administration of parish charity, such as the St. Vincent de Paul Society and the Ladies of Charity. However, he must remain the ultimate source of the Church's assistance. Vincentians and Ladies of Charity look to him for leadership, and there are those among the poor and unfortunate who will seek him out in preference to the lay groups.

There was a time when parish funds were adequate to meet all charitable needs. With the mounting cost of living and the increasing complexity of problems presented, this is no longer the case. It is now an absolute necessity to invoke the cooperation of public welfare agencies—local, state and federal. Such contacts are usually the responsibility of the parish charitable organization, and for this reason the value of a lawyer on its membership is apparent. However, the pastor must have at least a general familiarity with these sources of public assistance in view of the leadership required of him in this area. The following is a brief resume of situations where public agencies may be invoked for efficient service to the poor of the parish:

1. Unemployment Compensation

There is a nationwide program of unemployment compensation, administered jointly by the states and federal government and financed through a tax on employers. The amount and duration of benefit payments differs from one state to another, and in all states they are in proportion to earnings during prior employment.

2. Workmen's Compensation

In all states there are statutes under which most employers, particularly those in hazardous industry, are financially responsible for the death or injury of a worker while on the job. Ordinarily, the law requires payment of reasonable medical and surgical costs and continuance of a reduced rate of compensation during disability. In the event of death there is provision for compensation to the widow and minor children. In most states the employer is required to carry insurance to cover his responsibility under this law.

Most employees know about the unemployment and workmen's compensation laws. However, there are some, particularly among the poorly educated, who are unaware of them. Any person applying for parish charity who is entitled to benefits under either of these programs should be required to apply therefore and, if necessary, be assisted in preparing the necessary forms.

3. Public Welfare

Under liberalized public welfare laws in all states, cash grants, food allotments, medical service, and other forms of assistance are furnished to families lacking an income because of the absence or disability of the breadwinner. This might be the case, for instance, where the father is disabled by illness or injury not qualifying for workmen's compensation. It would be financially impossible for the average parish to carry such a family, unassisted, indefinitely on its relief rolls, and any available public assistance benefits must be sought. Coordination with officials of the local public welfare department is often necessary in these situations.

4. Social Security[1]

Under federal social security laws a worker who has been employed in "covered employment" for five years or more is entitled to monthly compensation during total and permanent disability. The amount of such compensation will depend on the extent of his previous earnings and the number of his dependents. It may be greater or less than that available under the local public welfare program. In some instances local welfare agencies will supplement the social security benefit in order to obtain a minimum living standard for the family.

5. Veterans' Benefits

A variety of benefits is available for veterans of the armed services, including particularly, monthly compensation for permanent disability and hospitalization. Eligibility depends on the circumstances of the case, the benefits being more generous and the right thereto more nearly absolute, where the disability is service connected. For nonservice connected disability, a needs test must be met. It should always be ascertained if an applicant for long-range parish assistance is a veteran, and if so, all possibilities for assistance from this source should be exhausted. Widows and minor children of deceased veterans may, in some situations, be entitled to pension.

6. Delinquent Fathers

A frequent and pathetic applicant for parish charity is the mother, married or unmarried, who complains that the father of her children fails to support them. In every state there are statutes under which a delinquent father can be compelled to meet his obligations in this regard, under penalty of imprisonment. The mother should be referred to the public prosecutor with instruction to initiate necessary action. In parishes where there is a heavy incidence of such delinquency, it might be advisable for the pastor, either in person or through his lay assistants, to establish liaison with proper public officials to expedite action on such cases.

---

[1] Other aspects of the Social Security program, not directly connected with welfare, are discussed elsewhere in this chapter.

7. The Federal Anti-Poverty Program

The welfare activities of the pastor are becoming progressively enmeshed with government programs, especially with the anti-poverty legislation. The community action title of this law provides for participation of non-profit agencies. One aspect of it, the Neighborhood Center, is particularly adapted to parish activity. The neighborhood center may concentrate on adult education or Head Start Programs, on the establishment of Credit Unions, the training of volunteers, and many other diverse projects. Vitally important to the success of the Center is the development of a sound relationship with the poor. The pastor is in a unique position to encourage this working relationship, and as a community leader can bring other groups together into coordinated attack on like problems of the poor. This activity can be federal funded, though obviously a great deal of volunteer work is needed for more complete development of the role of the parish in the war on poverty. Reference is made to a pamphlet entitled *Poverty and the Parish,* copies of which may be obtained by writing to the National Catholic Community Service, 1312 Massachusetts Avenue, N.W., Washington, D. C. 20005.

SOCIAL SECURITY

The ability of the pastor to give advice with respect to the welfare of his parishioners today demands at least a general knowledge of that pervasive socio-economic legislation, the Social Security system.

For the next few years, considerable emphasis will be placed upon that aspect of Social Security which relates to Medicare. Briefly, this legislation provides substantial hospitalization and medical care benefits for persons sixty-five years of age or older who are covered by the Social Security or Railroad Retirement systems.

Under the terms of the law, an eligible participant is entitled to 90 days hospitalization for a "spell of illness." The program pays for 60 days of hospital care with a deductible of $40 during a "spell of illness." If a participant is hospitalized for additional days, he must pay $10 daily. From the hospital, the patient may be sent to a nursing home where he is entitled to 20 days of care. If necessary, this care may be extended for an additional 80 days with a payment of $5 a day. Finally, the program will pay for the cost of post-hospital home health care services. Under this program, the government will pay for the cost of 100 visits during the 365 days following the discharge from a hospital or extended care facility.

In addition to institutional care, the legislation provides for a medical insurance program. Any person, whether covered by Social Security or not, may enroll for the medical insurance program by contacting the Social

Security Office and paying the small premium of three dollars a month. The medical insurance program pays 80% of the reasonable cost for services. There is a deductible of $50 in each calendar year. Those who are under Social Security or Railroad Retirement receive a card from the Federal Government. When they sign it they automatically authorize a deduction of $3 a month for medical care benefits. It would be well to encourage participation under this plan. Those who are not under the Social Security or Railroad Retirement System must apply to the local Social Security Office during the three-month period just before reaching the age of 65 or for a three-month period thereafter.

A special provision in the law states that all persons who become 65 on or before December 31, 1967, are entitled to hospitalization, extended care, and home care coverage. They should register with the Social Security Office and secure an appropriate identification number.

The other provisions of this legislation extend to an expanded medical care program for the medically indigent. By 1970, all states must submit to the federal government an improved plan according to which all "medically indigent" persons will be entitled to general hospitalization and medical care. Some states, as a stop gap measure, are already purchasing Medicare insurance for the medically indigent. This program should have a profound effect on the poor people of the parish and undoubtedly the pastor will be called upon to give advice with respect to this program as it unfolds. Critically important is that eligible persons register within the periods specified. This can be determined at local Social Security Offices.

The extension of Medicare benefits under the Social Security Program has again raised the advisability of priests being covered by Social Security. This basically is an issue of policy to be decided by the Ordinary and advice of chancery is the preliminary essential.

At present, the law provides that a clergyman may come under the Social Security law on a self-employed basis. In order to do so, he must file Form 2031 with the local Social Security office. Young clergymen may file for Social Security within two years from the date of their ordination; others must have filed by April, 1966. This currently is the terminal date but it has frequently been extended. At present, the rate of taxation is 5.8% of the self-employed's annual income which is currently $5,600. An additional tax of 0.35% is imposed to cover the cost of Medicare.

In determining income for Social Security purposes, the priest may evaluate his board and lodging. The suggested figure is about $75 per month. Fees, stipends, and the like also constitute income upon which the Social Security tax applies. Currently, the benefits are retirement allowances after the age of 65, disability payments before that age in the event that a priest should become disabled, Medicare benefits outlined above and, finally, burial expenses.

Uninsured diocesan priests and members of religious orders subject to the vow of poverty may secure Voluntary Supplementary Medical Insurance provided they pay a monthly premium of $3 and make appropriate application at the Social Security Office. It is obvious that the benefits to older priests are quite limited. On the other hand, younger priests may reap substantial benefits. One factor should always be considered and that is that the survivors' benefits which are available to the majority of those covered by Social Security are not available to priests unless they have dependent parents.

These, very briefly, are the essentials of the expanding Social Security program which directly or indirectly affects every individual. Another phase which we have not dealt with is the public assistance provisions of the law. Some of these are embodied in the new programs for the care of the medically indigent. Others involved are aid for crippled children and the blind.

ZONING

Zoning legislation and regulations must be considered in determining the nature and extent of parish development. This is especially true in suburban areas.

Despite restrictive language of a zoning ordinance, the courts will not uphold a ban on churches from the entire community (*Mooney* vs. *Orchard Lake*, 53 N.W. 2d 808). Moreover, the prevailing authority prevents an ordinance from excluding churches from a residential community. In the case of *Board of Zoning Appeals of Meridian* vs. *Schultz*, 172 N.E. 2d 39, the Indiana Supreme Court upheld the right to erect a church and school in a residential area. In so holding it observed:

> We judicially know that churches and schools promote the common welfare and the general public interest.

Other courts have refused to exclude churches on the basis that it would amount to a violation of religious liberty. On occasion, the courts have carved out an exception to the general rule where the presence of a church would occasion serious traffic congestion (*Jehovah Witnesses* vs. *Mullen*, 330 P. 2d 5). The opinion on this point is by no means unanimous and the municipality will have to present a very strong case in order to take advantage of this exception.

Similarly, parochial schools may not be excluded from a community or from a residential area if public schools are permitted in the same zone. In the case of the *Roman Catholic Welfare Corp.* vs. *Piedmont*, 289 P. 438, the Supreme Court of California said:

> It is settled law that children may be educated in schools of their parents' choice and that having this basic right no reasonable ground for permitting

public schools to be constructed in Zone A and prohibiting all other schools teaching the same subjects to the same age groups can be suggested.

Other courts have predicated this position on religious liberty. On the other hand, churches and schools must comply with certain reasonable restrictions. Churches are frequently required to provide parking lots and schools must provide playgrounds. In the case of secondary schools, parking lots are frequently required. In a very few States courts have permitted prohibition on nonpublic schools in areas where public schools are permitted. *State* vs. *Sinar,* 65 N.W. 2d 43 (Supreme Court of Wisconsin, 1954). This probably represents a definitely minority viewpoint.

One of the most difficult aspects of zoning involves the erection of a convent to house the sisters teaching at a parochial school. Many communities prevent houses of multiple occupancy in residential zones. The courts now tend to regard the convent and school as a single package and have allowed a variance for the convent to accommodate the building of a school.

Generally speaking, litigation can be avoided if the pastor, the architect, and the attorney consult with the zoning authorities substantially in advance of the building date.

15

The Pastor, the Lay Teacher, and the Catholic School

MOTHER BERNADETTE NEVILLE, O.S.U.

This Sacred Council of the Church earnestly entreats pastors and all the faithful to spare no sacrifice in helping Catholic schools fulfill their function in a continually more perfect way, and especially in caring for the needs of those who are poor in the goods of this world or who are deprived of the assistance and affection of a family or who are strangers to the gift of faith.[1]

FIFTY YEARS AGO CATHOLIC PARENTS WERE REMINDED FROM THE PULPIT of their serious obligation to give their children a Catholic education. Today, they are reminding us of their obligation.

The wonderful work which our priests and religious have been carrying out for many generations in the field of education is recognized as one of the outstanding achievements of the Church in recent times.

In our education-minded age, an increased understanding and appreciation of the value of Catholic education has developed. This happy circumstance, together with the accelerated birth rate and the relatively high birth rate among Catholics, has brought Catholic education at all levels in the United States to face an urgent need for expanded facilities. More schools and classrooms must be provided, and above all, many more teachers. The Catholic education system is faced with a serious problem, a crisis in fact, arising in part, ironically, as a result of its own prosperity.

The rising tide of enrollments, the rapid expansion of our schools, and

---

[1] Vatican Council II, *Decree on Christian Education* (trans. N.C.W.C.), pp. 9–10.

the inadequacy of religious vocations have suddenly made us aware of a vast, untapped reserve of teacher material among the Catholic laity.

There was a time when the lay person teaching in the Catholic school was a rarity. Today the proportion over the entire nation is five religious to three lay people. By 1970, the proportion will be the same; only the personnel will have changed. The projection, including the increase in vocations, is five lay people to three religious.

It should be obvious that the acceptance of laymen on our faculties must be on a partnership basis. We can hardly expect competent laymen to apply for membership on our staffs, or, if they do, to remain for any length of time, if they feel that they are little more than auxiliaries or substitutes, performing such services as the religious teachers are unable at the moment to discharge, and holding their positions precariously — at the whim or pleasure of pastors or school authorities. It is necessary, therefore, that these lay co-workers be thoroughly integrated into our educational system, that they be given sound professional status, and that they be made to feel that there is a future for them in Catholic education at all levels.

William H. Conley spoke frankly about the acceptance problem in our Catholic Schools in an address at the NCEA Convention in 1962 when he said:

> We must not give the false impression that in every situation the Catholic lay teacher has an ideal status in Catholic schools. The layman in some Catholic schools is still looked upon as a paying boarder is looked upon by some families. He is necessary to the welfare of the household, and the family could not get along without him, but he is never accepted as a full member of the family. This condition is inherent in the concept of ownership, responsibility, and control of our schools either by a religious community or by a diocese. In matters of policy formation, and in the government of institutions, the layman has a long way to go before he is an equal partner.[2]

Priests and religious generally feel strongly that the lay teacher's presence on our staff is a much desired and necessary element in the training of our Catholic youth. Allied with this feeling is the conviction that certain phases of our school program are best handled by the lay members of the faculty, provided they have a sound idea of Catholic principles of education.

It is no news to anyone concerned over Catholic life in our country today that the relationship between religious and laymen engaged together in professional work needs clarification. The problems involved in this relationship under modern conditions are becoming increasingly acute, and particularly so, perhaps, in the field of education.

---

[2] W. Conley, "The Lay Teacher in Catholic Education," *The National Catholic Educational Association Bulletin,* 59, August, 1962, pp. 26–27.

A popular assumption governing education used to be that the function of teaching belonged primarily, and some would have said exclusively, to persons with religious vocations. Once this is accepted as a controlling principle, then the only justification for the lay professor is expedience; that is, he is needed only when there is a shortage of religious vocations. Under a scheme which envisages a faculty composed exclusively of religious, the ultimate function of the layman is to become superfluous.

If our approach to lay teachers is such, is it not highly possible that their contribution to our educational program— instead of being the vital, life-giving contribution it could be — will be niggardly and restricted? If we insist on looking on them as unwelcome but unavoidable additions to the staff to be gotten rid of as soon as possible, will they develop the sense of belonging?

We think not. We feel strongly that since we must admit that the future of our Catholic school system depends heavily on the contribution to be made by lay teachers, we must learn to adopt, appreciate, and welcome that Providence-needed contribution.

Our lay teachers must be encouraged to feel that our school is their school; our job, their job; our students, their students; they must be made to feel wanted. Do they?

Oscar Perlmutter recently asked a group of lay professors what they thought of the situation of the layman in Catholic higher education. An experienced, brilliant, deeply dedicated professor responded at once: "Unwanted, unpaid, uncared for, and unpersoned."

Many religious educators may respond to these observations with indignation, and some may even be offended. Lay professors, they will say, are respected, cherished, and even loved.

And it is true. "In fact we always make them feel at home." But the layman is not at home in the *bona fide* sense of the term. He is more like a long-term guest, like the man who wandered in on the family one day, and just stayed on.

The layman does not want to be just like a member of the family. He wants a proprietary interest in his labors justly commensurate with his status; he craves the rights and dignities of a person that one should expect to find in a community of free and equal persons and he is prepared to accept concomitant burdens and obligations.

Though, in the following quotation, Gerald E. Sherry is talking about the lack of a "sense of belonging" among parents in their relationship with the Catholic school, what he says very often applies to our lay teachers:

> Few lay people have the feeling that there is any "sense of belonging" in their relationship with the parochial school. For years and years they have been drilled to believe that their function is to pray and pay and that is the extent of their responsibility. Somewhere along the line there

has been a failure of communication and understanding. Yet one reads constantly in the speeches and writings of our bishops and educators of the great sacrifices of the laity in establishing the Catholic school system. In these same speeches and articles we are also reminded of the necessity of parent-teacher cooperation, and herein lies a major problem. Too many of these parent-teacher groups and home and school associations are nothing more than "tokenism" in relation to the principle of cooperation. Too often the decisions have already been made, be it on enlarging the school, hiring lay teachers, fixing their salaries, deciding on school uniforms, and a host of other items of school life which affect the pocketbook and the social life of families (as well as their spiritual formation).

Very often there is no lack of information about what is going on or what is to be done. The catch is that there is no prior discussion with the people most involved. Most parent-teacher meetings are run very efficiently with the treasurer's report being the most important item. The regulations are nearly always to accommodate the school and the teachers, hardly ever the parents. Who could possibly have any real sense of interest or belonging in such a situation? Yet, without the parents, without their generosity, without their sacrifices, without the innumerable inconveniences which they willingly accept in the interest of parish harmony, where would the Catholic school be? . . .[3]

It should be clearly understood that the present unsatisfactory situation of the layman is not the result of design, deliberate neglect, nor, certainly, of malice. No one intended that the layman should suffer: the layman's part in the educational system was simply not thought through. The story is told of a nineteenth-century British ecclesiastic who said that the layman's role was "to shoot, to hunt, to entertain — nothing more." In an equally famous, though probably apocryphal story, still another prelate proclaimed that there were only two proper positions for the layman — on his knees in prayer, and in his pew to receive instruction. To these, of course, one of his listeners promptly added a third: with his hand in his purse to contribute.

The days when such stories could be told as anything more than jests are past. For decades now the popes have been asking, even begging for greater participation by the laity in the work of the Church.

This can be seen clearly in the fact that the Church asked laymen to express their views on and be observers at the historic Ecumenical Council, and in the fact that one of the most beautiful and inspiring documents issued by the Council is the *Decree on the Lay Apostolate* which in its very introduction states that:

In its desire to intensify the apostolic activity of the People of God the holy Council turns its attention to the Catholic laity whose specific and entirely necessary role in the mission of the Church it has already mentioned in other contexts. For the apostolate of the laity, flowing from their very vocation as Christians, can never be lacking in the Church. The Sacred

[3] G. Sherry, "To Whom Do the Schools Belong?" *The National Catholic Educational Association Bulletin,* 62, August, 1965, pp. 417–418.

Scriptures themselves excellently prove how spontaneous and profitable this activity was in the early days of the Church (cf. Acts 11:19–21; Rom. 16: 1–16; Phil. 4.3).

Our own times demand no less zeal on the part of the laity. In fact, conditions today call for a completely more intense and broader lay apostolate. . . .[4]

It is not primarily because there are not enough priests and religious to take care of the work, nor is it because the needs of the time are so urgent, that the Pope is asking for a lay apostolate. It is because the apostolate is the normal function of the laity. It is their birthright, and the hierarchy are only reminding them of the fact.

The work of the Church has to be done by the clergy — and the religious — and the laity — each in a different way. Christianity is not a case of just receiving the grace of God, the sacraments, and the teaching of the clergy. Christianity is not a passive religion; but is active and dynamic. After having received, the Christian has the obligation and the right to do something.

We received this obligation to be apostles by becoming members of the Church in baptism. This obligation is consecrated in the sacrament of confirmation, in somewhat the same way that a man is consecrated to the priesthood in the sacrament of holy orders. Every Catholic who has received the sacrament of confirmation has been ordained, in a way, to be an apostle. Bishop Blomjous draws this interesting conclusion: When a priest exercises certain aspects of the apostolate, he exercises them, not fundamentally in virtue of his priesthood, but by the fact that he is a confirmed Catholic. Of course, because he is a priest, because he is in a position of authority in the Church, he has to direct the apostolate and to give the example of being a zealous apostle, but he is not an apostle because of his priesthood — but simply because he is a Catholic.

> The Church was founded for this purpose: to make all men partakers in the Saviour's redemption by extending the kingdom of Christ throughout the world for the glory of God the Father, and to direct the whole universe to Christ through the instrumentality of men. As in the structure of the living body no member is merely passive but with its life shares also in the function of the body, so in the body of Christ, which is the Church, the whole body "according to the functioning in due measure of each single part makes bodily growth" (Eph. 4:16). Indeed, so great is the organic unity and so intimate the relation of the members (Eph. 4:16), that the member which does not contribute its due measure to the development of the body must be said to be useful neither to the Church nor to itself.
>
> In the Church there is a diversity of ministry but a oneness of mission. Christ conferred on the Apostles and their successors the duty of teaching, sanctifying, and ruling in His name and power. But the laity, made sharers in the priestly, prophetic, and royal office of Christ, discharge their own roles in the mission of the whole People of God in the Church and in the

---

[4] Vatican Council II, *Decree on the Lay Apostolate* (trans. N.C.W.C.), pp. 1–2.

world. They exercise the apostolate in fact by their work for the evangelization and sanctification of men and the penetrating and perfecting of the temporal order through the spirit of the Gospel, so that their activity in this order openly bears witness to Christ and promotes the salvation of men. Since this is a characteristic of their state of life, to live in the midst of the secular business of the world they are called by God to exercise their apostolate in the world like a leaven, with the ardor of the spirit of Christ.[5]

The work of the lay teacher in the Catholic school is a real collaboration in the apostolate of the Church. The lay person shares in the teaching office of the Church itself, which delegates this authority to religious and lay persons alike when these are specially trained to aid the clergy in carrying out the teaching mission of the Church in the schools.

The function of the lay teacher in the Catholic school is basically an apostolic function. The heart of the lay teacher's work in the Catholic school, like the heart of the religious work there, is a work of sanctification — and without sanctification education is vanity for everyone.

The need of the Catholic school is not just for the lay teacher per se, but for the lay teacher who is an apostle. It is only through an acceptance of his vocation in its full meaning as apostolate that the lay teacher will ever be able to fulfill his special function in the Catholic school. Until the lay teacher's "job" is seen as purposeful activity in the Mystical Body of Christ, the lay teacher's work in the Catholic school remains largely meaningless. It should be pointed out that our realization that Catholic laymen can help us solve the impending teacher shortage, along with a growing conviction that there is a definite, permanent place for the lay teacher in the educational apostolate, represents neither a rationalization nor a sharp reversal of policy. Already a quarter of a century ago, Pope Pius XI declared that it filled his soul "with consolation and gratitude toward the Divine goodness to see, side by side with religious men and women engaged in teaching, such a large number of excellent lay teachers."

When the religious and the lay teacher alike value their own respective contributions for what they really are, then many of the tensions that now hamper and frustrate teaching in Catholic schools will be dissolved. The special contribution of religious, as such, to the work of education, their special "witness to the modern world of the mystery of Christ," is an invaluable element in the total Christian formation of young people. And it will become clear also that the special contribution of a lay teacher as a layman, that his "involvement" as a Christian layman in the life and work of the world and the experience he gains thereby, is also a necessary element in the Christian formation of youth. We will develop just this one aspect of the lay teacher's contribution.

Since he will be molding the ideas, ideals, and values of his students, his

[5] *Ibid.*, pp. 3–4.

own character must be firmly rooted in the teachings of Christ. He must
not only know his religion; he must live it. He must not only talk good
example; he must be a good example. Actually, a Christian lay teacher can
have a tremendous influence on the young. Our students expect religious
to be good examples, to exhort to virtue, to condemn vice. When they see
laymen and laywomen giving equally good example, being equally enthusiastic about virtue and hostile to vice, they are even more deeply impressed.

There is ever present in the Catholic school the danger that the student
may come to identify religion exclusively with the habit — and everything
beyond a mediocre degree of piety exclusively with the "religious." This is
the actual situation which every lay teacher uncovers for himself sooner
or later, and is precisely the one which the lay teacher is providentially
ordained to change.

Catholic education must put more emphasis on the positive attitude
toward the world, for it seems that we need to get back to the idea that the
world is good, that God loves it even though we do not seem to. We need to
emphasize that the Christian has a proper and genuine interest in the
world's prosperity, has a duty to help solve the world's problems.

Perhaps it sounds paradoxical to say that the problem of the world is
not that men love the world too much, but that they do not love it
enough.

It is for the Catholic educator to establish in the minds of the next generation that the world and the peace of the world are worth their time and
effort and loving care, for precisely the same reason that the next world is
— because it is God's world.

Perhaps the challenge is to raise up a generation that will not despise
the world with its problems, but love it for what it is, and at the same time
relate the truths of this world to the truths of the next in their own person.

Because the lay teacher knows at first hand the problems a practicing
Catholic must face, the temptations he will meet and must overcome, the
difficulties of living a moral, upright life in a world where moral principles
are considered out-dated — when indeed they are considered at all — the
lay teacher can come into the classroom and relate his subject matter to
today's problems and offer Catholic solutions to problems he has had to
work out in his own experience. He can prove by his own example that it
is possible to be a good Christian in the second half of the twentieth
century.

Until the student is inspired by the example of the integrated lay
Christian, he will not even begin to understand what the ideal Christian life
in the world is.

Until he sees what he must BE, he will not BE it.

Until he sees what he must DO, he will not DO it.

The Christian ideal in lay life will not be "caught" by any amount of abstract depiction, or even of ardent exhortation. For this there is needed a flesh and blood embodiment, a veritable incarnation of this ideal, an inspiration that is at once constant, close, tangible, and above all, true to facts.

The lay teacher and the lay teacher alone is put in a providential position to provide this particular example and inspiration. The respective positions which the lay teacher and the religious occupy in the Catholic schools are not mutually exclusive, but mutually necessary. The religious can no more fill the essential role of the lay teacher than the lay teacher can fill the essential role of the vowed religious.

The Council Fathers, in the *Decree on the Lay Apostolate,* certainly confirm and strengthen this position when they say that:

> As sharers in the role of Christ as Priest, Prophet, and King, the laity have an active role to play in the life and activity of the Church. Their activity is so necessary within the Church communities that without it the very apostolate of their shepherds is often unable to achieve its full effectiveness. Truly apostolic-minded laymen like the men and women who helped Paul in spreading the Gospel (cf. Acts 18:18, 26; Rom. 16:3) supply what is lacking to their brethren and refresh both the spirit of their shepherds and of the rest of the faithful (cf. 1 Cor. 16:17–18). Strengthened by active participation in the liturgical life of their community, they eagerly play their role in the apostolic works of that community. They bring to the Church people who perhaps are far removed from it, earnestly cooperate in presenting the word of God especially by means of catechetical instruction, and by offering their skill make the care of souls and the administration of the temporalities of the Church more effective.
>
> The parish offers a clear example of the apostolate on the community level. It brings together many kinds of people within its boundaries and merges them into the universality of the Church. The laity should accustom themselves to working in the parish in union with their priests, bringing to the Church community their own and the world's problems as well as questions concerning human salvation, for study and solution by concerted effort. As far as possible the laity ought to provide helpful collaboration for every apostolic and missionary undertaking sponsored by their ecclesiastical family.[6]

Furthermore, the words of the Council Fathers to teachers in the *Decree on Christian Education* apply as much to our lay teachers as they do to priests and religious, when they say:

> But let teachers recognize that the Catholic school depends upon them almost entirely for the accomplishment of its goals and programs (27). They should therefore be very carefully prepared so that both in secular and religious knowledge they are equipped with suitable qualifications and also with a pedagogical skill that is in keeping with the findings of the contemporary world. Intimately linked in charity to one another and to their students and endowed with an apostolic spirit, may teachers by their

---

[6] *Ibid.,* pp. 13–14.

life as much as by their instruction bear witness to Christ the unique Teacher. Let them work as partners with parents and together with them in every phase of education give due consideration to the difference of sex and the proper ends Divine Providence assigns to each sex in the family and in society. Let them do all they can to stimulate their students to act for themselves and even after graduation to continue to assist them with advice, friendship and by establishing special associations imbued with the true spirit of the Church. The work of these teachers, this Sacred Synod declares, is in the real sense of the word an apostolate most suited to and necessary for our times and at once a true service offered to society.[7]

Are we using this situation which is all in the Providence of God? Are we developing to the fullest the tremendous potential latent in the rich field of our Catholic schools, where perhaps, not just five personal talents are wasting, but rather 500 talents of dedicated, intelligent, educated, zealous lay and religious teachers? The unanimity which bears fruit consists not so much in being together in one place, or belonging to a group with a label, says Sertillanges, but rather that each one should labor with the feeling that others also are laboring, that each one in his place should concentrate on his work while others also are concentrating; so that *one task* be accomplished, that *one principle of life and activity be its guiding spirit: and that the parts be put together by God.* We don't have to go looking for Catholic Action activities; in a sense we have only to accept the natural solidarities springing from our surroundings, our works in the schools. The highest form of love consists simply in being part and parcel of a given human situation, in sharing loyally the same destiny as others. Hasseveldt says that the great temptation consists in escaping from such situations, in looking for alibis. We must be part, and not apart, and so imitate the Incarnation of the Son of God who made himself one with all human existence, including the consequences of our sins and death. But it is precisely this example of Christ that invites us to a part in the Christian way.

Up to this point, among other things, we have considered two problems which confront the lay teacher in our Catholic schools. The first of these was the problem of acceptance or what some would call the problem of partial segregation, and the second is the problem that derives from the fact that so often the layman — parent and teacher — has little to say about what goes on in our schools. However, there are other problems, perhaps equally serious, with which the pastor should be acquainted. Let us briefly consider these before bringing this chapter to a close.

The first of these concerns the problem of advancement in positions of leadership in the Catholic school system. If we are to attract qualified, interested laymen to our schools, they must be given opportunities for advancement to supervisory and administrative positions. Such advancement

---

[7] Vatican Council II, *Decree on Christian Education,* pp. 8–9.

is necessary if there is to be a career for the lay teacher in the Catholic School, for as William H. Conley observes, "Restricting these positions to the clergy or to a member of the religious community leads to the attitude that there is no future for the talented layman in the system."[8]

Another problem which pastors and school authorities must face is the salary problem. Though there has been considerable improvement in this area in recent years, much more remains to be done. Many teachers, but especially men teachers who have families to support, who would otherwise prefer to remain in the system are forced to accept employment elsewhere because of the salary problem.

Furthermore, few Catholic schools provide adequate fringe benefits. To many lay teachers such fringe benefits as health and surgical insurance, free tuition for their children, and the total payment of annuities are at least as desirable as an equivalent raise in salary.

Finally, the burden of heavy class loads is another question which pastors and school administrations must consider. Too frequently, the teaching loads which all teachers — religious and lay — are expected to bear all but rule out the possibility of intellectual growth and personal development. As a result, many teachers cannot acquire or maintain the professional standing which is expected of them, and which would qualify them to participate in policymaking and long-term planning which is so essential to the layman who seeks a career in our Catholic schools.

Perhaps there is no more fitting conclusion to this chapter than to quote the closing paragraphs of William H. Conley's paper, for he surely puts things in their proper perspective when he says that:

> Our Catholic schools have grown to their present state of excellence and their scope because of the dedicated service of priests, brothers, and sisters for more than a century. The foresight and the concern of the bishops and the sacrifice of the laity have made possible American Catholic education. In the recent past there has been a rapid expansion of a new force in these schools — the Catholic lay teacher. More than fifty years ago, a French bishop stated, "Everywhere there is discussion of the delicate question of coordinating the two apostleships, ours hierarchical, yours lay."
>
> Understanding within our schools by the clergy and religious of the laity and understanding by the laity of the clergy and religious, must be brought about. To do so requires a positive effort on the part of each group, and of the two groups together, to gain this understanding. Each has an important role to play in building and perfecting the Mystical Body through education. Recognition that each is a part of the Mystical Body, and that together they have a common mission, is the starting point for the mutual understanding which will effect the unity that is necessary and permit our schools to reach even greater heights. Together they should communicate knowledge, develop understandings, and stimulate motivation which will result in the total development of their students, and will help to produce the conditions in which Divine Grace will effect a return to Christian unity.[9]

---

[8] W. Conley, *op. cit.*, p. 29.   [9] *Ibid.*, p. 30.

16

The Priest and
Parish Organizations of Men

DANIEL J. KANE — MARTIN H. WORK

WE LIVE IN SUCH A PERIOD OF CHANGE IN THE CHURCH THAT PERHAPS IT should be stated at the outset of this chapter that what was written in late 1965 may be increasingly out of date as the months and years of Post-Council History and experience pass by.

From the late thirty's through the post-World War II period to Vatican II, much was written and spoken about Catholic Action and the work of the layman in the Church. The "new" ideas of those years prepared many priests and laymen to experiment with new forms of apostolic action. Alongside the more traditional general membership Catholic societies for men, there began to appear groups more specialized as to membership, programs, and objectives. The efforts of these latter groups to pioneer in new techniques of apostolic work disturbed the *status quo* in certain places and, as might be imagined, caused frictions to develop with the "old line" societies. But in time these aspects were overshadowed by the growing realization that the Church in the United States had to make a "break-through" in the matter of lay leadership which was sorely needed in many areas of crucial concern to both Church and nation. Accordingly, we could no longer afford hit and miss methods of lay leadership training; we could no longer afford asking men to respond to minor needs of a parochial nature; we could no longer afford the use of weak or outmoded lay organizations to meet contemporary challenges. The decree of Vatican II on the Apostolate of the Laity sums this situation up tersely; "We also waste our resources when we keep in existence organizations and ways of doing things which are obsolete" (Ch. IV., Par. 19). What is today's pastor to do? Should he hold on to the old parish men's organizations and try to revive them? Should he "throw out" the old and bring in some new organizations or movement? Should he think in terms of a single parish organization in which both men *and* women can function? Across his desk in the rectory come the mailings of many lay groups and organizations with claims for their programs — to which should he respond? In this matter, a pastor's "lot" is not "an easy one" either!

Perhaps one way to begin working at a solution would be for the pastor to consider the "why" for change in his parish men's society so that he will be acting on a firm understanding of the problem. One of the main reasons for change is that the times have changed and the needs of the layman of today are different from say, those of the layman of 1925 or 1930 or 1940 when the old-line men's societies were in a more flourishing condition.

Thirty or forty years ago the parish men's society was a haven for the Catholic man where he could meet and socialize with his fellow Catholics, where he could be told by his pastor what the pastor wanted done in the parish, where he could feel a certain strength in being a Catholic in a land where the Church was a minority group. Monthly corporate communion deepened this sense of solidarity, and in many localities, the solidarity was given public witness in the annual men's parade or rally.

The men who constituted these societies were for the most part working men with relatively little education beyond grade or high school. They were the men who were raising the families which in a generation or two were to make of the American Church a congregation of over forty million persons. They were the men whose financial contributions were helping to build the churches, schools, hospitals, and seminaries for the growing spiritual and educational needs of the Church here. They were the men whose contribution to the American Church must never be forgotten.

Today there is a new generation of Catholic men in our parishes, more educated than their fathers, less dependent on the social strengths of an all-Catholic organization, more desirous of functioning as laymen in areas of concern to the Church and society. This generation of Catholic men can sustain a more mature, a more responsible clergy-lay relationship and wants to give witness to its faith not only in the parish but in the community as well. And this generation of men comes of "apostolic age" when the Church herself is desirous of its contribution, when the Church looks to renewed, strengthened parish life as well as to new, vital, and fruitful contacts with the modern world — and in both actions has great need of the layman. In the new era upon which the Church is entering, it is reasonable to conclude that the old forms of organization for men will not be totally adequate.

There is yet another question for the pastor to consider in this matter and it is of more delicate nature than seeing the differences between the parish men's societies of 1925 and today. This is the matter of the pastor's understanding of the layman in the Church, his competence, his sacramental dignity, his part in the Apostolate. In truth it can be said that in the past, for many pastors, the layman was seen as one to be directed, to be used, to be consulted rarely, if at all, and then usually on matters of temporal or financial concern. This situation can be documented historically and now is of such general knowledge that it does not require further comment. That there were historical as well as social and cultural reasons for such a clerical attitude cannot be denied. There was some deliberate discrimination against the layman but most of the clerical attitude toward the layman was more benign, more an acceptance of a *status quo* which no one questioned, least of all the layman. Living in the midst of such an atmosphere it almost seemed the "natural, Catholic" way of clergy-lay relations. Today, in historical retrospect and in the welcome light of Vatican II, we can see how much lay participation in the life of the Church was never sought or, if called on, was of a minimal nature.

Though we are witnessing a new, more positive, more mature clergy-lay relationship, traces of the old remain. Pastors still find it difficult to see the layman in a new light, to believe that he should be consulted on matters of importance in parochial life, and can be trusted with serious responsibility, that he, too, cares for the Church and desires to give full witness to his concern for her — and, often it is equally difficult for the layman to see himself in this light.

The pastor will find in his parish increasing numbers of men who are college graduates and who possess professional competences different from his own. Quite often these laymen are also well read in Catholic matters, abreast with current literature on social thought, Scripture, ecumenism, liturgy, and theology as well as on local, national, and international matters of politics, economics, and the like. These men, in whose ranks the pastor is likely to find his parish leaders, will not respond to the "old approaches." They expect a certain recognition of the gifts they have to offer — and desire to offer — to the parish societies. They will respond to the invitation to parochial activity when they see it couched in terms of collaboration and, as we shall note later, of collaboration in meaningful programs of important consequence to the life of the parish.

A third point for the pastor to consider relates to the area of spiritual formation in the men's organization. The experience of most men who belong to the traditional type of parish society is that "religion" is kept to a minimum in the business of the day. In part this was (and is still in many societies) due to the prevailing American theories that "religion is a private affair" and that men shy away from "religion" in their activities outside of church itself. Most of us, priest and layman, grew up in such an atmosphere and even when we recognized it wasn't a healthy atmosphere we were uncertain how to change it for the better.

One hesitates to state the following lest it seem too idealistic, but experience today in many parts of the country points to the appearance of increasing numbers of men who desire mature, positive spiritual formation and who welcome participation in parish programs on scripture, catechetics, liturgy and family life. These men, however, want a spirituality that has a contemporary expression which reflects the spirit of the decrees of the Vatican Council. Furthermore, such laymen desire a spiritual formation which will assist them in their professional and work life as well as in their family life, in their community life as well as in their parish life. Helping the men of his parish organizations to receive such spiritual formation is one of the most exacting and rewarding challenges confronting the parish priest today . . . and the major responsibility that is his in the development of the lay apostolate.

One more point of a general nature before we consider the possible specifics of parish men's organizations in this new age of Vatican II. In the past, most men's organizations saw their purposes fulfilled in a monthly meeting consisting for the most part of "a business section," "the program," and "the social." If there was some consistent form to it, "the program" consisted of a series of isolated topics usually treated by "guest speakers" at each monthly meeting. "Religious" themes were mixed with programs of a non-religious nature, the latter being scheduled so "we don't drive the men away with too much religion." Many priests succumbed to this rationalization and supported it while privately wishing the situation were otherwise.

Today such a concept of "programs" for parish men's societies is outmoded, unsuited to the needs of the Church and unable to enlist the time, talents, and energies of the laymen the priest ought to be seeking for apostolic work in the parish. Men today want study and discussion material concerning the many serious problems faced by themselves, their families, their parish and their community and nation. Men want to hear speakers at parish meetings who can help further their religious education, who help form their consciences on the complex social problems of our society, speakers who give them insights into programs which call for *participation* and *action,* programs which are meaningful to their lives as modern men. At such meetings the men also desire the opportunity to discuss matters with their priests not in the old, "now Father is going to explain it and tell you what to do" attitude, but in the new type of exchange which can take place when priest and layman talk together as people of God, each with definite responsibilities in the Church. Today, parish meetings should increasingly result in meaningful dialogue between priest and layman, both bringing their particular competences to bear on common concerns.

With these preliminary but important observations in mind we may now consider the wide area of types of organizations possible in parish life.

The "old" idea of just one parish society for men and one for women seems to be giving way to variety in parish organizations but variety based on actual parish needs. Together priest and laymen can survey the parish to discover what societies it possesses and how they are achieving their goals, and what must be done to modernize their purposes and functions. Unfulfilled needs in such areas as adult religious education, catechetics, liturgy, family life, social action, ecumenism and the parish school may call for the establishment of new groups in the parish. Possibly these may begin with just a few men or women who share important areas of Catholic life and who receive the "green light" from the pastor to go ahead and explore the area for parish action. Possibly they may begin in a more highly organized manner when priest and laymen decide to call on a national organization for help in setting up a unit of the national group in the parish.

National Catholic organizations, movements, and federations have much to offer the parish society especially in the professional competence of their national office staffs. Today while we desire and seek true "grass-roots" action on a parish level, we know that the parish society does not always have the necessary expertise in its membership nor the facilities for in-depth studies of areas of action that are found in national offices.

In recent years the consideration by parish societies of study-action programs in such complex but vitally important areas as civil rights, federal aid to Church related schools, Church-state relations, international relations, has significantly been aided by materials prepared by staff members of such groups as the National Council of Catholic Men, which for some years has been reprograming and reorganizing for the new lay apostolate. From such national offices as The Liturgical Conference, the Christian Family Movement, the National Catholic Conference for Inter-racial Justice, the Confraternity of Christian Doctrine, the National Catholic Rural Life Conference, the National Council of Catholic Women, have come similar program materials which the parish society, of itself, could rarely supply. Possessing authoritative documentation, study guides, and the like, the parish society adapts such material to its particular needs.

The national office staffs, of course, deal with more than program materials on weighty issues of the day. These offices also are ready to serve many other needs of the parish society, such as formation and leadership training, organizational techniques, and the like. The pastor who is burdened with many other responsibilities will find great assistance in the wise use of the knowledge and experience of national offices such as the National Council of Catholic Men. Too often too many priests and laymen try to "go it alone" and lose valuable time, for instance, in attempting to work out their own program ideas and secure program materials.

The use of national program material, however, is meant to aid and supplement "grass-roots" action in the parish and diocese. Such parish action is more than ever called for as we enter the time of renewal in the Church following Vatican II. The Church desires to see this renewal effective in the parish. In the parish the people of God gather to worship and to be formed spiritually. In the parish, the people of God serve one another's spiritual and corporal needs. In the parish the people of God are spiritually energized for their life in "the city of man" and for their cooperation in the pursuit of the common good of the community. In the spirit of this new vision of the parish, of the "living parish," the parish men's society has both internal and external responsibilities. In another age the society may have limited itself to its internal life but the challenges of today thrust the society's membership into vigorous concern for the external areas of neighborhood, city, nation and world. Lacking this external concern the parish men's society of today does not truly reflect the spirit of the modern age of renewal in the Church.

Earlier we wrote that the priest must embrace the work of positive spiritual formation of the men in the parish society. From the priest also, principally must come an interpretation of the renewal taking place in the Church in liturgy, catechetics, scripture, ecumenism, education, and other areas. This presupposes not only knowledge of Vatican II and its documents but the communication of such knowledge by the priest to the laymen. If such communication did not take place regularly during the progress of the Vatican Council sessions (and many laymen state they heard relatively little of Vatican II in sermons or at parish meetings), it must now be seen as a prime pastoral responsibility. The scope and depth of the various decrees of the Council do not make for easy discussion, but it is incumbent on priests to grapple with the material and having absorbed it and made it a part of their thinking, to give it to their laymen. The entire parish must be caught up in the spirit of renewal and a good beginning will be made if parish priests stir the hearts and minds of the men of their parish societies with the vision of the Church and the work of the Church in the world which is found in the documents of Vatican II.

The size of the parish, its age, its physical and spiritual needs, the educational and professional background of the parishioners, its location in the community and its relations with that community, all will determine the purpose and functions of its parish societies. A creative attack on the organizational problem should result in a healthy diversity of operation. If the parish has and desires to retain one of the old-line mass membership societies such as the Holy Name Society, it should be modernized, its spiritual goals restated for contemporary needs (e.g. monthly Communion might now become weekly, and when possible, daily Communion) and its program shorn of attachments that have been added "down through the years." Let other groups or committees run festivals, bingos, "sports nights," smokers et al! Within the mass-membership society of the parish (that organization to which *all* men can belong), careful planning can result in special study-action committees which will introduce the members to the areas of particular concern to the Church and the community which we mentioned earlier. The programs of the Holy Name Society then become a type of adult education for the men, bringing them into contact with new ideas abroad in the Church, helping them to form their consciences on complex social problems such as race, poverty, housing, peace, and assisting them to relate to the neighborhood and community where they are called today to give meaningful witness to Christ. Such emphases in a modernized program for a mass-membership parish society will greatly aid in raising the apostolic level of the entire parish.

As was mentioned in nearly all parishes there are men today who want and need to go beyond participation in the mass-membership society. These are men who possess a similarity of interest, education, work, or professional life and who are ready to commit themselves to a deeper participation in the life of the Church. These men will be ready for the invitation from the priest to come together in small groups or committees to work on specialized areas of parish life. From these men can come members for a parish school board, teachers in the catechetics program for children and adults, parish representatives to such local social action groups as those on race, housing, poverty, the aged, participants in ecumenical study groups, or men to help train other laymen for apostolic work in the parish. These are the men the priest ought to motivate with great care and loving concern for they can become a spiritual force of inestimable value in the parish.

In recent times considerable evidence has pointed to the desire of men and women to work more closely together in apostolic programs. For many, this desire is best fulfilled in participation in a couples' movement or organization (Christian Family Movement, Cana, Mr. and Mrs. Groups, etc.) and for others it means at least close cooperation of their particular men's and women's organizations. In the case of the latter situation, periodic meetings of officers of both organizations can be held. At such time plans of cooperative action can be agreed upon. Both approaches are possible in most parishes.

In addition to the types of lay organizations we are discussing in this article, many parishes contain units of the Legion of Mary, the Sodality, P.T.A., St. Vincent de Paul, etc. Given the busy pastoral life of our day, the pastor is hard-pressed to keep in touch with each group and its activities. The development of what are known as Parish Coordinating Councils is a boon for pastors in this situation. Generally speaking, the coordinating Council consists of the presidents of *all* parish organizations who meet regularly with the pastor to report to him on their particular activities and in turn to receive from him requests for assistance on parish matters. The pastor is the head of the coordinating Council and through the Council is able to get the advice and suggestions of key parish lay leaders on current parish developments, needs, and problems, and is able also to keep abreast of the activities of the various parish societies represented on the coordinating Council. Through one meeting with the heads of such societies the pastor can reach larger numbers of parishioners and this channel of communication can be of great assistance to him in maintaining and strengthening parish unity.

Another form of the Parish Coordinating Council includes the participation not only of the heads of lay organizations but the assistant priests, the principal of the parish school, youth leaders, choirmaster, etc.; but most importantly of these, laymen who do not "belong" to the organized life of the parish but find their apostolic commitment in the life of the civic community. It is also possible to have as two constituent elements of this coordinating Council a Parish Council of Men and a Parish Council of Women. This breakdown is especially helpful where existing lay organizations for men and women are inadequate or non-existent. Here every facet of parish life is represented and a full dialogue is possible and, as a result, a more total involvement in the life of the parish. Of particular gain here is the opportunity for priest, religious and layman and laywoman to meet and discuss common problems and together to work at solutions. At this stage of American Catholic history we cannot have too much of such dialogue for by it greater unity can be achieved for the Church and deeper respect can develop both for the Church and for the respective witness that priest, religious, and lay person give to Christ.

The formation of a Parish Coordinating Council does not mean the amalgamation of all societies and groups into one large organization. Each group retains its autonomy. Each group continues to pursue its goals. Hopefully, however, the coordinating Council will benefit all groups because of their closer ties with one another and with the pastor. Cooperation in programs will also make for more effective use of manpower in the parish and bring about greater participation in the total mission of the parish.

In the case of the coordinating Council as in that of the men's organizations we discussed, new leadership is required from the priest. The growth of the Church in the United States was marked by the openness of the clergy, especially of the parish priests, to the tasks of the day. Today a new openness is called for — an openness to change, to change in the Church, in the spirit of the Vatican Council. This means openness to new ideas, to new directions in thought and action, to the exploration of new pastoral methods, to new relationships within and without the parish. The evidence of this openness in the lives of priests will be the major factor in leading more laymen to a commitment to apostolic work in the parish and the community at large. The revivification of older forms of parish lay groups and the development of new ones needed to meet contemporary problems can best be built under the leadership of a new "team" — of priest and layman, who have opened themselves to the Spirit who is renewing the Church of our time.

17

The Priest and His Relationship to Lay Organizations of Women

MISS MARGARET MEALEY

ANY CONSIDERATION TODAY OF THE RELATIONSHIP OF THE PASTORAL ministry and the lay ministry, at the parish level, is contingent upon an understanding of the apostolate of the laity as defined by Vatican Council II, notably in the *de Ecclesia* Constitution and *The Decree on the Apostolate of the Laity.*

The Pastoral Council, as its founder Pope John XXIII called it, was convoked in October, 1962, to help the hierarchy to become better shepherds of their flocks. With a threefold theme and strategy — reform, renewal, and reunion — this *aggiornamento,* as it came popularly to be known, set out to reaffirm the spiritual mission of the Church. Where the laity is concerned, it resulted in revolutionary new concepts and a redefinition of our missionary vocation.

How this came about deserves our study. Whenever the dialogue of the Council Fathers centered around the achievement of their foremost desire, to make the contemporary world aware of the resplendent light and joy that is Christ, it became apparent that any such aspiration would have to be premised on an intensified and broadened role for the laity. The much-spoken-of bridge to the twentieth century, the much-needed dialogue with the world, the tenacious efforts to achieve peace, would have to be, the Fathers realized, the work of the laity. By the beginning of the second session, change was inevitable.

In opening the second session in September, 1963, Pope Paul stressed this need in advocating a four point discussion: self knowledge of the Church; its reform; the bringing together of all Christians in unity; and communication with the world. Advocating the need for self-awareness in the Church, Pope Paul told the Council to honor tradition by stripping the Church of what was superfluous, unworthy, or defective. The Church was a mystery, he continued, a reality imbued with the divine presence and, for that reason, susceptible of deeper investigation. The principal concern of the Fathers should be to examine the intimate nature of the Church and to express in human language a definition that would best reveal the Church's fundamental constitution and, moreover, manifest its manifold mission of salvation.[1]

With these directives, the Ecumenical Council began its lines of consideration that were to produce new perspectives for the lay ministry. As the Council Fathers undertook the first step of analysis of the Church itself, a new role, an added dimension for the laity began to appear. As the bishops reexamined their traditional roles, a shaft of light penetrated the darkness of centuries; the fundamental concept of the Church as a pyramid of power was seen to be archaic. The four hundred-year-old concept of a structure with the pope at the top, the clergy in the center, and the laity at the base, was seen to be outdated. Here, in the second session, came the long-awaited and long-needed breakthrough. Here, for the first time in Conciliar history, the laity was to be acknowledged as a positive force. Here, once again, as in the beginning, the Church was conceived of as living concentric circles around its center and head, Jesus Christ, with all members held to him by the sacrament of the episcopacy in which all priests share.[2]

Enlightened by this new vision, the Council inaugurated a policy change, a change from the structure of vertical authority to the structure of horizontal authority. As a result, no longer would ordination constitute the recipient as an expert in all areas. With the breakthrough a redefinition of the Church became necessary. The Church, said the Council, is the People of God. The People of God is composed of the pope, the bishops, the priests, and the laity. In *De Ecclesia* it is stated thus: "The People of God . . . is used by Him [Christ] as an instrument of redemption for all, and is sent forth into the world as the light of the world and the salt of the earth."[3]

Thus it can be seen that a new and basic theology of the laity emerged from the Ecumenical Council. Let us consider it as it is set forth in *De*

---

[1] Pope Paul VI to Second Vatican Council, 2nd session, September 29, 1963.

[2] "The People of God," address of the Most Rev. Stephen A. Leven, Aux. to the Archbishop of San Antonio. *Proceedings* of the 32nd national convention, National Council of Catholic Women, November 11–14, 1964, Washington, D. C.

[3] *De Ecclesia,* Chap. III, paragraph 9.

Ecclesia, in order that we may better comprehend the relationship between the laywomen and the priests. Any study of this relationship must be posited on this new theology. All people, the Council Fathers declare, are called to worship God, to do his will, and to carry his order into the world. The laity, too, says the document, are called to salvation-bringing, to apostolic life, to participation in the universal priesthood and liturgy, to the testimony of Christ, and they, if the Holy Spirit wills, share in all charisms, except those which demand orders or jurisdiction and with these they are invited to cooperate.[4]

Moreover, the Fathers say they are well aware that they themselves were not consecrated by Christ to take on themselves alone the whole of the Church's mission of salvation to the world. Therefore, the laity have the duty to make their opinions known in matters concerning the welfare of the Church. Pastors are instructed to recognize and uphold the dignity of the laity and to respect their responsibility in the Church; to employ the laity's prudent advice, and trustingly assign to them duties in the service of the Church, allowing them initiative and freedom for their tasks.[5]

Since its establishment in 1920, the National Council of Catholic Women (which together with the National Council of Catholic Men forms the Department of Lay Organizations) of the National Catholic Welfare Conference, has worked unceasingly to assist the Church in its spiritual mission. Today, it is a federation of approximately 14,000 national, state, and local organizations, representing 10 million Catholic women. With over forty years of experience in working to promote and further Christian life in this nation, NCCW has experienced unfailing assistance and benefits from the spirit of fatherly love so generously bestowed on us by our parish priests and the moderators of our local organizations. We well realize that many of our wishes, aspirations, and desires could never have become reality without the priests' guidance and support.

What, then, does *De Ecclesia* imply in the way of a new relationship for the women and priests working together in the parish and on other levels? What does it mean to us? It is a challenge to us, a challenge in that we are now expected to offer to the priests and bishops even greater assistance, new ideas, and new approaches. We are looking forward to our enlarged role with enthusiasm and a great sense of responsibility, and already we have embarked upon broader and deeper courses of action, knowing that the Council encourages our newly-expanded freedom to which, they say, "everyone in the earthly city is entitled."[6]

What do we foresee from the innovations? With the Council encouragement of initiative, the consolidation of lay-clerical strength, we can

---

[4] *Ibid.,* Chap. IV, paragraphs 30, 33, and 34.
[5] *Ibid.,* Chap. IV, paragraphs 30 and 37.
[6] *The Decree of the Apostolate of the Laity,* Chap. III.

predict a more permeating spirit of good will, a greater sense of lay responsibility, and outstanding achievements. The Council Fathers believe, and so do all women's organizations, that the experience of the laity will help the pastors to make more appropriate judgments in both spiritual and temporal matters thereby making more effective the whole collection of human activities.

At what level will this alliance be most successfully implemented? From our experience, we believe that it will be at the basic unit in Church operations, the parish level, and at the basic unit in the temporal world, the community. At these levels the layman can most successfully exert his beneficial influence in initiating the new basic theology of the laity. The parish can become a base, a fortress, from which the women can help intensify their spiritual and temporal contributions. Women want to be wholeheartedly involved with Christ's flock and his vine. The combined strength of illuminating leadership of our own women and of the priests — that is, the living Christ, Christ the head and his members — will bring hope, instill courage, and sanctify his field, the Church.

Women, through the now-opened windows of the Church, can look out upon all categories of humanity with particular solicitude — the needy, the afflicted, the sick, the ignorant, and the forgotten. Where is our Christian horizon, our perspective? *The Decree on the Apostolate of the Laity* lists as fields of the apostolate the following: church communities, the family, youth, the social environment, the nation, and the international community. Here is Vatican Council's answer to our question.

How can our parish priest help us to bring the light of Christ to all men as the *Decree* proposes? The answer is by giving fatherly counsel and support to our work. This counseling and support are needed in four areas: personal sanctification; understanding of the mission of Christ and his Church; spiritual and temporal programs; and, in some cases, the operation of priestly functions.

First, as individuals, we realize that for all of us, especially for the responsible and devoted Catholic woman, there is a primary task; the task of personal purification and personal apostolate. It is here, more than any other, that we look to the priest for guidance. Every woman of this generation, if she is to overcome the world's contagion, must sanctify herself. There is no substitute in the lay apostolate for the personal warmth and magnetism that glow from a soul that is intimate with God.[7] It is in this endeavor of ours — personal sanctification — that we need the help of the priest, lest we forget in our eagerness to assist others, what we are about, why we are here.

---

[7] "The Catholic Laywoman and the Apostolate of Our Time," address of Rt. Rev. Msgr. John Tracy Ellis to National Council of Catholic Women, 31st National Convention, Detroit, Michigan, November 6, 1962.

The individual apostolate must manifest Christ living in those who believe in him. All of us in our time, in the time of the Council, are a testimony of him. By our lives, by our words, by our teachings, we all announce Christ. The individual apostolate can flow generously, but it flows from only one source, one fountain — a truly Christian life. We can give only from the fountain of life that we ourselves have. Therefore we turn to the priests to help us apply within our own lives the image of Christ. Out of our own self-awareness will follow a fruitful renewal, and a flourishing reunion with our brothers and sisters in Christ. Our dialogue with others may even, on occasions, be a quiet one, yet does not the saint preach sermons merely by his presence?

We see the second area of pastoral ministry as that of helping the lay woman develop a sense of the universal mission of Christ and his Church. We need our horizons broadened — always. The priest can help us understand the theology of the laity, the directives of the Ecumenical Council, the social teachings of the Church. He can help protect us from doctrinal errors or imprudent action; he can help inspire enthusiasm for the new liturgy, Scripture reading and studies, and so on. And common worship services will be, in the future, something he can interpret to us. He can even, on occasions, redirect our goals and suggest new ones. In summary, how indispensable is a priest in his canonical mission to preach the Gospel! In this sphere, his authority is dominant.

Before considering the third area, that of spiritual-temporal activity, let us return to *De Ecclesia* for a guideline. According to the document, our apostolate is not only doing what we are told to do by the hierarchial authority, but our apostolate is doing what the Church needs, according to the gifts the Holy Spirit has given us.[8] And we understand, further, that we will have to answer, each one individually, for not carrying out that apostolate as we can. What a ministry this is! What a vast and enormous enterprise confronts us!

What is the role of the clergy in our spiritual-temporal activities? In considering ways and means in our undertakings here, we do expect the advice of the clergy. Yet, as all laymen know, Vatican Council II has assigned to us the solution of the problems. The burden is ours! We welcome it! In this most practical sphere, the Council says that the priest serves us in a subordinate capacity. The day of the imposition of an edict on non-approved lay activities has passed. Mutual cooperation has replaced opposition, as was unfortunately the case on a few occasions.

In this third area, the Council has given to the Catholic laywoman what all women want in any field of endeavor — the right to give — to give a life of love and sacrifice to the Church, to the family, to the individual, to the whole of humanity, to Christ in every being. And it is to the priests

[8] *De Ecclesia, op. cit.,* Chap. IV, paragraph 37.

that we look for a partnership in our plans of giving. In doing God's work here, we have no wish to take away, nor even to diminish in the slightest, priestly responsibility, priestly talents, priestly authority. What we want, as mature, capable adults, is to lead. And if Catholic lay leaders are going to develop, priests must let them lead. Nothing stifles leadership or initiative more than having to get the stamp of clerical approval on every project, or having to wait until the pastor decides the harvest is ready. We dread repression, for we see its fruit as a docile, submissive, ineffective laity; and its harvest as a barren parish life. Therefore, our belief is that a good moderator, a good priest, is one who is a guide and counselor, one who praises our initiative and encourages our plans.

With a responsibility all her own, today's laywoman needs to engage in activities that are intellectually stimulating, naturally attractive, and truly apostolic. The priest and the future priest, the seminarian, would do well to prepare themselves for their counseling role, then, by understanding the psychology of women, the psychology of leaders, and group dynamics. Thus a more effective counseling dialogue could take place. Mutual understanding would result in the rewards of high accomplishments, and the fulfillment that comes from successful work.

Priests and laity today both know that magnificent accomplishments for God and country can be attained only by leaders, not followers. And the clergy of today know, too, that if they allow the lay leaders to test their new apostolate, the result will be a genuine, flourishing, and vigorous type of Catholic operation, particularly in those parishes where the priest himself has a rapport with twentieth-century Catholicism.

What other factors enter into a good priest-laymen relationship? Great prudence on the part of both the laity and the clergy in selecting personnel leaders; open-mindedness; willingness to listen; understanding of human nature and of the psychology of the sexes; recognition of leadership characteristics; knowledge of parish economy; and an understanding of modern life. These elements will ensure the proper reception of ideas and constructive thoughts and will result in better personal relationships.

With a qualified personnel base, the work of renewal and reunion will succeed immensely. The complementary roles of the priest and the laywoman will bear fruit in an effective dialogue with each other and with our Christian brothers and sisters. Women's moral stake in human society can be expressed and expressed well — particularly in the areas of Christian example, education, racial equality, unemployment, poverty, world-wide starvation, physical and mental retardation, and in assisting displaced or forgotten persons, children in particular. These are the challenges of our century.

The Council Fathers have assigned us a special activity; that of sharing in the priestly office. Why is this? Because, as the document states, in the

Church there is a diversity of ministry, through a singleness of mission. Christ conferred on the Apostles and their successors the duty of teaching, sanctifying and governing. But the first two of these, evangelization and sanctification, belong also to the laity because they derive these rights and duties from their union with Christ.

> Incorporated into Christ's Mystical Body through Baptism and strengthened by the power of the Holy Spirit through Confirmation, they are assigned to the apostolate by the Lord Himself. They are consecrated into the royal priesthood not only that they offer, through all their activities, spiritual sacrifices in everything they do but that they may offer witness to Christ through the world.

The *Decree* more explicitly states that renewal in the temporal order is the special obligation of the laity.[9]

The document also states,

> that the hierarchy is to entrust to the laity certain functions which are more closely connected with pastoral duties, such as the teaching of Christian doctrine, certain liturgical actions, and the care of souls. However, the laity are fully subject to higher ecclesiastical control in the performance of this particular work.[10]

In some areas there is a very urgent need for this individual apostolate, particularly where the liberty of the Church is seriously restricted (or probably also, due to the lack of priests, almost nonexistent). The laity are to do, then, what they can to take the place of priests, training others in a religious way of life and a Catholic way of thinking, leading them to the sacraments frequently, especially to Eucharistic devotion.[11]

It would seem at first reading that here is meant the Communist-controlled countries or the no-priest areas of Latin America or Asia; yet we know that in many parts of the United States, particularly the South and the Southwest, priests are few and, therefore, many are Catholic only in name. They have known the grace of baptism and perhaps confirmation, but little of Catholic doctrine and, owing to conditions, only an occasional Mass. We feel that the Decree applies here also.

Evidently, then, the ministry of the laity is not only the witness of one's way of life, but the taking of whatever opportunities there are to announce Christ by words, addressed either to nonbelievers with a view to leading them to faith, or to the faithful with a view to instructing, strengthening, and encouraging them to a more fervent life. The words of the Apostle should echo in all hearts, "Woe to me if I do not preach the Gospel" (1 Co 9:16).

In conclusion, both documents show that the lay ministry admits of

---

[9] *Decree, op. cit.,* paragraphs 2 and 3.

[10] *Decree, ibid.,* Chap. V, paragraph 24.

[11] *Ibid.,* Chap. IV, paragraph 17.

different types of relationships with the pastoral ministry. In spiritual affairs, the laity are to be fully subject to ecclesiastical authority, but in the temporal, "there are many apostolic undertakings which are established by the free choice of the laity and regulated by their prudent judgement . . . [and] therefore they are . . . praised and recommended by the hierarchy."[12]

There is a great variety of associations in the lay apostolate, but what we have said here applies to all. Some associations are concerned with the broad apostolic purpose of the Church; others aim to evangelize and sanctify in a special way. Some purpose to infuse a Christian spirit into the temporal order; others bear witness to Christ in a special way through works of mercy and charity.

Yet for all, the apostolic dynamism of any organization depends on its conformity with the goals of the Church as well as on the Christian witness and evangelical spirit of every member and of the whole association. This is why the individual priest, pastor, or women's organization moderator, is of such great importance. His contributions can be inestimable, and he himself is indispensable.

Let us again stress, and it can never be too often, that what made the Council such a success was open lines of communication. Dialogue is the best way to avoid a disintegration in human relations.

Also, let us finally say, that we believe one of the most important directives of the Decree was that

> special care should be taken to select priests who are capable of promoting particular forms of the apostolate of the laity [and] who are properly trained. . . . They should promote proper relations between the laity and the hierarchy . . . they should devote themselves . . . to an apostolic attitude in the Catholic societies entrusted to them; they should contribute their wise counsel . . . and promote the undertakings of the laity.[13]

---

[12] *Ibid.*, Chap. V, paragraph 24.
[13] *Ibid.*, Chap. V, paragraph 25.

18

The Challenge of Working With Youth

PHILOMENA K. KERWIN

"Catholic Youth . . . You are a source of spiritual and moral energy; you possess Christian and human values which can make of you strong, generous, free men from whom society has nothing to fear but everything to hope for" (Pope Paul VI — in a message sent to the National Catholic Youth Organization Federation Convention in Chicago, November, 1965).

No greater challenge can come to those engaged in pastoral life than that of working with youth. This calls for the foundation stone of stability in a climate of constant change. The often repeated *aggiornamento* of Pope John as it reechoed in the halls of the Ecumenical Council placed a new emphasis on the importance of youth in the Church today. Cardinal Joseph Cardijn of Rome, founder and Chaplain General of the United Christian Workers and one of the world's greatest leaders of youth, said at one of the concluding sessions: "The youth of today are not the same as they were in the past. They cannot remake the world by themselves and they need the help of the Church."

Spiritual leaders recognize that the foundation of a happy and fruitful life is set in the souls of men during the formative years of childhood and young adulthood. What they will be in life usually depends upon the training they have received not only from their parents and teachers but also from those who plan their leisure time activities and their "off-duty" hours. The molding of the future of youth is important *individually* as every priest realizes because of the preciousness of their immortal souls *and collectively* because the youth of today will be the leaders of the Church of tomorrow. In their hands will be placed the greatest of all treasures — the Faith, and to them will be given the twofold command — to preserve the Faith and to teach it to "all nations."

The distinguishing mark of a good program for youth should be that it brings them to the center of their lives — the parish — and provides a setting whereby spiritual values permeate all their activities. Spiritual life for youth begins with the parish but other phases of their life can be developed from this source as well.

Vibrant and active parish programs for youth do not just happen. They are the result of concentrated and well-thought-out planning. It is not possible to blend into a smooth pattern of operation a group of youngsters who are pulling in all directions at the same time. This is achieved only if there is proper motivation for specific programs and suitable planning. No matter how great the program appears to be which comes from a diocesan or national level it is up to the youth in a parish group to put it into operation. A youth program lives or dies on the parish level. This is the acid test.

The most effective program for parish youth group is that developed by the National Catholic Youth Organization Federation. Established as an integral part of the Youth Department of the National Catholic Welfare Conference it bears the approval of the Administrative Board of the Bishops of the United States. The NCYO Federation is composed of two sections, the Teenage and the Young Adult Sections, and develops program suggestions for each. It is made up of affiiliated diocesan youth councils which reflect the pattern of parish youth councils.

In the light of the Ecumenical Council the National Catholic Youth Organization has reevaluated its goals with the *Constitution on the Church* serving as a basis. In pinpointing these goals, Monsignor Frederick J. Stevenson, the Director of the Youth Department of the National Catholic Welfare Conference, said

> The Catholic Youth Apostolate is a participation in the salvific mission of the Church itself. It seeks to make youth aware that in virtue of the very gift bestowed upon him he is at the same time a witness and living instrument of the mission of the Church itself. There are certain things which pertain in a special way to young people in their leisure hours namely "all their works, prayers and apostolic endeavors, their family life, their daily occupations, their physical and mental relaxation" . . . all these become spiritual sacrifices acceptable to God through Jesus Christ. Thus, the immediate goal of the CYO apostolate is the consecration to God of the leisure hours of youth and the sanctification of youth through a well balanced leisure time program. The CYO apostolate seeks also the development of all youth's potentialities, especially the qualities of leadership by which "they may work for the sanctification of the world from within as a leaven."

The priest who is in charge of the parish youth group will find it a variety of assignments. As Moderator of the youth group his parish work will take on a new dimension. His role as spiritual director of these young folks will keep him alert to the needs and problems which are peculiarly theirs. He will be considered an encyclopedia of information on all matters pertaining to the Church. He will be regarded as an authority on the morality of the latest dance craze and on the classification of the movie in the neighborhood theater. He will be questioned about the latest in paper backs and asked for his opinions on the current best sellers list. He will be expected to know all the social customs and to be alert to the changing pattern in etiquette. The Moderator who takes time to listen when the young folks feel like discussing their problems will become their confidant and friend. In this latter role he could well be rendering his greatest service.

The moderator will receive his greatest assistance from the parish youth council and the senior volunteers who serve as adult advisors. A parish youth council forms the ideal background for the efficient functioning of a parish youth group. This is made up of four officers, namely the president, vice president, secretary, and treasurer. If the youth group is in the process of being organized it is advisable for the moderator to appoint the officers and chairmen to serve on a temporary basis. However, in due course of time, elections should be held for these offices with all the membership participating. The chairmen of the various program activities should be appointed by the Moderator. Adult advisors should be selected also from among the parishioners to assist in all the activities of the CYO unit. The number and quality of adult volunteers can spell success or failure in an undertaking of this kind.

Monthly meetings of the officers, chairmen, and adult advisors should be held with the priest-moderator to plan the program and to discuss future events. Through this parish council the youth of the parish assume responsibility for arranging and carrying out their own program while having the benefit of the guidance of the moderator and the assistance of the adult volunteers. Planning and conducting their own program is important in teaching youth to assume responsibility and in training them to become leaders.

Youth as a group is endowed with more virtues than faults. The secret of success in working with them is to find the key to each one and to treat him as an individual. Recognize in each one his individuality and work with him as a person and not as part of the crowd. Each one of them will rise to this challenge and respond in kind. The ideals of youth can easily become confused and frequently they develop a mixed sense of values. They stand squarely at the crossroads of sharply dividing paths — the right way or the wrong way. The duty of those who endeavor to help them to choose the right way will not be an easy one.

The primary objective is to get all the young people involved in some phase of the program. No matter how good the activities look in print, unless the program appeals to them, unless they participate, it is all lost motion. All programs need to be translated into action. This is where leadership comes in. The officers and chairmen should take the lead in starting the activities and assist in promoting them. Other members should be asked to take over the lead from time to time in different events to insure greater participation and to divide the responsibilities. The life of any program is measured by the interest of the youth for whom it is planned and the extent of their participation.

The objectives of the CYO organization determine the content of the program and the parish resources provide its local adoption. The size of the parish and of its teen-age population is frequently a determining factor in the program makeup. Obviously what is successful in a large city parish may not work in a small parish or rural community. Originality and ingenuity are the indispensable attributes of a good program for youth, but flexibility is its hallmark. Allowances must be made for a happy medium in program changes to meet the changing needs and interests of the young people it serves.

Parish youth programs can be divided into four phases, namely, spiritual, cultural, social, and physical. A well rounded parish program for youth should contain all these and be planned so as to highlight a special one from time to time during the course of the year. It is wise to plan for the year instead of on a seasonal basis.

SPIRITUAL PROGRAMS

The spiritual program would include a retreat either on a weekend or during the week, a day or an evening recollection, special communion day, communion breakfast, religious vocation day, prayer vigil, observance of the special days of the year on which indulgences are granted to the CYO members, particular days of prayer, Advent and Lenten programs, discussion groups or study clubs featuring the new liturgy, talks on the role of teenagers in the Church of renewal and reform, and the usual parish activities.

Strange as it may seem, the spiritual program in a youth group sometimes has rough going. It does not always receive the same enthusiastic response as the other programs do. The secret is to keep it simple but attractive. Keep it short but alive. Have it reflect joy. Teach the youth that religion means happiness and that the joy of serving God is beyond all comprehension. Let it not have any association with gloom and melancholy attitudes. The spiritual program should have a soundness about it and should demonstrate that religion is good common sense. Consult the group as to what they are interested in and let them help in the selection of activities. Stress the importance of getting involved. Emphasize that spirituality can flourish in everyday life and that all activities can become a prayer. Try to find the factors that make a particular program unsuccessful and eliminate them if possible. Have the courage to drop an unsuccessful event temporarily but try it again at another opportune time.

CULTURAL PROGRAMS

The performing arts take priority in any cultural program. Art and music appreciation programs, creative dramatics, one act play contests, concerts, little theatre groups, summer theatre programs, oratorical contests, historical tours, visits to state capitals, poetry contests, arts and crafts classes, hobby groups are but some of the many activities that can be included in this program.

A survey of the resources of the parish and of the community will help to decide what types of cultural programs to undertake and the reaction of the youth themselves will determine the advisability of continuance or repeat performances. After the decision has been made as to the nature of the programs request the help of the best authority available on that particular subject in the community in putting it on. Star performers in any activity generally like to be associated with youth work, if they are not called upon too often.

SOCIAL PROGRAM

The social program can be the most popular and best attended phase of the entire CYO operation. It can also become routine and monotonous. It calls for detailed planning and constant alertness with special attention being given to features such as holidays, season events, and community customs. Leading the list of items in this group are dances, parties, social mixers, picnics, hayrides, boating and sailing parties; all of which take on the added significance of the particular day or time of the year on which they are held. Community customs often set the pace for social programs in many areas.

Social events can also present the greatest number of problems. Who gets in and who must be kept out, the dating and dress, smoking and drinking problems must be faced squarely in the beginning and regulations and controls established as safeguards. Every social event must be carefully planned and all problems must be anticipated. The method for solving each one should be worked out in advance. Social events are the balance-wheel in any parish program as they can make or break it. To achieve a happy medium in keeping them well attended and conducted properly is not easy. The priest who is the Moderator will need the help of well experienced adults, especially the parents, as well as the wholehearted cooperation of the officers and chairmen to keep these events running smoothly. A brief evaluation meeting after each event with those involved in running it helps in avoiding future mistakes.

Adequate supervision at all parish affairs for youth is a must and should be carefully planned for. Requests for special assistance at these affairs could be channeled through the existing parish societies. The best results are obtained when there is a regularly organized group of volunteers from among the parents for this purpose. This establishes a continuity in senior volunteers, helps them to get to know the teenagers in attendance and to be continually alert to the problems that may arise.

PHYSICAL PROGRAMS

This is by far the easiest and often the best attended phase of the program. It includes all kinds of sports activities, such as basketball games, baseball, softball, football, volley ball, soccer, hockey, swimming meets, track meets, table tennis, badminton, and other team games. It inspires competition and develops rivalry. It can be used to emphasize the importance of the rules of fair play and of consideration for others. Fostering the will to win is fine but fairness and justice must always be the traveling companions.

Other activities in this category include hikes, camping expeditions, skiing, toboganing, bowling, roller skating, ice skating, and sledding. There could be other activities which would be peculiar to special areas which would take precedence because of local customs and popularity.

The physical program for any parish group offers a good opportunity to participate in the President's Physical Fitness Program. Excellent material on this program can be obtained from the President's Committee on Physical Fitness in Washington, D. C.

Community Service

Any program for today's youth should include some activities devoted to community service. The admonition "To love thy neighbor" never had more opportunities for fulfillment than in the present era. Today our neighbors are everywhere. They live in the ghettos of poverty, in the slums of our neighborhoods, in the streets of racially torn towns and in the hospitals and institutions of all communities. They are the underprivileged children who practically live in our streets; the boys and girls in the orphanages who too frequently are remembered only at Christmas, and our senior citizens in homes for the aged who often enough are not remembered at all.

Most teenagers do not want to spend most of the day in church but they will not object to giving most of their day to a worthy cause. Early in life they must learn the lesson of giving and the truth that the most precious gift which they have to give is the gift of themselves. Some of the community projects should include service to the sick, the dying, the handicapped, the old, and the very young. Planning a party for crippled children, presenting a musical program geared to the youngsters at an orphanage, taking the men from the home for the aged to a baseball game, reading to the blind and writing letters for them, teaching catechism to mentally retarded children; these are services which teenagers will perform eagerly and successfully.

Doing regular volunteer duty at a veterans' hospital or community hospital, sponsoring a party for the underprivileged youngsters in the parish, taking flowers to the ladies in the home for the aged, giving birthday-card showers to the patients at a mental hospital, teaching arts and crafts to the youngsters in needy neighborhoods, sponsoring bicycle safety campaigns for young riders and teaching them the rules of the road, participating in safe driving campaigns for teenagers are but a few of the community projects which youth groups can consider. One that will certainly attract their interest and gain momentum as it progresses is collecting and repairing toys for needy children at Christmas time. In all of their projects the young folk are learning the valuable lessons of unselfishness and charity while they carry out the role of the Church in their own application of the works of mercy.

The world needs good neighbors and the time to acquire the qualities of neighborliness is in the younger years. The parable of the Good Samaritan will never have more interest for youth than when they are practicing that role themselves to the needy people around them. Every parish and community has persons who are in need, and every parish has youth who will respond to that need if it is properly presented to them.

Adult Advisors

Since the Moderator is unable to devote as much time to the youth program as he may desire, it is essential for him to enlist the aid of interested and capable adults. These people serve as advisors working with the young people and provide guidance and supervision at meetings, special events, and program activities. Because of the importance of these responsibilities the advisors should be carefully selected and thoroughly trained for their duties. A staff of well trained volunteer workers can insure a continuing youth program in the event that the moderator has to become involved in other duties.

Qualified volunteers willing to serve as adult advisors can often be found among members of the congregation, especially among those already active in parish societies. Personal contact is probably the most effective procedure in recruiting them. A person is more inclined to accept an appointment when he is personally asked by the moderator. This method also provides the opportunity for a personal conference with the selectee wherein the program objectives and job responsibilities can be presented in detail and questions concerning his duties and responsibilities answered.

If the personal approach is not feasible, the moderator might make a general request in person at meetings of parish societies and clubs. Announcements from the pulpit should be the last resort as this indirect approach involves the task of getting professional joiners who may not have the interest or the ability which this job requires. It also uses up valuable time in interviewing the undesirable.

1. Qualifications

An Adult Advisor should:
a. Be a practicing Catholic so that he may serve as an example to youth.
b. Have emotional stability and a reasonable level of intelligence.
c. Have a sympathetic understanding of youth and a knowledge of the factors which affect their development as lay apostles.
e. Have, or be willing to acquire a thorough knowledge of the CYO program and its application to his particular parish.
f. Know the potential of the parish resources and those of the community in regard to youth work.

2. Duties

An Adult Advisor should:
a. Assume responsibility for a special phase of the program.
b. Offer suggestions to youth but not commands.
c. Exercise control with his group — not *over* it.
d. Be prepared to stimulate, encourage, praise or prod, as the occasion warrants, and supervise when necessary.
e. Develop leadership in his group.
f. Interpret the youth program to other adults and other organizations.

3. Training

A thorough training course can transform a group of volunteers into an effective, coordinated team of adult advisors. Material for a training course for adults who will work with teenagers can be obtained from the National Office of the National CYO Federation in Washington, D. C. It has been developed on the basis of the following four topics:

1. The Modern Adolescent.
2. The CYO — What is it?
3. An Adult Advisor and the CYO.
4. The Four Part Balanced Program of the CYO.

Parish youth programs can benefit greatly if they are in a diocese affiliated with the National Catholic Youth Organization Federation in Washington. There is a wealth of program resources and materials which can be channeled to them from the National Headquarters through their diocesan offices. Among the special programs offered to affiliated dioceses or parish groups is participation in the following:

1. The National Oratorical Contest

This contest is conducted to enable young Catholics to develop skills in speaking publicly on Church-related topics. Contest regulations are based upon the standards of the National Catholic Forensic League. Entrants compete in one of two divisions: (1) Teenage, or (2) Young Adults. Tuition scholarships to leading Catholic colleges are awarded to the winners. Contestants are entered through their diocesan CYO office.

2. Outstanding Catholic Youth of the Year

The purpose of this selection is to spotlight active young Catholics who are contributing their time and talents to the betterment of their Church, community, and country by active participation in the lay apostolate. One is selected for the Teenage group and one for the Young Adult group for each calendar year.

3. National Catholic Youth Week

National Catholic Youth Week is celebrated annually from the Feast of Christ the King, the last Sunday in October, until the following Sunday. Its purpose is to focus attention on the accomplishments of youth in modern society. This project is sponsored by the National Council of Catholic Youth and has as its permanent aims:

1. To foster frequent reception of the sacraments and more intense prayer among Catholic youth.
2. To reveal modern Catholic youth's depth of spirituality.
3. To encourage youth by making them aware of their opportunity for good.
4. To emphasize youth's potential by demonstrating their willingness to assume responsibility by a display of their talents, abilities, and resources.

4. Catholic Youth Week Kit

The Catholic Youth Week Kit contains individual items for use during this particular week. It includes such items as: posters, fact sheets, prayer cards, a sermon and editorial, newspaper mats and reproduction proof of the Youth Week poster, and other promotional material. Publicity campaign aids are also available. These include: TV slides and Youth Week messages from famous personalities which are adaptable for local use on radio and television.

5. Communion Crusade

The Communion Crusade has had enthusiastic response from Catholic youth. This Crusade begins during Youth Week and moves from parish to parish. Its purpose is to increase religious vocations in every diocese of the country. The Crusade is usually concluded on the first Sunday in May.

Youth Adoration Day

Youth Adoration Day is held on the first Sunday in May. All Catholic youth of the United States are invited to receive Holy Communion and to spend a part of the day in private adoration before the Blessed Sacrament. To encourage the latter it is recommended that the Blessed Sacrament be exposed after the last Mass in the morning until late afternoon. This day concludes with Benediction or a youth Holy Hour. Fact sheets explaining the observance of this day, posters, and prayer cards may be obtained from the National Office.

6. Youth Government Day

The municipal officials of a locality relinquish their offices on this day to certain elected and appointed CYO members who assume authority for the day. The purpose of this special day is to encourage civic officials to reflect upon their moral and civic responsibility, and to display confidence in the ability and character of youth by entrusting them with the direction of the local government for a day.

Youth Government Day is not scheduled at the national level because local circumstances may prohibit observance of the event on a specific date. Most communities conduct this observance during March or April.

7. Youth Leaders' Course

This course is designed to develop young Catholic leaders as active lay apostles. The youth who are selected for the course discuss their responsibilities as leaders in promoting apostolic action and as Catholics in living their faith on a daily basis. They study concepts dealing with the lay apostolate, the qualities and duties of leaders, and evaluate programs for youth. These courses can be conducted during a weekend or on a weekly basis.

8. Workshops

Several workshops are available for Moderators, adult advisors, and officers and chairmen. These include:

1. One-day workshops are conducted for parish youth moderators by diocesan youth directors. The parish plan of organization is discussed and techniques and programs are evaluated.

2. Workshops of several evenings a week are held for adult advisors on their responsibilities. This is in addition to the initial training course for them.

3. Weekend workshops on programs and procedures are suggested for the officers and chairmen. These are periodic ways of revitalizing the program and of bringing those responsible for carrying it out up to date. The workshop can be a shot-in-the-arm, as it were, for the entire program as it affords a good opportunity to do some often needed face lifting.

Affiliation with the National CYO Federation gives parish youth groups an opportunity to participate in the organized apostolate of the Bishops of the United States. It gives official status to delegates at diocesan and national Conventions and unifies the work of youth in the field of the apostolate.

HELPS WITH PROBLEMS

Young people have problems whether there are programs for them or not. Good planning and foresight regarding their activities help to eliminate some of these problems, and the anticipation of them is often an aid in their solution. In any activity the usual factors which can spell difficulty and trouble for those conducting the affairs and which can be disastrous to the youth involved will always be present. These are the signs of our times — drinking, improper dress, steady dating, unbecoming conduct, and the presence of the uninvited.

Some ways in which these problems may be solved are:

1. Develop a set of ground rules regarding conduct, dress, drinking, and attendance, and adhere to them.
2. Organize a committee of youth to help enforce these rules.
3. Keep the parents advised as to the schedule of events for youth.
4. Publicize the activities in the parish bulletin.
5. Have the adult advisors present at all social events.
6. Insure proper supervision by having extra senior volunteers to serve as hosts and hostesses.
7. Keep the local police advised of the social events as an added precaution in case of gate crashers.
8. Appeal to the youth themselves concerning the importance of proper conduct at all times.
9. Find the troublemakers and give them extra chores during the event.

10. Give special attention and time to those continually causing trouble.
11. Show your appreciation for the good behavior and attendance of all at these affairs.
12. Emphasize the positive by stressing the do's and not always stressing the don'ts.
13. Be flexible in your planning and do not hesitate to make changes that will improve the program.
14. Take youth into your confidence in planning and in discussing problems.
15. Accept their suggestions and give them credit for their ideas and opinions when they are right.

The youth of today are growing up in difficult times. They have never lived in a more confused and chaotic age than the present one. It is not easy for them to live peacefully in an unpeaceful world. These times are filled with uncertainty, and the tension of the older generation is often reflected in their young lives. Patience, kindness, and understanding should be the order of the day in dealing with them.

Leaders of youth are entrusted with a great responsibility. They need to develop an optimistic attitude toward the vast potential of teenagers. Remembering what is *right* with them instead of stressing what is wrong with them helps to develop a positive attitude in working with them. The objective of fashioning the image of Christ in the youth whom they guide is worth all the blood and sweat and tears expended in the total effort. Youth's happiness and salvation and also the hope of our society for peace and progress lie in conformity to Christ.

Youth needs to be taught the qualities of leadership for this is their role in tomorrow's world. A parish program which shows them the values of prudence, justice, purity, and charity, and which makes them want to translate these values into actuality in their own life is an excellent program, indeed. Youth wants to be shown the difference between right and wrong despite their frequent outward protests to the contrary. A dance where the rules of good conduct are adhered to will eventually be the popular one and the coach who insists upon fair play at all times will be the one they will respect.

THE APOSTOLATE OF YOUTH

The sacrament of baptism commits Catholic youth to the apostolate by making them citizens and missionaries of the Church. The sacrament of confirmation obliges them to the apostolate and henceforth they are to consider the cause of the Church as their own. It is their task to bring something supernatural into the lives of their associates; to be an influence for good. This apostolate is something personal, exercised by each one in its own natural medium of daily life. Since members of each social group become apostles in their own sphere, the commission of youth is to those of their own group — youth to youth. The field of action of this apostolate is wherever youth are found — in classroom, shop, or office; at a party, dance, or game. This apostolate could be exercised by individual youths, but through the medium of parish youth CYO programs they are organized with other apostles. In this way more can be accomplished by the united efforts of several than by the isolated efforts of the individual.

Our youth received special mention in the decree of the Ecumenical Council on the Apostolate of the Laity which Pope Paul VI solemnly promulgated at one of the concluding sessions. In this *Magna Carta* for the future activity of laymen this decree acknowledges the role that young people can and should have in the lay apostolate, for it states that "they should become the first to carry on the apostolate directly with other young persons concentrating their apostolic efforts within their own circle according to the needs of the social environment in which they live."

Serving youth is a mission unto itself, for, with the proper understanding and guidance they will become tomorrow's stalwart citizens. With the past experience of the Church as its prologue the program of renewal begins with youth. The fresh air of change was meant in a special way for them.

19

The Parish Mission to Non-Catholics

Joseph V. Gallagher, C.S.P.

THE APOSTOLATE WE CALL "CONVERT WORK" BELONGS TO THE PARISH AS a major part of its mission. The Church of Christ lives in parishes and she lives among people who for the most part do not consciously belong to her. This basic fact alone is a providential sign that a large part of the Church's mission must be to those who are outside her visible boundaries. The Lord's charge to his Church is to "make disciples of all nations" and today in the United States these "nations" live in our parishes. If the Church is ever to reach them, she will have to do so, at least in part, through the parish.

Outside the so-called "mission countries," this sign has not always been read aright, but Vatican II has given new stress to the missionary responsibility of all Catholics, and this should awaken in American Catholics renewed interest and zeal in the evangelization of their fellow countrymen.

Like everything else in the Church that is now under scrutiny, the non-Catholic apostolate must be seen as part of a total picture of the renewed Church. This means that, like the whole Church, the whole parish must somehow be involved in this work. It means, also, that the former philosophy and practices of "convert work" must undergo the test of the Gospel. It means that new perspectives — ecumenical, liturgical, and scriptural — must enter into this mission and be reflected in its programs and spirit. And finally, it means that as with so many other activities of the Church during this time of transition, mistakes and ragged edges will occur and must be accepted as the Spirit breathes new life into the dry bones of parish structures in order to raise up new forms of life and mission for his Church.

BEYOND THE INQUIRY CLASS

Until quite recently any discussion of "convert work" would probably center on techniques for organizing an inquiry class and instructing those who came to it. Today, such a discussion scarcely begins to address itself to the subject, and I do not propose to approach it in these terms. Such a framework was previously acceptable because the inquiry class used to be the main tool of the non-Catholic apostolate. Non-Catholics were circularized by mail, phone, or doorbell, and those who showed interest were politely invited to attend a class that would reveal to them without cost or obligation the things that Catholics believe. A lot of factors have been at work causing this simple procedure to become outmoded. For one thing, the number of converts has been decreasing even though the population has been increasing. For another, the ecumenical movement has raised serious questions over the propriety of indiscriminate recruiting. For a third, the parish itself has been undergoing a change in self-understanding and mission. And finally, catechetics has advanced to the point where we have begun to appreciate that mere instruction in religion is not enough. A Christian must be formed in the process as well as informed, and so elements other than instruction in doctrine and morals are now accepted as a necessary part of "convert work." We see now that Scripture, liturgy, and the witness of Christians must also be brought to bear upon the inquirer and when this is carried out in practice the inquiry class becomes only one element of a larger whole.

It is now generally recognized that the introduction, instruction, and preparation of an inquirer for baptism is a very complex task which involves every major aspect of the Church. For that reason, there can be no such thing as a "handbook" for this apostolate, i.e., a book that will tell the pastor how to establish and execute a successful convert program step by step. Anyone who is looking for this kind of guidance will not find it here. However, there are certain truths that history and scholarship have brought home to us about religious education and the life of the Church and it is the congruence of these with the Church's missionary effort to the non-Catholic that seems to promise the most realistic approach to the subject. This, at any rate, is the approach that I am going to take. We will be speaking, then, of "convert work" within the context of the total life and mission of the Church. The term itself will continue to appear but in quotation marks, because (1) it is ambiguous, and (2) no one has yet come up with an acceptable substitute. We will be speaking, too, in terms of the parish because the bulk of non-Catholic work in the United States is parish-based. Such situations as the downtown information center, the Catholic Center on the secular campus, and the military chaplaincy present special conditions and provisions have to be made to suit the circumstances. These do not always admit of the kind of comprehensive approach we will follow; so we will treat "convert work" as a parish apostolate.

KEY ELEMENTS

Today, three considerations seem basic to our thinking about "convert work," and most of what follows will be developed in terms of them.

1. The different objectives to be achieved in bringing people to the Church.
2. The relationship of "convert work" to the rest of parish life.
3. The religious characteristics of non-Catholics.

These considerations should be the foci around which the apostolate takes shape. They should exercise a decisive influence not only upon the structures that are chosen for this work, but also on both content and teaching methods. I am following this approach because it does not call for an exclusive method of procedure, such as the inquiry class, the cursillo, or the like. In this time of transition it would be presumptuous to impose any single technique as the final solution. Rather it seems wiser to stress the important elements of this apostolate and leave it to the ingenuity of those concerned to work out programs and procedures that best incorporate them. In situations where the inquiry class is still the convention, the assimilation of more of these elements into the inquiry class is not only possible but will help its evolution toward something broader and more adequate to the task. It was from the experience of the inquiry class that we have learned its shortcomings and when steps are taken to compensate for these, we will find ourselves with a new but not unrelated form of initiation into the Church.

In addition to the basic considerations listed above, special attention must also be given to the content of instruction and the integration of liturgy, Scripture, and Christian witness into the apostolate.

THREE BASIC OBJECTIVES

"Convert work" has always had multiple objectives. It has always been recognized that the first thing necessary is that the non-Catholic be favorably disposed to listen to what the Church has to say. This perhaps did not require all the formal attention it received because the presence of the inquirer in the class presupposes a certain amount of good will. Nevertheless, the recognition of this step has always affected our choice of material and explains the traditional weight given to apologetics. It was believed that certain obstacles had to be cleared away and that the Church appear reasonable to the inquirer. This is still true for many inquirers; some people still have to be disposed to listen.

Secondly, after a person is so disposed the Church's message must be presented to him so that he can come to believe — a much greater response on his part than good will. To reach this objective another kind of material is offered, viz., the data of Catholic faith.

Finally, when a person comes to believe and wants to enter the Church, there is a certain preparation required so that he may live a full and responsible Catholic life. This third objective is distinct from, though related to, the other two, and it calls for its own content and method.

Traditionally, all three of these objectives were included in the inquiry class and, because they were combined, the material and emphases peculiar to each could never be fully developed. Now that we see the importance and the distinct nature of each of these stages, there is ample reason for adjusting our treatment of them so that we can do full justice to each.

The inquiry class technique is suited to the first and, with some modification, to the second, but the preparation for Catholic life is something that cannot be taught in the classroom alone. More is required. We must get outside the classroom, and as soon as we do, we step into the parish and bring a non-Catholic along with us. At this point, if not before, the parish involvement in "convert work" becomes more than the priest who has been conducting the inquiry class. Thus, the relationship of the parish to "convert work" and its role in this apostolate becomes critical.

THE PARISH'S ROLE

The science of catechetics tells us that instruction is only one of the means through which a person is introduced into the mystery of the Church. There are three other elements or signs by which the Christian mystery is made evident to him. They are the liturgy, Scripture, and the living witness of Christians. Instruction is adequately taken care of in the classroom, but it is obvious that the other elements must be sought elsewhere. We don't have to look far because they include practically everything important in the life of a parish. They are the hallmarks of Christ's Church and if a person is going to be truly initiated into the mystery of the Church then all of these signs must be scattered around his landscape. They already exist in the parish; the problem is to bring them to bear on the inquirer. This is why the relationship between "convert work" and the total parish has grown so important.

The liturgical sign should not be something that is simply put on for the benefit of the catechumen. Rather, it is best seen in the total worship life of the parish — the Church at prayer — and this means that the quality of liturgy in the regular Sunday worship will have a great bearing and influence upon the parish catechumenate. As far as the living witness of Christians goes, we have always realized that the so-called good example of Catholics was a great power in attracting nonbelievers to the Catholic Church. Hence, the importance of maximum participation of the laity in the catechumenate. However, today we are no longer satisfied with this simple notion of personal good example, important though it may be. Today the world is concerned with building communities, and this means that the parish must give a witness as a Christian community working together and exhibiting a truly Christian spirit of charity and concern for those both within and outside the Church. These two examples go to the heart of catechetics and point up the vital connection between the overall life of the parish and a successful apostolate to non-Catholics. The place of the scriptural sign will be taken up when we get to content.

It is probably true to say that the success of any missionary program in a given area will depend in direct proportion upon the degree to which the parish experiences a true renewal. If the basic Christian elements present in the Church in every place are truly brought to the surface so that they become visible in the lives of its members, then the mission will flourish. If a parish continues to drag along, divorced from the spirit of renewal brought about by Vatican II and wedded to old forms without appreciation or understanding of their meaning, then the non-Catholic apostolate, as all other apostolates in that parish, can only limp. In the Church all things work together unto good — or bad.

CLASSES OF NON-CATHOLICS

Closely related to the objectives of "convert work" outlined above, are the different categories of non-Catholics who approach the Church. It is always dangerous to classify people and we have a tendency to lean too heavily upon the labels we so freely bestow, yet there is some basis for grouping people and it is necessary to take some measure of the audience in choosing subject and style of presentation. So, we will probably go on categorizing non-Catholics and, as long as we realize we are describing characteristics rather than people, it should continue to be helpful.

Of vital concern to the Church are those non-Catholics who can still be described as nonbelievers — those who have not yet heard in a meaningful way the good news of salvation. Some or most of them may have a belief in God, but they are unaware of the new and eternal covenant offered in Jesus Christ. These persons still await conversion and when one of them completes the passage from nonbelief to belief in Jesus Christ, he can truly be described as a "convert."

Persons in this group may or may not be favorably disposed to hear the Christian message. If the catechist finds a lack of disposition he must, of course, concentrate on this as his first objective. In many cases this will not be necessary. But in all situations where the audience consists of non-believers the essential task is to confront them with the Gospel. No amount of apologetics or doctrinal explanation can by itself reveal the Savior in whom they can believe. Only the saving events of his passage as proclaimed by the Church make him present to the nonbeliever.

However, this does not take care of all non-Catholics. There are the Protestants and Orthodox who are already converted. They believe in Jesus Christ as Lord and Savior and have heard and responded to the Gospel. This segment of non-Catholics cannot, then, be dealt with in the same way as the nonbelievers. It would be an affront to their faith and conscience if we did so deal with them. Vatican II has told us how to meet this situation in the decree on Ecumenism. These people are not subjects for conversion; rather, their community and ours have a common mission of unity. They are already in a special relationship with us through baptism and our approach to them is one of mutual dialogue and support as together we help each other toward the full visible unity Christ wills. The apostolate to this group of non-Catholics is the ecumenical apostolate and has its own forms and style. It must never be confused with "convert work" and there is no reason for the two to be in conflict if we are aware of the distinction between conversion to Christ and unification of Christians.

There are others besides nonbelievers and believing Christians. Perhaps in the United States this third force is the largest of all. These are the nominal believers, uncommitted to any particular Church, occasional churchgoers or nonpracticing for the most part, yet possessed of a Christian background and a personal faith and piety that takes them out of the category of nonbelievers. There are many in this group who are nominally or originally Catholic, and for practical purposes should be classified with the others. This group is not the object of ecumenical activity since they are not identified with any Church and ecumenical activity is always between churches. They are legitimate subjects for the evangelizing activity of the Church and, even though they have heard the Gospel, it has not confronted them in a meaningful way, so the message we must offer them is still the basic Gospel message.

Allowing for a few other smaller categories such as the confirmed atheist, the agnostic, and the secular humanist, as well as those with special problems, these three main categories pretty well define, as much as categories can, the non-Catholics who are the concern of our apostolates. There are also a relatively small number of believing Christians, i.e., Protestants or Orthodox, who have come to see the divinity of the Church and seek entrance. They thus take themselves out of the ecumenical arena and identify themselves with the Catholic Church. They should be prepared for reception according to their particular needs. Often this means a full course of instruction or at least a modified review of the Christian message. At very least, it will mean a period of formation and preparation for life as a Catholic.

STRUCTURING A PROGRAM

A review of these basic considerations gives us the key to a "convert" program and the structure to carry it out. Our objectives tell us that there must be three different types of presentation — one that disposes, one that converts, and one that forms and instructs. Our survey of non-Catholics tells us that not every one who comes to the Church requires all three, and that some selectivity of forms is desirable. Both of these considerations indicate that all three presentations have to be somehow available if the needs of all inquirers are to be met. They suggest that the form of this apostolate be broad enough to include all three.

Finally, the third consideration, viz., the interrelation of parish life and non-Catholic mission, gives us the basic tools for the presentations. These tools are not only instruction and explanation of the faith, but, equally important, all the basic elements of the Church — parish, liturgy and preaching, reading of Scripture, the witness of the Catholic laity who assist in the catechumenate, and the Christian witness of the parish community as a whole.

The pastoral task is to create some kind of framework that will provide room for all these key elements and at the same time be practically operable. For want of a better term, we can describe this form of the apostolate as the "parish catechumenate."

A PARISH CATECHUMENATE

A criticism which could be leveled at our effort toward the non-Catholic in the past is that it was too peripheral. By this I mean that our permanent parish institutions were shaped exclusively to Catholic needs and purposes. Whatever attention was given the non-Catholic came in the form of programs and activities that were "tacked on" to the real life of the parish. If our parishes are to become truly apostolic and missionary, it will be necessary for these qualities to be reflected in permanent parish structures. Fortunately, there is no need to create something entirely new. We have only to turn back to the early Church and there discover that time-honored institution known as the catechumenate. As we know from early Church history, this was once a regular part of the Church's program. It consisted of preparing, generally during Lent, the catechumens for reception into the Church. It had a regular procedure, traditional forms, and a constant spirit. When we speak of restoring the ancient catechumenate in the Church today, this does not necessarily mean that it has to be restored with all its original features. Times have changed, and along with this change have gone changes in the needs of the Church. However, it is possible to retain the general features of a parish catechumenate and at the same time to develop it along the lines that seem best adapted to the needs of modern man. This will entail some difficulties in the beginning, since materials and programs are not immediately available. However, with a little experimentation it should be possible to devise a suitable catechumenate for every parish situation that will incorporate all the features necessary to prepare a person for life in the Church. In any such program at least two basic things must be achieved. First, there must be an adequate program of preparation for baptism, and secondly, there must be a presentation of the Christian message in such form that people are led to desire baptism. The different purposes of these two phases of a catechumenate have already been stressed. It must constantly be borne in mind that they are aimed at achieving different results, and for that reason must contain different material. The catechumenate proper presumes faith. It presumes that a person has come to see and accept the revelation of Jesus Christ and is willing to act upon this acceptance. Necessarily, this will involve a small number of the non-Catholics within any given parish. However, these catechumens did not come to that position unaided and there will be many more non-Catholics who will be interested and receptive to the Christian message but who are not in a position to commit themselves for baptism. For these persons, full exposure to the preaching of the Church must first be had. We might call this part of the program a precatechumenate, or evangelization. The purpose here is to move a person to conversion, to move him to accept Jesus Christ as Lord and Savior and to be willing to make such adjustments in his life as are necessary to become a disciple.

In the renewed parish, then, we would expect to find a regular preaching of the Gospel outside the liturgy and outside the church building itself. This would be the modern equivalent of the missionary going out into the marketplace or into the village where the nonbelievers dwell and there introducing them to the mystery of the Kingdom of God. If the circumstances and appearances of the situation are somewhat different in the modern American parish, this is only an accidental difference. The overall purpose and content of this missionary effort is essentially the same. If this truth is borne in mind, then the non-Catholic apostolate in the parish will never be allowed to become peripheral, but will remain an integral part of the main parish apostolate.

At least once a year it should be possible for any person within the environs of a given parish to hear the entire Gospel preached within a fixed period of time. It should also be possible at least once a year in that same parish for those who have been so moved by what they have heard as to desire baptism, to undergo a period of methodical preparation and spiritual formation to prepare them for the reception of the sacraments and the initiation into Christian life. In order to fulfill these expectations a parish should be able to offer a course, not simply of instructions nor an explanation of what Catholics believe, but rather a presentation in installments of the basic Christian message as it is lived and experienced in the Catholic Church. In technical terms this means the history of salvation. It does not have to be very long and involved. Actually it can be accomplished in approximately twelve to fifteen sessions, which is about half the time usually required by the inquiry class. During this series, all of salvation history is unfolded, beginning with God's revelation to Abraham in the Old Testament and continuing up through the life, death, and resurrection of Jesus Christ, the Church and the sacraments, to the second coming and the final establishment of all things in Christ. We will go into the content of this presentation in more detail later.

Naturally, many things that are important for the Catholic to know will not be covered in such a presentation. However, there is no reason why they should be. Some of the people who are taking this series will not, as a matter of fact, become Catholics, so there is no reason why they have to be exposed to all of the detailed instruction which is of value and meaning only to one who is a practicing Catholic. For those who will become Catholics there will be ample time during the subsequent catechumenate to cover these important matters with those concerned.

The catechumenate proper is geared only to those inquirers who show signs of faith and who now wish to become Catholics. It should be scheduled each year and during Lent when that is possible. In this way at least once a year a person who has come to believe in Jesus Christ, as he has revealed himself in the Church, will know that there is a regular period of spiritual formation and preparation that will begin sometime after the first of the year. He will know, too, approximately in what it consists, namely, a series of liturgical actions in which he is both exposed to the word of God, instructed in things necessary for the life of the Catholic, and drawn deeper and deeper into the life of the parish. Stress is placed upon the liturgy because the catechumen is now in a position where he can appreciate the liturgy and experience its saving action. The liturgy used here is both the liturgy of the sacrament of baptism in stages, and also the general liturgy of the Church — Mass, the sacraments, and Bible services. During the present stage of transition a Bible service is perhaps the easiest liturgical vehicle for the catechumenate. Later on, we ought to look forward to a baptismal Mass, or a special Mass for catechumens during Lent, at which time they would receive their instruction and participate in the liturgy to the extent that it is possible.

Experiments have suggested that the catechumenate may be best laid out as follows: Each week from Septuagesima until Easter the catechumens, i.e., those who have committed themselves to enter the Church, will meet. This weekly meeting will last approximately two hours. During the course of it a liturgical action, such as those mentioned, viz., a Bible vigil or one of the stages of baptism, will form the focal point of the weekly session. In this Bible service there will be a reading of the word of God, a homily by the priest, and some prayers and responses. All of these will be united around a single theme each week, such as faith, charity, worship, etc. The materials used will be drawn from Scripture. Its relevance and application to everyday life will be stressed in the homily. The purpose is to strengthen the faith of the catechumen by showing him how the great truths of salvation which he has heard proclaimed in the precatechumenate are relevant to his own personal life with God.

In addition to the liturgical action, each session of the catechumenate will include a brief instruction and discussion period. The instruction should not be more than half an hour and can be given by a lay catechist. It will cover such things as the practice and preparation for confession, prayer, the structure of the Mass, and any other important aspects of the Church that have not been treated elsewhere. It would be well to have the instruction before the liturgical action so that the discussion period will center on the homily rather than the instruction. Another half hour can be allotted for discussion and the active participation of lay catechists as discussion leaders will bring the catechumen into contact with practical examples of how these Christians have related to the Gospel.

The accent in the catechumenate is on spiritual formation, not intellectual. It aims at strengthening the commitment each of the catechumens has already made. The atmosphere is one of prayer, Scripture, and community and it radiates from the liturgical action that is the heart of each session. If these sessions are actually held in Lent, greater parish participation can be achieved by scheduling them as the parish Lenten devotions and inviting everyone to attend and participate.

The format here described is one possible way that has been successfully used. It is not meant to exclude others. However, whatever style is settled upon, if it is actually to prepare the catechumen for the life of faith, it should employ the traditional tools of the Church — preaching, prayer, Scripture, and the life of the Christian community.

PREACHING THE CHRISTIAN MESSAGE

Before we can have a catechumenate we must have catechumens. That is to say we must have people who have come to believe in God's revelation of himself in Jesus Christ. This presupposes a preaching of the Christian message, for St. Paul tells us that faith comes through hearing. I say "preaching" rather than instruction, because even though this phase of "convert work" be done in the classroom, the style should be more that of announcement and affirmation than of explanation. Explanation has its place both in elaborating upon the proclamation of what God has done and, especially in the preliminary stages, of disposing a person to listen to the proclamation. But we are here concerned with a presentation that will convert and the best argument for this approach is the fact that it imitates God's own approaches to man. God confronted man with events and persons over the centuries and it was their impact upon him that enabled God to break through man's self-enclosure and make himself known. Man's first experience with God was in these events and persons. The modern nonbeliever should be given the same opportunity to discover God in these same persons and events. That is why Scripture is the best presentation the Church can make when her objective is conversion, for Scripture is where we first learn about the acts of God.

Going back to the Bible we have great examples before us of God's approach to the nonbeliever. We have the examples of Abraham, the Israelites, and the Apostles. In considering how we should go about preaching the message of the Kingdom of Heaven to the modern non-believer or nominal believer, we can find no better way to begin than by following the pattern laid out for us in Scripture. For God is trying to do for these people today the very same kind of thing he did for Abraham, the Israelites, and the Apostles. Today, what God is trying to do through the Church for a particular person is to reveal himself to this man as the saving God and to call him to enter into permanent personal relationship with him. This is a truth of which we have always been aware, but at the same time it has not always been reflected in our teaching. If this is what we are actually trying to do, then it becomes imperative that God's revelation show through whatever it is that we present to this person. It means that our presentation must be simple and clear, uncluttered by details of theology, morals, and devotion. It means that this person must be able to see without undue difficulty the fact that here is a message to him from the saving God. It means also that there must be a spiritual and formational content in our presentation so that the person coming to God will be moved to an affirmative response.

If we follow the pattern of God's action, we will make our presentation in terms of salvation history. This history shows that God began in a simple and rather superficial way to prepare man for his great destiny. He approached him originally in material terms of land and earthly blessings. He continued to speak in these terms to successive generations of men in the Old Testament, and only when they had lived in the climate of these promises for centuries and adapted their life to meet them, did he begin to fill them with deeper meaning. So many non-Catholics today who have no particular religion of their own are in a position where only such a simple and, at first superficial, approach is understandable to them. Consequently, in conveying the Christian faith to a nonbeliever it may be best simply to follow the pattern God has laid out for us in the Old Testament. Only in this way will the nonbeliever really have an adequate preparation for the coming of Christ into his life just as only through the centuries of the Old Testament did mankind get the kind of preparation needed to receive the Savior when he came.

THE CONTENT OF PREACHING

In teaching salvation history to inquirers it is best to begin with Abraham rather than Adam and Eve. Abraham typifies the man of faith. In the Old Testament we see him both before and after he believed. He is a sympathetic figure with whom the inquirer can readily identify. As he confronts the Church and her preaching he can interpret to himself what he is experiencing in terms of Abraham.

In the story of Abraham, the major outlines of religion are to be found. First, God discloses himself to someone, and in this act reveals something about himself. Secondly, he promises man something good and invites him to come closer. Thirdly, this invitation involves a challenge to man which demands decision on his part. And finally, there is some symbolic action by which this encounter is solemnized. In these four elements — revelation, invitation, response, worship — all of which are found in Abraham's encounter with God, we see all of the major elements of religion. By beginning with Abraham, these can be established at the outset, Subsequent developments in salvation history can be described so as to bring out these same elements in their makeup. After Abraham, this same kind of encounter is illustrated by the cases of Isaac, Jacob, Moses and the Israelites in Egypt.

By this time the pattern should be clear to all. Then something is added. The idea of covenant. The exodus story is the vehicle for this. The covenant can be described as an institutionalizing or elaboration of the elements of religion that have been present from the time of Abraham. These are now formalized and developed in detail in the life of a people, and religion as we usually think of it is established.

At this point, it is well to go back to Adam and Eve and from that account teach why there is a history of salvation. It must be established why such a thing as salvation is necessary. When this is clarified a final look at the Old Testament stresses God's preparations for his coming in Christ.

At this point in the presentation, it is pretty well established in the minds of the inquirers that God has made some progress. At the same time it will be obvious to the instructor that he has also made some progress with these inquirers. Still following the pattern of God's approach to man, the next step is to introduce the inquirers to Christ. Again, this is best done through picturing him as he is found in the Gospels. The major points of his life and his teachings are first covered in a factual and quite superficial way. Then these same things are interpreted in the light of the faith of the Apostles who have given us the New Testament. In reviewing the beginning of Christian faith, the Apostles can be used as examples. The Gospels can be reviewed in terms of the effect of Christ's teachings and actions upon his followers, and the dawning realization on their part of who he really is. In this process the resurrection emerges as the key that revealed the divinity of Christ, and Pentecost as the culmination of the Apostles' journey toward faith.

Again, the divinity of Christ is described in terms of persons and events — Christ, the Apostles, and the acts surrounding his death and resurrection. This is the way it happened; this is the way God revealed the divinity of Christ to the Church, and this is the best way by which the Church can channel this truth to the inquirer.

Following the resurrection, it would be well to interrupt the course of salvation history and offer a reflection upon its meaning. This is to say, a lesson on redemption would be in order at this point. Strictly speaking, this is not salvation history, as the events of the redemption have already been covered. Rather this is a doctrinal explanation and interpretation of these events. It is a good opportunity to recapitulate salvation history from the beginning, showing why redemption was necessary, how it was accomplished, and looking ahead, how it is offered to the contemporary inquirer.

This last aspect naturally leads to the subject of the Church. As an event in salvation history it is best seen in the persons and incidents from which Christ constructed his Church. In this matter such things as the call of the Apostles, the election of Peter, the mandate to teach and baptize, the Christian law of love, and Christ's promise of the Spirit — all enter into the essential structure of the Church and can be taught from the Gospels. The key event is then shown by the Acts of the Apostles' account of Pentecost, when all of these ingredients were welded together through the coming of the Spirit and the manifestation of his actions in the Christian community.

Salvation history is then continued into the present so that it becomes clear to the inquirer that he too is involved in its mainstream. The principal way by which God presently acts in salvation history is through the actions and teachings of the Church, i.e., through word and sacrament. These are the current events in salvation history. So they are treated next. Baptism, confirmation, and holy orders can be presented together as they express different functions within the community of the people of God. The Eucharist can be used to tie together all of salvation history, past, present, and future. In this presentation stress should be laid on mystery, i.e., that power of Christianity to make present in material signs all of God's saving events. All the essential themes of salvation history can be illustrated in the Eucharist — the themes of liberation, covenant, worship, and reconciliation — all these can be shown in the Eucharistic act.

The sacrament of penance is best treated within the context of Christian morality. A brief overall picture of Christian morality as part of the Good News may serve as an introduction. The key points here are the law of love, the presence of the Holy Spirit, and the whole Christian life as a loving response to the gift of God. Within this context the sacrament of penance can be given its rightful position as the way in which the Christian, who is still a human being and subject to sin, can find himself once again reconciled to the loving God within his community.

The subject of Christian marriage naturally flows out of the Christian way of life because Christian marriage is the most common frame of life within which Christians express humanly and religiously what they are. The emphasis here should be on the sacramental aspect of marriage, namely, marriage as a meaningful way of living the life of love that has been given to the Christian. When the relationship between marriage and the Christian vocation is established, then the primacy of love in the Christian life emerges quite clearly, and it is well worth spending a little time on this most important subject because of the good teaching opportunity marriage presents for this basic Christian theme.

The sacrament of the anointing of the sick can be treated in the presentation on the Last Things. While it does not, strictly speaking, belong here, still it can at least be related to the fact of death. The Last Things should be treated as the final event of salvation history, final not only for the individual, but more important, final for the achievement and fulfillment of God's plan for mankind. The second coming of Christ should receive as much attention as heaven and hell used to get, for man lives his life within salvation history and the parousia is its term.

If salvation history is presented in this fashion, then all of the core elements of the Christian faith will have been communicated to the inquirer. Not only will they have been communicated to him in their substance, but also they will have reached him in somewhat the same fashion and order in which they happened. They will come to him as events — events which he can recognize as having a place in his own personal history. If he enters the Church, he enters the life of a people and their entire history becomes personal to him. It becomes his background and his inheritance and it is best to teach it to him in just this fashion.

The older way of instructing inquirers was largely a topical matter — the central elements of Catholic belief were singled out, explained, made reasonable, and fitted into a picture of the Church. This method is good as far at it goes, but it is largely an intellectual process, and if there is one thing we have learned in this generation it is that religion is far more than an intellectual act. It is a confrontation with the saving God, and this takes place in a much larger arena than we can find in books. The Church is the vehicle of that confrontation and her presentation of the saving God must be in such a fashion that a man can respond with that total commitment which we know God expects of believers.

THE ROLE OF DISCUSSION

The pattern laid down by God in his dealings with man contains another element which can be exploited for the benefit of the inquirer. It was pointed out above that the basic elements of religion include revelation, invitation, and response. Using the format of salvation history to present the revelation and invitation of God as it unfolded is one benefit to be derived from the pattern. The other is to begin to elicit an affirmative response from the inquirer, just as God elicted responses from men throughout both testaments. Although most people who are facing the Church formally for the first time will not be in a position to make the response of faith immediately, we should not overlook the value of a series of lesser responses. The most primitive and obvious type of response we should seek is interest and some involvement in the material of salvation history. One of the best ways by which such a response can be made practical is through group discussion. It seems almost necessary today that if adults are going to come to grips with religion in any kind of responsible way, they must begin from the very outset to discuss its meaning for their own lives. In this presentation of salvation history, then, there should be an opportunity afforded at the end of each session for the inquirers, under the leadership of lay instructors, to discuss in small groups the matters which they have heard from the Bible. The purpose of this discussion is to take the raw materials of salvation history and try to relate them to their own lives. In this way — and whether the attempt is successful or not is unimportant — the inquirer begins to look at God's plan for mankind in personal terms. He becomes involved in it from the outset and, as time goes on, granted the necessary conditions of good disposition, prayerful search, and a humble docility to the action of God, he will come to a personal realization of his role and destiny within that history. Experience has demonstrated that the interest of the inquirer is that much enhanced when discussion is used. It has shown that the rate of attendance remains high. Above all, discussion conveys to them better than words that salvation history is something not solely to be learned but to be lived.

In this type of discussion, carried out for these purposes, it is not important that it follow the exact subject matter of the presentation. The important thing in discussion is not so much learning as involving the participants with a religious issue. It is enough that the discussion be of a religious nature and that people are concerned enough to explore its meaning for themselves.

The choice of discussion leaders is important in order that the discussion may proceed freely and in orderly fashion. Persons who have a tendency to dominate conversation or who are dogmatic in their approach do not make good discussion leaders. Some experience in group dynamics is helpful but not absolutely necessary. The person who is open and really interested in other people and has the capacity to listen makes a natural discussion leader. Every parish has its share of these. Experience shows that in the beginning particularly, the presence of a priest in a discussion or even in the room at the time discussion is going on, very often hinders the discussion. Sometimes in the beginning too, it is quite difficult, especially in small groups, to get strangers to talk to each other. To take care of this situation it would be well to supply the discussion leaders with key questions for each presentation to be used in such emergencies. However, it should be stressed once again that the main purpose of the discussion is to get the inquirers involved and no discussion leader should feel chained to a set of discussion questions.

PRE-EVANGELIZATION

Most of this chapter has been concerned with helping inquirers to conversion and preparing them for sacramental life. Little has been said about disposing people to believe, and yet this is probably the most challenging task of all. It is a fact that the Church does not touch the majority of people, and it is also a fact that most people are not practicing Christians. So it would appear that pre-evangelization, or the initial steps by which the Church establishes contact and cultivates an audience for her message, is the most pressing need of our time.

The most pressing and the most difficult. The difficulties are such that all we can do is recognize the problem and affirm the need for action. This is not very helpful but it is senseless to outline programs and structures and pretend that they are the answer. The truth of the matter is that missionary work in the parish still depends upon people coming to us. This is perhaps its greatest weakness and the area in which most new ground must be broken. Whoever heard of a missionary waiting at home for the heathen to come to him? The very word "missionary" means "one who is sent," and this means that he goes out somewhere. Actually, this is still somewhat true in the parish. Even though the bulk of any program is to be found within the walls of the "plant," what brings the inquirers to the plant is the contact and example of the members of the parish who have been out among them in their daily lives. This is the witness of Catholic living and it remains the biggest single factor in bringing people to the Church. However, this approach is always indirect. There is need also for a much more direct going out by the Catholic laity and to some extent, too, by the clergy. There is need to bring the Church to where people are. Perhaps, as parish renewal grows and with it house liturgy, living room discussions, community projects, and other kinds of "extra-plant" activity, there will also be a development in direct evangelization of non-Catholics on their home ground. This would represent a real break-through in the apostolate. Meanwhile, however, our structures are still within the building and can achieve but limited results.

Some non-Catholics who come to the Church need a period of acclima-tization during which they can get used to the Church and quietly listen to what she has to say. There is no special way of bringing this about. Such things as a shortened form of inquiry class, discussion clubs, apolo-getical dialogue, a parish forum or lecture series, are all useful tools for this purpose. Where the number of inquirers is small, the approach can be as limited or as comprehensive as their particular needs require. In every case, this phase of the apostolate is only a preparatory one in which the ground is made ready so that the Gospel has a fair chance of taking hold. Anything that will achieve this is good.

Obviously, such activities will not effect the real pre-evangelization of a whole population, so they have received only cursory attention. That kind of missionary effort awaits the flood tide of Catholic renewal with the kind of Pentecostal vitality that will catch fire beyond the Church's borders. When the dynamisms released by Vatican II have taken hold of the Christian people, the Church will come up with the forms of mission that belong to this age. Meanwhile, we build on the past and, like the house-holder in the parable, take from our storehouse things old and new in order to meet the needs of the present.

20

Ecumenism and the Clergy

JOHN A. HARDON, S.J.

IT IS DOUBTFUL IF ANY SUBJECT IN CHRISTIAN THOUGHT HAS BEEN treated more extensively in recent years than the ecumenical movement. At least ten full-sized books are published annually in English on Church unity, and the number of monographs and articles runs into the hundreds. A spate of new periodicals has come into existence: *Unitas, Ecumenist, Journal of Ecumenical Studies, Christianity and Crisis, Ecumenical Review.* Members of the hierarchy have come out with pastorals, encouraging the faithful to become ecumenically involved. One of the last public statements of the late Cardinal Meyer of Chicago was his 1964 Lenten letter on "Ecumenism, the Spirit of Christian Unity."

Finally the Second Vatican Council issued its decree on ecumenism, that will hopefully open a new era in the Church's apostolate and offer unheard of possibilities for the extension of Christ's kingdom in the hearts of men.

But all of this can remain sterile theory unless the Catholic clergy, bishops and priests, and those studying for the priesthood catch the vision of Pope John XXIII who summoned the Vatican Council to reform the Church and to reunite a dismembered Christian world. There have been unity councils before, notably II Lyons in 1274 and Florence, which closed in 1445. Yet nothing much was done, partly because the clergy of those days were not prepared and the laity were as apathetic as their priests.

I do not believe the clergy today are apathetic, but I am sure they are not prepared to meet the challenge of an ecumenical age. I am also certain that this preparation will not come inevitably, like a sort of infused gift of wisdom. It calls for reexamination of our whole outlook on the Christian religion and reassessment of our role in the upbuilding of the Mystical Body of Christ.

For the sake of convenience, I shall treat the subject under the aspects that I consider most important for the clergy of today and tomorrow: knowledge, holiness, cooperation, and communication — where knowledge has to do with understanding what ecumenism is, holiness with becoming what ecumenism needs, cooperation with working together with our fellow Christians, and communication with striving to share the spiritual riches we possess.

UNDERSTANDING ECUMENISM

We may define the ecumenical movement with the Vatican Council as "the initiatives and activities planned and undertaken, according to the various needs of the Church and as opportunities offer, to promote Christian unity."

The essence of ecumenism, then, is the promotion of Christian unity. And no one with a spark of faith or after a moment's reflection would desire anything but an end to this scandal of Christian division. What is less obvious is the exact meaning of disunity, and the corresponding effort to change a divided Christianity.

Clarity here is indispensable, and whatever success the ecumenical movement will have in the Catholic Church depends on her clergy's especially knowing what they are being urged to promote at the risk of falling into one of two extremes: either taking ecumenism as just another fellowship program, a kind of let's-get-along technique; or thinking it means a concerted effort to convert people to Catholicism, a back-to-Mother-Church crusade.

Unfortunately some of the literature on the subject is not very helpful. Enthusiasm is no substitute for theology, and zeal in any cause, even in the cause of Christ, should be founded on the solid rock of faith and firmly balanced on the level ground of Catholic tradition. Otherwise what offers such hope of benefit to souls may burn itself out before it gets a chance to set the Church aflame with an apostolic spirit that has been unknown since the time of St. Paul.

Our best guide is the document of the Vatican Council, which must be studied with care and, under scrutiny, will reveal the basic principles of the ecumenical movement.

Heading the list of these principles is the fact that two kinds of division among Christians are implied in the word "disunity." The first and most serious is separation from unity with the Roman Catholic Church, which the Council describes by the use of such terms as "separated brethren" (*fratres a nobis sejuncti*) and "outside the visible boundaries of the Catholic Church" (*extra visibilia Ecclesiae catholicae saepta*). The crucial words *sejuncti* and *extra saepta* mean "being disjointed" and "outside the enclosure." They state that our fellow Christians, who are not professed members of the Catholic Church, are somehow separated from that communion with the Body of Christ which the late Pius XII identified as the Roman Catholic Church.

Another division in Christendom is the variety of churches and denominations that are not professedly Catholic, and whose differences range across the gamut of doctrine, ritual, and moral precept. It was this kind of disunity that first gave rise to the ecumenical movement in the last century and that even now is the main preoccupation of the leaders in the World Council of Churches.

The Vatican Council is at pains to balance both types of division. In spite of separation from Catholicism and among themselves, those who are baptized and profess belief in the Trinity and the divinity of Jesus Christ are united in a way that we have not sufficiently considered before. I was pleased to see the early mistake in the translation of the phrase *in quadam communione* changed from "real communion" to simply "communion with the Catholic Church." But the word *quadam* is vital. The correct rendering is, "Men who believe in Christ and have been truly baptised are in some kind of communion with the Catholic Church even though this communion is imperfect." By implication, such persons are also united with one another by the mystical bonds of grace which flow through all who are incorporated into Christ by baptism and belief in His sacred name.

A second principle logically follows from the first. If disunity is undesirable it can only be because of its effects, which the Council spells out in plain terms.

> Our separated brethren, whether considered as individuals or as Communities and Churches, are not blessed with that unity which Jesus Christ wished to bestow on all those who through Him were born again into one body, and with Him quickened to newness of life — that unity which the Holy Scriptures and the ancient Tradition of the Church proclaim.
>
> For it is only through Christ's Catholic Church, which is "the all-embracing means of salvation," that they can benefit fully from the means of salvation. We believe that Our Lord entrusted all the blessings of the New Covenant to the apostolic college alone, of which Peter is the head, in order to establish the one Body of Christ on earth to which all should be fully incorporated who belong in any way to the people of God.

Thus we see that disunity is harmful because it deprives those who are disunited from that fullness of participation in the means of salvation which are to be had in their entirety only in the Roman Catholic Church,

All through the decree on ecumenism the Catholic Church "of which Peter is the head" is described as normative of the means of salvation, so that where its full-fledged members enjoy access to the abundance of God's blessings, those not so privileged (through no fault of their own) have only an approximation of the depository of grace.

This position is not arrogance. It is a statement of fact which several times has been solemnly defined by the magisterium, that whoever is saved is saved by and through the one Mystical Body which Christ established on earth and of which the Roman pontiff is the visible head. In the degree that a person vitally professes the faith which has its fullness in Catholicism, he is more or less internally united with Christ and more or less in contact with his saving instruments of salvation.

Lastly the third principle. At its center the ecumenical movement is a coordinated effort to bridge the gap which still separates other churches than the Catholic from access to the plenitude of divine goodness that God became man to confer on the human race.

It is at this delicate point that a clear distinction must be made. Ecumenism as such is not a convert movement. Its driving power is not the terminal effect of bringing as many people as possible into the Catholic fold. On a broader base, it seeks to reduce disunity among Christians by having them grow in the possession of a common faith, common worship, and a common acceptance of moral laws which, *ex hypothesi,* are fully present in the creed, cult, and code of the Roman Catholic Church. But every growth in the profession of this faith, use of these sacraments, and obedience to these norms of conduct is unitive in the deepest and most ontological sense of the term.

Here we touch upon the secrets of Divine Providence. Why such disunity almost from the dawn of Christianity? Why does God permit such divergence and, by Catholic standards, deviation from the *pleroma* found in the one visible society which calls itself Catholic because it is the universal sacrament instituted by the Savior to redeem fallen mankind?

We do not know the reasons why, except to suggest that in this way those who possess more are sanctified by faithfully using what they have and sharing it with others, and those who possess less by also faithfully using and sharing what they have — besides receiving from others what they need.

Viewed in this way, ecumenism has a definite purpose: to increase in the Christian world the stock of faith, worship and conduct, established by Jesus Christ, on the assumption that all Christians have some degree of these spiritual gifts, but they can also grow in their possession and fidelity to what they possess.

Less obvious and more difficult for some to admit is that individuals outside Catholicism may possess certain gifts of grace which professed

Catholics do not have, and in their own way may be more responsive to what they profess than are nominal members of the Catholic Church. I am reminded of Augustine's famous remark that he would prefer a good catechumen to a bad Christian, and that the Spirit of God was more active in the faithful centurion than in the faithless Judas who betrayed Christ.

In view of the crucial importance of this subject, it will be useful to explain that ecumenism does not imply any real change in the Church's traditional concept of her nature. A superficial reading of the *Constitution on the Church* of the II Vatican Council might lead to the conclusion that Pius XII's definition of the Church in *Mystici Corporis* had been superseded. In that document, he said,

> If we would define and describe this true Church of Jesus Christ — which is the holy, Catholic, apostolic, Roman Church — we shall find no expression more noble, more sublime or more divine than the phrase which calls it "the Mystical Body of Jesus Christ." This title is derived from and is, as it were, the fair flower of the repeated teaching of Sacred Scripture and the holy Fathers.

Some have suggested that a radical change has taken place since *Mystici Corporis,* with regard to the historical existence of Christ's Church. No doubt if we assume that Pius XII began with the premise that body-equals-social-body, then the Mystical Body would be identified mathematically with the Roman Catholic Church; so that only professed Catholics would in any way belong to the Body of Christ. If we further assume that the Vatican Constitution begins by identifying the Mystical Body with communion of life in Christ, a different conclusion is reached and we have the II Vatican Council not only making explicit what Pius XII implied, but correcting *Mystici Corporis.* It is no help either to suppose that the Mystical Body is merely in the Catholic Church but, at the same time, transcends it.

A careful study of the two documents shows that Pius XII stated in essence what the Constitution *De Ecclesia* elaborated in detail.

Pius XII clearly distinguished between full-fledged members of the Mystical Body and those who are Christians, indeed, but not fully incorporated in the Body of Christ. He spoke, on the one hand, of unbelievers who, "not yet enlightened by the truth of the Gospel are still without the fold of the Church," and, on the other hand, of those who are truly Christians but, "on account of regrettable schism are separated from Us who, though unworthy, represent the person of Jesus Christ on earth." Moreover, he specifically stated that all mankind, even those who are not Christians, "may have a certain relationship to the Mystical Body of the Redeemer" (*ad mysticum Redemptoris corpus ordinentur*), depending on how faithfully they correspond with the interior movements of grace.

If anything, the Vatican Constitution is more incisive about the liability under which those labor who are not in full communion with the Church "of which Peter is the head." Basing itself on the Bible and Tradition, it teaches that "the Church, now sojourning on earth as an exile, is necessary for salvation . . . Whosoever, therefore, knowing that the Catholic Church was made necessary by Christ, would refuse to enter it or remain in it, could not be saved."

Spanning Pius XII and II Vatican was the ecclesiology of St. Robert Bellarmine (1542–1621), which both authorities used, as indicated in the *Acta* of the Council and the reference sources of *Mystici Corporis*.

In Bellarmine's theology, those are to be considered members of the Church who profess the Christian faith, use the same sacraments, and are obedient to the same rightful pastors under the Roman pontiff. He was even willing to admit that a minimum of interior faith along with external profession of Catholicism constituted membership in the Mystical Body.

By the same token, however, he allowed for a whole spectrum of incorporation in the Mystical Body: from "putative membership" of a man who had no internal virtue at all but gave external adherence to Catholicism, through the range of incorporation with various levels of exterior profession together with interior virtue, to the highest kind of ecclesiastical communion where a Christian is intimately joined to Christ because he fully professes the visible norms of Catholicism and interiorly possesses all the supernatural virtues.

Bellarmine's analysis is based on the familiar analogy of body and soul, consecrated by the recent Constitution *On the Church*.

> The Church is a Living Organism, composed of body and soul. This composition means that the soul are the gifts of the Holy Spirit, that is, faith, hope and charity, and the internal, infused virtues. The body is the external profession of faith, submission to the Pope and participation in the same sacraments.
>
> Some people belong to both the body and the soul of the Church, which means they are united to Christ, the Head, interiorly by the virtues and exteriorly by professing the faith and sharing in the sacraments. They belong most perfectly to the Church, like living members of the human body. They can further be subdivided into three categories: those who have more of the life of the Church in their souls because they have more faith and charity; those who have less of this life because they have less faith and charity; and those who have only the beginnings of this life because they have only faith, internal and external, and no charity, that is, no sanctifying grace.
>
> Other people belong to the soul and not to the body of the Church, like catechumens and those who are excommunicated. However, not all belong to this group but only those who have internal and external faith, and charity or sanctifying grace.
>
> Finally, there are persons who belong to the body and not to the soul of the Church, namely those who have no internal virtue, but yet externally profess the true faith and share in the sacraments, under obedience to the

Pope, from hope or fear or some other temporal motive (*De Ecclesia Militante,* caput 2).

Accordingly, in theological terms, incorporation in Christ varies immensely, as between one person and another or within the same person at different times. It is possible, as Augustine and Bellarmine submit, that a Christian who is not Catholic may be more closely united with Christ by internal virtue (pertaining to the soul of the Church) than a Catholic whose external profession (pertaining to the body of the Church) contradicts his internal dispositions because he is not in the state of grace.

Yet the objective norms remain. By the will of Christ who founded the Church, those who fully profess the Catholic faith, worship, and obedience have access to the fullness of God's blessings. If their state of soul corresponds to what their lips and body proclaim, they are incorporated most completely in Jesus Christ and enjoy the plenitude of membership in his Church.

Approximations of this standard are all but infinite: depending first on how much of Christian revelation is known, and which Catholicism concedes is in some measure available outside its visible organization; but mainly depending on how generously a person responds to what God has revealed to him of divine truth and cooperates with the graces he receives.

Objectively, then, the divine will is that all men should come to the full knowledge of God's revelation, communicated by Christ through his one visible Church, and be daily more responsive in living up to whatever divine light they have obtained.

In the pursuit of this ideal, Christian unity becomes not so much an early goal to be attained as a sign that God's plan for the human family is being achieved. Unity among men should be evidence that some unity between men and God has been reached. There is no true unity among creatures unless it reflects the communion between creatures and their Creator.

HOLINESS IN THE CATHOLIC CHURCH

It is not surprising that the Vatican Council should cut through the trappings of a complicated subject and identify the heart of the ecumenical movement as a reformation of morals in the Catholic Church.

A paradox has plagued the Church since the beginning of her existence. She has been endowed with all divinely revealed truth and all the means of grace, yet her members fail to live by them with all the fervor they should. This creates the spectacle of a society that claims to be the *una sancta,* while often failing to give the world that image of Christ's sanctity which he expects of his chosen flock and that scandalizes those who are not Catholic and (most tragically) professed members of the Church.

Disunity has been the fruit of this disloyalty. If we want Christian unity, we must pay the price of ecumenism worthy of the name. In the words of the Council, there must be a change of heart.

> For it is from renewal of the inner life of our minds, from self-denial and an unstinted love that desires of unity take their rise and develop in a mature way. We should, therefore, pray to the Holy Spirit for the grace to be genuinely self-denying, humble, gentle in the service of others, and to have an attitude of brotherly generosity towards them. St. Paul says: "I, therefore, a prisoner for the Lord, beg you to lead a life worthy of the calling to which you have been called, with all humility and meekness, with patience, forbearing one another in love, eager to maintain the unity of the spirit in the bond of peace" (Eph 4:1–3).

This exhortation is directed especially to those raised to sacred orders precisely that the work of Christ may be continued. He came among us "not to be served but to serve" (Mt 20:28).

A new term has been coined, "spiritual ecumenism," which the Council calls the soul of the ecumenical movement, and which consists in holiness of life achieved through reformation of conduct and assiduous prayer.

It is not a platitude that we have no more effective way of reuniting a dismembered Christian world than by professing our faith in deeds. One of the main causes of the Reformation was the conduct of the clergy, religious, and laity who professed to be Catholic but belied that profession by their lives. To reverse history the opposite must be done. Catholic people, beginning with their priests, must show forth to the world the good fruits of the faith they believe in and prove what no argument alone can confirm, that the Sermon on the Mount is being lived out as Christ would have it, by those who are in communion with Rome.

No amount of exposition can take the place of this visual proof of God's presence. If example be lacking, the most convincing logic fails and looks suspiciously hollow. "If the Gospel you preach," says the Protestant, "is so effective in making people good and holy, why has it been wasted on you?" It is a modern application of Christ's words to His followers, "You are the light of the world. Even so let your light shine before men, in order that they may see your good works and give glory to your Father in heaven" (Mt 5:14–16).

Among the good works we perform to merit reunification from God none stands higher in the scale of value or will have more effect on those whom we are trying to help than the practice of unity among ourselves. If the world of apostolic times was drawn to Christ by the evidence of mutual charity — canonized in the phrase, "See how the Christians love one another" — the same law of attraction still obtains today.

Before we can sell unity to others we must love and practice it ourselves. Within the framework of our Catholic life, so often torn by discord over temporal and trivial things, we must profess the harmony which better than rhetoric proves that the Church is animated by the Spirit of God. If we are truly united in affection as befits members of the one Body of Christ, we shall be disposed to work and pray for those who worship the same Lord as we but are separated from us in the Christian community; we shall merit the graces we both need, and call them into fellowship by the one language that all men understand, the language of charity.

Public and private prayers for unity are indispensable. In this we are joined by millions of Christians in the ecumenical movement. The World Council of Churches in its second international assembly agreed that "the measure of our concern for unity is the degree to which we pray for it. We cannot expect God to give us unity unless we prepare ourselves to receive this gift by costly and purifying prayer." Particularly valuable is communal prayer, for "to pray together is to be drawn together." The World Council recommended public prayers for Christian unity, to coincide, where possible, with similar devotions in the Catholic Church. It would be tragic if we showed less interest in praying for the reunion of Christianity than those whom we call separated brethren.

MUTUAL COOPERATION

Cooperation among Christians is less familiar in a pluralistic society than most of us are willing to admit. The clergy on both sides form an enclave that seldom ventures beyond the fold, and, despite all the publicity to the contrary, most priests are not on easy speaking terms with their Protestant confreres in the ministry.

Yet unless the clergy get together, and come to understand one another, it is fatuous to expect the laity to rise above the dead level of a studied formality. Cooperation under these circumstances will be sporadic, ineffectual, and worse — it may hide deep prejudices because the relationship is superficial and never gets beneath the surface of external or purely social amenities. Some time ago I had dinner with the pastor of the First Congregational Church in Kalamazoo. He told me it was the first time in the forty years of his ministry that he had a meal with a Catholic priest or engaged him in any sort of conversation.

The result of this exclusivism has been to stifle anything like collaboration on a spiritual basis between Catholics and Christians of other churches. I put the blame for racism in America at the door of the Christian clergy who for more than a hundred years have raised only weak voices against mass injustice to the Negroes and until the last hour could not agree on a common platform to denounce this crime against humanity.

The breakdown of family life in America is the worst in the nation's history and, some would say, of all times. Some large cities have a divorce rate of one for every two marriages annually, and the end is not yet in sight. Nothing can hide the fact that our country is socially sick and the malady is spiritual anemia which religious leaders have done little to cure or even alleviate. Occasional sermons on the evils of divorce, there are, and private consultations with young couples in trouble, but nothing like a joint effort to study and try to solve what the bishops of the United States have said is one of the blackest stains on the dignity of American life.

Our crime rate is fantastic, and a growing number of criminals are people in their teens. Most often they are products of broken homes and victims of a family tragedy. Crime is a moral issue, and the custodians of morality are the clergy. Not unlike the responsibility for the race problem, I cannot forbear blaming the Catholic and Protestant ministry for doing so little cooperatively to stem the flood of America's youthful crime, which is juvenile only in the age of those who steal and kill and violate women's chastity.

One area of ecumenical cooperation deserves strong emphasis: the teaching of moral and spiritual values in public education.

Many Catholics, including priests, are unaware of the crisis. Yet no problem is more deeply critical for American Protestantism than the gradual secularization of public schools.

It is one of the paradoxes of history that the United States, where human liberty is specially prized and religious institutions have flourished as nowhere else in modern times, should yet be the only great country in the West where teachers have to defend their claim to transmit the religious heritage on which the existence of America depends.

About a century ago, a Princeton theologian, Dr. A. A. Hodges, argued that "if every party in the state has the right of excluding from public schools whatever he does not believe to be true, then he that believes most must give way to him that believes least, and then he that believes least must give way to him that believes absolutely nothing, no matter in how small a minority the atheists or the agnostics may be." It is self-evident, Hodges concluded, that on this scheme, if it is consistently and persistently carried out in all parts of the country, the United States system of national popular education will be the most efficient and wide instrument for the propagation of unbelief which the world has ever seen.

Much has happened since Hodges wrote just after the Civil War. His fears about public education becoming "the most appalling enginery for the propagation of anti-Christian and atheistic unbelief" have not been verified. On the contrary, public schools have become the bulwark of American democracy and one of the principal instruments of unity in a melting pot of nations. They have done much to safeguard American traditions, including religion, and have helped to produce some of the greatest of this country's spiritual leaders. But a new element has entered the scene. Certain interests, influential in shaping national opinion, are now opposed to any semblance of religious values in public education.

Aroused by such pressure groups, the Protestant Churches of America have awakened to the crisis. They declare themselves unequivocally in favor of integrating religion with the regular curriculum and warn against any shibboleths about mixing Church and State.

> We believe that religion has a rightful place in the public school program [officially declares the Methodist Church] and that it is possible for public school teachers, without violating the traditional American principle of separation of church and state, to teach moral principles and spiritual values. Such teaching would afford a background for further and more specific instruction on the part of home and church. The home and church must carry the chief responsibility for nurturing vital faith which motivates life, but the home and church must have the support of our public schools.

And most recently the National Council of Churches has completed its own five-year analysis of religious values in public education to publish a second report to the forty million Protestant and Orthodox membership of the Council. It concluded that "the public school should recognize the function of religion in American life, and maintain a climate friendly to religion, doing its share to assure to every individual the right to choose his own beliefs."

These are not passing sentiments but the grave judgment of most of our fellow citizens. They need our help in this competition for the soul of America. Currently two forces are struggling for mastery of the public school system: high-minded religionists in every denomination who are deeply concerned for the spiritual welfare of the country, and straddling or confused secularists who place selfish and doctrinaire interests before what they call "ethical theism," deriving from the acceptance of a personal God.

In the years to come it will make a world of difference whether Catholics are alert to this tension and place their influence on the side of believing educators or allow naturalism to win by default. The reward of generous labor on the side of religion is not to be measured in dollars and cents, or even in terms of this-worldly compensation, where human souls are involved. A child, we are told, is a pledge of immortality, for he bears upon him in figure those eternal excellencies in which the joy of heaven consists, and which would not thus be shadowed by the all-gracious Creator, were they not one day to be realized. It is our privilege to cooperate in this realization.

There are no hard and fast rules governing the active cooperation of Catholics with other Christians in solving problems of common social concern. But one idea must be emphasized because it has special relevance to the Catholic clergy.

In dealing with persons of other religious affiliations, I have to know what their commitment means. The better I understand our common affirmations, the more confidently I can cooperate with people in matters involving moral and religious values. By the same token, the more clearly I understand where we differ, the less likely will I offend and perhaps lose a collaborator. The background of knowledge which this presupposes will be dealt with later. Enough here to say that Catholics often do not collaborate with other Christians for lack of confidence (born of study and experience) in just how to deal with people who believe otherwise than they.

COMMUNICATING THE FAITH

The Vatican Council clearly states that ecumenism is not the same as conversion. "When individuals wish for full Catholic communion, their preparation and reconciliation is an undertaking which of its nature is distinct from ecumenical action." However, and this should be underlined, "there is no opposition between the two, since both proceed from the marvelous ways of God."

Indeed, the Council tells Catholics in their ecumenical work to be concerned for the spiritual welfare of their separated brethren, by praying for them and keeping them informed about the Church — "making the first approaches toward them."

No matter how we understand the ecumenical movement we cannot lose sight of the fact that one of the duties of a Christian is to give witness of his faith, not only by the example of a holy life but by the teaching of the Gospel and its communication to those who either do not have it or know it only partially.

Prudence and kindness are the watchwords in communicating the faith to other Christians. The principle set down at the beginning still stands: ecumenism is not technically conversion, if by conversion we mean only entrance into the Catholic Church. But ecumenism emphatically implies conversion, if conversion means the change of mind and heart that I can effect in my fellow Christian by sharing with him my own religious convictions. From his side this does not exclude a similar contribution to me, but from mine I cannot refuse to communicate my knowledge and love of Christ (nurtured in the Catholic faith) without betraying a primary law of charity, which is to share with others the good things that God has undeservedly given me.

Priests must teach the people that clergy have no monopoly on the apostolate. One of the most urgent statements on the duty to share the faith was Pius XII's complaint about isolationists who are unaware that to be a Catholic means to have a sense of mission.

How many young people and adults, who call themselves Catholic, are satisfied to fulfill their immediate duties and meet the obligations strictly necessary for their own salvation. They betray how imperfect is their concept of the nature and demands of the Catholic religion. This religion is essentially apostolic (*essenzialmente apostolica*). It would gain all souls for Christ, the humble and the mighty, the rich and poor, young and old. It would make the Lord known and loved always and above all. Whoever does not have this burning desire, this constant impulse to communicate the rich treasures of the faith to others, is not living up to what the Church expects of her devoted children (*Discorsi e Radiomessaggi,* 17, 454).

The end product of the Catholic dialogue with other Christians is to reunite a dismembered Christian world. The Vatican Council, wrote Pope John XXIII, "will surely be a wonderful manifestation of truth, unity, and charity. It will be a manifestation that we hope will be received by those who behold it, but who are separated from this Apostolic See, as a gentle invitation to seek and find the unity for which Jesus Christ prayed so ardently to His heavenly Father."

I realize that this attitude is not shared by many Protestants when they engage in ecumenical conversation with Catholics. When they foresee organic unification as the final stage of the ecumenical movement, they shy away from admitting that this means integration in the Catholic Church. As one theologian expressed it, "The only kind of unity Rome believes in is the unity of Jonas and the whale, where Protestants are swallowed up by the Catholics!"

Yet, knowledgeable Protestants are not offended by this attitude. They respect it in their disagreement with its premises, and they are frank in admitting that, from the Catholic standpoint, no other position is possible.

In a touching letter addressed to Pope John by an American member of the World Council of Churches, the writer said, "By God's grace, Your Holiness has been called to the See of Rome at a time when Christians of every communion are notably sensitive to division and ardently desirous of unity." He admitted, "It is clear to us that the Roman Catholic Church asserts unequivocally that the fulness of unity can be attained only by conversion to herself. It is equally clear that many of us, who may be willing to consider certain modifications of our faith if required for the sake of the truth of the Gospel, cannot conceivably accept the gracious invitation extended" to the Protestant world.

From an ecumenical viewpoint this desire to communicate covers the spectrum of what I, as a Catholic, possess of divine revelation and what I understand my separated brother in Christ does not have. It is not a question of "selling him" Catholicism. It means sharing with him what I believe to be a great treasure; and no greater disservice can be done the ecumenical movement than to stifle this divine instinct or fear to communicate to others the love of Christ that burns in my own heart.

ROLE OF THE SEMINARIES

The greatest hope of the ecumenical movement lies in the seminaries. If the adaptations recommended by the Council are carried into effect, the next generation of priests will be grounded in the spirit of ecumenism, which for us is the spirit of Christ. At the present writing, Canon Law states in prosaic terms that bishops in their diocese and pastors in the parish should look upon non-Catholics as "committed to them in the Lord" (Canon 1350, § 2). I hesitate asking how this provision has been interpreted in practice, but I think not very effectively.

My first recommendation, then, is that seminary training should be adjusted to the ecumenical times, above all by instilling in candidates for the priesthood a desire to help all Christians, and not only professed Catholics, to grow in the knowledge and love of God. We often speak of a narrow parochialism that hardly knows there are souls to be saved outside a given diocese or parish boundary. But there is another, more grievous domesticism that has never learned to see in all men, above all in every Christian, an object of priestly ministrations.

One of the graces for which I specially thank God is the opportunity I have to teach at a state university where half my students are not Catholic. Their desire to learn from a priest was a revelation to me that I wish to pass on to you. This mere fact that one is a priest for every Christian who enters his life can change a man's whole attitude toward souls, with consequences in the apostolate that are startling. I have in mind a Methodist minister who took one of my classes to help him discover the divinity of Christ. He found that faith and is now preparing to pass it on to others as teacher in a seminary.

The seminary curriculum, and not only in theology, should gradually be adapted to meet the new needs. In the words of the Council, "We must get to know the outlook of our separated brethren. To achieve this purpose, study is of necessity required, and this must be pursued with a sense of realism and good will. Catholics, who already have a proper grounding, need to acquire a more adequate understanding of the respective doctrines of our separated brethren, their history, their spiritual and liturgical life, their religious psychology and general background." If this advice pertains to educated Catholics generally, it is mandatory for future priests.

I like the expression, "with a sense of realism and good will," to describe how the study of other religions should be done. The realism means that I do not ignore or underestimate the differences that divide Catholicism from other religious systems. Such realism will protect me from falling prey to the naïve irenicism that Pope Paul excoriated when he charged some priests and theologians, with criticizing the Church for its "ghetto mentality," as though Catholic unity were something imposed by external tyranny and not a divine gift of interior piety. At the same time, "the good will" preserves me from looking for defects in those who are not Catholic, instead of finding what we have in common and on which they can build an edifice of spirituality.

A good example of this "new approach" is the sacrament of orders. Ingrained in Reformation Protestantism was the notion of a universal priesthood of all believers. But much has happened since Luther's Appeal to the German Nobility, when he branded as an "artful lie" Catholic belief in the real distinction between the clerical and lay states.

For some time now, two different trends are seen among Protestant theologians in reacting against the *status quo*. Some are indignant that after four hundred years the Churches still show the practical recognition of a secondary status of the laity in comparison with the ministry, the breeding of passivity in the laity as a whole, and stressing the importance of "office" and "ordination" among the clergy. This reaction is most prominent in the Free Church and Congregational traditions, where creedalism is least important and the local churches have ultimate authority.

Another and more dominant reaction has been to recognize the facts of history, admit that persistence of a clerical order answers to an inner religious need, and seek to restore the meaning of the ministry to something of its status before the Reformation.

This trend is visible in practice by the amazing proportion of transfers from non-episcopal Churches (Baptists, Disciples of Christ, Congregationalists) to Protestant Churches which maintain a historic episcopate (Methodists and Episcopalians). Fully one half the clergy of the Protestant Episcopal Church have come to it from other denominations, whereas one seldom hears of the reverse. Observers see in this a clear sign of restlessness throughout the Protestant world for some adjustment to traditional, i.e., pre-Reformation, positions on a historic episcopate.

In the light of these and similar reappraisals of the centuries-old theology of the Reformation on the universal priesthood of the laity, it would be a pity if the seminary courses in history and theology did not reflect corresponding changes in curricular structure, content, and stress in manner of treatment. The Council of Trent cannot be too well known and there is no question of minimizing the value of its decree on justification or definitions of the sacraments. But they are not enough. Today's priests ought to be familiar with the broad sweep of four centuries of Church History — Catholic, Protestant, and Orthodox — since the Council of Trent. They have a right to know how Catholicism has affected the mainstreams of Protestantism since that fateful October 31, 1517; and how they, in turn, have influenced the Catholic Church.

I believe also that seminarians should have personal contact with Protestant students for the ministry. In Protestant divinity schools many voices are calling for faster adjustment of the curriculum to meet the realities of the ecumenical spirit. This is becoming almost a matter of survival. Seminary graduates assume ministerial roles in a society where large numbers of Protestants, at least forty percent, change denominations when they change residence. Informal relations with Catholic seminarians in the course of their training would extend the horizons of both sides. Future priests would be more understanding of the difficulties faced by ministers and be more appreciative of their work; and ministers would learn what motivates Catholic divinity students to follow a priestly vocation. My own experience in sponsoring inter-seminary groups has been uniformly good. In fact, unless some such rapport is cultivated long before ordination, the chances of any serious ecumenical effort afterward are notoriously slim.

We return where we began: to see that among the most powerful means of fostering ecumenism is holiness of life that no one can deny is a reflection of God's presence.

Protestants have a long memory, and their classic authors are being studied as never before. In the latest (1960) critical edition of Calvin's *Institutes* is a graphic description of the condition of the clergy that, in his own words, cried to heaven for reform. It was the only cogent argument Calvin gave to disprove the divine origins of the Catholic priesthood.

> What if we proceed to their morals? Where will that "light of the world" be that Christ requires? Where will that "salt of the earth"? Where that holiness which is, so to speak, an abiding standard of life? Today there is no order of men more notorious in excess, effeminacy, voluptuousness, in short, in all sorts of lust.
> There is scarcely a bishop, and not one in a hundred parish priests who, if his conduct were to be judged according to the ancient canons, would not be subject to excommunication or at least deposition from office. I seem to be saying something unbelievable — so far has that former discipline fallen into disuse which enjoined a more exacting censure of clergy; but this is entirely so.
> Let those who serve under their banners and protection of the Roman See go now and boast among themselves of the priestly order. The order that they have is neither from Christ, nor from the Apostles, nor from the Fathers, nor from the ancient Church (*Institutes,* IV, 5, 14).

It should be a source of inspiration to the clergy to grow in the likeness of Christ to know that more than ever today the eyes of the non-Catholic Christian world are looking with close scrutiny at the conduct of priests, either to confirm their suspicions or change their ideas of Rome. Nothing else in the ecumenical movement is more necessary than a generation of priests who expiate the sins of their forbears and help restore what only divine grace can truly achieve — divine grace, that is, won by the sanctity of God's chosen ones.

21

The Priest and
Modern Communications

Vincent A. Yzermans

SINCE THE DAWN OF THE TWENTIETH CENTURY OUR WORLD HAS WITNESSED a communications revolution which many sociologists have called the most revolutionary event of modern times. In the relatively short span of sixty years mankind has witnessed:

1. The advent and universal expansion of the motion picture industry.
2. The diffusion of radio broadcasting.
3. The creation of photo-journalism with the appearance of *Time* in 1923 and the resultant mass circulation magazines.
4. The invention of television and its first commercial telecast in 1941.
5. The orbiting of Telstar in 1962 with the possible instantaneous coverage of every major news event in the world.

The American public is almost a glutton when it comes to the use of the mass media. In 1965 in the United States alone there were 1754 daily newspapers with a total daily circulation of over sixty million copies being delivered into the nation's forty-eight million homes. There are also 22,130 weekly and monthly publications, including over 100 diocesan weeklies and 375 magazines with a total combined circulation of over twenty-eight million. The nation's 5201 radio stations beam their broadcasts into almost 160 million receivers and the 651 television channels are servicing over sixty million television sets.

Globally, the statistics are equally staggering. There are over 8000 daily newspapers with three hundred million copies printed daily. There are 22,000 other periodicals with 200 million copies printed either weekly or monthly. There are 170,000 movie theaters visited by over 17,000 billion customers each year who view the 2500 films produced annually. There are over 6000 radio stations broadcasting over 400 million receivers and over 1000 television stations beaming out programs to 120 million television sets that are used over 200,000 billion hours every year by young and old, wise and foolish, mighty and lowly.

The point is this: The *media* of communications are everywhere. They are vitally important. They are influencing the thoughts and actions of countless millions. They cannot be ignored. Cardinal Bea stressed the same point when he said:

> First of all it must be realized that these media of communication have come to stay. They cannot be suppressed, even if one wanted to; and if there is danger in them, danger is never a reason for refusing the use of means which can be of real and immense service in the cause of good.[1]

Nothing, perhaps, has so dramatically awakened the Catholic Church to the importance of the mass media of communications as Vatican Council II. Press, radio, and television combined to make that greatest religious event of our times the best-reported religious story of all time. The Council Fathers themselves gave witness to the importance of mass communications by approving the *Decree on the Media of Social Communication* which was promulgated by Pope Paul VI on December 4, 1963.

The Church's official attitude toward the mass media was best expressed in the opening sentence of that conciliar decree. There we read:

> Among the wonderful technological discoveries which men of talent, especially in the present era, have made with God's help, the Church welcomes and promotes with special interest those which have a most direct relation to men's minds and which have uncovered new avenues of communicating most readily news, views and teachings of every sort.[2]

The pervasiveness and the persuasiveness of the mass media make them, in a very particular manner, the object of every pastoral ministry. They will not go away; on the contrary, they will increase in influence and importance more and more as the years go on. The priest who meets them with condemnatory sermons or shrugs them off as of little importance is acting more foolishly than the proverbial ostrich. They form, in more ways than we care to admit, the thought processes and the action patterns of the vast majority of people today. The importance of the mass media has

---

[1] Augustin Bea, *Unity in Freedom* (New York: Harper & Row Publishers, 1964), p. 29.

[2] *Decree on the Media of Social Communications* (trans. N.C.W.C.), p. 3.

brought about in recent years a growing awareness on the part of Church leaders of two necessary areas for Catholic leadership. These two great needs, namely, a healthy public opinion and a flourishing intellectual creativity, we should examine briefly.

A HEALTHY PUBLIC OPINION

We must not forget, much less deny, that there exists a fundamental human right to information — be this within or without the Church. Pope John XXIII enunciated this right in *Pacem in Terris* when he wrote: ".... man has a natural right . . . to freedom in investigating the truth and — within the limits of the moral order and the common good — to freedom of speech and publication . . ." Taking up the same theme, Pope Paul VI, in his address of April 17, 1964, stated: "Information by this time is unanimously recognized as a universal, inviolable and inalienable right of modern man." He went on to say, "Information must be true, honest, and faithful to facts, to fulfill its social role, and it will never be so unless he who gives information is always anxious for objectivity. That is to say that information must before all else correspond to truth."

The communications decree of the Second Vatican Council also discussed the importance of man's right to information. It declared:

> The prompt publication of affairs and events provides every individual with a fuller, continuing acquaintance with them, and thus all can contribute more effectively to the common good and more readily promote and advance the welfare of the entire civil society. Therefore, in society men have a right to information . . . about matters concerning individuals or the community.[3]

Man's right to information exists in the Church as well as civil society. We should like to think that the right to information is cherished and granted even more readily and willingly in the Church than in other spheres of man's activities.

In the Church today there are many dangers to healthy public opinion. The cleric endowed with the siege mentality, as well as the layman with the pay-and-pray complex, are serious threats to healthy public opinion. Both represent weaknesses described by Michael Novak in *The Open Church* as ".... an uncritical use of abstractions; the loss of honesty and candor; and undue admiration for uniformity with a lack of esteem for diversity; and a blindness to the spiritual values promoted in the secular world."[4] If we are ever going to begin correcting the threat of the totalitarian mind within the Catholic Church, we must restore among ourselves a dedication to healthy public opinion within the Church.

---

[3] *Ibid.*, p. 5.
[4] Michael Novak, *The Open Church* (New York: Macmillan Company, 1964), p. 349.

Pope Pius XII in his February 17, 1950, address was the first supreme pontiff to use the term "public opinion" in relation to the Church. He then described public opinion "as a natural echo, a more or less spontaneous common resounding of acts and circumstances in the mind and judgment of people who feel they are responsible beings, closely bound to the fate of their community." At the same time he warned of the dangers if public opinion is thwarted. He said:

> When so-called public opinion is dictated or imposed . . . [it] makes a mockery of the just rights of men to their own judgments and their own convictions. Then it creates a heavy, unhealthy, artificial atmosphere which in the course of events . . . compels [men] to give their wealth and their blood for the defense and triumph of a false and unjust cause. In truth, where public opinion ceases to function freely, there peace is in danger.[5]

We are not surprised today to know that there is room for public opinion in the Church. There is not only room for it; on the contrary, it is a necessary condition of the Church's life. Amazingly, this was not always recognized by churchmen. Yet, Pope Pius said it most directly: "Because the Church is a living body, something would be wanting in her life if public opinion were lacking — and the blame for this deficiency would fall back upon the pastors and the faithful."[6] Public opinion, then, is not merely a relish, or the frosting on the cake. Without public opinion, let us repeat, something would be wanting in the Church's life.

This statement of Pius XII prompted Father Karl Rahner to spell out further corollaries in his essay on *Free Speech in the Church*. Thus he admonishes clerics and ecclesiastical superiors:

> If [the clergy and hierarchy] do not allow the people to speak their minds, do not, in more dignified language, encourage or even tolerate, with courage and forbearance and even a certain optimism free from anxiety, the growth of a public opinion within the Church, they run the risk of directing her from a soundproof ivory tower, instead of straining their ears to catch the voice of God, which can also be audible within the clamor of the times. . . .[7]

Further, Father Rahner issues a warning:

> Apart from anything else, the Church today should be more careful than ever before not to give even the slightest impression that she is of the same order as those totalitarian states for whom outward power and sterile, silent obedience are everything and love and freedom nothing, and that her methods

---

[5] Vincent A. Yzermans, ed., *Major Addresses of Pope Pius XII*, Vol. 1, "Public Opinion," Address of February 17, 1950, p. 136 (St. Paul, Minn.: North Central Publishing Co., 1961).

[6] *Ibid.*, p. 137.

[7] From *Free Speech in the Church* by Karl Rahner, S.J., © (New York: Sheed and Ward, Inc., 1959), p. 26.

of government are not those of the totalitarian systems in which public opinion has become a ministry of propaganda.[8]

In his pastoral letter of 1963, entitled "The Church and Public Opinion," Cardinal Cushing attaches an apostolic dimension to public opinion, thereby making it an aspect of priestly ministry. He wrote:

> Besides the role that public opinion plays within the Church specifically on Church life, it has, we know, a wider function in reference to the world and those common goals all other men share with Christians. The responsibility of the member for the Church is a real one . . . but just as real and, in a sense, equally compelling is his responsibility to society and the general welfare of humanity. Church authority cannot be unmindful of this larger burden, nor can it act as if the common good of the Church is somehow unrelated to the common good of mankind.[9]

INTELLECTUAL CREATIVITY

Not every priest is a creative genius. As a matter of fact, most are not. But in one way or another every priest is a guide and counselor and thus in a position to encourage creativity. In this sense he must be sympathetic both to the need of creativity in the Church today as well as to those under his charge in encouraging creative thought and action.

Creativity demands a noble mind, a generous heart, and willing hands. Suffering will be, as it always has been, the beginning of every creative endeavor.

This type of creativity demands, in other words, a pure heart, a loyalty to Christ and His Church, and a prudence that will, by all means, act and act with reason and love. Creativity demands, too, that one be willing to take a chance, that one be not too proud to make a mistake, that one be willing to seek guidance and direction from those who are best qualified to aid the cause of Christ.

Nor must it be thought, as some people think, that there is a conflict between creativity and authority. On the contrary, the two are but aspects of divine love. Every act of creation, beginning with that primeval *fiat* uttered by God, is essentially an act of love. It is only love that can create, just as hate destroys.

The exercise of true authority is likewise an act of love. Pope Paul expressed this thought in these words: "Authority in the Church is a vehicle of the divine gifts. It is a service of charity by means of love on behalf of salvation." If one is willing to make the effort to create, one must not fear authority. It is there to be a service and if it does not serve the creative forces at work in the Church it cannot hold claim to a genuine Catholic concept of authority.

---

[8] *Ibid.,* p. 137.
[9] Richard Cushing, *The Church and Public Opinion* (Boston: Daughters of St. Paul, 1963), p. 14.

There is yet another compelling reason why we all must stir up our creative energies. That reason is the very world in which we live. That world has engaged in its most staggering revolution since the dawn of our century. John Gunther observed, "There have been more changes in the past sixty-five years than in all other centuries put together." He also pointed out that "the great coin of the globe has become a dime."

Pope Paul has referred to our world today as going through "the evolution of civilization" and in this process "an immense and overwhelming process is changing the face of the earth as if man today were accomplishing fully the very first biblical precept: 'Fill the earth and subdue it.' " If we are going to develop the kind of Christians the world demands, we must be servants of mankind, using every creative urge and impulse that God has shared with us.

At the turn of the century Leon Bloy wrote: "Present events are certainly hideous, but not vulgar, as to their tendencies. I therefore again think that we are at the prologue of an extraordinary drama, the like of which has not been seen for twenty centuries, and I invite you to a certain degree of recollection."

The creativity we must exercise will be successful to the extent that we preserve a spirit of recollection. A spirit of recollection will enable us to be the true inaugurators of creative forces under God. It will also force upon us a commitment to creativity. This type of commitment will be, as it always has been, the direct consequence of vital Christianity. No one, perhaps, expressed this better than Father Isaac Hecker when he wrote almost a century ago: "It is for this we are created: that we may give a new and individual expression of the absolute in our own peculiar character. As soon as the new is but the re-expression of the old, God ceases to live."

Father William Lynch, in his excellent work, *The Image Industries,* makes this observation: "The Church has refused to stay within the sanctuary in the areas of economics and politics. Here is another area, the area of the creative image of man and of human sensibility, in which it must refuse to be contained within 'transcendent' and pious boundaries."[10]

THE PRIEST AND THE PRESS

The priest of the twentieth century must realize these needs of the mass media and, to the best of his ability, make the press, radio, and television an integral part of his apostolic life. He need not be a specialist; he need only exhibit that minimal degree of charity in dealing with newsmen that enables him to communicate. This, admittedly, takes a bit of effort for, as Edward Fischer remarked:

---

[10] William F. Lynch, *The Image Industries* (New York: Sheed & Ward, 1959), p. 39.

The Church can issue all the decrees it wants about communications, but all of it will be just so many words until people within the Church work hard at learning how to communicate. Communication is not the same as information. Dictionaries, encyclopediae, and textbooks inform, but they do not communicate. Communication is one human spirit reaching out and touching another.[11]

If communication is encumbent upon every Catholic it is especially vital to the ministry of the priest. He must be able to overcome, and sometimes overlook, the failings of the past as well as the present. At the same time he must know what is expected of him and how he can co-operate in serving the media of communication. The priest of tomorrow must be able to put the ax to the indictment expressed in a letter to this author. Wrote a very respected religious editor of a large metropolitan newspaper:

Working as a Catholic news writer for a secular paper is not the easiest job in the world, as I am fast finding out. Probably the hardest part of this job is working with priests. Many of the pastors and a good percentage of the assistants, I am afraid, have prejudged all newsmen by what they have heard or seen and maybe from a long-ago personal experience. I have the nasty job of trying to break down this barrier.

Experience with many distinguished members of the general press forces the conclusion that this is an all too frequent criticism. The average cleric's treatment of newsmen is often far from courteous. Few groups, in my judgment, have projected a poorer image nationally as far as the general press is concerned than the Catholic priesthood.

This is not flattering. It is both discouraging and disheartening. If time has not already run out, if there is still hope for recovery, then we must ask ourselves two questions. First: Why has the Catholic clergy generally projected such a negative, if not antagonistic, attitude toward the general press? Secondly: What can we do to improve the situation?

Our Past History

As an immigrant people we were forced to fight our way up from the bottom. Our forefathers who built neo-gothic churches, laid the tracks of countless railroads, and plowed the fields of virgin territory were by and large poor, unlettered, hardy people. They fought mightily to preserve the faith, and they did an excellent job. But in preserving the faith they had enemies. Among the chief antagonists were the lords of a so-called "secular" press who were suspiciously hostile to everything that smacked of popery or Romanism. In all honesty this press was often dishonest and bigoted.

---

[11] Edward Fischer, "If Seminaries Don't Teach Communication," *Ave Maria,* February 13, 1965, p. 9,

But that was generations ago. As the nation grew, as journalism matured, the old canards whispered like old wives' tales behind rectory curtains lost — or should have lost — their meaning. As Catholics, we emerged from the ghetto. We became respectable and acceptable. We began to enter into the mainstream of American society. We were both newsworthy and newsmakers.

The past is dead; a new era has been ushered in. Still, too many failed to recognize the writing scrawled across the battered walls of the world, breaking down centuries-old barriers and propelling us, as the ministers of God's people, into the forefront of events that are news.

Secondly, in the early days of our American history we were forced to build around us a protective wall which we called the Catholic press. For decades bishops have supported, promoted, and almost canonized the Catholic press. This, we must recognize, was a necessity. In an era of violent bigotry and vicious calumny against the Catholic Church the most logical defense was a press that would refute the charges, set the record straight, and — unfortunately, not to be overlooked — create a reassuring atmosphere of triumphalism, exaggerated greatness and glory, and unwarranted clericalism within the Catholic body.

These observations are made with no intention of slighting the Catholic press. We still need a Catholic press, but it should be quite different from what we grew up with and find all too often even today. We are still supporting the Catholic press, as we should. But there is another world "out there" which also needs our support.

Finally, I believe our clerical education has made us oblivious to both the pervasiveness and persuasiveness of the mass media. American corporations spend literally millions of dollars every year on advertising in radio, television, and the general press; this is done quite successfully by public relations people who realize where the message is being heard and seen and how it will affect the dividends the stockholders receive at the next annual meeting. According to one study, the average American family spends at least thirty hours a week watching television.

The image makers are busily and successfully at work creating a mass media culture. By and large this world of mass culture is one that has passed by the Catholic Church. We have not studied it; generally we do not analyze it. When confronted with its enormous influence and power our tones are too often hostile, our stance too often indifferent, and our utterances too negative. Generally speaking, as clerics we have made ourselves Public Enemy Number One for the majority of newsmen, radio announcers, and television commentators. They would, however, like to be our friends. Too often the rebuff they get from the average chancery, rectory, and Catholic institution is enough to make them question our commitment to the divine command: "Little children, love one another."

All of us know some reporter, editor, newscaster who did not give the Catholic Church a fair shake. There are white hats and black hats in every profession, and journalism is no more an exception than the Catholic clergy. But my defense of the newsmen, the editor, the columnist is this: the zealous, assiduous search for truth and facts among respected journalists at least equals the efforts of many clerics.

In this age of renewal in a reforming Church we must be in the forefront of the ranks of reformers. As the priest molds his parish by his own living and thinking, so he will also help mold the mass media by his attitude toward the working press.

First, then, I believe we must develop in our mental outlook a healthy respect for the general press. We can follow no better example in this regard than that of Pope Paul VI. Speaking on April 30, 1966, to delegates of the International Federation of the Periodical Press he said:

> . . . You are the eloquent manifestation of the very elemental need of man, which he rightly claims against all totalitarianism: the right to think freely, the right to express himself freely. . . . You are also the living expression of man's right to think and express himself in freedom.

At the same time Pope Paul presented two cautions to the group which might also be taken to heart by each of us in our dealings with the press. "Now more than ever," he said, "it is necessary not to degrade information into propaganda." In other words, reporters seek news that is truthful, not a party line or a pious plug. Reiterating the same thought Pope Paul went on to say that "the exercise of freedom, which you rightly claim, must never go against the rights of truth and against demands of the common good." Journalists rightly expect truth from the clergy and too often they are disappointed.

This leads to the second observation. As the conciliar decree on social communications underlines, man has a basic, fundamental human right to information. As ministers of God's people we have a duty to supply information when it is legitimately sought and respectfully requested. This means that priests have no right to withhold or deny information about matters that pertain to the public domain. The most damning statement uttered by clerics to newsmen is: "No comment."

For the good of the Church, we should encourage public information in order the better to assess public opinion. The more that people know about the activities, policies, and directives of God's Church, the better able will they be to fulfill their roles as the people of God and the friends of his Church. Members of the press, whom Pius XII called "valiant heralds of truth," serve the Church valiantly when they make known to the general public the vital issues of the Church. When a reporter comes seeking information he is doing the cleric an infinitely greater favor than Church officials do him by taking the time to help him with his story.

Not the Enemy

The priest is responsible for everyone within the boundaries of his parish. A good number of people in many parishes are concerned with mass communications and they have special problems. They need more attention, guidance, and friendship, perhaps, for the very reason that they are influencing countless numbers of people. Radio, television, and newspaper people tell me frequently that they are rebuffed by their parish priests. They, to repeat, are not the enemy.

Not every priest is an expert in the field of the mass media, nor is he expected to be. Kindness, understanding, honesty, and integrity, however, are demanded by his calling. The average newsman does not look for expert professional advice from his parish priest but only the simple amenities expected among Christian gentlemen.

But in most dioceses there are priests and laymen who are experts in the area of mass communications. These are the diocesan directors of bureaus of public information, radio and television, and the diocesan newspaper. The press, radio, and television form their specific field of apostolic activity. Their office is to serve the general press which is designed to serve the priest-pastor, priest-educator, priest-official, and the priest assistant. When questions arise, when a priest wants to get a story out, when he wants the right image projected, he should contact his diocesan public information director. This man knows the media, the men, and the techniques; and he is competent. If he is allowed to help, he will do the job a hundred times better than the priest himself could hope to do.

The diocesan bureau of information is by nature a public relations office, but definitely not in that sense which is odious to most clerics. Public relations in the Church must eliminate the gimmicks, the subtle sophistications, the deception and dishonesty of many well-known hidden persuaders foisted upon a weary public by some slick Madison Avenue agencies.

Cardinal Cushing, in the same pastoral letter we quoted before, made very much the same observation. He wrote:

> . . . in its basic sense the Church must be aware of what is called "public relations," that effort by which a reciprocal interpretation can be made by the Church and the world. It should be superfluous to say that we do not speak here of that manipulation of public opinion and mass suggestions, sometimes called public relations, which has been raised to so specialized a craft as to include distortion, misrepresentation and deception. This has no place in the interpretation of the Church to men which is in its essence a work of truth.[12]

In my mind the best public relations will be built on an effective diocesan program of public information. The Church's image will need no glossy veneer if we are true to our mission as servants of the Church. Our best

---

[12] Cushing, *op. cit.*, p. 23.

public relations will be, as they were from the days of the Apostles, a burning desire to tell all men the truth and a ceaseless love for all men in the unity of the all-embracing love of Christ. This was stated exceptionally well by Father Bernard Cooke, S.J., when he said:

> Genuine communication takes place when the person who is doing the communicating is himself open to communication — when he lets people get at him. He has to say what he means, what he's really convinced of. That doesn't always happen in the Church. Some priests and religious are always *telling* people, but we never let them know who we are.

Finally, information and public relation entail money. It is the word that creates the problems that haunt many pastors' sleepless nights. But the simple fact is that a diocesan bureau of public information needs money. A source of constant wonderment is how the Church spends untold millions each year on Catholic schools, hospitals, organizations, conventions, Communion breakfasts, and banquets.

Comparatively, we do not spend so much as a widow's mite on building up a healthy relationship with the mass media. We spend our money too often in a Catholic ghetto where we glow with a feeling of security and fraternity. We begrudge the few pennies we might very easily spend for a vigorous diocesan public information and public relations program to serve those who will tell our story to the majority of American people in the general press, radio, and television. In accord with the directives of the conciliar decree on social communications, there should be more serious attention given financially to promoting and fostering Catholic participation in the area of mass communications.

Catholic priests are rightly involved in the liturgical apostolate, the civil rights movement, the war on poverty, the education of youth, the care of the aged, infirm, and delinquent, the family life movement, the administration of parishes. It is high time that we become more realistically involved in the field of communications arts. As priests this would be the greatest good we could bring to the areas of the general press, radio, and television, namely, to be priests not afraid to study seriously, to meditate frequently, and to speak intelligently the good theology at work in our Church today, telling the Good News to those dedicated men Pius XII called "the valiant heralds of truth."

22

The Apostolate to the Businessman

THOMAS F. MCMAHON, C.S.V.

We have a true respect for what you are: leaders of industry, as you are called today, entrepreneurs, managers, producers of wealth, organizers of modern businesses. . . . It is you who create opportunities for work, employment, professional skill, and who thus provide jobs and bread for large numbers of workers and collaborators. It is you, therefore, who transform society through the deployment of labor forces which science, technology and the industrial and bureaucratic structure place at the disposal of modern man. Together with teachers and doctors you are in the forefront of those who transform society, who have the greatest influence on living conditions, and who open the way to new, undreamt-of developments (Paul VI, June 8, 1964, Address to "Christian Union of Employers and Managers").

Like a diamond, the apostolate to the businessman has many facets. The person of the businessman, his spiritual and moral problems, and the vocational aspects of his profession require investigation, discussion and delineation. This paper proposes to investigate a few of these points to suggest possible methods of approach to this apostolate; the apostolate *of* the businessman; the apostolate *to* the businessman; the role of the priest in this apostolate; what is understood by "businessman" in terms of the apostolate; the needs of this apostolate; the history of business morality; preparation for the apostolate to the businessman. In the past, seminary training did not ordinarily make students sufficiently aware of this apostolate and its potentialities. It is my hope that these points will stimulate further discussion that might ultimately lead to general recognition of this apostolate as part of the priestly ministry and to a more widespread participation in its activities.

THE APOSTOLATE OF BUSINESSMEN

The decisions of businessmen affect the whole socio-economic structure to such an extent that Pope Paul VI places businessmen in the same category with doctors and teachers. They are men "who transform society, have the greatest influence on living conditions, and who open the way to new, undreamt-of developments." In a sense, each businessman has a "vocation"; that is, a "mission that God has assigned to him," as Pius XII stated in an address to the Chambers of Commerce.[1] Bearing the imprint of religion, the businessman in his mission "aims and strives to circulate worldly goods, destined by God for the advantage of all, and takes them where they must serve and in a manner to make them serve well." He is then "a good and true servant of society, a guarantee against misery, a promoter of general prosperity." Accordingly, the businessman properly fulfills his function as a lay member of the Church in seeking "the kingdom of God by engaging in temporal affairs and by ordering them according to the plan of God." The very secular nature of his professional activities and the "transforming" role of his decisions offer the businessman the opportunity to "work for the sanctification of the world from within as a leaven."[2] The "mission" of the businessmen, then, is truly the apostolate of transforming society through greater productivity and more equal distribution of material goods among mankind.[3] In a word, the production and distribution of goods and services is the apostolate *of* the businessman.

A personal experience of an executive might clarify these points:

Several summers ago, a young college student worked in my office as a stenographer. After graduation the following June, she volunteered for the Peace Corps, and was assigned to teach in Ethiopia. During her three-month training period which, incidentally, took place in a city where one of my plants is located, I happened to have a business appointment in this city and suggested that we have dinner together.

During dinner, she recalled a few incidents of the previous summer when she had worked for me. She remarked that it had been a revealing experience and then commented, "I think it is perfectly awful that your salesmen are concerned only with getting an order and earning a commission. They are only interested in dollars." This statement came as a real shock to me. Further conversation revealed that she had a very dim view of our operation as a whole, since, insofar as she could see, it was

[1] Pius XII, "Address to the Delegates of the World Congress of Chambers of Commerce," April 27, 1950, *The Catholic Mind*, 48, August, 1950, p. 511.
[2] Vatican Council II, *Constitution on the Church* (trans. N.C.W.C.), p. 35.
[3] Vatican Council II, *Decree on the Church in the Modern World* (trans. N.C.W.C.), p. 40.

motivated solely by the desire to make a profit — in other words, money. Additionally, she felt a great sympathy for "those poor men at your factories who have to stand at a machine for eight hours a day doing the same old thing over and over." To me it is inconceivable that anyone could go through four years of college and still have such a complete misconception of the fundamentals of economic life and of the motives that cause people to function. True, a salesman's motive in getting an order is largely the income he derives from his work. But what other motivation could there be? What happens to these orders after they have been secured? How many other *people* — not just money — are really involved? These orders, when translated into products that are shipped and paid for, provide employment for approximately 3200 people. This, in turn, provides the livelihood for about 700 families. In other words, these orders represent food, housing, clothing, medical care, education, and any other service required by the American family.

As I pointed out to my former stenographic employee — who apparently was completely unaware of this reality — these orders, the goods they produce, the money exchanged in the process, and the taxes paid, are currently paying for her training course in the Peace Corps. And will also pay for her two years in Ethiopia. In effect, a share of the salesman's services was given to her in exchange for her services to a foreign country.

Besides, I believe it is another misconception to say that the average factory worker does not enjoy his work under present working conditions. Furthermore, his income is sufficient to give him the feeling of accomplishment in providing comfortably for his family. When I asked her if the same point didn't apply to Ethiopia, she admitted that the purpose of the Peace Corps in that area was, in general, to raise the standard of living. She also admitted that although she would teach children, other volunteers were being trained to introduce efficient, productive farming methods and to help establish some basic industries in certain areas of Ethiopia. She mentioned that there is practically no industry. In fact, in some areas, the natives do not even use the wheel; they still drag things along on a sled. Obviously the building of wagons, wheelbarrows, and other means of transportation will be one of the first Peace Corps projects. It will not be very long before a number of native Ethiopians will spend eight hours a day in a wagon factory doing what my young friend described as "that awful monotonous work" of repeatedly hammering nails into boards in the process of wagon-building. Such is the price of progress, in the United States or in Ethiopia. But more significantly, if we had not discussed these points, she would have misrepresented the functions of businessmen, their part in the economic life of a country, and the real opportunities for good that their profession provides. But most important of all, she could not have explained how taking raw materials from the earth, transforming them into products, and distributing them among mankind makes a businessman a "co-creator" with God.[4]

This experience clearly illustrates the need for understanding the apostolate *of* businessmen. Is there an apostolate *to* businessmen?

---

[4] From the unpublished notes of Richard Sunderland, President, General Meters and Controls (Chicago) and currently president of a local chapter of the National Conference of Christian Employers and Managers.

THE APOSTOLATE TO BUSINESSMEN

The so-called "labor priest" was common a few decades ago when labor unions became the protectors of workingmen. The impact of this clerical zeal is still felt when clergymen act as arbitrators at the bargaining table. Such priests as John A. Ryan, John W. Maguire, C.S.V., Leo Brown, S.J., John Cronin, S.S., and George G. Higgins have fearlessly defended labor's rights against the pressures of corporate power, managerial techniques, and advancing technology. Educated to establish a more progressive socio-economic structure and guided by the principles elucidated in Pope Leo XII's *Rerum novarum* and Pope Pius XI's *Quadragesimo anno,* these great men responded dynamically to a need of the American Church in crisis.

Notwithstanding the Church's continuous concern for the laborer, sociological change in the American Church and technological change in industry suggest a further point of emphasis — an apostolate to the businessman. A number of factors warrant this change. More Catholic college graduates plan to move up the managerial pyramid, especially in large corporations that had previously favored the so-called WASP [White Anglo-Saxon Protestant] of American literature. Complaints of religious discrimination against Jews and Catholics qualified for top echelon jobs in business have reached the ears of the U. S. Department of Labor. If the government acts on these complaints, then those managerial positions that had previously been closed will now be available to ambitious, qualified Catholic executives. In addition to the educational advancement of Catholic businessmen and the opening up of positions, automation is possibly the most important factor in establishing the apostolate to the businessman. News magazines, television documentaries, and popular journals have, for the most part, limited their coverage to the effects of automation on "blue collar" laborers. Natural attrition, geographical relocation, and retraining of personnel are just a few of the problems that accompany automation. Less newsworthy but perhaps more important to the apostolate to the businessman is the use of automated systems in office procedures, inventory control, and lower-to-middle echelon managerial decision-making. With the increasing use of automated systems in offices and banks, employees who are not generally protected by labor unions are at the mercy of top executives. Consequently, top executives up to the present have reluctantly introduced automation at the management level. But sound economics (in the broad sense of the word) may require more intensified automated systems for planning and organizing as well as for controlling (where it is currently employed most effectively). If this is true, then the decision-maker in the middle level of management will develop other talents, for his work will probably involve greater creativity and fewer repetitive tasks.

The efficient running of an automated corporate structure will almost certainly require the centralization of corporate authority. Intensified competition inside and outside the corporation, increased personnel layoffs, geographical relocation of plant and personnel are just a few by-products of automation that affect managers as well as laborers. And decisions in these areas involve moral problems, both for top executives and for their subordinates.

With an increasing number of Catholics entering executive ranks of corporations that must automate to survive the battle of competition, the clergy have a challenge that at least rivals that of the "labor priest" of thirty years ago. It is the apostolate *to* businessmen.

WHO ARE BUSINESSMEN?

When Pope Paul VI calls businessmen "leaders of industry . . . entrepreneurs, managers, producers of wealth, organizers of modern business,"[5] he seems to limit his description to top level decision-makers, structurally considered as "top management." True, their decisions have widespread effect on the whole economy, for opening and closing plants, introducing new products and taking other goods off the market, setting higher production goals, and raising prices are top management decisions that can have staggering effects. However, the term *businessman* can be applied equally to a corporation president with 50,000 employees and a billion dollars in assets and to the manager of a laundromat with no employees and $1000 in assets. It includes professional managers on every level of corporate structure and in every functional area (e.g. marketing, production, research). Business theorist and management consultant Peter F. Drucker places foremen in the ranks of management. Controllers of finance (e.g., bankers) may also be considered as businessmen. Shareholders (who generally as individuals do not make decisions on company policy) are not ordinarily called businessmen. Stockbrokers, on the other hand, do qualify as businessmen. In an extended sense, salesmen and their counterparts, purchasing agents, are *businessmen* inasmuch as their activities directly affect the behavior of the whole corporation, because sales are required for profits just as material is necessary for the production of goods and services.

Not all *executives,* however, are necessarily businessmen. They are rather managers, or decision-makers who affect the behavior of others in their planning, organizing, motivating, and controlling. Government officials, deans of schools, directors of charitable institutions or foundations, bishops of dioceses, and provincial superiors are executives rather than businessmen. To be businessmen, they must have profitability built into their

5 Paul VI, "Address to the Christian Union of Employers and Executives," June 8, 1964, *The Pope Speaks,* 10, 1964, p. 46.

operations. Without profit or "a reasonable return on investment" a business venture will soon collapse from financial anemia. In the so-called "non-profit" organizations, profit becomes a by-product of effective management. The apostolate to businessmen, then, would exclude executives or managers who look upon profit as merely a *conditio sine qua non* of an enterprise. It would include those whose decisions are directed to earning a profit, either as a means or as an [intermediate] end.

NEEDS OF THE APOSTOLATE

It is a common experience of life that other people like to tell us what we should do. Others seem to know what is good for us. And it is a common experience of businessmen that clergymen like to tell them what they should do. Businessmen, such as the "enlightened" Catholic layman, resent *a priori* solutions to their spiritual, moral, and psychological problems. Perhaps priests would be more effective in their apostolate if they asked businessmen this question: "Just what kind of guidance do you expect from the clergy?" Father Raymond C. Baumhart, S.J., in his Harvard Graduate School of Business survey,[6] did just that. He received answers from businessmen, of whom 228 were Catholic. In general, the respondents felt that preaching and writing are the best means of helping businessmen. What should sermons and literature cover? Businessmen prefer, first of all, clear explanations of ethical principles; secondly, applications of ethical principles to typical business situations; thirdly, motivation for ethical behavior. Businessmen were also enthusiastic about meeting with the clergy in small groups for discussion and were interested in having a clergyman available at church or rectory for consultation. But they did not respond enthusiastically to the suggestion of having in-plant "pastors" for consultation.

Is there a difference between the approach expected of the clergy in assisting businessmen and the methods used in "labor priest" movement? I suggest that there should be. The latter generally stressed personal involvement (sometimes emotional) in strikes, boycotts and marches. For the most part, "social action" became an effective instrument for promoting the rights of labor. Recent civil rights demonstrations are somewhat reminiscent of social action for labor's rights in the 1930's. Even as arbitrators who are supposed to judge objectively, priests appear — at least to some businessmen — to favor the labor side of the dispute. One Catholic busi-

---

[6] Raymond C. Baumhart, S.J., "How Ethical Are Businessmen?" *Harvard Business Review,* 39, July-August, 1961, p. 6. For reports on Catholic businessmen, cf. *America,* 106, January 6, 1962, pp. 436, 106; February 3, 1962, pp. 589, 107; April 14, 1962, p. 47. From his survey, Father Baumhart concluded that Catholic businessmen do not differ substantially from non-Catholics in their approach to moral problems in business.

nessman I know refuses to accept priests as arbitrators. "They are the worst," he claims, "because they quite rightly must preserve the image of protecting the 'downtrodden' — sometimes to the point of inequality." Notwithstanding dubious indictments of this sort, the priest interested in the labor movement historically has been for the most part an "action" priest.

Although the respondents of the Baumhart study were not given the opportunity to accept or reject explicitly an action-type priest for their needs (except for "plant pastors" which they did not accept enthusiastically), they explicitly desired assistance of the priest as an *educator*. That is, they want clear explanations of principles. They want discussions. They want motivation. They want some help in problem-solving from qualified clergymen. None of these roles even suggests an "action priest." Nor is this conclusion surprising. Almost two thirds of the respondents had no formal training in philosophy or in business ethics. In order to make business decisions that are morally correct, these men recognize the need for further education in moral principles and practices. Father Baumhart suggests the possibility of developing "medial norms" that can be adapted to the particular circumstances of the businessman, his company, or the industry. In the apostolate to businessmen, the executive, the manager, or the salesman is the instrument for "social action." The priest assumes the role of professional educator.

A further explanation of the priest's role as educator seems appropriate at this time. The National Conference of Christian Employers and Managers, a continuing education group of executives who meet each month to discuss the ethical problems in business, distinguish between *moral theologians* and *priest counselors*. Priest counselors work directly with small groups; their role is primarily consultative. They are also expected to provide spiritual motivation, to uncover higher values in the temporal order, to clarify moral principles, and to suggest scriptural texts and themes, philosophical insights, and theological dimensions for consideration. On the contrary, moral theologians prepare research papers on various moral problems. Their in-depth studies are made available to the general membership through "program packages" that specialists adapt to the needs and capabilities of the members. The moralist also investigates such topics as the theology of work and the vocation of businessmen, and he attempts to develop, or he suggests, "medial norms" for particular problems. In a word, the priest counselor is a *resource* man for the spiritual and moral needs of a small group to which he ordinarily acts as chaplain. The moral theologian is a *research* man who provides the resources both for the general membership and for chaplains. The priest in either role is still an educator. His apostolate to businessmen is essentially teaching.

It is almost a truism that a good teacher "leads" his students. Only the insecure or unqualified teacher is apodictic. Similarly, "pat" solutions to complex business problems, hostile attitudes toward businessmen, authoritarian pronouncements on cases and principles tend to broaden the gap between clergy and businessmen. How many priests are qualified to pass judgment on the business aspects of moral problems? A priest might know his moral principles, but does he know which ones pertain to this situation? Unless a priest shared the experiences of the "business fraternity" before entering the seminary or unless he experienced the pressures of administration in his priestly life, businessmen hesitate to rely on his solution. For them, it is frequently "unrealistic." Seminary training *does* qualify a priest to present clearly general and particular moral principles that businessmen may apply to their problems.

From what I have written so far, one might conclude that the apostolate to businessmen is identical with the teaching of business morality or business ethics. I suggest that the apostolate includes more than teaching business morality. Moral behavior is one aspect of any vocation; it is not its totality. Similarly, the moral problems confronting businessmen comprise but one aspect of their vocation as Christians and businessmen. There is more to a Christian businessman's vocation than the moral problems he faces each day. His daily decisions cover the whole gamut from the completely moral to the totally amoral, for as part of his vocation he "transforms society" through production, services, distribution of goods, employment, conversion of raw materials to usable tools. Moral problems necessarily arise in the salesman's desire to top his quota, the executive's drive for a higher rate of return, for the purchasing agent's temptation to force a lower bid. These are particular problems.

Some moral problems are even industry-wide. The question of building fertilizer plants in communist satellite countries, the social problem of plant closure in one-industry Southern mill towns, price-fixing in the manufacturing of electrical products, and the pressures, pricing, and questionable advertising of the drug industry revealed in the Kefauver Committee hearings are examples of industry-wide moral problems. But these same industries provide the material goods for mankind. And businessmen in these same industries should recognize in their labors the opportunity to transmit the "good news" of the Gospel in a contemporary setting:

> I was hungry and you developed fertilizers and farm machinery to produce abundance. I was thirsty and you built dams and irrigation projects. I was naked and you built textile factories to produce clothing at low cost. I was weary and you built power plants and transmission lines and distributed electricity. I was sick and you developed and produced drugs and powerful medicines.[7]

---

[7] Cited in *Social Digest*, 8, May-June, 1965, p. 132.

Nonetheless, businessmen are preoccupied with the moral problems they face in their decision-making. The situation is somewhat analogous to a doctor whose primary concern is treating patients in a manner consistent with professional ethical norms, but who realizes at the same time that he is effectively fulfilling his vocation and professional commitment. Emphasis on medical ethics has in no way lessened the vocational aspect of the medical profession. By recognizing the ethical demands of his profession, a doctor can more easily relate his daily activities to the precepts of divine law, both natural and supernatural, which in turn safeguard the sacredness of human life, and can acknowledge the need for the supernatural and see himself as the image of the Divine Physician.

Although businessmen should recognize the ideals of their vocation, they usually experience first of all those moral problems that force them to choose between the "economic must" and the "ethical ought." The Christian commitment reveals a new dimension when the challenge is presented in the concrete situations of daily decision-making. Projected within the Christian framework and its goals, these decisions, both ethical and unethical, have far-reaching effects on society, as the history of business ethics shows. It is no wonder that contemporary businessmen show concern for raising the moral standards of industry.

History of Business Morality

Writers and lecturers frequently refer to the Judaeo-Christian tradition as the norm of business morality in the United States.[8] This tradition, they claim, preserves the sacredness of the human person, the right of private property, a "just" return for investment and labor, and concern for the commonweal. Our American forefathers, however, incorporated these values as European Jews and Christians expressed and hopefully, lived them. Further development of the European Judaeo-Christian tradition occurred in the eighteenth and nineteenth centuries in the United States. Based on middle-class English Protestant mores, it stressed the values of the individual, thriftiness as virtue, and temporal prosperity as a sign of divine benevolence. This development also expanded the concept of "excess" which was a dominant trait of the American Puritan.

With the factory system came what Leo D. Stone calls the "divine right

---

[8] The Business Ethics Advisory Council, encouraged by the U. S. Department of Commerce under Luther Hodges, published *A Statement on Business Ethics and a Call for Action* (Washington, D. C.: U. S. Government Printing Office, 1962) which refers to "those high ethical standards that derive from our heritage and traditions." Explicitly rejecting the feasibility of the Judaeo-Christian concept for international ethical problems, Robert W. Austin, in his "Code of Conduct for Business," *Harvard Business Review*, 39, September-October, 1961, p. 60, offers four basic principles as a common denominator for all men, regardless of religious traditions and customs.

of businessmen."[9] In this practical philosophy the rights and the interests of the laboring man would be protected and advanced by the good Christian men to whom God in his wisdom had given property rights. This gave rise to such sincerely religious entrepreneurs as Daniel Drew and John D. Rockefeller who saw a source of holiness in wealth gathering and in the stewardship of the unfortunate. And Adam Smith's economic theories, so well-received in the United States, contributed immensely toward making a virtue out of big business. The pre-established, iron-clad economic "laws of nature" were free of Church control. And by the end of the nineteenth century God was no longer recognized as a "claimant" in the business world. The low point in American business ethics came with the "robber barons," for whom "business is business." Their double standard of morality — one for the family, another for business — still perdures. The age of excess led to social reforms in the form of laws and permanent commissions — the Sherman Anti-trust Act, the Clayton Act, the Interstate Commerce Commission. It is no wonder that morality at times becomes synonymous with legality. Recovery from the depression of the 1930's stressed social legislation favoring the working class; these laws might also have contributed toward accepting the legal minimum as the moral maxim in business.

Post World War II business theorists began to depart from the legal formulation of the corporation and its exclusive responsibility to shareholders. In their place, they substituted a new form of stewardship, the "gospel of service," that attempts to balance, through "enlightened self-interest," the different claims of shareholders, consumers, suppliers, and employees. It is a step from the legal minimum to self-regulation, and it augurs hope for more effective ethical decisions.

Notwithstanding the electrical manufacturers' conspiracy and other industry-wide unethical practices prevalent in an oligopolistic structure — or perhaps because of these well-known problems — businessmen are becoming more concerned with the ethical dimensions of their decisions. The Business Ethics Advisory Council, endorsed by the U.S. Department of Commerce, could become a powerful source of revitalizing ethics in business.

THE CATHOLIC TRADITION

Obviously absent from the above history of business ethics in the United States is Catholic social doctrine and the traditional view of moral theologians on the virtue of justice. The reasons for this omission are almost as obvious as the omission itself.

First of all, the Catholic notion of economics and business ethics, as part of the Judaeo-Christian tradition, evolves from principles and conclusions

---

[9] Leo D. Stone, "The History of Ethics in American Business," *Ethics in Business,* ed. Robert Bartels, Bureau of Business Research Monograph, pp. 111, 31.

found in the writings of the Scholastic period. From them, the precepts of the natural law determined by the relations between God and man, man and God, and man and his fellow man, were the criteria for economic policy. For the Physiocrats, pre-established, iron-clad economic "laws of nature" — the "hidden hand" concept — leading to laissez-faire policy became the norm. For the English classical economist (with whom Americans identified themselves), the Utilitarian principle of the greatest happiness of the greatest number directed economic behavior. Catholic economists ultimately accepted the "pure theory of economics" (that is, *economic analysis*) as an explanation of what men actually do when certain assumptions are given. But they never accepted laissez-faire or utilitarianism as the criterion for *economic policy,* which is concerned with what *should* be the relationship between economic means and ends. The latter — not the former — requires moral judgment. Since the criterion for economic policy is ultimately based on philosophical and ethical (moral) systems, moral value judgments on the ethical aspects of business practices, except for basic concepts contained in sections of the Constitution, tend to follow either the Protestant adaptation of philosophical positivism or the Catholic tradition of the Scholastic natural law approach. Establishing a common norm of behavior is still one of the principal difficulties in the study of business ethics. The development of foreign markets, the demand for international cooperation in the distribution of products and services, and the emergence of non-Western nations makes the search for an acceptable norm all the more difficult — and necessary.[10]

Secondly, Catholic moral theologians have traditionally related business ethics to particular aspects of the virtue of justice. They applied the principles of commutative, distributive, and legal (general) justice to such problems as private property, just price (from St. Augustine) and competitive market, just wage, usury and interest, profit and merchandising. Additions and refinements due to changing conditions (e.g., discovery of the "new world" and its markets) led ultimately to a cadre of practical norms that, indiscriminately applied from the circumstances of time and place, could produce the worst kind of inequality — inequality under the guise of justice.

Another factor in the Catholic tradition has been the manuals of moral theology of the eighteenth and nineteenth centuries. Directed primarily to the needs of confessors, the manuals (some refer to them as "peccato meters") preserved both principles and applications in necessarily concise and apodictic form. Published for the European market, these confessional guides failed to consider the American democratic structure, its law based primarily on English common law (not the Roman law of most European nations), and consequently its socioeconomic structure. A notable excep-

---

10 Robert W. Austin, *ibid.*

tion was Archbishop Kendrick's *Moral Theology,* which incorporated existing Federal and State law into its treatises on justice and law.

Pope Leo XIII's *Rerum novarum* confirmed the social revolution already taking place in the United States and gave theologians an added impetus in their efforts to the social needs of an immigrant minority. The pontificates from Pope Leo XIII to John XXIII showed a continuous development of social doctrine which Vatican II crystalized in its decree "On the Church in the Modern World." Over the years the American bishops and priests effectively applied this body of social doctrine to their flock. They looked at labor from labor's viewpoint.

The current need — to look at management from management's viewpoint for a study in ethics and morality — is an anomaly for most priests and moral theologians. Although a change in values is not appropriate, a thorough understanding of corporate structure, business management, functional procedures, and financial workings of an enterprise is the "key" that opens the door to the moral problems of the executive suite. Pioneering efforts have been made through the writings of Dr. Herbert Johnston of Notre Dame University, Fr. Henry Wirtenberger, S.J., of Loyola University (Chicago), Fr. Thomas M. Garrett, S.J., of the Cambridge Center for Social Studies. Fr. Raymond C. Baumhart, S.J., received national attention in his survey on the ethics of businessmen, published in the *Harvard Business Review.* On the institutional level, Loyola University (Chicago) sponsored monthly meetings for executives; St. Joseph's College (Philadelphia) has established The Council on Business Ethics as a continuing project to assist business enterprises in the Greater Philadelphia Area; The Viatorian Seminary (Washington, D. C.) has a biennial Conference on Business Morality that attempts to serve the needs of moral thologians, college instructors and seminary professors. Furthermore, business leaders are beginning to invite priests as lecturers on business ethics in executive training programs, sales trainees indoctrinations, and trade association conventions. In a word, the gap between businessmen and clergymen is narrowing. Why not? One Catholic executive remarked to a priest: "You *have* the goods and the market. All you need is attractive packaging"

"PACKAGING" BUSINESS MORALITY

Attractive packaging sells products. Supermarkets operate on the principle that a customer will be attracted to more products than he originally intended to buy. Salesmen know that an "eye catcher" package gives them a competitive advantage. Quality is only one aspect; many brands are of the same quality. The package — design, shape, color, message — sells the product.

The "product" is business ethics — or is it business morality? If this distinction embodies the usual formal viewpoints of "reason" for the first and of "revelation" for the second, then it seems that business-related problems, as part of the apostolate, should be seen in the light of revelation as a part of moral theology. Scripture, the Fathers, papal social doctrine, conciliar decrees, and theological reasoning could hardly be separated from an apostolic approach to business problems. But if the distinction between business ethics and business morality refers to an approach that might be acceptable to all groups, non-Christians as well as Christian, then "reason" becomes the final arbiter. In the study of ethics, reason is a true, but imperfect, norm of conduct. "Moral theology," the Jesuits John C. Ford and Gerald Kelly write, "includes ethics and goes beyond it — absorbs it, so to speak."[11] Similarly, business morality as a part of moral theology goes beyond business ethics and "absorbs" it. Although many of the moral problems of businessmen seem to relate more directly to the precepts of natural law, the solutions themselves in the form of decision-actions can be supernatural through the extrinsic denomination of efficient and final causality.

If business morality is part of moral theology, does it really differ from the treatise on the virtue of justice? Essentially, it does not. From the apex of the pyramid to the base, management is characterized by decision-making. Management theorist Paul M. Dauten, Jr., in *Current Issues and Emerging Concepts in Management,* states,[12] "His (business manager's) ultimate criterion for successful decision-making is impartiality" in reconciling the interests of many individuals and groups. For that reason, Dauten concludes "justice is the ultimate standard for evaluating the appropriateness of managerial decisions." Without doubt, business morality uses the principles of justice. It seems to be a question of *how* to apply these principles to business-related situations. This statement calls for an explanation.

In a dialogue between priests and businessmen on the problems of business morality, a well-known moral theologian stood up and pleaded with the businessmen: "Give us the facts and we will solve your problems of business morality!" This is hardly the type of "packaging" that attracts or sells.

Different styles of packaging attract different customers. Some packagings are distinctive; others are merely prosaic. But they are all in the market for sales. How does a priest "package" such general principles as double effect, commutative justice, scandal, voluntary in cause and restitution? Profit, price justice, and interest are familiar terms in the business

---

[11] John C. Ford, S.J., and Gerald Kelly, S.J. (Westminster: Newman, 1958), *Contemporary Moral Theology,* pp. 2, 3.

[12] Paul M. Dauten, Jr., *Current Issues and Emerging Concepts in Management,* p. 45.

world, but will priests and executives communicate their ideas within a scholastic framework or in the many varieties of business concepts? No one can be certain of the answers to these and related questions. Nonetheless, I believe that certain procedures will be "attractive" to both priests and businessmen.

First of all, terminology is more than semantics. Among businessmen, the word "profit" has many technical meanings. When a priest quotes from manual of moral theology that any profit exceeding 8% to 12% is excessive, he had better realize that such a standard does not categorically apply to all business situations.[13] When a businessman speaks about "ethics," he might actually mean the requirement for the "ideal" business decision; or he might identify ethics with legal demands. The first point, then, is an understanding of terms used in morality and in business.

When priests gather together for class reunions, Forty Hours, and retreats, personal pastoral experiences set the tone of the conversation. Businessmen are no different. Formal papers and informal discussions among participants at trade association meetings are filled with problems and solutions — the successful ones. They appear to be more interested in practical cases than in theoretical excursions. Businessmen appear to approach this in the same way they make business decisions — the here-and-now situation, its possible solutions, and its overall effects appraised in light of past experiences, current practices, and future contingencies. In the American Management Association's several hundred seminars and workshops each year, a "practical" faculty composed of active businessmen present their viewpoints and solutions to problems that they faced. Many, if not most, of the articles in business magazines and trade journals quote liberally from the experiences of businessmen. Underlying any approach to business (or moral) theory and problems is the question: "This sounds good, but does it work?"

Since businessmen frequently lack formal theoretical training in moral principles, they prefer to have principles and norms presented in a manner consistent with their own *modus procedendi*. I suggest that the "handle" to the cup will be short, pertinent illustrations that bridge the gap between pure theory and pure practice. In a word, then, the second point for attractive packaging is the frequent use of interesting examples.

The third point for attractive packaging is taken from Fr. Thomas Garrett, S.J.'s address to the Direct Mail Advertising convention in Pittsburgh a few years ago.[14] Father Garrett delivered the keynote speech on "The Anti-Business Ethic" which he defined as "an ethic that denies value to both business and businessmen." Referring to the need for responsible

---

[13] For an excellent clarification on the notion and morality of profit, cf. John F. Cronin, S.S., *Social Principles and Economic Life,* pp. 148–156.

[14] Reported in *Printer's Ink,* October 18, 1963, p. 22.

business activity, Father Garrett suggested that a general climate of responsibility be further developed by treating others as humans (and not as things) and by exacting the same sense of responsibility from employees, suppliers, dealers and clients. Nothing short of a general climate of responsibility in business and society "can defeat the anti-ethic which lies behind the anti-business ethics," he concluded.

Unwittingly, priests might betray an "anti-business ethic" in their attitudes toward businessmen in general and to executives in particular. Although the *caveat emptor* is more often a vestige of history, the "Sons of Business" buttons of the Kennedy administration imply that a "business-over-all" attitude still lives in certain industries. The labor conditions of the '20's, the depression of the '30's, the war of the '40's (didn't it save business?), the recession of the '50's, and the skirmishes of the '60's tend to remind priests and parishioners of the unscrupulous conduct of some businessmen. Furthermore, the efforts of "marginal" businessmen to use moral theology in order "to succeed in business while avoiding implication in practices which conscience has already instinctively and correctly judged to be patently wrong"[15] could easily occasion a skeptical, or even a cynical, attitude toward all businessmen, including those who are seriously trying to live according to their Christian vocation and commitment.

If priests manifest an anti-business attitude, they might further unwittingly contribute to the "anti-business ethic" by default. Unless priests take time and effort to clarify principles through realistic illustrations, unless priests are capable of discussing problems and solutions on a tentative basis, and unless priests are willing to assume an attitude of good-will in those who seek their assistance, the possibility of "attractive" packaging is seriously limited and the apostolate to businessmen becomes a matter of social lionizing for the priest rather than the development of socially responsible businessmen for the Church.

TYPES OF ORGANIZED APOSTOLIC ACTIVITY

The distinction between moral theologian and priest counselor becomes useful to delineate the role of priests in the different types of apostolic activity now available. Preparation for these different roles will be considered afterward.

Among existing Catholic organizations, the one most specifically directed to the needs of businessmen is the National Conference of Christian Employers and Managers (NCCEM), founded in 1957 by a group of dynamic laymen. An independent organization, NCCEM has for its purpose:

1. To aid the spiritual and moral formation of its members;
2. To study Catholic social teachings, moral and ethical principles;

---

[15] John J. Lynch, S.J., "Notes on Moral Theology," *Theological Studies,* 23, June, 1962, p. 249.

3. To exchange views on the application of these principles to complex business situations;
4. To promote individual action of members in their own businesses, trade associations, and politics.
5. To encourage and promote interest in sound moral and ethical principles among businessmen in general.

A continuing education organization for businessmen, NCCEM employs local monthly meetings, annual national conventions, specialized seminars, and active participation in other employer-management groups to fulfill these purposes. It currently has local chapters in Chicago, St. Paul, Minneapolis, Detroit, and Cleveland; it has extensive plans for expansion.[16] Not limited to the needs of professional businessmen as such, the National Council of Catholic Men and the Serra Clubs have in the past shown interest in business morality in their meetings, publications and conventions. On a more limited basis, Newman Centers, Holy Name Societies, parish study clubs, CCD training corps, and other similar organizations have invited priests and businessmen to speak on business morality or the vocation of the businessman. However, these three types of organized activity differ in their approach to Catholic lay activity. NCCEM is continuous and requires long-range commitment. NCCM and Serra usually work on a "project" basis for a determined time or within a definite scope; e.g. NCCM's closed session workshop on business ethics at its 1963 Biennial Convention, or Serra's series of articles on ethics in business. The other groups usually have "one-shot" approaches, e.g., Holy Name, breakfast talks, Newman Center guest speaker, etc.

It seems to me that another type of activity might possibly be useful. For the past twenty years or more, Cana and Pre-Cana Conferences have produced informed Catholic engaged couples and married partners. Using the "team" approach with doctor, family economist, and priest, the Cana Conference prepares engaged couples for married life and offers married couples the opportunities to re-evaluate their lives together in light of spiritual, moral, psychological, physiological, and economic principles and practices. It is diocese-centered at the inter-parish level, and its teams are ordinarily composed of doctors, priests, and businessmen-economists from the locality.

Could not some sort of business-oriented "team approach" to the apostolate of the businessmen be established along similar lines? Dioceses that have universities or colleges could supply professors of management or economics to explain some of the theory behind business decision-making. Local successful businessmen — known for their ethical conduct — might act as a panel for discussing the solutions they reached in solving certain

---

[16] Information may be obtained by writing to: National Conference of Christian Employers and Managers, 109 North Dearborn Street, Chicago, Illinois 60602.

business problems involving morality. The priest, from either a Catholic college or the diocesan seminary, could act as a resource man for the discussion and could also elaborate on the spiritual dimensions of the vocation and apostolate of businessmen. A team of this sort could move from town to town or from parish to parish throughout the diocese. And the team might even include a manager and his wife to help recognize and suggest solutions to family-related business moral problems. Perhaps one session of the business apostolate conference should include both husbands and wives. Where a diocese or city has one major industry (e.g., steel, rubber, automobile, textile, coal, farm machinery, etc.), specific problems might need expert help. Personnel and public relations departments of management, unions, and trade associations often welcome the opportunity to represent their point of view to outside groups, such as a business apostolate conference.

PREPARATION FOR THE APOSTOLATE

The initiative for a more thorough understanding of moral problems in business has not been restricted to the laity. A few dioceses and religious communities have had clerical conferences (monthly or quarterly) on business morality. Seminaries have invited NCCEM members or other businessmen to address their student bodies. Colleges and seminaries have instituted courses or "exchange programs" that include economists, professors of management, and moral theologians or ethicians who are familar with businessmen and their problems. Others find seminars on business morality an effective way to cultivate the seminarian's interest in this apostolate. Most of these methods are geared to the priest counselor approach.

An interested priest has many opportunities close at hand. However, for professional recognition a Master in Business Administration is the minimum. Part-time evening courses leading to a degree not only prepare him theoretically but also practically insofar as his fellow students hold regular full-time jobs that provide interesting points for class discussion and for after-class coffee. If formal courses at a university are not feasible, sometimes correspondence courses provide the necessary impetus for study.

Public libraries frequently contain many volumes covering business topics. And libraries in major cities operate special business sections. Frequently enough, public libraries also provide trained librarians to assist in selecting basic sources, in securing books concerning a particular problem, and in evaluating current literature. For the priest who cannot follow an academic program of business administration, the public library with its trained staff and reference sections is probably the most useful single source of information and background materials for studying current business and economic problems.

The business section of a public library also contains current general business periodical literature (e.g., *Harvard Business Review, Fortune, Business Week*, American Management Association publications, etc.) and trade journals (e.g., *Purchasing, Steel, Advertising Age, Printer's Ink, Sales Management*, etc.) that cannot be purchased at newsstands. The *Industrial Arts Index*, a guide to periodical literature in business, saves time in searching for articles on business ethics.

Government publications provide another important and inexpensive source of helpful information. They cover almost every conceivable aspect of business. But the highly technical nature of some and the precisely delineated areas of others limit their usefulness.[17]

In the past, moral theologians urged seminarians to familiarize themselves with cases and solutions written up in books and periodicals. A purposeful study of cases and solutions gives the seminarians a "sense" or a "feeling" for approaching, questioning, and solving different situations. It also helps to develop an "attitude" toward certain problems. And it frequently opens up new viewpoints, perspectives, and aspects of a problem. Perhaps the same type of case-study would contribute toward an understanding of those problems that have moral implications. Johnston's *Business Ethics* and Wirtenberger's *Morality and Business* have a variety of interesting cases and solutions. George Albert Smith's *Business, Society and the Individual*, a textbook for a course on social responsibility of management at the Harvard Graduate School of Business Administration, offers actual case histories for serious study.

These suggestions point to just a few of the possibilities for developing competence as a priest counselor. Other ideas might be more useful. Regardless, the end is the same — a priest who is a more effective instrument in the ministry.

Conclusion

If the economic inequality of the world is to be balanced and the sacredness of the human being is to be acknowledged in business decisions, if the future history of business morality is to be written exemplifying Christian principles and Catholic social doctrine, if the businessman is to assume the responsibility of transforming society through production and service, if — in other words — the apostolate *of* businessmen is to bring Christ effectively into the marketplace, then, it seems to me, the apostolate *to* businessmen becomes an equally important correlative.

---

[17] Pertinent material is available under the following topics (with price lists): "Law, Rules, and Regulations" (PL 10); "Finance" (PL 28); "Labor" (PL 33); "Occupations" (PL 33A); "Tariff and Taxation" (PL 37); "Interstate Commerce" (PL 69); "Commerce" (PL 62); and "Farm Management" (PL 68). Subscription (free) to the Government Printing Office biweekly "Selected United States Government Publications" covers current useful topics.

23

The Priest in the
High School Classroom

LEON McKENZIE

THE PASTORAL AIMS OF THE MODERN PRIEST ARE ESSENTIALLY THE SAME as the aims of the priest of the primitive Christian community. From apostolic times priestly energies have been directed toward the sanctification of the world and the salvation of men. While these aims have remained constant through the centuries, pastoral approaches employed to achieve these aims have been various. St. Paul takes note of the diversification of ministries in his letter to the Corinthians. "Now there are varieties of gifts, but the same Spirit; and there are varieties of ministries, but the same Lord; and there are varieties of workings, but the same God" (1 Co 12:4 f).

Today we find priests engaged in a multitude of ministries ranging from parochial missions and military chaplaincies to social work endeavors and labors in the communication arts. No area of our complex world is, or should be, isolated from the presence of Christ's priests.

> . . . the priesthood cannot in any way procure the full effects which are demanded by the needs of the present time unless the priests shine forth among the people with marks of sanctity, as worthy ministers of Christ, faithful dispensers of the mysteries of God, God's helpers, and ready for every noble work.[1]

Historically, one of the most noble of pastoral works has been exercised in the schools. In his enumeration of the various activities of the priest in the encyclical *Ad Catholici Sacerdotii,* Pope Pius XI emphasized that the priest ". . . is, both by vocation and divine commission, the chief

---

[1] Pius XII, *Menti Nostrae* (New York: The Paulist Press, 1951), p. 6.

apostle and the tireless furtherer of the Christian education of youth. . . ."[2] One of the most valuable approaches of our times concerns the Christian education of youth and the apostolate of the classroom. It is of capital importance that we be vitally aware of the authentic pastoral dimensions of priestly ministry in the high school classroom.

Quite regularly a zealous young priest embarks on the adventure of teaching with high spirits. But soon he hears voiced what I have called "the heresy of parochialism" — the opinion that identifies pastoral activity with parochial endeavors to the exclusion of all else. In their enthusiasm to state the undeniable pastoral greatness of parish work the proponents of "the heresy of parochialism" maintain that priest-teachers are a diocesan luxury in the face of the shortage of priestly vocations; that the role of teaching is of secondary and dubious value when compared to the role of parish priest; that the diocesan priest who serves on a full-time basis in the parish can alone glory in the title of pastor of souls.

When the young priest-teacher realizes that he is regarded in some quarters as something less than an authentic shepherd of the flock, he begins to wonder if his presence in the classroom is appropriate. He becomes dismayed and disheartened at the thought that he could be rendering a more valuable service to Christ and His Church were it not for the fact that he has received from his bishop an appointment to a classroom.

After he has taught for a few years the priest-teacher begins to appreciate that in many ways he is more authentically a pastor of souls than some of his brother priests who labor in the parochial vineyard. Only after serious reflection on his experiences in the classroom is the priest-teacher able to overcome his initial doubts about the value of his ministry. He begins to realize that any definition which limits the meaning of "pastoral activity" to parochial activity is unrealistically narrow, a definition that does not take into account the complex needs of the Church in twentieth century America. The priest-teacher understands that if there is to be a balanced distribution of priestly personnel in each diocese, it is necessary that priests enter the high school classrooms.

What is needed today is personal contact between the shepherd and his flock. Father Goldbrunner has written:

> In his intercourse with men and women today the priest realizes that the influence of his work is decreasing because the legacy of a Christian atmosphere from the centuries of faith is gradually dwindling away. The people in the pews are no longer a body of Christian "people" but mere individuals, a multiplicity of individuals who wish to be addressed as individuals.[3]

---

[2] Pius XI, *Ad Catholici Sacerdotii* (Garden City: Doubleday and Co., Image Book: *The Church and the Reconstruction of the Modern World,* 1957), p. 175.

[3] Josef Goldbrunner, *Cure of Mind and Cure of Soul* (Notre Dame: The University of Notre Dame Press, 1963), p. 12.

The opportunity for what modern personalist philosophers call a "personal encounter" between priest and individual Catholic does not present itself too often in most large parishes in the United States. A parish priest can exert every effort to encounter personally the members of his parish for the purpose of getting them involved in parish life, yet he can expect to achieve only a nodding acquaintance with the preponderance of his people. In large parishes the majority of the people will inevitably remain faces in the Sunday crowd. Many Catholics go through life without ever establishing anything but a remote and distant relationship with a priest of God. Many of the faithful in every parish view their priests as little more than liturgical functionaries.

In offering a vindication for the existence of priest-teachers I have no wish to overstate the case in such a way that the value of parochial endeavors is lessened. One form of priestly ministry is never served by underestimating the value of another form of priestly ministry. The parish is the basic canonical unit of the Church. The parish is, or should be, the center of every Catholic's liturgical life. The parish should serve as the axis of every Catholic's involvement in the challenges of Christ's apostolate to the world. But before the parish becomes this center of liturgical life and axis of apostolic action the people must be educated. Youth must be educated so that they make take their places in the future as active and involved members of the parish. And it is through the instrumentality of the priest-teacher that young people are encountered, educated, and oriented toward a more fruitful participation in parish life.

There can be no doubt that the adolescent is "reached" most effectively in the Catholic high school. The psychological center of the student's religious life is not the parish but the Catholic high school. Willis D. Nutting addresses this point incisively when he writes:

> The school is an institution in which rather large groups of young people are taught by professional teachers. . . . We can see that such a situation establishes a life pattern which cannot help having a great effect on most young people. The fact that the school, with all that accompanies it, occupies the most significant part of a child's time during the most impressionable part of his life means that it is hard for him to escape the education that the school gives. . . . The basic fact in a young person's education, the fact that explains what happens to him during his years in school, is this: in these years he spends the most significant part of his life in school — not the largest part but the part that looms largest in his consciousness. . . .
> It is an acknowledged fact that teenagers form a little world of their own, with their own sanctions, their own styles, their own values, and even their own language. . . . They have their world; we all grant that. Some of us approve of it and some of us don't. But what most of us fail to realize is the more important fact that *the world of teenagers, caused by their isolation in school, is an abnormal world. It is a thoroughly artificial society.* . . .[4]

⁴ Willis. D. Nutting, *Schools and the Means of Education* (Notre Dame: Fides Publishers Association, 1959), pp. 20–22.

The priest-teacher who is able to contact his students at a personal level over a relatively prolonged period of time is provided with the opportunity of "getting to know" the sheep of Christ's flock at an extremely critical time — the time of youth when character is formed and when impressions are registered that will profoundly influence adult life.

And who is better able than a priest-teacher to make use of the adolescent artificial society created by the school situation in order to orient his students toward a profitable entrance into the more stable Christian society of the parish? Who is more informed about the parish society than the priest who lives at a parish and who associates daily with brother priests who are exercising and discussing parochial ministries?

Rather than weakening the effectiveness of the parish unit because he is away from the parish teaching classes, the priest-teacher is the foremost instrument for the development of the parish-minded youth who will someday become a parish-minded adult. The role of the priest-teacher is complementary to the role of those who are engaged full time in parochial activities. Some may never see the propriety or the pastoral significance of the ministry of the priest-teacher, but given enough time, experience, and sober reflection the priest-teacher will eventually discover that he plays a *necessary* part in the *total* pastoral mission of the Church.

The Priest-Teacher and Profane Subjects

If the priest-teacher who leaves his parish to teach religion in a classroom outside the territorial boundaries of his parish is sometimes dismayed over the thesis that he is inappropriately employed, the priest-teacher of profane subjects is liable, *a fortiori,* to develop a sacerdotal inferiority complex.

While some will admit that the priest-teacher of religion is necessary for the soundness of a religion program, they will balk at any plan which calls for a priest to be an instructor of profane subjects. "Priests are ordained to preach the Gospel, not geometry," runs the argument.

At first hearing the argument is impressive. But a more careful analysis of the meaning of Catholic education leads one to the irrefutable conclusion that Catholic education demands the presence of at least a limited number of priests in areas of study and teaching commonly known as profane. The Catholic educational system is founded on a principle of Catholic educational philosophy which maintains that nothing of genuinely human value is foreign to the interest of the Church, and that the Church is a sacramental presence which should influence all aspects of life and every human endeavor. Humanism, to be a true humanism, must be a Christian humanism. The profane and secular values of life become ultimately valuable in the light of Christian revelation. Where Christian secularity and true humanism is unemphasized, secularism and counterfeit humanism thrive.

Catholic education recognizes the truth that everything profane is potentially sacred and can contribute to the formation of "the supernatural man who thinks, judges, and acts constantly and consistently in accordance with right reason illumined by the supernatural light of the example and teachings of Christ."[5] Father Teilhard de Chardin has restated, in a masterful manner, the thesis of Christian humanism that is also a central thesis of Catholic educational philosophy: ". . . by virtue of the Creation and, still more, of the Incarnation, *nothing* here below is *profane* for those who know how to see. . . . Try, with God's help, to perceive the connection — even physical and natural — which binds your labour with the building of the Kingdom of Heaven. . . ."[6]

Priests, since they eminently manifest the presence of the Church in the world, must be involved in some way in profane studies.

> Today it could hardly be hoped that the clergy could hold . . . a primacy in every branch of knowledge; the range of human science has become so vast that no man can comprehend it all, much less become distinguished in each of its numberless branches. Nevertheless wise encouragement and help should be given to those members of the clergy who by taste and special gifts, feel a call to devote themselves to study and research, in this or that branch of science, in this or that art; they do not thereby deny their clerical profession; for all this, undertaken within just limits and under the guidance of the Church, redounds to the good estate of the Church and the glory of her divine Head, Jesus Christ.[7]

There has been much comment in recent years about the apparent divorce of religion from life and the apparent lack of interest manifested by the Church in human endeavors. "All you ever talk about is pie in the sky," say some youthful critics of the Church. "You are so interested in the other world that you don't realize *we* live in *this* world."

These exaggerated criticisms are, of course, unwarranted. The papal pronouncements concerning the great social questions of the day are evidence that the Church is extremely interested in the affairs of this world. In attempting to dispel the notion that the Church is totally extramundane Pope Paul has stressed, on many occasions, the position of the Church. As Cardinal Montini he stated:

> The fundamental attitude of Catholics who want to convert the world is loving it. We shall love our neighbors and those far afield. We shall love our country, we shall love other peoples. We shall love Catholics, the schismatics, the Protestants, the Anglicans, the indifferent, the Moslems, the

---

[5] Pius XI, *Divini Illius Magistri* (Garden City: Doubleday and Co., Image Book: *The Church and the Reconstruction of the Modern World*, 1957), p. 106.

[6] Pierre Teilhard de Chardin, *The Divine Milieu* (New York: Harper and Row, 1960), p. 35.

[7] Pius XI, *Ad Catholici Sacerdotii*, in *op. cit.*, p. 197.

pagans and the atheists. We shall love our time, our civilization, our technical science, our art, our sport, our world. . . .[8]

But however forceful the words of the sovereign pontiffs and the declarations of Christian humanists, the Church must project an image of its involvement in and with the world by its deeds. And the deeds of the Church are manifested primarily through the deeds of her priests.

When I refer here to projecting an image of the Church I do not mean that Catholic education must project an image as a mere expedient or as an exercise in hypocrisy. Any person or institution inevitably projects an image. This is an unavoidable fact of life. The Church must project an image that is true to her divine mission in the world and that is in conformity with the teachings of the sovereign pontiffs. The most direct way to project an image to youth that the Church is uninterested in the world and in what Pope Paul, in his Easter message of 1965, called the technological and social "energies of progress," is to restrict priests from areas of profane teaching in our high schools. The demon of the apparent irrelevance of religion to life haunts many young people today. The strategic placement of priests as teachers of profane subjects would go a long way to deprive this demon of the vitality it now enjoys in many places. The priest, above any other person, by reason of his education and what he stands for, is capable of fitting all secular and profane values into the perspective of the Christian world view.

The priest-teacher, even the priest-teacher of profane subjects, is far more than a substitute for Sisters or a means of cutting the cost of teacher salaries in our high schools. His presence in the classroom pertains intimately and directly to the essence of Catholic educational philosophy.

THE PRIEST AS CLASSROOM CATECHIST

In the encyclical *Ecclesiam Suam,* Pope Paul turned his attention to what he termed the "inescapable mission" of the Church: The evangelization of mankind.

> The duty consonant with the patrimony received from Christ is that of spreading, offering, announcing it to others. Well do we know that "going therefore, make disciples of all nations" (Mt 28,19) is the last command of Christ to His Apostles. By the very term "apostles" these men define their inescapable mission. . . . The Church has something to say; the Church has a message to deliver; the Church has a communication to offer."[9]

The obligation to "sound forth" the message of Christ and to teach His truths is an obligation that is shared by all members of the Mystical Body

---

[8] Paul VI, Statement to the World Conference for the Lay Apostolate, 1957. Recalled on the occasion of Cardinal Montini's elevation to the Papal throne, *Life,* July 5, 1963.

[9] Paul VI, *Ecclesiam Suam* (Huntington, Ind.: Our Sunday Visitor Inc., 1965), p. 25.

of Christ. But this obligation weighs most heavily upon priests "since they are representatives of Christ as well as teachers and rulers in the Church."[10]

The priest-teacher of religion in the secondary school is blessed with ample opportunities to plan and execute a comprehensive and intensive program of religious instruction. In the classroom situation he is able to take the time to explain the teachings of Christ in fine detail. Perhaps nowhere else save in the classroom is the priest able to draw out the many implications of Christian teaching and apply these to the contemporary scene. The classroom situation offers the opportunity for continuity in the presentation of the message of the Gospel. The priest is with his students almost daily for the better part of a year. He is presented with a set of circumstances that enables him to spend time profitably in the pursuit of the knowledge, wisdom and vision that comes from faith.

While the academic aspects of religion class must not be de-emphasized, the catechist must also attempt to form Christian attitudes in his students and initiate them into the apostolic and liturgical life of the Church. The priest-teacher is furnished with the background and the necessary time to accomplish the threefold aim of modern catechetics. In the classroom he can be an effective agent of information, formation, and initiation.

> That we are obliged to *instruct,* that is, to transmit the content of Faith, is a truism beyond any need for discussion. . . . But we must not overlook the fact that a well-grounded catechesis will also form pupils by initiating them into the ways of Christian life. For, even though belief presumes knowledge, knowledge is not belief. Instruction can all too easily terminate in mere religious knowledge and not in a living faith. . . . Though didactic instruction gives content and articulation to a living faith, it is still necessary that this faith be aroused, grow and expand. The considerable role that religious formation must have in the pedagogy of faith should be evident.[11]

At this point a rather harsh fact must be granted. Most priests who have had classroom catechetical experience will admit this fact. The fact is this: Four years of theological preparation in the major seminary does not necessarily qualify a priest as a good catechist. Students expect more from a teacher of religion than a condensed version of seminary theology. Catechizing is not quite the same as theologizing. It is a fatal mistake to enter a classroom with the intention of teaching fundamental theology and equipping high school students with abstractions that are necessary and valuable only for priests, religious, and other catechists.

If he sincerely wishes to become a good catechist, the priest-teacher

---

[10] *The Constitution on the Church of Vatican II, De Ecclesia* (Glen Rock, N. J.: The Paulist Press, 1965), p. 138.

[11] Francois Coudreau, P.S.S., "Introduction to a Pedagogy of Faith," *Shaping the Christian Message,* Gerard Sloyan, ed. (Glen Rock, N. J.: The Paulist Press, 1963), p. 136.

must be well-grounded in the principles and practices of good pedagogy. The sovereign pontiffs have consistently urged catechists to employ the latest methods and tactics of education, to grasp the insights of modern psychology, and to avail themselves of every pedagogical tool in the transmission of Christian truths and in the shaping of Christian attitudes in their students.

> Although the case of a teacher who does not know what he should teach his student is inconceivable, it is not impossible to notice in some teachers a certain lack of preparation as to the manner in which such teaching should be imparted or as to the purpose it should have. . . .[12]
>
> Religious instruction, especially when it is directed to young minds, cannot be satisfied with expounding in abstract lessons the truth of the Faith and the norms of Christian morality. It must go further and guide ceaselessly in the most adequate and concrete way possible all the activities of the child and the adolescent, suggesting to him how he must conduct himself in difficult circumstances, drawing him by example and emulation toward what is best, sustaining him in his endeavors so as to prevent fatigue and discouragement. . . . Try to acquire at the same time a good technical preparation. Look for ways to perfect your methods without flagging, and to increase their efficiency.[13]
>
> The teacher must make his teaching live, make his students think, and uncover for each of his students the talents he has at his disposal.[14]

Because of this age of rapid transition in which we live seminarians do not have sufficient training in modern catechetics. Nor do priests who have studied before them possess the "know-how" of modern catechetics. This is not an indictment of seminaries; only a frivolous critic would expect the catechetical training offered there to be updated immediately in the wake of the catechetical renewal.

> Seminaries generally are performing a creditable service in educating holy, dedicated priests. Out of our seminaries have come numerous priests who have patiently prepared the ground for the present renewal in the Church by their pioneering in the biblical, liturgical, ecumenical and catechetical movements, to name a few.
>
> While heartening progress has been made, it must be recognized that much remains to be done if seminaries are to produce priests who are not only personal witnesses to Christ in the world but also animators of zealous laymen.[15]

Until such time as the seminary curriculum is fully renewed in the

---

[12] Pius XII, An Address to the Italian Association of Catholic Schoolmasters, 1955. Quoted in *The Modern Challenge to Religious Education,* G. Emmett Carter (New York: William H. Sadlier, Inc., 1961), p. 387.

[13] Pius XII, An Address to the Teachers Affiliated with the Center of Roman Oratories, 1955. Quoted *ibid.,* p. 388.

[14] Pius XII, An Address to the Italian Association of Catholic Teachers, 1953. Quoted *ibid.,* p. 388.

[15] *Apostolic Renewal in the Seminary,* James Keller and Richard Armstrong, eds. (New York: The Christophers, 1965), pp. 11–12.

area of catechetics, it is imperative that seminarians read as many catechetical works as they are able. This suggestion for self-education applies also to the priest-teacher, even if he has been teaching religion for years. No one can rest on what has been accomplished in the past. The need for every priest engaged in proclaiming the Gospel to keep abreast with the gains of modern catechetics is urgent.

THE QUALITIES OF A GOOD TEACHER

Any priest who hopes to be successful in the high school classroom must possess or acquire several qualities that will assure his success. Different enumerations of these qualities of a good teacher appear in various books, and if all these recommended attributes were listed, they would number in the thousands. But it is possible to narrow the basic general qualifications of the good teacher to five, without which the teacher cannot be effective.

First of all, the priest-teacher must realize and appreciate the immense importance of his position in the classroom. The teacher exerts a momentous influence on his students and can shape the future for good or for ill. He deals in the most precious of commodities: Truth. He is dedicated to the overthrow of the tyrannies of ignorance, error, and prejudice.

Etienne Gilson asks, "What life . . . could be more noble than that of a teacher, if it achieves in perfection the unity of action and contemplation? . . . to act is not as noble as to contemplate, and it is true that to teach is to act, but to act in view of imparting to others the fruit of contemplation is more noble than contemplation alone."[16]

The second quality of the good teacher flows directly from the first. (To be sure, all of the qualities of the successful teacher are interrelated.) The priest-teacher must be enthusiastic. If one is fully aware of the nobility of his work and of the magnitude of his contributions to individuals, society, and the Church, it will necessarily follow that he will be charged with enthusiasm about his work. This enthusiasm cannot remain bottled up. It will express itself in the dynamic presentation of truth. The enthusiastic teacher will inspire in his students a love for truth. His enthusiasm will be contagious. Enthusiasm for his work will also motivate the priest-teacher to gain deeper insights into the content of the material he presents to his class.

Nothing can substitute for zeal or enthusiasm on the part of the teacher. Enthusiasm is an imperative requirement for anyone who hopes to break the bread of truth to youthful minds.

In some places young priests are assigned to teaching positions without regard to their personal sensibilities and feelings about teaching. Such

---

[16] Etienne Gilson, "The Eminence of Teaching," *A Gilson Reader*, Anton C. Pegis, ed. (Garden City: Doubleday and Co., 1957), p. 311.

assignments are grievous mistakes. It does not take too many days in a high school situation to discover the harm done by the priest-teacher who lacks enthusiasm for his work. He enters the classroom, assigns twenty pages of reading from the text, and then proceeds to read his divine office. It were better that this man had not been born into the pedagogical world.

The priest-teacher who lacks enthusiasm for his work and finds himself assigned to a teaching position should meditate frequently on the nobility of teaching and the immense good he could possibly accomplish as a teacher. If a cup of cold water will not go unrewarded on judgment day, how much more of a reward will he receive who reveals some aspect of reality to young people. Should he even then find his presence in the classroom an intolerable burden, he should approach the diocesan authorities and make his feelings known. Priests in administrative positions in education know the futility of forcing anyone into a classroom. If the exigencies of the diocese allow it, the diocesan superintendent of education will exert every influence to gain a change of appointment for the unenthusiastic priest-teacher.

However important and necessary enthusiasm is for the priest-teacher, nothing takes the place of adequate knowledge and scholastic competency. Not even the most enthusiastic of teachers can hope to accomplish anything worthwhile if he is ignorant of what he should be teaching. The third quality, therefore, of the good teacher is knowledge.

His enthusiasm for his work should prompt the priest-teacher to become more proficient in his scholastic field. One cannot divorce teaching from learning. The teacher who is content to remain three pages ahead of his class may be putting in time in the classroom, but he is not teaching. Docility and the eagerness to learn is a virtue of the teacher long before it is a virtue for the student.

Perhaps it may seem obvious that teachers should possess a mastery of what they are teaching and that what is written here should go without saying. But there are teachers who do not have a firm enough grasp on the subject matter they present to their classes. Classroom experience and the sometimes pointed and complex questions of students reveal to most teachers their own need for continued study. Tragically, however, some teachers never recognize the need for continuing study. They rely on evasions or pull clever non-answers from the top of their heads when confronted with a penetrating question asked by a precocious student.

The priest-teacher in particular must exert caution that he never forsake good study habits. Since the priest is accorded an almost universal respect, he may sometimes be tempted to employ authoritarian methods and to rely on *ex cathedra* pronouncements when a student asks a question he cannot answer immediately. If the priest-teacher is asked a question he cannot properly answer, he should tell his students he does not know the answer. After he researches the matter he will be able to give a good answer at a later date. No student has ever been scandalized by the admission on the part of the priest-teacher that he is human and fallible.

The fourth quality of the good teacher is ability to communicate. Teaching is concerned fundamentally with communication. It profits a group of students very little if they have for a teacher a genius who is unable to communicate his ideas to them. Such a situation is frustrating for both students and teacher. Most students who have experienced the predicament of a teacher who is unable to convey ideas have neither learned in the classroom nor felt challenged to set out on their own in quest of knowledge. Gilbert Highet writes of communication:

> After the teacher has prepared his subject, he has to communicate his knowledge of it to his pupils. If he fails in this, he has failed as a teacher. He may still be an inspiration for a few youngsters because of his selfless devotion to scholarship or the charm of his character; yet that will scarcely make up for his central failure. But let him be good at communication, and even if he is a mediocre scholar, he can be an excellent teacher. . . . Communication is an essential function of civilization. Teaching is only one of the many occupations that depend upon it, and depend upon it absolutely.[17]

The ability to communicate is possessed, at least in some degree, by every mature rational creature. But when we speak of communication in education we refer to a special and peculiar talent by which the teacher conveys the content of education or a corpus of academic truths to the student. This talent is largely an acquired skill, an art. Few teachers are born; most are made.

Education courses offered in most colleges and major seminaries today are extremely helpful in assisting the future priest-teacher to gain his skill of communication. These courses equip the seminarian with sufficient pedagogical insight to enable him to continue enriching any native proclivity for communicativeness he may have. It is not rare, however, that seminarians and/or priests who have been assigned to pursue further studies in education look upon these courses as mere frills in the academic curriculum. Such a viewpoint underestimates the intellectual gain and practical skills that can accrue from the study of the psychology of learning, educational methodology, and similar courses. Even if the priest never enters a classroom after ordination, what he learns in education courses can be put to good use in his parish ministry.

The fifth quality necessary to the good teacher is concern. Unless a teacher is truly concerned about his students as persons he will never be able to communicate with them, he will never be able to influence them

---

[17] Gilbert Highet, *The Art of Teaching* (New York: Vintage Books, 1950), pp. 86–87.

for good. Students must be recognized not as mere faces in a schoolroom or as names on a class list, but as real people with hopes and fears, dreams and apprehensions, illusions and insights. They must be appreciated by the teacher as persons who are uniquely individual and who live in a very real world filled with very real problems.

Concern, as the word is used here, means many things. It means understanding and patience; it means sharing the joys and discouragements of students; it means respecting the student however unattractive, immature, or dull-witted that student may be. Concern prompts a teacher to be interested in football scores and dances, basketball games and class projects, however fatuous these things may appear to him. This does not mean that the teacher must become a teenager among teenagers and enter adolescent society as a full-fledged member. But it does mean that the teacher keeps himself in contact with the situations in which his students are involved. The teacher cannot be a remote Olympian figure any more than he can be "just one of the group."

Perhaps the most difficult challenge for the concerned teacher is the challenge of patience. It does little good for a teacher to wring his hands in exasperation when he is disappointed in a student. Nor does it do any good to bemoan the fact that students are sometimes immature and given to "uncivilized" actions. The teacher must begin his endeavors with the knowledge that his students are immature and prone to "uncivilized" judgments. This is precisely why they are in school. It is the teacher's task to lead them from immaturity to maturity; from "uncivilized" and egocentric judgments to a state where balanced and unselfish judgment prevails. This takes patience.

Brother Luke Grande, F.S.C., writes:

A teacher with patience is well on the way to leading students in good, since he does not expect perfection from imperfect strivers. They are allowed some leeway with time to get where they are going. In their slow progress as weak human beings, students are prone to taking one step backward for every two steps forward; but eventually with a teacher's coaxing and confidence, they seem, amazingly enough, to get to the goal he wants them to reach.[18]

Appreciation of his role, enthusiasm, knowledge, the ability to communicate, and concern — these are the five central hallmarks of the good teacher. No teacher possesses them in a perfect degree; all good teachers strive to attain them.

PROFESSIONAL TRAINING OF THE PRIEST-TEACHER

The curricula of most seminaries in the United States offer courses in the philosophy of education, the history of education, the psychology of

---

[18] From *Twelve Virtues of a Good Teacher* by Brother Luke M. Grande, F.S.C., © Sheed and Ward, Inc., 1962, New York, p. 132.

learning, and the general principles of pedagogy. These courses provide an excellent basis for further study on the part of the priest-teacher. I would suggest, however, that the education courses offered in the seminary do not fully prepare the priest for classroom experiences. Complete formation of the priest-teacher should include specific courses in adolescent psychology, methods and techniques of secondary education, the use of audio-visual aids, and the central principles of the counseling process.

If it is not practicable to offer these courses in the seminary, those who are preparing to be teachers should be allowed to take these courses at a nearby teacher's college or university. If this is not possible, the courses can be taken during the summer vacation either before or after ordination to the priesthood. Certainly this is quite a bit to demand of the priest-teacher. But it must not be forgotten that teaching is a highly specialized occupation that requires highly specialized training. Each of the courses listed above, in addition to seminary courses in the field of education, is invaluable to anyone who must enter the classroom as teacher.

A few years ago adolescence was considered a mere transitional period between childhood and adulthood. Today psychologists are beginning to see ever more clearly that adolescence is an age in its own right. "In primitive societies entrance into the adult world of the tribe was achieved abruptly and quickly," writes Father Pierre Babin. "It was sufficient to know how to hunt and fight with simple weapons. Today, this entrance into adulthood is considerably delayed for the majority of young people."[19]

This prolongation of the period of adolescence coupled with an ever increasing number of young people under twenty years of age (70 million in 1960) has led to the formation of a truly adolescent society within society at large. The priest-teacher must become familiar not only with the psychological makeup of the individual adolescent; he must become aware of the values and patterns of adolescent society.

> The problems of youth can be approached constructively only when the classroom teachers, as well as administrators and specialists, know their students thoroughly. The knowledge required includes far more than that supplied by testing programs, previous grades, and health records. The religious, social, ethnic, and economic backgrounds of the homes, the degree of permisiveness in family discipline, the relationships of parent and child, and the ideals and status symbols of the community are among the forces teachers must understand and interpret if they are to contribute to the solution of youth problems.[20]

The study of adolescent psychology equips the priest-teacher with sufficient insight that he may see and understand this student in the light of his environment and social milieu.

---

[19] Pierre Babin, *Crisis of Faith* (New York: Herder and Herder, 1963), p. 124.
[20] William H. Conley, "The Many Problems of Youth," *Catholic School Journal,* February, 1965, p. 4.

Knowledge of *how* to teach is just as important as knowledge of what to teach and knowledge of the subject of education. This "how to" knowledge is of the practical order and contains the various norms and directives, the various pedagogical methods and techniques that must be employed to foster teacher-student communication.

Generally we can say that the methods and techniques of secondary education — the tricks of the trade — are developed by individual teachers who profit from their classroom experiences. Nevertheless, a good course in methodology can be quite helpful to the neophyte priest-teacher. Concerning methods courses in education Dr. John F. Travers has written: "Critics of teacher education have overlooked the catastrophic consequences that ensued before state departments of education insisted upon this phase of a teacher's training."[21]

The priest-teacher who has studied the methods and techniques of secondary education is well on his way to the discovery of what it takes to maintain a well-ordered classroom. He has been furnished with concrete approaches to effective classroom communication and a basis upon which he can build his individualized complexus of methods and techniques. The methods and techniques described in books may not work for this teacher or that teacher. But what is described in books of methodology can be adjusted according to the needs of the class and the personality of the priest-teacher.

A specific methods course of undeniable value is the course that prepares the teacher in the use of audio-visual equipment. The modern Catholic secondary school is ordinarily well-equipped with a library of audio-visual materials. These pedagogical tools can be employed to maximum effect by a teacher who knows how and when to use them. Unfortunately, it sometimes happens that the priest-teacher who has not been trained in audio-visual approaches is either hesitant to employ such aids or utilizes them indiscriminately outside the perspective of his lesson plans. In the prior case nothing is accomplished; in the latter case little more is achieved than a pleasant diversion for the students. Training in the use of audio-visual aids will assist the teacher to integrate such materials into his program of instruction. These marvelous tools that have been placed at the disposal of the modern educator can be instruments of profound value only if they are employed correctly.

The recommendation that the priest-teacher be trained in counseling is a recommendation of almost vital urgency. Every teacher is confronted occasionally by a student with a personal problem. Students sometimes feel at ease with no other adult save a trusted teacher. When that teacher is a priest the student is even more inclined to confide personal problems and

---

[21] John F. Travers, "A Blueprint for Catholic Teacher Education," *The Catholic Educator*, June, 1965, p. 912.

troubles. "I didn't know where else to go, Father," is a familiar phrase to the ears of the priest-teacher, even if that priest teaches nothing more than mathematics.

The technique of efficient counseling is not easily mastered. This is especially true of the nondirective and indirective types of counseling which are most satisfactory at the secondary level of education. In addition to the knowledge of counseling principles the priest-teacher must possess a firm grasp on the practical procedures of the counseling process. Although every counselor develops an individual counseling "style" and learns much from counseling experiences, it must be admitted that competency in counseling derives just as much from a solid academic course in counseling as it does from experience.

PRACTICAL PROBLEMS OF THE PRIEST-TEACHER

In the United States the diocesan priest-teacher ordinarily teaches at a diocesan high school and resides in a neighboring parish. Immediately he encounters the problem of deciding how much time and energy he should expend at the school and in the parish at which he resides. It is the unusual man who is able to conduct classes all day and then come home to a full schedule of instructions, parish meetings, and innumerable other activities related to his position in the parish.

Experience has taught priest-teachers that they cannot possibly engage in a regular schedule of parish activities while at the same time devoting themselves to their work in the high school classroom. Victory is always illusive for the man who attempts to fight the good fight on two fronts.

The priest-teacher also finds that one of his most vexing problems is lack of time for recreation. To be engaged daily at work in the classroom and on weekends in the parish is an exhausting situation. The priest-teacher must have two or three days a month he can call his own. Everyone needs time for recreation and rest; the priest-teacher is no exception to this rule.

Solutions to these problems are not easy to discover and generally must be formulated in the context of the exigencies of a particular locality. However, a few suggestions, general enough to be almost universally applicable, can be made here.

First of all, there is a need for a stipulated diocesan policy regarding the extent and limits of the activity of the priest-teacher both in the high school and in the parish at which he resides. Much misunderstanding can be obviated if the episcopal letters of appointment to residency at a parish definitely outline the duties of a "part-time" assistant pastor. Clearly stipulated diocesan policy serves as a protection for the priest-teacher and as a basis for the many practical judgments relating to the assignment of parish work that must be made by the pastor.

Diocesan policy should allow the priest-teacher one or two free Saturdays per month. This means that he would not be required to help with confessions on these Saturdays. He would be free, therefore, to plan a full day's schedule of recreation with other priest-teachers. Diocesan policy should also limit the number of classes taught by priests. What is even more important is the limitation placed upon the number of daily preparations for class. If a priest is teaching Religion IV all day in the high school, he has but one preparation for class. The number of preparations is equal to the number of different courses taught to different levels of students. The number of preparations should never exceed three each evening.

Should the priest-teacher discover that he needs more recreation than one or two Saturdays per month, especially in those months that lack holidays in the school calendar, he should not hesitate to take a day off from the routine of the classroom. There is an old saw that runs: "A teacher cannot afford to get sick or to take a day off." However noble sounding this may be, it is highly unrealistic. Every teacher, including the priest-teacher, is heir to the physical and mental limitations of his human nature. Not to recognize these limits of human endurance is something less than wise.

If the priest-teacher is fortunate enough to reside with a pastor and assistants who are considerate; if he is blessed with an understanding principal or administrator, then he will have little difficulty in so arranging his schedule as to find time for recreation and relaxation. Nor will he find himself burdened with work he cannot do. If circumstances are less than ideal, the priest-teacher should quietly do the best he can. If circumstances are intolerable, the priest-teacher should notify the proper authorities. His work and his health are too important to the Church to be endangered by those who are inconsiderate.

Perhaps it appears that I am going out of my way to make things easy for the priest-teacher. Such is really not the case. Those who have spent some time in the high school classroom on a regular basis know that this ministry is as exhausting as it is necessary. It is not uncommon to find young priest-teachers in a constant state of fatigue due to those who unwittingly demand too much of them.

THE SPIRITUAL LIFE OF THE PRIEST-TEACHER

The spiritual life of the priest-teacher is not pronouncedly different from the life of the priest who does not teach. Meditation, spiritual reading, daily examen, and prayer: All of these spiritual exercises are necessary for the spiritual development of the priest-teacher.

The particular danger faced by every priest-teacher is the temptation to postpone or cancel the exercises of the spiritual life on the grounds that papers must be corrected and classes prepared. The road that leads to the neglect of daily spiritual exercises can be a very wide one for the priest-teacher who is not conscientious. It is quite easy to convince oneself that preparation for schoolwork supercedes the importance of daily meditation or spiritual reading. The priest-teacher must exercise caution lest his awareness of his duties as a teacher mitigate his realization of the fact that he is first of all a priest.

It usually takes several months for a beginning priest-teacher to devise a schedule of spiritual activities that is workable. Much of his time is already structured for him. He must be in such and such a place at such and such a time. The schedule of private spiritual exercises, therefore, must be built around his school schedule.

It would be a serious mistake to think that conformity to Christ, the goal of every priest, is something that takes place by itself without any effort on the part of the priest. Unless the priest-teacher attempts to conform himself to Christ daily by means of the recommended spiritual activities; unless he tries to become personally what he is by reason of ordination, his labors in the classroom will be in vain. It is not enough for a priest-teacher to be a Socrates or a Mr. Chips in the classroom. He must be "another Christ." This is what his students need more than anything else. The words of Dom Hubert van Zeller, taken from his essay, "Mainly for Schoolmasters" apply here:

> Young people are not shepherded by Providence into our sphere of influence to be taught out of a book or to be won to the admiration of our personalities. Both these elements may come in, must come in, but they are not primarily what education is for. . . . What is our stock in trade? No one can give more than he has got, and if one in authority is spiritually impoverished, the work which he does for souls will be impoverished accordingly. We can't awaken enthusiasm by pretending to be enthusiastic, we can't point to a beauty which we don't see. Only if Christ is a reality to us, only in the measure we live the Christ-life can we effectively teach it to others. . . . What is remembered by those who come under you is *you*, and if you are, like St. Paul, an *alter Christus*, you are training minds as they are meant to be trained. They will remember Christ. They will remember you too, but that does not matter. Even the fact that they will remember you for the best you had to give them instead of for the worst, must not, for you, be allowed to matter. The only thing that weighs with you is the memory which you give to them of Christ.[22]

Strict attention to the matter of personal Christian formation is demanded for another reason. The process of teaching is, ideally, one continuous act of charity. "Teaching is a process that goes on between living men" writes Josef Pieper. "The teacher looks not only at the truth of things; at the same time he looks at the faces of living men who desire to know this truth. Love of truth and love of men — only the two together

---

[22] Hubert van Zeller, O.S.B., *We Live With Our Eyes Open* (New York: Sheed and Ward, 1963), pp. 79–80.

constitute a teacher."[23] The priest-teacher's love of truth and love of men depends on his love of God. This love of God, which is the source of the priest-teacher's devotion to truth and men, must be an ever deepening love that derives its vitality from the proven practices of the spiritual life.

Finally, it must be noted that the spiritual handbook best suited for the priest-teacher is the New Testament, particularly the four Gospels. It is here that the priest-teacher will find his exemplar, the first and foremost priest-teacher, Jesus Christ. The majority of scenes in the Gospels frame Jesus in teaching situations. The Gospels reveal the Divine Teacher; they reveal his wisdom and patience, his enthusiasm and kindness, his concrete methods of instruction and his approachability. If the priest-teacher reflects frequently on Christ as he is presented as teacher in the Gospels; if the words of the Gospel are always present in the memory of the priest-teacher, then these words and the example of Christ will always be present in the heart of the priest-teacher and in his actions. He will grow day by day in the virtues. He will become, over the years, a better priest, a better teacher, and a better person.

---

[23] Josef Pieper, *The Silence of St. Thomas* (New York: Pantheon, 1957), p. 23.

24

The Newman Apostolate

CHARLES W. ALBRIGHT, C.S.P.

IN HIS PREFACE TO A MANUAL FOR NEWLY APPOINTED NEWMAN CHAP-
lains, Archbishop Paul J. Hallinan of Atlanta, speaking with an authority
born of fruitful experience, observed,

> The Newman Apostolate is underway and the Newman chaplaincy will
> provide the continuity that gives it direction, inspiration and steadfastness.
> Let our Newman priests be men of broad vision and big hearts — not
> narrowly provincial or parochial. Let them put the excellence of the intel-
> lect first, confident that if students humbly seek truth, God will give the
> increase. Let them be patient in the formation of the Christ-life in the
> student, confident that these students will be our best leaders. Perhaps, best
> of all, may we ask that the chaplains never lose that spirit of adventure
> and excitement, that frontier mentality, that will spend and be spent in a
> real sacrifice of time, talents and temperament that has marked our mission
> since 1893.

The excellence of the intellect and the formation of the Christ-life in
the student, conceived and carried out in the spirit of adventure native
to the frontier — this is the substance of the Newman Apostolate: an
apt summary of its goals, an authentic expression of its best spirit.

It is, however, a challenge to try to formulate a "theology of the
Newman Apostolate." In isolating even the most basic principles and
policies one runs the risk of being contradicted by the first Newman
chaplain who might pause to read. It is not that there has not been time
enough to test what is good, nor able men capable of establishing the

right approaches, it is simply that there is such extraordinary diversity in what the term "Newman Apostolate" embraces. It has been thoughtfully defined as "the work of the Church in the secular campus community." But think what tortures of analogy are required to encompass in the term "secular campus community" the mobile thousands of the metropolitan university, the highly disciplined cadet corps of a service academy, the serious sophisticates of the Ivy League, the casual informality of the midwestern agricultural college, the small handful of uneasy Papists in a Southern Baptist college, the autocratic democracy of our better State Universities, not to mention what have almost become relics of a pre-freudian age — the all men or all women colleges!

However, with due stress on the overriding primacy of that ancient principle revived by the Constitution on the Sacred Liturgy — adaptation — it is worth the risk to set up some broad basic principles, policies, and practices, and with due caution, describe broad categories of situations to which these must be applied.

THE BASIC GOALS

In the summer of 1962 a representative and experienced group of chaplains, students, alumni, and faculty were called together by Archbishop Hallinan, then episcopal moderator for the National Newman Apostolate, for a special meeting at the University of Michigan in Ann Arbor. In one of those hard-working, lively, far-into-the-night sessions that has characterized national Newman organization at its best, this group hammered out a statement of basic aims and broad goals. Enlarging on the brief definition given above (The Newman Apostolate is the work of the Church in the secular campus community), these goals were enumerated:

1. The intellectual and moral development of the Catholic on the secular campus.
2. The religious education of the Catholic.
3. The apostolic formation of the Catholic.
4. The contribution of Catholic culture to the academic community.
5. The responsible participation of Catholics in the academic and civic communities.

Religious education and moral guidance have always been recognized as goals of this apostolate since the first Newman Club was founded at the University of Pennsylvania in 1893. The apostolic formation of what will, of necessity, be the few, has gained common acceptance more recently. It has only been since World War II that there has developed a consensus which sees the Newman Apostolate as an *opportunity* for the Church to become incarnate in the university community, to influence in a positive way the academic world. Too often in the past Newman work was seen as only a protection against evil, as something unfortunately necessary "to preserve the faith" endangered by the secularism, atheism, and communism of "godless universities." And equally often there was the tendency to isolate Catholic students as far as possible within the Newman Club as the best means of such protection. That day has passed.

Intellectual Development

The intellectual development of Catholics is the goal first enumerated in the Ann Arbor statement mentioned above. In the spirit of an incarnational theology, this goal of the Newman apostolate is seen as something far deeper and broader than urging students to study so as to get good grades or just to "learn their religion." It aims to instill in students an understanding that they cannot separate "going to college and studying" from "serving God and practicing their religion"; that one becomes good and holy just as much by serious study, active concern for campus life, and sensible recreation as by attendance at Mass, reception of the sacraments, and active participation in the Newman program.

The Newman chaplain should appreciate and encourage, in whatever way possible, not only good study habits in the undergraduate, but sound scholarship and intellectual initiative among graduate students and faculty. He will find that good scholarship and a real commitment to the ideals of the intellectual life are never the obstacles to religion that shoddy scholarship and intellectual indifference are. In the Catholic faculty member sound scholarship is a positive asset for Christian witness, and in the agnostic professor it insures at least an *honest* challenge to religious values.

The group at Ann Arbor, in formulating these goals, studiously avoided limiting the work of the Newman Apostolate to the Catholic *student*. It is concerned with the whole academic community, professors and administrators as well as students. It goes without saying that concern for students will and should have a special place and a particular importance. But, *in the long view,* the work of the Church for the student will be successful only to the degree that the Newman Apostolate has reached effectively the faculty and administration of the university. We have complained too long about the "godlessness" of both public and private secular universities while doing very little to bring sound theology to the campus, to Christianize what is secularistic, even to enlist those of good will who have always been potential supporters of our best efforts on campus. On its lowest level, for example, any time a chaplain can influence — say a professor of European history — so that he presents fairly and objectively the Church's role in medieval Europe (including things we wish hadn't happened, but did) rather than malign the Church and distort Catholicism, then, to that degree, the chaplain is no longer needed as someone who must "protect" a young Catholic's faith from historical falsity, because the student will no longer be exposed to false history.

In all this, of course, there is the implication that the chaplain himself needs intellectual preparation. This is true, though academic status and intellectual brilliance are not the only qualifications for a chaplain on the secular campus. Indeed, if I had to choose between the priest with an outgoing personality, able to establish rapport with students and others (as long as he was not *anti*-intellectual), and the scholarly Ph.D. who was an introvert and unable to get along with people, I would not hesitate to choose the personable cleric who couldn't understand Teilhard de Chardin and hadn't even tried to read Paul Tillich. Other things being equal, however, the priest who goes to the secular campus with that status symbol of the academic community — the Ph.D. — has that much better chance of wielding influence within the university community. If the chaplain has both the academic degree and intellectual competence, with at least a modicum of personality, he can make a lasting impact on the whole university. Should bishops not be able to find such a happy combination in one man, there is no law against appointing two priests to the campus (or even more) whose combined talents might include the desirable characteristics.

Granted the value of a graduate degree — in what, from where? I'm not sure it matters. It is probably true that the secular campus will set greater store on a degree from one of the respected secular universities, but "status-wise" the degree is more important than the institution. Graduate work at a good secular university, however, can be an excellent way to get to know the inner workings of the secular campus, and there are many fields of study that can prove relevant to a priest's work as chaplain: psychology, philosophy, almost any of the social sciences, even English literature. The talents and interests of the priest should probably be the determining factor. But whatever competence one might have in any of these fields, the one competence that will be expected of the chaplain will be that of theology. Many chaplains feel that if a priest could have at least a licentiate in sacred theology plus a doctorate from a secular university in some non-theological field, this would be near ideal preparation, as far as formal academic qualifications are concerned. Others are of the opinion that a doctorate in religious education such as Father Gerard Sloyan has developed at Catholic University is the answer to academic training for this apostolate. It is obviously still an open question: the one concensus being the value of graduate study and the added prestige of the Ph.D. or its equivalent. It must be stressed, however, that the really important consideration is that a priest be prepared to take his place on a footing of equality with the best in the academic community, and that he will be concerned to promote the best values of that community.

Moral Development

In most ways, the means for helping others to achieve moral excellence within the academic community will be no different from those used in any other pastoral situation in the Church: sound liturgical and sacramental practices, preaching of the Word of God rooted in Scripture and the liturgy, help with personal problems through enlightened counseling, and a lively sense of Christian concern for the social problems of the day.

These accepted and ancient basics of the Christian life, must, however, be carried out in an atmosphere that is sensitive to the particular needs and special values of the university community. For example, whatever the discrepancies between theory and practice, the academic world sets strong store on academic freedom, honesty, and integrity. These are values and virtues that can be ardently defended and respected with no compromise of Catholic principles. One finds students and faculty alike keenly observant and quick to be critical, particularly of anything smacking of hypocrisy or lack of candor. The university community runs the gamut of conviction and commitment, but its members are more apt to be open in expressing their doubts and dislikes, as well as their certainties and likes. If the Church has always been poorly served by trying to conceal or deny the presence of human weaknesses and sin in the Church, it is disastrous to try it on campus.

The Liturgy. As in all pastoral endeavor, the liturgy is central to the development of a Christian community within the university. Few places have been more open to the recent changes in the liturgy or more readily appreciative. Because of this openness of the college community, diocesan liturgical commissions could hardly choose a better location for liturgical experimentation than the Newman chapel. Such a measure of freedom would not only play its role in liturgical development, but would have its pastoral importance for an age group always somewhat resentful of regimentation, and often prone to see the Church in an overly authoritarian role.

There could be other areas for fruitful pastoral experimentation. For example, much discussion is being carried on concerning the effectiveness of our present practices in the use of the sacrament of penance. Here again the college community, relatively more open to new ways of doing things, might well be chosen by bishops as a testing ground for developing more effective sacramental practices. The suggestion that general absolution might become a somewhat normal practice, not as a substitute for private confession, but as a means of making private confession more effective in healing the roots of sin, might be tested by the campus community. My point here is not to argue for or against such a practice, but to underline the advantages to the campus in trying new methods.

The principle of adaptation, accepted by the Fathers of the Second Vatican Council as a necessary principle if the Church is going to have a living liturgy, should be brought into play just as surely on the secular campus as in the developing nations and cultures of Asia and Africa. The adaptations may be less "exotic" — to our way to thinking — than bongo drums, different colored vestments, or quarter-scale musical modes, but they may be just as essential to bringing the university community to Christ in meaningful worship. It is in being sensitive to discover areas where something new may be needed that today's chaplain will maintain that "frontier mentality" praised by Archbishop Hallinan.

Counseling. Simply in terms of time, counseling will usually be the chaplain's biggest job. Any priest who has spent much time struggling with the problems of today's collegians will often wish that he had professional training as a psychotherapist. The student needing psychotherapy, however, is still the exception — or at least in the minority. The priest does need to be able to recognize those who may need psychiatric care, but for the most part his own training, with a sympathetic readiness to *listen,* will be adequate for the demands. Availability and patient kindness are indispensable: availability at all hours of the day and night, patience and kindness for whatever brand of perverted, inconsiderate egomaniac who takes two hours to tell a ten-minute tale. They won't all be like that, and few other areas of a chaplain's work will offer the satisfactions of knowing he has helped.

Religious Education

For many years chaplains argued about which was their more important role: educational or pastoral? Which was their distinguishing role? The question is seldom asked today, at least in those terms, partly because the Second Vatican Council has given us a much broader concept of what is meant by "pastoral." Chaplains who "put the excellence of the intellect first" will likely be the very ones who hold that pastoral concern is primary in the Church's apostolate on the secular campus. For it is soon learned that in terms of a living Catholicism the formal educational program — classes, lectures, seminars, discussions — gains relevancy from a living liturgy. Or to put it from another perspective, the good pastor soon finds that the Mass, the sacraments, devotions, works of the social apostolate will have relatively little relevance to campus life and to the academic community unless offered in conjunction with an educational program and in an atmosphere of intellectual concern.

There are a growing number of chaplains who would prefer to see the university itself accept responsibility for theology as an academic discipline. Whether in a school or department of religion or theology, or, less desirable, in some interdepartmental program, there is a value in having theology taught and studied in the normal framework of other university disciplines. In the interesting symposium sponsored by a group of priests and laymen in England, and reported in the volume *Theology and the University,* edited by John Coulson, many varied opinions were expressed on many points, but there was one well established concensus which summarized the conclusions of the conference:

> Theology can choose; it can remain dead and neglected, or take the pressure of the times and live; but if it chooses life it has need of three things: a university setting, lay participation and the ecumenical dialogue.

I think most Newman chaplains would be in substantial agreement with such a conclusion.

Earlier fears on the part of Catholic authorities that the university could not be trusted to teach Catholic theology are disappearing; the standards of academic responsibility give reasonable assurance that only those qualified will be asked to hold a chair of Catholic studies. Partly as a result of the changes wrought by the two Johns, there seems a greater openness on the part of the university to see the value of theology courses; there is undoubtedly less inclination on the part of university authorities to push that once popular educational theory — that only the "uncommitted" could teach religion objectively — which led in the past to some almost unbelievably distorted versions of "Catholicism" in an otherwise innocuous course of comparative religion. Not all universities are yet ready to follow the example of the State University of Iowa and establish a School of Religion, offering majors, minors, and graduate degrees, nor are many ready to develop a department of religion after the fashion of Western Michigan University, but where religion or theology *is* introduced into the curriculum today, it is much more likely to be in an academically responsible manner than once was true.

However, even where there are acceptable theology courses offered by the university, there will still be a need for a Newman educational program: supplementary courses, special lectures, and, highly important, those more informal means of learning: small discussion groups, symposia pertinent to special fields (law, medicine, business, etc.), speakers on matters pertinent to the day: racial problems, work of the Council, whatever might be the particular interests of the moment.

Equally important will be the opportunities for the Newman Center to cooperate with various individuals and departments in the university in such things as bringing a speaker to campus, sponsoring special conferences (say on "control of nuclear weapons," with the political science department), as well as joint programs of this type with other religious groups on campus.

Many avenues of education are open and worth being sponsored or encouraged by the Newman chaplain: a Catholic library, either at the Newman Center or by donation to the university library — or both (or perhaps today an Ecumenical religious library), a well stocked rack for paperbacks, college level pamphlets, periodicals, or perhaps even a bookstore of selected current books and some good religious art.

There is a wealth of good educational material in films, easily available at low cost. Educational television also gives promise of soon being able to provide valuable educational tapes for closed circuit TV, or cinescopes that can be used on a movie projector. Knowledge of such developments will usually be brought to the attention of chaplains by the Newman national office and at national meetings of Newman chaplains.

A special point should be made in this context concerning the importance of enlisting the active help of all segments of the university community in the planning and carrying out of the educational program: students (reflecting all the major facets of the student body: town students, dorm students, foreign students, graduate students, students from each college of the university), faculty, and representatives of any other groups that might be organized from the Newman Center (women's guild, alumni, foundation). A "Board of Education," with special status in relation to the overall operation of the Newman Center, will not only involve more people in a meaningful way in the work of the apostolate, but will help create the right image of the importance given to education and culture as central to the Newman program.

Apostolic Formation

There is perhaps no area of a chaplain's concern in which there is less satisfaction that one "has the answer" than in the matter of a program for apostolic formation. The techniques and programs of various apostolic groups, YCS, Legion of Mary, Sodality, the Christophers, third orders — all have been used in one place or another, but none have been found to fully meet the needs of today's campus apostolate. Many experiments have been made, with varying degrees of success, in adapting and modifying these various apostolic programs, particularly YCS and Legion of Mary. In searching for a "Newman Way" of apostolic development and spiritual formation there is at least concensus as to some of the elements that must be included: an integration of the intellectual life and the spiritual life, a respect for the values of the secular campus, the central role of the liturgy and of Scripture in forming the Christian conscience. The one source for optimism in this area is the wide variety of experimentation going on, with efforts to share the results through the various media of the national apostolate. An experimental program developed by one of the Dominican chaplains at the University of New Mexico is available through the office of the National Newman Apostolate at the National Catholic Welfare Conference in Washington, D. C.

CONTRIBUTION OF CATHOLIC CULTURE TO THE ACADEMIC COMMUNITY

Where there is an atmosphere of ecumenical concern, much of the educational program directed primarily to the Catholic community may well serve the broader interests of the university. Particularly the special lectures, panel discussions on current problems, and other of the more informal educational techniques can be used in programs open to the entire university community. For many years, on a number of campuses, the Newman Center has made a major contribution to the cultural life of the university through a first class lecture program, known in many places as "The Newman Forum." Under the auspices of the Newman Center, speakers of such caliber as Martin D'Arcy, Philip Sharper, Eugene McCarthy, C. J. McNaspy, Claire Booth Luce, John Courtney Murray, Thomas Stransky, and John Cogley are brought for public lectures to the whole university community, with special opportunity for members of various departments of the university to meet the speaker who might have a scholarly reputation in some particular field.

An open field for development lies in the media of the printed word. Many Newman Centers publish some kind of paper, but only a few to date have published a journal on a regular basis that is directed to the whole university community. Of the few instances where it has been done, a notable example has been the quarterly *Newman Review* at Wayne State University, now in its eighteenth year of publication, and more recently at Harvard, *The Current*. *The Newman Annual* published by the Newman Center at the University of Minnesota has also had a university-wide orientation, and ably demonstrates that the Catholic university community can produce writing of high literary caliber.

RESPONSIBLE PARTICIPATION IN THE ACADEMIC AND CIVIC COMMUNITIES

For many years the Newman Club too often served as another Catholic agency for developing the ghetto spirit. Chaplains were inclined to see the Newman Club in competition with university organizations in attracting student members, and were prone to discourage students they could influence from getting involved in other campus activities since they would not then have time for the Newman Club. An unfortunate effect of such a policy was to strengthen the idea that the priest was just there as chaplain for those who joined the Newman Club, rather than as the Catholic chaplain to the university. Though such attitudes and actions have not completely disappeared, few chaplains would any longer openly defend them. Without doubt, the Council and its influence on the ecumenical movement, as well as Pope Paul's goal for the council of "dialogue with the world" will continue to be the major force in encouraging a spirit of cooperation and involvement of the Church with all aspects of university life, as well as in the life of the larger community of which the university is a part.

Without detracting from the narrower goals of academic accomplishment and preparation for the future, students can still find time for many worthwhile concerns. The involvement of college students in the civil rights movements in the country has in many instances been a decisive factor in interracial progress: Catholic participation in these varied activities for civil rights has not always been evident.

Valid criticism might well be made that student involvement in outside programs can interfere with the legitimate demands of their academic responsibilities. Some excess in this direction might be preferable, however, to an inaction that betrays a totally unchristian lack of concern for others. At least those who in the name of "prudence" caution against such involvement might be more open to such programs as do not militate against college life itself, such as tutorial programs for high school "drop-outs," and others that can be fitted into an academic schedule. The irony is that at times the chaplain who has cautioned against involvement in other university and civic activities because it will interfere with studies is the last to see that he himself often asks more time of students than they can give and still keep up with their academic responsibilities. It has not been unknown for a student to "major in Newman" — and fail to graduate.

Even more important than the specific instances of whether or not it is advisable to "get involved" in outside interests, is the general *attitude* of interest and concern for the whole of university life, and to a more limited extent, the entire civic community. Prudence must guide in the decision of how much and when, but there should be no question that the Church's concern extends to the welfare and advancement of the entire university community, and the chaplain will seek to implement this concern by encouraging participation in any of the various organizations, activities, and programs that give promise of benefiting the university.

There is a sense in which every Newman chaplain should seek to realize all the objectives here enumerated. Circumstances, however, will dictate that now one, now another of these goals will have priority — and at times some must simply be neglected as far as practical implementation goes. There is a variety of these determining circumstances, but the primary ones are the type of institution in which the chaplain is working and the personnel available.

THE SECULAR CAMPUS COMMUNITY

As indicated earlier, there is a great variety in the kinds and types of institutions. As it affects the Newman program, the distinction of greatest moment is between the *residential* and the *commuter* college.

The Commuter College

Since World War II, there has been a tremendous growth in the urban college and university, both as to the number of institutions and as to their size. We can anticipate an even greater percentage of our students attending such universities. For the most part, students at these schools are characterized by being almost wholly commuters, largely part-time students, with a significant percentage enrolled in the evening division. Since most or all of the students are living at home, their liturgical and sacramental lives will normally be centered in their own residential parishes. Some might argue that because of this there is no need for a Newman program. If every parish were a vibrant center of Christian life, the argument might have a point, but would still be only partly true. Apart from the fact that not every parish is the ideal dynamic Christian community, there are still needs and problems peculiar to the university campus that very few good parishes would meet. And such an argument misses the more positive aspect of the matter: the opportunity for the Church to enter into dialogue with this important segment of the world, the meaning of the apostolate of presence, the apostolic imperative of the Incarnation in the university.

Given the need for the Newman program in such an institution, how will it differ from the Newman program on the residential campus? It will differ in emphasis, in extent, and somewhat in the tools and techniques used.

The difference in emphasis will lie primarily in the greater amount of time given to the educational program and the proportionately fewer liturgical and sacramental activities. For example, on most commuter campuses there will be no need for Sunday Mass since all live at home; on the others there may be fewer students at Sunday Mass than at daily Mass. If the daily Mass can be held on campus it can be a most important part of the Newman program at the commuter college. It will often be the only means whereby a sense of community can be established; it can be a highly valuable means for Christian education through the daily homily; and, in a way somewhat hard to define, it has an importance because it identifies the chaplain as a *priest*. The chaplain at the commuter college should also be easily available for the sacrament of penance; college life is still an age of uncertainties and the trials of adolescence have not all been conquered. There will rarely be occasions for other sacramental practices at the urban college.

The Newman program at the commuter college will differ in extent, in that it will always reach a smaller percentage of the students. The universal problem facing the chaplain(s) at the urban college or university is how can he reach so many students, so widely scattered, spending (so many of them) so little time on campus? In many instances, of course, the answer is simply, he can't, primarily because of inadequate personnel, the physical impossibility of one chaplain meeting the two to eight thousand Catholics on campus. But even with the somewhat ideal staff of one chaplain (or chaplain's assistant — priest, sister, brother, layman) for every five hundred students, not all students on this kind of campus will ever be reached. Many students must leave for work as soon as their last class is finished, with no free time between classes. For many others, the energy involved in returning to campus for participation in any extracurricular activity (including Newman) is more than they can muster — these apart from the purely nominal Catholics who will go to any length to keep away from anyone representing organized religion. Not that you don't sometimes reach them — despite their efforts.

The relevant factor for the chaplain in meeting this problem is not to confuse numbers with success — or failure. The chaplain who knows he is only reaching ten to fifteen percent of the Catholics on campus has sound reasons for not being complacent, and for using all his energy and ingenuity in trying to reach many more. He has no reason, however, for discouragement. There is meaning simply in the fact that he is there on campus, making the Church visible in a way that perhaps only the clergy can do and which will always be one of the services of the clergy to the People of God. Those the Newman program is not reaching directly may still be influenced for good because the Church is at work on campus: through the "reached" Catholic student, or faculty member, or counselor or advisor or someone in the Dean's office who has felt the influence of Newman on campus.

The Newman program at the commuter college will also differ somewhat in the tools and techniques the chaplain uses, at least in the relative value found in means to reach students. Communication through the mails is of value on any kind of campus, but it is absolutely essential for the commuter campus. Some kind of bulletin or newsletter, at least, is essential for informing the Catholics on campus of the Newman program, and a periodical with thought content will be even better. Here again one should not try to measure success by the amount of identifiable response. Sometimes there may be none; other times it's obvious you have "come through." For example, I wondered if anyone read my fall letter of welcome, but since our last monthly newsletter went out two weeks ago, I have had over a dozen students come in to see me with relatively serious problems, as a result of something I had said in the chaplain's column. New faces keep turning up at daily Mass, again as a result of the paper's reminder that Mass was being offered on campus. The chaplain on the residential campus can make an announcement from the pulpit at Sunday Masses and reach a large percentage of the students; the chaplain on the commuters' campus has only the mails. Or almost. Don't forget the campus newspaper, whether weekly or daily. This is valuable at both types of school, and spot checks have shown that students read and learn of Newman activities from their campus paper.

Another area of difference one should note at the urban university is the timing of activities. Noon hour is especially good most places, but classes, discussion groups, committee meetings, almost anything can be scheduled for any hour during the *day*. Most students will be in class, of course, but there is always a sizable number who in any given class period have a free hour. Again — face it — only a few of this sizable number will show up for the Newman activity, but five or ten are better than none. If something can be scheduled during every school hour, five or ten times eight or nine begins to add up. Some checking may show some hours more favorable than others; a few schools will have free hours in the schedule for extracurricular activities. If such favored hours exist, be sure to make use of them.

Most of this adds up to the fact that there will be less response to fewer things by fewer people on a commuters' campus than at the residential college. To the degree that this is true, let the chaplain offer thanks that, as a result, he will have more time to spend in the faculty lounge, dropping in for a chat with the Dean of Students, having lunch with a history professor. If, despite the relatively less response he gets on the commuters' campus, the chaplain still finds his hours filled with student interviews, classes, discussion groups, committee meetings, then he would do well to schedule into his day some time in the faculty lounge, morning coffee with a group from the psychology department (or English or chemistry), with weekly lunch (at least) with some faculty group. The emphasis one gives to these contacts with faculty should not differ from one kind of campus to another.

The Residential Campus

Though some (perhaps Pope John's "prophets of doom") have predicted that the residential campus will one day disappear, it is presently very much with us, growing in size, increasing in number, at least the publicly supported ones, and for any chaplain who has served on a variety of campuses, certainly the most satisfactory on which to work among God's academic people. Its greatest natural asset, perhaps, is that there *is* a community, and sometimes a sense of community. This is something on which the Christian community within the university can build, making the chaplain's work not only easier and more satisfying, but probably more fruitful as well. The pressures of the community, particularly some of the smaller units of the community such as fraternities and sororities, can also create problems for the Newman program, but on the whole the advantages outweigh the drawbacks.

The emphasis at this type of campus is, of course, on the liturgical and sacramental aspects of the apostolate, at least in terms of time. Particularly on the large residential campus, where the chaplain is most likely not only to be full-time, but to have a staff of assistants and a Newman Center, the distinguishing mark of Newman work is that it will be a campus parish — whether it has that canonical status or not. A full liturgical program, incorporating all those elements envisioned by the Council's decree on the liturgy, can be carried out with relative ease. Equally important is the possibility of experimenting with those paraliturgical forms of worship recommended by the council, of having as well, some part of the Office said in common in the vernacular, and in general of developing a living Christian community centered in the worship of the Church. It seems to me that the special value in this for the Newman program is that much of the educational and cultural program can develop from and grow in relation to this living liturgy. The possibilities of this have been illustrated in a singular way by the Dominican Father Blase Schauer in his work at New Mexico State University. He has been unusually successful in encouraging the development of talents in arts and crafts among members of the college community, and then incorporating the fruits of their efforts into the liturgy — even to the point that the Newman Center and chapel were almost completely built by students.

In extent, the Newman Apostolate at the residential university reaches a much larger percentage than the small percent noted as to be expected at the commuter college. This is done, however, through the pastoral program, primarily by reaching members of the university community at Sunday Mass. Without having scientifically verifiable statistics, there is reason to believe that the percentage of college students attending Sunday Mass is higher than in an "average" parish. With the advantages of a relatively homogeneous group, the Newman Chaplain will find the Sunday homily can be most effective as a tool for Christian education. The pulpit can also be used effectively to encourage reading magazines and books as a means of developing their religious literacy. When the writer was at the University of California in Berkeley we were selling one hundred copies of *The Catholic World* each month by mentioning a particular article with an appeal to the college community. The Newman Center Library is also more likely to get good use on the residential campus than at the commuter college, though this may represent a temporary phase related to new colleges still in the process of developing high scholastic standards, and the serious reading that goes with such standards.

Other Types of Schools

There are other factors besides whether the college is residential or commuter that will dictate adaptations and different emphases. For example, there are scholastic demands that create an atmosphere of serious study in our Ivy League colleges that are seldom matched elsewhere, though our better state universities have achieved the same standards of scholarship in their graduate schools, while many smaller private colleges have standards almost as exacting. In these schools there will be serious study and discussion groups that most major seminarians would have difficulty keeping up with, students who are reading Karl Rahner, Hans Küng, Teilhard de Chardin, Paul Tillich, as well as Dan Callahan, Michael Novak, and the latest discussion on the morality of contraception. Such students also have their problems with sex, but the problem may be philosophical as well as practical, and both will need to be faced with honesty and candor as well as with patience and compassion.

Technical and professional schools will also dictate particular programs in answer to their needs, and may call for one to become a specialist in some particular field such as medical or legal ethics.

Other Determining Circumstances

If difference in type of school will demand differences in type of approach, the other circumstances most affecting the Newman program will be the *talents* and *time* of the chaplain. I may see a need for a course in medical ethics, but if I am not capable of giving such a course, I will do better to give no course than a half-baked one. The answer may be to find someone who is qualified to teach the course, or start some serious studying on my own until I am qualified. Meanwhile, I plan a program I am capable of handling.

The chaplain's available time will also do some dictating as to what he will do, as well as how much. Though the number of full-time chaplains has more than doubled — almost tripled — in the past ten years, there are still many colleges needing a full-time chaplain. Or, as one student put it, "We only have a some time chaplain." Other colleges may need more than one full-time chaplain or other full-time personnel. There are still several instances where one chaplain is responsible for more than 6500 Catholic students. A knowledge of this is not in itself pastoral theology, but when a priest finds himself assigned to such a position, he should realize that he cannot do the things that are done on a nearby campus where there are four or five full-time people on the staff of the Catholic Center. Nor should he become discouraged trying to do the impossible. When the situation demands a full-time chaplain or additional personnel, the overburdened chaplain should bring this to the attention of his bishop with all the force he can — total statistics, predictions of future growth, detailed description of demands already made on his time — but once done, it is the bishop's responsibility before God, and all the chaplain can do after that is his best.

THE NEWMAN CLUB

It may have been noted that up to this point the term "Newman Club" has seldom been used in speaking of the work of the priest so often called the "Newman Club Chaplain." This is no mere accident or oversight. The term "club" has perhaps done more to hinder the proper growth and development of this apostolate of the Church than even the lack of enthusiasm of bishops in earlier days. It is somewhat ironic that just about the time bishops started being in favor of Newman Clubs, the Newman Club Chaplain wanted to do away with the Newman Club — or almost. Nor is this some perversity on the part of priests, being against anything the bishop is for. Once bishops started appointing full-time chaplains and these chaplains were able really to give themselves completely to this work they soon realized that very few people would take a *club* seriously — even if it was a club whose purpose was "to deepen the spiritual and enrich the temporal lives of its members through a balanced program of religious, intellectual and social activities." Parents usually thought it a "nice thing" for students to belong; some students (almost always the minority) also thought it was a nice thing, but very often for the wrong reasons, and those who didn't think it was a nice thing proceeded to absolve themselves from any participation in the religious and educational program for Catholics on the campus — save Sunday Mass. Newman *Club* perhaps need not, but too often has produced a ghetto mentality. The big problem has been to drop the "Newman Club" without losing what had been and can still be the good in it. This good is primarily the potential for developing lay leadership, and American culture being what it is, one will find it almost impossible to do this without organization. Much experimentation is still going on. A recent report on developments at the University of Colorado quoted the experienced chaplain there, Father Charles Forsyth, O.S.B., as saying:

> "Center" will be used in place of "Club" because the Newman Center has truly become a Center of the Apostolate of the Church on this secular campus. . . . When we had nothing — no facilities, no staff — we tried to give the students something, to be preserved through a club. Now its goals have matured. The club word and mentality have become a barrier to what really is the Apostolate of the Church on campus. We used to be a refuge for the unattached independent and the maladjusted "greeks." Now with our facilities and our staff, we are involved in the formation of the Christian community. Club committees have given way to a Parish Board and Commission. . . . Now the Newman Center is really a personification of two things: *aggiornamento,* a renewal of ourselves individually and as a Christian community. We also are an "open window" to Catholicism on the secular campus.

Catholic Center, University Parish, Newman Foundation: these are all terms and concepts replacing Newman Club, at least Newman Club as the total concept of the Church's work on campus. However, the urban university chaplain and the small college part-time chaplain may still find a positive value in both the term and the concept of Newman Club, shorn at least of some of its uncatholic characteristics. Certainly the part-time chaplain, able to meet with students only once or twice a week, will still see value in the Newman Club. But even here, if Newman Club is to represent the Church on campus, club must not become "clique," and the chaplain must take definite precautions that everyone in the college realize he is chaplain to all Catholic students, not just to those who join the Newman Club.

The Ecumenical Movement on Campus

Since the goals of the Newman Apostolate were formulated at the Ann Arbor meeting referred to toward the beginning of this chapter, the Second Vatican Council has set in motion some trends few would have envisioned at that time, particularly the change of stance of the Church toward the Ecumenical Movement. This is going to have a significant effect on the Church's work on campus. The secular campus has long been the *locus* of the greatest cooperation by Catholics in interreligious affairs, and almost every campus has evolved some sort of Religious Council. Some bishops have forbidden Catholic participation in these councils, but most have not, so that a structure for ecumenical programming is in most places already at hand on the secular campus, and needs only the impetus that fuller Catholic participation can now give to develop it into a significant area for ecumenical progress. A small and unofficial group of Catholic and Protestant chaplains met for discussion of common concerns during the summer of 1965 in Atlanta. A statement representing a consensus of those present has been received with much interest by other chaplains. It may not represent a consensus of thinking among Newman Chaplains, but the ideas it presents are certainly going to be discussed in the years ahead. It is perhaps fitting then, that my observations on the Newman Apostolate as it has developed from the past and is being realized in the present should close with presenting these ideas looking so largely to the future:

The Atlanta Statement

Because the University is a significant institution in the shaping of our world, the Church must be concerned about its relationships with it.

As chaplains we are concerned with the University, meaning not simply the administration but the whole collective of persons and structures. We respect the integrity of the University's own life, without seeking to impose on it preconceived religious images.

We seek to cooperate with the University in its continuing search for self understanding. We seek to cooperate with it in providing occasions for inter- and intra-disciplinary dialogue. At times we must be creative critics of the University, without standing over against it. We see the teaching of theology as an academic discipline to be the responsibility of the University.

It is not necessary to define but to develop our position in the structure of the University, though in many instances the position we are seen to occupy hinders and frustrates the vitality of our work.

A Christian ecumenical ministry is not only possible now but imperative, and we are committed to it. We can no longer tolerate sectarianism, and we should work to modify the structures which perpetuate a sectarian stance. This does not suggest that we are all of a single mind regarding revelation as it relates to belief and practice, but it does suggest that we must continue to be responsible to one another. In such matters as religious counselling there is already a climate for mutual acceptance to each other's work.

As we seek within the University a ministry consonant with our possibilities in an ecumenical age, so we seek from the Church freedom to discover forms of the Church which best serve the campus community and freedom to experiment with forms of worship and service which best celebrate the presence of Christ there.

Though the precise forms of the Church on campus are not clear, it is clear that they cannot be along denominational lines. They will more than likely be flexible enough to follow natural University groupings which suggests small communities which may be brought together on occasion.

We must seek from the community of scholars the ideas, insights, and research which can and should be reshaping the life of the Church.

College and University chaplains must be intellectually and academically competent.

25

Preparing the Retreat Master

THOMAS M. BREW, S.J.

. . . And let us ask God to continue to make it a blessed oasis of prayer and recollection where in the light of the Blessed Sacrament all classes of workers may attain peace, serenity, comfort and spiritual refreshment, renewal and pardon, and holy resolutions to persevere in faithfulness to the Divine law.

(Pope John XXIII. To members of
Retreat Movement, Jan. 21, 1959.)

NEARLY ALL PRIESTS, AT ONE TIME OR ANOTHER, BECOME INVOLVED IN retreat work in some way. Hence, it is almost inevitable that someday, not too long after your ordination, you will receive a letter or phone call requesting you to give a retreat. More and more people in this country are making retreats. Besides, it is assumed that every priest is ready and able to give a retreat.

Retreats are far from new in the Church. They go back to the time of our Lord. Not content with the long years of quiet in the home of Nazareth, Jesus Christ spent forty days in prayer and fasting on a retreat in the desert before he went forth to teach the people publicly. He would occasionally invite the Apostles in the midst of their labors into the friendly silence of a retreat — "Come aside into a desert place and rest a little" (Mk 6:31). During the ten-day interval between the Ascension and the coming of the Holy Spirit on Pentecost Sunday, the Apostles together with the Blessed Mother were gathered in the

Upper Room "persevering together in prayer so that they might be worthy to receive the Holy Spirit." Never was there a retreat so explosive in its effects. After the coming of the Holy Spirit the Church came forth in power and strength. The Apostles had overcome their fear and timidity and were filled with zeal, courage, and the desire to preach the Gospel to the whole world.

The strange thing about the assumption that every priest can give a retreat lies in the fact that all through the regular seminary course there are few, if any, formal courses on the preparing and giving of retreats. For the most part, this preparation has to be on a do-it-yourself personal basis.

This chapter aims to give some idea of the work and functions of the retreat master and of the basic preparation that needs to be made by the young priest or seminarian. It is not a technical treatise on the mechanics and techniques of giving or preaching a retreat. Neither is it an attempt to explain or analyze any particular system of retreats. The purpose is to offer suggestions and guidelines that will enable the neophyte to make a start in preparing himself for retreat work. Once the start is made, his own interest and zeal should lead him further into the considerable literature on the subject of retreats. For that reason, whatever is suggested in the way of books to be read and studied is intended merely to be a starting point.

NEED AND PURPOSE OF RETREATS

For an understanding of the need, purpose, and place of retreats in the life of the Church, the best starting point is the encyclical *Mens Nostra* (1929) of Pope Pius XI wherein he states: "We esteem retreats to be a special safeguard for eternal salvation . . ." and then continues:

If you consider, Venerable Brethren, the times in which we live, you will see that the importance, usefulness and timeliness of retreats are brought home by manifold considerations. The worst disease which afflicts our age, the most pregnant source of evil, is its lightness and thoughtlessness, through which men lose their way. Hence arises that continual and eager distraction in external things, that insatiable desire for wealth and pleasure which slowly extinguishes in the minds of men the inclination for things that are more excellent. It implicates them so deeply in outward and passing things as to prevent all thought of eternal truths, of divine laws, and even of God Himself, the beginning and end of all. God, it is true, in His infinite goodness and mercy, no matter how far the evils penetrate, does not cease to give the largess of His grace, and to draw men to Himself. Yet we must fight against this sickness of the human race. And what better help and remedy can we propose than the invitation of those weakened and careless souls to the devout quiet of the Spiritual Exercises? In these Exercises an opportunity is given to a man to get away for a few days from ordinary society and from strife and cares, and to pass the time, not in idleness, but in the consideration of those questions which are of perennial and profound interest to man, the questions of his origin and his destiny, whence he comes and whither he goes. If no more than this were attained, surely no one will deny that the Spiritual Exercises would justify their existence.

In this country today, more people than ever before are making closed retreats. Consequently, the need for retreat masters grows apace. For lay people alone there are more than two hundred retreat houses. A large number of priests, diocesan and religious, are assigned to retreat work on a full-time basis. Every year more priests are needed to help on a part-time basis or to give an occasional retreat.

Canon law requires that diocesan priests, religious priests, nuns and brothers, make an annual retreat of several days. Some religious orders require an eight-day annual retreat. A small number of retreat houses provide retreats only for priests. They make available to the priest who wants it a longer retreat than is ordinarily required as well as the opportunity to make a retreat with a much smaller group. Retreats for priests and religious require older and more experienced retreat masters. Many religious orders have priests who are assigned to this type of retreat work on a full-time year-round basis. Your first retreat assignment will hardly be in this area.

It is more likely that you would first of all be asked to give a retreat to one of the many groups of laymen and laywomen who make an annual retreat in one of the many retreat houses for laymen in the United States. No accurate figures are available but it is estimated that nearly half a million lay people make a retreat each year.

The Laymen's Retreat Movement

This remarkable and encouraging phenomenon of the Laymen's retreat movement of our times deserves the understanding and active interest of every priest and future priest. Bishop John J. Wright of Pittsburgh, Episcopal Adviser of the National Laymen's Retreat Conference, describes it this way:

> The retreat movement not only builds up the supernatural life of the Church in America; it also projects a most attractive image of the nature and function of the Church. The lay-retreat movement is without any element of controversy; it has neither rightist nor leftist tendencies; it takes no positions of any kind on questions that divide, even legitimately, Catholics or Americans. It is concerned with the basic, inescapable question: What must I do to possess eternal life? It presents the image of a people at prayer pondering those eternal questions which transcend the categories of time, place, or partisan interest.

Why, in the midst of today's secularist culture and environment, have retreatants and retreat houses been growing in number? Jesuit Father L. Chiuminatto, after years of experience in directing retreats for laymen at the White House Retreat in St. Louis, explains it thus:

> For the same reason that hospitals, schools, and supermarkets are springing up all over the United States. They fulfill a material need and a great bodily want. People need and want better health, better education, and better food and clothing; hence the major phenomenon of expanding hospital, educational, and welfare facilities. The same is true for closed retreat houses. People have a great personal want and need for better spiritual health, a deeper understanding of religion, and a greater abundance of religious vitality. More and more men and women are finding that closed retreats satisfy this need by giving them a deeply moving personal spiritual experience. They return to their daily work and responsibilities with renewed courage, a sense of spiritual purification, a deeper realization of purpose in their lives, and a feeling of inner peace and joy.

Someone has well said that what this country needs is tranquility without tranquilizers. More lay people are discovering, in a much deeper and more effective way, that closed retreats bring this "tranquility without tranquilizers." In addition to rest and quiet for the body, closed retreats offer men and women the opportunity to think out quietly, prayerfully, and at leisure, under experienced guidance and direction, the great meaning of life itself.

In the stress and strain of today's pressures, tensions and feverish activity, the need for quiet, thoughtful evaluation of life's meaning becomes greater than ever. Psychiatrists are discovering every day that in many cases of breakdowns in adult life — i.e., after thirty-five — the cause lies so often in the failure of the patient to find or to hold on to his religious beliefs and outlook. If a person is to be able to keep his life on an even keel, realization and conviction about the meaning of his life are essential.

This need for a time and place for reflection was expressed by a retreatant this way:

> The pace keeps building up, the pressure gets heavier and heavier, things get noisier and more confused all the time. A place like a retreat house is just about the only place where I can be quiet enough, long enough, to figure out how I am going to get straightened out with a lot of this stuff that is bothering me.

Despite the benefits to be derived from closed retreats, the number of laymen who do not make a closed retreat is far greater than the number who do. There are many reasons for this. Some are good, some bad. Any retreat captain trying to recruit retreatants soon becomes familiar with the litany of excuses offered. Someday as moderator of the parish retreat group, you may find yourself trying to "sell" the idea of a retreat to your Holy Name Society or some other organization.

An unusual pamphlet written by Father D. F. Miller, C.S.S.R., entitled, *Ten Reasons For Making a Retreat* (Liguori, Missouri: Liguorian Pamphlets) will be of great help in your efforts to offset the basic fear and the excuses usually offered for not making a retreat.

During and immediately after World War II, the remarkable growth in the number of laymen who make retreats on an annual basis began. With the emphasis on lay activity and apostolate given by the Vatican Council II, it is reasonable to assume that retreats will play an even larger part in the spiritual training of the laity. Your first retreat could well be to one of these groups in a retreat house for laymen over a weekend.

And what of that group? What can and should you expect to find? Actually, you will find Catholics and often some non-Catholics, persons of many trades and professions, of all ages and walks of life. You will find deeply spiritual men and women as well as other persons whose religious beliefs and practices have worn thin or lapsed altogether. Some retreats may be for special groups or occupations, such as doctors, lawyers, firemen, policemen, office workers, farmers, or salesmen. Many are for men only or for women only. There are special retreats for engaged couples, married couples, teen-agers, university students. Most retreat groups, however, are made up of a good cross section of any ordinary parish or community. The retreatants all have one thing in common: they are human beings seeking rest, guidance, peace of mind, and spiritual strength. Even though the retreat groups are very diversified, retreats can be very effective because they are not just get-togethers with religious overtones. Nor are they religious workshops or even study clubs. They are spiritual exercises engaged in by each retreatant personally to renew his own personal sense of direction and communication with Almighty God. The final purpose of a retreat as stated by St. Ignatius is: "to seek and find the will of God concerning the ordering of life for the salvation of one's soul." Any group and every group of retreatants has this basic purpose and objective.

Many Catholic colleges require or urge that the students in their senior year make a closed retreat before graduation. Some colleges even require or at least recommend such a retreat each year from the Freshman year on. Many Catholic high schools for some years have required a closed retreat for their graduating classes. To accommodate the increasing number of student retreatants, a number of retreat houses exclusively for students have come into being in recent years. The first such in the eastern United States was the Gonzaga retreat house at Monroe, N. Y. The example of Gonzaga has led to the opening of other youth retreat houses in Narragansett, Rhode Island; St. Louis, Missouri; Milford, Ohio; Gloucester, Massachusetts; Ridgefield, Connecticut; Shelter Island, New

York; and Sparks, Maryland. With a youth retreat house in Illinois and a newer one in Maryland, the Christian Brothers are undertaking to provide retreats and retreat houses for the students of their schools. Your first retreat could quite possibly be to one of the many student groups. Nearly all retreat houses for adult laymen have mid-week retreats on their schedules for high school and college students.

RETREAT METHODS

As regards the "systems" to be followed, Pope Pius XII clearly stated that there should be no monopoly. However, in his encyclical *Mediator Dei* he did point out that "it is well known that the spiritual exercises according to the methods and norms of St. Ignatius have been fully approved on account of their admirable efficacy." The suggestions, given in this chapter for the preparation of a retreat, are based on the *Spiritual Exercises.*

Other methods and other approaches to spiritual renovation and renewal are available and are being used today with good results. Two such are the *cursillo* and the seminar type method.

The Cursillo

The *cursillo* (*Cursillos de Cristiandad*) is a short course in Christianity. It is a three-day period of intense prayer and study about the basic truths of the Catholic Church. The *cursillo* is like a retreat inasmuch as the participants leave their ordinary activities for a time. It differs from a retreat in that it involves the participants in group study, prayer, meditation, singing, and pious conversations to a greater extent than does the usual retreat. The *cursillistas* (participants) assist each other to arrive at personal conclusions and resolutions to improve their life in Christ.

The aim of this dynamic movement, as explained by its founder, Most Reverend Juan Hervasy Benet, Bishop of Ciudad Real, Spain, and reported in the magazine *Christ to the World* is:

> To impress deeply, to burn in, as it were, what is fundamental in the Catholic religion. To have those who make the *cursillos* live for three days in a joyful atmosphere of real Christianity, steeped in faith and grace, joy and charity. To fill the participants with the conviction that they can continue their contact with Christ and with their brothers only by an inner life of team solidarity. To arouse in the *cursillistas* a fervent apostolic concern for others. In this, the *cursillistas* are prepared, even before they leave the *cursillo,* to work as a team under the Church's hierarchy.

This movement, which has spread over four continents and into more than ten countries, started in Spain in 1959. During the early years of the program, Bishop Benet was assisted by a group of priests and laymen who helped him perfect this method of spiritual renewal.

Though the *cursillo* may be in some respect similar to a retreat, it is not intended to take the place of a retreat. In fact, the two movements are separate though complementary means of spiritual renovation. Writing on retreats and the *cursillo* in *The Sign,* Father Bertin Farrell, C.P., discussed some of the differences between the two movements:

> . . . Some of the differences are: (1) the cursillo has a definite doctrinal program while the retreat may vary with the spiritual director. In a retreat, much is left to the originality and personality of the retreat master. In the cursillo, the doctrine and structure of the experience is all planned out in advance. (2) Laymen must help in giving a *cursillo.* If a layman doesn't give the talks proper to him, there is no *cursillo.* Whereas it is a priest who gives all the talks on a retreat. (3) The *cursillo* is deliberately filled with music, songs, and laughter; the retreat is carried out in silence and recollection. (4) The *cursillo* emphasizes participation and conviviality; the retreat asks for quiet and solitude. (5) A *cursillo* is made only once; retreats are annual. It is precisely this last point which indicates that there is no conflict between a *cursillo* and a retreat. The *cursillo* is not here to take over the layman's retreat movement. As a matter of fact, every *cursillista* is encouraged to make an annual retreat, on the assumption that what was begun in the *cursillo* needs to be brought to fruition. The retreat movement might easily integrate the *cursillo* movement and go on to take a vital role in *post-cursillo* apostolic formation. This latter formation is a vital factor in the *post-cursillo* movement.

The Seminar Method

Young priests, engaged in giving retreats to high school and college students, have found the seminar approach well-suited to the needs of young people.

The seminar approach for teen-agers was developed by Father Joseph L. Baglio, Director of the Catholic Youth Center in Minneapolis. These programs include the week-end seminar, the new daylight seminar and seminar II for students in Catholic high schools, and the twilight seminar for students attending public high schools.

The weekend seminar is a three-day combination of prayer, work, recreation, and discussion all focusing on the theme: "Love — essence of Christianity." The basic ingredient of this program is "involvement of the whole person," and the purpose of the seminar is to permit those attending to discover the meaning and relevancy of Christianity through a family experience. To achieve this purpose, each seminar invites an equal number of high school or college students to live a family-type experience and to become brothers and sisters for the weekend.

Each group spends the weekend at Fiat House where activities are arranged so as to form a social weekend as well as an opportunity to relate Christianity to real life. During this period, six discussion sessions form the framework for the development of ideas. Along with these sessions, there is a meditation period, play, and work periods, and some socializing. During these weekend seminars, there is "much fun, much much humor, much laughter," and apparently too, there is "much commitment to Christianity." "Many experience the notion of Christian love for the first time," says the director, because this spiritual experience is planned to "give them an opportunity to decide for themselves that they wish to commit themselves to Christ and to Christianity."

In the first of the six discussions, the group asks such basic questions as: "What is a Christian?" "What things bother you today — in school, in the community, at home, around the world?" "Are Christian answers being given to these problems?" The following five discussions are concerned with the more specific aspects of modern living: "Home and Family"; "Sex and Chastity"; "The Mass"; "Your Vocation — How do you fit into the world today?" and "The Catholic — Lethargic or Apostolic?" In all discussions, the guiding principle is the idea that love should permeate these areas and the decisions to be made — that love marks the Christian.

The new seminar II program is intended for those who have made at least one previous seminar. This program is aimed at helping teenagers develop self-understanding. Therefore, like the other programs it is not a time of self-centered contemplation, but rather a time to discover one's self through varied experiences — cultural, liturgical, and social.

The Scriptural-Liturgical Method

Another method or approach which seems ideally suited for adult retreatants is the scriptural-liturgical program which includes formal and informal discussion. In this approach the conferences are scriptural and liturgical in the fullest sense. What Father Leon A. McNeill says about this approach, in a discussion of priest's retreats in *Pastoral Life,* may be said of retreats for laymen, for he points out that the retreat master

> began by reading the first paragraph of the *Constitution on the Sacred liturgy*, . . . (and) spoke of the aggiornamento which is taking place in the Church under the direction of the Holy Father and the Bishops; . . . truly the work of the Holy Spirit, . . . and its impact is being felt in every field of study and action.

He then explains that the retreat master went on to explain that the retreatants

> must be docile to the promptings of the Holy Spirit and readily obedient

to the call of the Church for reform and renewal: not only for the salvation of our own souls but also, and especially, for the the spiritual welfare of all the People of God.

To assure active liturgical participation on the part of all of the retreatants, the community Mass would be celebrated *versus populum,* in the late forenoon of each day. Whenever possible, a lector-commentator would carry out his full role. The retreatants would be invited to pray and sing together, and appropriate hymns would be sung during the *Introit* Procession, the Offertory, the Communion, and at the end of the liturgical celebration. There would, of course, be a brief homily and an Offertory Procession. A Bible service would be held each evening.

Formal and informal discussions would be another outstanding aspect of this method of giving retreats. Each afternoon the participants would meet in an appropriate place such as the library or the lounge for a brief conference to be followed by general discussions presided over by the retreat master. Informal discussion of the conferences and of the work of Vatican Council II, or the liturgical renewal, or the lay apostolate might be encouraged during the after-dinner recreation period. Of course, the appropriate silence would be kept at all other times.

The Spiritual Exercises

Though there are other new approaches to recollection and renewal that might be discussed at this time, something needs to be said about the *Spiritual Exercises.* The *Spiritual Exercises* of St. Ignatius Loyola are an approved and time-tested instrument for bringing about the salvation and perfection of Christian souls. Though several centuries old, their remarkable adaptability is an added recommendation for their study and use in these times of change. "Of the several laudable methods for conducting retreats for the laity, the method based on the *Spiritual Exercises* of Saint Ignatius Loyola is, since their approval by Pope Paul III in 1548, the most widely used. Retreat Directors, however, must never cease to deepen their understanding of the doctrinal and spiritual riches of the Ignatian text, and to express those riches in terms of the theology of the Second Vatican Council. The retreat is not to become a study of conciliar documents, but the director should present the insights of the *Exercises,* or of any other method he may use, in a theological context with which modern laymen will be familiar." (From the message of His Holiness, Pope Paul VI, to the National Laymen's Retreat Convention in Boston, Mass., August, 1966.)

Priests in general have a deep appreciation of the value of these *Spiritual Exercises.* They have at various times made the Exercises. In larger numbers each year, they come to retreat houses for priests for the same purpose.

They urge their parishioners to go for a few days to retreat houses where they will be able to make the *Spiritual Exercises*. However, priests in general do not sufficiently realize that the *Spiritual Exercises* of St. Ignatius are an instrument that they may themselves use for the salvation and perfection of the souls committed to their care.

In the encyclical *Mens Nostra* Pope Pius XI urged all to use this method of spiritual exercises. While praising all forms of true retreat, His Holiness singles out the special method of St. Ignatius:

> Lastly it is of great moment for making spiritual exercises properly and deriving fruit from them that they should be conducted in a wise and appropriate method.
> Now it is recognized that among all the methods of spiritual exercises which very laudably adhere to the principles of sound Catholic asceticism, one has ever held the foremost place and, adorned by the full and repeated approbation of the Holy See and honored by the praises of men distinguished for spiritual doctrine and sanctity, has borne abundant fruits of holiness during the space of well nigh four hundred years. We mean the method introduced by St. Ignatius of Loyola, whom We are pleased to call the chief and peculiar Master of Spiritual Exercises, whose "admirable book of the Exercises" . . . ever since it was solemnly approved, praised and commended by Our Predecessor Paul III of happy memory, already, to repeat some words We once used before our elevation to the Chair of Peter, already, We say, 'Stood forth and conspicuous as a most wise and universal code of laws for the direction of souls in the way of salvation and perfection; as an unexhausted fountain of most excellent and most solid piety; as a most keen stimulus, and a well-instructed guide showing the way to secure attainment of morals and to attain the summit of the spiritual life.'

It should be understood that the Society of Jesus claims no monopoly or exclusive rights to the *Spiritual Exercises* of St. Ignatius. It would be regrettable if the faithful were deprived of the benefits to be derived from the Exercises because of any such notion. The *Spiritual Exercises* of St. Ignatius are an instrument of the universal Church and therefore a legitimate tool in the hands of every qualified priest. No diocesan priest, no religious priest, should ever feel that he is infringing on a Jesuit spiritual copyright when he puts people through the *Spiritual Exercises* of St. Ignatius.

It is to be hoped that more and more priests and those studying for the priesthood will undertake the study and work necessary to use the Exercises effectively. First of all, it has to be presumed that one giving the Exercises has made them himself and can therefore give the retreatant something of his own experience of them. The ability to give the real thing is acquired only by serious preparation. There is no shortcut to attaining the art of giving them. The retreat master must strive to grasp something of the tradition of the Exercises.

He must realize that there is more to them than just the printed book. He has to be familiar with their closely knit structure along with the progressive advance each exercise makes toward the goal of the whole. There are certain principles in the book which he must master along with the art of directing retreatants in the application of these principles. If possible, it is highly recommended that the prospective retreat master make the full Exercises, i.e., for the space of thirty days and that he become familiar with the better commentaries and study carefully the various directories.

For a start on the study of the *Spiritual Exercises,* these books could be helpful to the beginner:

The Spiritual Exercises of St. Ignatius, translated by Louis J. Puhl, S.J. (Westminster: Newman Press, 1951).

CALVERAS, I., *The Harvest Field of the Spiritual Exercises of St. Ignatius,* translated by J. G. Gense, S.J. (Bombay: St. Xavier College, 1949).

IGNATIUS IPARRAGUIRRE, S.J., *How To Give A Retreat,* practical notes (Westminster: Newman Press, 1961).

ALOYSIUS AMBRUZZI, S.J., *A Companion To The Spiritual Exercises of St. Ignatius* (Westminster, Md.: Newman Press, 1961).

W. H. LONGRIDGE, *The Spiritual Exercises of St. Ignatius Loyola with Commentary and Directory* (London: Robert Scott, 1919).

As previously stated, the Jesuits do not claim exclusive rights to the *Spiritual Exercises.* Other groups, notably the Religious of the Cenacle, have made extensive and effective use of them in their work of retreats for women. In fact, the Religious of the Cenacle were founded precisely to give the Spiritual Exercises to women. In recent years, The Program To Promote The Spiritual Exercises, 144 Grand Street, Jersey City, N. J., 07302, directed by Father Thomas A. Burke, S.J., has been operating to make available material and information about the *Spiritual Exercises.*

PREPARING TO GIVE A RETREAT

Whether one plans to base his retreat work on the *Spiritual Exercises* of St. Ignatius or some other system, one thing is necessary. The study, planning and working on a retreat should begin as early as possible in the seminary — no later than the start of the course in theology. It would be presumptuous to attempt to give any directions or suggestions on the methods of study, taking notes, gathering material, organizing it, and finally putting on paper at least a rough draft of a retreat. Each has his own method of doing these things. Likewise, one may prefer to do it all alone. There are some obvious advantages of working with others, at least occasionally. What better way is there of testing out one's ideas and obtaining the reaction and opinion of others?

Gathering Material

A man facing his first retreat is usually painfully aware of his ignorance of the field. The ignorance may be more apparent than real. Let him take courage and remember: (1) that he is a priest, with training in moral and dogmatic theology; hence the ways of virtue and vice are not unfamiliar; (2) that he has been something of a teacher, who has had some practice in guidance; (3) that he has learned to think with some ease along the lines of human conduct; (4) that he knows in a practical way something of different types of character; (5) that he can speak on his feet. If previous preparation has provided him with ample material, there will be little to fear then — and much to hope for. With immediate preparation in view these suggestions and guidelines are offered.

Grist for your mill (retreat material) will be coming your way from many sources all through your theology course. Keep your eyes and ears open and your notebook close at hand. Most of the material will not come in finished form. It will need to be sifted, analyzed, adapted, prayed over, worked over, and synthesized.

Main Sources

1. Your spiritual training — everything that has gone into your spiritual formation such as your annual retreats, the days of recollection and renovation, the conferences, exhortations and consultations plus your own private spiritual reading and daily meditation and prayers will be helpful.

In all these exercises of piety, especially the annual retreat, you will be under the guidance of experienced priests and retreat masters. No one ever sincerely made a retreat or any spiritual exercise without benefit to himself. Each retreat master has something to give you personally for your own spiritual progress and possibly for your own retreat work. It is suggested that at the end of each annual retreat you make a careful review of how the retreat master did his job. From each of these experienced retreat masters you can learn something in the way of presentation of spiritual ideas, use of examples and anecdotes, and overall, general impression and techniques used. Write down what most impressed and helped you and study over what you might be able to adapt to your own use in giving your retreat.

2. Your theological studies — a good test of your knowledge of any subject is the ability to explain it to someone else in such a way that he also understands it. Much of your dogmatic theology is presented to you and studied by you in thesis form, clothed in scholastic terminology which is meaningless to most people today. Yet these are the great truths that as a priest you will have to explain and communicate

to the faithful through your preaching and writing. Your understanding of these truths will be helped and at the same time you will be preparing yourself for retreat work by putting yourself to such tests as these: How best can I present clear notions of hell, sin, the Incarnation, the Resurrection, grace, and the like to young people in high school or college who are making a retreat given by me? How can I present these same ideas to groups of novices or professed sisters or to lay people?

Study the Scriptures well, keeping in mind the new approach to Scripture and its possible effects on giving retreats. The good retreat master must present his own ideas and then be able to follow them up with clear references from Scripture. Among Catholics today there is a greater knowledge of and interest in Scripture. What you say has much more meaning if it is built on and around the Scriptures. The retreat master must be able in his own words, words that the retreatants can understand, to present our Lord and his life and his views and then be able clearly and accurately to quote Scripture to show that his ideas are Christ's ideas.

To do his work effectively the retreat master needs a rich fund of knowledge about many things. Like the sanctity he daily strives with the help of God's grace to acquire, his knowledge is not acquired for himself but to be used prudently and completely in behalf of the men and women retreatants who are trying to lead Christian lives in a de-Christianized atmosphere. Sociology courses bring a knowledge of the environmental setting of the retreatants' lives, financial status and problems, housing situation, the atmosphere of their group whether it be an urban group striving to keep up with the Joneses, or rural groups.

It is necessary to be familiar with the findings of modern psychology and the field of psychiatry so that you will be able to recognize emotional problems and to be able to recommend competent psychiatric treatment. You are not trained to be a psychologist or psychiatrist but by working with the psychologist or psychiatrist you may be able to do much good because many psychological problems have spiritual ramifications.

For retreats to young people, a knowledge of the psychology of adolescence is essential. For any retreat, knowledge of the differences between the masculine and feminine temperaments is extremely valuable.

If you expect to be able to give retreats to nuns and religious brothers, you need to make a theoretical and practical study of the religious life; its obligations, aims and objectives. You will also need to have some understanding of canon law and the religious life, and some knowledge of the history and the spirit of various Congregations, as well as confessional practice for Religious and priests.

For any retreat, it is necessary to know something of the spiritual life, and of ascetical and mystical theology. As a retreat master you will be expected to be able to deal with such problems in the spiritual life as scrupulosity and vocational difficulties, and help and guide younger retreatants in discovering their vocations in life.

There is much more to giving a retreat than preaching a number of meditations. It is in the confessional that the retreat master will often do his most effective work. When a priest is spoken of as a good retreat master, it is taken for granted he is also a good confessor. That should be kept in mind in your study of moral and pastoral theology. The work and qualities of the good confessor are discussed in another chapter of this book.

Retreats for married couples are becoming more common. For these the retreat master must be versed in the spirituality of married life. A number of books have appeared lately on this subject. They provide fine insights into the helps that married life affords for true holiness. The retreat master must be prepared to help married couples see and value the dignity of marriage, so that they will be better able to use spiritually the opportunities of their vocation. If possible, take courses in marriage guidance or at least read books on this subject.

Spiritual Reading

In search of material for retreat talks, well-known contemporary writers, as well as those of an earlier period will show the way to adaptation. Some of the more modern writers include: L. Blosius, *A Book of Spiritual Instruction;* E. Boylan, O.Cist.R., *This Tremendous Lover;* J. P. De Caussade, *Abandonment; or Absolute Surrender of Self to Divine Providence;* M. Day, C.O., *Prayer and the Present Moment;* F. W. Faber, *Growth in Holiness;* L. A. Fenn, *Particular Examens for Seminarians and Priests;* A Goodier, S.J., *The Meaning of Life;* G. Kelly S.J., *Modern Youth and Chastity;* L. O'Brien, O.P., "Frequent Confession," *Cross and Crown* XII (1960); O'Driscoll, S.M., *The Holy Spirit and the Art of Living;* F. J. Sheen, *Go to Heaven;* L. J. Trese, *More Than Many Sparrows;* H. Trindade, O.F.M., *Recollections, the Soul of Action;* and H. Van Zeller, O.S.B., *The Choice of God.* Other helpful works can be the writings of Raoul Plus, Marmion, Tanqueray, Pere Charles: *Prayer for All Times,* and Karl Rahner, S.J.: *Spiritual Exercises* (trans. Kenneth Baker), and *Encounters With Silence* (trans. James M. Demske).

Try to find time to read the Fathers of the Church. From them you can learn much on how to speak to the people in language that is forceful, simple, and clear. At the same time, study the presentation and development of spiritual ideas by present-day writers such as Father

Leo J. Trese and the Irish Jesuit, Father Robert Nash. Among the works of the late Monsignor Ronald Knox that should be studied are his retreat books, (1) for beginners, (2) for lay people, and (3) for priests.

Other Reading

Even the most eloquent explanation of a religious principle will be greatly helped by as many examples as possible, either from what you have read or from your own experience. As you read the daily newspapers or news magazines, or history and biography and light literature, be on the lookout for suitable and worthwhile examples to drive home your lesson.

There is no shortage of material and to give direction to the gathering of it the list of twelve basic retreat topics, suitable, with the necessary adaptations, for every kind of retreat may be helpful. Before you begin to write, keep in mind that a retreat is the time when the individual strives to realize the fundamental obligation he has to God — to love Him with his whole soul and to love his neighbor. It is essential that a retreat deals with fundamentals. Hence, the retreat talks must consider the purpose of our creation; those things which militate against this purpose, principally sin and its consequences; the means to overcome ourselves for union with God; Christ's place in our life; his life and teaching; the means he has given us for union with God. It is up to the retreat master to inspire the retreatant to think over these fundamentals, to realize more deeply their truth until they become strong convictions that will guide his life.

MATTER AND PRESENTATION

Twelve basic retreat talks:

1. Introductory — Plan and purpose of retreat — How and What of retreat? Dispositions needed.
2. Toward God — End of Man.
3. Self-control — Purpose and use of Creatures.
4. Christian Life — Faith, Hope, and Charity.
5. The Three Sins — Our Own Sins.
6. Hell, Eternal Failure.
7. The Prodigal — Divine Mercy.
8. Call of Christ.
9. Nazareth — The Hidden Life.
10. The Public Life — A Program of Life for the Retreatant.
11. Passion and Death.
12. Resurrection and Risen Life — Final Victory.

Whether these talks are to be written out in full will have to be determined by each individual. They should, at least, be completely outlined with sufficient material for a talk of no less than 30 to 40 minutes on each. Above all, in the use of his material and the giving of his talks, the retreat master should keep in mind the need for adaptability and flexibility, fully aware that the presentation of the meditations to a group of high school seniors must differ from those given to a group of adult laymen even though the same subjects are treated. In other words, know as far as possible the special needs of the group to whom the retreat is to be given and arrange your material and its presentation accordingly.

This is not the place to try to say anything definitive about the delivery of your talks other than that you should be yourself. Have something to say and say it with as much clarity and conviction as you possibly can. In delivering the talks, refer to notes if you wish but do not read them or even parts of them even though some of your good material may be lost. Retreatants, whatever their age or educational background, want you, not your words. They can get those elsewhere. They will often mention the feeling of intimacy, "Father was talking right to me," or they will ask with a smile, "How did he know that?" Animated delivery is the most effective. Convey to the retreat group your desire to "sell" your own personal conviction.

How long should a retreat talk be? For most lay groups, talks less than 30 minutes in length do not seem to give most retreatants enough to "get their teeth into." Talks of more than 45 minutes tire them. Usually talks of about 40 minutes' duration seem best. However, the specific needs of the group have to be considered. For priests and religious, a talk of 25–30 minutes is ordinarily sufficient.

The foregoing suggestions have been offered with the basic or traditional type of retreat in mind. There is and will always be a need and demand for this type of retreat. Here, the retreat master gives a series of talks or meditations. The retreatant listens and then thinks over privately what the retreat master has said. Other devotions such as the rosary, stations, spiritual reading, question-box, occupy him as he moves from one exercise to the other with his fellow retreatants. Sometime during the retreat he may have a personal conference with the retreat master or one of the other priests. His free time is devoted to personal reflection and to preparation for his retreat confession. This type of retreat emphasizes retirement for a few days or a week-end from the world and ordinary occupations. Electronic and scientific devices are being used extensively in this type of retreat: spiritually oriented motion pictures, slide lectures of high quality with sound effects, readings professionally recorded on tapes with high fidelity.

As the needs of the laity and the requirements of the Church change, departures are being made from the traditional retreat form. Retreats must keep pace with the deepening spirituality of the layman and the needs of the lay apostolate. With sufficient knowledge of the framework of the spiritual exercises plus some experience in the traditional type of retreat, the retreat master should be ready and able, when desirable, to make the necessary adaptations required for the newer forms of retreat that have been developing over the past ten years, such as:

The Directed Retreat

With a group of people used to the practice of mental prayer and following a systematic spiritual life this form makes it possible for the retreat master to direct the activity of the retreatants through various considerations, meditations, and contemplations which they themselves make. The fruit of the retreat comes from the work of the retreatant. Points of meditation are given in common but they are not of obligation and are much shorter. Other devotions such as rosary and stations are left up to the individual. There is more free time during the day and silence is insisted upon.

THE COUNSELED RETREAT

This form represents a further step toward making the retreat more dependent upon the retreatant. Here, the main work of giving the retreat consists in holding frequent private conferences with the retreatants both in turn and on request. They make the retreat, each in his own way and each at his own pace. The whole retreat group gathers in the morning for one session at which the retreat master outlines the work of the day ahead. He points out the goal at which they are to aim and he makes some suggestions as to the method they are to use. Once the day begins, the retreat master remains in his consulting room. The retreatants call upon him if they have special needs. This method has been found successful for those who have made a number of retreats in the traditional way. It is too difficult for beginners.

The Private Retreat

This is an even further advance in personal spiritual enterprise. It involves retiring to a retreat house or monastery and performing the spiritual exercises by oneself with perhaps a daily conference with a retreat master. Father Hogan's recent book, *A Do-It-Yourself Retreat,* has been helpful to laymen making such a private retreat.

The Social Retreat

The growing social awareness of the Catholic has had an influence upon retreats. Many retreat masters believe that retreatants should be given the opportunity to express what happens to them interiorly during the retreat. In this form of retreat each exercise is done in three phases: in the first, the retreatants listen to a talk on the subject matter of the retreat; in the second, each retreatant makes his own personal and private mental prayer and reflection on the subject; in the third, the group gathers together again, and by way of discussion the retreatants share with each other the results of their individual efforts. At the end of the third phase, there is time for each to spend in personal prayer summing up his own net profit from the exercise.

The Bible Service Retreat

The Bible service retreat originates from the liturgical movement and the urge growing in the faithful for corporate worship as well as from the revived interest in and esteem for Sacred Scripture. This form of retreat consists in a series of exercises based on alternating reading, prayers, and hymns in a succeeding series, based respectively upon the subjects of the Spiritual Exercises. (Father John Gallen, S.J., in *Scripture Services* [The Liturgical Press, Collegeville, Minn., 1963] has prepared eighteen such Bible themes with readings and group and private prayers, suitable for such exercises.) Parts of the Divine Office are also said or sung as the day goes on. The retreat master prepares the half-hour Bible-reading service. It consists of a reading from the Old or New Testament on the theme of the meditation and is read aloud by one of the retreatants. Then all pray, saying together a prayer composed in response to the content of the Bible reading. A liturgical hymn or one of the psalms is sung.

The time between Bible sessions is occupied with personal prayer, some instruction or discussion, and private devotions. In this form of retreat, much is made of the Holy Sacrifice of the Mass; and the greatest possible solemnity and active participation by all is expected. Offertory processions are common. These Bible services or vigils, as they are sometimes called, are often used to supplement other forms of retreat, including the traditional. They are frequently used in days of recollection to maintain the fruit of the annual retreat throughout the year.

The Part-Time Retreat

Not everyone who would like to do so can get away for a closed retreat. For these, various part-time plans have been devised and put into operation. For example, workingmen seeking the benefits of a retreat have the opportunity of coming to the St. Joseph Retreat League center in Charlestown, Mass., for three hours each Wednesday evening for the space of a month. Youth in public schools come once a month for a semester to a retreat house for what are called Twilight Retreats.

Still another form of retreat is that inspired by the *Exercitations* of the Better World Movement originated by Father Lombardi. In this the subject is society rather than the individual person. The exercises consist in discussion rather than meditation. The retreat aims primarily at the reform of society, secondarily at the reform of the individual.

After the points for meditation-discussion are given, the retreat group breaks up into small gatherings of six or eight members. With a mimeographed set of questions to guide and stimulate them they set about the discussion of the matter and attempt to come to some conclusion as to what corporate or individual action they might perform as they strive to specify their activity in the social apostolate. Lay apostolate groups have found this form of retreat helpful.

QUALITIES OF A RETREAT MASTER

No matter what the form of retreat, the retreat master soon discovers that much of his time during the retreat must be spent in the individual direction and guidance of the retreatants. It will not be possible to solve all their problems but it is necessary to listen attentively and to give the individual all the time needed to unburden himself of the problem or worry that has been troubling him. Hence, one of the prime requisites of the retreat master is that he be a willing and sympathetic listener.

Some other qualities that people like to find in the retreat master are:

1. Availability — A good retreat demands that the retreat master place himself entirely at the service of the retreatants. This requires a spirit of self-denial. The retreat master must make it a full-time job, putting aside all other work to devote himself completely to the retreatants and their needs.

2. Approachability — For some it will be the first time that they have ever talked to a priest about a personal problem. It has taken a little while for some to get up sufficient courage to do so. Your whole manner should be such that the retreatants will approach you without fear and with the feeling that they will receive from you the sympathetic understanding and encouragement they need.

3. Prudence — The prudent man will always be mindful of what *is* the fact rather than what it should be. By asking the right questions he learns the true circumstances before attempting to inform or guide. He is prepared to use the door left open by the retreatant rather than to force an entrance.

4. Gentleness — After the example of the gentle Christ, he gives all the time necessary to unburden. He encourages by a glimpse of the heights rather than weighing down by emphasis on the depths.

5. For the retreat master there can be no compromise with principle. The teachings of the Church and religious authority must be upheld by him.

In *The Serran* of July-August 1962, these words of Most Rev. John J. Krol, Archbishop of Philadelphia, appear:

> The priest is but an instrument of God's grace and power. He must strive to be a worthy instrument by developing a perfect blend of virtue. The priest must derive energy for his external apostolate from an interior life of prayer and meditation. . . . The priest's faith must be firm, his prudence must exclude compromise with evil. His purity must include sensitivity to the weakness of others. His humility must exclude pride and ambition. His character must combine the gentleness of a mother, with the firmness of a father. His mercy and compassion for the sinner and the errant must be as strong as his intolerance of sin and error. His obedience, like Christ's, must be perfect, even unto death. He must be a reservoir, not merely a channel, of God's Grace.

Now reread the Archbishop's words, substituting "retreat master" for "priest" and you have the picture of the ideal retreat master. Keep that picture before you constantly as you prepare yourself for retreat work.

26

The Hospital Chaplain

JAMES G. WILDERS

NOW WHEN HE HAD ENTERED CAPHARNAUM, THERE CAME TO HIM A
centurion who entreated him, saying, "Lord, my servant is lying sick in
the house, paralyzed, and is grievously afflicted." Jesus said to him, "I
will come and cure him" (Mt 8:57).

Though every priest, following in the footsteps of his divine Master,
should have a special solicitude for the sick and the dying, some priests
will be assigned by their superiors to enter this apostolate on a full-time
basis; they will be assigned as hospital chaplains. This chapter is addressed not only to those priests who will enter the hospital apostolate,
but also to those whose task it is to make such assignments and to
those hospital administrators who also share some responsibility for the
spiritual well-being of the hospital clientele.

In the past it was possible and, perhaps, even acceptable to assign a
semi-invalid or a "problem-priest" to the hospital apostolate. Today,
however, when hospital administrators are striving to assemble superbly
qualified staffs, it is neither possible nor desirable to assign the unqualified or the unfit to this important work. Today's hospital chaplain must
meet certain standards as regards age, health, personality, and freedom
from other burdensome duties. Furthermore, he must be regarded as a
specialist (or one who will soon become a specialist) in his field, and
be properly and adequately trained for this vital apostolate.

However, before discussing in detail the various aspects of the hospital
apostolate, it seems fitting to say a word or two about the deep

satisfaction and the great sense of accomplishment that comes to those who serve as hospital chaplains and make daily visitations to the patients. Perhaps this can be best achieved by letting a chaplain speak from personal experience:

Mr. X, a man of 85 years, came into the hospital with a rapidly advancing cancerous condition. For 60 years, I learned later, he had been an avowed Communist who had turned completely against the Church. On my first visit he showed his hatred for the Church by the way he looked at me, and I know he would have thrown me out of the room bodily if he were able. On the second day he again showed his bitterness and hatred, but I wished him well and gave him my blessing. On the third day he seemed slightly less bitter; on the fourth day he talked to me; and on the fifth day he received the sacraments. On the sixth day he died and was buried three days later with a solemn requiem mass.

The daughter of this former bitter enemy of the Church, herself converted from Communism, wrote to me after her father's death in these grateful words: "I wanted to thank you again for all that you did for my dad during the past week, and for myself as well. It is very difficult to put into words all that you sent our way, but I think you know without my saying so just how much it meant to have my dad return to the sacraments. I cannot thank you enough for your considerateness, your consistent visits to his bedside. But most of all, for the understanding that made it possible for him to receive the last rites and to be one with Our Lord at the hour of his death."

Mr. J. H. was an elderly newspaperman who had long been away from the Church and the Sacraments. He was terminally ill with cancer at one of our large hospitals. I visited him day after day for a number of weeks before he went to confession and received Holy Communion and the last sacraments of the Church. He told me that the daily visitation impressed him so much that he just had to make his peace with God. He died a few days later.

The chaplain of a large hospital found a dying man of Catholic birth many years away from the Church who refused the Sacraments and said he wanted no part of the Catholic religion. The priest visited him every day for 34 consecutive days, sometimes just offering him a cold drink of water or making his pillow more comfortable for him, each time speaking a few kindly words. On the thirty-fourth day the man received the Sacraments. He died the following day.

ROLE OF THE CHAPLAIN

The primary role of the Catholic chaplain in both Catholic and non-Catholic institutions is that of caring for the religious needs of the Catholic patients. His secondary role — one which he should perform in a truly ecumenical and charitable spirit — is concern for the religious needs of all patients. Since more and more physicians and hospital administrators are coming to realize that the well-trained chaplain can make a vital contribution to the total program of patient care, it is important that the chaplain look upon himself as a member of a highly qualified staff and realize that his effectiveness will almost certainly be in direct proportion to his willingness to cooperate with the other members of the hospital staff — administration, physicians, psychiatrists, other Catholic chaplains, chaplains of other denominations, personnel, and the institution itself.

In his consideration of the role of the Catholic chaplain, Father John W. Mullally observes that inasmuch as he is charged with the care of souls, the hospital chaplain has much in common with all other priests engaged in the various phases of the pastoral ministry. However, he also notes that there are several striking differences between the priest involved in the hospital apostolate and those who are laboring in other fields. He isolates eight differences every chaplain should keep in mind if he hopes to be successful in his work. These are:

1. The chaplain is a specialist in his profession, and must be convinced of the dignity of his apostolate if he expects others to respect him.

2. The hospital chaplain will spend a large part of his time working privately with individuals.

3. The hospital patient is in an abnormal environment away from his home, his family, and his ordinary associations. The hospital patient is not a normal person; he is a sick person.

4. The hospital chaplain carries on his apostolate in an unusual environment and frequently must follow a somewhat burdensome schedule; he must frequently deal with unusual problems and make immediate decisions.

5. As a member of a team, the hospital chaplain must carry on his ministry in accord with the overall hospital program. Though he does not compromise in matters of faith or morals, he must adjust his ideas, activities, etc., in accord with the needs of the institution and the team.

6. The hospital chaplain not only assumes the privileges, but also the responsibilities of the hospital and is therefore bound by the same general rules of conduct, deportment, and procedure that bind other members of the hospital staff. Therefore, it is of the greatest importance that he assiduously observe all rules and regulations and follow established procedures as he goes about his task of caring for souls.

7. The hospital chaplain is neither a physician nor a psychiatrist and therefore should not attempt to perform the functions of either. Though his pastoral efforts will certainly assist the medical staff, his sole task is that of serving the religious needs of the patient.

8. The hospital chaplain must be interested in the "whole man," and strive to understand the patient's physical and mental needs as well as his spiritual needs.[1]

THE FOUR AIMS OF THE APOSTOLATE TO THE SICK

The priest who is assigned to a hospital chaplaincy should strive in every way possible to be an *"alter Christus"* to the sick, the afflicted, the troubled of heart and, like the divine Master whom he serves, should continually strive to be a good shepherd to his suffering "flock." As a hospital chaplain he must not merely sit in an office and wait for calls. Rather, he must be willing to labor zealously for the cure of souls by going daily from bed to bed to bring Christ's love and mercy to all, but particularly those long away from the Church and the sacraments, and by tending to the spiritual needs of the patients in other ways. Actually, the priest engaged in the apostolate to the sick in hospitals should have four aims toward which he will continually strive. These are:

1. To make a daily visitation to every Catholic patient.
2. To spend time each day with the critically ill, especially during those hours and days when they need most the real comfort of Christ.
3. To bring Holy Communion daily to those who wish to receive.
4. To arrange Sunday and Holyday Mass, and, where possible, weekday Mass in all hospitals.

Though at times it may be difficult for a hospital chaplain to achieve these aims, their value and importance is obvious. Almost any priest who has worked in a hospital will acknowledge the great benefits resulting from the daily visitation of all Catholic patients, and the testimony of the patients themselves will substantiate his position.

One of the great joys of every hospital chaplain should be that of bringing Christ in the Eucharist to the sick each day. Though many patients are not daily communicants when they are well, they eagerly seek the consolations of the Sacrament of Love during a period of hospitalization. They should not be denied. On the other hand, while the hospital chaplain should afford the opportunity to receive daily, he should not pressure patients into doing so. But, almost every hospital chaplain can describe instances of the fact that daily Communion during a period of hospitalization often brings the patient to a greater love for the Eucharistic Christ and, consequently, to a much more frequent reception of the Sacrament after dismissal.

The zealous hospital chaplain soon realizes that his priestly obliga-

---

[1] J. Mullally, "The Priest and Hospital Work," *All Things to All Men,* (ed. Joseph F. X. Cevetello), pp. 211–213.

tions are not over once he has brought the sacraments to the seriously ill. For, another very important part of his apostolate is the spending of time daily with the critically ill. This is the time when the patient most needs the consolation of the priest, and it is during this time that the priest has the most to give. Along with his words of encouragement and assistance in preparing for death, if that be God's will, the priest can pray with and for the patient, and bestow upon him his priestly blessing. The chaplain, during these difficult hours and days can also be of considerable assistance to the patient's family, for they too need the comforting and reassuring words of the kindly priest. Perhaps the great value of spending time with the critically ill and of consoling the members of their family is best illustrated in the following two stories:

> A 16-year-old girl, terminally ill after an operation for a brain tumor, said to the priest who visited her daily, "How wonderful it is that you come to see me each day. When one is as sick as I am and doesn't know whether she is going to get better, she has to know that someone loves her. I know you do because you are here every day, and I know God does because you bring him to me."

> The parents of a 24-year-old nurse who died of Lupis, a terrible kidney disease, said, "Father, we could never have endured this period of trial without your daily visits to Terry and ourselves." This is a part of the apostolate to the sick where truly Christ-like, priestly compassion plays a very special role.

The Catholic chaplain, whether he is assigned to a Catholic or a non-Catholic hospital should make every effort to have Sunday and Holyday Mass *for the patients*. The words "for the patients" are emphasized because too frequently, even in our Catholic hospitals, little effort is made to provide Mass for the patients. The problem of moving the patients from their hospital rooms to the chapel can be readily solved by having volunteer groups — The Legion of Mary, Altar and Rosary Society, Holy Name men, the St. Vincent de Paul Society — assist. A Mass scheduled during the afternoon or evening visiting hours would allow family and friends the opportunity of bringing their loved ones to and of assisting at Mass with them. By using volunteer groups and/or family and friends, Masses *for the patients* can be scheduled without interfering with overall hospital routine or without taking the hospital personnel away from their stations during duty hours.

Though it would not seem desirable for the priest to prolong the time that the patients must spend in the chapel for fear of retarding their recovery, it is certainly desirable for the priest to give a short homily. As Father Roy Aiken in another chapter of this book points out:

We Catholics are emphasizing these days the power of the Word of God as contained in the Scriptures. But, unfortunately, we have yet to go on from there to see and appreciate the importance of the preached word. The homily is an important and integral part of the fore-Mass. It should have power, it should say something relevant and specific to man and his present needs. It should be substantial fare. . . .[2]

Whenever possible, provisions should be made for hearing confessions before and even during the patients' Mass, if that be necessary. It might even be desirable to distribute Communion to the patients in their places (pews, wheelchairs, or stretcherbeds) rather than place upon them the added burden of approaching the Communion rail or station.

Under those circumstances where it is extremely difficult, if not impossible, to have a patient's Mass even on Sundays and Holydays, the hospital chaplain might hold short Bible Vigils in the hospital chapel or in other suitable places throughout the hospital. These services need not be lengthy, but could merely consist of a reading of a few selected passages from the Bible, a brief homily based on the readings, and the recitation of a few psalms or liturgical prayers. These short services can be of great spiritual benefit to the patient. Furthermore, in the spirit of ecumenism, patients of all faiths might be invited to participate in the Bible service.

While it is extremely desirable that the hospital chaplain provide religious services for the patients, it is important for the chaplain in a Catholic hospital to remember that he bears a special responsibility to religious sisters or brothers who staff the hospital. Therefore, one of his major considerations must be to care for the spiritual needs of the religious. Their long schedules and frequent lack of opportunities for rest and recreation make it doubly important that they receive the spiritual care that is appropriate to their vocation. Aside from providing for their ordinary religious needs — Mass, sacraments, conferences, etc. — the chaplain should, from time to time, speak to them about the many wonderful opportunities that religious engaged in hospital work have to share vitally in the spiritual care of their patients. On this point, Father Jerome F. Wilkerson speaks eloquently when he writes:

First, every hospital sister needs an abiding awareness of the reality of Divine Providence — in which there are no accidents; an awareness that for any given soul with whom she is in contact she may well be the very closest this soul will ever come to the elixir of immortality coursing within her — the life of Christ.

Second, the hospital sister needs an awareness of the power of her example of dedication and devotion to the sick, and that in time of sickness a soul has the greatest vulnerability to the sword of kindness.

Third, and probably one of the most significant of apostolic opportunities

[2] R. Aiken, "The Proper and Fruitful Celebration of the Sacred Liturgy."

for hospital sisters, is that of harnessing suffering. Bishop Fulton J. Sheen has echoed so frequently and effectively what others have said before him, that every soul has a price tag and that life's greatest tragedy is not suffering but rather the wealth of wasted suffering.

Fourth, in a discussion of the sister apostolate, there comes the idea of the sister visitor. This sister, a trained and alert apostle, supplements the work of the chaplain by visiting — with warmth, tact, and intelligence — on a full-time basis. She is the embodiment of the sisters' supernatural concern for their patients.

A fifth apostolic opportunity can be realized through the use of the prayer card prepared by the late Monsignor Raphael J. Markham in his "Apostolate to the Dying Non-Catholic." This remarkable prayer, available in braille and in approximately 35 languages, covers essential theological points plus an act of perfect contrition without using the words "Catholic Church." It is a prayer that even those most unaccustomed to prayer can easily use and, for the most part, unhesitatingly recite.

The sixth suggestion is the idea of the book cart, the apostolic and mobile division of the hospital library that features materials carefully chosen and appealingly displayed.

The seventh and final suggestion is this: the day is fast approaching when the potentialities of the hospital sister as a catechist will be discovered. The sister catechist and her office could become a center for coordinating the apostolic work of the whole institution. And her professional competence and awareness of the newest and best thinking in her field could rival any other department in the hospital.

But great as is the actual and potential role of hospital sisters, they are handicapped when there is not a well and able chaplain to direct the work. At times such a chaplain is unavailable because of the shortage of priests. At other times the reason appears to be that the implications of this apostolate are not clearly understood.[3]

EDUCATION OF THE HOSPITAL CHAPLAIN

As a specialist in his field, the hospital chaplain must have special training in the ancillary pastoral sciences of pastoral medicine, pastoral psychology, pastoral counseling, and even marriage counseling, for as we have already noted, he is frequently called upon to solve unusual problems and make immediate decisions on matters that would rarely confront priests active in the other apostolates. Therefore, by all means available to him — institutes, workshops, lectures, private study, and the like — the hospital chaplain should acquire an adequate knowledge of these fields. In view of the importance of these subjects to those in this apostolate, it seems appropriate to present a brief outline of the basic knowledge of these areas which the chaplain should possess.

A. Pastoral Medicine

Since the turn of the century, but more so in the past twenty-five or thirty years, pastoral medicine has attracted considerable attention.

---

[3] J. Wilkerson, "Patient Care — Spiritual Needs," *Hospital Progress,* (December, 1965), pp. 79–80; Cf. *Hospital Progress* (July, 1965), p. 75.

In recent years, more and more priests, but especially those in hospital work, have been called upon to solve complicated medico-moral problems, and to counsel both physician and patient in matters involving medical ethics. As a consequence, there is an ever increasing need for special training in pastoral medicine to prepare young priests to meet their responsibilities in this vital area.

Pastoral medicine is classified as both a branch of medicine and a branch of theology. As a branch of the science of medicine, it deals with medical questions in their relationship to moral theology, canon law, and the other branches of theology. As a branch of pastoral theology, it is concerned with that part of medicine which is of concern to a priest in fulfilling the duties of his ministry. In other words, pastoral medicine is that science which supplies the priest with reliable and up-to-date anatomico-physiologico-clinical data and guides him so that he can rightly discern and judge in particular cases that have medical implications. It also forms and guides the physician so that he can form his conscience on those aspects of his medical practice that have moral equality. In their explanation of the term "pastoral medicine," Austin O'Malley, M.D., and James J. Walsh, M.D., point out that pastoral medicine

> . . . presents that part of medicine which is of import to a pastor in his cure, and those divisions of ethics and moral theology which concern a physician in his practice. It sets forth facts and principles whereby the physician himself takes on a moral quality, and it also explains to the pastor, who must often minister to a mind diseased, certain medical truths which will soften harsh judgments, and other facts, which may be indifferent morally but which assist him in the proper conduct of his work, especially as an educator.[4]

Since the subject matter of pastoral medicine is continually developing, just as medicine itself is continually developing, it is all but impossible to outline a typical course in pastoral medicine for hospital chaplains. However, if a course is to be of value to them, it should include a discussion of such problems as the medical aspect of obstetrical problems, mental hygiene, drug addiction, surgical operations, marriage problems, mental deficiency, psychoneuroses, psychoses, etc. In a word, this course should be designed to orient the chaplain in the medical background of those problems which are likely to confront him in his work.

In an address to the NCEA Convention several years ago, Father M. Scheuer, O.Carm., made several remarks which give some indication of the content of this science:

---

[4] A. O'Malley, M.D., and J. Walsh, M.D., *Essays in Pastoral Medicine,* V.

. . . The priest who has some acquaintance with psychic and somatic studies comes to these life situations with an appreciable advantage.

Moral principles connote more to a student, the more varied the realistic applications he comes to know. Who of us after years in the priesthood does not find his moral principles becoming an ever more living outlook. They have been concretized time and time again. When pastoral medicine is incorporated into the curriculum, moral principles take on life for they are worked out in real life facts of medicine.

Often it is the young priest who carries the Church's reputation into public hospitals where he functions as chaplain. His knowledge or lack of it reflects upon the Church. Thanks to his seminary training he should see the need of keeping abreast in his reading on medico-moral problems. It frequently happens that, as a new medical finding or treatment appears, new moral questions are posited. It takes some time before the matter is adequately thought out morally and medically. Then there comes the refined answer of the theologians. This latter will from time to time supplant earlier solutions without, however, any change in principle. Usually this final solution is thought workable by doctors. Should a chaplain not be familiar with these developments, he may insist upon an earlier judgment with which a doctor finds it difficult to work. He may insist too strongly and his ignorance may reflect unfavorably upon the Church in a secular environment.

The younger clergy are regularly called upon to give moral advice to nurses. The man who understands the medical aspects of the operation or treatment of which he is speaking morally, speaks with greater security. Does not the very tract on emergency baptism presuppose some knowledge of pathology?

From time to time doctors of repute speak as though immoral operations and treatment were necessary for therapeutic reasons. To those who know, however, they are giving personal opinions or speaking unscientifically. If a priest knows they are speaking out of turn medically and why, he can answer them effectively and to the satisfaction of listeners who might otherwise be overawed by medical terms.[5]

In his consideration of pastoral medicine as it affects handling of souls, Father Scheuer pointed out that pastoral medicine is not intended to prepare the priest "that he may prescribe or diagnose. That is not within his competence. He is primarily instructed in these matters that he may recognize when a doctor is needed, that he may give intelligent answers to a doctor seeking medico-moral advice, that he may know what to expect in the disease he is witnessing, and that he may know what not to do."[6]

B. Pastoral Psychology

Dr. Francis J. Braceland points up the importance of special training in pastoral psychology for the hospital chaplain when he writes:

Whether we like it or not this is an age of psychology, just as it is an age of guided missiles, and if people are to take their every day psycho-

---

[5] M. Scheuer, O.Carm., "Instructions in Pastoral Medicine for Seminarians," *The National Catholic Educational Bulletin,* 49 (August, 1952), p. 73.

[6] *Ibid.,* pp. 73–74.

logical problems to their family doctor or priest, they have a right to expect from these sources either proper direction or referral to others who can provide them with efficacious help. Our social and economic life and our culture have changed. People have lost their moorings. As Wheelis says, it is no longer the inner man who is the measure of things, it is the other man. People have changed, disease processes have changed, and the ways of treating them have changed. The professional man be he priest or doctor, must keep abreast of these external changes if he is to fulfill his function completely.[7]

In the preface of his book, *Personality and Sexual Problems,* the editor, Father William C. Bier, S.J., states that "In 1955 the psychology department of Fordham University inaugurated a series of pastoral psychology institutes intended to acquaint the members of the clergy with the findings of psychology, psychiatry, sociology and allied disciplines in the belief that the insights provided by these relatively new and fast developing behavioral sciences would prove helpful to clergymen in their pastoral work."[8] In setting forth the purpose and scope of these institutes, Father Bier has also set down an excellent definition of pastoral psychology. For, pastoral psychology is that branch of pastoral theology which presents those parts of psychology, psychiatry, and other related disciplines which are of value to a chaplain in the care of souls, and those divisions of ethics and moral theology which are of concern to a psychologist or a psychiatrist in his practice.

From what has been said, it becomes immediately evident that the basic purpose of pastoral psychology is to make available the contemporary findings of the behavioral sciences to seminarians and priests, and to develop in these men trained in philosophy and sacred theology a conception of the dynamic nature of personality and of the social processes to aid them in the effective discharge of their priestly role with parishioners. Just as pastoral medicine can be classified as a branch of two sciences, so pastoral psychology is also classified as both a branch of psychology and psychiatry and a branch of theology. Inasmuch as it is a branch of theology, it deals with psychological questions in their relationship to the various branches of theology; inasmuch as it is a branch of psychology and psychiatry, and their allied sciences, it prepares the cleric to handle those cases that have psychological implications. Therefore, hospital chaplains should be conversant on such topics as: religion and moral development in childhood, adolescence, and adulthood; individual and group differences; persons of exceptional intelligence; conflict and adjustment; behavior problems, alcoholism, drug addiction, masturbation, homosexuality; psychosis and psychoneurosis,

---

[7] F. Braceland, M.D., "A Psychiatrist Examines the Relationship Between Psychiatry and the Catholic Clergy," *Pastoral Psychology,* 10 (February, 1959), p. 19.

[8] W. Bier, S.J., *Personality and Sexual Problems,* p. ix.

including scrupulosity; mental health and readjustment techniques; psychoanalysis; client-centered counseling, and marital counseling.

When considering the training in psychology that a hospital chaplain ought to receive, perhaps the observations of Father James H. Vander-Veldt, O.F.M., and Dr. Robert P. Odenwald are pertinent here. They point out that priests are not only moral theologians, but also moral psychologists, and therefore ought to have a knowledge of the various classes of mental diseases and the theories which attempt to explain them. Consequently, from what they say, it is evident that they would favor a course that would present a description of the main forms of mental disorder, and explain what pastors can do when confronted with mental cases, and what they should avoid. They would also include a discussion of the counseling procedure and symptomatic method of psychotherapy, and a rather detailed treatment of the principles which, according to Catholic philosophy and theology, should be employed in solutions to problems of mental disease.[9]

C. Pastoral Counseling

Even though a hospital chaplain will receive some training in counseling in pastoral psychology, additional training in this area can be of great benefit to him in his work in this apostolate.

Earlier in this chapter, it was pointed out that medicine and all the behavioral sciences have both philosophical and theological aspects or overtones; these, of course, include counseling. Therefore, it is important to note that the relationship established between the counselor and the counselee involves the same moral and ethical responsibilities that are involved in the relationships of doctor and patient, or priest and penitent.

Pastoral counseling does not differ from counseling in general, except that the primary aim of the pastoral counselor is to establish a relationship that will draw the counselee closer to God. On this point, Father Vander-Veldt, O.F.M., and Dr. Odenwald state that

> . . . After establishing the necessary rapport between himself and the counselee, the priest attempts to understand his client's problem and to help him solve it according to the latter's personality structure, in view of making a better Christian and thereby a better man out of him. Pastoral Counseling, therefore, is decidedly psychagogic; it is of such a nature that it should not only help the parishioner with his present problem, but also give him the rules with which he can help himself in similar and even different situations.[10]

True pastoral counseling must be genuine counseling. It must help people to help themselves by developing an understanding of their

[9] J. Vander-Veldt, O.F.M. and R. Odenwald, *Psychiatry and Catholicism* (New York: McGraw-Hill, 1952), p. 419.   [10] *Ibid.*, p. 208.

inner conflicts. Therefore any worthwhile course in pastoral counseling must prepare the student to help the client develop new insights which will show themselves in improved personal and behavioral relationships. The course in pastoral counseling must train the student in those counseling procedures which are useful in bringing the individual closer to God and assisting him in the salvation of his soul. On this point Father William C. Bier, S.J., observes that:

> Pastoral counseling is to be considered as part of the larger domain of pastoral care, which is the chief work of the clergyman. As a Catholic, I consider this care to be first of all of a spiritual nature and to be exercised through the spiritual ministrations of the priest, consisting in the celebration of Mass, the administration of the Sacraments, instructions, and so forth. Though some clergymen would express their pastoral functions somewhat differently, a clergyman would think of himself as being dedicated principally to the *religious* care of those entrusted to him. In my judgment it would follow then that, if the clergyman employs counseling, he does so as an aid in the attainment of over-all pastoral goals. These latter, I assume, are fundamentally of a religious nature. In other words, if the clergyman becomes a counselor he must remain a *religious* counselor. . . .[11]

Therefore, a course for hospital chaplains should include a discussion of the principles and practices of pastoral counseling, and of pastoral counseling cases, including the nature, scope, and limitations of self-integrative counseling; counseling in relation to personality growth; basic counselor attitudes and techniques; development of the counseling relationship, and special problems of counseling and the priest counselor.

In a proposed curriculum for chaplain's institutes, the N.A.C.C. listed the following topics under pastoral counseling:

1. The nature of the pastoral counseling approach. Its limits; its place in the different pastoral functions; possible case studies.
2. Important attitudes for the pastoral counselor. Primacy of attitudes over approach or techniques; counselor attitudes related to method; counselor attitudes related to personality.
3. Initial stage of pastoral counseling. Receiving the problem(s); letting the client grow; gathering data for decision as to appropriateness of counseling approach, etc.; possible case studies.
4. Later stage of pastoral counseling. Collaborative; how to proceed. Or if teacher is entirely Rogerian — developments such as shift of emphasis on the part of the client; possible case studies.
5. Deciding on the appropriate helping relationship (I place this here so as not to break up the ongoing consideration of the counseling process and because the counseling approach itself helps to make a more sound decision). Clues to consider in making decision-type of problem and level of maturity of client. Different

---

[11] W. Bier, S.J., "Goals in Pastoral Counseling," *Pastoral Psychology*, pp. 9–10.

possible pastoral relationships consisting of one or more pastoral functions. Consultation and referral. Personality theory related to counseling. Different pastoral relationships might replace 5 partially.

6. Special problems of the pastoral counsel approach. Unwilling client; transference and counter-transference; moral consideration.
7. Consideration of frequent personal problems brought to the pastoral counselor.
8. Scrupulosity, sexual problems, alcoholism, etc.; facing death, etc.

Though it is difficult to describe in any detail the expanding role that pastoral counseling will have in future years, it can be said with certainty that the more extensive the chaplain's training in pastoral counseling, the more effective will be his ministry.

D. Marriage Counseling

Though the hospital chaplain is certainly not expected to become a professional marriage counselor, he should have some training in this area also. Therefore, a hospital chaplain should have some knowledge of the following aspects of marriage counseling: the role of the clergy in marriage counseling; marriage problems and the spiritual life of the couple; marriage counseling as a tool in pastoral effort; principles and practices in interpersonal counseling; joint and separate interviews; diagnostic procedures in marriage cases, and the use of inventories, background schedules, the role of the priest in family life education; the importance of family life education; the divine plan for marriage; the integral nature of the supernatural and natural in marriage; the various family relationships; content, and techniques of family education, and family life movements operative in Catholic circles.

Certain states are now requiring a period of clinical training in order that a minister of religion be appointed to one of their hospital chaplaincies. In line with this, the Bureau of Health and Hospitals of the National Catholic Welfare Conference has mapped out the following steps in the preparation of a priest for a hospital chaplaincy:

1. Lectures in the seminary on the care of the sick.
2. Use of the Deacon's Holy Orders to bring Communion to the sick in hospitals, to preach to the sick in hospital chapels, and to aid in the baptism of babies in the hospital.
3. After ordination, to volunteer some hours or days each week for visitation of the sick outside of and apart from parochial duty.
4. When appointed to a hospital chaplaincy, to spend two weeks in intensive training at a center designated for this purpose.

The National Association of Catholic Chaplains has also suggested other areas for inclusion in a program for training hospital chaplains. These areas are:

1. The relation of the chaplain to nursing personnel. (What assistance and cooperation can he expect from them; willingness to accept opinion of nurses; and what services can he render.)
2. Relation of the chaplain to medical personnel.
3. Special problems connected with obstetrics-gynecology.
4. Special problems connected with pediatrics.
5. Special problems connected with general medical and diagnostic patients.
6. Special problems connected with surgery and intensive care.
7. Special problems connected with cardio-vascular disease.
8. Special problems connected with the geriatric patient.
9. Special problems connected with the emergency room; fire and disaster programs, and cardiac arrest.
10. The chaplain and volunteer services. (How can he utilize volunteers in his chaplaincy program; assisting in recruitment of volunteers; a source of good public relations with the community.)
11. The chaplain as teacher. (Participation in the orientation of all new employees, nursing school, local clergy of all faiths, pastoral training for seminarians, especially in deacon year.)
12. Admission information and the chaplain's records. (How notified of new admissions; patient's religious affiliation; what records are to be kept: baptisms, confirmations, marriages, anointings; where ought records to be kept; notification of proper parish, parish in which hospital is located.)
13. Baptism and the reception of converts. (Infant, adult, instruction required, emergencies.)
14. Faculties for sacrament of penance; various methods used in the distribution of Holy Communion.
15. Sacraments of the sick. (Viaticum; faculties for confirmation.)
16. Matrimony. (Delegation.)

THE CATHOLIC CHAPLAIN AND NON-CATHOLIC PATIENTS (ECUMENISM)

Earlier in this chapter it was noted that the Catholic chaplain must be concerned not only about the religious needs of Catholic patients but also about the spiritual needs of all the patients. Therefore, it is important that he know the religious needs of Protestants and Jews, so that, should the need arise he can meet his responsibilities in this regard. However, perhaps his most important function in this matter will be that of instructing Catholic nurses and hospital personnel regarding the spiritual needs of patients of other faiths,

Since the most important contribution that the administration of a Catholic hospital can make to the proper spiritual care of patients of other faiths is a sure method for guaranteeing prompt and accurate notification of the patient's pastor, or another clergyman of his faith, the Catholic chaplain should make every effort to cooperate with this procedure, and even seek ways to improve it when it is seen to be less than adequate.

There are also occasions when the Catholic chaplain, in a true ecumenical spirit, can quite effectively cooperate with clergymen of other faiths. Father Wilkerson gives one example of this when he writes about the team approach for mixed marriages:

> Another particular ecumenical aspect of providing for the patient's spiritual needs is the occasional care of those in a mixed marriage. When, for example, a distraught Catholic wife is summoned to the bedside of a gravely ill Protestant patient, the Catholic chaplain should be notified. Something of a team approach is then set up in caring for the spiritual need of this patient and his family.[12]

The zealous pastor of souls, the chaplain who is truly concerned about the spiritual well-being of all his patients, will quickly discover other areas for cooperation with the clergy of other faiths.

Perhaps a word should be said here about the importance of recognizing the chaplains of other faiths as members of the hospital team who also have a responsibility to minister to the spiritual needs of the members of their faith. Catholic chaplains, therefore, should extend to these clergymen the same courtesies and cooperation that he would extend to all other members of the hospital staff.

The Catholic hospital chaplain has a special job to do in the secular hospital in his meeting with doctors, nurses, and other personnel of all faiths. He must be most cordial, kindly, and cooperative, and realize that their thinking, because of different religious and moral backgrounds, is not always the same as his as regards things dealing with the sick, the hospital, surgery, and medicine in general. The hospital chaplain must meet them with understanding; he will usually find that they will return the same. They will notice in him the Christ-likeness that cannot help but be attractive to anyone of any faith. All that a priest has to remember is that when he goes into the sick room Christ goes — Protestant, Jew, and pagan, as well as Catholic; nurse, doctor, administrator, visitor, and patient are watching him. He is ever on display. Therefore, it is of the greatest importance that priests who work with the sick be real priests, and be kind. Kindness, above all, is so important; everything else follows.

---

[12] *Op. cit.,* p. 78.

Conclusion

Though the life of the hospital chaplain can be a very rewarding one, especially when the priest functions as a member of the hospital team and carries out his various duties to the best of his ability, it can also be a very confining life. It is no small task to visit every single patient every day and to know the spiritual health of each patient. If he is to remain vigorous and enthusiastic about his job, he cannot ignore the needs of his personal life, especially his prayer life and his recreational life. Therefore, to the extent that this is possible, his schedule should be so arranged as to leave adequate time for prayer, rest, and recreation. As Father Wilkerson observes, "A chaplain who is feted to a full day off every week, a full vacation, who is sent to relevant meetings and programs, will understandably be more physically vigorous and mentally stimulated than the chaplain who can 'never get away.' " He also has a point when he remarks that ". . . the chaplain who is always tired and under pressure from innumerable demands cannot meet the spiritual needs of his patients to the fullest satisfaction."[13]

---

[13] *Ibid.*, p. 80.

27

The Convent Chaplain

JOHN E. FOLEY

A POWERFUL AND DEDICATED GROUP IN THE CHURCH IN THE UNITED States is the many and varied congregations of Sisters. The 1965 *Catholic Almanac* lists 180,015 Sisters in America who are engaged in most aspects of the apostolate. They are an influential group of women who have been a tremendous force for good in almost every area of Catholic life. If the Church is flourishing today, much of the credit must go to the work of all these generous women. We must appreciate and realize their great contribution in order to discuss, in proper perspective, the role of the convent chaplain.

The Church has always been solicitous for the welfare of religious women. Pius XII said: "The apostolate of the Church today is scarcely conceivable without the cooperation of religious women in works of charity, in the schools, in assistance to the priestly ministry, in the missions." John XXIII and Paul VI have frequently expressed these same opinions.

It seems true that many priests demean the ministry to religious women, and many come poorly equipped to serve them. In March, 1949, the French Bishops issued the following statement regarding Religious Congregations: "The ministry to religious is to be esteemed as a select ministry, which may not be discharged without preparation and attention." It further urged greater understanding and respect of the religious life and work of sisters.

Only those priests who have an interest in this special ministry should be selected as chaplains. Assignment to this work ought not to be made because of the physical or other incapacities of the priest, which often seems to be the case. The chaplain should have a knowledge of the religious life, as well as the origin and the rules of the Congregation which he is serving.

The chaplain is not the canonical pastor of the religious, even though the bulk of his work borders on that of a pastor. The local ordinary may communicate certain pastoral rights and duties. In the *Canonical Commentary* of Abbo and Hannon, the chaplain's position is outlined:

> It is the chaplain who exercises the sacred ministry in behalf of the members of a religious household (for example, by celebrating Mass for them and distributing Holy Communion to them.) Generally speaking, his office is a wonderful form of pastorate, lacking the rights and duties peculiar to pastors.

His duties and obligations should be clearly defined by his ecclesiastical superiors. A clear agreement between the Congregation and his superiors will render the chaplain's work more effective. His role may be considered a species of contract.

The chaplain has the obligation to offer Mass and provide other services for the Sisters. In the practical realm, because of the pressing schedule of the convent, and the school or institution, all service must be on time. Many a Sister's day has ended disastrously because morning Mass was fifteen minutes late. It is absolutely necessary that the horarium be observed as much as possible.

Most priests are aware that the Sisters hold the priesthood in the greatest esteem and, therefore, it should be easy for the chaplain to set up his priestly program. However, he should conduct all business with the Superior and not with a particular Sister. Occasional talks with the Superior will make for better communication, a virtue often missing in priest-sister relationships. In the past, formalism has created a barrier between the chaplain and the Sisters, resulting in a strained and artificial relationship.

In conveying a functional view of the chaplain, it is necessary that many priestly prejudices toward religious women be overcome. Some priests might feel that the Sisters are concerned with the minutiae of life and will make incessant demands upon them.

When contrasted with his previous apostolic life, the role of chaplain is a complete reversal for most priests. An adjustment is required in his thinking when he is suddenly confronted with the obligation of ministering to those who themselves have removed him from some of his most vital responsibilities. The priest is commanded by Christ to administer the sacraments, and to teach the faithful the "Good News" of salvation. His removal from parish life reduces his ministry to a more passive role. He will no longer be concerned with parish societies and organizations, or associated with (and teach) the young. In great part, the religious perform these works for him, leaving him on the perimeter of loneliness.

What, then, is he expected to do? Now he must adjust to this reversal of his priestly office among the religious. It is to him, as another Christ, that the religious must look for the spiritual assistance that will sustain them in performing their duties.

He must be available at suitable times to direct, to nurture, and to form the generous oblation of the religious toward greater spiritual maturity in the service of the Lord. In every spiritual or social contact, he should exemplify the classical qualities of prudence, knowledge, experience, confidence, kindness, understanding, and genuine sympathy. Reverend Felix M. Kirsch, O.F.M.Cap., in his book, *The Spiritual Director of Sisters* writes: "Fundamentally, the attitude of the priest towards Sisters should be one of reverence."[1]

Saint Teresa of Avila tells us that "if all these qualities cannot be found in the same man, prudence and sound understanding are the more important." "Because," she continues, "it is always possible to find learned men to consult when necessary."[2]

The chaplain is not without an adequate education. His training has been professional with graduate and post-graduate academic studies. The concentration in his education on the needs of the laity and the lack of competent texts on the subject of religious women present a difficulty to any newly-appointed chaplain. His life has been male-oriented, without too much emphasis on the relationship to the distaff side. There are a few things he must remember in dealing with women. Most important, perhaps, is the fact that virtue in a woman takes on another form than it does in a man. St. Teresa of Avila admitted that there may be secrets in a woman's soul unknown even to the man who has years of knowledge of her. This places an initial burden on the chaplain. If he possesses a negative attitude, he must change his thinking.

The emotional side of a woman is God's gift to her and is an invaluable aid to a Sister in her work; generally, she will be inclined to obey the promptings of her heart rather than the reasonings of her mind. The fact that Sisters are women cannot be ignored. Consequently, they will possess whatever qualities, both desirable and undesirable, are to be found in all women.

The chaplain should be most prudent in his corrections and suggestions concerning his personal living quarters, meals, his needs for

---

[1] (New York: © Benziger Brothers, Inc.), p. 13.
[2] *Autobiography.*

sacristy and altar. Presented with less than tact, the sensitive nature of woman, personified in the sacristan or cook, will promptly think: "Father doesn't like me!" Women are apt to take a manly reproof or correction on a personal basis.

Father Kirsch also states that "the priest will experience that what the Sisters will respect in the long run is his reserve and manly dignity."[3] He should be above any sort of pettiness.

His knowledge and appreciation of the congregation's rule and customs must influence him sufficiently so that he will be prevented from making any drastic internal changes. Communal living may well be something new to him and as a result should make him feel inadequate to compose a rule for women. It would be insolence on his part to think that he could improve a way of life that has weathered many storms, saved many souls, and guided many to sanctity. He should be very hesitant about suggesting change or reformation, either by intervention or indirectly by non-compliance. The Church is very strong in her legislation on this matter regarding confessors and others in the Code of Canon Law.

Canon 524 states plainly: "The confessor of religious women should beware of interfering in any way with the internal or external management of the community." This applies to the chaplain. Father Kirsch recommends: "It would be well for priests to reread from time to time the 154 canons (No. 487 to No. 681) of the Code of Canon Law in which the church expresses unequivocally her esteem and solicitude for the religious."[4]

A chaplain should never criticize the rules or customs of the community since they are beyond his competence and jurisdiction. The rights of a superior in a convent should be treated with the same respect as the head of any other family. In speaking of obedience, Sister Bertrande Meyers, D.C., writes in her perceptive book, *Sisters for the Twenty-First Century:*

> Obedience will always be the *sine qua non* of the religious life.
> The principle of obedience is based upon the conviction that the will of God is made known to a religious through her lawful superiors.[5]

All business, suggestions, and the like, therefore, should be communicated through the Superior.

As a general rule, the chaplain should not take sides either with the Superior or her subjects, and it is most certainly not his position to act as a "pipe-line" between the Superior and her subjects, or vice-versa. His is a neutral role akin to that of a spiritual director in a seminary.

---

[3] Kirsch, *op. cit.*, p. 26.
[4] *Ibid.*, p. 14.
[5] Meyers, *op. cit.*, p. 89.

The community is a religious family and the rights of all are to be respected. This can be accomplished by mutual love and esteem. In this family, there will be members who are young and old. They should be treated equally.

Religious penitents have perfection as a goal and minor deviations from that dedication are significant to them. This calls for patience and kindness on the priest's part. In this modern and exciting period of transition in the Church, he can be an effective instrument in quieting the anxieties of the old and tempering the enthusiasm of the young. In conferences, sermons, and homilies, he can help to clarify the issues and ease the tensions between the older members of the community and "the new breed."

The chaplain can practically implement the Constitution on the Liturgy in the liturgical life of the Congregation. He should endeavor, for instance, to carry out the full liturgical program of Holy Week. Neighboring parishes could supply the necessary servers and the nearby seminary could supply the ministers. The riches and significance of the Holy Week ceremonies are a great spiritual inspiration to the Sisters. He should extend himself to provide those "extra" spiritual services.

In his conferences and homilies, and even in his informal talks, the convent chaplain must be aware that Sisters are mature persons. They resent being "talked down to." In their maturity, they can appreciate and savor sound theology and Sacred Scripture. Homilies should be brief and based on solid spirituality.

Sisters are familiar with ascetical theology in their reading, and many convent libraries would easily rival the average reading material of some priests. He should be able to cite from the professional journals, such as *Homiletic and Pastoral Review, Theology Digest, American Ecclesiastical Review,* those articles and essays that can help the Sisters in their formation in theology, particularly pastoral theology.

Many changes have taken place in the convent during the fresh spirit of renewal and rejuvenation since John XXIII opened that famous window. A great change has taken place in the Sisters themselves, in their increased awareness of themselves as persons and of their mission to the world. They have become articulate in their apostolates. There is a growing ease and a most welcome naturalness in their relationship with others, with superiors, with Protestants, with the ecumenical movement as a whole, and most happily, with the laity.

With his practical background in parish life, the chaplain's clinical knowledge of the laity can be a force to direct any misguided zeal. This requires continued communication between him and the community.

He should judge each religious individually, and be careful not to fall into the philosophical error of making general conclusions from particular premises. From time to time, he will be asked for advice in personal areas, that is, problems in a sister's own family, such as broken marriages, alcoholism, illness, disagreements. The priest who is experienced in the pastoral counseling of the typical rectory-type problem will be able to calm anxieties and solve problems that divert a Sister from her life of dedication.

In line with individual counseling, the chaplain will occasionally be asked to advise a Sister who wishes to leave the convent and go back into the world. A Religious who is chronically disgruntled, or a habitual trouble-maker, should be encouraged to leave her community since the Church cannot move forward with personalities of this kind. But one should not be quick to make this judgment, since Sisters may be emotionally or psychically disturbed and require medical or psychiatric treatment at that particular time.

If an infirmary is attached to the convent, the chaplain should be ready to make a decision concerning a sick Sister and her reception of the sacrament of the anointing of the sick and viaticum. Sister should have the benefits of the Church at this hour.

Concerning his personal life, the convent chaplain should be free to have guests in his room or to invite guests to dine. Sisters understand his need to socialize with fellow priests or laymen in his own living quarters. However, he should notify the Superior in sufficient time that extra guests have been invited for a particular meal, and these events should in no way interfere with the good order of the community.

We are all poignantly aware of the great need for more vocations in the Religious Communities. Priestly zeal and interest can be a factor in aiding the Sisters in this regard. Knowledge of the Sister Formation Movement which, today, is revolutionizing every community is vital. This movement will lead to an increase of vocations since it makes the religious life more tolerable and meaningful.

The Sister Formation Movement had its beginning in 1952 at the National Catholic Educational Association, (N.C.E.A.) in Kansas City. The Holy See, in 1956, established formally the Conference of Major Superiors and, finally, in August of 1964, the Sister Formation Conference was placed under the direction of a Committee of the Conference of Major Superiors. Thus, the two organizations were melded into a clearly defined relationship. The purpose of the Sister Formation Movement is to develop a sister as a *whole* person. Sister Mary Emil, I.H.M., a pioneer in the movement, defines the program:

> Sister Formation, a rather unfamiliar expression, was chosen to stand not only for the education of sisters in a formal and informal sense, but also for all of the influences, pre-service and in-service, which go to make a better religious, and a better professional person.

The Sister Formation Bulletin (Summer — 1956) states:

> This movement is the remedy for Sister shortage; it upholds the dignity of religious vocation, all the essential facets of a Sister's formation, spiritual, intellectual, social, and apostolic are considered.

If a chaplain is to be a success, he must be familiar with this movement and have a working knowledge of the program. A quarterly, *The Sister Formation Bulletin* will keep him up to date on current advances made by the religious communities.

Sisters are troubled, not to say aggravated, by the many articles appearing in magazines and periodicals questioning the value of religious life. A vociferous minority of pseudo-liberals believes that religious can be replaced by the laity. They would do well to familiarize themselves with the mind of the Church in this matter. Father Gregory Baum, O.S.A., in his commentary on *The Constitution on the Church* says:

> Though all Christians are called to follow the Lord, religious men and women who have consecrated themselves to the imitation of Christ in a community or some other stable form of life, have a special place in the Church.[6]

He further comments that "religious life is characterized by a total consecration to God that draws all areas of a man's life in a new way into the service and worship of God."[7] Finally, he states:

> Chapter VI also defends religious life against an accusation which, today, is sometimes raised against it. We are told that even if the renunciation in religious life is considerable on one level, this does not frustrate, but liberates man for greater self-possession and creativity. Through religious profession, men do not become immature and estranged from the brothers in the world, but, by opening their hearts to the love of Jesus in a special way, they are united to all men in a deep and abiding fashion.[8]

There is no substitute for a personality totally dedicated to God. Religious cannot be replaced by the laity. Both have their proper place in the Mystical Body of Christ.

The religious life is defined by Archbishop Phillipi, Secretary of the Sacred Congregation of Religious, as "a state which constitutes a system of life, organized to form and to train religious to Christian perfection. The religious life is this privileged way of perfection because it is essentially constituted by the three vows of religion. The vows free the religious from the obstacles which might hold back the impulse of his love toward God, and insofar as they consecrate him to God, they make his life a divine service."

Divine Service needs underscoring in theory and practice.

---

[6] (Glen Rock, N. J.: Paulist Press), p. 47.
[7] *Ibid.*, p. 48.   [8] *Ibid.*

The purpose of each religious community — teaching, nursing, missionary works — is service to their fellow man; by reason of their religious vows, they are a divine service bearing witness to Christ. Our Lord laid down the first principle: "If you would be perfect, go, sell what you possess and give to the poor, and you will have treasure in heaven; and come, follow me" (Mt 19:21).

Sisters are essential to the Church, not in the hierarchical or sacramental order, but in the moral historical order, so that our Lord's commands may be fully carried out. Since he recommended the evangelical counsels, there must always be some members of the Church who observe these counsels, otherwise the Church would not be fully in accord with his wishes.

Shakespeare realized the efficacy of the prayers of religious women dedicated to God. In *Measure for Measure* he says:

> Not with fond shekels of the tested gold,
> Or stones, whose rates are either rich or poor
> As fancy values them; but with true prayers,
> That shall be up at heaven, and enter there
> 'Ere sun-rise — prayers from preserved souls,
> From fasting maids, whose mind are dedicate
> To nothing temporal. (Act II, Sc. II)

A convent chaplain should brief himself on the importance of his assignment. His tenure will not be barren, for he will share in the molding of basically generous people. His is a most important task and he can make a most valuable contribution to the Church in his capacity as chaplain. Too long have these and similar chaplaincies been held in low esteem by priests themselves, and by their superiors. This is a specialized work that should be given to talented men, ascetical in outlook, and practical in reality. Less talk about Sisters changing their garb today and more action in changing our attitudes toward them would be ideal.

Father Bernard Häring in *Christian Renewal in a Changing World* says in his introduction:

> Contemporary man is reminded of the stupendous transformations apparent in all phases of his material existence. Impressive signs of a new age have appeared in the second industrial revolution with the introduction of automation, the smashing of atoms, the utilization and control of atomic energies, and man's daring venture into space. All these epoch-making achievements are unmistakable indications of a "new era — a new world."

Sisters are a great part of this new era, and are in tune with the times. They are helping to make this new world. We must be the symbol of Christ to them, to lead and to guide, and they will follow.

28

The Military Chaplain

CHAPLAIN, LT. COL. FRANK J. GILCHRIST

CADET CHAPLAIN

UNITED STATES AIR FORCE ACADEMY, COLORADO

We have granted many most gratifying audiences in the past few weeks; but this one, as you will easily understand, fills Our paternal heart with a particular joy and consolation, for you are Our beloved sons in a very special way.

Just now, in this tragic hour of human history, called from the regular life of the parish or from the calm of retirement of the student or professor, you have been caught up in the maelstrom of war and thrown into the perils of battle and the temptations of a soldier's life. No ordinary shepherds of souls are needed here. Your Bishops and religious Superiors know how immensely important and how arduous is this apostolate and they have given of their best for it.

It is arduous and very trying at times for the soul as well as the body. At such times renew your resolution to devote yourselves wholeheartedly to your sacred trust. Win the hearts and the souls of your men by the integrity and the holiness of your lives, and a devotion to their spiritual good that does not count the cost. Keep your eyes ever on the Divine Shepherd, that most ardent Lover of Souls; take inspiration and courage from the great Apostles, Peter and Paul; and as you continue your magnificent apostolate for your dear men, be assured that Our prayers are accompanying you.

(*Words of Pope Pius XII to Sixty-four American Catholic Chaplains received in Audience a few weeks after the fall of Rome*)

MILITARY CHAPLAINS OF ALL DENOMINATIONS PERFORMED ADMIRABLY during World War II. They wrote a heroic chapter in American history.

Yet, despite this outstanding performance at home and abroad, at the end of the war, a prominent army general and a former Catholic chaplain differently appraised the Catholic chaplain and his work. The general said: "You have to give the Roman Catholic Church credit. When the War Department requests a bishop to supply twenty priests for chaplains, he looks over his diocese and picks out the twenty best men."[1]

On the other hand, the former Catholic chaplain stated that the Catholic Church was sending its "plough horses" into the military service and keeping its "thoroughbreds" at home. The records show that both were wrong.

Catholic chaplains who entered the service during World War II and since then, have done so voluntarily. Without exception, they were and are volunteers for this unique spiritual work. They are motivated — or should be — solely by a desire to serve God and country. Any prospective volunteer whose motive is otherwise would do well to reconsider his decision. And it is undoubtedly better that they are volunteers, because if ordinaries and religious provincials supervised prospective candidates, it would result in the chaplaincy getting better than the average run-of-the-mill American priest who distinguished himself both in peacetime and in combat, one who has been a credit to his Church and country and an example to his men. Some sort of selection of the volunteers, however, is desirable, both on the part of bishops and provincials and on the part of the military ordinariate, which ultimately is responsible for the quality and quantity of chaplains. This choice results in the military service getting the best possible chaplains in a field which unquestionably demands much — both spiritually and physically.

Concerning the matter of military chaplains, the scheme on bishops specifically mentions:

> Since, because of the unique conditions of their way of life, the spiritual care of military personnel requires special consideration, there should be established in every nation, if possible, a military vicariate. Both the Military Vicar and the chaplains should devote themselves unsparingly to this difficult work in complete cooperation with the diocesan Bishops. Diocesan Bishops should release to the Military Vicar a sufficient number of priests who are qualified for this serious work. At the same time they should promote all endeavors which will improve the spiritual welfare of military personnel.

Because the military service makes so many spiritual and physical demands on the chaplain, he should keep himself in good physical condition and, by all means, not neglect his spiritual life. For this reason, his prayer life is essential. It should be adequate and well planned; it is, perhaps, more important in military than in civilian life. Temptations, I think, are

---

[1] *Time Magazine,* National Affairs, September 1, 1945, and *New York Times,* October 6, 1954, p. 16.

never more frequent or violent in one place than another, but they are perhaps more subtle and varied in military life. An annual retreat is a *must* for all chaplains. Military regulations generously allow adequate time, other than leave, for this all-important spiritual obligation.[2] If the chaplain takes his retreat with priests of his own diocese or with his religious community, it can serve a double purpose. It not only recharges his spiritual batteries, but also links him with the priests who in the long run will mean most to him. During overseas tours of duty, such a retreat is not practicable, but an annual retreat is usually arranged for all the chaplains in the area by the chaplain delegate of the military ordinariate. And in most areas, there are also monthly days of recollection which keep the chaplain on the spiritual beam. In ordinary circumstances, daily Mass, meditation, visit to the Blessed Sacrament, spiritual reading, rosary, and private devotions round out the day of the chaplain just as they round out the day of the civilian priest. The breviary, needless to say, cannot be ignored in military life and there is no dispensation from it for military chaplains. Without exception, the best chaplain, when the chips are down, is still the good zealous priest who is firmly rooted spiritually and who is happy in his apostolate of serving God and souls.

The physical side, however, cannot be overlooked. While it is true that almost any priest can do the work of a chaplain, it is still true that there are certain qualities which make for a successful chaplain. A chaplain should make a good appearance, should have above-average health, and should have an appealing personality. A chaplain should be friendly to all men at all times, for he never knows when he is talking to a man or woman aching with a problem to be solved. Military men quickly size up their chaplains. Soldier or sailor, marine or airman will unburden his troubles, sometimes in the most unlikely place and at the most inconvenient time, to the priest who seems outgoing and interested. A priest may be scholar or saint, but unless he deeply sympathizes with all men and can communicate this desire to help, he is better off not entering the military service. He must see Christ in every soul and every soul must be able to see Christ in him. Every priest must preserve his public image, but a chaplain can never be excused if he is untidy in appearance. Parishioners on a military installation do complain if their chaplain, as the representative of the base and the Church, does not spend more money on haircuts, laundry and dry cleaning and shoe polish, and less on large and sporty cars. As one airman put it, "The chaplain should be neither a dapper Dan nor a sloppy Sam."

Whether in uniform or mufti (many experienced chaplains insist that

---

[2] AFR 265-1, AR-630-20, Sec. 2. Nav. Pers. 15664 B — Sec. 1209.

their parishioners like to see them in a Roman collar on Sundays and on other occasions), the chaplain must always be conscious of his public image. Although he must "ex officio" fulfill his social obligations and be familiar with the rules of etiquette and the social amenities, he cannot tarnish that image by too frequent appearances at the bar of the officers' club or at other places of public amusement. If a chaplain appears every Saturday night at some social activity, his parishioners will quickly suspect that he is not spending too much time preparing his Sunday services and sermons, and may wonder who is hearing confessions. At the same time, a good chaplain makes himself readily available at any time of day or night for emergencies and keeps the base telephone operator and officer of the day advised as to where he can be reached at all times, especially when he is off post or ship. He is not expected to live like a recluse, anchored to the rigors of monastic discipline, but then again his quarters should be in keeping with the ordinary degree of priestly poverty expected of a priest today.

As to poverty, the newly commissioned chaplain will find his income considerably increased in military life; and at the same time, he will find that he has greater expense and more financial obligations. Both the diocesan and the religious priest should maintain the spirit of poverty expected of all priests, and this can be done in military life as well as civilian life. There must be a degree of flexibility in the application of the vow of poverty for the religious but he should understand that he is not dispensed from it while in the military. Nearly all religious superiors leave the amount of income the chaplain sends the community to the discretion of the individual, since personal expenses will vary with each priest; but for a religious to make no return whatever to his community would be difficult to explain in view of his vow of poverty. Clearly, the military chaplain should maintain himself in accordance with his professional status as an officer and, at the same time, live in accordance with the religious state. These standards are neither impossible nor incompatible. Each religious, at the outset of his military apostolate, should be reminded by his superior that the matter of poverty is something better left to individual conscience; nevertheless, the religious should take his actual and legitimate living expenses from his salary, maintain a modest bank account only for this purpose, and return the remainder to his community. The bank account is almost a necessity for the modern-day chaplain. Indeed, some chaplains solve the community-religious problem by having a joint account from which both the individual and the superior can draw as needed. In general, then, both the religious and diocesan priest in the service should guard against cupidity and avarice, which can very easily creep into the life of an American priest who must handle money in fairly large amounts.

A great spiritual safeguard against materialism for the chaplain, especially one at an isolated post or base, is the company of other priests.[3] Friendly relations with neighboring clergy sustain a chaplain. He should visit the local priests frequently and accept invitations to diocesan functions and such local religious exercises as Forty Hours Devotions. Not only does this help the chaplain himself but it will also benefit his military parishioners, some of whom look to the local pastors to provide parochial schooling, Catholic boy and girl scouts, and other help which the military chaplain cannot provide. Also, the chaplain will want to have contacts with the clergy of other denominations. His relations with them should be cordial and guided by Christian charity. Although at times Catholic chaplains can be distant and even smug with their separated brethren, this aloofness usually dissolves upon acquaintance. Friendliness and gentlemanliness are expected of a chaplain at all times. Bigotry, no matter where it appears, is unforgivable; in a military chaplain, it is totally reprehensible.

In these days of reaffirmation of the ecumenical spirit, the military chaplain can be a strong focal point for ecumenism. The young chaplain of today will find many opportunities for cooperation with his Protestant and Jewish brethren, without having to worry about *"cooperatio in divinis."* He might have to review his theology on this matter, however, for he will be asked often to participate in interfaith ceremonies of one kind or another and to give invocations and blessings at semi-military and semi-religious functions, frequently difficult to classify. If a chaplain has any doubt about whether a particular invitation is an interfaith activity, he should consult with the military ordinariate.[4] An invocation or blessing may be requested for anything from a mass funeral to a marble tournament. The average Protestant chaplain seems to be better at giving invocations and blessings than the average priest, probably because it is part of his seminary training or because he is called upon more frequently for this activity. Then again, and perhaps closer to the truth, it might be that he takes the time to compose prayers for these occasions. A good idea for the Catholic chaplain is to keep a file of prayers and blessings for all occasions, rather than to fall back on some stereotyped prayers, prayers whose language is frequently archaic and often unfit for the occasion. For him to run through or to mumble some prayer of the *Raccolta* at a high school graduation, or to dash through the "Bless us, O Lord," at some formal banquet, does not impress the listener as well as some of the well composed and well delivered prayers of our Protestant chaplains. Invocations should be brief, appropriate to the occasion, suitable to all denominations, and more in the nature of a self-prepared prayer to God than a sermon.

---

[3] "The priesthood and celibacy," *Review for Religious,* Vol. 24, No. 6, 935, November, 1965, p. 9.

[4] Cf. *Vademecum,* 1965, Sec. 22, p. 43.

At the outset of his military service, the new chaplain will frequently be transferred. Indeed, at times he will suspect that he is being arbitrarily shifted from pillar to post. At first, the young chaplain welcomes change, but as he gets older in the service, he can find it irksome and irritating. The old Army maxim, "Volunteer for nothing and take what comes along," is a good philosophy for a chaplain to adopt. Rare is the assignment in the service that is not left without a certain amount of regret and nostalgia, despite an initial dislike for it.

Some chaplains sometimes make life difficult for themselves and others by trying to choose their own assignments or by always trying to request assignments near their home. Actually, assignments are better left to chance, at least in the beginning, since one of the advantages of military life is its broadening influence from work in other dioceses and in foreign countries. The chaplain may find it difficult to equate with the will of God special orders that assign him to an isolated post, but he will be better off if he can think of them this way. At the beginning of their military service, new chaplains are usually assigned to a post or base where there are several older chaplains. In this way, they can benefit from previous experience and can receive invaluable on-the-job training, especially in the regulations and customs of the service, administration, and the management of funds. There are times, however, when the young chaplain will find himself on his own. In such a situation he should make friends of someone who can help him to help himself.

All branches of the service have schools for the chaplains where they receive about six weeks of basic training. Here a new chaplain is first introduced to the chaplaincy. He learns the necessary regulations, how to make out reports, fill in forms, write military correspondence. Obviously, a good secretary or assistant is invaluable; as a rule, a chaplain rates either one or the other.

The military chaplain will be asked to participate in civic and social functions with far greater frequency than his civilian counterpart. When requested, the chaplain should be ready to fulfill his community obligations and should take time to prepare for them, for he never knows or realizes the picture he can present of the Church and the Catholic priesthood. An Oblate of Mary Immaculate missionary, for example, liberated at last from Santo Tomas prison camp in Manila at the close of the Pacific war, remarked that he never realized how important softball could be in convert-making until he became the star shortstop on the prison camp baseball team. "A good solid double to left field at a crucial moment in an important game," he said, "very often was more convincing to a prospective convert than all the argument of the seminary course in apologetics, especially if it happened to drive in the wininng run."

PERSONNEL

It may sometimes be difficult to know whether commanders are for or against you. Most of them, however, recognize you as a valuable member of their staff. They respect your professional status and actively seek your advice on matters of morals and morale. Your commander is like a mayor of a town; as such, he has responsibility for everything except the off-duty social life of the troops, and often enough he may even become involved in that. Become acquainted with him, but don't wear out your welcome. Invite him to your important social functions, but remember he is generally overloaded with social obligations. Keep him informed about your work but do it through his executive officer; if it is something of great importance, then ask to see him personally.

Even if you should find that a commander is distant or even unfriendly, make it a point to be cordial with him at all times. Occasionally, a priest can have a seemingly haughty attitude toward a commander or even toward the men of the installation, expecting perhaps the same deference and respect from them as from the faithful back home. While it is true that military chaplains have considerable status — earned undoubtedly by the heroic and saintly efforts of chaplains who served during World Wars I and II and in Korea — yet the new chaplain must in turn earn individual respect, by exemplary charity, industry, and friendliness.

So much for the officer relationships. But what about the enlisted men, from noncommissioned officer to private, basic airman, and seaman? The chaplain must know a unit's sergeants and petty officers. Usually, they are most eager to help a young chaplain and have a remarkable talent for getting things done. A chaplain should never overtly question how they "do things," but should be prudent lest he become a part of anything that is contrary to the regulations. These men of high enlisted rank provide an excellent link between the chaplain and the enlisted men and between the chaplain and the officers. Many successful Holy Name Societies have NCO's that run them and run them well.

The NCO opens his heart to the young chaplain and welcomes opportunities to keep him informed and to teach him the ways of service life. Although the chaplain, because he is a commissioned officer, will most often go to the Officers' Club for his meals and relaxation, he should remember that he is also welcome at the NCO Club, where he will find a warm and genuine hospitality awaiting him.

Officers, commissioned and noncommissioned, are relatively easy to know; but a group of men probably most neglected in military life is that of the single enlisted men. Yet, ironically, it is the group most in need of help. These young men are just a few months or years away from home, church and school. They are hard to pin down and very unpredictable, difficult to accurately assess in their morals, their interests, and their needs, frustrating to work for and with. Nevertheless, you must show the enlisted man that you are interested in him, for your interest is the key to his response. Such little practices as visiting the mess hall or the snack bar, as well as attending sporting events or other affairs where enlisted men gather, will pay off handsomely. Your work necessarily extends to all men — enlisted and commissioned. As St. Paul tells us of priests, the chaplain must be "all things to all men."

The final and most important class of men is those who will assist you in your work — the chaplains' assistants. Called clerks, yeomen, or welfare specialists, depending on the branch of the service in which they serve, these men have chosen to work with you and for the chapel program. Generally, they are volunteers and have been carefully screened by a senior chaplain at the indoctrination centers. They are carefully trained in administration and are given a course in the basic requirements of the worship services of all faiths. They can be a very strong arm in a chaplain's program.

Remember, their calling is not a religious vocation. If they are not as devout as you would like them to be, it may be they lack a sound religious education and upbringing. Always give them the best example and resist any temptation to work off your frustrations on them. They are trained in a special administrative field; and generally, they know their job better than you ever will. Lean on them and place responsibility in them. Perhaps a Protestant or Jewish boy may be assigned you, and you may be surprised: he will work harder for you if you treat him as a human being worthy of your kindness, charity, and consideration. Such should be your guideline in working with all men, up and down the military ladder.

PROGRAMS

The happiest aspect of military life for a priest is that he can try almost any program. Very little tradition, if any, and a constantly changing congregation challenge the chaplain; he can accept or reject new devotions, societies, novenas, Bible vigils, and other methods of worship or devotion on their individual merit. Some branches of the military service have, by regulation, very definite guidelines; but the zeal and ingenuity of the chaplain usually determine that program which best fits the needs of his people. In some instances the Holy Name Society and Sodality flourish; in others, they inexplicably wither and die.

One program, however, was tailor-made to aid religion in the military: The Confraternity of Christian Doctrine. Founded in Milan, Italy, in 1518, and still possessing its original goal, the CCD is an indispensable feature of parish life in America. Located on most military installations where large groups of children need religious education, the CCD is required by regulation in at least one of the services — the Air Force (AFR 265-1).

Probably the outstanding feature of the CCD is the manner in which it channels the skills, time, and zeal of laymen. Because military chaplains are even more mobile than their transient parishioners, the gap created when Father leaves and sometimes is not replaced for weeks or months, is partially filled by the CCD Executive Board. It provides the necessary continuity. The new priest will find a parish board of men and women experienced in running "this" parish, with all its peculiarities; thus he is spared the painstaking, and frequently the trial-and-error, method of having to find out for himself.

Every military installation, no matter how large or small, where there are dependents, will have a number of former professional teachers, both men and women. These people often work in one or more of the six facets of the CCD. And there are many others to help them. A mother with a large family can be on a telephone committee, a grandmother can do all sorts of clerical work, shut-ins can be praying members, eager young teen-agers can be Fishers, and retired people can do a number of time-consuming jobs. There is no end to the possibilities when the CCD program is fully presented.

The priest who thinks CCD means only the Sunday morning catechizing of the children who do not attend the local parochial school, will soon find that CCD will help him in many other ways: with his convert classes, the annual religious survey, non-Catholic spouses of Catholics, fallen-aways, sick and needy, and with hospital visits. He will see that in the Apostolate of Good Will he has a place even for the "dreamers" in his parish.

High on the priority list of religious programs should be some form of nocturnal adoration. Grace flows abundantly where men in a parish make the sacrifice to come in the small hours of a cold morning to spend an hour before the Eucharistic Master. Women and children enjoy sharing the daytime hours, and you will be delighted to see the teen-ager respond to the challenge of an hour or less. Local priests or the diocesan office or the National Nocturnal Adoration Society can help you to organize your group.

Beneath your officer's tunic, you will be very Christlike if you visit the hospital and guardhouse from time to time. In both institutions you will find troops whom you might not otherwise meet, especially those in the guardhouse. Those who are sick and those who are in trouble need a priest more than those who are healthy or not in trouble. A special Mass can be arranged for both guardhouse and hospital on a weekday. Many a good soldier comes away spiritually healed from both.

In military hospitals you will find a great deal of generous help. Doctors, nurses, and corpsmen should be formally instructed on the subject of religious care of the sick. This can be arranged through the hospital commander, surgeon, or the chief nurse, who are usually happy to give you some time from their periodic meetings or conferences for such an explanation. It should not have to be said but Communion calls to the sick must never be neglected. A priest, through the healing grace of the sacraments, is a doctor of the soul.

Concerning the guardhouse or stockade, you should keep in close touch with the chaplain assigned; if there is none, then you should inform the officer in charge that you wish to be notified when a Catholic man is confined.

The Second Vatican Council has turned the spotlight on preaching. This aspect of the pastoral life of a chaplain, as with the priest in civilian life, is a most important contact with the souls entrusted to you. Sometimes it is your *only* contact. Sunday sermons can be the most effective mission talks your people will ever hear. As to the quality of your talk, you will be judged severely. Many of your men are in the business of communicating with troops and know when a speech is properly prepared; they will turn away disappointed when it is just a few thoughts gathered out of thin air at the last minute. Others of your congregation have been subjected to many talks — good and bad — and they expect something worthwhile from the chaplain. Work and pray that God will help you make the most of this precious ten to fifteen minutes every Sunday.

On the matter of religious instruction for adults, the field is unlimited. The CCD has discussion groups and the CFM movement grows daily in the military; but the individual chaplain, once again, has to tailor his program to the needs of his particular military parish. In one training installation, for example, religious instruction classes were given on Friday nights, and premarital classes on Sunday afternoons — both with great success, as unlikely as these days and hours might seem. And new chaplains should realize that, in working in a pluralistic society, they cannot use government facilities to proselytize. Their work of spreading the Kingdom of God will depend as much on a prayerful preparation for a new class as on the right location, as much on good teaching as on effective publicity.

On the credit side in heavy black ink the new chaplain will be delighted to discover that he doesn't have to run bingo, manage a fashion show, or conduct a raffle to pay for the heat and light. His socials for the parish will be conducted purely for the social good of his people. A gigantic parish picnic will introduce you to Catholics you never met before; as will the get-together for the altar boys and choirs. Here again, the wise chaplain will delegate most of the work for socials to his laymen for they are eager to help.

Depending on where you are stationed, you may find a retreat house close by. Or you may devise ways and means of getting your people to yearly retreats and to days of recollection. In either case don't overlook them; they have become part of parish life in America and your people have heard about them and expect them. Military personnel, unlike their civilian brothers, can be granted a few days each year, not chargeable as leave, so that they may have this spiritual treat. Also, it is helpful to bring in a team for a Cana Conference; better still organize one of your own at your installation, because you, the doctor, the lawyer, and others who make up the team, are more sensitive to the problems which are peculiarly military.

Another practice, called "Clergy Day" has become an annual feature of the chaplains' program at most installations. In many cases, ministers, priests, and rabbis are invited to the installation for a tour of the facilities, for briefings on the mission of the base, and for good fellowship. Occasionally a Catholic chaplain will have only priests, or sometimes nuns, while the Protestant and Jewish chaplains will have their own clergy for a similar function. Such a practice has many ecumenical advantages and much public relations value.

MISSIONS

Legendary is the word to describe the aid given by American men to mission activities. Only God himself has a computer capable of toting up the funds and counting the tons of good will given by the chaplains and men of the armed forces. Orphanages in the Orient; food, clothing, and medicines in the early post World War II period in Europe; buildings at missions in Alaska; these plus the yearly contribution to the military ordinariate appeal for funds for the various American charities, as well as the response to many personal appeals, all add up to an overwhelming American generosity.

The chaplain has a unique opportunity to guide the charity of his men, and a certain obligation, too, to educate his parishioners about their responsibilities. For the fact is that military men and their dependents do not have to support their military priests and parishes. The U. S. Government pays the chaplain an adequate salary, builds the church and maintains it, assigns clerical help, provides materials for the catechetical program, and gives him an administrative assistant. Everything a priest needs, save vestments and pamphlets, is provided; even these can sometimes be obtained through funds other than those from the Sunday collection. What can the priest do, therefore, to keep alive in the hearts of his military parishioner the obligation stemming from his vocation as a Christian to share his abundance with the less fortunate?

He can do a number of things. If he is overseas, where needs are obvious, he organizes his people and goes to work. He mentions the need in the pulpit on Sunday morning so that those who cannot contribute intelligence or skill, may contribute funds. The chaplain works *with* people and for them. He guides their enthusiasm and their zeal. At stateside installations he channels American generosity into various mission fields. Happily, some chaplains have discovered that when they have a monthly mission collection, their parishioners respond by trebling and quadrupling their ordinary Sunday offering. On these Sundays, he might invite representatives of different missionary orders to speak to his people. Some chaplains have even adopted parishes overseas, a practice which could be adopted in many American parishes, civilian as well as military.

The chaplain is careful also, to train in charity the children of military personnel. Unless they attend Catholic schools they may never hear of the foreign missions. In CCD classes and in sermons to the children, the priest appeals to their zeal and their sense of sacrifice. At Christmas, Thanksgiving, and Easter, especially, he arranges ways or means for them to help others. Such acts of charity and self-sacrifice from parents and children of the military cannot but help bind them to the Mystical Body of Christ.

VOCATIONS

Unlikely though as it might seem to most people, the military has produced more than its share of candidates for the priesthood, the brotherhood, and even to the sisterhood. Bishop Arnold, World War II chief of army chaplains, used to tell with delight his surprise in seeing the nuns at a Florida airbase marching children to the accompaniment of crisp military commands. Interested, he inquired, and discovered that five of the eight nuns were ex-WACS and WAFS and they marched the children regularly during recess from CCD classes. Only God knows how many men and women have heard in their hearts the whisper of a religious vocation while on active duty.

Certainly, the chaplain will have many opportunities to foster and encourage those who are obviously interested in religious life, and he should be alert for overt signs. First of all, he should remember that every unmarried enlisted man or officer who shows a special devotion to Mass and Holy Communion, and to other devotions, may have a vocation. The chaplain must realize that the affability which he enjoys with some of his men may be a boon to a vocation or, on the other hand, it may discourage a vocation. This is true primarily because in no other aspect of the priesthood is the life of the priest such an open book. In the happiness of his holiness, the priest is his best advertisement.

The chaplain who is constantly on the lookout for the signs, mundane and mysterious, of a vocation, can gently but realistically offer the young man greater responsibility in the Catholic program. Among the many ways he may serve are training the Knights of the Altar, teaching other military men to serve Mass, becoming active in the CCD, and helping the priest with religious instruction. Opportunities are limited only by the imagination and zeal of the chaplain and the available time of the young man.

When a young man approaches a chaplain to talk about a vocation, the priest should point out obvious concrete guidelines. Daily Mass when possible, spiritual reading, learning church history, and taking a correspondence course in Latin are among the practices the aspirant to the priesthood or religious life can begin.

Always, the chaplain should keep the ideal of a religious vocation before the eyes of his men and their dependents. He will urge prayer for vocations. He will invite and welcome priests and sisters who request the opportunity to talk on vocations. He will speak on vocations himself. Should the need arise, regulations provide that a young person can leave the service short of the normal tour to enter a seminary or convent.

The step from military life to religious life was an easy one for Ignatius Loyola; so can it be for others: both lives demand dedication, discipline, love, and sometimes self-sacrifice. And a smiling, happy priest best advertises his vocation for others.

COMBAT CHAPLAIN

In these days of brush-fire warfare, of the Korean, Vietnam, and Dominican crises, to say nothing of even more horrible possibilities, the combat chaplain stands tall, for the need for him is great indeed. Many of the things a combat chaplain should know, he can learn only from actual combat, and in actual combat he *must* learn them. But there is a body of experience to guide him.

At this very moment, chaplains are serving our men in the Vietnam war. Whether at isolated outposts or at large base camps, their problems are physical and logistic, social and climatic, and above all, moral and spiritual.

A chaplain entering a combat zone must be well equipped. Indispensable and basic to his needs is a Mass kit. As a matter of utmost practical fact: *never get separated from your Mass kit.* Carry it yourself. Don't leave it in the hands of your assistant or another chaplain. If the climate and terrain are such as to make it difficult to keep the kit clean, then have another Mass kit and alternate them occasionally, sending one back to the rear area, now and then, to be cleaned. If the Mass kit supplied to you is too bulky and heavy, there is nothing in the liturgy to prevent you from improvising. Some chaplains, for example, have used a Mass kit which fits into a musette bag, a lightweight carryall type of bag which is slung over the shoulder. The kit was devised by obtaining a very small chalice, reducing the size of the vestments, and eliminating all but the necessities for saying Mass.

Keep as well supplied with hosts and wine as you can. In tropical climates, preserving hosts may be a major problem for the combat chaplain, since they mildew quickly. To guard against this, hermetically sealed containers can keep them fresh indefinitely. Altar wine also presents a logistical problem; very often it cannot be obtained locally.

Should the priest reserve the Blessed Sacrament in combat zones? Some chaplains have been liberal in doing so and others are very conservative. Some chaplains carry a number of consecrated Hosts with them at all times, while others have kept the Blessed Sacrament in their Mass kits. Some chaplains prefer not to run the risk of either losing the Sacred Host or of its desecration; consequently, they give Communion only at Mass. Not reserving the Blessed Sacrament and offering the Holy Sacrifice more frequently may be a safe solution. With the liberal laws concerning bination on week days and trination on Sundays, a chaplain could easily offer as many as fifteen Masses in a week and thus bring Holy Communion to a great number of men, even if they are scattered over a wide area.

The entire question of Holy Communion, reservation of the Blessed Sacrament, the Eucharistic fast, and the principles of administration of the sacraments in general should be carefully reviewed occasionally by the combat chaplain. Too strict an interpretation of law will deprive men of the sacrament when they most need God's help, while too free an interpretation may result in serious abuses. Nevertheless, "the sacraments are for men," and if a mistake has to be made, perhaps it is better to make it on the side of leniency.

Another very important practice, which because of various interpretations has caused confusion to the chaplain newly arrived in a combat zone, is that of general absolution. Some chaplains have never made use of it; others have seemed to use it too frequently and then in circumstances where its use might be questioned. Although of great value at times, it is a practice which should be sparingly used, carefully explained to the penitents at all times, and frequently reviewed to ascertain whether it is still justified. The danger is always this: such a practice can be justified in certain circumstances and at given times, but later when the circumstances change, the practice persists because it has almost become a custom or a habit.

Under combat conditions, the chaplain should announce — and this should be done carefully and clearly *each time it is done* so as to avoid any misunderstanding — under present conditions he is giving general absolution to all who are properly disposed to receive it. The absolution is valid for all who are truly sorry for all grave sins and determined to avoid sin and its occasion in the future, and on condition that they *will* confess any grave sins not previously confessed as soon as they can *conveniently* do so.

The wise chaplain has found it helpful to announce publicly that if there are any men not accustomed to confessing in English, he will help them make a valid confession. He should urge them not to stay away from confession for this or any other reason. A timid or reluctant Spanish-speaking, Polish-speaking, or Italian-speaking soldier, sailor, or airman could easily be encouraged to confess by such an announcement. A fine Polish-American boy, for example, went through several years of World War II and months of combat without the sacraments, because he thought he could never confess or say his prayers in English, even though he spoke it as well as the next man. Such myths must be dispelled, and soon.

For confessions in foreign languages, new chaplains should know that polyglot confession cards are available. Though hearing a confession by means of an interpreter is rare, the procedure is quite safe and simple. The interpreter stands in a corner of the room with his back to the confessor and penitent. Through the interpreter the confessor asks the penitent to indicate whether or not he is guilty of a specific sin by a position or negative shake of his head, and if guilty to indicate the number of times with his fingers. Since the interpreter cannot see or hear the penitent, the seal of confession is safeguarded. It would be most unusual for a chaplain to be required to hear confession in such a manner but the possibility is interesting and the difficulty can be overcome.

Mass, communion, and confession: these are the spiritual sustenance that the combat chaplain offers the soldier in combat. If Christ through his death gave life to the world, then the priest, through the Mass, can give life everlasting to a soldier in combat.

CONCLUSION

The military chaplaincy offers a priest an exciting and fruitful life. Not since Constantine removed the eagles from the shields of his soldiers and replaced them with crosses has a civil government so encouraged and aided the practice of religion as does the American military establishment. In addition to all the things he needs to carry on his work, the chaplain has enviable status. Forged in the tragedies of World Wars I and II, gloriously tempered in the Korean Conflict and in the present engagement in Vietnam, the sword of honor and respect which the military chaplaincy enjoys in all branches of the service seems guaranteed for long service. When a young priest either answers the invitation of his religious superior or offers his services as a chaplain, he becomes part of a proud and grand tradition.

He joins a team, a band of brothers, even a fraternity of heroes, a group of real men devout and loyal to the Church, led by the late Father Joseph T. O'Callahan, S.J., the first chaplain to be awarded the Congressional

Medal of Honor, whom his commander called: "The bravest man I ever saw." A steady parade of decorated chaplains from many battles marches through the official histories of all branches of the service.

At present, 925 commissioned chaplains care for the spiritual needs of over two million servicemen and their families. Of these chaplains, 76 currently serve the war effort in Vietnam. Under the spiritual guidance of Francis Cardinal Spellman, Military Vicar, with headquarters in New York City, this group of priests is comprised of men from most of the dioceses and religious orders in America.

The satisfaction in the chaplaincy is great. The "Hi, Father" which so often accompanies a smart salute thrills new and veteran chaplain alike. The easy camaraderie one feels upon entering active duty continues long afterward. Only God knows the exact number of converts and marriages validated, as well as men brought back to him, because of the close contact enjoyed by priests with their men in service. To a priest, these are more than statistics; these are the joys of his daily life. The close association with chaplains and men of other faiths has proved a broadening influence with many ecumenical results. Indeed, the respect and love which a priest has enjoyed in his home parish can continue and grow with his service parishes.

As in the vineyard where the work is great and the laborers few, so in the service the need for chaplains is great. Young laymen march off from home, church, and community to a larger world. Most of them have good moral training. In the service they meet other fine young men, but they also meet those others who are morally bankrupt. In the military as in civil life, the good get better, the bad get worse, and the ones in between react to those they meet first. A chaplain can steer these latter in the right direction and help them when they meet the wrong people. He is not only their spiritual father, but becomes their father-away-from-home as well. Especially is this true in the first few months of service before the recruit finds his place in the community. Therefore, the young soldier needs to be sure that the chaplain is available, ready and willing and able to listen to his problems and to help him in their solutions.

The military service also offers many benefits, especially to one who enjoys travel. Assignments can send a chaplain across the nation and around the world. In his travels he can meet and become friendly with priests of different cultures and racial backgrounds from all parts of the world.

The chaplaincy, then, is a vocation within a vocation. It is a call to the service of country within the call to the service of God. Thousands of men have answered that call. Of the thousands who have served their country as chaplains, hundreds have been killed in action, or wounded. In World War II 1,178 chaplains received 2,453 decoration; in the Korean Conflict, 567 earned 683. This is commitment of the noblest kind.

In their article, "The Vocation of Arms," Major Paul L. Briand, Jr. and Captain Malham M. Wakin have said: "The man who voluntarily puts on the . . . uniform of the service, implicitly, if not explicitly, commits himself to the principal view that there are some values in life worth more than life itself. There *is* something worth the risk of life. That something is the way life is lived."[5] Certainly the chaplain implicitly *and* explicitly holds to the same belief. As an ally of Christ, the chaplain-priest is allied to that kind of soldier; and he is willing like him to pay, if necessary, the price of death so that others may live.

Clearly, therefore, the vocation of arms requires the same kind of dedication, courage, and selflessness as the religious vocation. Pursued together, they can give a depth and breadth to a priest's life he could never attain anywhere else. It is a life eminently worth living.

---

[5] *Air Force Magazine,* July, 1963, pp. 41–43 ff.

29

The Catholic Correctional Chaplain

JOHN J. FREEMAN

All men are called to belong to the new people of God. Wherefore this people, while remaining one and only one, is to be spread throughout the whole world and must exist in all ages, so that the decree of God's will may be fulfilled. In the beginning God made human nature one and decreed that all His children, scattered as they were, would finally be gathered together as one. It was for this purpose that God sent His Son, whom He appointed heir of all things, that He might be teacher, king and priest of all, the head of the new and universal people of the sons of God. For this too God sent the Spirit of His Son as Lord and Life-giver. He it is who brings together the whole Church and each and every one of those who believe, and who is the well-spring of their unity in the teaching of the apostles and in fellowship, in the breaking of bread and in prayers (*De Ecclesia,* November 21, 1964).

This quotation taken from the *Constitution on the Church* reflects the spirit of its Founder, Jesus Christ, who commissioned his Apostles and their successors to instruct all men regardless of race, color, or condition of life, in the truths of the Catholic Church. This commission includes our incarcerated brethren —- the thousands of men and women, boys and girls — who are now locked behind prison walls in punishment for their crimes. It is therefore, the duty of the Church, as part of her mission in the modern world, to bring to these miserable souls the Good News of Salvation and the benefits of the sacraments. It is her duty to send her priests behind the prison walls to labor for the salvation of souls.

THE CORRECTIONAL CHAPLAINCY

It is only within recent years that the pastoral ministry has been extended to our correctional institutions. Prior to the end of the nineteenth century, prisoners were almost completely deprived of the ministrations of the clergy, and even when the idea won acceptance the prison chaplain was required to perform many other duties besides those of ministering to the spiritual needs of the inmates. Frequently, because of their superior education, chaplains were assigned to many secular duties, such as teaching, acting as librarian, or supervising recreational activities. As a consequence, the chaplain had to find time in between his other duties to carry out the responsibilities of his apostolate. However, the priests of these days were zealous men, and, therefore, they were willing to make almost any sacrifice to labor for the salvation of their unfortunate flock.

OLDER CONCEPTS OF PENOLOGY

The theories of penology of the previous century were almost entirely punitive in character. Those who were responsible for the operation of our correctional institutions were convinced that prisons must be dark, uncomfortable places where inmates would be made constantly aware of their guilt and of the vindictive punishment they must receive. The very institution itself was designed for punishment. It was a dismal place and surrounded the prisoner with specters of impending doom which overwhelmed him with horror and remorse. In almost all of our prisons the cells were small, dark, airless cubicles having only one small window some eight or nine feet above the floor. From these cells the prisoners never had a view of the outside. Some prisons were even worse, for they included "jugcells," small cubicles dug in the ground with only a small opening at the top large enough to allow a prisoner to enter. Even the meager accommodations in the cell contributed to the prisoner's discomfort. The bucket, which was used for natural functions, remained in the cell throughout the entire day, and was emptied only once in every twenty-four hours.

Unfortunately, the professional penologists of the nineteenth century were so imbued with the idea that law offenders must be severely punished for their crimes, that they seldom if ever thought of the harmful effects of the kind of treatment they were meting out. As a result of this kind of thinking, our prisons returned to society living corpses broken in spirit and body. In this condition, they were, for the most part, unable to take their place in society and make a worthwhile contribution to it. Instead, they became an added burden to society, often reverting to the very crimes that had resulted in their imprisonment. Even in the light of the many advances that have been made in the science of penology in recent years, some few career men still favor these older theories.

According to journals in the field of correctional work, it was toward the end of the last century when a clergyman from the eastern part of the country was finally able to persuade a warden to allow him to conduct a religious service for the inmates. Though the warden granted the clergyman's request, it was only after due preparations had been made that the services were held. These preparations included extreme measures of security and isolation. In the room that was to be used for the services, the warden ordered that a cannon pointed at the inmate congregation be mounted next to the pulpit, and that a guard be stationed nearby with a lighted torch, ready to fire it in case of disturbance. Furthermore, each seat in the "chapel" was equipped with blinds so that each inmate was isolated from all the other members of the congregation. Needless to say, the religious services were conducted without a single incident.

In recent times, things have changed considerably in our correctional institutions. Modern theories of penology tend toward rehabilitation rather than punishment. The modern prison exists to provide the criminal with the education and training necessary to make him a useful member of society who can find his rightful place in the world after he has served his sentence. Throughout the length and breadth of our land, the "medieval approach," which was so popular only a few decades ago, is rapidly disappearing. Today, those in charge of our correctional institutions have developed a more Christian and humane approach to the problem, which is certainly in accord with the advances of modern civilization. It is in this modern and encouraging atmosphere that the office of the correctional chaplain was born.

NEW THEORIES OF PENOLOGY

Modern penology concentrates on the rehabilitation of the lawbreaker. It aims at correcting those aspects of the prisoner's behavior which are offensive to society and contrary to the laws of God and man. Penology also strives to instill in the residents of the correctional institution those basic principles essential if he is to become a useful and productive member of society. Even new prison terminology more in conformity with the aims of modern penological theories has been adopted. In recent years, the term "prison" has been disregarded in favor of the new and more meaningful term, "correctional institution." The prison chaplain of yesteryear exists no more. He is now referred to as "the correctional chaplain attached to a correctional institution." The word "guard" too, with all of its punitive implications, has been replaced by the term, "custodial officer." Needless to say, this is certainly more in keeping with his duties and responsibilities, since his office is to detain in a society that detains. Even the prisoners themselves are no longer referred to as inmates, but rather as "residents." Now, the prison inmate is a "resident of a correctional institution." As in the past, these terms are no longer mere names but rather they are descriptive, for they explain the aims of our modern institutions, pointing out that these institutions exist to correct the reprehensible behavior of those detained, while maintaining the human dignity of the person, who is, after all, a creature made to the image and likeness of God.

THE CORRECTIONAL CHAPLAIN

When a priest is first assigned to a correctional institution, his first impression may be one of dismay and confusion. Everything about his new assignment is unfamiliar. Now, to carry out his ministry effectively, he must be willing to labor within the framework of the institution. This means, of course, that his sphere of activities is considerably limited and circumscribed by the restricted setting of the correctional institution. This includes as well the permissive facilities of the institution.

This latter point — operating within the permissive facilities of the institution — is of extreme importance. In fact, the success of his apostolate is directly proportionate to his willingness to recognize that he now has two superiors, his ecclesiastical superior, the bishop, and his secular superior, the warden. A successful chaplain cannot operate independently of either the one or the other. Needless to say, the environment of an institution of detention is far different from that of the average parish. It is, therefore, important that the correctional chaplain recognize this fact, and be willing to accept and familiarize himself with the differences. To do this, he must realize that his new field of pastoral activity must be carried out within the limits of a restricted society, and that this necessarily places restrictions on his pastoral activities. It also means that he must abandon "parochial" approaches in favor of new methods more suited to his surroundings.

In an address to the general assembly at the Congress of Correction, Portland, Oregon, His Excellency, Bishop Andrew G. Grutka, D.D., Episcopal Adviser to the Catholic Correctional Chaplains,[1] illustrates the point when he said:

> A Catholic Chaplain in a correctional institution must be first, last and always a priest. The life of a Chaplain in a correctional institution is perhaps the most difficult of all lives in the Church. His life has to be lived amidst all the difficulties, frustrations and despairs prevalent in these institutions and very much in striking contrast to the high holiness to which a priest is called in the eminent sanctity of the office which he fulfills.

At the conclusion of his address, the bishop also reminded the chaplains of the purpose of their assignment:

---

[1] In the annual meeting of Bishops in fall of 1965 the Most Reverend Leo T. Maher, D.D., Bishop of Santa Rosa, Calif., was appointed to succeed Bishop Grutka as Episcopal Advisor to the Catholic Correctional Chaplains. His term of office began January 1, 1966.

The Church, like Christ Himself, is primarily interested in the salvation of men's souls. The Chaplain in fulfilling the expectations of the Church must, as St. Paul puts it, become "all things to all men." He must therefore be familiar with the overall work in the correctional institution and be as much a source of edification to the executive, administrative, treatment, and security personnel, as to the residents. His faith must be strong enough to strengthen the weakest in belief, his hope radiant enough to resurrect the hopeless, and his charity bright enough to dispel the gloom of disappointment, depression, and sorrow, and reveal a vision of divine beauty. Finally, his holiness must be joyful and saintly enough to leave behind a fragrance unmistakably heavenly. The Church considers the Chaplain as a spiritual leader completely devoid of all stage effects. Dedication and not external signs best define and describe him.

On another occasion in an address to the Catholic Chaplains, Bishop Grutka came directly to the crux of the matter when he declared that "The Church does not need an amateur psychologist, an amateur psychiatrist in the person of her Chaplain in a correctional institution. The Church needs a good priest as do the residents in the institution." No truer words were ever spoken regarding the duties and responsibilities of the chaplain of a correctional institution.

THE AMERICAN CATHOLIC CORRECTIONAL CHAPLAIN'S ASSOCIATION

Prior to 1951, many chaplains felt that they were merely tolerated in our state and federal correctional institutions. They felt that the government permitted chaplains in its institutions only as a means of providing the free exercise of religion as guaranteed by the Constitution, and because it believed that chaplains might be useful in the rehabilitation of the residents. In those years, the office of chaplain did not receive the recognition required for the proper care of souls.

In 1951, in an effort to solve these problems, a group of experienced chaplains met during the Congress of Corrections in Atlantic City, New Jersey, and formed the American Catholic Correctional Chaplains' Association. Its first task was to seek affiliation with the American Correctional Association, the parent body, and to obtain the approval of the American hierarchy. The new organization was quickly affiliated with the parent group, and episcopal approval soon followed; it was placed under the auspices of the Social Action Department of the National Catholic Welfare Conference in Washington, D. C. The Most Rev. Martin McNamara, D.D., Bishop of Joliet, Illinois, was named as its first adviser.

The organization quickly set to work to improve the situation of the correctional chaplain. One of its first activities was the publication of a directory listing all Catholic correction chaplains and the institutions to which they had been assigned. The Association Secretariat also published a newsletter for distribution to correctional chaplains. This organization quickly won the support of all priests engaged in correctional work, for they realized the many advantages that a group such as this could offer. Now, the office of chaplain would take on greater meaning in the eyes of penologists, the opportunities for increasing the spiritual programs would be more numerous.

After these initial efforts, and as the organization began to expand, the group divided the country into regions and a chaplain was appointed vice-president in each region. As a result of this action, five regions were established. Within a short time after these divisions were made, the organization decided to publish a *Manual of Directives* for use of Catholic chaplains. The manual was published in 1955, and soon won the whole-hearted approval of both federal and state correctional officials, and has proven to be of great value in clarifying the duties of a Catholic correctional chaplain.

On June 22, 1952, an indult of the Sacred Congregation of Rites permitted the Solemn Votive Mass of the Good Thief on the second Sunday of October in all correctional institutions of the United States. The celebration of the Feast of St. Dismas has been an inspiration to many residents, and a ray of hope to many who are despondent. This feast day has also occasioned a greater reception of the sacraments in correctional institutions.

In recent years, special faculties have been obtained for all Catholic chaplains, and the organization has drawn up a constitution and by-laws to govern its activities. The manual, first published in 1955 has been revised and retitled. It is now called *Orientation Guidelines for the Use of the Catholic Correctional Chaplain*. As this chapter is being written, nearly 500 priests are engaged in correctional work.

WORKSHOPS FOR CATHOLIC CORRECTIONAL CHAPLAINS

Each year, the five regions offer workshops for correctional chaplains. These workshops are designed to afford the correctional chaplain the opportunity to keep abreast of recent developments in penology. Through an exchange of ideas and the opportunity to participate in discussions and policy-making decisions, the chaplain shares his many unique experiences with others, and profits from the experiences of others. Furthermore, all members of the association are encouraged to attend the week-long Congress of Correction which is held in different parts of the country each year. The congress is sponsored by the parent body, the American Correctional Association. This congress is attended by federal and state wardens of correctional institutions throughout the United States, state directors of correction, federal and state parole officers, members of the various professions on institutional staffs, chaplains representing all three major faiths, and other persons who are interested in correctional work. The National Catholic Correctional Chaplains' Association also holds its national meeting at this time.

Membership in the Catholic Chaplains' Correctional Association requires that a priest take an active part in the various programs and activities of the association. To become a certified member of the association, a chaplain must attend at least one regional or national meeting annually. If this organization is to achieve its purpose of promoting professional growth and increased proficiency in the chaplaincy, and if it is to continue to receive federal and state recognition for its members, the organization must include among its members only those men who are willing to be active in the association and in the American Correctional Association.

APPOINTMENT TO A CHAPLAINCY IN A CORRECTIONAL INSTITUTION

Catholic priests are appointed to chaplaincies in correctional institutions either by their Ordinary or their religious superiors. Upon receiving his appointment, a priest should present himself to the warden of the institution to which he has been appointed. After examining his qualifications, the institutional authorities will then arrange for final approval of his appointment by the State Department of Corrections. Once he has received final approval from the state, the new chaplain should contact the American Catholic Correctional Chaplains' Association and enroll in an orientation program which leads to certification. This program is designed to familiarize the new chaplain with every phase of his work in a correctional institution. Under the supervision of a certified instructor, the new chaplain spends two weeks with the head of each of the institution's facilities so that he may acquire a thorough knowledge of institutional procedures. After he has completed this phase of the program the trainee spends the third week familiarizing himself with the role of the Catholic chaplain in an institutional setting, and observes or conducts, under supervision, the religious or educational activities that will later be assigned to him. These usually include Mass and homily, the administration of the sacraments, religious-instruction classes, etc. During the fourth and final week of the program, the fledgling chaplain, still under supervision, conducts interviews with the residents. During the final two weeks of his training, the chaplain must also visit other correctional institutions and report to his instructor concerning the value of these trips. At the conclusion of this training period, the new chaplain is evaluated on the basis of written examinations on the areas covered during the training period. Certification follows the successful completion of these examinations. Aside from his training for the priesthood, the Chaplains' Association has established certain qualifications that are essential for institutional work. Along with the usual physical, mental, and spiritual qualifications, the Catholic Chaplains' Association requires that those assigned to this apostolate have an aptitude for the special duties of correctional institutional work. The association suggests that only those men be chosen for this apostolate who possess to a high degree such qualities as patience, firmness, emotional stability, an agreeable and approachable personality, good judgment, initiative, and zeal.

ROLE OF THE CATHOLIC CORRECTIONAL CHAPLAIN

Priests are assigned to correctional institutions for the sacramental ministry. This role is defined in the *Orientation Guidelines* published by the American Catholic Correctional Chaplains' Association, and in the *Manual of Correctional Standards* published by the American Correctional Association. Therefore, the basic duties of any clergyman of any faith in a correctional institution is recognized by both the Church and the state as the sacramental ministry. For the Catholic correctional chaplain, this includes the offering of the Holy Sacrifice of the Mass on Sundays, and if permissible, on Holy Days of Obligation, Holy Communion, and frequent opportunity for the confessions of the residents. Moreover, it includes any other religious services such as the Stations of the Cross, Benediction of the Blessed Sacrament, Novenas, Bible Vigil, etc., and any other religious functions the chaplain may deem necessary for the spiritual growth of the residents. In scheduling such functions, however, attention must be given to other programs in the institution and care should be exercised that no conflicts of programs occur. The chaplain must remember that in a correctional setting all institutional programs are important, and that to institutional administrators all programs have the same value in the process of rehabilitation. In their view, no single program, religious or otherwise, will rehabilitate the resident, but all institutional programs are equally essential for rehabilitation. Thus, as mentioned previously, in a correctional setting the chaplain must frequently improvise, and learn to curtail and arrange his religious program to fit the framework of the institution.

In a correctional institution, preparation and consideration must be given to the sacraments of baptism and confirmation. Regular visits to the institution hospital will keep the chaplain informed of the spiritual needs in that area. Anointing of the sick is not to be overlooked.

One area in particular requires the chaplain's closest attention. This is Death Row where eternity hangs in the balance and seems so close to the resident. Here the Chaplain should make provision for the Sacrifice of the Mass whenever possible, and for frequent reception of the sacraments, always keeping in mind that *sacramentum propter hominem* may well apply to non-Catholics.

A case in point is that of the late Fr. Thomas J. Donovan, who, while he was chaplain at Sing Sing Prison, in Ossining, New York, once confided to this writer that as soon as a condemned man had been transferred to Death Row, he would devote an average of two hours a day to him, bringing him the consolation of the Church and the friendship of the Catholic priest during the most lonely hours of his last days on earth. Frequent visits to the condemned residents can become most fruitful. On the occasion of his death, the *Catholic News* of New York reported that Father Donovan had brought the sacraments of the Church to some fifty-four condemned residents in the hours before their deaths and had assisted them at the time of their execution. So thoroughly convinced of the sincerity of their Dismas' conversions was Father Donovan that he would say somewhat complacently: "I have many friends waiting for me up there." No doubt, there was a happy reunion "up there" when Father passed to his eternal reward a few years ago. Truly, as our episcopal adviser, Bishop Grutka, observed, the Catholic chaplain is the spiritual leader of his flock in the correctional institution.

THE CORRECTIONAL CHAPLAIN AS TEACHER

Teaching is one of the most important functions of the pastor of souls. In a correctional institution the chaplain will reach his greatest audience at Sunday Mass. Consequently, his homily, though it must be brief, must be to the point and meaningful. The residents do not expect their chaplain to come down to the level of prison jargon. They expect respectability from their chaplain. Institutional slang during the Sunday homily would be offensive to the residents. Moreover, it is advisable to confine sermons to dogmatic rather than moral themes in a correctional setting. Berating the residents for their flagrant disobedience to God's law will produce disastrous results in a correctional institution whereas the doctrinal theme will in time produce the desired moral reform. The chaplain should use every occasion to preach the Good News of Salvation. The Sunday homily should never be omitted. A short homily on the liturgy of the day is always appropriate and would at least certainly satisfy the obligation to teach on this important occasion. The new liturgy has been well received by the residents of our correctional institutions. They are impressed by it and take an active part in the Eucharistic celebrations; this includes the singing of hymns. Every effort should be made to carry out the liturgy as it is done in the average parish church.

GIVING RELIGIOUS INSTRUCTION

The correctional institution is a mixed society which includes a few illiterate residents, some of average intelligence and education, and still others who are quite gifted. Only a very few have a clear knowledge of God and of their purpose in life. In fact, a Protestant chaplain once complained that his Bible class was composed of the rejects of the churches on the outside. "They come to us with very little knowledge of God if any at all," he said.

Religious instruction classes, therefore, are a most important phase of the religious program. The new chaplain will soon realize that to be of greater service to the residents, he must give instruction on at least three levels. First, he must schedule an inquiry class for those residents interested in investigating the claims of the Catholic Church. Second, he must hold an advanced class for those Catholic residents who wish to review Catholic doctrines. And third, he will organize discussion groups similar to those offered by the Confraternity of Christian Doctrine. Finally, the correctional chaplain must be prepared to use all the modern teaching aids, including visual aids, tape recorder, records, library materials, etc. He should also distribute Catholic newspapers and periodicals to the residents after each Sunday Mass.

The Correctional Chaplain Is a Friend

Loneliness is one of the most serious problems for the resident of a correctional institution. He has lost his freedom; he feels rejected by society and by members of his family. He is alone. In these difficult times, he turns to his chaplain, for he sees him as a friend whom he can trust. For him, the chaplain is a friend who will not reject him, but rather accept him on his own merits. This acceptance of the chaplain as a friend frequently starts for the new resident when he meets the chaplain for the first time at the initial interview held during the resident's orientation period.

This initial interview is held as soon as possible after the arrival of the resident. Mutual impressions obtained during this procedure are of the utmost importance to both chaplain and resident. Their relationship will depend on this initial interview. The basic purpose of this interview is to meet the resident personally, obtain his religious history and to inform him of the religious program sponsored by the chaplain, and to encourage him to participate actively. During this interview, all formalities must disappear and a friendly and warm atmosphere must permeate this initial meeting. The genuine interest which the chaplain shows in the new resident's situation during this initial interview will, for the most part, determine the future relationship of the chaplain and the resident. Dr. James V. Bennett, former Director of the Federal Bureau of Prisons, illustrates the function of the chaplain in these words: "Frequently, the chaplain is the one official who can establish a personal contact based on understanding and good will. He has no product to manufacture, no marks or grades to give, no demerits to assess, no pills to offer; his sole object is the spiritual welfare of the new resident. In an organized religious program, this relationship is based on the understanding engendered in the initial interview."

HANDLING REQUESTED INTERVIEWS

The chaplain, in the words of St. Paul, is "all things to all men." As the most trusted member of the institutional staff, the chaplain will be approached by the residents of all faiths to discuss every conceivable problem affecting life in the institution, the lives of their loved ones at home, domestic problems, etc. In such interviews, the chaplain will always exercise prudence, especially in regard to secular matters. If, in his prudent judgment, the problem should be referred to another agency, he will do so. However, he should never refer a problem to another agency unless he first informs the resident of his actions. In all of his work with the residents, the chaplain must always work within the framework of institutional policy, and never allow himself to become emotionally involved with a client. Even in those instances where the chaplain can do little to help the resident solve his problem, he should always be willing to extend the hand of friendship and be an interested listener.

THE CHAPLAIN AS COUNSELOR AND SPIRITUAL DIRECTOR

In most instances, it is desirable that counseling be done by a qualified layman, and that spiritual direction be given by the priest. However, in the correctional situation, this is seldom possible, for both counseling and spiritual direction become the functions of the chaplain. Frequently, these two closely related functions overlap to such a degree that it is sometimes difficult for the chaplain to see where direction begins and counseling ends.

The experienced chaplain continually tries to keep the unique goals of each in mind, realizing that whereas counseling is a natural function employing natural means to achieve its end, namely the maximum growth or actualization of the individual, spiritual direction is essentially directed toward the supernatural, that is, spiritual growth and maturity. However, even when these points are kept in mind, the role of the priest as counselor and spiritual director can become a complex one. The chaplain's success depends largely on his knowledge, science and skill, and on the amount of patience he is willing to exercise. It is important for the chaplain to keep in mind that rejection of the resident at this point for any reason whatsoever will jeopardize his chance of ever reaching him. Obviously, this area is a rather sensitive one. For this reason, correctional chaplains are urged to read the latest works on counseling and to obtain specialized training in these fields whenever possible. Each summer, Catholic colleges and universities throughout the country offer institutes and workshops in the field of pastoral counseling.

One last but important observation. Once the resident has opened up to the chaplain in counseling, he may become dependent on the counselor. Therefore, it is important to remember that the chaplain accepts the person but not the burdens. It is perfectly good psychology and, as well as good Christian charity, for the chaplain to help the resident solve his problems, and aid him to shoulder his own cross, but not his duty to carry it for him.

OTHER DUTIES OF THE CORRECTIONAL CHAPLAIN

There are many other areas in a correctional institution in which the chaplain will come in contact and cooperate with institutional authorities in order to serve his parishioners more effectively. Though these are secondary functions of the chaplain, they do have a bearing on his work. The religious program alone will not rehabilitate a resident. To do his work, a chaplain will need the cooperation of both the professional and the institutional services. It is important for him to remember that only the resident who has achieved some degree of adjustment with appropriate emotional stability and is willing to accept assistance on the road to rehabilitation, can be helped. A resident who is disgruntled, whose personality clashes with his superiors and perhaps with the other residents, is hardly a fit subject for rehabilitation. Emotional blocks will have to be removed first. The continued good will and cooperation of the chaplain in all areas of the institution is a vital ingredient for the rehabilitation of the resident.

The chaplain should be aware of the various custodial problems and always conduct his religious program according to institutional policy and with the proper permission. The Treatment area in a correctional institution comprises many other subdivisions, including that for the classification of residents, which is the most important. It is important for the chaplain to familiarize himself thoroughly with the various areas and to cultivate good relations in them so that his referrals may be more quickly expedited and the residents encouraged by his efforts on their behalf. The chaplain should also be informed about the work schedule of the residents, the ways in which he can effectively cooperate with the parole board, the clemency board, and other interested agencies; his responsibility to the institution's administration, his right to access to institution records, and the institution's regulations with regard to the residents' mail, etc. In short, to be effective, the chaplain must be familiar not only with his own area of religious programming, but also with all the other activities both inside and outside the institution. The chaplain will receive much of this information during his orientation period prior to being certified by the Chaplains' Association.

AREAS OUTSIDE THE CORRECTIONAL INSTITUTION

There are areas outside the institution where the chaplain will want to maintain good relations. For one thing, he should inform his ecclesiastical superior of his activities, of the time spent in the institution, the extent of his religious program, etc. He will also want to associate with the pastor of the parish in which the institution is located and be careful not to infringe upon parochial rights, although in nearly all cases, the chaplain in a correctional institution is given parochial rights. A true spirit of friendship and cooperation should exist between pastor and chaplain. Needless to say, this relationship could become a delicate matter if not handled in a priestly and thoughtful manner. The chaplain will come in contact with many professions and organizations outside the institution, such as Alcoholics Anonymous, social workers, family counselors, etc. In his relationships with these groups, he must keep in mind that involvement in these outside fields may be time consuming and that he will do well to assist only when his efforts contribute to his primary responsibilities as chaplain.

The Chaplain and the Families of the Residents

Because of his position in the institution, the Catholic chaplain will frequently be contacted by the families of the residents. An anxious mother, or a wife residing in a distant city will often consult the chaplain by mail in an attempt to allay her anxieties, on any number of things. For example, the resident may have been delinquent in corresponding with his loved ones, or may be far too brief in his letters. In such cases, the chaplain will communicate promptly with the relatives, reassuring them, correcting any possible misconceptions concerning correctional treatment, and emphasizing in particular the religious program which is made available to all residents. Many families are unfamiliar with the Church behind the correctional walls. The chaplain should list the services afforded residents: Sunday Mass, opportunities for the reception of the sacraments, instruction classes, etc. He will point out that because of the difficulties in adjusting to the life in a correctional institution, regular correspondence with the resident becomes more meaningful and visits, if at all possible, will assist him in maintaining his morale under these conditions. The chaplain should be careful not to offend the family by mentioning certain character weaknesses of the resident, for it is hoped that these difficulties will be corrected in time. It is wise to inform the resident that the family wrote to the chaplain. The resident will appreciate this interest, be reminded that he is still wanted in the family circle, and be moved to greater achievement in his spiritual life.

The World Outside

Man was created by God to attain his final destiny — eternal life. Social institutions were established to assist him in reaching this goal. Like other institutions, the correctional institution is also a real society providing all the services of society in assisting its residents to attain their final destiny — eternal life. While this correctional society affords all the advantages of a regular society on the outside, it has an additional duty; it must detain. It then becomes the duty of the custodial officers to impose detention on the residents and to provide the proper amount of security demanded in this area.

The residents are acutely aware of this aspect of their society which adds greatly to their anxiety of mind. Confinement, enforced celibacy, regimentation, lack of privacy, and constant supervision, along with numerous other aggravations which crop up in a restricted society, are the cause of pressure in the life of a resident. The chaplain will always be mindful of these difficulties in his relationship with the residents. He will endeavor to understand how vitally significant freedom becomes to a person who suffers its loss and will make allowance for this in his dealings with the residents. Along with the problems mentioned above, the resident also experiences a sense of guilt at one time or another. The notion, so often publicized, that all criminals continually insist that they are innocent is not true. In fact, quite the opposite is true, for most residents do experience feelings of guilt. This guilt complex may come either at an early stage of their incarceration, or at some later date. But, it will come. It usually begins with the realization of a sense of shame: the shame a person brings down upon himself by committing a crime, or the shame that one brings to one's family. The difficulties little Joey experiences with his classmates in and out of school, because his dad is a "con"; the unkind remarks heard in the market where his wife goes shopping; the many uncharitable acts the family suffers from its neighbors, because one of its members is behind bars; all of these embarassing situations and many more torture the minds and souls of the residents, and as a consequence, they develop a keen sense of shame.

Contrition will soon follow shame, especially when the resident discovers that the laws of society are based on the Ten Commandments and that to forge a check or to steal a car is an offense not only against the laws of society but also against the commandment of God. As the resident progresses in his religious program, and gives more time to serious thought, he becomes increasingly aware of his immoral conduct. Through the grace of God shame and contrition follow in regular pattern, sooner or later.

Therefore, the chaplain, mindful of his role as a spiritual leader, teacher, and friend, will always carefully weigh the difficult problems of incarcerated life in his relationship with the residents.

Pope Paul VI sums up the working of grace in the souls of correctional residents in these encouraging words:

"I want to say everything and conclude with one single word: I would instill in your hearts the capacity for good thoughts, of right thinking, yes, of joyful thinking. There is a word which encompasses everything in religious and Christian language: it is a current word even in profane language, but here it acquires a beauty and a force full of sunshine: it is the word hope.

Keep it in your hearts, beloved sons. *I would say there is one sin only that you can commit here: despair.* Remove from your soul this chain, this real imprisonment, and allow instead your heart to expand and to find again, even in this construction which deprives you of physical, exterior liberty, the liberty of expanding in hope. I open to you the skies of this hope, which are those of your reinstated dignity, of this reinstated humanity of yours, of this future of yours which is not closed off, of this elevation of yours to the higher destiny to which Christ calls and leads you.

Learn at this hard school of Regina Coeli, to hope in the name of Christ. And let my eyes, my soul, while I look at you, beloved sons, extended to the beholding, I would say to the panorama, of all the prisons in the world, and, let me send from this place, from the altar of the Lord, this greeting of affection and invitation to christian hope to all those who suffer and to all those who are capable of listening to the echo of my voice. It is the voice of Christ, which urges them to be good, to begin again, to resume life, to rise again, my sons, to hope. Amen (Conclusion of sermon delivered by Pope Paul VI to residents of Regina Coeli Prison, Rome).

30

What Is Pastoral Theology?

Eugene J. Weitzel, C.S.V.

SINCE THIS BOOK IS INTENDED TO BE A VERY PRACTICAL BOOK — SOME might even classify it as a practical manual of pastoral theology — for aiding seminarians and priests to acquire a basic knowledge about the pastoral ministry and the various apostolates, all the chapters up to this point have, for the most part, avoided theory and have dealt with those practical matters which will make the pastoral ministry more fruitful. In fact, in inviting the various priest and lay experts to contribute to this book, I specifically asked each of them to consider the following question when outlining his chapter: "If you were invited to speak to a group of seminarians or priests regarding the stituations and problems they will encounter in that phase of the pastoral ministry or the apostolate in which you are regarded as a specialist, what would you want to tell them?" However, since few will deny that effective practice is the result of sound theory, it seems appropriate, as this book draws to a close, to include at least one theoretical or speculative chapter.

However, there is another reason for attempting at this point to answer the question: "What is pastoral theology?" Though this book has been written and edited as much for priests as for seminarians, it may well be that some seminaries and professors of pastoral theology may choose to use it as a classroom text. If this be so, it would seem that a chapter on the nature and function of both traditional and contemporary pastoral theology would be most valuable for professors and students alike.

Furthermore, many priests though interested are not aware of the developments in this science in recent years, especially in the area of "existential ecclesiology." Therefore, it is the purpose of this closing chapter to bring them up to date in this regard.

Pastoral theology, the science of the care of souls, is that branch of theology which has grown out of and is based upon dogmatic, moral, and ascetical theology and canon law. Though the name is relatively new, pastoral is as old as Christianity itself. Christ practiced it during the years of his public life, and taught it to his disciples. It is both a practical and a theoretical science. As a practical science, its primary and pervading purpose is to give to the priest of tomorrow, as part of his professional preparation, a practical theology that will enable him to be effective in the pastoral ministry of mediating in a unique manner between God and man. For the priest of tomorrow, like those who have served before him, must be totally dedicated to the apostolate so that he can be a true witness to Christ, the sacrament of man's encounter with God.

Therefore, as a practical science, it must, in the words of Pope Pius XII, not only ". . . draw attention to the fact, that over and above sanctity and proper science (i.e., intellectual knowledge), the priest needs a detailed and absolutely complete preparation for the dutiful performance of his apostolic ministry," but, ". . . must beget and nourish a real skill and dexterity in properly carrying out the manifold duties of the Christian apostolate."[1] For the people of God, if they are ever to experience a "three-cornered Christianity" involving God, self, and neighbor, need priests who can bring to them a theology that is in harmony with the times, participate with them in a living liturgy, provide pastoral counseling as well as sacramental absolution, and inspire them with sermons and homilies filled with divine revelation and human wisdom.

Inasmuch as pastoral theology is a speculative science, it has another purpose as well; one that it alone can effectively achieve. For it falls to pastoral theology to consider the Church as a dynamic entity and to establish the basis of her self-awareness in a scientific manner. More specifically, it is the task of this discipline as a speculative science to discover and formulate the basic principles and pressing activities that the Church needs for her contemporary fulfillment. For, the Church can only hope to succeed in her continuing mission to make Christianity relevant to all mankind when she can plan and develop her various activities in a methodical and scientific manner. In this role, pastoral theology may be properly called "existential ecclesiology."

---

[1] Pius XII and the Sacred Congregation of Religious, *The Apostolic Constitution Sedes Sapientiae and the General Statutes Annexed to it* (trans. by The Catholic University of America Press), p. 12.

Though much more remains to be said regarding the question, "What is pastoral theology?" even these brief remarks about this science are sufficient to justify the importance which the Church attaches to its study, and to justify a thorough consideration of this question. Furthermore, any program of study formulated to facilitate the pastoral ministry of the priest and to contribute to the self-realization of the Church must be based on sound theory. But sound theory, from which effective practice flows, cannot be achieved unless there is a clear and unequivocal presentation of the nature and function of this discipline.

Other reasons as well urge a more profound study of the nature and function of pastoral theology. Chief among these is the Church's understanding of the priesthood itself. Throughout the whole of her existence, the Church has continually taught that the priesthood is a social sacrament, and that those who embrace it must be faithful "dispensers of the mysteries of God,"[2] and "ready for every noble work."[3] Consequently, she requires that her priests, "chosen by our brethren to be helpers in the ministry,"[4] be possessed of knowledge and skill sufficient to meet the ministerial obligations that flow from the social character of this sacrament. Though many popes in every age of history have strongly emphasized the social character of the sacrament of orders, none has been more articulate on this point than Pius XII, who in his encyclical letter wrote:

> Priests are the "stewards of the mysteries of God" (1 Cor 4:1); therefore they must serve Jesus Christ with perfect charity and consecrate all their strength to the salvation of their brethren. . . . (They) are apostles of grace and pardon; therefore they must consecrate themselves entirely to the salvation of men and draw them to the altar of God in order that they may nourish themselves with the bread of eternal life.[5]

While all branches of theology must reflect, at least to some degree, the social character of orders, it is the task of pastoral theology to provide the practical and pragmatic training and preparation for the ministry. But this vital task can never be fully accomplished unless there is first a comprehensive and penetrating understanding of the nature and functions of this science.

Two other factors also make the consideration of the nature and function of pastoral theology a timely one. Canon 1365 § 3 requires that major seminaries offer lectures in pastoral theology, and practical exercises especially on teaching catechism to children, hearing confessions, visiting the sick, and assisting the dying. In 1926 and again in 1929, the Sacred Congregation of Studies issued letters urging that

[2] 1 Co 4:1.
[3] 1 Co 3:9.
[4] *The Rite of Ordination* (trans. A. Biskupek, S.V.D.), p. 76.
[5] Pius XII, *Menti Nostrae* (trans. by N.C.W.C.), p. 21.

seminaries give special attention to a program of catechetical instructions.[6] Other documents also stress the importance of professional preparation for the pastoral ministry and establish certain norms and goals for this branch of theology.

Thus, the Apostolic Constitution, *Sedes Sapientiae,* issued by Pius XII and the Sacred Congregation of Religious also points up the importance of obtaining a more profound understanding of the nature and function of pastoral theology. For, not only does it continually stress the need for seminary education that is essentially pastorally thrusted for all priests, diocesan as well as religious, but also establishes the Pastoral Year for newly ordained priests who are members of religious communities.

> In order to profit rightly from the pastoral training, the students, immediately upon finishing their theological studies must spend a year at least in a special apprenticeship. During this period, while they practice more carefully the priestly virtues and exercise some priestly ministry, they will strive, under capable teachers, to extend and to complete their theoretical and practical knowledge of pastoral theology in accordance with the Apostolic provisions and instructions.[7]

The many constitutions and decrees issued by the Second Vatican Council also place great stress on the pastoral formation of seminarians and priests, and have established clear and definite norms and goals for the pastoral training of all seminarians and priests. Thus, in the *Decree on Priestly Training,* they state:

> That pastoral concern which ought to permeate thoroughly the entire training of the students also demands that they be diligently instructed in those matters which are particularly linked to the sacred ministry, especially in catechesis and preaching, in liturgical worship and the administration of the sacraments, in works of charity, in assisting the erring and the unbelieving, and in the other pastoral functions. They are to be carefully instructed in the art of directing souls, whereby they will be able to bring all the sons of the Church first of all to a fully conscious and apostolic Christian life and to the fulfillment of the duties of their state of life. Let them learn to help, with equal solicitude, religious men and women that they may persevere in the grace of their vocations and may make progress according to the spirit of their various Institutes.
> In general, those capabilities are to be developed in the students which especially contribute to dialogue with men, such as the ability to listen to others and to open their hearts and minds in the spirit of charity to the various circumstances and needs of men.
> They should also be taught to use the aids which the disciplines of

---

[6] Sacred Congregation of Studies, *Catechetical Training in Seminaries, AAS* 18 (1926), p. 453; *Oriental Studies and Catechetical Instruction in Seminaries, AAS* 22 (1928), p. 146. A translation of these documents will be found in *Canon Law Digest,* vol. I, pp. 664 and 666.

[7] Pius XII, *Sedes Sapientiae, op. cit.,* p. 66.

pedagogy, psychology, and sociology can provide, according to correct methodology and the norms of ecclesiastical authority. Likewise let them be properly instructed in inspiring and fostering the apostolic activity of the laity and in promoting the various and more effective forms of the apostolate. Let them also be imbued with that truly Catholic spirit which will accustom them to transcend the limits of their own diocese, nation, or rite, and to help the needs of the whole Church, prepared in spirit to preach the Gospel everywhere.

But since it is necessary for the students to learn the art of exercising the apostolate not only theoretically but also practically, and to be able to act both on their own responsibility and in harmonious conjunction with others, they should be initiated into pastoral work, both during their course of studies and also during the time of vacations, by opportune practical projects. These should be carried out in accordance with the age of the students and local conditions, and with the prudent judgment of the bishops, methodically and under the leadership of men skilled in pastoral work, the surpassing power of supernatural means being always remembered.[8]

However, if these norms are to be fully observed and these goals achieved, a thorough study of the nature and function of pastoral theology is essential.

A close examination of the various manuals of pastoral theology immediately brings to light the variety that exists in these books. While it is by no means extreme, it is sufficiently evident to indicate that the question of nature and function has not been thoroughly thought out and an agreement reached among theologians. In view of what has already been said above, it is important that this problem be solved, if for no other reason than to avoid overlapping with other disciplines such as moral theology, canon law, liturgy, and homiletics in the seminary curriculum.

This same examination also strongly indicates that divergences exist as regards the content and the divisions of this science. These exist, first, because theologians disagree as to what exactly is to be understood by pastoral theology, and secondly, because many authors tend to arrange their material along practical lines, but without scientific consideration of the function of their science or the basis of its divisions.

As far back as 1912, A. M. Micheletti, a highly respected authority in the field of pastoral theology, recognized this problem, for in the preface of his *Summa Theologiae Pastoralis* he writes of the differences he has found among authors concerning the understanding of pastoral theology:

> Some authors do not believe in a systematic study of Pastoral Theology, and content themselves with a brief reference to it in the textbooks of Moral Theology. Others limit it to the consideration of the right administration of the sacraments, being guided in this by the principles of Moral Theology, and the directions of the Ritual. Thus, I might remark, Merkelbach's *"Questiones Pastorales"* deals almost uniquely with the sacraments.

---

[8] Vatican Council II, *The Decree on Priestly Training* (trans. by N.C.W.C.), p. 9.

A few authors, on the other hand, would make Pastoral Theology the principal course in the seminary. Since the aim of the seminary is, according to Saint Charles Borromeo, to form good pastors of souls, these authors believe that every subject in the curriculum should be studied with a practical viewpoint and method, and thus Pastoral would become an encyclopedia of Theology, Philosophy, Liturgy, and all the other subjects. Such a broad understanding of Pastoral Theology as that held by these last authors might be in order in a university course in Pastoral, but it would be out of place in the ordinary seminary.[9]

Furthermore, though at one time or another considerable efforts have been made to demonstrate the necessity and importance of pastoral theology, as well as to collect its sources and write its history, little has been done to understand its nature and function either as a clerically oriented discipline, or as "existential ecclesiology." Or to look at it in another way, few efforts have been made to examine not only the traditional concepts developed by such outstanding authorities as Stang, Schulze, Micheletti, Blout, and Lithard, but also the new approach being developed by such men as Rahner, Arnold, Weber, Schurr, and Schuster.

Finally, few would deny that considerable progress would be made in converting the world to Christ if the apostolic principles that are inherent in divine Revelation permeated the whole teaching of theology including pastoral theology in universities, seminaries, and special institutes. For the divine truths which have been revealed to us by the patriarchs and prophets of the Old Testament, and by Jesus Christ and his Apostles in the New Testament, contain all the power needed to inspire in future priests a picture of Christian life which includes not only man's final end, but also his responsibility to labor continually for the improvement of the temporal order in accord with God's entire plan.

Therefore, it is my first purpose in this chapter to contribute in some small way to the task of reevaluating and reshaping the science of pastoral theology by examining the nature and function of both traditional and contemporary pastoral theology so that the apostolic principles inherent in Revelation can more effectively permeate the teaching of this discipline in schools of sacred theology.

Secondly, I hope to show that contemporary pastoral theology, that is, pastoral theology as it has been envisioned and defined within the past five years, but especially since the opening of the Vatican Council II, unlike traditional pastoral theology, is a dynamic science capable of adapting itself to serve the needs of the Church in the modern world. For it is the position of this author that while traditional pastoral theology has always shown some interest in the need of the times, for the most

[9] Cited in M. Larkin, "The Pastoral Theology Course: Its Content and Method," *National Catholic Educational Association Bulletin,* 36 (August, 1939), pp. 489–490.

part, it has tended to become a somewhat static discipline, content to restrict itself to the needs of the individual pastor and his pastoral activity, and to collect and transmit norms, regulations, and pastoral experiences for his use. Furthermore, this science, as it has been traditionally understood and taught, has never fully grasped the contemporary reality and the accompanying social changes. In fact, as Heinz Schuster observes, it has too frequently regarded them as ". . . superficial, refractory matter that free pastoral care must oppose and must change, and if necessary, against its will, with the help of traditional forms and tactics, in such a way that it fits in with the accustomed, 'unchanging' image of the Church."[10]

My third purpose is to demonstrate that pastoral theology, in the true sense of the word, is both a speculative and a practical science. That is to say, pastoral theology is capable not only of providing a truly theological, methodical, and scientific treatment of the Church as a contemporary phenomenon, but that it is also capable of providing the practical and pragmatic preparation for the various apostolates in a manner that is truly scientific and theological.

Finally, I want to point out that contemporary pastoral theology has two aspects or goals, which have their own primary material object. To the extent that contemporary pastoral theology is clerically orientated, it must have for its subject matter not only the sacred, but also the social functions and duties of the pastor of souls whose task it is to lead men to God in a world where the social structure of society and the functions of culture are continually changing. To the degree that contemporary pastoral theology is "ecclesially" oriented, it must have for its subject matter the Church established by Jesus Christ as a dynamic entity having a communal structure and existing in a world where the social structures of society and the functions of culture are continually changing. This distinction of aspects or goals is essential if pastoral theology is to possess a truly dynamic character, which can meet the needs of Church and churchmen in the modern world, and continue to train priests for the various apostolates, while at the same time dealing with the fulfillment of the Church as contemporary.

A. WHAT IS TRADITIONAL PASTORAL THEOLOGY?

1. Traditional Pastoral Theology Defined

In *Clerical Studies,* an important work on seminary education published toward the end of the last century, the author, the Very Reverend J. B. Hogan, S.S., D.D., said that in his opinion, "Pastoral Theology is

---

[10] H. Schuster, "The Nature and Function of Pastoral Theology," *The Pastoral Mission of the Church* (ed. K. Rahner, S.J.), pp. 9–10.

the crowning, for the pastor of souls, of all other forms of knowledge, the connecting link by which all ecclesiastical science is placed in contact with its ultimate object."[11] Other authors have defined pastoral theology as the science of the care of souls, and treated it as a branch of theology concerned with the principles regulating the life and conduct of the parish priest. However, the definition formulated by Cornelius Krieg is, perhaps, the most specific of all. He defines traditional pastoral theology as "The science which treats about those activities which the priesthood carries on in the name of Christ and the Church in order to mediate the work of redemption to individual souls."[12] This definition is even more meaningful when the words "and guides the future priest in acquiring proficiency in these activities" are added to it.

But, even though theologians have formulated definitions of pastoral theology that are clear and precise, many problems concerning its nature, function, content, and even its method still remain. For example, some writers question whether or not pastoral theology is theology at all. Others maintain that pastoral is a study or an art rather than a science. Furthermore, as A. M. Micheletti observes, some authors do not believe in a systematic study of pastoral theology, but prefer to make a brief reference to it in the textbooks of moral theology. One such author is Henry Davis, S.J., who contends that ". . . since Moral Theology is closely connected with Pastoral Theology, some attention should be given to the duties of pastors, and this practical aspect of the work should be emphasized in Moral Manuals."[13] At the opposite extreme, a few writers favor making pastoral theology the principal course in the seminary. They argue that inasmuch as the aim of the seminary is to form good pastors of souls, every subject in the curriculum should be taught from a practical viewpoint and method, and that pastoral should be an encyclopedia of philosophy, theology, canon law, and all the other subjects.

Perhaps as a result of these different views, there is considerable variety in the content and method of the pastoral courses in seminaries throughout the country. While these differences are not great, they do indicate that certain basic questions remain to be answered and that the program has not as yet been completely determined. A survey conducted by Father John A. Boere, M.S.C., in 1963 in cooperation with the National Catholic Educational Association supports this contention. Under the heading "Subject Offerings," the author lists the various subject offerings in the departments of theology and indicates the number of seminaries that offer or do not offer each course, as well as those

---

[11] J. Hogan, *Clerical Studies,* p. 302.
[12] C. Krieg, *Wissenschaft der Seelenteitung,* p. 1.
[13] H. Davis, S.J., *Moral and Pastoral Theology,* pp. vii, 1.

which make it a required course or offer it as an elective. Of the 101 seminaries that reported, 71 include a course in pastoral theology in their curriculum, while 30 do not; 66 seminaries require that students take the course, whereas five offer it as an elective.[14]

Later in this survey, under the heading "Semester Hours Devoted to Dogma and Moral Theology," John A. Boere indicates the number of hours devoted to dogma and moral combined, and in combination with related subjects. The minimum number of hours devoted to the combination of dogma, moral, pastoral, and introduction to Sacred Scripture is 62 hours per semester; the maximum is 101 hours per semester, and the average is 77.55 hours per semester.[15] This computation of the total number of hours per semester devoted to these four related subjects reveals remarkable differences. Another computation presented under the title "Summary of Data on Semester Hours" is equally revealing. According to these statistics, the minimum number of semester hours devoted to pastoral theology is 1; the more frequent number is 2; the maximum number is 5, and the average number is 2.29 semester hours.[16]

Though these statistics as well as those that concern the other pastoral subjects — homiletics, catechetics, liturgy, ceremonies, pastoral psychology, pastoral counseling, etc. — do not present a complete picture of the status of pastoral in the American seminary, they do show the variety to be found in the pastoral courses of the different seminaries, and give added proof of the need for answers to questions about the nature and function of the pastoral science.

2. Nature and Function of Traditional Pastoral Theology

Before the seventeenth century, theologians usually treated dogmatic and moral theology, pastoral, and Sacred Scripture as different aspects of the one science of theology. However, since that time there has been a tendency to treat them separately. As a result, many are left with the impression that the various branches of theology are distinct sciences, each having its own formal object. But such a view is incorrect, for theology, whether speculative or practical, is one science, since its formal object is the same; it treats of God and creatures in their relations to God in the light of reason elevated and guided by faith.[17] Nevertheless, because the material objects of the various branches of theology are quite different, they can be treated in different courses in the seminary.

Pastoral theology, like the other branches of theology, is part of the one science of theology. However, it has traditionally been regarded a

---

[14] J. A. Boere, *A Survey of the Content and Organization of the Curriculum of the Theological Departments of Major Seminaries in the United States of America,* p. 37.
[15] *Ibid.,* p. 75.
[16] *Ibid.,* p. 89.
[17] T. Aquinas, *Summa Theologica,* 1, Q. 14, a. 16.

practical science rather than a speculative one. Nevertheless, to some extent, it includes all the theological sciences inasmuch as they have for their ultimate purpose the salvation of souls and aim to make priests fit dispensers of the mysteries of God. Pastoral strives to show how the various branches of theology and the related subjects can be effectively used for the salvation of souls. While its immediate end is to assure that every cleric will be properly prepared to carry out his apostolate, its ultimate end is to lead souls to eternal salvation. The purpose of this science is to state and explain the norms, regulations, and pastoral experiences which direct the pastor of souls in carrying out the duties of his apostolate. In other words, this science provides techniques designed to make abstract and theoretical principles concrete and practical and thus productive of spiritual good.

Though pastoral most closely resembles moral theology, it is not to be identified with this science or with any other branch of theology. Nevertheless, it does depend on them and borrow from them. This relationship with the other sciences stems from the fact while they speculatively teach about the threefold function of teaching, ruling, and sanctifying, pastoral considers these matters concretely. Thus, whereas dogmatic theology establishes the Church as the depository of revealed truth, and systematizes the deposit of faith which Jesus Christ entrusted to his Church to transmit to all mankind, pastoral theology teaches the priest his specific role in the transmission of this message. Whereas, moral theology not only deals with human acts inasmuch as they are obligatory, but also treats of works of counsel and acts of virtue, pastoral teaches the importance of these to the daily life of the priest, alone and in contact with his people. While canon law collects, correlates, and coordinates the laws of the Church, and treats of them to the extent that they are enforceable in the external form, pastoral applies these laws to the care of souls, by showing not merely what must be done, but also what can be done, and by pointing out the means of doing it. Pastoral also presupposes and borrows from casuistry. For while casuistry, which is most frequently associated with the fields of moral theology and ethics, is merely the reasoned application of law to concrete cases, so that the limitations or the applications of law in particular cases can be determined with all possible exactitude, pastoral goes far beyond this point, and strives to show not merely what is obligatory but what is an appropriate course of action for the true Christian. Though pastoral theology is clearly distinct from ascetical and mystical theology, it does use the principles of these sciences to encourage and direct souls capable of attaining the higher states of the spiritual life. From all this, then, it is evident that pastoral theology actually begins where the other theological sciences leave off, taking the results of these sciences and rendering them effective for the salvation of souls through the ministry of the priesthood instituted by Jesus Christ.

Thus, the primary *objectum materiale* (that which constitutes its proper subject matter) of traditional pastoral theology is the various functions of the pastor of souls, for this science is uniquely interested, for their own sake, in the duties and offices of the priest in leading souls to God. Though pastoral does have a speculative side, and is responsible for collecting norms and regulations for the use of the clergy, it is not directly concerned with principles as such. The formal object of this science is the same duties and functions of the pastor of souls, but inasmuch as they lead to God, and not merely from a natural viewpoint, and the light under which it considers these duties and functions is practical reason illumined by faith and guided by the principles and norms derived from theology, philosophy, and the other sciences.

Many centuries ago, Gregory the Great declared that pastoral theology is the art of arts — *"ars artium, regimen animarum."* Most theologians agree, though they maintain that pastoral is both a science and an art. They argue, on the one hand, that it is a science because it is part of the one science of theology, and because it is an exact, scientific systematization of all the questions about pastoral functions and duties of the individual priest as well as all of the various aspects of actual pastoral care, with its own research and methodology; and, on the other hand, that it is an art because it applies the principles of theology, canon law, Sacred Scripture, and the other theological studies in the pastoral care of souls.

However, some theologians, including J. B. Hogan, M. J. Larkin, S.M., and a number of German theologians, contend that pastoral theology is merely a function of theology and that "the relatively young discipline of pastoral theology only meant to fill a gap in clerical training and not in theological thought as a whole."[18] This argument as to whether pastoral theology is a science, an art, or merely a study is an old one and the "problem of the place of pastoral theology in the scientific theory of theology as a whole and . . . the problem of its specific theological function"[19] have still not been fully answered.

Defending his position, M. J. Larkin maintains that since pastoral, in its fundamental meaning, is an art, and pastoral theology is the study of this art, pastoral theology is more of a study than a science. He also argues that if it were considered strictly as a science, it would logically be absorbed in the general science of theology and that, furthermore, it is practical rather than speculative. Father Larkin sums up his position by saying that "It is not, however, just an art, nor the exercise of the

---

[18] H. Schuster, *op. cit.,* p. 5.
[19] *Ibid.,* p. 4.

priestly ministry, but it is the study of this art with a view to the acquiring of this art, and hence it is not fully a science nor an art."[20] J. B. Hogan held a similar position, for he says that "Pastoral Theology is not so much a science as an art."[21] The German born theologian, Heinz Schuster also claims that a study of pastoral theology textbooks written before the middle of the nineteenth century, and even many written in the present century accept this concept of pastoral theology, and stress the "art and study" concept of pastoral rather than the scientific concept.[22]

However, even though traditional pastoral theology is primarily practical, it is also partially speculative since it does present a truly theological, methodical, and scientific treatment of the pastoral ministry by formulating the principles and defining the duties of priests in the various phases of the apostolate. Therefore, pastoral theology must be regarded as a science rather than merely an art or a study, though it certainly encompasses both of these, and it seems best to define it as a science.

B.   WHAT IS CONTEMPORARY PASTORAL THEOLOGY?

Contemporary pastoral theology, if it is to meet the needs of the Church in the modern world, must have two well-defined aspects or goals. The first of these must be to continue and expand the work of traditional pastoral theology by renewing and reforming old approaches to the various apostolates and by developing new ones. Secondly, in the words of Heinz Schuster, pastoral theology must deal with "the Church's self-fulfillment in the ever new contemporary situation,"[23] that is, "its special task is to work out and to formulate the principles and urgent duties that the Church needs for her contemporary fulfillment."[24]

In striving to attain its first goal, contemporary pastoral theology must continue to consider the various questions about the pastoral function of the individual priest, and all the forms and norms of the pastoral ministry. To this extent, it must remain clerically oriented. However, if contemporary pastoral theology is to achieve its second goal, it must consider all the members of the Church and all those functions which, in one way or another can contribute to the self-fulfillment of the Church. Furthermore, "it must subject the constantly changing contemporary situation to an equally constant theological and sociological analysis."[25] In this role, it is "practical theology" in the true sense of the word.

---

[20] M. Larkin, *op. cit.,* p. 491.   [21] *Ibid.,* p. 491.
[22] H. Schuster, *op. cit.,* pp. 3, 5.   [23] *Ibid.,* pp. 3, 7.
[24] *Ibid.,* p. 8.
[25] K. Rahner, S.J. and H. Schuster, "Prefact," *The Pastoral Mission of the Church* (ed. K. Rahner, S.J.), pp. 3, 1.

Both goals are equally important. For while it is quite evident that pastoral theology can no longer limit itself to the mere transmission of norms, regulations, and pastoral experiences for use by the clergy, but must deal with many decisive issues that are outside the realm and beyond the capacity of the individual priest or pastoral theologian, the fact remains that the individual priest, first and foremost, is charged with the care of souls. Even lay leaders are aware of the need to strive for the first goal, for as Daniel Kane and Martin Work in an earlier chapter in this book point out:

> . . . new leadership is required from the priest. The growth of the Church in the United States was marked by the openness of the Clergy, especially of the parish priest, to the tasks of the day. Today, a new openness is called for — an openness to change, to change in the Church, in the spirit of the Vatican Council. This means openness to new ideas, to new directions in thought and action, to the exploration of new pastoral methods, to new relationships within and without the parish. The evidence of this openness in the lives of priests will be the major factor in leading more laymen to a commitment to apostolic work in the parish and community at large. The revivification of older forms of parish lay groups and the development of new ones needed to meet contemporary problems can best be built under the leadership of a new "team" — of priest and layman, who have opened themselves to the Spirit Who is renewing the Church of our time.[26]

The second goal derives its importance from the fact that all Catholics living at this point of history have been given a special kind of challenge and opportunity to change the world. As Joseph H. Fichter, S.J., points out:

> . . . Perhaps only two or three times in the history of Christianity has the Church enjoyed an opportunity like this. In the momentous transition at the breakup of the Roman empire the Church successfully met the challenge of change, and the consequence was centuries of Christians. At the time of the Reformation the opportunity slipped out of our hands; and at a later time, in the era of colonialism, the adaption of Catholicism to the various indigenous cultures was not properly understood. The whole Far East might today be Catholic if the modern principle of cultural adaptation had been understood and applied.[27]

Karl Rahner, S.J., also stresses the importance of this goal when he says:

> . . . For example, how often has pastoral activity in the Church always [had] the character of service? Or, how far can the Church plan its activities? What is the state of the Church's contribution to developing countries? What kind of situation has the Church to deal with in various continents, countries or racial groups?[28]

---

[26] D. Kane and M. Work, "The Priest and Parish Organizations of Men."

[27] J. Fichter, S.J., "The Priest and His Work," a paper delivered at a symposium for priests of Chicagoland, pp. 11–12.

[28] K. Rahner, S.J., *op. cit.*, p. 2.

Furthermore, as Father James Keller, M.M., and Richard Armstrong, M.M., observe, the Constitution on the Church stresses the need for the Church "to unfold more fully to the faithful and to the whole world its own inner nature and universal mission," and point out that "present day conditions of the world add greater urgency to the work of the Church so that all men, joined more closely today by various social, technical and cultural ties, might also attain fuller unity in Christ."[29]

Each of these goals of contemporary pastoral theology must be the object of detailed study by pastoral theologians, and serious efforts must be made to demonstrate the close connection that must exist between these two goals.

1. Clerically Oriented Pastoral Theology

a. Contemporary Clerically Oriented Pastoral Theology Defined

Since the Second Vatican Council was essentially a pastoral council, most, if not all, of the constitutions and decrees provide valuable data for those seeking to revitalize the old approaches to the various apostolates and to discover and develop new ones. However, before the pastoral theologians can set about this task, it is important that they have a clear and concise definition of contemporary pastoral theology. One of the most meaningful definitions of this science, one which is certainly contemporary, is that proposed by His Holiness Pope Paul VI in an address to the Thirteenth Pastoral Updating Study Week held in Rome in 1963. On this occasion, the Pope said, in the course of his address, that "There comes to mind one of the most flowering branches of practical theology, pastoral theology, which is the Church's own art and science, enriched by special gifts and charisms, of the salvation of souls."[30] He then defined pastoral theology as "the science by which the Church knows souls, approaches them, instructs and educates them, guides them, serves them, defends, loves and sanctifies them."[31]

From the opening paragraph of Chapter 6, "The Promotion of Strictly Pastoral Training," of the *Decree on Priestly Training,* it is possible to develop an excellent descriptive definition of contemporary pastoral theology. Thus, contemporary pastoral theology is the science which is concerned with "those matters which are particularly linked to the sacred ministry, especially in catechesis and preaching, in liturgical worship and the administration of the sacraments, in works of charity in assisting

---

[29] J. Keller, M.M. and R. Armstrong, M.M., "Aim of Christopher Study Week," Apostolic Renewal in the Seminary (ed. J. Keller, M.M. and R. Armstrong, M.M.), pp. 1–2.

[30] Paul VI, *Address to the 13th Pastoral Updating Study Week, AAS* 55 (1963), pp. 752–753.

[31] *Loc. cit.*

the erring and the unbelieving, . . . as well as the art of directing souls,
. . . and helping religious men and women that they may persevere in
the grace of their vocation. . . ."[32]

b. Nature and Function of the Clerically Oriented Phase of
   Pastoral Theology

When pastoral theology is considered from the viewpoint of its
clerical orientation, its nature and function are basically identical to
those of traditional pastoral theology. However, if there is to be a true
aggiornamento in this discipline, its nature and function must be restated
to include the notions of expansion and development expressed above.

Thus, the traditional primary material object — the various functions
of pastors of souls — should be restated to include the social as well
as the sacramental aspects of the pastoral ministry. For, according to
Pope Paul's definition of pastoral theology, and the other points he
discussed, the priest in the modern world must be as well trained for
the world in which the sanctuary exists as he is for the sanctuary. As
Hartzel Spence expressed it, "Today's clergy must be literally all things
to all men — preacher, teacher, pastor, counsellor, advisor, administrator, architect and financier. To accomplish all these vocations the minister
must be a sociologist, a humanitarian, a businessman, as well as theologian
and public speaker."[33]

Furthermore, it would seem that the primary material object of this
phase of pastoral theology should reflect the prophetic function of the
pastoral ministry. Pope Paul himself has pointed out that the very
structures of society and the functions of culture are being altered in
many ways, and that it is of the greatest urgency that the priest of
today have a place in this dynamic culture and adapt to the cultural
needs and social change of today's world.

Finally, the primary material object should reflect the fact that the
occupation of the priesthood is a profession which requires, among other
things, specialized knowledge and technical training, a lifelong commitment to the pastoral ministry, and an awareness that the priest's main
motivation must be his service to others rather than profit to himself.

The primary material object of clerically oriented contemporary pastoral theology now becomes the sacred and social duties and offices of
the present-day priest — a professional possessed of knowledge and skills,
imbued with a lifelong commitment to the pastoral ministry, and motivated to service to others — in leading to God souls living in a world
where the social structure of society and the functions of culture are

---

[32] Vatican Council II, *The Decree on Priestly Training, op. cit.,* p. 9.
[33] H. Spence, "Do You Want Your Child To Be A Clergyman?" in J. Fichter, S.J.,
op. cit.

constantly being altered. Such an expression of the material object of pastoral not only adheres to the definition and guidelines established by the present Pope and the Council, but also avoids the static character of the traditional statement of the material object, while emphasizing its dynamic aspect. While the clerically oriented phase of pastoral does have a speculative side, and is concerned with the collecting, reforming, and renewing of norms and regulations for the use of the clergy, it is not directly concerned with principles as such. The formal object of pastoral is the same sacred and social duties and functions of the pastor of souls in the contemporary situation, but inasmuch as they lead to God, and not merely from a natural point of view and the light under which it considers these duties and functions is practical reason illumined by faith, and guided by the principles and norms derived from theology, philosophy, anthropology, sociology, psychology, and the other sciences.

2. Pastoral Theology As "Existential Ecclesiology"

a. "Existential Ecclesiology" Defined

Toward the middle of the past century a number of theologians, especially those from Tübingen, proposed a new concept of pastoral theology. This new concept involved expanding pastoral theology so that it would have as its object the planning of the Church's self-fulfillment in the present and in the future. Though these theologians were able to establish this concept scientifically and theologically within Catholic theology, it has, for the most part, remained a fond desire of theology. In fact, the concept and the theme of what might well be called "practical theology" has been supplanted by a growing preference for traditional pastoral theology. However, within the last few years, a number of well-known and respected theologians have striven with considerable success to solve this difficulty by restudying and reevaluating the nature of "practical theology."

Nevertheless, before the advocates of this concept of theology (or what has been called in this chapter the second goal of contemporary pastoral theology) can investigate the nature of practical theology, it is essential that they have a precise and meaningful definition of it. According to Karl Rahner, S.J., pastoral theology must be understood as "practical theology" in the sense that it seeks "to lay down the basis of the Church's self-awareness in a scientific manner" in a way that this science will not "limit itself to the mere unfolding of the permanent factors in the history of the Church."[34] In other words, as Rahner explains it, pastoral theology is the science which studies the present and future of the entire Church and arrives at "conclusions reached by practical-theological research; with the analysis of the contemporary situa-

---

[34] K. Rahner, S.J., and H. Schuster, *op. cit.*, p. 1.

tion; with the relationship between kerygma and dogma, etc."[35]

Heinz Schuster defines this aspect of pastoral theology as "that branch of theology which deals with the Church's self-fulfillment in the ever new contemporary situation."[36] Undoubtedly this definition will become more clear and meaningful when theologians determine more precisely the scope or subject matter of this science, and when they determine the specific angle or approach from which it will be studied. The meaning of this aspect of pastoral theology will be better understood as theologians develop a greater understanding of the aim of this science as well as its specific method.

This aspect of pastoral theology can also be called "existential ecclesiology" inasmuch as it studies the Church as a dynamic entity with a communal structure, which is subject to the vicissitudes of history, and "which must express itself here and now in present actuality in order to be concretely what it ought to be, and do concretely what it ought to do."[37]

In a word, this aspect of pastoral theology is to be understood as the scientific-theological teaching concerning the fulfillment of the Church, a fulfillment always relinquished for the present. The need for such a forceful theological contemplation of both the lasting nature of the Church and of its specification through its contemporary situation, a situation which for historical-theological reasons must be seen as God-willed and therefore willed by the Church itself, may be derived a priori from the enduring mandate of the Church, which is to actualize the salvific work of God in man for each generation. Furthermore, this need is being increasingly felt within the confines of pastoral theology itself, and even though there may be historical and scientific-theoretical reasons why pastoral theology should not assume this task, the fact remains that the present situation requires that it take it over.

b. Nature and Function of the "Existential Ecclesiology" Phase of Pastoral Theology

To the extent that contemporary pastoral theology considers the Church's self-fulfillment in the present situation, its nature and function are somewhat similar to those of basic ecclesiology, that branch of theology which is primarily concerned with Christ's Church, a visible society to which he entrusted his doctrine and bestowed his own divine mission of saving souls, and which has different hierarchical ranks, and an infallible *magisterium*. However, there is a significant difference between basic and existential ecclesiology in that whereas basic ecclesiology is concerned with the enduring transcendental and sacramental nature

[35] *Ibid.*, p. 2.
[36] H. Schuster, *op. cit.*, p. 8.
[37] *Ibid.*

of the Church, existential ecclesiology treats of the Church as a dynamic institution which must carry out its mission in the present age.

Therefore, the primary material object of basic ecclesiology must be reformulated to include the whole Church's mission in contemporary reality, including the various principles and duties that the Church needs if she is to achieve contemporary fulfillment. From this point of view, the primary material object of practical theology is Christ's Church as a dynamic entity having a communal structure and existing in a world where the social structures of society and the functions of culture are continually changing, as well as the duties and functions which the whole Church must perform to attain contemporary self-fulfillment. Systematic theology or ecclesiology presently considers several basic demands and assumptions which must be included in this aspect of pastoral theology. The more important of these are: (1) the responsibility for carrying on Christ's redemption by the pastoral activity of all members of the Church, not merely by the individual priest; (2) the primary object of this branch of pastoral theology is the whole Church with all its members and all its functions; (3) the secondary object of this ecclesially oriented branch is the structure of the contemporary society in which the Church proclaims its message, which must be evaluated and interpreted so that the Church can attain its self-fulfillment in the present age.[38]

This goal of pastoral theology definitely has a speculative side, in that it treats of the Church of Christ as a contemporary phenomenon in a manner that is truly theological, methodical, and scientific.

The formal object of existential ecclesiology is the whole dynamic Church existing today and the duties and functions which the Church must perform to attain contemporary self-fulfillment, but inasmuch as these lead to God, and not merely from a natural point of view and the light under which it considers the whole Church as a dynamic entity and its duties and functions is practical reason illumined by faith, and guided by the principles and norms derived from theology, philosophy, anthropology, psychology, and sociology.

In view of the fact that the Church as a whole is the subject-matter of this aspect of pastoral theology, this science must treat each of the following four points:

1. As existential ecclesiology, pastoral theology must restudy and rework in terms of the needs of the Church today the complete dynamic nature of the Church, including her permanent basic structures, the total membership — faithful, deacons, priests, bishops, pope — who are the bearers of salvation-conveying self-fulfillment, and the basic functions of the Church — worship, the dispensing

---

[38] *Ibid.*, pp. 6–7.

of the sacraments, preaching, discipline, charity, and Christian life
of fulfillment.

2. This aspect of pastoral theology must research and develop the
   anthropological suppositions for the Church's self-fulfillment in
   such areas as unity, freedom, personality, sociality tradition and
   personal decision, national character, and the historical constitution of men.

3. Ecclesially oriented pastoral theology must reflect the formal basic
   fulfillment, including a respect for the various aspects of piety,
   racial difference, the elite and the masses, age differences, gradual
   initiation, proportion of witness and teaching, theoretical and practical ethics, and the like.

4. The various communal and sociological aspects of the Church's
   nature and activity, inasmuch as these are most subject to structural
   changes.[39]

C. PROBLEMS FACING THE PASTORAL THEOLOGIAN

This chapter, and even the works quoted in it, evidence only the
most embryonic attempts to examine the nature and function of contemporary pastoral theology. Much more work needs to be done before
all the problems connected with this science can be solved, for not
only must the theologians of today and tomorrow consider the nature
and function of the science, but they must also evaluate methods and
content so that pastoral will always remain a vital and effective speculative
and practical science.

Though an important start has been made, much of the success of
the work that will be carried on by future theologians will depend, in
this writer's view, on the theologians' willingness to see that the two
aspects or goals of contemporary pastoral theology explained above are
not poles apart, but are truly interdependent aspects of the one same
discipline. Concerted efforts must be made to synthesize the clerically
oriented goal and the ecclesially oriented goal so that the interdependent
relationship that does exist will become even more evident and fruitful. Though some present-day theologians seem inclined to exclude altogether the clerically oriented aspect of theology in favor of the ecclesially
oriented one, work done up to the present time seems to indicate the
need for a synthesis of the two, rather than an abandonment of either.

Furthermore, in view of the fact that the subject matter of this science
has so expanded that it cannot be adequately covered in one or two
courses in the major seminary, pastoral theologians must devise new
ways of integrating some pastoral topics in other disciplines, and must
develop long-term programs that can be inaugurated in the minor

---

[39] H. Schuster, "Praktische Theologie," *Lexikon für Theologie und Kirche* (2nd
ed.), pp. 8, 685.

seminary at the college level, continued in the major seminary, and extended to the early years of the priesthood.

Finally, pastoral theologians must be aware of the fact that the problems of contemporary pastoral theology are only one segment of the problems that all theologians and educators must consider regarding the preparation of candidates for the priestly ministry, and be willing to make a contribution to the whole question of renewal and reform in seminary and post-seminary education. They too, must clearly see the need to take a new look at the entire seminary curriculum, and to seek answers to such questions as: "What is the principal purpose of seminary education?" "Does the traditional seminary curriculum meet the needs of today's seminarians?" "Do our seminaries reflect the idea of renewal that has become increasingly evident in the life of the Church?" Though these questions and many similar ones are still under consideration, and perhaps will never be answered fully and finally, the information that has been garnered so far has enabled those concerned to develop some new and profound insights regarding curriculum and teaching in seminary education. These new insights will touch every course in the seminary curriculum, including pastoral theology.

Perhaps the most important insight developed thus far concerns the purpose of seminary education. On this point, most agree that the principal purpose of the seminary is to give to candidates for the priesthood a professional preparation for the pastoral ministry. Father Timothy Manning stated the purpose of the seminary quite succinctly when he wrote that the role of the seminary is to prepare "general practitioners — men who are destined for the normal offices of the priesthood in the care of souls."[40] The *Decree on Priestly Training* elevates these insights on the primary purpose of the seminary to the level of official Church teaching, for it declares that "Major seminaries are necessary for priestly formation. Here the entire training of the students should be to the formation of true shepherds of souls after the model of our Lord Jesus Christ, teacher, priest, and shepherd."

The answers to these other questions and more like them concerning seminary education will surely be resolved as more and more seminaries, under the guidance of the hierarchy, experiment with various types of curricula, course content, methods of teaching, number and length of class hours, etc. But, at this time, it is impossible to predict, even in a general way, what the future holds for the total process of seminary education, or, for that matter, for any course of study, including pastoral theology. The questions have been posed; the goals are clear. It remains now for seminary administrators, and theologians, to develop programs that are intimately related to the pastoral ministry.

[40] T. Manning, *Clerical Education in Major Seminaries,* p. 11.

The Contributors

FATHER ROY FRANCIS AIKEN has been for the past fourteen years pastor of St. Anthony's Church, Walterboro, South Carolina. Before assuming this position, he was vice-chancellor of the diocese of Charleston, editor of the diocesan newspaper, the *Catholic Banner,* and chairman of the diocesan liturgical commission. He was born on November 28, 1920, and ordained to the priesthood on June 15, 1946. Father Aiken received his B.A. degree from Spring Hill College, Mobile, Alabama, and took his theological studies at St. Mary's Seminary, Baltimore, Maryland. Though he has not previously written for national publication, he has contributed numerous articles for local publication in newspapers. Over the years, he has organized and conducted numerous study days, institutes, etc., on the liturgy, and has given many retreats and parish missions. Father Aiken is a former member of the Board of Directors of the North American Liturgical Conference. He has also been active in the social and civic life of Walterboro since his appointment there.

MR. EUGENE F. KENNEDY, JR., F.A.I.A., A.N.A., is an architect with the firm of Maginnis, Walsh, and Kennedy in Boston, Massachusetts. He was born in Brooklyn, New York, on January 31, 1904. He studied architecture at the Boston Architectural Center. Mr. Kennedy was a regular contributor to the *Architectural Forum* in the late 1920's. He is a member of the American Institute of Architects, the Boston Society of Architects, the National Academy of Design, and the National Sculpture Society.

MR. VIGGO F. E. RAMBUSCH is chairman of the Board of Rambusch — Designers, Craftsmen, and Lighting Engineers, a position he has held for the last two years. Mr. Rambusch, who was born in New York City on April 17, 1900, received his higher education at Columbia College, where he received a B.A. degree. He then enrolled at Columbia University to study architecture, and earned his B.A. degree in Architecture in 1926. He also attended The Catholic University of America where he received his M.A. degree in Architecture. Mr. Rambusch has written a considerable number of articles in the field of arts and crafts. He is a member of the Architectural League of New York, The Liturgical Art Society, St. Ansgar's Scandinavian Catholic League, the American Scandinavian Society, and the Columbia University Club. Mr. Rambusch served in the United States Army during World War I.

FATHER JOHN EDWARD CORRIGAN, who is presently an assistant pastor of the Church of Christ the King in Silver Springs, Maryland, was born in Newark, New Jersey, on April 16, 1931. He holds a B.A. degree from Seton Hall University and an M.A. degree from The Catholic University of America. For the past four years, he has contributed articles to such well-known publications as *America, Worship,* and *U. S. Catholic,* including such articles as, "Bless Me Father," Self Denial," "Pastoral Renewal of Penance," "Induction of Lay Lectors," and "Preparing for First Communion." Father Corrigan is a member of the National Liturgical Conference and the National Catholic Educational Association.

FATHER BERNARD A. MEYER is an assistant pastor at Sacred Heart Church in Springfield, Illinois. Before coming to Springfield in 1963, he was an assistant at St. Thomas Church in Decatur, Illinois. He was born in Effingham, Illinois, on September 29, 1932. Father Meyer, who was ordained in 1959, received his theological training at St. John's Home Missions Seminary in Little Rock, Arkansas. He is a member of the Priests' Lecture Forum of the Diocese of Springfield in Illinois, and of the Urban League, Springfield and Sangamon County Community Action, Inc., and the Community Action Advisory Committee on Head Start.

FATHER WILLIAM TOOHEY, C.S.C. is a professor of preaching and catechetics at Holy Cross College, Washington, D. C. and a chaplain at the National Training School for Boys. Before coming to Washington, he was a student chaplain at Notre Dame University. He has also done parish and retreat work. Father Toohey was born in Racine, Wisconsin, on June 2, 1930. He received his B.A. degree from Notre Dame University. He is the holder of two M.A. degrees; one from Holy Cross College, Washington, D. C., and another from Northwestern University. Since 1962, he has contributed to a number of periodicals, including the *American Ecclesiastical Review, Homiletic and Pastoral Review, Ave Maria, Marriage,* and *The Yearbook of Liturgical Studies.* He is a member of the American Correctional Association, the American Correctional Chaplains' Association, the American Correctional Catholic Chaplains' Association, the Catholic Homiletic Society, and the Speech Association of America.

FATHER CARL JAMES PFEIFER, S.J. is an instructor in religious education in the department of religious education at The Catholic University of America, and a consultant to the National Confraternity of Christian Doctrine Center in Washington, D. C. At the present time he is also a doctoral candidate in the Department of Religious Education at The Catholic University of America. Before coming to Washington, he taught at the St. Louis University High School and was a part-time chaplain at the Kansas State Boys Industrial School in Topeka, Kansas. Father Pfeifer was born in St. Louis, Missouri, on June 22, 1929. He is the holder of four degrees from St. Louis University, including a B.A. degree, an M.A. degree, a Licentiate in Philosophy, and a Licentiate in Sacred Theology. He has also carried on his studies at Georgetown University, Laval University, Quebec, and Universität Innsbruck, Innsbruck, Austria. Father Pfeifer published an article entitled "An Evening Service for Thanksgiving Day," in *Review for Religious* in 1961 and an article entitled, "Popular Devotions: A New Look," in *Homiletic and Pastoral Review* in 1963. He is a member of the Liturgical Conference.

FATHER JOHN HENRY YANNONE is the pastor of St. Margaret's Church in Seat Pleasant, Maryland. He is also a judge of the Washington Archdiocesan Tribunal and a member of the Archdiocesan Ecumenical Commission. Father Yannone, who was born on January 1, 1912, received his higher education at Fordham University and at the Gregorian University in Rome, where he received his Licentiate in Sacred Theology. Several years ago, this active parish priest directed the translation into English of the Second Italian Edition of the *Dictionary of Moral Theology,* an excellent work that provides in each entry a summary of the traditional teaching of the Church, useful clarifications of important issues, and the fullest available information that modern scientific studies can offer in areas relevant to human morality. He is a member of the Health and Welfare Organization of the Washington Metropolitan area.

BROTHER LEO V. RYAN, C.S.V. is the deputy director of Peace Corps programs in Nigeria. Before accepting this position, Brother Ryan was Chairman of the Department of Management at Loyola University in Chicago, Illinois, a position he held since 1965. Prior to his coming to Loyola he was director of Continuing Education at Marquette University in Milwaukee where, from 1961 to 1965 he also coordinated Peace Corps activities and directed three Corps Brazil training programs. Born in 1927 in Waukon, Iowa, he was an infantryman in World War II. He received a B.S. degree in business administration from Marquette University, an M.B.A. in marketing from DePaul University, and Ph.D.'s in management and education from St. Louis University in 1958. He was a member of the faculty of the School of Commerce and Finance of St. Louis University from 1954 to 1957. In 1957 he joined the faculty of Marquette University as assistant professor of general business. He was appointed assistant dean of the College of Business Administration in 1958 and Director of Continuing Education a year later. In 1964, he was named professor of industrial management. He has been visiting professor and lecturer at The Catholic University of America, University of San Francisco, and Bradley University in Peoria, Illinois. He also has taught at Spalding Institute in Peoria and Cathedral Boys High School in Springfield, Illinois. He is a former national president of the Catholic Business Education Association. He holds a "Young Man of the Year" award from the Milwaukee Junior Chamber of Commerce; a Distinguished Service award from Alpha Kappa Psi, national business fraternity; and a B'nai B'rith interfaith award for work in the field of human relations. He has written extensively for both professional journals and popular publications.

MR. WILLIAM R. CONSEDINE, has been, for the past ten years, the director of the legal department of the National Catholic Welfare Conference. He was born in Olean, New York, on August 18, 1910. He received his B.A. degree from St. Bonaventure University and his LL.B. degree from Georgetown University School of Law. He is also the holder of an honorary LL.D. degree from Siena University, Albany, New York. Mr. Consedine served in the United States Navy from 1942 to 1945 and is presently a Lt. Commander in the United States Navy Reserve. He is also a member of the American Bar Association.

SISTER M. BERNADETTE NEVILLE, O.S.U. is an instructor at the Ursuline Academy in Bethesda, Maryland. Before assuming her duties at the academy, she was principal of Our Lady of Mercy Elementary School, Bronx, New York, of St. Joseph's Elementary School, Middletown, New York, and of St. Philip Neri Elementary School, Bronx, New York. She was also supervisor of the elementary schools of the Eastern Province of the Ursuline Nuns of the Roman Union. Sister Bernadette was born in New York City on January 7, 1927. She received her B.A. degree from the College of New Rochelle in 1951, and her M.A. degree from The Catholic University of America in 1966.

MARTIN HAVERTY WORK, the executive director of the National Council of Catholic Men, is a native-born Californian. He received his A.B. degree from Loyola University in Los Angeles, California, and his M.A. degree from the University of Southern California. He is also the recipient of an LL.D. degree from Springhill College in Alabama. During World War II, Mr. Work served in Washington as special consultant to the Secretary of the Army and later as an army colonel. Immediately after the war, he entered the business world and served as an account supervisor with the well-known Madison Avenue advertising agency, Young and Rubicam, and as sales and advertising manager for a national manufacturing company. He later became a consultant to the Office of Military Government in Germany and special consultant to the Executive Office of the President through the National Security Resources Board. Convinced that the layman has an inescapable responsibility to contribute to the mission of the Church, Mr. Work responded to a request of the Bishops of the United States to take on the task of building the National Council of Catholic Men into a coordinated, unified, effective Catholic Action federation of all Catholic men's organizations in the United States. As executive director of NCCM, he has represented Catholic men in countless national and international meetings. In 1954, Pope Pius XII made him a Knight of St. Gregory. In 1960, Pope John XXIII named him to an eight man Board of Directors of the Permanent Committee of the World Congress of the Lay Apostolate. Pope Paul VI named him an auditor at Vatican Council II, and he is a member of Post Conciliar Commission of Vatican II and the vice-president of the International Federation of Catholic Men.

MR. DANIEL KANE is the assistant executive director of the Archdiocesan Council of Catholic Men and Women, and the assistant executive director of the Archdiocesan Bureau of Information of the Archdiocese of Cincinnati, Ohio. He has been a member of the official family of the Archdiocese since 1957. Before assuming his present position, Mr. Kane worked with a number of Catholic organizations including the Rural Life Conference and other Catholic Action groups. Since his graduation from St. Joseph's College in Philadelphia, Pennsylvania, where he received the B.S. degree in administration, he has been an active lecturer, addressing many local and National Catholic groups. He was born in Philadelphia on March 31, 1917. In 1962 he was the recipient of the *Pro Ecclesia et Pontifice* medal from His Holiness Pope John XXIII for his outstanding service to the Church in Cincinnati. Mr. Kane is a member of the Catholic Interracial Council of Cincinnati.

MISS MARGARET JOSEPHINE MEALEY is the executive director of the National Council of Catholic Women, a position she has held since 1949. Before coming to this post, Miss Mealey was a case worker in Alameda County California Charities, director of Labor Relations for the W.P.A. in Alameda County, director of the U.S.O.-National Catholic Community Services Club, Bremerton, Washington, program consultant West Coast Area, U.S.O.-N.C.C.S. Club, regional supervisor for Washington and Oregon, U.S.O.-N.C.C.S. Club, director of U.S.O. Community Directed Club in Oakland, California, executive secretary of the National Catholic Community Services, Oakland, California, and director of the National Services to Women and Girls. She was born in San Francisco on December 21, 1911, and received her higher education at the College of the Holy Name where she received her B.A. degree *cum laude*. She is also the recipient of an honorary doctorate from Seton Hill College in Greensburg, Pennsylvania. Miss Mealey has written for both *The Sign* and for *St. Joseph the Worker*. Her articles include: "Is the Catholic Church Lagging Today in the Use of the Talents of Women?" and "The New Pentecost." She is a member of Citizens' Advisory Council on the Status of Women, a consultant for the World Union of Catholic Women's Organizations, a member of the National Safety Council's National Committee of Religious Leaders for Safety, Pan American Liaison Committee of Women's Organizations, Kappa Gamma Pi, International Federation of Catholic Alumnae, American Association of Group Workers, Adult Education Association, Catholic Press Association, and the National Catholic Adult Education Commission.

PHILOMENA KELLY KERWIN is the executive secretary of the National CYO Federation of the National Catholic Welfare Conference. She was born in Wiconesco, Pennsylvania, on December 21, 1907. Miss Kerwin holds a B.A. degree from College Misericordia in Dallas, Pennsylvania. From 1936 to 1940 she was employed as a newspaper reporter, and in 1947 she became the editor of the N.C.C.S. — Veterans' Administration Hospital Service, a position she held until 1965. In 1963 she also became the editor of *News and Views*, a publication of the Catholic Daughters of America. Miss Kerwin has contributed articles to the *Messenger of the Sacred Heart; Today's Family*, a publication of the Veterans' Administration; to the *Auxiliary Newsletter*, a publication of the American Hospital Association; to *N.C.W.C. Feature Service*, and to *Hospital Management*. She is a member of the Catholic Press Association and the Professional Writers Club of Washington, D. C. She is also National Chairman of the Public Relations Committee of the Catholic Daughters of America and a member of the National Academy of Certified Social Workers and the Catholic Association of Mass Media.

FATHER JOSEPH V. GALLAGHER, C.S.P. is the director of the Paulist Institute for Religious Research in New York City. Before coming to this post, he was a member of the staff of the Catholic Information Center in Boston, Massachusetts. He was born in New York City on March 5, 1923. He received his B.A. degree from Notre Dame University and his LL.B. degree from Fordham University Law School. He also holds an M.A. degree from St. Paul College, Washington, D. C. Father Gallagher, who served in the United States Navy from 1943 to 1946, has contributed articles to *Catholic World* and to *Guide*.

FATHER JOHN A. HARDON, S.J. is an associate professor of comparative religion at Western Michigan University, and an associate professor of systematic theology at Bellarmine School of Theology. Prior to assuming these positions in 1962 and 1965 respectively, he was an assistant professor at West Baden College and an instructor in philosophy and theology at John Carroll and Detroit Universities. Father Hardon, who was born in Midland, Pennsylvania, on June 18, 1914, received his B.A. degree from John Carroll, his M.A. degree from Loyola University, Chicago, Illinois, and his D.S.T. degree from the Gregorian. His writings in the periodical field concentrate on religious history and current problems arising from the pluralistic society in America. About one hundred articles have been published in the United States and Europe, in such magazines as *Theological Studies, Catholic Mind, Saturday Review, La Civilta Cattolica* (Rome), *Le Christ au Monde* (Lille), and *Ecclesia* (Madrid). The books he has published include *The Protestant Churches of America* (1956), now in its third edition and eighth printing, and a Spanish edition (1959) as *Las Eglesias Protestantes de America; All My Liberty* (1959), a theological analysis of the Spiritual Exercises of St. Ignatius; *Christianity in Conflict* (1959) as a sequel to the earlier volume on Protestantism; *For Jesuits* edited (1963) as a manual of prayer and meditation; *Teaching the Devotion to the Sacred Heart*, co-authored (1963) with Thomas Diehl, S.J., and *Religions of the World* (1963), which is in its second edition and fourth printing, with a German edition (1965) published at Zurich. He also has two volumes in progress toward publication in 1966: *Christianity in Dialogue* on the ecumenical movement, and *The Hungry Generation,* a study of religious attitudes and needs in a state university. Father Hardon is also actively cooperating with national agencies like the American Council on Education to promote the teaching of moral and spiritual values in public schools. He has lectured on religious and ethical issues at Indiana, Purdue, Michigan, Michigan State, Washington, and Minnesota Universities. He is a member of the American Academy of Religion, American Association of University Professors, Catholic Theological Society, Religious Education Association, and the Michigan Academy of Arts, Sciences, and Letters, and a consultant and contributor for the *New Catholic Encyclopedia* and the *Catholic Encyclopedia for School and Home.* Contributor in theology to the *Encyclopedia Americana, Encyclopedia International, Collier's,* and *Universal Encyclopedias.*

MSGR. VINCENT A. YZERMANS is the director of the Bureau of Information of the National Catholic Welfare Conference, a position he has held since July of 1964. Prior to coming to this position, Msgr. Yzermans was an assistant pastor at St. Boniface Church, Melrose, Minnesota, and at St. Mary's Cathedral, St. Cloud, Minnesota. In the mid-fifties he was an instructor at Cathedral High School, in St. Cloud. Later he was named pastor of St. John's Church, in Swanville, Minnesota. He was also editor of the *St. Cloud Visitor,* the official diocesan newspaper, and director of the St. Cloud Diocesan Bureau of Information. On December 6, 1962, he was named a *peritus* at the Second Vatican Council. He was born in St. Paul, Minnesota, on December 2, 1925. He took his theological studies at St. Paul Seminary and did graduate work at both Notre Dame University and Fordham University. He holds an M.A. degree in journalism and communications arts from Notre Dame. Msgr. Yzermans is the author of a number of books including: *The Popes Speak of Mary, 1854–1954; Valiant Heralds of Truth; All Things in Christ; Pius XII and the American People; Catholic Origins of Minnesota; Major Addresses of Pius XII,* and *The New Pentecost, Vatican II, Session I.* He is a member of the Minnesota Newspaper Association, National Press Club, Public Relations Society of America, Catholic Theological Society of America, Catholic Historical Association, Catholic Press Association, and the Catholic Broadcasters' Association.

FATHER THOMAS F. McMAHON, C.S.V. is dean of studies and professor of moral theology at the Viatorian Seminary in Washington, D. C. He was born in Chicago, Illinois, on September 4, 1928. In October of 1947 he made his first vows as a cleric of St. Viator, and was assigned to St. Ambrose College where he received his A.B. degree. After completing his studies at the "Angelicum" (University of St. Thomas Aquinas) in Rome, Father McMahon was awarded his doctorate in sacred theology. He is the author of *Imperfect Supernatural Happiness of This Life: a Definition,* which was published in 1962, and has contributed to a considerable number of professional journals, including: *The Priest, Homiletic and Pastoral Review, Catholic Business Education Review, Social Order, Social Digest, American Ecclesiastical Review, Proceedings of the Catholic Theological Society of America,* and *The National Conference of Christian Employers and Managers Program Extra.* He is a member of the Catholic Theological Society of America and the American Management Association. Several years ago, Father McMahon and Brother Leo V. Ryan, C.S.V., organized a biannual conference on business morality which provides theologians and businessmen with an opportunity to consider the moral aspects of business and management functions. Father McMahon is presently program director for the Conference on Business Morality.

FATHER LEON R. McKENZIE is the director of religious education at St. Mary's High School, and an assistant pastor at St. Jude Parish in Wichita, Kansas. He was born in Chicago, Illinois, in 1932. He received his higher education at Kenrick Seminary in St. Louis, Missouri, where he received his B.A. degree. After his ordination to the priesthood in 1958, he has done graduate work at Kansas State Teachers' College in Emporia, Kansas, and will continue his graduate work at Fordham University. In 1964 Father McKenzie published a book entitled *Minitations for Teens,* and has also written a number of articles for various publications, including: *Pastoral Life, Ave Maria; The Bible Today, Catholic School Journal; Youth; Sunday Visitor;* "The Cathedral," *Advance Register North American Journal of Numismatics.* He has had considerable classroom experience, having taught at the elementary, secondary, and college levels. His college teaching was done at Sacred Heart College in Wichita.

FATHER CHARLES W. ALBRIGHT, C.S.P. is presently Catholic chaplain at Louisiana State University in New Orleans, and director of the Newman apostolate there. Before coming to this assignment two years ago, he was assistant director, Newman Hall, the University of California at Berkeley, and at the Newman Foundation, Wayne State University, Detroit, Michigan. Father Albright was also executive secretary of the National Newman Apostolate, Washington, D. C. He was born in Craig, Colorado, on December 18, 1920. His A.B. degree is from St. Paul's College, Washington, D. C. Father Albright has published articles in both *America* and *Ave Maria,* and has written several articles for the *New Catholic Encyclopedia,* and *The Catholic Youth Encyclopedia.* He is presently a member of the Advisory Board of the National Newman Chaplains' Association, and is a member of the Religious Education Association, the Association for the Coordination of University Religious Affairs, and the National Catholic Educational Association.

FATHER THOMAS M. BREW, S.J. is the retreat director at the Loyola Retreat House, Faulkner, Maryland, a position he has held since August, 1964. Before coming to this assignment, he was retreat director at Manresa-on-Severn, Annapolis, Maryland, and an instructor at Loyola High School, Towson, Maryland. Father Brew, who was born on October 17, 1909, received his higher education at Mount St. Mary's College, Emmitsburg, Pennsylvania, the Columbus Law School of The Catholic University of America, and Woodstock College. He is the holder of a B.A. degree from Mount St. Mary's, an LL.B. degree from the Columbus Law School, and a licentiate in sacred theology from Woodstock. From 1951 to 1964, Father Brew was the editor of *The Manresan,* and he is the present editor of *The Loyolan.*

MSGR. JAMES G. WILDERS is the director of the hospital apostolate of the Archdiocese of New York, a position he has held for the past fourteen years. He was born in New York City on December 26, 1914. He attended Manhattan College where he received his B.A. degree. He was ordained to the priesthood in 1939. During his twenty-five years in the priesthood, Msgr. Wilders was five years in parish life at the churches of St. James and Blessed

Sacrament in Manhattan; five and one half years as a Chaplain in the United States Air Force, retiring in 1949 with the rank of major; nearly three years as associate director of the Society for the Propagation of the Faith in New York — and twelve years in his present capacity as chaplain of the Mary Manning Walsh Home and director of the hospital apostolate of the Archdiocese of New York. Monsignor is also on the religious advisory board of the nursing administration; a member of the nursing advisory board at the hospital for special surgery, chaplain of the Cornell University — New York Hospital Medical Center Newman Club, a member of the American Legion, and honorary chaplain of the Coyle Council, Knights of Columbus. Msgr. Wilders has also contributed articles to the New York State *Medical Society Journal* and to *Hospital Progress*. Msgr. Wilders was elevated to the rank of papal chamberlain in 1955 by Pope Pius XII, and to the rank of domestic prelate in 1958 by Pope John XXIII.

FATHER JOHN E. FOLEY is the pastor of St. John's Church in Cambridge, Massachusetts. Before assuming his duties as pastor, he taught theology at Aquinas College in Newton, Massachusetts. He was born in Framingham, Massachusetts, on August 1, 1912. He is a graduate of Boston College where he received his B.A. degree and of St. John's Seminary in Brighton, Massachusetts. Father Foley is a member of the Catholic Theological Society.

FRANK J. GILCHRIST is presently the Catholic chaplain at the United States Air Force Academy in Colorado, a position he has held for the past thirteen months. He has been an airforce chaplain for the past eighteen years, having entered the service in 1949. Father Gilchrist was born in Troy, New York, on April 9, 1920. He attended Siena College, Loudonville, New York, and St. Bernard's Seminary, Rochester, New York, and holds a B.A. degree from this latter institution. He was ordained to the priesthood in 1945. For two years, Father Gilchrist was military editor of the magazine *Catholic Men*, a National Council of Catholic Men publication.

FATHER JOHN JOSEPH FREEMAN is a correctional chaplain at the Illinois State Farm, Vandalia, Illinois, and pastor of St. Joseph Church in Ramsey, Illinois. He has held both positions for the last thirteen years. He was born on March 30, 1910. Father Freeman received his higher education at the Marist Scholasticate, Poughkeepsie, N. Y., Fordham University, and Montreal University, and holds a B.Mus. in liturgical music degree from Montreal University. He has also done considerable work in the field of education. Before assuming his present positions, Father Freeman taught Latin and English at the secondary level, and practical psychology at the School of Nursing at St. Joseph Hospital, Alton, Illinois. During the years 1963–1964, he was president of the American Catholic Correctional Association, and has contributed to the revised section on chaplains in the *Manual of Standards of American Correctional Association* and to *Guidelines for Catholic Correctional Chaplains*. Father Freeman is also a member of the liturgical commission of the Diocese of Springfield, Illinois, and deanery director of the Confraternity of Christian Doctrine. He is a member of the American Correctional Association, the American Correctional Chaplains' Association, and the American Catholic Correctional Chaplains' Association.

Selected Bibliography

by EUGENE J. WEITZEL, C.S.V.

1. THE PASTORAL MINISTRY

Benedictines of St. Meinrad, ed., *The Popes and the Priesthood*. St. Meinrad, Ind.: Grail Publications, 1960.

Bertrams, Wilhelm, S.J., *The Celibacy of the Priest, Meaning and Basis* (tr. Rev. P. Byrne, S.M.). Westminster, Md.: Newman Press, 1963.

Caemmerer, Richard R., and Fuerheinger, Alfred O., eds., *Toward a More Excellent Ministry*. St. Louis: Concordia, 1964.

Cafasso, Joseph, St., *The Priest, the Man of God*. St. Paul, Minn.: Radio Replies Press Society, 1958.

Carré, A. M., O.P., *The Everlasting Priest*. New York: Kenedy, 1961.

Dalla Costa, E., Card., *Consider Your Call*. Derby, N. Y.: St. Paul Publications, 1951.

D'Arcy, Paul F., M.M., and Kennedy, Eugene C., M.M., *The Genius of the Apostolate*. New York: Sheed and Ward, 1965.

Dillenschneider, Clement, C.SS.R., *The Holy Spirit and the Priest* (tr. Sister M. Renelle, S.S.N.D.). St. Louis: B. Herder, 1965.

Doyle, C. H., *Looking Toward the Priesthood*. Derby, N. Y.: St. Paul Publications, 1961.

Gorres, Ida Friederike, *Is Celibacy Outdated?* (tr. Barbara Waldstein-Wartenbert). Westminster, Md.: Newman Press, 1965.

Hermand, Pierre, *The Priest: Celibate or Married*. Baltimore, Md.: Helicon, 1965.

Heston, Edward L., *Priest of the Fathers*. Milwaukee: Bruce, 1945.

Kenrick, E., "New Light on the Spirituality of American Priests," *The American Ecclesiastical Review,* 139:5 (November, 1958), 299–311.

Manning, H., Card., *The Eternal Priesthood*. Westminster, Md.: Newman Press, 1954.

Marmion, C., *Christ — The Ideal of the Priest*. London: Sands, 1952.

Montini, Giovanni Battista, Card., *The Priest* (tr. Serge Hughes). Baltimore, Md.: Helicon, 1966.

Nash, Robert, S.J., *Wisdom I Ask*. Westminster, Md.: Newman Press, 1965.

Nugent, F., ed., *The Priest in Our Day*. Westminster, Md.: Newman Press, 1954.

O'Neill, David P., *Priestly Celibacy and Maturity*. New York: Sheed and Ward, 1965.

Paul VI, *The Priest*. Baltimore, Md.: Helicon, 1966.

Rihn, Roy, *The Priestly Amen*. New York: Sheed and Ward, 1965.

Sellmair, J., *The Priest in the World*. Westminster, Md.: Newman Press, 1955.

Suhard, Emmanual Card., *Priests Among Men*. Notre Dame, Ind.: Fides, 1963.

2. THE PROPER AND FRUITFUL
CELEBRATION OF THE SACRED LITURGY

Athill, Mother Emmanuel, *Teaching Liturgy in Schools,* Notre Dame, Ind.: Fides, 1959.

Bouyer, Louis, *Liturgical Piety.* Notre Dame, Ind.: Notre Dame Univ. Press, 1954.

———— *Rite and Man: Natural Sacredness and Christian Liturgy* (tr. M. Joseph Costelloe, S.J.). Notre Dame, Ind.: Notre Dame Univ. Press, 1963.

Brasso, Gabriel, *Liturgy and Spirituality* (tr. L. J. Doyle). Collegeville, Minn.: Liturgical Press, 1960.

Dalmais, O.P., *Introduction to the Liturgy.* Baltimore, Md.: Helicon, 1961.

Diekmann, Godfrey, O.S.B., *Come Let Us Worship.* Baltimore, Md.: Helicon, 1961.

Gelineau, Joseph, S.J., *Voices and Instruments in Christian Worship* (tr. C. Howell, S.J.). Collegeville, Minn.: Liturgical Press, 1964.

Guardini, Romano, *The Church and the Catholic and the Spirit of the Liturgy* (tr. A. Land). London: Sheed and Ward, 1935.

Jungmann, Josef Andreas, S.J., *Pastoral Liturgy.* New York: Herder and Herder, 1962.

King, J., *The Liturgy and the Laity.* Westminster, Md.: Newman Press, 1963.

Leonard, W., S.J., ed., *Liturgy for the People: Essays in Honor of Gerald Ellard.* Milwaukee: Bruce, 1963.

Liturgical Conference, The, *The Renewal of Christian Education.* Twenty-fourth North American Liturgical Week, 1963. Washington, D. C.: The Liturgical Conference, Inc., 1964.

McCabe, Fr., *The People of God, the Fullness of Life in the Church.* New York: Sheed and Ward, 1964.

McManus, Frederick R., ed., *The Revival of the Liturgy.* New York: Herder and Herder, 1963.

Magner, Johannes, ed., *The Church and the Liturgy. Concilium,* Vol. II. New Jersey: Paulist Press, 1964.

Marshall, Romey P., O.S.L., and Taylor, Michael J., S.J., *Liturgy and Christian Unity.* Englewood Cliffs, N. J.: Prentice-Hall, 1965.

Martimort, A. G., *Signs of the New Covenant.* Collegeville, Minn.: Liturgical Press, 1963.

Meyer, Leonard B., *Emotion and Meaning in Music.* Chicago: Univ. of Chicago Press, 1957.

Miller, John H., C.S.C., *Fundamentals of Liturgy.* Notre Dame, Ind.: Notre Dame Univ. Press, 1959.

Schillebeeckx, Edward, O.P., *Christ, the Sacrament of the Encounter With God.* New York: Sheed and Ward, 1963.

Sloyan, Gerald S., *Liturgy in Focus.* Glen Rock, N. J.: Paulist Press (Deus Books), 1962.

———— *Worship in a New Key, What the Council Teaches on the Liturgy.* New York: Herder and Herder, 1965.

3. ARCHITECTURE: THE ARCHITECT AND THE PRIEST
4. THE LITURGICAL ELEMENTS
OF THE CHURCH INTERIOR

Amency, J., "Architectural Aggiornamento," *Catholic World,* 190 (August, 1964), 279–285.

———— "Architecture in Print; Books," *America,* 112 (February 6, 1965), 204–205.

Bandas, Rudolph G., "Modernistic Art and Divine Worship," *American Ecclesiastical Review,* 142:4 (October, 1960), 228–235.

Baumann, C., "Liturgy, Art and Architecture," *Friar,* 22 (July–August, 1964), 25–29: Reply and Rejoinder, 23 (January, 1965), 38–39.

Biéler, André, *Architecture in Worship: The Christian Place of Worship* (tr. Donald and Odette Elliott). Philadelphia: Westminster Press, 1965.

Boccia, E., Heigerg, J., and Rambusch, R., "The Visual Liturgy," *Sign,* 44 (March, 1965), 46–49.

Carey, G., "Sermons in Stones," *Good Work,* 26 (Summer, 1963), 82–91.

———— *Church Architecture.* Washington, D. C.: The Liturgical Conference, 1965.

Crichton, J., "Building Churches; University of Birmingham Institute," *Clergy Review,* 48 (May, 1963), 279–285.

De Blas, A., "Planning the Structure: the Process," *Priestly Studies,* 30 (September, 1964), 28–42.

Diekmann, Godfrey, O.S.B., "The Place of Liturgical Worship," *The Church and the Liturgy (Concilium,* Vol. 2). New York: Paulist Press, 1964.

Dillenberger, Jane, *Style and Content in Christian Art.* New York: Abingdon Press, 1965.

Dimock, G., "Architecture and Liturgy," *Dominicana,* 49 (Summer, 1964), 130–140.

Dixon, Jr., John W., *Nature and Grace in Art.* Chapel Hill, N. C.: Univ. of North Carolina Press, 1964.

Dom David, "Coming to Terms With the Fine Arts," *Good Work,* (Winter, 1965).

Hammond, Peter, *Liturgy and Architecture.* New York: Columbia Univ. Press, 1960.

Hazo, S., "Art and the Liturgy," *Catholic World,* 199 (August, 1964), 287–292.

Lowrie, Walter, *Art in the Early Church.* 2nd rev. ed. New York: Harper and Row, 1965.

McNaspy, Clement J., "Expression of Faith and Religion Through Art and Music," *National Liturgical Week,* 23 (1962), 192–195.

Obata, G., "How to Design Meaningless Churches," *Catholic Property Administration,* 27 (April, 1963), 44–45.

O'Connell, J., *Church Building and Church Furnishing.* Notre Dame, Ind.: Notre Dame Univ. Press, 1955.

Pavia, R., "Modern Church Building Problems of Sacred Space," *Liturgical Art,* 31 (May, 1963), 74–76.

Quinn, P., "Real Determinants of Significant Church Building," *National Liturgical Week,* 23 (1962), 121–125.

———— "Refurnishing Churches," *Homiletic and Pastoral Review,* 65 (March, 1965), 518–520.

Sablé, S., "Project for a Church and a Convent," *Liturgical Art,* 33 (February, 1965), 50–51.

Seasoltz, Kevin, *The House of God.* New York: Herder and Herder, 1963.

Smith, George Everard Kidder, *The New Churches of Europe.* New York: Holt, 1964.

———— *The New Architecture of Europe.* New York: Meridian, 1961.

Tegels, A., "The Church as a Figure of the New Jerusalem: Need for Symbolism as Well as Function," *National Liturgical Week,* 23 (1962), 127–130.

Tomkins, H., "Music, Bricks and Mortar," *Worship,* 38 (November–December, 1964), 644–651.

White, James F., *Protestant Worship and Church Architecture.* Fair Lawn, N. J.: Oxford, 1964.

Wright, L., "Church Design: A Reappraisal," *Month,* 29 (March, 1963), 133–139.

5. THE VIRTUES OF A GOOD CONFESSOR

6. THE CONFESSOR FOCUSES ON THE ADOLESCENT

7. THE CONFESSOR OF NUNS

8. CO-WORKERS IN THE LORD

A. The Sacrament of Penance:

Anciaux, P., *The Sacrament of Penance.* New York: Sheed and Ward, 1962.

Emerson, James G., Jr., *The Dynamics of Forgiveness.* Philadelphia: Westminster Press, 1964.

Grossouw, W. K., *Spirituality of the New Testament.* New York: Herder and Herder, 1961.

Haring, Bernard, C.SS.R., *The Law of Christ.* Westminster, Md.: Newman, 1963, I, 387–478.

Jean-Nesmy, Claude, *Conscience and Confession* (tr. Malachy Carroll). Chicago: Franciscan Herald Press, 1965.

McAuliffe, C., "Penance and Reconciliation With the Church," *Theological Studies,* 26 (1965), 1–39.

Martimort, A. G., *The Sign of the New Covenant.* Collegeville, Minn.: The Liturgical Press, 1963.

Poschmann, B., *Penance and the Anointing of the Sick.* New York: Herder and Herder, 1964.

Rahner, Karl, S.J., *The Church and the Sacraments* (tr. W. J. O'Hara). New York: Herder and Herder, 1963.

——— "Forgotten Truths Concerning the Sacrament of Penance," *Theological Investigations,* Vol. II. Baltimore, Md.: Helicon, 1963.

Ranwez, P., S.J., "Forming a Moral Conscience in the Very Young Child," *Lumen Vitae,* 15 (1960).

Riga, Peter, *Sin and Penance.* Milwaukee: Bruce, 1962.

Roguet, A. M., O.P., *Christ Acts Through the Sacraments,* Collegeville, Minn.: The Liturgical Press, 1953.

Schillebeeckx, Edward, O.P., *Christ, the Sacrament of the Encounter With God.* New York: Sheed and Ward, 1963.

Von Speyr, Adrienne, *Confession.* New York: Herder and Herder, 1966.

B. Scrupulosity and Anxiety:

Allers, Rudolph, *The Psychology of Character.* New York: Sheed and Ward, 1940.

Bier, William C., S.J., ed. *The Adolescent: His Search for Understanding.* New York: Fordham Univ. Press, 1963.

——— *Personality and Sexual Problems in Pastoral Psychology.* New York: Fordham Univ. Press, 1964.

Hagmaier, George, C.S.P., and Gleason, R. W., S.J., *Counselling the Catholic.* New York: Sheed and Ward, 1959.

Kelly, Gerald, S.J., *Guidance for Religious.* Westminster, Md.: Newman, 1956.

Mora, G., "The Psychotherapeutic Treatment of Scrupulous Patients," *Cross Currents,* 7 (1957), 29–40.

O'Flaherty, Vincent, S.J., *How to Cure Scruples.* Milwaukee: Bruce, 1966.

Oraison, Marc, *Illusion and Anxiety.* New York: Macmillan Co., 1963.

Terruew, A. A. A., M.D., *The Neurosis in the Light of Rational Psychology.* New York: P. J. Kenedy and Sons, 1960.

Weisner, Wayne M., and Riffel, Pius, S.J., "Scrupulosity: Religion and Obsessive Compulsive Behavior in Children," *American Journal of Psychiatry,* 117 (1960), 314–318.

C. Adolescence and Chastity:

Archambault, P. and Boddeti, R., *Jeunesse d'aujourd'hui, ses problems, ses conflicts.* Paris: Editiones Fleurus, 1962.

Babin, Pierre, *Faith and the Adolescent* (tr. David Gibson). New York: Herder and Herder, 1965.

Berrigan, Philip, S.S.J., "Living the Mystery of Marriage," *Worship,* 36:7 (July, 1962), 437–444.

Blees, Robert A., and Staff of First Community Church, Columbus, Ohio. *Counseling With Teen-agers.* Englewood Cliffs, N. J.: Prentice-Hall, 1965.

Bouyet, Louis, *Woman and Man Before God.* London: Darton, Longman, and Todd, 1960.

Conway, J. D., *What They Ask About Marriage.* Chicago: Fides, 1955.

Cooke, Bernard J., S.J., *Formation of Faith.* Chicago: Loyola Univ. Press, 1965.

Ellard, Gerald, S.J., *Christian Life and Worship.* Milwaukee: Bruce, 1933.

Filas, Francis L., S.J., *Sex Education in the Family.* Englewood Cliffs, N. J.: Prentice-Hall, 1966.

Hildebrand, Dietrich von, *In Defense of Purity.* New York: Longmans, Green, and Company, 1931.

Kerns, Joseph E., S.J., *The Theology of Marriage.* New York: Sheed and Ward, 1964.

Kilgallon, James J., and Weber, Gerard, *Beyond the Commandments.* New York: Herder and Herder, 1964.

Landis, Paul H., *Understanding Teen-Agers.* New York: Appleton-Century Crofts, 1955.

McCabe, Herbert, S.P., "Sex and the Sacred," *Life of the Spirit,* 16:182 (August–September, 1961), 70–80.

Rouille, M. August, *Catholicisme et Sexualité.* Paris: Editions de Levain, 1953.

Suenens, Leon Joseph, Card., *Love and Control.* Westminster, Md.: Newman, 1961.

Thomas, John L., S.J., "Family Life and Sex Relations," *Religious Education,* 58:2 (March–April, 1963), 96–105.

D. Adolescence:

Ausubel, David, *Theory and Problems of Adolescent Development.* New York: Grune and Stratton, 1954.

Babin, Pierre, *Crisis of Faith.* New York: Herder and Herder, 1963.

Bier, William C., S.J., *The Adolescent: His Search for Understanding.* New York: Fordam Univ. Press, 1963.

Bridwell, Mabel M., "From Dependence to Independence — The Role of Parent-Child-Teacher Relationship," *Childhood Education,* 24 (1948), 219–223.

Connell, William, S.J., *The Adolescent Boy.* Notre Dame, Ind.: Fides, 1958.

Fromm, Erich, *Escape From Freedom.* New York: Rinehart and Co., 1941.

Giese, Vincent J., *Patterns for Teenagers.* Notre Dame, Ind.: Fides, 1956.

Greeley, Andrew M., *Strangers in the House.* New York: Sheed and Ward, 1961.

Guelluy, Robert, "What Kind of Christianism Should Be Put Before Youth?" *Lumen Vitae,* 19/1 (1964), 77–92.

Heider, F., *The Psychology of Interpersonal Relations.* New York: John Wiley and Sons, 1958.

Helping Teachers Understand Children. Washington, D. C.: American Council On Education, 1945.

Horrocks, John E., *The Psychology of Adolescence,* 2nd ed. Boston: Houghton and Mifflin Co., 1962.

Jersild, Arthur T., *The Psychology of Adolescence.* New York: Macmillan, 1963.

Liccione, J. V., "The Changing Family Relationships of Adolescent Girls," *Journal of Abnormal and Social Psychology,* 51 (1955), 421–426.

McCullough, Marygrace, "Liturgy in Adolescent Personality Growth," *Insight,* II/1 (Summer, 1963) and II/2 (Fall, 1963).

Riesman, D. *et al., The Lonely Crowd.* New Haven: Yale Univ. Press, 1950.

Rogers, Carl R., *Client-Centered Therapy.* Boston: Houghton Mifflin Co., 1951.

Schneiders, Alexander, *Personality Development and Adjustment in Adolescence.* Milwaukee: Bruce, 1960.

Schutz, W. C., *FIRO — A Three-Dimensional Theory of Interpersonal Behavior.* New York: Rinehart and Co., 1958.

Seidman, Jerome M., ed., *The Adolescent — A Book of Readings.* New York: Holt, Rinehart and Winston, 1960.

Sloyan, Gerard, *Christ the Lord.* New York: Herder and Herder, 1962.

Strang, Ruth, *The Adolescent Views Himself.* New York: McGraw-Hill, 1957.

———— *Group Work in Education.* New York: Harper and Brothers, 1958.

Sullivan, Harry Stack, *The Interpersonal Theory of Psychiatry.* New York: W. W. Norton and Co., 1953.

Symonds, P. M., *The Psychology of Parent-Child Relationships.* New York: D. Appleton-Century Co., 1939.

Varillon, Francois, *Announcing Christ.* Westminster, Md.: Newman, 1964.

E. Religious Sisters:

Biot, Francis, *The Rise of Protestant Monasticism.* Baltimore, Md.: Helicon, 1963.

Dondero, Austin, F.S.C., *No Borrowed Light: Mental Health For Religious.* Milwaukee: Bruce, 1965.

Donnelly, Gertrude Joseph, Sister, C.S.J.C., *The Sister Apostle.* Notre Dame, Ind.: Fides, 1964.

Evoy, John H., S.J., and Christoph, Van F., S.J., *Maturity in the Religious Life.* New York: Sheed and Ward, 1965.

Gambari, Elio, S.S.M., *The Religious-Apostolic Formation of Sisters.* New York: Fordham Univ. Press, 1964.

Harmer, Mary Fabian, Sister, S.C.M.M., comp. *Books for Religious Sisters: A General Bibliography.* Washington, D. C.: Catholic Univ. of America Press, 1963.

Herr, Vincent V., S.J., *Religious Psychology.* Staten Island, N. Y.: Alba House, 1964.

Huyghe, Gerard, B.P., *Tensions and Change: the Problems of Religious Orders Today* (tr. Sister Marie Florett, S.C.H.). Westminster, Md.: Newman, 1965.

John XXIII, "To Religious," *Sister Formation Bulletin. VI* (Spring, 1960), 18–21.

———— "Il Tempio Massio," *Sister Formation Bulletin. VI* (Spring, 1960), 1–5.

Klimisch, Sister Mary Jane, O.S.B., *The One Bride.* New York: Sheed and Ward, 1965.

Legrand, M. E. P., Lucien, *The Biblical Doctrine of Virginity.* New York: Sheed and Ward, 1963.

McGoldrick, Desmond, C.S.Sp., *Independence Through Submission.* Pittsburgh: Duquesne Univ. Press, 1964.

Meissner, W. W., S.J., *Group Dynamics in the Religious Life.* Notre Dame, Ind.: Notre Dame Univ. Press, 1965.

O'Brien, Michael J., C.S.V., and Steimel, Raymond, J., eds., *Psychological Aspects of Spiritual Development.* Washington, D. C.: Catholic Univ. of America Press, 1964.

O'Flaherty, V. M., S.J., *How to Cure Scruples.* Milwaukee: Bruce, 1966.

Paul VI (as Cardinal Montini), "Discourse to Sisters — 1961," *Sister Formation Bulletin. X* (Autumn, 1963), 1–6.

———— *Magno Gaudio.* Washington, D. C.: National Catholic Welfare Conference, 1964.

Pius XII, *Annus Sacer. Acta Apostolicae Sedis* 43 (1951).

———— *Provida Mater. Acta Apostolicae Sedis* 39 (1947).

———— *Sponsa Christi. Acta Apostolicae Sedis* 42 (1950).

———— *Holy Virginity.* New York: Paulist Press, (1954).

9.   THE MODERN RENEWAL OF PREACHING

Dodd, C.H., *Apostolic Preaching and its Development*. London: Hodder and Stoughton, 1963.

Drury, Ronau, ed., *Preaching*. New York: Sheed and Ward, 1962.

Burghardt, Walter J., S.J., *All Lost in Wonder*. Cincinnati, Ohio: Pustet, 1962.

Crossan, Dominic M., O.S.M., *Scanning the Sunday Gospel*. Milwaukee: Bruce, 1966.

Donne, John, 1573–1631, *Sermons on the Psalms and Gospels with a selection of prayers and meditations* (ed. Evelyn M. Simpson) Berkeley: Univ. of California Press, 1963, 244.

Fuller, Reginald, *What is Liturgical Preaching?* London: SCM Press, 1957.

Grasso, Domenico, S.J., *Proclaiming God's Message*. Notre Dame, Ind.: Notre Dame Univ. Press, 1965.

Hitz, Paul, C.SS.R., *To Preach the Gospel* (tr. Rosemary Sheed). New York: Sheed and Ward, 1963, 209.

Hunter, A. M., *Interpreting the Parables*. Philadelphia: Westminster, 1960.

Jungmann, Josef, S.J., *The Good News, Yesterday and Today*. New York: Sadlier, 1962.

Keir, Thomas, *The Word in Worship*. London: Oxford, 1962.

Knox, Ronald, *The Epistles and Gospels for Sundays and Holydays*. (Translation and Commentary). New York: Sheed and Ward, 1946.

———— *The Window in the Wall*. New York: Sheed and Ward, 1957.

Lawrence, Emeric, O.S.B., *Homilies for the Year*. Collegeville, Minn.: Liturgical Press, 1965.

McBride, Alfred, O.Praem., *Homilies for the New Liturgy*. Milwaukee: Bruce, 1966.

Martimort, A. M., *et al.*, *The Liturgy and the Word of God*. Collegeville, Minn.: Liturgical Press, 1959.

Miller, Donald, *Fire in thy Mouth*. Nashville: Abington, 1954.

Murphy, R. T. A., O.P., *The Sunday Epistles*. Milwaukee: Bruce, 1961.

———— *The Sunday Gospels*. Milwaukee: Bruce, 1960.

Murphy-O'Connor, Jerome, O.P., *Paul on Preaching*. New York: Sheed and Ward, 1964.

Mussner, Franz, *The Use of Parables in Catechetics*. Notre Dame, Ind.: Notre Dame Univ. Press, 1965.

Ott, Heinrich, *Theology and Preaching* (tr. Harold Knight). Philadelphia: Westminster Press, 1965.

Parsch, Pius, *Sermons on the Liturgy for Sundays* (tr. Philip T. Weller). Milwaukee: Bruce, 1963 (4th prtg. 1965).

Philibert, Michel, *Christ's Preaching — and Ours* (tr. David Lewis). Richmond, Va.: John Knox Press, 1964.

Pittenger, W. Norman, *Proclaiming Christ Today*. Greenwich: Seabury, 1962.

Priest's Guide to Parish Worship. Washington, D. C.: Liturgical Conference, 1964.

Putz, Louis J., C.S.C., *The Lord's Day*. Notre Dame, Ind.: Fides, 1963.

Rock, Augustine, O.P., *Unless They Be Sent*. Dubuque: Brown, 1953.

Selner, John C., S.S., *Fundamental Course in Sacred Eloquence*. Toledo: Gregorian Institute of America, 1960.

Semmelroth, Otto, S.J., *The Preaching Word: On the Theology of Proclamation* (tr. John Jay Hughes). New York: Herder and Herder, 1965.

———— *The Preaching Word* (tr. John Jay Hughes). New York: Herder and Herder, 1965.

Sharp, John K., *Our Preaching*. Philadelphia: Dolphin Press, 1936.

Von Allmen, Jean-Jacques, *Preaching and Congregation*. Richmond: Knox, 1962.

Weber, Gerard, and Killgallon, James, *Witness to the World*. Staten Island, N. Y.: Alba House, 1965.

Whitesell, Faris D., Comp., *Great Expository Sermons*. Westwood, N. J.: Fleming H. Revell, 1964.
—— *The Word*: *Readings in Theology*. New York: Kenedy, 1964.

Books on the Bible for Teaching and Preaching

Alonso Schökel, Luis, S.J., *Understanding Biblical Research* (tr. Peter J. McCord, S.J.). New York: Herder and Herder, 1963.
Anchor Bible Series. (A continuing series combining the most up-to-date scholarship and translation available). New York: Doubleday, 1965.
Anderson, Bernhard, *Understanding the Old Testament*. Englewood Cliffs, N. J.: Prentice-Hall, 1957.
Brown, Raymond E., S.S., *New Testament Essays*. Milwaukee: Bruce, 1965.
Bruns, J. Edgar, *Hear his voice today; a guide to the content and comprehension of the Bible*. New York: P. J. Kenedy and Sons, 1963.
Congar, Marie Joseph, O.P., *The Mystery of the Temple; or, The manner of God's presence to his creatures from Genesis to the Apocalypse* (tr. Reginald F. Trevett). Westminister, Md.: Newman, 1962.
Ellis, Peter F., C.SS.R., *The Men and the Message of the Old Testament*. Collegeville, Minn.: Liturgical Press, 1963.
Flanagan, Neil, O.S.M., *Salvation History*. New York: Sheed and Ward, 1964.
Grant, Robert M., *A Historical Introduction to the New Testament*. New York: Harper and Row, 1963, 447.
Gray, John, *Archaeology and the Old Testament World*. New York: Nelson, 1962.
Guillet, Jacques, *Themes of the Bible*. Notre Dame, Ind.: Fides, 1964.
Gutzwiller, Richard, S.J., 1896–1958. *Day by Day With Saint Matthew's Gospel* (tr. I. T. Hale). Chicago: Regnery, 1964.
The Interpreter's Dictionary of the Bible, an illustrated encyclopedia. New York: Abingdon Press, 1962.
Joy, Charles R., comp., *A Concordance of Bible Readings*. Cleveland, Ohio: World Publishing Company, 1965.
—— *Harper's Topical Concordance*. Rev. and enl. ed. New York: Harper and Row, 1962, 6128.
Kopp, Clemens, *The Holy Places of the Gospels* (tr. Ronald Walls). New York: Herder and Herder, 1963, 424.
Kraeling, Emil Gottlieb Heinrich, *The Clarified New Testament, Vol. I: The Four Gospels*. New York: McGraw-Hill, 1962.
McGoey, John H., S.F.M., *Speak, Lord!* Milwaukee: Bruce, 1966.
McKenzie, John L., S.J., ed., *The Bible in Current Catholic Thought*. New York: Herder and Herder, 1962.
—— *Dictionary of the Bible*. Milwaukee: Bruce, 1965.
—— *The Power and the Wisdom: An Interpretation of the New Testament*. Milwaukee: Bruce, 1965.
Maertens, Thierry, O.S.B., *A Feast in Honor of Yahweh* (tr. Mother Kathryn Sullivan, R.S.C.J.). Notre Dame, Ind.: Fides, 1965.
Maly, Eugene H., *The World of David and Solomon*. Englewood Cliffs, N. J.: Prentice-Hall, 1966.
May, Herbert Gordon, ed., *Oxford Bible Atlas*. New York: Oxford University Press, 1962.
Pawlikowski, John, O.S.M., *Epistle Homilies*. Milwaukee: Bruce, 1966.
Plastaras, James, C.M., *The God of Exodus*. Milwaukee: Bruce, 1966.
Quesnell, Quentin, S.J., *This Good News: An Introduction to the Catholic Theology of the New Testament*. Milwaukee: Bruce, 1964.
Schnackenburg, Rudolf, *New Testament Theology Today* (tr. David Askew). New York: Herder and Herder, 1963.
Tos, Aldo J., *Approaches to the Bible: The Old Testament*. Englewood Cliffs, N. J.: Prentice-Hall, 1963.

Weiser, Artur, *The Psalms, A Commentary* (tr. Herbert Hartwell). Philadelphia: Westminster Press, 1962.

Wollman-Tsamir, Pinchas, ed., *The graphic history of the Jewish heritage; an encyclopedia presentation with illustrations, charts, vignettes and tables: the Biblical period.* New York: Shengold Publishers, Inc., 1963.

Worden, Thomas, *The Psalms are Christian Prayer.* New York: Sheed and Ward, 1962, 219.

Wright, George Ernest, *Biblical Archaeology.* New and revised ed. Philadelphia: Westiminster Press, 1962.

Zurcher, E., *Buddhism: Its Origin and Spread in Word, Maps, and Pictures.* New York: St. Martin's Press, 1962.

10.   CONTEMPORARY CATECHETICS

A. General Catechetics

Collins, Joseph B., *C.C.D. Methods in Modern Catechetics.* Milwaukee: Bruce, 1966.

St. Augustine, *First Catechetical Instruction.* Westminster, Md.: Newman, 1958.

Australian Bishop's Committee, *Catholic Catechism,* Book II. Sydney, Australia: E. K. Dwyer Publishing Company, 1963.

Babin, Pierre, *Crisis of Faith.* New York: Herder and Herder, 1964.

Bandas, Rudolph G., *Catechetical and Confraternity Methods.* St. Paul, Minnesota: C.C.D. of Archdiocese of St. Paul, Inc., 1957.

Carol Frances, Sister Mary, B.V.M., "Teacher as Mediator," *Perspectives,* VI (December, 1961), 10–13.

Carter, Most Rev. G. Emmett, D.D., *The Modern Challenge to Religious Education.* New York: Sadlier, 1961.

———— *La question Mariale.* Paris: Seuil, 1963.

Delcuve, George, S.J., "The Teacher's Faith and its Radiation," *Lumen Vitae,* IX (April–June, 1954), 209–216.

———— and Meilhac, Louis, "Dispositions Unfavorable to the Faith," *Lumen Vitae,* XVI (September, 1961), 449–464.

Ecumenism and Religious Education. Chicago: Loyola Univ. Press, 1965.

Gettys, Joseph M., *How to Teach the Revelation,* 56. *How to Study the Revelation.* Richmond, Va.: John Knox Press, 1963.

Gilleman, Gerard, S.J., "The Educator, Witness to Charity," *Lumen Vitae,* IX (April–June, 1954), 556–568.

Goldbrunner, Joseph, gen. ed., *Contemporary Catechetics* Series:
    a. Filthaut, Theodor, ed., *Israel in Christian Religious Education.* Notre Dame. Ind.: Notre Dame Univ. Press, 1965.
    b. Goldbrunner, Joseph, *New Catechetical Methods,* 1965.
    c. Mussner, Franz, *Christ and the End of the World,* 1965.
    d. ———— *The Use of Parables in Contemporary Catechetics,* 1965.

Grasso, Domenico, S.J., "The Catechist as Witness," *Worship,* 38 (February, 1964). 157–164.

Hofinger, Johannes, S.J., *The Art of Teaching Christian Doctrine,* Notre Dame, Ind.: Notre Dame Univ. Press, 1962.

———— *Imparting the Christian Message.* Notre Dame, Ind.: Notre Dame Univ. Press, 1961.

———— *Teaching All Nations: A Symposium of Modern Catechetics.* Notre Dame, Ind.: Notre Dame Univ. Press, 1961.

Hofinger and Reedy, *The A B C's of Modern Catechetics.* New York: Sadlier, 1962.

———— and Stone, Theodore C., eds., *Pastoral Catechetics.* New York: Herder and Herder, 1964.

Jungman, Joseph, S.J., *Handing on the Faith.* New York: Herder and Herder, 1959.

McBride, Alfred, O.Praem., *Catechetics: A Theology of Proclamation.* Milwaukee: Bruce, 1966.

McMahon, John T., O.P., *Building Character from Within.* Milwaukee: Bruce, 1940.

Sister Michael, O.L.V.M., *Communicating the Mystery.* Huntington, Ind.: Our Sunday Visitor Press, 1963.

Opdenaker, Theodore A., "Humility, Patience, Justice, Truthfulness," *Catholic School Journal,* 52, No. 2 (February, 1952).

Pius XI, *On the Christian Education of Youth* (*Divini Illius Magistri*). New York: Paulist Press, 1929.

Raphael, John, O.S.A., "The Teacher: A Good Shepherd," *Catholic School Journal,* 60 (April, 1960), 59 f.

Sloyan, Gerard, ed., *Modern Catechetics.* New York: Macmillan, 1963.

B. Catechizing on Our Lady

Carol, Juniper., ed.. *Mariology,* 3 Vols. Milwaukee: Bruce, 1954–57–61.

Congar, Yves, *Christ, Our Lady and the Church.* Westminster, Md.: Newman, 1957.

Davis, Charles, "The Starting Point of Mariology," *Theology for Today.* New York: Sheed and Ward, 1962.

De Lubac, Henri, "The Church and Our Lady," *Splendor of the Church,* Glen Rock, N. J.: Deus Books (Paulist Press), 1963.

Diekmann, Godfrey, "Mary, Model of Our Worship," *Worship,* 34 (October, 1960), 579–586.

Dillenschneider, Clement, *Le sens de la foi et le progres dogmatique du mystere marial.* Romae: Academic Mariana Internationalis, 1954.

Laurentin, Rene, *Queen of Heaven* (*A Short Treatise on Marian Theology*). Dublin: Clonmore and Reymonds, Ltd., 1956.

———— *Structure et theologie de Luc I–II.* Paris: Gabalda, 1957.

Mary in the Liturgy. Proceedings of the Liturgical Week, 1954. Elsberry, Mo.: The Liturgical Conference, 1955.

"The Mother of God," *Lumen Vitae,* 8 (April–June, 1953), 169–347.

Papal Teachings — Our Lady (Arranged by the Benedictine Monks of Solesmes). Boston: St. Paul Editions, 1961.

Rahner, Karl, S.J., *Mary Mother of the Lord.* New York: Herder and Herder, 1963.

———— "Mary and the Apostolate," *The Christian Commitment.* New York: Sheed and Ward, 1963.

Rahner, Hugo, *Our Lady and the Church.* New York: Pantheon, 1959.

Scheeben, M. J., *Mariology,* 2 Vols. St. Louis: Herder, 1948.

Schillebeeckx, E. H., *Marie mere de la redemption, approches du mystere marial.* Paris: Cerf, 1963.

Semmelroth, O., *Mary, Archetype of the Church.* New York: Sheed and Ward, 1963.

Thurian, Max, *Mary Mother of All Christians.* New York: Herder and Herder, 1963.

11. and 12.   NEEDS AND PROBLEMS
OF THE MODERN PARISH — PART I
NEEDS AND PROBLEMS
OF THE MODERN PARISH — PART II

Berard, Aram, S.J., *Preparatory Reports: Second Vatican Council.* Philadelphia: Westminster Press, 1965.

Blöchlinger, Alex, *The Modern Parish Community* (tr. Geoffrey Stevens). New York: P. J. Kenedy and Sons, 1965.

Casey, Thomas F., H.F.D., *Pastoral Manual for New Priests*. Milwaukee: Bruce, 1962.

Chautard, J., *The Soul of the Apostolate* (tr. J. A. Moran). New York: P. J. Kenedy and Sons, 1933.

Courtois, Gaston, *Before His Face*. New York: Herder and Herder, 1961–1962.

———— *The Young Priest*. New York: Herder and Herder, 1965.

Cunningham, James V., *The Resurgent Neighborhood*. Notre Dame, Ind.: Fides, 1965.

Fichter, Joseph H., S. J., "What's Wrong With Sunday School?" *Catholic World*, 185 (1957), 246–251.

———— *Social Relations in the Urban Parish*. Chicago: Chicago Univ. Press, 1954.

Franz, J., *The Parish Priest's Examen*. Springfield, Ill.: Templegate, 1955.

Frazier, E. Franklin, *The Negro in the United States*, rev. ed. New York: Macmillan Co., 1957.

Gauthier, Paul, *Christ, the Church and the Poor* (tr. Edward Fitzgerald). Westminster, Md.: Newman, 1965.

Greer, Scott, *The Emerging City*. New York: The Free Press of Glencoe, 1962.

Hanrahan, N., "Cardinal Vaughn and the Secular Clergy," *The Clergy Review*, 47:12 (December, 1961), 715–733.

Hofinger, Johannes, S. J., "The Catechetical Apostolate of Lay Teachers," *Lumen Vitae*, 12 (1957), 650–656.

———— "The Formation Our Catechists Need," *Shaping the Christian Message* (G. Sloyan ed.). Glen Rock, N. J.: Paulist Press, 1963.

Jacobs, W., "Lest We Wait With Bubbles Burst," *Worship*, 38 (1964), 151–156.

Kelly, John E., "You and Your Parish — The Strength of the Church," *Catholic Action*, 32 (1950), 68.

Klink, Thomas W., *Depth Perspectives in Pastoral Work*. Englewood Cliffs, N. J.: Prentice-Hall, 1965.

Masure, E., *Parish Priest* (tr. A. Bouchard). Chicago: Fides, 1955.

Meyer, B., *Lend Me Your Hands*. Chicago: Fides, 1955.

Michonneau, G., *Revolution in a City Parish*. Oxford: Blackfriars, 1950.

Neighbor, Rev. Russell, "CCD–Lay Apostolate for the Young," *American Journal of Catholic Youth Work*, 3 (1962), 15–18.

———— "CCD. A Matchless Aid," *Homiletic and Pastoral Review*, 63 (1963), 580–585.

O'Neill, J. H., *A Pastor's Point of View*. Milwaukee: Bruce, 1963.

Prindiville, Raymond, C. S.P., *The Confraternity of Christian Doctrine*. Philadelphia: American Ecclesiastical Review Press, 1932.

Retif, Louis, and Retif, Andrea, *The Church's Mission in the World*, Vol. 102. *The Twentieth Century Encyclopedia of Catholicism*. New York: Hawthorne Books.

Reum, E., "Rich Little Poor Kids," *Worship*, 38 (1964), 219–224.

Ryan, Mary Perkins, *Are Parochial Schools the Answer?* New York: Holt, Rinehart and Winston, 1964.

Schmitz, Walter J., S.S., *Learning the Mass*: The New Liturgy; Handbook for Priests and Seminarians According to the Latest Decree of the Sacred Congregation of Rites. Milwaukee: Bruce, 1965 (rev. 1966).

Schneider, Rev. Nicholas, "The Priest as Catechist in the Parish School," *AER*, 148 (1963), 389–397.

Sellmair, J., *The Priest in the World* (tr. B. Battershaw). Westminster, Md.: Newman, 1954.

Sister Marie, O. L. V. M., *How to Organize and Conduct High School CCD Classes*. Elm Grove, Wis.: Hi-Time Publishing Co., 1963.

Staff, National Center, "A High School Confraternity Unit," *Catholic School Journal*, 53 (1953), 115–116.

Stone, Theodore C., "Bringing Christ to Public School Youth," *Modern Catechist*

(G. Sloyan, ed.). New York: Macmillan, 1960.
Younger, George D., *The Church and Urban Renewal.* Philadelphia: Lippincott, 1965.

13. MANAGEMENT RESPONSIBILITIES OF THE PARISH

"Accounting for Charitable Organizations," *JA,* Vol. 104 (July, 1957).
Boutell, W. S., "Implementation of National Standards of Reporting for National Voluntary Organizations," *Accounting Review.* Vol. 37 (July, 1962), 406–409.
—— "Centralized Financing Plan for Construction in New Orleans," *Catholic School Journal,* 63 (May, 1963), 6.
Cullather, J., "Parish Income Tax: a Reply to W. Guerin," *America.* 109 (August 3, 1963), 118–119.
Daniel, William S., "Church Finance and Accounting — Their Relationship to Church Management," *N. A. A. Bulletin,* Vol. 40, sec. 1 (August, 1959), 19–28.
Editor's forum: "Role of the Priest in Modern Society," 100: 13-15 (January 29, 1966). Discussion held at Notre Dame by:
  Father William Lewers, C. S. C.
  Father Simons
  Father David B. Burrell
  Father John S. Dunne, C. S. C.
Esposity, F. L., "Planning and Control Through Budgeting," *Bulletin,* Vol. 35, No. 7 (March, 1954).
Feyerharm, Robert W., "Budgetary Accounting Procedures and Accounting Forms for Small Colleges and Universities," *AR,* Vol. 30, No. 1 (January, 1965).
Foster, Chandler H., "Accounting for Charitable Educational and Religious Organizations and Similar Endowed Institutions." Transcript, 16 (July, 1959), p. 1, 6–8. *Massachusetts CPA Review,* (September, 1959).
Guerin, William L., "Tithing: Toward a Clarification," *America,* 108 (March 16, 1963), 354–355.
—— "Handling of Parish Funds Seen As Part of Lay Role," *Catholic Messenger.* 82 (March 26, 1964), 6.
Hewitt, LeRoy A., "Aiding Church Administration by Fund Accounting and Budgeting," *N. A. A. Bulletin,* Vol. 40, sec. 1 (November, 1958), 43–48.
Kaletta, P., "How To Finance Diocesan Growth: St. Louis Seminar," *Catholic Property Administration,* 27 (February, 1963), 32–33.
—— "The Lord's Way and Father Moore's Way: Method Used at St. Agnes Church, Arlington, Va.," *Catholic Property Administration.* 26 (November, 1962), 36–39.
Larson, Lowell E., "Church Accounting," *JA,* Vol. 103 (May, 1957), 28–35.
Moonitz, Maurice, Accounting Research Study No. 1, *Basic Postulates of Accounting,* AICPA, 1961.
Pace, Homer St. Claire and Koestler, Edward J., "Income and expenditure statements of membership plan organizations," *Specialized Accounting,* 1957, 301–308.
—— "A Pattern for Parish Upkeep; Volunteers," *Catholic Property Administration,* 28 (January, 1964).
Ryan, Leo V., C. S. V., "Accounting for School Funds," *Catholic Property Administration,* 26 (December, 1962), 32–33.
—— "Challenge of School Costs," *Catholic Property Administration,* 26, (November, 1962), 40–41.
—— "Efficient School Management Demands Data Processing," *Catholic School Journal,* 64 (September, 1964).
—— "Diocesan Foundation Plan," *Catholic School Journal,* 64 (May, 1964), 76–78.
—— "15 Problem Areas in School Finance," *Catholic Property Administration,* 27 (July, 1963), 26–27.

––––––– "Introducing an Accounting Manual for Catholic Schools," *National Catholic Educational Association Bulletin,* 59 (May, 1963), 13–18.

––––––– "The Many Meanings of Business," Cf. issue of *Catholic Business Education Review,* (Fall, 1963).

––––––– "Pastor Computes Per Pupil Costs," *Catholic Property Administration,* 27 (February, 1963), 26.

––––––– "Prorating Parish Expenditures," *Catholic Property Administration,* 27 (January, 1963), 25–26.

––––––– "Purchasing Pointers," Cf. issues of *Catholic Property Administration,* Beginning September, 1963.

––––––– "Reporting School Costs to the Parish," *Catholic Property Administration,* 27 (March, 1963), 68.

Sage, Paul, "The Accountability of Charitable Organizations," (September, 1965) 88. Discussion of an article published in N. Y. CPA, April, 1965, p. 269.

Slade, Felice V., Audit., *In Church Accounts,* 1960, 152–158.

Trainor, P., "Way to Improve Parish Support," *Catholic Property Administration,* 27 (February, 1963), 36–37.

Whitey, Howard A. and Holman, Guy, "Standards of Accounting for Voluntary Health-Welfare Agencies," (August, 1965) 47.

14. PASTORAL LAW

Antieau, Chester James, Downey, Arthur T., and Roberts, Edward C., *Freedom From Federal Establishment.* Milwaukee: Bruce, 1964.

Antieau, Chester James, Carroll, Phillip Mark and Burke, Thomas Carroll, *Religion Under the State Constitutions.* 850 De Kalb Avenue, Brooklyn: Central Book Co., 1965.

Bayne, David Cowan, S. J., *Conscience, Obligation, and the Law; the Moral Binding Power of the Civil Law.* Chicago: Loyola Univ. Press, 1966, 287.

Bishop, Crawford M., *Missionary Legal Manual.* Chicago: Moody Press, 1965.

Brassell, V., "Matrimonial Cruelty in Civil and Canon Law; Review of The Concept of Matrimonial Cruelty," *Heythrop Journal,* 6 (January, 1965), 46–54.

Buehner, Andrew J., ed., *Law and Theology.* Addresses at the Dedication of Wesemann Hall, Valparaiso University, and Essays on "The Professional Responsibility of the Christian Lawyer," St. Louis, Mo.: Concordia Publishing House, 1965.

Cong. of the Consistory, "Decretum circa praescripta cann. 534 par. 1 et 1532 par. 1, n. 2 C.I.C.," *Acta Apostolicae Sedis.* 55 (August, 1963), 656. (Tr. in *Canon Law Digest, Supplement 1963,* under c. 1532.).

Connery, J. R., "Religious Pluralism and Public Morality," *America.* 100 (February 21, 1959), 597–599.

––––––– "Gambling and Public Policy; Law and Morality in a Pluralistic Society," *Ave Maria.* 97 (May 25, 1963), 16.

Giannella, Donald A., ed., *Religion and the Public Order.* Chicago: Chicago Univ. Press, 1964.

Gustafson, G., "Moral Values," *Priest.* 19 (January, 1963), 21-24.

Howe, Mark DeWolfe, *The Garden and the Wilderness; Religion and Government in American Constitutional History.* Chicago: Chicago Univ. Press, 1965, 180.

Howes, R., "The Church and Zoning," *Priest.* 19 (April, 1963), 336–339.

McNicholas, T., "The Influence of Christianity Upon American Civil Law," *Jurist.* 23 (July, 1963), 327–332.

"Pro and Controversy, Your Life Insurance"; replies, *Ave Maria.* 92 (August 6, 1960), 8–11.

Whalen, W., "Your Life Insurance," *Ave Maria,* 91 (June 11, 1960), 5–8.

Wright, Bishop John, "Law Must Recognize Sovereignty of God," *Catholic Messenger.* 77 (September 24, 1959), 143–146.

15. THE PASTOR, THE LAY TEACHER, AND THE SCHOOL

"About Lay Teachers in Catholic Schools," *Liguorian.* 48 (August, 1960), 31–33.

Barber, G., "The Lay Teacher in the Catholic High Schools," *Today.* 20 (March, 1965), 14–15.

Carolyn, Sr., "Lay Teachers Have a Spiritual Role," *Catholic School Journal.* 63 (January, 1963), 43–44.

Conley, William, "Lay Teacher Responsibility," *Catholic School Journal.* 63 (October, 1963), 6.

———— "Lay Teachers Obligations," *Catholic School Journal.* 63 (November, 1963), 4.

Deters, L. J. (Mrs.), "Recruiting and Training of Lay Teachers;" summary, *National Catholic Educational Association Bulletin.* 56 (August, 1959), 306–308.

Donovan, Paul M., "Lay Teachers Are a Blessing," *Catholic World.* 191 (April, 1960), 15–18.

Fitzsimons, M. J., "Lay Teachers of Youth," *Messenger Sacred Heart.* 94 (May, 1959), 10–13.

Flannery, H. W., "Jane Doe, Lay Teacher," *Ave Maria.* 91 (April 23, 1960), 9–12. Reprinted in *Family Digest.* 15 (September, 1960), 22–26.

Jencks, B., "Lay Teachers Will Out-Number Religious," *Way.* (US) 19 (December, 1963), 15–18.

Joachim, Sr., "Help for Our Lay Teachers," *Catholic School Journal.* 59 (June, 1959), 37.

Kearns, F., "Handkerchief Heads and Clerical Collars; Relationship of Lay Faculty to Clerical Administration," *Ramparts.* 2 (Winter, 1964), 18–24.

"Laien als Lehrer in den USA," *Herder-Korrespondenz.* 18 (March, 1964), 283–284.

"Lay Teachers in Catholic Schools," *Liguorian.* 52 (July, 1964), 51.

Le Boeuf, R., "Sister Act," (some practical suggestions on how to work with Sister), *Ave Maria.* 89 (January 31, 1959), 24–26.

McDevitt, J., "The Layman and the Schools," *National Catholic Educational Association Bulletin.* 61 (August, 1964), 29–36.

Mapelli, G., "How Parents Evaluate Lay Teachers," *Catholic School Journal.* 63 (March, 1963), 64–65.

Mary Irenaia, Sr., "The Lay-Teacher; Partner," *Catholic Educator.* 35 (January, 1965), 458.

O'Keefe, W., "Conditions of Service of Lay Teachers in Catholic Elementary and Secondary Schools in the State of Connecticut; Abstract," *Catholic Educational Review.* 42 (January, 1964), 48.

Pflaum, W., "Lay Teachers: How Many in the Elementary Schools?" tabs., *National Catholic Educational Association Bulletin.* 60 (November, 1963), 17–23.

"Planning and Caring for Lay Teachers," *Sign.* 40 (September, 1960), 2.

"The PR Method For Better Teachers," *Ave Maria.* 92 (October 15, 1960), 17.

Reedy, J. L., "Explosive Buried in Catholic Schools," *Ave Maria.* 92 (September 10, 1960), 16–17.

Riegert, N., "Attitudes of Lay and Religious Faculty: Psychology of Relationships," *Catholic School Journal.* 63 (March, 1963), 64–65.

———— "The Relationships of the Lay Teacher," *Catholic School Journal.* 64 (January, 1964), 84–85.

Ryan, Leo V., C.S.V., "Written Contracts for Lay Teachers," *Catholic School Journal.* 60 (February, 1960), 63–65.

Ryan, M. P., "The Problem of Religious and Lay Teachers," *Catholic Educational Review.* 68 (April, 1960), 248–255.

Statistics of Lay Teachers in Catholic Schools, *Catholic Eductional Review.* 61 (May, 1963), 344–345.

Thorman, D. J., "Healthful Effect on American Catholic Education," *Ave Maria*. 90 (November 14, 1959), 18.

Trapani, Sr. M. C., "Status in 4 Southern Dioceses; abstract," *Catholic Educational Review*. 58 (April, 1960), 268.

Treacy, John P., Ph. D.; Driscoll, Justin A., Rt. Rev. Msgr.; Corcoran, Sister M. Jerome, O.S.U., *The Pastor and the School*. Milwaukee: Bruce, 1966.

"Underpaid Lay Teachers," *Liguorian*. 47 (October, 1959), 36.

"You and Lay Teachers," *Ave Maria*. 90 (October 10, 1959), 18.

Wagner, J. F., "The Laity and the School Boards," *Catholic Educator*. 29 (February, 1959), 385.

"What Do We Pay Our Lay Teachers"; survey, *Catholic School Journal*. 60 (September, 1960), 81.

16. THE PRIEST AND PARISH ORGANIZATIONS OF MEN

17. THE PRIEST AND HIS RELATIONSHIP TO LAY ORGANIZATIONS OF WOMEN

Acker, Bro. William G., F. S. C. H., *You Are God's Chosen People*. New York: St. Paul Publications, 1960.

Alberione, Giacomo Giuseppe, S.S.P., *Woman: Her Influence and Zeal as an Aid to the Priesthood* (tr. The Daughters of St. Paul). Boston: St. Paul Editions, 1964.

Berger, A., "What Lay Organizations Can Contribute to Parish Liturgical Life," *National Liturgical Week*. 23 (1962), 171–174.

Congar, Yves Marie Joseph, O.P., *Lay People in the Church: A Study for a Theology of Laity* (tr. Donald Attwater). Westminster, Md.: Newman, 1965.

Eastwood, Cyril, *The Royal Priesthood of the Faithful*. An investigation of the doctrine from biblical times to the reformation. Minneapolis, Minn.: Augsburg Publishing House, 1963.

Geaney, Dennis, O. S. A., *You Shall Be Witnesses*. Notre Dame, Ind.: Fides Press, 1963.

Gerken, John D., S. J., *Toward a Theology of the Layman*. New York: Herder and Herder, 1962.

Greenspun, William B., C.S.P. and Norgren, William A., eds., *Living Room Dialogues*. Glen Rock, N. J.: Paulist Press, 1965.

Guiton, Jean., *The Church and the Laity* (tr. Malachy Gerald Carroll). Staten Island, N. Y.: Alba House, 1965.

———— *Feminine Fulfillment* (tr. Paul J. Oligny, O. F. M.). Chicago: Franciscan Herald Press, 1965.

Guinan, J., "New Approaches in Lay Organization," *National Liturgical Week*. 23 (1962), 160–162.

Hanssler, Bernhard, *The Church and God's People* (tr. Gregory Roettger, O. S. B.). Baltimore, Md.: Helicon, 1963.

Harris, Paul T., ed., *Brief to the Bishops; Canadian Catholic Laymen Speak Their Minds*. Ontario, Canada: Longmans Canada Limited, 1965.

Jansen, G. M. A., O. P., *An Existential Approach to Theology*. Milwaukee: Bruce, 1966.

Killgallon, James J. and Weber, Gerard P., *Beyond the Commandments*. New York: Herder and Herder, 1964.

Leclercq, Jacques, *Christians in the World*. New York: Sheed and Ward, 1961.

Liege, P. A., O. P., *What is Christian Life?* New York: Hawthorne Books Publishers, 1961.

Meyer, Bernard F., M. M., *The Whole World is My Neighbor*. Notre Dame, Ind.: Fides, 1964.

Mosshamer, Ottilie, *The Priest and Womanhood* (tr. Robert J. Voigt). Westminster, Md.: Newman, 1964.

Mourous, Jean, *I Believe*. New York: Sheed and Ward, 1959.

Newman, Jeremiah, *The Christian in Society: A Theological Investigation*. Baltimore, Md.: Helicon, 1962.

Novak, Michael, *Belief and Unbelief: A Philosophy of Self-Knowledge*. New York: Macmillan, 1965.

O'Connor, William R., *The Layman's Call*. New York: P. J. Kenedy and Sons, 1942.

Papali, C., "The Apostolate of the Laity," *Theology Digest*. 7, 3 (August, 1960).

Quigley, Martin, Jr. and Connors, Msgr. Edward M., *Catholic Action in Practice: Family Life, Education, International Life*. New York: Random House, 1963.

Rahner, Karl, S. J., *The Christian Commitment*. New York: Sheed and Ward, 1963.

Richards, Hubert J. and De Rosa, Peter, *Christ in Our World*. Milwaukee: Bruce, 1966.

Schauinger, J. Herman, Ph. D., *Profiles in Action*. Milwaukee: Bruce, 1966.

Suenens, Leon Joseph Card., *Christian Life Day by Day*. Westminster, Md.: Newman, 1964.

Thorman, Donald J., *The Emerging Layman: The Role of the Catholic Layman in America*. Garden City, N. Y.: Doubleday, 1962.

Vatican II, *Decree on the Apostolate of the Laity*. Dogmatic Constitution on the Church.

18.   THE CHALLENGE OF WORKING WITH YOUTH

Carroll, T. P., "Formation Programs for Youth-Workers Needed," *Homiletic and Pastoral Review*. 63 (March, 1963), 509–513.

Conway, P., "Why Professional Training?" *American Journal of Catholic Youth Work*. 5 (Winter, 1964), 20–24.

――――― (CYO challenges teen-agers to undertake a five-week course to give them a greater awareness of their lay vocation), *Catholic Layman*. 78 (January, 1964), 21.

Deleclos, F., "Leisure and Christian Character-Formation in the Parish," *Lumen Vitae*. 18 (December, 1963), 639–650.

Fischer, D., "Parish Life for High Schoolers," *Catholic Property Administration*. 26 (November, 1962), 29.

Fischer, G., "Where CYO Really Works; St. John the Baptist Parish, Kenmore, N. Y.," *Catholic Digest*. 28 (January, 1964), 14–17.

Gladych, E., "CYO: A Progress Report," *Catholic Digest*. 27 (June, 1963), 63-66.

Hagmaier, G., "Recommends CYO Merger with YMCA," excerpts. *Catholic Messenger*. 82 (June 4, 1964), 1.

――――― "YMCA — Catholic Youth Organization Merger Suggested," excerpts. *U. S. Catholic*. 30 (August, 1964), 58.

――――― "Insurance Perils and Coverages," *Catholic Property Administration*. 23 (April, 1959), 162.

Kathleen, Sr., "The Seminar; Leadership Training Program in Diocese of Sacramento," *American Journal of Catholic Youth Work*. 5 (Winter, 1964), 38–42.

Kennedy, P., "The Hungry Hoods of El Pasto," Our Lady's Youth Center, *Catholic Layman*. 77 (September, 1963), 32–41.

Libersat, H., "To Enhance Work With Youth Achieve Unity Within the Diocese," *American Journal of Catholic Youth Work*. 3 (Fall, 1962), 24–29.

Mannion, D., "New Approach to Delinquency," Arriba Juntos Program in Brooklyn Diocese, *Lamp*. 61 (July, 1963), 4–7.

McGloin, J., "Light a Candle for Teenagers," *American Journal of Catholic Youth Work.* 5 (Winter, 1964), 52–56.

McGowan, E., "Contact Leaders' Corps," leadership training program at Minneapolis Catholic Youth Center, *American Journal of Catholic Youth Work.* 5 (Winter, 1964), 43–47.

McKeone, S., "The Catholic Youth Club," *Clergy Review.* 48 (June, 1963), 369–374.

McNeil, T., "We Must Involve the Teen-agers; Race Problems," *Interracial Review,* 37 (April, 1964), 85–87.

Monnaie, J., "Missionary Work-Yards: Discovering a Mission for the Church," *Lumen Vitae.* 18 (December, 1963), 651–658.

——— "Newark CYO Athletic Program," *American Journal of Catholic Youth Work,* 4 (Summer, 1963), 25–31.

O'Connor, V., "Junior Vincentianism," *Pastoral Life.* 11 (September, 1963), 21–24.

——— Our Mother of Sorrows Youth Club (Cincinnati, social work projects), *Extension.* 58 (November, 1963), 55.

Putz, L., Favors CYO and YMCA Staff Exchanges; excerpts, *Catholic Messenger,* 82 (June 18, 1964), 7.

Rogers, W., "Teen-agers and the Parish," *Mary.* 24 September–October, 1963), 8–12.

Scanlan, J., "The CYO Sports Program," *American Journal of Catholic Youth Work.* 4 (Summer, 1963), 46–49.

Watson, R. E., "Organizing a Newly-Affiliated Diocese," *American Journal of Catholic Youth Work.* 1 (Fall, 1960), 36–41.

Witte, E. E., "The Objectives of Social Security," *Review of Social Economy,* 17 (March, 1959), 23–33.

19. THE PARISH MISSION TO NON-CATHOLICS

Allan, A., "Convert Making Our Apostolate; Convert Makers of America," *Apostle.* 42 (April, 1964), 26–28.

Allen, W., "Decline in Converts," *Pastoral Life.* 12 (July–August, 1964), 53.

Baillie, John, 1886-1960, *Baptism and Conversion.* New York: Scribner, 1963.

Beckman, J., "We're Losing Ground in Conversions; sermon," *Homiletic and Pastoral Review.* 63 (March, 1963), 519–521.

Blanc, H., "Evaluating Apostolic Work," *Priest.* 19 (January, 1963), 44–48.

Bradet, A., "Feu les retraites paroissiales," *Maintenant.* 3 (February, 1964), 40–41.

Connell, F., "Should We Try to Convert Good Protestants?" *American Ecclesiastical Review.* 150 (March, 1964), 209–213.

Corbishley, Thomas, S. J., *Roman Catholicism.* New York: Harper and Row, 1964.

Farrell, B., "One Convert Guarantees Heaven?" *Sign.* 44 (August, 1964), 54.

Fischer, G., "The Big Boom in Lay Retreats," *Catholic Digest.* 28 (February, 1964), 20–24.

Gallagher, W., "The Class Method With Inquirers," *Guide.* 175 (February, 1963), 8–12.

Gleason, Robert W., S. J., ed., *In The Eyes of Others; Comon Misconceptions of Catholicism.* New York: Macmillan, 1962.

Gotz, I., "Retreats for Non-Christians," *Clergy Monthly Supplement.* 6 (December, 1963), 338–340.

Granfield, P., "The Dialogue and Converts," *American Ecclesiastical Review.* 151 (August, 1964), 133–135.

Hanbury, M., "Baron von Hugel and the Ecumenical Movement; His Attitude Towards Conversion Work," *Month.* 29 (March, 1963), 140–150.

——— "Housewife Apostolate; Housewife Gives Out Booklets on Catholic Faith to Salesmen," *Liguorian.* 52 (April, 1964), 54.

Hurley, M., "Ecumenism and Conversion," *Irish Theological Quarterly*, 31 (April, 1964), 132–149.

Hyland, L., "Retreats for Shut-Ins," *Liguorian*. 52 (March, 1964), 40–41.

Keating J., "Conversion and Christian Unity," *Guide*. 188 (April, 1964), 16–17.

——— "Survey on a Slump: Conversions," *Guide*. 188 (May, 1964), 16–17.

Kelly, G., "Catholic Ladies' College Retreats," *Sursum Corda*. 7 (December, 1963), 558–566.

Kennedy, P., "Only God Counts His Converts; Arthur Hughs," *Guide*. 188 (May, 1964), 11–13.

Killgallon, J., "The Art of Giving Instructions," *Guide*. 174 (January, 1963), 10-12.

Küng, Hans, *That The World May Believe* (tr. Cecily Hastings). New York: Sheed and Ward, 1963.

Le Joly, E., "Are We Trying to Lead Non-Catholics to Christ?" (excerpt from Witnesses of Christ), *Christ to the World*. 9 (1964), 110–118.

Leeming, B., "Conversions? Ecumenism?" reprint from *Catholic World* (January, 1964), *Catholic Mind*. 62 (March, 1964), 24–29.

——— "Ecumenical Dialogue and Conversions," *Catholic World*. 198 (January, 1964), 222–229.

——— "Ecumenism and Converts," reply to F. J. O'Brien's article in *Lamp* (January, 1964), *Lamp* 62 (March, 1964), 29.

——— "Lessons To Be Learned from Case of Dutch Princess, *Ave Maria*. 99 (May, 1964), 16–17.

Loh, J., "Retreats for Non-Catholic Clergymen;" reprint from *Columbia* (November, 1962), *Guide*. 184 (January, 1964), 11–13.

McGinn, J., "Why fewer converts?" *Guide*. 189 (June–July, 1964), 2.

Meyer, A., "Ecumenism and Conversion," *Guide*. 188 (May, 1964), 3–4.

——— "A Modern Conception of the Salvation of Infidels Which Hampers Apostolic Zeal According to Fr. Karl Rahner," *Christ to the World*. 8 (1963), 421–428. Replies (1963), 543–544; 9 (1964), 84–86, 166–168, 272, 364–365.

Mickerman, N., "I Never Talk Religion," *Liguorian*. 52 (March, 1964), 37–39.

Muller, A., "Conversion Is Not Obsolete," *Columbia*. 45 (January, 1965), 17–19.

Nebreda, A., "Conversion: Key-Stone of the Missionary Process, " *Lumen Vitae*. 18 (December, 1963), 661–678.

O'Brien, J., "Ecumenism and Conversions," *Pastoral Life*. 12 (September, 1964), 17–21.

——— "Extending Christ's Mystical Body," *American Ecclesiastical Review*. 151 (July, 1964), 41–46.

——— "Good Example Wins Converts," *Pastoral Life*. 11 (January, 1963), 11–15.

——— "Is Making Converts Ecumenic?" *Lamp*. 62 (January, 1964), 8–9. Condensed in *Mission Digest*. 22 (February, 1964), 29–33.

——— "Make Your Parish Convert-Minded," *Pastoral Life*. 11 (March, 1963), 5–10.

——— "Room for Improvement; reply to H. Blanc," *Priest*. 19 (April, 1963), 370–373.

——— "Why Fewer Converts," condensed from *America* (October 5, 1963), *Catholic Digest*. 28 (February, 1964), 10–11.

——— "Winning 84 Converts a Year: A Convert-Minded Parish; St. John's Parish, Waterloo, Iowa," *Priest*. 20 (March, 1964), 217–220.

——— "Our Losses Are Showing," *Priest*. 20 (July, 1964), 589–592.

Owens, J., "Relaxation That Re-Creates; Family Retreats at Carmel Retreat House, Chicago," *Columbia*. 44 (February, 1964), 21-22.

Pauwels, C., "Ecumenical Theology and Conversions; Proselytism vs. Ecumenical Fellowship," *Thomist*. 27 (April–July–October, 1963), 570–598.

Peter, K., "Is There a War Between Ecumenism and Conversion?" *Ave Maria*. 99 (April 11, 1964), 18.

Pitrone, J., "You Can Be a Convert-Maker," *Friar.* 23 (March, 1965), 41–45.
——— "Religion and Logistics; Religious Information Bureau of K. of C.," *Columbia.* 43 (November, 1963), 14–15.
Ripley, F., "Why the Drop in Converts?" *Homiletic and Pastoral Review.* 64 (June, 1964), 774–781.
St. John, H., "Reunion or Conversion," *Blackfriars.* 44 (March, 1963), 98–107.
Sheed, F., "Catholics Won't Talk Religion With Me," *Catholic Messenger.* 82 (June 18, 1964), 6.
Sheen, Bishop Fulton J., "Conversion in the Mission World," *Worldmission.* 15 (Winter, 1965), 3–7.
——— "The Spirit and Conversion; excerpt from the Priest is not His Own," *Guide.* 183 (December, 1963), 7–12.
——— "Why Only Individual Conversions? Role of the Laity," *Worldmission.* 13 (Winter, 1962), 3–7.
Sontag, J., "A Grave Obstacle to Evangelization: Religious Subjectivism," *Christ to the World.* 9 (1964), 152–156.
Vebelmesser, J., (Fr. D. Sontag), "God's Letter Writer; condensed from Jesuit Missions October, 1963," *Mission Digest.* 21 (November, 1963), 24–26.
Whalen, W., "Are Catholic Parishes Too Large?" *Catholic Layman.* 77 (November, 1963), 5–10.
Wheel, B., "Let Laymen Instruct," *Catholic Layman.* 78 (June, 1964), 25–31. Concluded in *Mission Digest.* 22 (July–August, 1964), 2–7.

20. ECUMENISM AND THE CLERGY

Bamberger, Bernard J., *The Story of Judaism.* New York: Schocken Books, 1964.
Baum, Gregory, *Progress and Perspectives.* New York: Sheed and Ward, 1962.
Bea, Augustin, Cardinal, *The Unity of Christians* (ed. Bernard Leeming, S. J.). New York: Herder and Herder, 1963.
Berkouwer, C. G., *The Second Vatican Council and the New Catholicism.* Grand Rapids, Mich.: Eerdmans, 1965.
Bevan, R. J. W., ed., *The Churches and Christian Unity.* New York: Oxford Univ. Press, 1963.
Bogolepov, Alexander A., *Toward an American Orthodox Church; The Establishment of an Autocephalous Orthodox Church.* New York: Morehouse-Barlow, 1963.
Brown, Robert McAfee, and Scott, David H., eds., *The Challenge to Reunion; the Blake Proposal Under Scrutiny.* New York: McGraw-Hill, 1963.
Carson, H. M., *Roman Catholicism Today.* Grand Rapids, Mich.: Eerdmans, 1965.
Cooley, John K., *Baal, Christ, and Mohammed; Religion and Revolution in North Africa.* New York: Holt, Rinehart and Winston, 1965.
Dunn, Helfer, and Shusterman, *To Promote Good Will.* Baltimore, Md.: Helicon, 1965.
Gaines, David P., *The World Council of Churches; a Study of its Background and History.* Peterborough, N. H.: Richard R. Smith Co., 1966.
Gaustad, Edwin Scott, *Historical Atlas of Religion in America.* New York: Harper and Row, 1962.
Guitton, Jean, *Unity Through Love: Essays in Ecumenism* (tr. Brian Thompson). New York: Herder and Herder, 1965.
——— *The History of American Methodism* (ed. Emery Stevens Bucks and others). New York: Abingdon Press, 1964.
Hardon, John, S.J., *The Protestant Churches of America.* Westminster, Md.: Newman Press, 1965.
Jackson, Joseph H., *Many But One; The Ecumenics of Charity.* New York: Sheed and Ward, 1964.

Jaeger, Lorenz, Cardinal, *A Stand on Ecumenism; the Council's Decree* (tr. Hilda Graef). New York: P. J. Kenedy and Sons, 1965.
Karrer, Otto, *The Kingdom of God Today* (tr. Mrs. Rosaleen Okenden). New York: Herder and Herder, 1964.
Kegley, Charles W., *Protestantism in Transition*. New York: Harper and Row, 1965.
Küng, Hans, S.J., *Ecumenical Theology (Concilium)*. Glen Rock, N. J.: Paulist Press, 1965.
Lackmann, Max, *The Augsburg Confession and Christian Unity*. New York: Herder and Herder, 1963.
Landis, Benson Y., *Religion in the United States*. New York: Barnes and Nobel, 1965.
———— *World Religions* (rev. ed.). New York: E. P. Dutton, 1965.
Linn, William Alexander, *The Story of the Mormons from the Date of Their Origin to the Year 1901*. New York: Russell and Russell, 1963.
Lipman, Eugene J., and Albert Vorspan, eds., *A Tale of Ten Cities; the Triple Ghetto in American Religious Life*. New York: Union of American Hebrew Congregations, 1962.
Martin, Walter R., *The Kingdom of the Cults; an Analysis of the Major Cult Systems in the Present Christian Era*. Grand Rapids, Mich.: Zondervan Publishing House, 1965.
Marshall, Romey P., O. S. L. and Taylor, Michael J., S. J., *Liturgy and Christian Unity*. Englewood Cliffs, N. J.: Prentice-Hall, 1965.
Meyer, Carl S., ed. *Moving Frontiers*: *Readings in the History of the Lutheran Church — Missouri Synod*. St. Louis: Concordia Publishing House, 1964.
Miller, Rabbi Milton, and Schwartzman, Rabbi Sylvan D., *Our Religion and Our Neighbors*. A study of comparative religion emphasizing the religions of the western world. New York: Union of American Hebrew Congregations, 1963.
Miller, Samuel Howard and Wright, George Ernest, eds., *Ecumenical Dialogue at Harvard*: *the Roman Catholic Protestant Colloquium*. Cambridge: Belknap Press of Harvard Univ. Press, 1964.
Noss, John B., *Man's Religions,* 3d ed. New York: Macmillan, 1963.
Persson, Per Erik, *Roman and Evangelical; Gospel and Ministry* (tr. Eric H. Wahlstrom). Philadelphia: Fortress Press, 1964.
Pol, William Hendrik van de, *Anglicanism in Ecumenical Perspective*. Pittsburgh: Duquesne Press, 1965.
Romeu, Luis V., ed., *Ecumenical Experiences*. Westminster, Md.: Newman, 1965.
Ross, Floyd Hiatt, *Shinto: The Way of Japan*. Boston: Beacon Press, 1965.
Sandmel, Samuel, *We Jews and Jesus*. New York: Oxford Univ. Press, 1965.
Saunders, E. Dale, *Buddhism in Japan; with an Outline of its Origins in India*. Philadelphia: Univ. of Pennsylvania Press, 1964.
Schmemann, Alexander, ed., *Ultimate Questions: An Anthology of Modern Russian Religious Thought*. New York: Rinehart and Winston, 1965.
Solomon, Victor, *A Handbook on Conversions to the Religions of the World*. New York: Stravon Publishers, 1965.
Tavard, George, *Protestant Hopes and the Catholic Responsibility*. Notre Dame, Ind.: Fides, 1964.
Sourdel, Dominique, *Islam* (tr. Douglas Scott). New York: Walker, 1964.
Thurian, Max, *Visible Unity and Tradition* (tr. W. J. Kerrigan). Baltimore: Helicon (dist. New York: Taplinger), 1962.
Tillich, Paul Johannes Oskar, *Christianity and the Encounter of the World Religions*. New York: Columbia University Press, 1963.
Vassaday, Bela, *Christ's Church; Evangelical, Catholic, and Reformed*. Grand Rapids, Mich.: Erdmans, 1965.
Vatican Council 2. *The Decree on Ecumenism* (tr. The Secretariat for Promoting Christian Unity). Glen Rock, N. J.: Paulist Press, 1965.
Weber, Max, *The Sociology of Religion* (tr. Ephraim Fischoff). Boston: Beacon Press, 1963.

Whalen, William J., *Faiths For The Few: A Study of Minority Religions.* Milwaukee: Bruce, 1963.
World Council of Churches, 3rd Assembly, New Delhi, 1961. *The New Delhi Report.* New York: Association Press, 1962.
Zaehner, R. C., *"Christianity and Other Religions"* vol. 146. *Twentieth Century Encyclopedia of Catholicism.*
———— *Hinduism.* New York: Oxford Univ. Press, 1962.

21. THE PRIEST AND MODERN COMMUNICATION

———— "Airwave First Amendment," *America,* 112 (February 13, 1965), 213.
Anderson, F., "Catholic Families Need the Catholic Press," *Family Digest,* 19 (February, 1964), 7–11.
———— "The Catholic Press," *Today's Family,* 38 (February, 1963), 2–7.
———— "Archbishop Beck on the Mass Media Commission, *Tablet,* 218 (June 20, 1964), 704.
Baum, G., "The Council, the Press, and Ecumenism," *Catholic Journalist,* 15 (July, 1964), 7–8.
Brophy, L., "Where Good News is no News," *Apostle,* 42 (February, 1964), 2–3.
Brown, R., "A Protestant Assessment; the Vatican Council," *Commonweal,* 79 (December 27, 1963), 369–398.
Callahan, D., "Candor Urged in Catholic Press;" excerpt, *Catholic Messenger,* 82 (May 28, 1964), 1.
———— "The Council, the Press and the Laity," *Catholic Journalist,* 15 (July, 1964), 15–17.
Cargas, H., "The Pen, Speech and the Sodalist," *Queen's Work,* 56 (February, 1964), 2.
———— "Catholic Press, Beware," *Commonweal,* 81 (March 12, 1965), 753.
Culkin J., Revolution in Communications, *Catholic Educator,* 33 (January, 1963), 466; (February, 1963), 549–550.
Cushing, Richard, Card., *The Church and Public Opinion.* Boston: Daughters of St. Paul, 1963.
Deedy, J., "The Catholic Press," *Commonweal,* 81 (February 19, 1965), 666–667.
———— "Laymen and the Catholic Press," *Social Justice Review,* 57 (February, 1965), 339–340.
Eller, J., "Not Always on the Day After Sunday," *America,* 108 (March 23, 1963), 391.
Ellis, J. T., Address at the Fall '62 meeting of the Catholic Press Association *Catholic Journalist,* 14 (March, 1963), 3–4; (April, 1963), 7–8.
———— "Catholic Press: Reflections on Past and Present," *American Benedictine Review,* 14 (March, 1963), 45–61.
Girard, W., Promotion by Professionals; Dayton's Ad Dexterum Guild, *Catholic Layman,* 77 (March, 1963), 40–47.
Gorman, R., "The Catholic Press; Improvement Over the Years," *Sign,* 42 (February, 1963), 10.
Hallran, J., "Mass Media and Mass Culture," *Doctrine and Life,* 12 (December, 1962), 633–651.
———— "Has the Catholic Priest Entered a New Era?" *Ave Maria,* 99 (May 23, 1964), 18.
Horchler, R., "The Catholic Press: A Balance Sheet," *Lamp,* 62 (February, 1964), 12–13.
Howard, D., "The Truth Beat"; editor Robert Hoyt of The Catholic Reporter, port., *Sign,* 42 (February, 1963), 19–20.
Hoyt, R., "The Issue Is Greatness," *Commonweal,* 77 (February 15, 1963), 534–538.
John XXIII, Pope (January 27, 1963), To Catholic journalists; the world sees the

significance of the Council; the role of the Catholic press and its responsibilities; the Pope's prayer for journalists.

Kedl, A., "Catholic Press and Roman Curia"; reprint from *Our Family* (March, 1964), *Social Justice Review,* 57 (June, 1964), 85–86.

Leo, J., "It's Not Your Duty to Support the Catholic Press," *U. S. Catholic,* 29 (February, 1964), 19–20. Replies 30 (July, 1964), 61–62.

────── "The Mass Media Decree Under Fire"; Catholic Press Convention, Pittsburgh, *Tablet,* 218 (June 13, 1964), 676.

Maly, E., "The Council, the Press and Biblical Study," *Catholic Journalist,* 15 (July, 1964), 18–20.

McCorry, V., "No Limit?" *America,* 112 (February 6, 1965), 195.

────── Names 20 Members to Mass Media Office, *Catholic Messenger,* 82 (June 18, 1964), 1.

Nevins, A., "Mass Communications and the Mission of the Church," *Catholic Messenger,* 81 (May 16, 1963), 5.

────── "More Readers Needed," *Ave Maria,* 97 (February 2, 1963), 17.

O'Connor, J., "The Diocesan Weekly: A Question of Purpose"; reprint from *Commonweal* (February 15, 1964), *Way* (US), 20 (January–February, 1964), 25–31.

────── "Question of Purpose," *Commonweal,* 77 (February 15, 1963), 538–541.

Paul VI, Pope, (April 2, 1964), In fructibus (motu proprio). Scope of the Pontifical Commissions for Motion Pictures, Radio and Television extended to cover the press, and its name changed to the Pontifical Commission for Mass Media.

"The Publication Explosion in the Catholic Press"; by P. Scharper, G. Shuster, B. Gallagher, W. Buckley, R. Wolseley, E. Walsh, *Critic,* 21 (May, 1963), 52–57.

────── (July 18, 1963), "Letter to Cardinal Silva Henriques for Inauguration of Radio Chilena; Value of Religious Radio Programs." (Spanish Text) *Acta Apostolicae Sedis,* 55 (September, 1963), 692–693.

Rahner, Karl, S.J., *Free Speech in the Church.* New York: Sheed and Ward, 1959.

Reedy, J., "Catholic Editors Disagree; Responsibility of the Catholic Press, and the Steubenville Register Criticism of the Apostolic Delegate," *Ave Maria,* 97 (May 4, 1963), 16–17. Reply by J. Adamo with editorial comment (May 25, 1963), 2–3.

Reynolds, R., "Heritage of Hope"; interview by S. DeLeon, port., *Today,* 18 (February, 1963), 3–5.

Ruppert, R., "Laymen in the Catholic Press," *Catholic Journalist,* 14 (February, 1963), 6. Replies (April, 1963), 3–4.

Tansey, A., "Charity in Print; Obligations of the Catholic Press," *Social Justice Review,* 55 (February, 1963), 334–336.

Tavard, G., "The Council, the Press and Theology"; address at 1964 CPA Convention, *Catholic Journalist,* 15 (July, 1964), 21–24.

────── "The Council, the Press and Theology"; reprint from *Catholic Journal, Catholic World,* 199 (September, 1964), 337–344.

────── "Three German Bishops signed anti-schema leaflets, *Tablet,* 217 (December 7, 1963), 1339.

────── "Too Many? Need for a Serious Depth Study of the Catholic Press," *Commonweal,* 78 (May 3, 1963), 155–156.

────── "Troublesome" Catholic Press, *Ave Maria,* 99 (February 1, 1964), 16–17.

────── "U. S. Journalists (Cogley, Kaiser, Novak) criticise schema (on communications media)," *Tablet,* 217 (November 30, 1963), 1302–1303.

Vatican Council, 2, "Decree on Media of Social Communication," (NCWC tr.), Washington, D. C.

Walsh, P., "Lack of Unity in the Broadcasts of Mass," *Furrow,* 14 (November, 1963), 23–26.

Walter, Sr., "Importance of the Catholic Press," *Magnificat,* 113 (June, 1964), 7–9.

Weigel, G., "Ecumenism and the Catholic Press," *Catholic Messenger,* 81 (February 7, 1963), 12.

——— "What is a Catholic Paper?" Archbishop Cody on the New Orleans *Clarion Herald, America,* 108 (March 30, 1963), 426.

Wilt, M., "Catholic Press Month, 1963," *Catholic Library World,* 34 (February, 1963), 277.

Wright, Bishop, John, "Distinguish Facts and Truth"; excerpts, *Catholic Journalist,* 15 (July, 1964), 1.

22. THE APOSTOLATE TO THE BUSINESSMAN

Arendt, Hannah, *The Human Condition.* (Anchor Books), Garden City, N. Y.: Doubleday, 1959.

Austin, Robert W., "Code of Conduct for Executives," *Harvard Business Review,* 89 (Sept.–Oct., 1961), 53–61.

Bartels, Robert, ed., *Ethics in Business.* Columbus, Ohio: Bureau of Business Research, Monograph No. 111, College of Commerce and Administration, Ohio State University, 1963.

Baumhart, Raymond C., S.J., "Ethics and Catholic Businessmen," *America,* 106 (January 6, 1962), 436; 106 (February 3, 1962), 589; 107 (April 14, 1962), 47.

——— "How Ethical Are Businessmen?" *Harvard Business Review,* 36 (July–August, 1961), 6–8.

Boulding, Kenneth E., *The Organizational Revolution.* New York: Harper, 1953.

Connell, C.SS.R., "The Priest and the Businessman," *All Things to All Men* (ed. J. F. X. Cervetello). New York: Joseph F. Wagner, Inc., 1965.

Cosby, Beverly Roy, *Business As a Christian.* Englewood, N. J., 1954. (Union Theological Seminary B.D. Thesis).

Cronin, John F., S.S., *Social Principles and Economic Life* (rev. ed.). Milwaukee: Bruce, 1964.

Dempsey, Bernard W., *The Functional Economy.* Englewood, Cliffs, N. J.: Prentice Hall, 1958.

Dondeyne, Canon Albert, *Faith and the World.* Pittsburgh: Duquesne Univ. Press, 1963.

Fatherwood, Henry F., *The Christian Industrial Society.* London: Tyndale Press, 1964.

Garrett, Thomas M., S.J., *Bibliography on Social Theory and Social Ethics.* Scranton, Pa.: Institute on Business and Social Ethics, Univ. of Scranton, 1964.

——— *Ethics in Business.* New York: Sheed and Ward, 1963.

Graham, Dom Aelred, O.S.B., *Catholicism and the World Today.* New York: David McKay Company, Inc., 1952.

Harlan, Homer Charles, ed., *Readings in Economics and Politics.* Fair Lawn, N. J.: Oxford, 1961.

Hayes, Arthur H., "Moral Problems in Business Practice," *Catholic Theological Society of America Proceedings,* 1961.

Hodges, Luther Hartwell, *The Business Conscience.* Englewood Cliffs, N. J.: Prentice Hall, 1963.

Johnston, Herbert, *Business Ethics,* 2nd ed. New York: Pitman, 1961.

Johnson, Harold L., *The Christian As a Businessman.* New York: Association Press, 1964.

Lenski, Gerhard, *The Religious Factor.* (Anchor Books), Garden City, N. Y.: Doubleday, 1963.

Lowery, Daniel, C.SS.R., "Moral Problems in Business Practice," *Proceedings of the Sixteenth Annual Convention of the Catholic Theological Society of America* (June, 1961), 121–146.

Marcel, Gabriel, *Man Against Mass Society.* (Gateway edition), Chicago: Henry Regnery Company, 1952.

Mason, Edward Sagendorfh, *The Corporation in Modern Society.* Fair Lawn, N. J.: Oxford, 1960.

McMahon, Thomas F., C.S.V., "Morality in Business," *Homiletic and Pastoral Review,* 63 (March, 1963), 501–508.

―――― "Professional Ideals for Business Executives — Sacramental Aspects," *Social Digest,* 8 (May–June, 1965), 162–168.

Messner, Johannes, *Social Ethics; Natural Law in the Western World,* rev. ed. (tr. J. J. Doherty). St. Louis, Mo.: B. Herder, 1965.

Montini, Giovanni Battista (Paul VI), *Man Against Mass Society.* Westminster, Md.: Newman, 1961.

Morgan, Everett J., S.J., ed., *The Social Conscience of a Catholic:* the social doctrine of the Church applied to problems in our contemporary society. Dstr. by Marquette University Bookstore, Milwaukee, Wisconsin, 1964.

Mulcahy, R. E., *Readings in Economics.* College Reading Series No. 5. Westminster, Md.: Newman Press, 1959.

Obenhaus, Victor, *Ethics for an Industrial Age; A Christian Inquiry.* New York: Harper and Row, 1965.

Paul VI, "Christian Concept of Economics," (Address, June 8, 1964), *The Pope Speaks,* 10 No. 1 (1964), 46–50.

Piper, Otto A., *The Christian Meaning of Money.* Englewood Cliffs, N. J.: Prentice-Hall, 1965.

Pius XI, "Vocation of Businessman" (Address, Mar. 7, 1957), *The Pope Speaks,* 4 No. 1 (1957), 85–89.

Samuelsson, Kurt, *Religion and Economic Action* (tr. Geoffrey French, ed. D. C. Coleman). New York: Harper and Row, 1964.

Schollgen, Werner, *Moral Problems Today* (tr. Edward Quinn). New York: Herder and Herder, 1963.

Smith, George Albert, *Business, Society and the Individual.* Homeward, Ill.: R. D. Irwin, 1962.

Spurner, William Atwell, *Ethics and Business.* New York: Scribners, 1962.

VanVlack, Philip W., Sewrey, Charles I., and Wielsen, Charles E., *Economic Ethics and Bibliography. Agricultural Experiment Station Brookings.* South Dakota: South Dakota State Univ., 1964.

Welty, Eberhard, O.P., *A Handbook of Christian Social Ethics;* vol. 2: The structure of the social order (tr. Gregor Kistein, O.P.). New York: Herder and Herder, 1963.

23.   THE PRIEST IN THE HIGH SCHOOL CLASSROOM

Bibin, Pierre, "What Youth Thinks of Priests and Religious Life," *Lumen Vitae,* 8:4 (October–December, 1953), 639–663.

Carpentier, R., "Priestly Vocation and Religious Vocation," *Review for Religious* (1962), 21, 206–226.

Cunnean, Joseph, "Catholics and Education," *Commonweal,* 7–14 (1953), 58: 437–441, 461–464.

D'Arcy, Paul F., M.M., and Kennedy, Eugene C., M.M., *The Genius of the Apostolate.* New York: Sheed and Ward, 1965.

Editorials, "Backtalk on Hyphen Priests," *Ave Maria,* 102:8 (August 21, 1965), 10–11.

Editorials, "Is There a Clergy Shortage?" *Ave Maria,* 97:25 (June 22, 1965), 16–17.

Fichter, Joseph H., *Religion as an Occupation.* Notre Dame, Ind.: Notre Dame Univ. Press, 1961.

Greeley, Andrew, *The Church and the Suburbs.* New York: Sheed and Ward, 1959.

Guerrero, E., "El sacerdote Como Professor de materias profanas," 161, *Razon y Fe,* 1960, 583–594.

Gulley, Anthony D., "Chalk on my Cassock," *Homiletic and Pastoral Review,* 64 (1963–64), 317–320.

Hassel, David, "Mediator Between the Church and Secular Learning," *Chicago Studies* (Fall, 1963), 229–246.

Hodges, Most Rev. Joseph H., D.D., "Bishops and the Distribution of Priests," *Homiletic and Pastoral Review* (Dec., 1965), 195–204.

Huyghe, Gerard, Rahner, Karl, Hamer, Jerome, Besret, Bernard, Harue, Rev. Uratsun, Joseph, *Religious Orders in the Modern World.* Westminster, Md.: Newman Press, 1965.

Kenning, Herman, "The Parish Priest as a High School Teacher," *Priest,* 14 (1958), 740–744.

Lamirande, E., "The Priesthood at the Service of the People of God According to St. Augustine," *The Furrow* (Aug., 1964), 501–507.

Leclercq, Jacques, *Christians in the World.* New York: Sheed and Ward, 1961.

―――― "The Priest-Expert: A Theological Philosophical Assessment," *Chicago Studies,* 3 (1964), 201–227.

Lord, Daniel, "The Changing Priesthood," *Meeting the Vocation Crisis,* George Kane. Westminster, Md.: Newman Press, (1956).

O'Connell, Matthew J., S.J., "The Priest in Education: Apostolate or Anomaly?" *Theological Studies* (March, 1965), 65–85.

Rahner, Karl, S.J., *Theology for Renewal.* New York: Sheed and Ward, 1964.

Sittler, J., "The Maceration of a Minister," *Christian Century,* 76, 23 (June 10, 1959), 698–701.

Thompson, Harold, "The Priest-Teacher and Secular Subjects," *Review for Religious,* 23 (1964), 79–87.

Toohey, William, "Hyphen Priests," *Ave Maria,* 102, 3 (July 17, 1965), 5–7.

24.   THE NEWMAN APOSTOLATE

Albright, Charles W., C.S.P. (ed.), *Newman Chaplain's Source Book.* National Newman Apostolate, 1965.

―――― "Building a Newman Club; Construction of Chapel and Center at Central Michigan University." il., *Catholic Property Administration,* 27 (January, 1963).

Butler, R., "The Catholic Chaplain in the American University," *Dominicana,* 48 (Fall, 1963), 187–192.

―――― "Catholic Education Redefined," *Ave Maria,* 98 (October 12, 1963), 10–12.

―――― "The Cultural Contribution of the Newman Apostolate to Secular Higher Education," *National Catholic Education Association Bulletin,* 61 (August, 1964), 148–155.

―――― *God and the Secular Campus.* New York: Doubleday, 1963.

―――― "New Directions on the Campus: The Newman Apostolate," *Priest,* 20 (February, 1964), 144–149.

―――― "The Newman Apostolate: Cultural Contribution to Higher Education," *American Ecclesiastical Review,* 150 (June, 1964), 405–416.

Clifford, R., and Callahan, W., "Catholics in Higher Education; a Study of the Next 20 Years," graphs, *America,* 111 (September 19, 1964), 288–291.

Coulson, John (ed.), *Theology and the University.* Baltimore, Md.: Helicon, 1964.

Donovan, E., "The Newman Apostolate and the High School Graduate," *National Catholic Education Association Bulletin,* 61 (August, 1964), 273–280.

Garrelts, G., "Liturgy and Cultural Development in Secular Colleges," *National Liturgical Week,* 23 (1962), 147–150.

Gray, A., "Development of the Newman Club Movement, 1893–1961," *American Catholic Historical Society Records,* 74 (June, 1963), 70–128.

Haas, W., "Counseling the Catholic Student for Secular Education; St. Thomas Aquinas Center at Purdue," *Catholic Counselor,* 8 (Spring, 1964), 79–83.

Kirvan, J., "Newman and a New Era," *Ave Maria,* 100 (August 29, 1964), 14–15,

———— Meeting Expenses at a Newman Club; Center at University of Minnesota, *Catholic Property Administration,* 27 (January, 1963), 22–24.

McMahon, L., "ELV in the Newman Apostolate; Extension Lay Volunteers," *Extension,* 58 (May, 1964), 28–29.

———— "The Need for Newman Clubs," *Liguorian,* 52 (January, 1964), 54.

———— "Newman and Communications: 'cor ad cor loquitur,'" *Ave Maria,* 100 (August 29, 1964), 18.

O'Gara, J., "The Newman Apostolate," *Commonweal,* 79 (October 4, 1963), 32. Reply by J. Duryea, (November 15, 1963), 228.

Phelan T., "I Am A Newman Chaplain; Rensselaer Polytechnic Institute, Troy," *Homiletic and Pastoral Review,* 64 (February, 1964), 403–409.

Sigur, A., "Catholics on the Secular Campus," *Lamp,* 61 (September, 1963), 14–15.

Somers, E., "Hectic Days Ahead for the Newman Chaplain," *Catholic Educator,* 33 (May, 1963), 801–803.

Stevens, C., "Aggiornamento on the Campus; New Mexico State University Newman Center," *America,* 112 (January 23, 1965), 122–123.

Swidler, L., "Catholic Colleges: A Modest Proposal," *Commonweal,* 81 (January 29, 1965), 559–562.

———— Two priests look at the Newman Apostolate, symposium: "Newman Centers: A False Hope," by E. Somers, "Newman in Focus," by R. Butler, *Catholic School Journal,* 65 (January, 1965), 53–56.

———— "University Catholic Chaplaincies; replies," *Tablet,* 217 (February 9, 1963), 146; (February 16, 1963), 173–174; (February 23, 1963), 204–205; (March 2, 1963), 229–230; (March 9, 1963), 264; (March 16, 1963), 290–291; (March 23, 1963), 403–404; (April 20, 1963), 436; (May 4, 1963), 493.

Whalen, William J., *Catholics on Campus.* Milwaukee: Bruce, 1965.

25. PREPARING THE RETREAT MASTER

Alvin, J. and J., "No previous experience necessary; Holy Family Retreat Association," *Marianist,* 54 (June, 1963), 2–8.

———— "The Annual Retreat; Readers' Comments," *Sursum Corda,* 8 (August, 1964), 166–170.

———— "Auriesville Retreat," *Priest,* 20 (May, 1964), 384.

Basset, Bernard, S.J., *The Noonday Devil.* Fresno, Calif.: Academy Guild Press, 1964.

———— "The Bible and the Retreat; Scripture Reading Outline," *Way,* 3 (July, 1963), 222–225.

———— "Biblical Retreats," *America,* 109 (November 2, 1963), 19.

Burghardt, Walter J., S.J., *Saints and Sanctity.* Englewood Cliffs, N. J.: Prentice-Hall, 1965.

Cheap, J., "Retreat Vacation Family Style," *Marriage,* 46 (June, 1964), 34–38.

Doty, William L., *Virtues for Our Time.* St. Louis, Mo.: B. Herder, 1964.

Duffy, A., "The Retreat Master," *American Ecclesiastical Review,* 151 (August, 1964), 112–118.

Edwin, Brother, F.S.C., *Retreat Conferences for Religious.* Milwaukee: Bruce, 1964.

———— *Examens for Retreat Time.* Milwaukee: Bruce, 1964.

Evely, Louis, *We Dare to Say Our Father* (tr. James Langdale). New York: Herder and Herder, 1965.

Farrell, B., "Retreats and Cursillo," *Sign,* 43 (April, 1964), 58.

Farrell, W., "The Spiritual Exercises and Contemporary Thought," *Review for Religious,* 22 (March, 1963), 218–224.

Gabriele Di Santa Maria Maddalena, Father, O.D.C., *Divine Intimacy; Meditations on the Interior Life for Everyday of the Year* (tr. Discalced Carmelite Nuns of Boston). New York: Desclee, 1964.

Geaney, D., "A Priest on Stage; the High School Retreat Master," *Today,* 18 (March, 1963), 11–13.

Hennessy, T., "Effects of a Closed Retreat on High School Students," *Catholic Counselor,* 8 (Spring, 1964), 94–98.

Kast, S., "No Silence, Please; Discussions at a Closed Retreat for Boys," *Today,* 20 (February, 1965), 16–17.

Lechner, R., "Rethinking the Annual Retreat; Renewal," *Review for Religious,* 22 (March, 1963), 211–217.

Loh, J., "Retreats for Protestant Ministers," reprint, *Catholic Digest,* 27 (February, 1963), 3134.

———— "Make a Retreat: Me?" *Catholic Messenger,* 82 (June 4, 1964), 10.

McEvoy, Hubert, S.J., *Work and Worship.* Springfield, Ill.: Templegate, 1964.

McNamara, William, O.C.D., *Manual for Retreat Masters.* Milwaukee: Bruce, 1960.

Mendiburu, N., "Orientation Day for Non-Christian Students," *Christ to the World,* 9 (1964), 326–332.

Montgomery, H., and M., "The Lame Are Not Halted; Retreats for Handicapped Women," Cenacle Retreat House, Wayzata, Minnesota," *Columbia,* 43 (September, 1963), 10–11.

Nimeth, Albert J., O.F.M., *Instant Inspiration, Add Only Good Will.* Chicago: Franciscan Herald Press, 1965.

Nolan, H., "Malvern's Golden Jubilee; St. Joseph in the Hills, Malvern, Pennsylvania," *Emmanuel,* 69 (October, 1963), 410–413.

O'Donnell, D., "The Annual Retreat: Another Look," *Sursum Corda,* 8 (June, 1964), 135–143.

Pathe, M., "Why Should I Make A Retreat?" *Liguorian,* 51 (October, 1963), 9–11.

Paulussen, L., "The Dynamic Growth of Closed Retreats," *Direction,* 10 (November, 1963), 4–9.

Rahner, Karl, S.J., *Spiritual Exercises* (tr. Kenneth Baker, S.J.). New York: Herder and Herder, 1965.

Raymond, Father, O.C.S.O., *The Mysteries in Your Life.* Milwaukee: Bruce, 1965.

Suhor, M., "Operation Public School; Sodality Program in Omaha," *Queen's Work,* 55 (June, 1963), 4–6.

Suenens, Leon Joseph, Card., *Christian Life Day by Day.* Westminster, Md.: Newman, 1964.

Taylor, T., "Enclosed Retreats for Boys," *Sursum Corda,* 7 (June, 1963), 421–429.

Teresa Margaret, Sr., "An Automated Retreat?" *Sponsa Regis,* 35 (November, 1963), 83–88.

Trese, Leo J., *You Are Called to Greatness.* Notre Dame, Ind.: Fides, 1964.

Vera Marie, Sr., Thoughts on Retreats for Nuns, *Review for Religious,* 23 (July, 1964), 473–480.

Yeomans, W., "Not My Will," *Way,* 4 (July, 1964), 187–198.

Zubeldia, F., "A Retreat for Non-Christian Students," *Christ to the World,* 8 (1963), 417–420.

26. THE HOSPITAL CHAPLAIN

Allen, W., "Confirmation by Chaplains," *Pastoral Life,* 12 (June, 1964), 52.

Cavanagh, J., "Courses for Chaplains; With Proposed Curriculum," *Guild of Catholic Psychiatrists Bulletin,* 10 (April, 1963), 120–123.

Davis, Charles, "Sacrament of the Sick or of the Dying," *Theology for Today.* New York: Sheed and Ward, 1962.

De Le Letter, P., "The Meaning of Extreme Unction," *Theology Digest* 4 (Autumn, 1956), 185–188.

Didier, Jean-Charles, *Death and the Christian,* Vol. 55, *The Twentieth Century Encyclopedia of Catholicism.* New York: Hawthorne Books, 1961.

Ellard, Gerald, S.J., *Christian Life and Worship*. Milwaukee: Bruce, 1933–34.

Giblin, G., "48 Hours at Metropolitan Hospital," *Catholic Digest*, 27 (August, 1963), 97–101.

Henry, A.M., O.P., E.D., *Christ in His Sacraments*, Vol. 6, Theology Library. Chicago: Fides, 1958.

Howell, Clifford, S.J., *Of Sacraments and Sacrifice*. (Engl. edn., *The Work of Our Redemption*.) Collegeville, Minn.: Liturgical Press, 1952 and Oxford: Catholic School Guild, 1953.

Jungmann, Joseph, S.J., *Public Worship: A Survey*. Collegeville, Minn.: Liturgical Press, 1957.

Jouvel, Francis, O.P., and Putz, Louis, C.S.C., *Signs of Life*. Notre Dame, Ind.: Notre Dame Univ. Press, 1953.

Laursen, E., "The Role of the Hospital Chaplain," *Linacre Quarterly*, 32 (February, 1965), 50–54.

Mullally, J., "CU Pastoral Institute; A Report," *Hospital Progress*, 45 (February, 1964), 44.

Palmer, Paul, "The Purpose of Anointing the Sick: Reappraisal," *Theological Studies*, 19 (1958), 309–344.

Palmer, Paul F., *Sacraments and Forgiveness*. Vol. 2, *Sources of Christian Theology*. Westminster, Md.: Newman, 1959.

────── *Sacraments of Healing and Vocation*. Englewood Cliffs, N. J.: Prentice-Hall, 1963.

Poschmann, B., *Penance and the Anointing of the Sick*. New York: Herder and Herder, 1964.

────── "Pointers for Hospital Chaplains," *Homiletic and Pastoral Review*, 65 (December, 1964), 193–194. Reply 65: (March, 1965), 449.

Rafferty, H., "Poor Little Rich Girl: M. Miller's Apostolic Work at City Hospital, St. Louis." ports. *Mary*, 25 (July–August, 1964), 16–28.

Roguet, A. M., O.P., *Christ Acts Through the Sacrament*. Collegeville, Minn.: The Liturgical Press, 1953.

Rowley, F., "The Psychiatrist, the Chaplain and Rehabilitation," *Guild of Catholic Psychiatrists Bulletin*, 11 (July, 1964), 161–165.

Wartenberg, G., "The Hospital Chaplain," *St. Anthony Messenger*, 71 (March, 1964), 38–39.

Watkins, A., "My Parish Is Sick," *Friar*, 22 (September, 1964), 26–30.

27. THE CONVENT CHAPLAIN

Angelica, Sr., "The Urban Nun," *Perspectives*, 10 (March–April, 1965), 45–53.

Barbeau, E., "What Is a Nun?" *Ave Maria*, 100 (July 4, 1964), 10–11.

"Bringing Nuns Up to Date; Spode House Conference," *Tablet*, 217 (March 2, 1963), 222.

Bouscaren, T., S.J., and O'Connor, James I., S.J., *Canon Law Digest for Religious*. Milwaukee: Bruce, 1964. Annual Supplements.

Celestine, Sr., "Every Event and Every Moment," *Sponsa Regis*, 35 (August, 1964), 355–363.

Charles Borromeo, Sr. M., *The Changing Sister*. Notre Dame, Ind.: Fides, 1965.

Claudia, Sr., "100,000 Can't Be Wrong; reprint," *Family Digest*, 18 (March, 1963), 23–28.

Daniewicz, C., "Occupational Therapy; Aged and Convalescent Sisters, Bethany Convent, St. Paul, Minn.," *Hospital Progress*, 45 (February, 1964), 78–80.

Dubay, T., "Psychological Needs in the Religious Context," *Review for Religious*, 21 (November, 1962), 522–530; 22 (January, 1963), 3–13.

Dunne, E., "Is There Anything in the Liturgy Constitution That Particularly Concerns Religious Women?" *Sursum Corda*, 8 (August, 1964), 172–174.

Eberle, J., "Sister's Health, a New Approach," *Ave Maria,* 100 (August 8, 1964), 13–15.

Elizabeth Ann, Sr., "Sister Cursillistas," *Review for Religious,* 24 (January, 1965), 87–90.

———— "Emancipation of Nuns and the Updating of Convent Life Are Long Overdue," *U. S. Catholic,* 30 (March, 1965), 2.

———— "Further Health Care Development for Nuns," *Linacre Quarterly,* 30 (May, 1963), 84.

Grosso, B., "How to Deal With Vocations; the Theresians," *Catholic Layman,* 78 (August, 1964), 49–56.

———— "Is It True That Some Priests Look Down on Pastoral Ministry Among Women Religious?" *Review for Religious,* 23 (January, 1964), 97–99.

Huyghe, G., "Understanding the Cross;" excerpt from *Equilibre et adaptation, Cross and Crown,* 16 (June, 1964), 166–178.

Jerome Marie, Sr., "The Way of Loneliness," *Review for Religious,* 22 (September, 1963), 559–561.

Judith Ann, Sr., "Theology for Sisters: An Imperative," *Catholic Educator,* 33 (April, 1963), 722–723.

Kirsch, Felix M., O.F.M. Cap., *The Spiritual Direction of Sisters.* New York: Benziger, 1961.

Kramer, M., "A Community Health Program for Sisters," *Hospital Progress,* 45 (April, 1964), 82–86.

McCormack, A., "A New Age in the Life of Religious; Review of Suenens' The Nun in the World," *Month,* 29 (June, 1963), 325–331.

Meyers, Sr. Bertrande, D.C., *Sisters for the 21st Century.* New York: Sheed and Ward.

Motte, A., "Concerning the Nun in the World;" review of Suenens' book, *Sponsa Regis,* 35 (February, 1964), 153–170.

O'Keefe, M., "The Sister in the Modern World; Summary," *National Catholic Education Association Bulletin,* 61 (August, 1964), 409–410.

Paula, Sr., "Bleak Image of Nuns Hinders Vocations; Excerpts," *U. S. Catholic,* 30 (June, 1964), 64.

Romans, M., "Negro Vocations and Religious Communities," *Review for Religious,* 23 (May, 1964), 329–334.

Schwarz, J., "The Charity of Interest," *Review for Religious,* 22 (September, 1962), 552–558.

———— "Sisters Experiment With Modern Dress," *U. S. Catholic,* 30 (March, 1965), 59.

———— "Sisters' Outfits; Ursuline's Experimental Habit," *America,* 112 (January, 9, 1965), 34.

———— "Sisters Pool Ideas; Sacred Science Classes," *America,* 112 (February 13, 1965), 213.

Smith, H., "Professional Enthusiasm vs. Religious Detachment," *Sponsa Regis,* 35 (May, 1964), 270–274.

Spae, J., "Japanese Psychology and the Religious Life," *Lumen Vitae,* 17 (December, 1962), 695–716.

Suenens, Leon J., Card., *The Nun in the World.* Westminster, Md.: Newman, 1962.

Tate, M., "Existentialism and the Religious Community," *Sponsa Regis,* 34 (August, 1963), 357–365.

Teresa Margaret, Sr., "Our Reasonable Service; Problem of Too–Heavy Assignments and Time for Prayer," *Sponsa Regis,* 35 (May, 1964), 247–254.

Vaughan, R., "Counseling the Former Nun," *NCGCJ,* 9 (Winter, 1965), 93–101.

28. THE MILITARY CHAPLAIN

Brey, L., "Interfaith on the High Seas;" reply to G. Rosso, *Priest,* 19 (April, 1963), 313–318.

Dimino, J., "Social Status of the Military Chaplain," *Homiletic and Pastoral Review,* 63 (September, 1963), 1042–1048.

Joel, K., "Father Gets His Wings; C. Loftus. ports.," *Columbia,* 44 (May, 1964), 14–15.

Kennedy, W., "View From the Brick Chapel (at Fort Knox)," *America,* 109 (August 24, 1963), 184.

McDonald, A., "Religion in the Service;" reply to L. Brey, *Priest,* 19 (July, 1963), 608. Reply, (November, 1963), 958–959.

McGowan, J., "I've Got the Blues; the Priest in the Air Force," *Priest,* 19 (July, 1963), 570–575.

"A Military Chaplain Sounds Off," *Ave Maria,* 100 (December, 1964), 5–7. Replies 101: (January 9, 1965), 3; (January 23, 1965–February 6, 1965); (April 24, 1965), 3; (May 15, 1965).

Moran, T., "The Military Parish," *North American Liturgical Week,* 23 (1962), 181–183.

Murphy, J., "A Crimean War Chaplain; Denis Sheahan," *Tablet,* 218 (August 29, 1964), 970–971.

Roche, S., "Reflections of a Monk Military Chaplain," *American Benedictine Review,* 14 (June, 1963), 342–345.

Spano, W., "Uncle Sam Needs Catholic Chaplains," *Catholic Layman,* 77 (October, 1963), 28–37.

29.   THE CATHOLIC CORRECTIONAL CHAPLAIN

Cassidy, T., "College in Prison;" program at branch of Illinois State Penitentiary, *American Benedictine Review,* 14 (June, 1963), 221–232.

"Catholics in Prison;" personal narrative, *St. Joseph Magazine,* 60 (July, 1959), 12–15.

Cook, B., "Portrait of a Prison Chaplain: Fr. Aidan Potter of Cook County Jail, Chicago." il., *U. S. Catholic,* 30 (June, 1964), 26–31.

Connell, F., "Duties of a Prison Guard," *Liguorian,* 51 (August, 1963), 53–54.

Dativus, Gabriel, Bro., "Catechism in a Manila Prison," *Lasallian Digest,* 5 (Spring, 1963), 58–63.

Duggan, M., "Father Charles Dismas Clark, He's Good to Hoods," *Queen's Work,* 53 (December, 1960), 16–17.

Egan, D., "Big Problem: Return to Society; Need for a Department of Correctional After-Care for Women," *Lamp,* 61 (April, 1963), 4–7.

"First Half-Way House for Women," *Magnificat,* 112 (January, 1964), 29.

Gabriel, Bro. D., "Brothers Initiate Prisoners Into the Catechetical Apostolate," *Christ to the World,* 8 (1963), 218–223.

Gladych, E., "SIG Members Don't Come Back; Self-Improvement Group, McNeil Island Penitentiary," *Catholic Digest,* 28 (August, 1964), 118–120.

Glazier, R., "No Ex-Cons Wanted," *New City,* 2 (August, 15, 1963), 7–8. Replies: (September, 1963), 15; (September 15, 1963), 13–14; (October 1, 1963), 15; (February 1, 1964), 14–15.

Haines, A., "Rehabilitation Work of Fr. Charles Dismas Clark," *Christian Family,* 54 (December, 1959), 13–15.

Jacobs, L., "A Police Chief Looks at the Crime Wave," *Today's Family,* 38 (November, 1963), 2–10.

McCabe, S. F., "The Sociology of Crime: Modern Theories of Personal Responsibility," *Tablet,* 213 (July 25, 1959), 629–630.

Montgomery, H. and M., "Ex-Convicts Halfway Home," Roncalli House, Minneapolis, Minnesota, *Catholic Digest,* 28 (March, 1964), 79–82.

Nord, M., "The Mental Element in Crime," *University of Detroit Law Journal,* 37 (June, 1960, 671–700.

Norman, J., "The Trickster of Islas Tres Marias; Fr. M. Martinez," *Catholic Digest*, 28 (December, 1963), 51–56.

Pius XII, Pope, (1954 December 5. English tr.). "Crime and Punishment," *Catholic Lawyer*, 6 (September, 1960), 92–109.

Pius XII, Pope, (1957 May 26. *Come Rappresentanti*. English tr.). "Christian Aid to Those in Prison: Guilt, Punishment, Suffering," *Irish Ecclesiastical Record*, 91 (April, 1959), 293–302.

"Prisoners on Release," *Tablet*, 214 (February 27, 1960), 194.

"Rights of Prisoners: Bailleaux V. Holmes," *Catholic Lawyer*, 6 (Summer, 1960), 249–252.

Shanahan, L., "Portrait of a Prison Chaplain; Fr. Thompson of Los Angeles County Jail," port., *St. Joseph Magazine*, 65 (January, 1964), 7–10.

Sullivan, E. J., "Ex-Con Husband," *Marriage*, 42 (November, 1960), 12– 15.

Twigg-Porter, G., "And You Visited Me;" the Apostleship of Prayer, *Sacred Heart Messenger*, 99 (March, 1964), 16–17.

"You and Ex-Prisoners," *Ave Maria*, 90 (November 12, 1959), 18.

"Why Violence?" *Sign*, 40 (October, 1960), 9.

Xavier, Therese, Sr., "The Convict's Letter;" condensed from the Reign of the Sacred Heart (October, 1963), *Family Digest*, 19 (February, 1964), 37–41.

30. WHAT IS PASTORAL THEOLOGY?

Abbott, M. M., *A City Parish Grows and Changes*. Washington, D. C.: The Catholic University of America Press, 1954.

Boere, J., *A Survey of the Content and Organization of the Curriculum of the Theological Departments of Major Seminaries in the United States of America*. Washington, D. C.: The Catholic University of America Press, 1963.

Bor Broen, W. E., "A Factor Analytic Study of Religion," *Journal of Abnormal and Social Psychology*, 54 (1957), 176–179.

Bruehl, C., D.D., "Pastoral Theology," *American Ecclesiastical Review*, 31 (1931), 909–916.

Davis, H., S.J., *Moral and Pastoral Theology*. 4 Vols. London: Sheed and Ward, 1945.

Early, I. D., "The Sociology of Religion in the United States," *Sociologia Religiosa*, 7 (1961), 85–100.

Fichter, J. H., S.J., *Southern Parish I: Dynamics of a City Church*. Chicago: Univ. of Chicago Press, 1961.

————— *Social Relations in an Urban Parish*. Chicago: Univ. of Chicago Press, 1954.

————— *Parochial School*. Notre Dame, Ind.: Notre Dame Univ. Press, 1958.

————— *Religion as an Occupation*. Notre Dame Ind.: Notre Dame Univ. Press, 1961.

Glock, C. Y. and Ringer, B. B., "Church Policy and the Attitude of Ministers and Parishioners on Social Issues," *American Sociological Review*, 21 (1958), 148–156.

Greeley, A. M., *The Church and the Suburbs*. New York: Sheed and Ward, 1961.

Hogan, John Baptist, *Clerical Studies*. Boston: Marlier and Co., 1898.

Houtart, F., *Aspects Sociologiques de Catholicisme Americain*. Paris: Economie et Humanisme, 1957.

Krieg, C., *Wissenschaft der Seelenteitung*. Freiburg: 1904.

Lacoste, N., *Les Caracteristiques Sociales de la Population de Grand Montreal*. Montreal, Can.: Univ. of Montreal, 1958.

Lambert, R. D., (ed.), "Religion in American Society," *Annals*, 332 (1961).

Larkin, M., "The Pastoral Theology Course: Its Content and Method," *National Catholic Educational Association Bulletin*, 36 (August, 1939), 485–505.

Moberg, D. O., *The Church as a Social Institution.* Englewood Cliffs, N. J.: Prentice Hall, 1960.

Nimkoff, M. L. and Wood, A. L., "Effect of Majority Patterns on the Religious Behavior of Minority Groups," *Sociological and Social Research,* 30 (1946), 232–289.

Nuesse, G., and Harte, T. J., *The Sociology of the Parish.* Milwaukee: Bruce, 1951.

Page, J. E., *Catholic Parish Ecology and Urban Development in the Greater Winnipeg.* Winnipeg: 1958.

Parsons, T., "The Cultural Background of American Religious Organizations," *Proceedings of the Conference on Science, Philosophy and Religion,* 1960.

———— "The Patterns of Religious Organization in the United States," *Daedalus,* (1958), 65–85.

Rahner, Karl, S.J., and Schuster, Heinz, "Preface," *The Pastoral Mission of the Church.* Glen Rock, N. J.: Paulist Press, 1965.

Schuyler, J. B., *Northern Parish: A Sociological and Pastoral Study.* Chicago: Loyola Univ. Press, 1960.

Schnepp, G. J., *Leakage From a Catholic Parish.* Washington, D. C.: Catholic Univ. of America Press, 1942.

Stang, W., *Pastoral Theology.* New York: 1897.

Schulze, Frederick, D.D., *Manual of Pastoral Theology.* St. Louis: Herder, 1944.

Schuster, Heinz, "Praktische Theologie," *Lexikon Fur Theologie Und Kirche,* (2nd ed.), 8 Vols. Frieburg: Herder, 1930–1938.

———— "The Nature and Function of Pastoral Theology," *The Pastoral Mission of the Church,* ed. Karl Rahner, S.J. Glen Rock, N. J.: Paulist Press, 1965.

Toward Bringing Out the Apostolic Potentialities of Theology in the Training of Seminarians, Special Christopher Notes No. 17.

Vatican Council II, *Decree on the Priestly Training.* (Eng. tr., Documentary Service, N.C.W.C.): Washington, D. C., 1965.

Index

in, 60; public, 59; in a retreat, 60 f;
services for, 59 f; in vigils of major
feasts, 59
Penance, sacrament of, 24 f, 46
   age of first reception, 61; awareness
   of effects of, 83; by children, 61;
   choice of, 53 f; community aspect of,
   59; completion of sacrament of, 55;
   first effect of, 59; preparation for, 49;
   private character of, 59; in religious
   life, 84; source of graces in, 89 f;
   spiritual direction in, 57 ff; symbolic
   reality in, 84
Penances, 53
Penitent, analysis of, by confessor, 69;
   guideline for, 50 f; relationship with
   priest, 58; teen-age, 64 ff
Penology, theories of, 404, 405
Persecution complex, development of, by
   adolescent, 71
Personnel administration, 180
Phillipi, Archbishop, definition of reli-
   gious life, 384
Pieper, Josef, on teaching, 322 f
Pittenger, W. Norman, on preaching, 116
Pius X, St., 115; and CCD, 149; and
   liturgy, 143 f
Pius XI, Pope, on lay teachers, 209;
   Mens Nostra, 343 f, 351; on priest
   as educator, 306 f; on priests in profane studies, 310 *n*; *Quadragesimo
   Anno*, 291; on spiritual exercises, 351
Pius XII, Pope, 31 *n*; on artists, 31; to
   Assisi Liturgical Conference, 43; on
   Church, 265; complaint about isolationists, 272 f; explanation of priestly
   ministry, 3; on importance of pastoral
   theology, 421; on members of press,
   285; on pastoral training of priest,
   419; on priests, 306 *n*, 420; on public
   opinion, 280; on religious women, 378;
   on retreat methods, 347; on teaching
   religion, 313
Poor, aggressive, problems with, 156;
   honest, problems of, 155; spiritually,
   problems with, 156, timid, problems
   of, 155
Poverty, vow of, in income tax obligation, 188 f
Power and the Wisdom, The, 122
Prayer, contemplative preconditioning
   for, 136; Sisters' desire for, 107
Prayers, in Mass arrangement, 18
Preacher, as mouthpiece of Christ, 110;
   word of, as personal call from God,
   112
Preaching, adaptation in, 118; apostolic
   tradition of, 112; appreciation of general principles of, 119; catechetical,
   119; the Christian message, 253; construction of theology of, 109; content
   of, 255; current renewal of, 116;
   deterioration in, 146; evangelization,
   119; fundamental truths in, 111; Gospel as starting point, 116; as grace of

faith, 112; imagery in, 116 f; importance of, 146 f; as incarnational activity, 113; interior testimony of, 112;
liturgical, 120; at Mass, 120; missionary, 119; modern renewal of, 109;
moralistic, 115; moralizing in, 114 f;
outward testimony in, 112; pitfalls in,
113; pre-evangelization, 119; as primary apostolate, 145 f; prophetical nature of, 110; purpose of, 115; relation
to audiences, 117; renewal of, in Catholicism, 111; selection of Mass texts,
120; signs of resuscitation in, 109;
special, 119; as speech by God, 112;
"springboard," 114; in suburban parishes, 146; thematic, dangers, 114;
topical, dangers, 114
Predella, size of, 40
Press, history of attitude toward, 283 f
Priest, anti-business attitude of, 302;
building problems of, 33; as classroom catechist, 311; as confessor to
Sisters, 101; as confessor and spiritual
director, 46; demands on, 108; diocesan information director, 286; as educator, 294; in field of communication
arts, 287; function of in apostolate,
99; as guide and counselor, 281; in
high school classroom, 306; information to press, 285; as Leitourgos, 99;
mass media needs, 282; ministry of,
in high school classroom, 307; and
modern communications, 277; molding of mass media, 285; molding of
parish by, 285; and parish organizations of men, 214; pastoral aims of,
306; pastoral function of, 429; as
patron of architecture, 28; preparation for hospital chaplaincy, 374; and
the press, 282; as real man of God,
108; relationship to architect, 27; relationship to lay organizations of
women, 223; responsibility for parishioners, 286; as retreat master, 103;
role of, as confessor, 62 f; selection
of architect by, 30; sensitivity to
Holy Spirit, 108; sensitivity to women,
108; as sign of divine mercy, 102; as
sign of forgiving Christ, 102 f; as
spiritual director, 104; spiritual exercises, study and work for, 351 f; treatment of newsmen, 283
Priest-confessor, as father and friend, 51;
as judge and physician, 51; as spiritual
director, 47
Priest counselors, consultative role of,
294; developing competence as, 305;
and moral theologians, distinction between, 294
Priesthood, preparation for, 1
Priestly training, value of, 7
Priests, aids for life of, 8; appreciation
of spiritual exercises, 350 f; and religious women as co-workers, 94; young,
restlessness among, 141 f